The Psychology of Sexual Orientation, Behavior, and Identity

The Psychology of Sexual Orientation, Behavior, and Identity

A Handbook

EDITED BY LOUIS DIAMANT AND RICHARD D. McANULTY

Greenwood Press
Westport, Connecticut • London

Library of Congress Cataloging-in-Publication Data

The Psychology of sexual orientation, behavior, and identity : a
   handbook / edited by Louis Diamant and Richard D. McAnulty.
      p.   cm.
   Includes bibliographical references and index.
   ISBN 0-313-28501-2 (alk. paper)
   1. Sexual orientation.   2. Gender identity.   3. Homosexuality.
  I. Diamant, Louis. II. McAnulty, Richard D.
  HQ16.P79   1995
  306.76—dc20   95-7512

British Library Cataloguing in Publication Data is available.

Library of Congress Catalog Card Number: 95-7512
ISBN: 0-313-28501-2

First published in 1995

Greenwood Press, 88 Post Road West, Westport, CT 06881
An imprint of Greenwood Publishing Group, Inc.

Printed in the United States of America

∞™

The paper used in this book complies with the
Permanent Paper Standard issued by the National
Information Standards Organization (Z39.48–1984).

10 9 8 7 6 5 4 3 2

Copyright Acknowledgments

The editors and publisher gratefully acknowledge permission to reprint excerpts from
the following copyrighted material:

American Psychiatric Association, (1994). *DSM-IV Casebook* (3rd ed. rev.).
Washington, DC: Author.

Contents

Contributors

Gene G. Abel, M.D., Professor of Clinical Psychiatry and Clinical Director, Behavioral Medicine Institute of Atlanta

Henry E. Adams, Ph.D., Research Professor, Department of Psychology, University of Georgia

Geary S. Alford, Ph.D., Professor of Psychiatry (Psychology), Department of Psychiatry and Human Behavior, University of Mississippi Medical Center

Howard E. Barbaree, Ph.D., C. Psych., Professor and Head, Forensic Division, Clarke Institute of Psychiatry

Andrew E. Behrendt, Ph.D., Psychologist and Lecturer, Human Sexuality Program, University of Pennsylvania

Anthony F. Bogaert, Ph.D., Postdoctoral Fellow, Gender Identity Clinic, Clarke Institute of Psychiatry

Vern L. Bullough, Ph.D., R.N., Distinguished Professor Emeritus, State University of New York

Michael P. Carey, Ph.D., Associate Professor, Department of Psychology, Syracuse University

Jessy G. Devieux, Ph.D., Research Associate Professor, Department of Family Medicine and Community Health and Department of Psychiatry, University of Miami

Louis Diamant, Ph.D., Professor Emeritus, Department of Psychology, University of North Carolina at Charlotte

Milton Diamond, Ph.D., Professor, Department of Anatomy and Reproductive Biology, John A. Burns School of Medicine, University of Hawaii

Stanley Ducharme, Ph.D., Professor of Rehabilitation Medicine and Assistant Professor of Urology, Boston University Medical Center

Frederick A. Ernst, Ph.D., Professor and Director of Research, Department of Family and Preventive Medicine, Meharry Medical College

Ruth E. Fassinger, Ph.D., Associate Professor, Counseling and Personnel Services, University of Maryland

Rupert A. Francis, M.D., Professor and Chairperson, Department of Family and Preventive Medicine, Meharry Medical College

Kenneth D. George, Ph.D., Professor and Chairperson, Human Sexuality Program, University of Pennsylvania

Kathleen M. Gill, Ph.D., Psychologist and Lecturer, Harvard University Medical School

Christopher M. Gordon, B.A., Doctoral Candidate, Department of Psychology, Syracuse University

Raul Goyo-Shields, B.A., Doctoral Candidate, Department of Communication, School of Communication, Information, and Library Studies, Rutgers University

Karen Hambright, Ph.D., Assistant Professor of Psychology, Division of Social Sciences, Macon College

Marjorie S. Hardy, Ph.D., Assistant Professor, Department of Psychology, University of North Carolina at Charlotte

Seth C. Kalichman, Ph.D., Assistant Professor, Center for AIDS Intervention Studies, Department of Psychiatry and Mental Health Sciences, Medical College of Wisconsin

Michael R. Kauth, Ph.D., Clinical Psychologist, Department of Veterans Affairs Medical Center, Psychology Service

Kelly B. Kyes, Ph.D., Research Psychologist, University of Washington, Department of Health Services

Larry M. Lance, Ph.D., Associate Professor, Department of Sociology, Anthropology, and Social Work, University of North Carolina at Charlotte

Kenneth Lewes, Ph.D., Clinical Psychologist

Bethany Lohr, M.S., Doctoral Candidate, Department of Psychology, University of Georgia

Patricia J. Long, Ph.D., Assistant Professor, Department of Psychology, Oklahoma State University

Richard D. McAnulty, Ph.D., Assistant Professor, Department of Psychology, University of North Carolina at Charlotte

Michael H. McGee, J.D., Attorney-at-law

Tavia L. McNair, M.S.W., Social Worker, Mississippi Baptist Medical Center, Chemical Dependency Center

Victor J. Malatesta, Ph.D., Director, Behavior Therapy Program and Clinical Associate Professor, Institute of Pennsylvania Hospital and University of Pennsylvania School of Medicine

Susan L. Morrow, Ph.D., Assistant Professor, Department of Educational Psychology, University of Utah

Candice Osborn, M.A., Director of Sex Offender Services, Behavioral Medicine Institute of Atlanta

Joyce Perkins, M.S., Instructor and HIV/AIDS Health Educator, Department of Family and Preventive Medicine, Meharry Medical College

Joseph J. Plaud, Ph.D., Assistant Professor, Department of Psychology, University of North Dakota

Matthew S. Robinson, M.A., Doctoral Candidate, Division of Clinical Psychology, Temple University

Nancy L. Roth, Ph.D., Assistant Professor, Department of Communication, School of Communication, Information, and Library Studies, Rutgers University

David L. Rowland, Ph.D., Professor, Department of Psychology, Valparaiso University

Michael C. Seto, M.A., Doctoral Candidate and Research Scientist, Impulse Control Disorders Program, Clarke Institute of Psychiatry

Kenneth J. Zucker, Ph.D., Head, Child and Adolescent Gender Identity Clinic, Clarke Institute of Psychiatry

Preface

There was a sexually explicit joke making the rounds during the young adult-hood of the senior editor. Its theme was sexual variations. Whether it was funny or not is not the main point. The crucial part is that, unknown to the editor at the time, this joke was inspired by the recently released findings of Alfred C. Kinsey. This marked the time that sexuality had come out of the closet and presaged an era of factual acquaintance with human sexual motivation and behavior. Prior to Kinsey, sexual knowledge was promulgated chiefly through doctrine and mythology. Kinsey gave the world an entry into the empirical study of sexuality. It was exciting and modern and promised to dispel the prevailing misconceptions.

In spite of continuing criticisms, Kinsey's work may be viewed as the spiritual parent of a prolific line of research and published work, including this handbook. Through their determination and creativity, many individuals have been instrumental in bringing the study of sexuality into the twenty-first century. Some of these individuals made direct contributions to this book; others are prominently listed in the references.

Empirical studies of sexual orientation and behavior have proliferated in recent years. Although attempts to synthesize historical and contemporary views have been made, we identified the need for an updated yet concise overview of the empirical findings. We further reasoned that such an overview would be meaningful and accurate only if placed within our cultural historical context.

It is the design of this handbook to be a comprehensive aggregate of topic chapters that bring together the individual expertise and styles of the contributors. In producing this work, we have sought to fill a void in the literature and create a scholarly yet concise volume. Despite the diversity in areas of expertise, all of the authors share a commitment to advancing our knowledge of human sexuality. All have adhered to accuracy, objectivity, and thoroughness in coverage.

We anticipate that this book will be of interest to several broad groups: academics and other researchers, professionals, and students of human sexuality. Through our choice of contributors and topics, we have attempted to meet the needs of these intended audiences. Topical coverage is founded on empirical data and organized around prevailing theories and perspectives. Whenever possible and pertinent, the historical and sociocultural context is discussed. For professional readers, applications and clinical issues and findings are summarized. For instance, the chapters on sex therapy provide a wealth of information that has rarely been offered in a single source. Students will find information on a wide variety of topics relating to sexual orientation, behavior, and identity.

The book is organized in five parts. In the introductory Part I, an overview of attitudes toward homosexuality throughout the history of psychiatry is offered. The changes in official views of homosexuality (e.g, the "disease" versus "variation" views) closely parallel the evolution of sociocultural perspectives. The relativity and subjectivity of our definitions of "disease" and "disorder" are both insightful and troubling. The psychobiological foundations of sexual arousal and behavior are summarized. This review reveals that many areas of human sexuality still remain largely unexplored (for example, studies of male sexuality have disproportionately outnumbered those of female sexuality). In Part II, the major theoretical approaches to sexual orientation are reviewed. An authoritative overview of the current biological research, including genetic and neuroanatomic findings, is offered. Data congruent with an interactive model of sexual orientation development are summarized throughout, and alternative, though not necessarily inconsistent, theories are discussed. Although frequently cited, Freud's original views on sexual orientation development remain frequently misunderstood. The learning and conditioning perspectives on sexual behavior have remained influential despite a relative lack of empirical support. Finally, the unique contributions from primate research broaden our understanding of sexual orientation and behavior.

Part III comprises research and issues in the treatment of sexual dysfunctions. The extensive research pertinent to heterosexual and homosexual couples is comprehensively reviewed. The authors explore and discuss research innovations and developments in this area since the pioneering work of Masters and Johnson.

Homosexuality had been linked historically with "sexual deviations" until the major mental health organizations elected to remove it from that category of disorders. In Part IV, the most common clinical disorders of sexual behavior and identity are reviewed. Issues relevant to the current diagnostic system and influential theories are summarized. The literature on pedophilia, incest, sexual sadism, and sexual masochism is critically reviewed. Additionally, the constructs of impulsive sexual behavior and hypersexuality are carefully examined. Finally, a developmental perspective on the gender identity disorders is proposed.

In Part V, social issues relating to sexual orientation and sexual behavior are identified and discussed. The roles of major social institutions in dealing with variations in sexual orientation are examined. The legal system, religions, and the military are considered. Other relevant topics, such as aging, gender roles, and disability, are also addressed. Existing cultural stereotypes and prejudices are reviewed in the context of gender role socialization, sex education, and disease prevention messages. A chapter is devoted to reporting the early misguided attempts to modify established sexual orientation. The important question of whether the sexual fantasies and behaviors of pedophiles can be altered is considered in the light of empirical data.

We are grateful to many individuals for their contributions to his project. George Butler, Mildred Vasan, and Cynthia Harris of Greenwood Publishing Group were instrumental in the planning and completion phases. A number of assistants and colleagues of the University of North Carolina at Charlotte provided invaluable help. We are especially indebted to Winnie Stinson, Betty Cook, Beth Cagle, Kim Buch, and Paul Foos. The reference staff at the Atkins Library, Alice Sigley, and April Bradshaw offered tireless assistance with much of the detail work. Mickey Diamond contributed at several levels. Beyond his authoritative review of the biological factors in sexual orientation, he offered advice and support throughout the project. As editors, we are deeply grateful to the contributors who shared their expertise and endured with us the customary frustrations of deadlines and revisions.

Part I

Introduction

1

Sexual Orientation: Some Historical Perspective

Louis Diamant

I open this precis on sexuality and psychology with an awareness and concern that much of what is written about here bears the stamp of politics, social notion, and convention more than the print of the physiological, behavioral, and genetic sciences—that is, what is specified as this or that in terms of personality, thinking, drives, or biology has often a tenuous and maybe more faddish existence than our idealistic construction of science should allow. Labels, nomenclature, etiology, and definitions have often been argued in committees and have been created and deserted by the rule of bureaucracy, constituent pressure—diagnoses by vote, in other words. Thus, designates representing the various aspects of sexuality have come, gone, and reappeared, sometimes meaning normalcy, sometimes disorder, sometimes sin, sometimes drive, sometimes illness. An additional meaning to an old word has evolved, and psychiatry has adopted it. It is a word used very parsimoniously in diagnosis and is ordinarily preceded by the modifier *ego-dystonic,* which roughly means that it goes against the grain of the patient (American Psychiatric Association 1980, 1987, 1994). The word is *orientation,* and though it remains undefined in the latest edition of the *Diagnostic and Statistical Manual of Mental Disorders* (DSM-IV; American Psychiatric Association 1994), it most likely refers to the propensity for homosexuality since that was the previous connection in DSM-III and DSM-III-R. It could, of course, also mean heterosexuality, falling as it does within the new "acceptable" usage, but heterosexuality has never in the history of the DSMs been designated a pathology. And although my notion that orientation indicates an individual sexual patterning in its nuances and focuses is steadfast, I have adjusted my thinking of those as propensities and have subsumed orientation under it—at least for now—for reasons that I hope will become apparent.

The wish that everything be in a tidy, well-defined place is strong and understandable. One will see this ardor for science, for postulating and making and testing of hypothesis, in the references that follow.

Perhaps no better example of the muddle can be found than in the titling of this book. Originally the publisher requested *Handbook of Sexual Orientation,* and this was the title for which a goodly number of authors were recruited. In order to do a new and comprehensive book, it would need to be somewhat encyclopedic and include the rainbow of orientations (more than gay, lesbian, and bisexual). Had we prepared this book as recently as the Johnson or Nixon presidential administrations, it could have been called *Psychology of Normal Sexual Development and the Perversions.* From the nonclinical side, assessment favored crime, sin, or both, while from the clinical perspective, the notion of disorder was the order of the day, and all but missionary sex was deviance. *The Diagnostic and Statistical Manual of Mental Disorders,* DSM-I (American Psychiatric Association 1952) dealt with it as follows:

Sexual Deviation 00-X63. This diagnosis is reserved for deviant sexuality which is not symptomatic of more extensive syndromes such as schizophrenic and obsessional reactions. The term includes most of the cases formerly classed as "psychopathic personality with pathologic sexuality." The diagnosis will specify the type of pathologic behaviors such as homosexuality, transvestitism, pedophilia, fetishism, and sexual sadism (including rape, sexual assault, mutilation). (p. 38)

The organization is somewhat similar for DSM-II (American Psychiatric Association 1968):

302. Sexual deviation. This category is for individuals whose sexual interests are directed primarily toward objects other than people of the opposite sex, toward sexual acts not usually associated with coitus or toward coitus performed under bizarre circumstances such as necrophilia, pedophilia, sexual sadism and fetishism. Even though many find these practices distasteful, they remain unable to substitute normal sexual behavior for them. The diagnosis is not appropriate for individuals who perform deviant sexual acts because normal objects are not available to them. (p. 44)

Homosexuality was rescued from this list in 1973 by a vote of the American Psychiatric Association, an action that Coleman, Butcher, and Carson (1980) called "an instant cure" for homosexuality and drew the opinion from Barnhouse (1977) that the political action by the National Gay Task Force had ended the illness classification of homosexuality. It may have been political or social action that forced the issue, but who would not have wanted out of any classification that included necrophiles and pedophiles. *Rescued* may not be too theatrical a term. The classification committee did not, however, completely let go of homosexuality. Rather, it modified the nomenclature and introduced for psychiatric classification the term *ego-dystonic homosexuality*—homosexuality that is unwanted by the individual (American Psychiatric Association 1980). Yet this act of classifying may indicate resistance to relinquishing while clinically clinging to homosexuality as a specially selected human condition or behavior needing to be indexed or listed as ego dystonic, that is, in itself not designated as pathology. Being old, stout, clumsy, homely, jobless, or ethnic comes quickly to mind as things that could bring about ego dystonia. I had gotten the notion of rainbow from a now-replaced encyclopedia. Realistically, however, some of its hues would now present difficulties for clinicians because it may be legally criminal not to report the patient or client to the proper government authority for certain proscribed behaviors.

Edwards (1972) reports on the psychoanalytic and assertiveness treatment of a physician who as a result of the therapeutic experience changed from a pedophile to an active homosexual. His pedophilic behavior was never reported; the failure to report such behavior today would be a criminal act. Now what has this to do with the reorientation of a book? Simply this: It was brought to my attention by a colleague at the American Psychological Association that the proposed title *A Handbook of Sexual Orientation* could be a volatile explosive with respect to his agenda for equal rights for gays and lesbians. "Orientation," he said, "has reached a linguistic place where it connoted heterosexuality, bisexuality and homosexuality, period, but the main issue for social and political reasons was homosexuality." In an earlier survey (Diamant 1990) I noted that terms, once almost exclusively used in clinical jargon, were defined by an average person much the same as in a professional description. It called for some concern that a status that has been normalized and decriminalized (in most states) would be back in that pool of pathology from which it had been freed. My colleague believes that the association of the term *orientation* with criminal and despised pathologies could work against equal employee status for the gay and lesbian community. We have accepted his premise as correct, whether or not a valid point could be made that all distinct sexual behaviors and identities could be promulgated as orientations. He thought that it would be "disastrous" if an influential lawmaker who has been opposed to equal opportunity for gays and lesbians and strongly opposed to their presence in the military would be enabled by my earlier proposed use of *orientation* to think or intimate that orientation rights would give entitlement to pedophiles, rapists, sadists, and others. In response to the old query, "What's in a name?" the answer could be, "Lots." Not too long after the consultation, the following appeared in the *Charlotte Observer:*

Washington Gay-rights Activists charge that Sen. Jesse Helms, R–NC was raising a dead issue just to be inflammatory last week when he got the Senate to take a stand against child molestation. But a Helm's aide said the Senate's 99–0 vote to deny $238 million to the United Nations was necessary because the United States wanted to send a strong message to the world organization that it must sever ties with pro-pedophilia groups.

"It makes it clear money won't be spent for it," said Helms's aide Darryl Nurenberg.

In a Senate speech last week, Helms charged that the U.N. Economic and Social Council had granted consultative status to the Brussels-based International Lesbian and Gay Association. One member of ILGA is the "notorious" North American Man Boy Love Association, a group founded in Boston in 1978 to promote sexual relations between men and boys. (Monk 1994)

ORIENTATION TODAY AND YESTERDAY

I will, in these pages, examine from time to time the conceptual linkage of orientation to a number of sexual behaviors and labels. This is, however, an exercise in the classification aspects of social and behavioral science. For political (and perhaps even scientific correctness) I have taken the liberty of using Diamond's (1994) terminology as it appears in the *Encyclopedia of Psychology:* "Sexual orientation refers to the sex of the erotic/love/affectional partners a person prefers," with a caveat about the use of the word *prefers.* Diamond further states that "heterosexual, homosexual and bisexual which are the three categories of orientations are better used as adjectives not nouns and better used applied to behaviors not people. Sexual identity, however, speaks to the way one views oneself as male or female, and gender or gender identity while related to orientation and identity are primarily concerned with the roles that males and females are societally assigned" (p. 199).

The diagnostic manuals used the term *orientation* for the first time in DSM-III (American Psychiatric Association 1980) when describing "ego-dystonic homosexuality" as a disorder. At this juncture, homosexuality per se had been removed from DSM-III as a disorder. Previously, in DSM-I and DSM-II, homosexuality per se was classified as a disorder. DSM-III-R (American Psychiatric Association 1987) indexes "ego-dystonic homosexuality," but the reference page states only that it is a persistent distress about one's "sexual orientation," and in DSM-IV (American Psychiatric Association 1994) "homosexuality" is not even included in the index and that volume's final statement in the section on sexual and gender identity disorders under "Sexual Disorders Not Otherwise Specified" is "3. Persistent and marked distress about sexual orientation" (p. 538).

HISTORICAL PERSPECTIVES

Actually there had been a gradual drift from the early clinical descriptions and classifications of homosexuality to an updated post–Greenwich Village riots outcome. The riots of 1969 started in a gay bar in New York City's Greenwich Village section. Kameny (1971) viewed this event as the beginning of gay liberation, and according to Bullough (personal communication, June 1986), these represented the rise to media attention of developments that had been taking place since World War II. The term *sexual preference* began to be used to designate heterosexuality or homosexuality by gay and lesbian advocate groups. But Money (1987a) warns: "*Sexual preference* is a moral and political term. Conceptually, it implies voluntary choice, that is, that one chooses or prefers to be homosexual instead of heterosexual or bisexual, and vice versa. Politically sexual preference is a dangerous term, for it implies that if homosexuals choose their preference, then they can be legally forced under threat of punishment to choose to be heterosexual" (p. 385). Money has also delineated sexual behaviors from sexual orientations in the sense that one may perform sexually, at times, in a manner inconsistent with one's orientation but under compelling circumstances. What begins to emerge in the scientific arenas are stronger cases for the developmental aspects of orientation construction, with the nature-nurture ingredients being argued as fixating variables (Byne 1994; LeVay & Hamer 1994) more than a cognitive predilection approach. The religious-moral view may look more to individual will.

Several of the categories of sexual propensities were originally intended for this book as "disorders of orientation." The heading was chosen because they were described and coded as mental disorders in DSM-IV. Most had been included as disorders along with homosexuality in DSM-I and DSM-II. Some, such as the paraphilias, have with homosexuality a lengthy history of being deviance, perversion, and disorder in psychiatric nomenclature. Other categories of sexuality status, such as sexual arousal and performance that may distress an individual, are recent inclusions made there with many of the above in DSM-III-R under the rubric "psychosexual disorders." Those problems of sexual performance and enjoyment had long before been drawn to our attention by Masters and Johnson (1970) but not, however, as being basically psychiatric in nature. From the historical perspective, sexualities that early in this century were designated perversions were launched onto the twentieth-century clinical stage largely upon the power of the words of Krafft-Ebing (1886) and Havelock Ellis (1915). Of these, Richard von Krafft-Ebing became associated with the notion of homosexuality as a disease with strong emphasis on hereditary defects and a concept of degeneracy. Ellis had a more benign view of homosexuality, pleading for tolerance and acceptability. These two physicians had, along with Sigmund Freud, predominant influence in bringing homosexuality into the domain of the modern clinician, along with Karoly Maria Benkert who, writing under the name of Kertbenny, originated the term *homosexuality* (Bullough & Bullough 1977).

There is not much doubt that Freud, for most of the twentieth century, commanded the attention of the Western psychotherapists. He is set apart from contemporaries and predecessors by the tenets of psychoanalytic theory, his major innovation and the first set of postulates to weave homosexuality and heterosexuality into the structure of personality theory (1905).

Although many clinicians who claim a theoretical kinship to Freud still view homosexuality as a treatable mental disorder, Freud saw it as a developmental aspect of all people. He proposed (1905) that psychoanalysis had found that everyone is capable of making a homosexual object choice and have in fact done it in the unconscious. In 1935, in a letter to an anguished American mother, he wrote: "I gather from your letter that your son is a homosexual. I am most impressed by the fact that you do not mention this term yourself in your information about him. May I question why you avoid it? Homosexuality is assuredly no advantage, but it is nothing to be ashamed of, no vice, no degradation, it cannot be classified as an illness; we consider it to be a variation of the sexual development" (p. 1951).

"Variation" is how homosexuality was defined by Alfred C. Kinsey (Kinsey et al. 1948), whose research became the prime for a salvo of scientific missives on sexuality and sexual variation that brought the topic up toward empirical and rational study (Siegelman 1987)—a far piece from its original site in biblical Western culture.

The ancient Greeks had had a rather accepting attitude toward the homosexual ethos. According to West (1967) love and sex between two men had been celebrated events important in Hellenic society. Homosexual roles were encouraged and developed as part of Greek cultural idealism, although the laws placed definite restrictions on homosexual relationships. Aspects of homosexuality and evidence of its acceptability as a male function were recorded in the art and literature of ancient Greece (Dover 1978). According to Dover, homosexuality, with little exception, was described in terms of male behavior. The main point of reference for discussing female homosexuality in classical Greece is the poet Sappho, who lived circa 600 B.C. It is from her celebration of female love on the isle of Lesbos that the term *lesbian* originates. Dover thought it doubtful that even with Sappho's highly erotic poetry, lesbianism, with its current behavioral connotation, could have existed under her aegis. It was highly unlikely that girls of prominent Lesbos families would have been sent to a school at which sexual techniques were practiced (Diamant 1987).

As the ancient Greeks appear encouraging or permissive in their acceptance of homosexuality, the Judeo-Christian ethic was restrictive in its interpretation of permissible sexual behavior. The Old Testament has some of the earliest recorded dictums on homosexuality without, of course, having the use of Kertbenny's coined term. The Jews, after their return from Babylon, emphasizing the philosophy of the procreative purpose of sex, placed proscriptions on sexual behavior that border on the paranoid (Pomeroy 1972). Certain scriptural passages have supported attitudes antagonistic to homosexuality throughout history. Examples include Leviticus 20:13 "If a man lies with a man as with a woman, both have committed an abomination; their blood is upon them." Of the account of Sodom and Gomorrah, St. Augustine writes in *Confessions,* "Shameful acts against nature as those committed in Sodom, ought everywhere and always to be detested and punished." According to Lovelace (1978), the position that admonitions regarding homosexuality in the Old Testament were arguable for Christians is invalid. According to a principle "which the reformers called the analogy of Scripture, the rest of the Bible confirms and reiterates the Levitical prohibition of homosexual practice.''

This is especially evident in the Pauline Epistle (Romans 1:26, 27): ''For this cause God gave them up into vile affections: for even their women did change their natural use for that which is against nature and likewise also the men leaving the natural use of women, burned in their lust toward one another. Men with men wanting that which is unseemly and receiving in themselves that recompense of their errors.''

Lovelace states that on the face of it, the text condemns both male and female homosexual acts as sinful: ''It also speaks of the homosexual orientation, the erotic drive behind these acts as 'dishonorable desires' (pathe atimias)'' (p. 91). He states further that ''Paul's statement that homosexual practice is 'against nature' does not mean that it is against the natural orientation or inner drives of an individual, for he says that those mentioned are homosexual and in harmony with one another. 'Against nature' simply means against God's intention for human sexual behavior, which is plainly visible in nature in the complementary function of male and female sexual organs and temperament.''

Pomeroy (1972) viewed this reference to women in Romans as the assumption of a sexual position in heterosexual intercourse rather than a comment on lesbianism. Szasz's (1970) view is that the emphasis on the prohibition of male homosexuality stemmed from the Bible, where God only addresses men. Further, the biblical omission is reflective of the biblical treatment of women as less than equal.

Perhaps because Western law has roots in the Judeo-Christian ethic, governments placed sexuality within a legal restrictive framework. Political control of sexuality certainly appears the consequence of such a history. In Europe, ecclesiastical law incorporated the ideas of Jewish tradition, Christian teaching, and Roman law as a basis for the punishment of behavior until the nineteenth century, when a liberalization of attitudes toward homosexuality was brought about by the Napoleonic Code. However, the prosecution of homosexual persons has been historically directed against males. Most European countries and most states in the United States no longer have laws against homosexuality, but when it was considered criminal, women were rarely prosecuted, while men were often imprisoned. Socarides (1965) found no recorded case of lesbian entrapment of women by police as was common with homosexual men. However, the tendency to persecute, if not to prosecute, in the military may be more aimed at lesbians than gays. According to Anderson (1993), ''The women we interviewed felt that women were abused more in investigations and that witchhunts more often involved women. Several possibilities for suspicion were suggested. . . . Whatever the reasons discharge statistics bear out that enlisted women are discharged for homosexuality at a rate disproportionate to their numbers in the military'' (pp. 80–81).

Wolff (1971) found the dynamics of homosexual orientation different for men and women, which may have something to do with the historical tolerance of lesbianism that is other than (or in addition to) woman's longstanding struggle with being viewed as less than consequential by church and state. She stated that there was no valid comparison between male and female homosexuality and then argued that most writers on the subject have not seen the real differences that exist, emphasizing only superficial similarities between men and female homosexuality.

I have not to this point found a chronological expository necessary. But in summing up this section we can see that there was a classical Greek view that, without much transition, gave way to the Judeo-Christian ethos, which was restrictive and controlling about most aspects of human sexual behavior and promotive mainly of sexual behavior for procreation only. Not much is cited biblically about other anomalous sexual behaviors, but some laws prevailed against pederasty and rape.

Biblical injunctions became civil codes as history took us to the formation of governments by law. So biblical injunctions became criminal injunctions, thus adding the second dimension to the nonheterosexual orientations. At the time that the criminal statutes against homosexuality were being reduced (especially in Europe by the Napoleonic Codes), medicine and psychology were pulling nonconventional sexual propensity and behavior into their domain. Much of the early medical speculation had to do with a misguided view of illness and sexuality (Bullough & Bullough 1977). Thus, we come to the third dimension, and illness, and the introduction to "perversions."

PSYCHOLOGICAL PERSPECTIVE

Perversions were publicized and spectacularized by Richard von Krafft-Ebing. The author of *Psychopathia Sexualis* (1922) collected more than 200 case studies of "abnormal" individuals, which he used to demonstrate the thesis that these "abnormalities" were the result of abuse of the sex organs and an abnormal central nervous system. More moderate voices were to follow the pronouncements of Krafft-Ebing, which were particularly noxious to homosexuality. He included homosexuality with other nonconventional, and to many abhorrent, sexual behaviors classified as perversions and sexual deviations, whether the etiology was considered physiological, social, or psychological. In Fenichel's 1945 classic work, a chapter is devoted to "perversions and impulse neuroses." Perversions included homosexuality, fetishism, voyeurism, coprophilia, oral perversions (fellatio and cunnilingus), extreme sexual submissiveness ("Falling in love as such is certainly no perversion, but it is a perversion of the only sexual exactment consistent in the feeling of one's own significance as compared to the magnificence of the partner"), sadism, and masochism. Fenichel stated that the aims of perverse sexuality are identical with those of infantile sexuality; the possibility for every human being to become perverse under certain circumstances is rooted in the fact that each of us was once a child.

According to Freud (1905), the person from whom sexual attraction proceeds is called the "sexual object," and the act toward which the instinct travels is called the "aim." Using Freud's view of personality, Fenichel (1945) stated "persons who react to sexual frustrations with a reaction to infantile sexuality are perverts" (p. 325). The implication for DSM is the possibility of cure through a psychological realignment of the narcissistic regression. Karpman (1954), using what must be one of the earliest clinical usages of the term *orientation,* stated under the heading "Perverts Must Live" "that a homosexual is not a pervert but the *victim* of a constitutional or psychological development which gives him a sexual orientation that is different from the established social pattern, has been a matter of scientific and clinical knowledge for many years but such knowledge has not affected the popular view which is guided more by unreasoning emotions than by rational thinking. From a scientific point of view, there is very little which differentiates a homosexual from any other individual except his *peculiar* sexual orientation" (p. 21, italics added).

As we have seen in tracing the evolution of terminology from Krafft-Ebing to DSM-IV, the classification of sexual perversions or sexual deviations has been modified to sexual and gender identity disorder. All this can appear an improvement because *pervert* and *deviate* have ugly connotations as compared to a more benign-sounding *sexual disorder* or *ego-dystonic orientation.* Freud had brought sexual motivation, sexual behavior, and sexual object and aim (object may be thought of in the same vein as orientation and if so conceptually embraces a myriad of behaviors) into a developmental explanation of personality.

Although Money (1987b) writes, "because heterosexuality needs no explanation, the homosexual component needs explanation," Freud could not have structured a view of homosexuality without one on heterosexuality, and this he does in *Three Essays on the Theory of Sexuality* (1905). Lewes (this volume) succinctly states, "[H]eterosexuality was as puzzling a phenomenon to Freud as homosexuality, and he thought that it required an explanation as much as homosexuality did. The theory he evolved to account for homosexuality formed part of his larger project of describing the psychic processes that, in their complexity, determined all variations in adult sexual orientation and behavior." It is the tenets of psychoanalysis that made the Oedipus complex central to human sexuality and in the understanding of the neurotic as well as the nonneurotic individual.

The psychoanalytic view of behavior splintered into a number of others, with the broader groups frequently labeled "psychodynamic." Variations on the theme of homosexual orientation were espoused by certain former and post-Freudian clinicians whose views started clinically significant schools.

Alfred Adler (1946) saw homosexuality as a neurotic type of behavior used to safeguard the individual and as an attempt at compensation for people with distinct inferior feelings. Homosexuality in both males and females was an attempt at feeling superior. Adler opined that female homosexuality could result from a brutal father, an interpretation of the female sex role, or the desire to be like a man to avoid an inferiority complex based on being "only a girl." Male homosexuality could result from a feeling of inadequacy for life and heterosexual performance.

To Carl Jung (1942), the persona, anima, and animus were unconscious elements in the development of homosexuality. Jung describes anima and animus as psychological bisexual components in each person. The animus is the masculine aspect of the woman, and the anima is the feminine aspect of the man; the persona is our role-playing archetype. That is, archetypes such as the anima, animus, and persona are our ancestral experiences contained in each generation in the form of imagery. Jung thought that such identifications "always involve a defective adaptation" to reality and a lack of relatedness to the object due to the homosexual subject's primary absorption into inner rather than interpersonal relationships. Perhaps his most elaborate discussion on homosexuality is reported in the analysis of a male patient who "has come to the physician in connection with a very disagreeable matter; namely to be healed for homosexuality" (p. 393). One of his concluding remarks on this analysis reads: "The malady to be cured is we know, homosexuality. The dreamer is to be brought out of his relatively infantile condition into a more mature stage of development" (p. 398). Jung's notion appears to be that homosexuality is not horrendous, is perhaps transient, and warrants treatment.

Harry Stack Sullivan (1953, 1970), a force in the history of American psychiatry, saw homosexuality, both male and female, in preadolescence as having an adjustive value. He viewed the development of intimate ties with "chums" in the juvenile era as facilitative of later socialization and heterosexuality. However, Sullivan designated a "homosexual syndrome" as being maladaptive and a category of maladjustment. This classification is for people whose earlier experiences result in a barrier to persons of the other sex.

Clara Thompson (1947) also postulated that homosexuality may serve an adjustive process. She concluded that a number of biological, personal, and interpersonal variables could lead to homosexuality. She posited that homosexuality could be a symptom in people who are afraid of the opposite sex, or responsibility, and of intimacy and who could have limited opportunity for heterosexual success. She found less pathology in female than in male homosexuals, which she related to a number of psychosocial variables.

CONCLUSIONS

By and large, modern psychiatry played a major role in creating a new dimension for sexuality differences. Very early historically, there was not much concern about paraphilias, but homosexuality was always an issue for religions and governments. Psychiatry had various speculations as to the etiologies and dynamics of the variety of sexual orientation, behavior, and identity problems, but eventually the modernizing forces behind a changed outlook may not have come from the clinical scene. I view Kinsey's data, now challenged by the comprehensive survey of Laumann, Gagnon, Michael, and Michaels (1994), which brought reality and reason to the demographics of sexuality as well as the Greenwich Village riots as having momentous impact on clinical and social thinking.

Actually much of psychiatry remained resistant to a nonpathological status for homosexuality. Fine (1987) states, "The reclassification of homosexuality by the American Psychiatric Association need not be taken seriously." Socarides (1974) has offered evidence to show that the conclusion was reached on the basis of political rather than scientific considerations: "The balloting of the American Psychiatric Association was carried on in a scandalously dishonest manner." Possibly. In a survey of American psychiatrists, Lief's often-cited paper (1977) observed that the majority of respondents believed homosexuality was a disorder and a pathological adaptation, and the chair of a major clinical psychology program told me that he still believed in the behavioral treatment of homosexuality, but this program dared not to use it: "Who wants to be picketed?"

While the psychiatric tug of war went on, many researchers turned to the laboratories for answers, searching out hormonal components to solve sexual riddles. Most recent is the work of LeVay and Hamer (1994), who point to the structure within the human brain (the hypothalamus) that was examined by autopsy on a number of human adult males, many who had died from AIDS. Some structural differences are noted in the homosexual and heterosexual specimens. The studies also emphasize a genetic link. The researchers make an eloquent argument for the genetic notion after stating that "a notion of gay genes might seem absurd." The LeVay and Hamer proposal has been responded to by Byne (1994) who questions their premise and reasons that even if genetic and anatomical links to gayness correlate, it does not prove causation. His paper supports others on interactional theory (Diamond 1965; Hambright, this volume; Money 1987; Whalen, Geary & Johnson 1990) and rejects a dichotomy of nurture-nature in the understanding of sexual orientation.

There is a perhaps surprising tendency for some gay men to welcome the biological origins hypothesis. Charles, a gay man, brought to my attention much of the current literature on the research supporting the neurologic bias. Of all the explanations of homosexuality, Charles seemed most satisfied with a biogenetic one. In response to wondering if that were generally true, he informally interviewed twelve subjects (gay men) with the overwhelming consensus that it was true. Why? Speaking for himself, Charles said that it relieved him of guilt and that it may relieve some of the pressure from parents and clergy who believe it to be a chosen style. The interactive explanation of orientation may not seem to affirm the fixedness of sexuality with the same ring of inevitability, yet it could produce this same certain resolution.

It is obvious that most research and theory presented in this chapter are not my own but belong to others—sometimes persons of renown, perhaps even of genius. The conclusions, summaries, packaging, and weighing of ideas belong to me at the time of this writing. Change of heart and change of view are possible; think of all who swapped Freud for Skinner and the small number who made the opposite swap. Early I had seen orientations described as the rainbow of sexualities (or variations as Kinsey might say) and had chosen that designation as all inclusive. But in time, the meaning of *orientation* has become such that for semantics and political and communication purposes, it is now and in this book necessary that *orientation* means heterosexuality, homosexuality, and bisexuality and that other propensities be considered as behaviors and identities. The chapter authors handling the various sexual dimensions will each pick up the brush and paint a canvas on subjects about which they are authorities and eminently qualified to present.

Still to me, a major conceptual task lies in the understanding of sexuality with its infinite nuances and their relationship to freedom and well-being. There are some long odds against two adults' producing identical Rorschach (ink blot) protocols, yet two persons may be diagnosed as "A" with many similarities and quite individually different responses and personality nuances. Two men may also be considered heterosexual and yet one sexually attracted by an older woman and the other not. There is probably something in our experiential shaping (or is it genetic?) that makes the idea of sex for or with the elderly repulsive or laughable. Older women are taboos for young males. Newspaper reports of an elderly woman's rape will often immediately reveal the age of that woman not simply to show her defenselessness (since women of any age are defenseless with a knife at the throat). Young women may not be as prohibited for old men, but a man must hear the modifier "dirty old." Yet many cross-age couples find each other in viable relationships that others would not touch with a ten-foot pole. And so on for ethnicity and race. Reports of older women's pregnancies draw many negative criticisms. Some of the negative comments have been published about the recent pregnancy of a 61-year-old woman, to which Dr. Mark Siegler, director of the Center for Medical Clinical Ethics at the University of Chicago, responds, "When men bear children in their old age it's looked on as a kind of a crowning achievement of their lives" (Chira 1994).

A furor about the age at which a woman should enjoy sex (and with whom) as well as her child-producing accomplishments may be a wasted anger from a humanities point of view. But the understanding of mind-behavior sets that get us to this rejection are relevant. It is not some subtlety of orientation? More dramatically challenging the usage of orientation occurs with pedophilia. Katchadourian (1989), in his thorough and erudite *Fundamentals of Human Sexuality,* describes pedophiles as heterosexual or homosexual pedophiles. However, if drive, aim, and object structure of orientation were permissible, these people might more appropriately be considered pedosexuals since the object of the drive is not a sexually developed person and the sexual aim is pregenital. Consider that some pedophiles are labeled "exclusive." Thus, use of *orientation* as applied by Katchadourian seems problematic both politically and clinically.

Finally, it might be noted that I have segued to different topics, themes, and labels while attempting to put orientation within a relevant historical framework. This has been done to reify the social, psychological, and biological linkage of all sexual propensities and leave the specificities to others who follow in this book. Like the commonness of the australopithicines to modern persons, this linkage concept holds within it the seeds of debate. We have it from no less an authority than S. Freud (1905) that all of us, even the most devout heterosexuals, have within us the ingredients that have been once and even recently described as perversions (Fogel & Meyers 1991). Stoller (1991) writes, "I think I am in agreement with Freud—which should make one feel good but should never be used to win arguments—that psychoanalysts should know better than to use the term *normal* to describe any piece of behavior, for once the underlying structure of the behavior (its dynamics, fantasies) is determined *normal* has no meaning. Yet in the discussions on perversions, analysts use that wondrous group of people labeled 'the normal' as a fixed point against which all others are measured'' (p. 43). Could it be that, like fingerprints or comprehensive personality profiles, there might be many similarities but rarely identicals? Will we not encounter heterosexuals (or homosexuals or nonsexuals) who are sexually constricted because of constitutional or nurturing or both and be thwarted in relationships, judged sexually dysfunctional, and offered treatment while others whose similar state of arousability present no special problem to them? DSM-IV requires that when a sexual dysfunction diagnosis be made that "B. the disturbance causes marked distress of interpersonal difficulty." For the paraphilias, the B qualifier is slightly more intricate: "The fantasies, sexual urges or behavior cause clinically significant distress or impairment in social, occupational or other areas of functioning."

It is quite a challenging adventure to address the countless questions about what is possibly a myriad of sexual dispositions that through the applications of the scientific process of classifying have been encapsulated within a manageable number of categories.

A CASE STUDY: PAULINE RÉAGE, A BRILLIANT NOVELIST

Dominique Aury who now, after forty years, is revealed in interview (De St. Jorre 1994) to be the author of the acclaimed and widely read French novel of erotic sadomasochism, *The Story of O,* "wrote that she frequently wondered about origins of her 'oft repeated reveries, those slow musings just before falling asleep ... in which the purest and wildest love always sanctioned, or rather demanded, the most frightful surrender, in which childish images of chains and whips added to the symbols of constraint.... 'Weren't those male fantasies'? I've always been reproached for that. All I know is that they were honest fantasies—whether they were male or female, I couldn't say."

At this point, I borrow from an earlier book the words of the incomparable John Money (1987b): "Read on!"

REFERENCES

Adler, A. (1946). *The practice and theory of individual psychology.* London: Routledge and Kegan Paul.

American Psychiatric Association. (1952). *Diagnostic and statistical manual of mental disorders.* Washington, DC: Author.

American Psychiatric Association. (1968). *Diagnostic and statistical manual of mental disorders.* (2nd ed.). Washington, DC: Author.

American Psychiatric Association. (1980). *Diagnostic and statistical manual of mental disorders* (3rd ed.). Washington, DC: Author.

American Psychiatric Association. (1987). *Diagnostic and statistical manual of mental disorders* (3rd ed. rev.). Washington, DC: Author.

American Psychiatric Association. (1994). *Diagnostic and statistical manual of mental disorders* (4th ed.). Washington, DC: Author.

Anderson, C. W. (1993). Stigma and honor: Gay, lesbian, and bisexual people in the military. In L. Diamant (Ed.), *Homosexual issues in the work place* (pp. 65–89). Washington, DC: Taylor & Frances.

Barnhouse, R. T. (1977). *Homosexuality: A symbolic confusion.* New York: Seabury Press.

Bullough, V. L., & Bullough, B. (1977). *Sin, sickness, and sanity.* New York: Garland Publishing.

Byne, W. (1994). The biological evidence challenged. *Scientific American, 270,* 50–55.

Chira, S. (1994, January 2). Of a certain age and in a family way. *New York Times,* p. E5.

Coleman, J. C., Butcher, J. N., & Carson, R. C. (1980). *Abnormal psychology and modern life.* Glenview, IL: Scott, Foresman.

De St. Jorre, J. (1994, August 1). The unmasking of O. *New Yorker 70,* 42–50.

Diamant, L. (1987). Introduction. In L. Diamant (Ed.), *Male and female homosexuality: Psychological approaches* (pp. 3–20). Washington, DC: Hemisphere Publishing.

Diamant, L. (1990). A note on the possibility of a paranoia of everyday life. *Psychoanalytic Review, 77,* 201–218.

Diamond, M. (1965). A critical evaluation of the ontogeny of human sexual behavior. *Quarterly Review of Biology, 40,* 147–175.

Diamond, M. (1994). Sexuality: Orientation and identity. In R. J. Corsini (Ed.), *Encyclopedia of psychology* (2d ed.) (Vol. 3, pp. 399–402). New York: Wiley.

Dover, K. J. (1978). *Greek homosexuality.* Cambridge, MA: Harvard University Press.

Edwards, N. B. (1972). Case conference: Assertive training in a case of homosexual pedophilia. *Journal of Behavior Therapy and Experimental Psychiatry, 3,* 55–63.

Ellis, H. (1915). *Studies in the psychology of sex.* Philadelphia: F. A. Davis.

Fenichel, O. (1945). *The psychoanalytic theory of neuroses.* New York: W. W. Norton.

Fine, R. (1987). Psychoanalytic theory. In L. Diamant (Ed.), *Male and female homosexuality: Psychological approaches* (pp. 81–95). Washington, DC: Hemisphere Publishing.

Fogel, G. I., & Meyers, W. A. (1991). *Perversions and near perversions in clinical practice.* New Haven: Yale University Press.

Freud, S. (1905). Three essays on the theory of sexuality. *The standard edition of the complete works of Sigmund Freud* (Vol. 7, pp. 125–245). London: Hogarth Press.

Freud, S. (1951). Letter to an American mother. *American Journal of Psychiatry, 107,* 786.

Jung, C. G. (1942). *Contribution to analytical psychology.* New York: Harcourt Brace.

Kameny, F. E. (1971). Gay liberation and psychiatry. *Psychiatric Opinion, 7,* 18–27.

Karpman, B. (1954). *The sexual offender and his offenses: Etiology, pathology, psychodynamics and treatment.* New York: Julian Press.

Katchadourian, H. A. (1989). *Fundamentals of human sexuality.* Fort Worth: Holt, Rinehart and Winston.

Kinsey, A. C., Pomeroy, W. B., Martin, C. E., & Gebhard, P. H. (1948). *Sexual behavior in the human male.* Philadelphia: W. B. Saunders.

Krafft-Ebing, R. von (1886). *Psychopathia sexualis.* New York: Putnams. (Reprinted in 1966.)

Laumann, E. O., Gagnon, J. H., Michael, R. T., & Michaels, S. (1994). *The social organization of sexuality: Sexual practices in the United States.* Chicago: University of Chicago Press.

LeVay, G., & Hamer, P. H. (1994). Evidence for a biological influence in male homosexuality. *Scientific American, 270,* 43–49.

Lief, H. I. (1977). Sexual survey #4: Current thinking on homosexuality. *Medical Aspects of Human Sexuality, 11,* 110–111.

Lovelace, R. F. (1978). *Homosexuality and the church.* Old Tappan, NJ: Fleming A. Revell.

Masters, W. H., & Johnson, V. E. (1970). *Human sexual inadequacy.* Boston: Little, Brown.

Money, J. (1987a). Foreword. In L. Diamant (Ed.), *Male and female homosexuality: Psychological approaches* (pp. xi–xii). Washington, DC: Hemisphere Publishing.

Money, J. (1987b). Sin, sickness or status? Homosexual gender identity and psychoneuroendocrinology. *American Psychologist, 42,* 384–399.

Monk, J. (1994, July 17). Man's transfer after remark on gays angers Helms. *Charlotte Observer,* 3B.

Pomeroy, W. B. (1972). *Dr. Kinsey and the Institute for Sex Research.* New York: Harper & Row.

Siegelman, M. (1987). Kinsey and others: Empirical input. In L. Diamant (Ed.), *Male and female homosexuality: Psychological approaches.* Washington, DC: Hemisphere Publishing.

Socarides, C. (1965). Female homosexuality. In R. Slovenko (Ed.), *Sexual behaviors and the law* (pp. 462–477). Springfield, IL: C. Thomas.

Socarides, C. (1974). The sexual unreason. *Book Forum, 1,* 172–185.

Stoller, R. J. (1991). The term perversion. In G. I. Vogel & W. A. Myers (Eds.), *Perversions and near perversions in clinical practice* (pp. 36–58). New Haven: Yale University Press.

Sullivan, H. S. (1953). *Conceptions of modern psychiatry.* New York: W. W. Norton.

Sullivan, H. S. (1970). *The psychiatric interview.* New York: W. W. Norton.

Szasz, T. S. (1970). *The manufacture of madness: A comparative study of the Inquisition and the mental health movement.* New York: Harper & Row.

Thompson, C. (1947). Changing concepts of homosexuality in psychoanalysis. *Psychiatry, 78,* 237–240.

West, D. J. (1967). *Homosexuality.* Chicago: Aldine Publishing.

Whalen, R. E., Geary, D. C., & Johnson, F. (1990). Models of sexuality. In D. P.

McWhirter, S. A. Sanders & J. M. Reinisch (Eds.), *Homosexuality/heterosexuality: Concepts of sexual orientation* (pp. 61–70). New York: Oxford University Press.

Wolff, C. (1971). *Love between women.* New York: St. Martin's Press.

2

The Psychobiology of Sexual Arousal and Behavior

David L. Rowland

Sexual arousal, as well as its end point, sexual behavior, involves a web of physiological, psychological, and cultural factors. Yet like most other biologically relevant behaviors, the personal experience of sexual arousal and response seldom reveals the complex mechanisms that underlie it. When a problem interferes with this mechanism, we are strongly motivated to analyze it, and only then are the intricacies uncovered.

CONCEPTUALIZATION OF SEXUAL AROUSAL AND RESPONSE

Various models of sexual arousal and response have been proposed over the past century. Contemporary models are more detailed than earlier ones and emphasize different aspects of sexual response depending on the disciplinary framework from which they emanated. Some, for example, take a clinical or medical orientation toward sexual arousal and response, others a psychophysiological or cognitive-behavioral approach.

Models for Sexual Response

The seed for the modern conceptualization of sexual response was planted by Masters and Johnson (1966), whose "sexual response cycle" attempted to provide descriptive labels for the sequence of physiological (mainly genital) events occurring during sexual arousal and orgasm. Thus, the sequential phases of sexual excitement, plateau, orgasm, and resolution corresponded to specific genital changes, beginning with increased blood flow to the genitalia, on to the muscular contractions of orgasm, and finally to the period of deactivation following climax. The model's strong focus on genital response (Rosen & Beck 1988), as well as the semantic problem of using discrete verbal labels (Robinson 1976) for a physiologically continuous process, has generated criticism.

Alternatively, Kaplan's (1974) model of sexual response incorporates three components: desire, excitement, and orgasm. Kaplan's model was important in that desire, an indisputably psychological construct closely connected to motivation, was added. This triphasic model has strong clinical appeal since its components coincide with the types of problems often encountered by the clinician. The dysfunctional individual may lack an interest in or desire for sex, may not be able to become sexually excited (e.g., get an erection or show vaginal lubrication), or may indicate a problem with orgasm (e.g., too soon in men or not at all in men and women). Indeed, Kaplan's approach to describing sexual response has been incorporated into diagnostic manuals for classifying sexual dysfunctions (American Psychiatric Association 1987). Like Masters and Johnson's model, Kaplan's was primarily descriptive, viewing sexual response as a ssequence of ordered events, each of which was requisite for the next ($R1 \rightarrow R2 \rightarrow R3$). This triphasic model not only separated the response into discrete units but also pointed out the interdependence among the response components. For example, problems with the orgasmic phase could result from insufficient arousal, or problems with arousal might actually be seated in the desire phase.

Focus on Sexual Arousal

While a model such as Kaplan's may be clinically useful, greater definition and detail are often required when empirical investigation of the model is desired. As a result, some theorists have restricted their focus to the "arousal" or excitement component of the sexual response cycle. At the same time, they have broadened the concept of sexual arousal to include its multiple facets: physiological (nongenital as well as genital), psychological, and behavioral. In addition, there has been interest in defining the context for sexual arousal by identifying those factors that stimulate or inhibit sexual arousal. Recent models, replete with bidirectional and interactive relationships among components, often bear little resemblance to the sexual problems brought to the clinician, and much less to the personal experience of sexual arousal. Nevertheless, such models suggest comprehensive and often novel ways of viewing sexual arousal and response. For example, a psychophysiological model of sexual response, which emphasizes the interactive relationship between psychological and physiological response, provides the advantage of linking the study of sexual arousal to research on emotion (Everaerd 1988).

Because models of sexual arousal have typically emerged from the psychological sciences (rather than the biomedical sciences), it is not surprising that one major element tying them together is their greater attention to the role played by informational, affective, and attitudinal factors. Bancroft (1989), for example, notes the importance of "central arousal," a term that refers to the attentional mechanisms that underlie the processing of information. Byrne (Byrne & Kelley 1986) offers a model of sexual response based on the classic S-O-R (stimulus-organism-response) paradigm. Here, both innate and learned stimuli operate on a number of central mediating processes, including those representing memories and images, beliefs and expectations, and emotions and subjective perceptions. These systems guide physiological responses and sexual activity. The end responses and activities are themselves evaluated and fed back to influence future sexual situations.

A model of male sexual arousal similar to Byrne's has been advanced by Barlow (1986; Cranston-Cuebas & Barlow 1990), who attempts to differentiate the response of sexually functional men from that of dysfunctional men. The chain of events begins with the expectation of sexual performance from the partner, which typically evokes a positive emotional response, directs attention toward erotic cues, and results in autonomic arousal and sexual performance. In some instances, expectations of performance may evoke a negative emotional response, which then focuses attention on performance or other nonerotic cues. Autonomic arousal under these conditions leads to dysfunctional sexual performance.

Synthesis of Models

Obviously no single model is universally accepted. Because various models differ in their focus or utility, some are frequently cited among clinicians, others with greater frequency among researchers. Clearly a comprehensive understanding of sexual arousal requires familiarity with the important aspects of all models. First, certain preconditions are necessary for sexual response to occur, including the appropriate external stimuli (partner, sexual situation, etc.) and internal conditions (desire, readiness, etc.). These internal conditions are mediated through both psychological and physiological influences and contribute to the ability to experience arousal. Second, a constellation of psychological factors influences and guides sexual response. These include affects, cognitions, attitudes, and beliefs. Third, sexual response itself consists of a series of events. Arousal, an important first step, is multifaceted, having both a central component and a peripheral (autonomic) component. The subsequent behavioral response (a sexual act) is maintained through ongoing psychological and peripheral physiological processes, which, through feedback mechanisms, may culminate in orgasm and resolution.

Further empirical investigation of these models is necessary to explicate cause-and-effect relationships, explain differences among individuals, and account for various kinds of sexual dysfunction. Furthermore, current models undoubtedly provide more valid representation of male than female sexual arousal (Tiefer 1991). More information is generally available regarding men's sexual response than women's, and there is a bias toward developing models that fit the masculine overrepresentation in the data. For example, evidence from a study on functional women in Denmark indicates that a third never experience spontaneous sexual desire (Garde & Lunde 1980). A similar percentage has been identified in a recent survey of sexual practices in the United States (Michael, Gagnon, Laumann & Kolata 1994). Yet desire is central to most sexual arousal–response models. Furthermore, there is evidence that women are more likely than men to engage in sexual behaviors even when they do not find them to be sexually arousing (Geer & Broussard 1990), suggesting a stronger role for sociocultural factors (e.g., pleasing partner) in determination of their sexual behavior.

PHYSIOLOGY OF SEXUAL AROUSAL AND RESPONSE

Physiological systems are involved in sexual response in three ways. First, noncentral physiological systems enable response to internal and external stimuli that produce sexual readiness (arousability) or induce sexual arousal itself. These systems may show seasonal or circadian fluctuations, they may convey information about general environmental conditions, or they may transmit specific sensory stimulation from a potential mate. In humans, where there are few rigid biological constraints regarding sexuality, the role of these systems is subtle, and their mechanisms of action are not fully understood. However, afferent neural systems that transmit visual and tactile information (e.g., stroking of the genitals) to the brain might fall into this category, as would endocrine factors that prime the organism for sexual action.

Second, central neuronal mechanisms underlie sexual arousal (central arousal). Presumably internal and external stimuli produce alterations in neural activity in specific brain regions, which in turn induce a state of central activation. Although there is substantial evidence from the animal literature, the mechanisms are primarily hypothetical in the human.

Finally, physiological systems are involved in the peripheral somatic and autonomic responses necessary for preparing and maintaining the organism's body, including the sex organs, for sexual behavior. These changes have been documented quite extensively in humans, although the mediating biochemical mechanisms are not well understood.

NonCentral Physiological Mechanisms That Prepare
for Sexual Responsiveness

A variety of physiological systems are responsible for maintaining the organism in a "motivated" (arousable) state and for mediating sensory information that induces arousal. Many species, for example, require specific photoperiodic stimulation, ambient temperature conditions for seasonal gonadal development, or both. Furthermore, olfactory, auditory, visual, and tactile cues from a potential mate often serve as releasers of sexual response in many mammalian species. In humans, the sexual meaning of most cues is the result of complex conditioning and socialization processes; the underlying processes are highly complex and idiosyncratic and therefore easily defy investigation. Nevertheless, some types of stimulation appear to be universally interpreted sexually, and therefore the physiological systems underlying them are likely to play an important role in sexual response. In men, for example, penile tactile stimulation, given the appropriate context, is reliably arousing (Rowland, den Ouden & Slob 1994).

Not only must the organism receive arousing stimulation, the organism must be arousable. Variation in arousability in humans has typically been attributed more to psychosocial than biological factors. Nevertheless, in most mammals, arousability is largely under the control of the gonadal hormones (see Baum 1992; Carter 1992a for reviews). These hormones, produced by the ovaries in the female and testes in the male, are secreted in response to stimulation from the pituitary gonadotropic hormones. In the postpubescent female or male, the hypothalamic region of the forebrain stimulates the anterior pituitary gland to release the gonadotropic hormones, luteinizing hormone (LH) and follicle-stimulating hormone (FSH). These pituitary hormones, in turn, stimulate the organism's gonads. The pituitary and gonadal hormones constitute a negative feedback loop, such that high amounts of circulating gonadal hormones feed back to inhibit further production of the pituitary hormones. When blood levels of gonadal hormones fall, the hypothalamus responds by stimulating the pituitary to secrete more gonadotropic hormones.

In the female, FSH stimulates follicle growth and estrogen production in the ovary during the first half of the reproductive cycle; accordingly during this part of the cycle (the follicular phase), estrogen is the predominant circulating gonadal hormone. Midway through the cycle, there is a surge in LH, which acts to stimulate ovulation and results in the formation of the corpus luteum in the ovary. The corpus luteum secretes progesterone, the predominant hormone during the second half (luteal phase) of the cycle. Thus, in females, there is a sequential nature to the secretion of gonadal hormones, with estrogen dominating during the first half of the cycle and progesterone during the second half. In males, the picture is simpler. Secretion of pituitary gonadotropins is tonic rather than cyclic. LH is mainly responsible for production and secretion of androgens. Of these, testosterone exerts a greater effect on the central nervous system and has been implicated most in sexual arousal and behavior. FSH in the male is responsible primarily for gamete (sperm) production.

In many nonhuman mammals, the relationship between gonadal hormones and sexual arousal has been well delineated. In males, circulating androgens cross the blood-brain barrier and act (probably after conversion to estrogen) upon hypothalamic and other forebrain structures to maintain the organism in a sexually prepared state. Without these hormones, sexually experienced males of some species show little or no interest in sexual behavior in the presence of a female. In the female, estrogens and progesterone serve essentially the same function as androgen in the male. This state of easy arousability controlled by the sex hormones in nonhumans is typically referred to as the motivational component of sexual response. The human counterpart, libido or desire, is not controlled by gonadal hormones but may be influenced by them. Specifically, testicular hormones (particularly testosterone) contribute to a man's interest in sex; the removal of these hormones is associated with diminished interest in and desire for sex (Bancroft 1989; Carter 1992b), whereas their reinstatement increases nocturnal erections, spontaneous sexual thoughts, and sexual desire. In this respect, testosterone appears to have much the same impact in both human and nonhuman males. Yet there is at least one important distinction between men and nonhuman males. Men with insufficient testosterone (e.g., less than 3 ng/ml serum) are quite capable of becoming sexually aroused in response to erotic visual stimulation (Davidson & Myers 1988), suggesting some independence between sexual arousal and androgen-mediated interest in sex. Thus, a lack of testosterone does not render a man "nonarousable," as is seen in most nonhuman males. Such men may rely more heavily on conditioned (erotic) stimuli than on an internally mediated (hormonal) state to trigger arousal.

Whereas gonadal hormones appear to play a significant role in male sexual response, their role in human female sexual response remains unclear. In most female primates, ovarian hormones influence but do not control the expression of sexual behavior. Furthermore, female primates may engage in sexual behavior even when gonadal hormones are minimal. In women, attempts to correlate desire, arousability, and arousal (measured through self-report and/or genital response measures) with different phases of the menstrual cycle, at points when different hormones dominate, have met with limited success (Davidson & Myers 1988; Meuwissen & Over 1992). Although postmenopausal women, who show declining levels of ovarian hormones, do exhibit slight decrements in genital response and sexual desire (McCoy & Davidson 1985; Sherwin 1991), the relationship of the latter to a decline in ovarian hormones is correlational. Any number of other age-related changes might be responsible for this decline in desire. Nevertheless, in some women hormone replacement therapy with estrogen does slightly increase sexual desire and enjoyment (Sherwin, Gelfand & Brender 1985). Estrogen is known to facilitate physiological responsiveness in women by enabling greater vaginal response, which increases enjoyment of and interest in sex.

Interestingly, androgens, not estrogens, probably play the more significant role in a woman's sexual desire. As levels of estrogen in the system increase, more becomes available for conversion to androgen by the ovary and adrenal glands, and in peripheral tissue. Levels of one androgen in particular, testosterone, correlate positively with genital and subjective arousal to erotic stimulation in women, and exogenous testosterone is quite consistent in its effect of increasing sexual desire and fantasy (McCoy 1991).

Central Mechanisms of Sexual Motivation and Arousal

Although models of human sexuality often distinguish among the desire, cognitive-affective, arousal, and response aspects of sexuality, such distinctions become blurred at the level of the central nervous system. For example, a physiological substrate in the brain for "desire" may be nonexistent. Desire might simply entail a state of high sensitivity (low threshold) in the pathways involved in arousal. Even in relatively simple animal models of sexual behavior (e.g., rats), the interaction of a number of structures is essential for sexual response, as sensory, information-processing, motivational, and consummatory aspects of sexual response are integrated to generate a "purposeful" action. Furthermore, the activity within these structures may be under the influence of multiple internal and external modulators. For example, many of the structures known to be involved in the control of sexual behavior are also sensitive to the presence of circulating steroid hormones (Pfaff & Schwartz-Giblin 1988). Specifically, hormone-sensitive cells have been found in the medial preoptic area, parts of the hypothalamus, extrahypothalamic limbic areas, and several midbrain structures.

In males of many species, several neural structures, particularly the medial preoptic area (MPOA) and other forebrain limbic areas, appear to play a central role in mediating sexual responses. Early research suggested that the MPOA, located just anterior to the hypothalamus, was the seat of sexual motivation and arousal. Recent studies, however, indicate that this conceptualization may be oversimplified. This center may be responsible for translating sensory input into appropriate behavioral output (Baum 1992; Sachs & Meisel 1988). The MPOA receives via cortical and limbic (e.g., amygdala) structures input about the external environment and internal motivational and hormonal condition, and it translates the resulting aroused state to motor output. Steroid hormones can modulate the activity of the MPOA, as can input from other brain areas. The presence of a particularly attractive stimulus (female) or a strong emotional or cognitive association (memory) based on a past experience, for example, could provide modulating input from various cortical and limbic regions. Ultimately, output to the motor systems, including those involved in penile response, would be affected by these modulators. Data from both humans and other species suggest that such output removes an ongoing inhibitory influence by the brain over the spinal mechanisms involved in erection.

The preoptic area is also involved in the regulation of sexual behavior in the female, but its role is inhibitory; MPOA activation inhibits sexual receptivity. The primary brain structure responsible for activating sexual behavior in the female appears to be the ventromedial nucleus (VMN) of the hypothalamus. Removal of this area interferes with sexual response in the female and reduces the tendency of the female to approach the male (Clark, Pfeifle & Edwards 1981). It is not clear whether the VMN is involved in the motivational or consummatory components (or both) of sexual response. However, as with the

MPOA in the male, the VMN may act to facilitate sexual response in the female by increasing the connection between sexual sensory stimuli and autonomic-behavioral output. This effect might be achieved by raising the aversion threshold to somatosensory stimulation arising from mounting by the male (thereby increasing receptiveness to the stimulation) or by activating the sympathetic nervous system in preparation for both precopulatory behaviors and copulation itself (Pfaff & Schwartz-Giblin 1988).

The extent to which the preceding findings apply to humans is an open question. Although ethical constraints preclude the possibility of addressing such questions directly, parsimony would dictate similarity in these mechanisms in humans, although with greater modulation by psychological variables. In fact, the few studies conducted on humans have suggested that hypothalamic and limbic structures are involved in sexual behavior. For example, pharmacological stimulation of the septal region in a woman apparently is capable of inducing sexual arousal and orgasm (Heath 1972). Nevertheless, important differences between humans and other species undoubtedly exist. First, hormone-sensitive structures relevant to sexual response in nonhumans, particularly those involved in sex-specific motor responses (e.g., lordosis in the female, pelvic thrusting in the male), may not be duplicated in the human brain. Second, the central roles that structures like the MPOA and VMN play in rodents may be much less critical in primates and humans, whose sexual response depends more on other factors, such as relationship, social behavior, and moral constraints.

Two conclusions relevant to understanding human sexual behavior may be drawn from animal studies. First, dissecting human sexual response into discrete phases or components (e.g., sensory, motivational, affective, cognitive) is largely based on introspective analyses. Such conceptualizations may prove useful for research and communication purposes, but discrete neural analogues (in terms of structures or activities within the brain) for these constructs are unlikely to exist. Second, although similar brain regions appear to underlie sexual behavior in the male and female of most species, substantial differences exist in the precise role that various neural structures play, as well as the way in which they interact with other structures. Such differences at the level of the rodent strengthen the possibility that the structures and mechanisms underlying sexual response may be quite different for men and women.

Peripheral Autonomic Response

During sexual arousal, the autonomic nervous system (ANS) is activated to prepare or maintain the organism for sexual behavior. Extragenital changes, which are similar across the sexes, include increased blood pressure, transient increases in heart rate, vasocongestion in the breast and pelvic regions, and ultimately an overall increase in muscle tension. Genital changes are different, although they follow parallel courses.

Mechanisms of Erection and Ejaculation

Evidence suggests that both divisions of the ANS, parasympathetic and sympathetic, contribute to penile erection (Benson 1988; Batra & Lue 1990). Traditional functional classification of these systems (a homeostatic role for the parasympathetic component and an emergency-arousal role for the sympathetic component) does not necessarily extend to the innervation of the genitals. A number of classical studies have demonstrated that stimulation of parasympathetic fibers of the pelvic nerve arising from the sacral (lowest) area of the spinal cord can generate an erection. Recent studies, however, suggest a possible role for the sympathetic nervous system in erection as well (Benson 1988). Blockage of sympathetic alpha-adrenergic receptors or stimulation of beta-adrenergic receptors produces penile engorgement (Siroky & Krane 1983).

The ANS influences erectile tissue through changes in the hemodynamics of the pudendal arteries, which furnish the blood supply to the corpora cavernosa, the two dorsal lengthwise chambers of the penis, and the corpus spongiosum, the ventral chamber that expands to form the glans penis. Erection is the result of increased arterial flow through vasodilation and shunting of the arterial blood away from immediate venal flow into the cavernous spaces of the penis. At first this increase in arterial flow occurs without an increase in blood pressure, and therefore it is probably the result of smooth muscle relaxation of the arterial walls. When full erection occurs, intracavernosal pressure is increased. Although restricted venal drainage presumably contributes to inducing or maintaining erection, its role has only recently received possible clarification (Batra & Lue 1990). During erection, when intracavernosal pressure is high, venules are compressed against the relatively unyielding walls of the chambers, known as the tunica albuginea, and the resulting occlusion may decrease venal outflow.

Ejaculation is generally viewed as the efferent (motor) component of a reflex process resulting from sensory stimulation of the coronal region of the penis. In some instances, it appears that the afferent (sensory) component is not critical to this process (e.g., spontaneous ejaculation). At the genital level, ejaculation involves several steps—seminal emission, bladder neck closure, and expulsion of fluid (Kedia 1983)—and requires involvement of the sympathetic, parasympathetic, and somatic motor systems. The spasmodic (clonic) contractions responsible for ejaculation are typically associated with the subjective experience of orgasm (Davidson 1980).

Since ejaculation involves a series of muscle contractions, models typically have presumed a mechanism at the level of the musculature (e.g., stretching of muscles to a point of vigorous contraction). Furthermore, there is evidence to suggest that the posterior pituitary hormone, oxytocin, may facilitate this process (Carmichael, Humbert, Dixen, Palmisano, Greenleaf & Davidson 1987). Unfortunately, models of ejaculation have ignored the role of central pathways and subjective arousal, both of which undoubtedly play a major role (Rowland, Haensel, Blom & Slob 1993).

Mechanisms of Vaginal Lubrication and Female Orgasm

Although a number of internal (vagina, uterus) and external (clitoris, labia) structures respond to sexual stimulation in the woman, the vagina and clitoris are most directly involved in sexual response (see Levin 1992 for a review). As with men, sympathetic, parasympathetic, and somatic pathways innervate the genital region and mediate these responses. Sympathetic and parasympathetic nerves connect via the pelvic and pudendal nerves and are known to produce increased pulse blood flow and affect smooth muscle tone in the vagina. It has been suggested that parasympathetic input dominates during the earlier stages of arousal, and the sympathetic component dominates during orgasm. Somatic pathways are responsible for controlling striate muscles around the vaginal opening and in the pelvic and abdominal areas.

During sexual arousal, vaginal smooth muscle shows a gradual increase in tone. In addition, autonomic input stimulates vasodilation, leading to vaginal vasocongestion. Vasodilation from increased arterial flow presumably produces vasocongestion in the lining of the vaginal wall as well as engorgement of the labia and clitoris. However, other factors are probably also involved. The gradual accumulation of blood in the vaginal epithelium in response to sexual stimulation provides the stimulus for vaginal lubrication, a process akin to sweating (transudation), from the blood circulating through the vessels underlying the vaginal lining.

As the woman approaches orgasm, the uterus elevates to produce a "tenting" effect in the inner third of the vagina, and the outer vagina forms the orgasmic platform, a state of maximal vasocongestion (Masters & Johnson 1966). As in the male, the trigger for orgasm itself is unknown but probably is the result of a reflexive muscle response to accumulating afferent input (Mould 1980). Presumably sympathetic control becomes dominant at this point. Without entering the debate about the anatomical locus of orgasm (clitoral versus vaginal), it is probably safe to say that several pelvic and genital structures (clitoris, uterus, cervix, etc.) contribute to the overall experience of orgasm in the woman. Clearly the clitoris, and possibly the periurethral glans (the area below the clitoris surrounding the urethra), are homologous to the penis and for most women are the epicenter of orgasm. There is no universally accepted homologue to ejaculation in the female, although in some women, the possible production of ejaculate-like fluid from the anterior wall of the vagina (G-spot) has been noted (Alzate & Hoch 1986).

Given these sex differences in structure and function related to orgasm, the mechanisms of orgasm may be sufficiently disparate in women and men so that the experience of orgasm is different as well. Specifically female orgasm tends to be more variable in its description, longer in duration, more dependent on learning factors, less reliable in its occurrence, and less sensitive to refraction than male orgasm. In reference to this last point, various studies have estimated that anywhere from 15 to 42 percent of women experience multiple orgasms

(Darling, Davidson & Jennings 1991). In contrast, even the mere possibility of multiple orgasm in men is still being debated. The traditional view of a prolonged male refractory period has recently been challenged by research suggesting that a subpopulation of men may be capable of achieving multiple orgasms, although each orgasm may not be accompanied by ejaculation (Dunn & Trost 1989).

PSYCHOLOGICAL FACTORS AFFECTING SEXUAL AROUSAL

Since physiological systems must underlie psychological processes, the distinction between these two domains is sometimes gray. Yet a number of sensory, cognitive, and affective processes affect sexual arousal, though they defy easy identification with a physiological mechanism.

The Nature of Erotic Stimulation

Psychophysiological laboratory studies have enabled investigation of self-reported sexual arousal and genital response under controlled, experimental conditions in which subjects are exposed to various sexual stimuli. Most controlled studies have used the presentation of erotica to the auditory, visual, or tactile senses. Despite some longstanding beliefs, men and women do not seem to respond differentially to romantic versus explicit sexual material. Specifically, a number of studies (see Rosen & Beck 1988 for a review) have demonstrated that the sexes show similar patterns in their response to different kinds of sexual materials—the more explicit the material is, the greater are the self-reported arousal and genital response.

Mitigating factors need to be considered as well. First, the context in which the sexual stimulation occurs appears to affect men's and women's arousal differently. For example, group sex situations are not as sexually arousing to women as they are to men (Steinman, Wincze, Sakheim, Barlow & Mavissakaliam 1981). "Women-friendly" films, which emphasize foreplay, stroking, enjoyment, and desire on the part of both male and female characters, are rated more sexually arousing by women, although genital response is not necessarily affected (Laan, Everaerd, van Bellen & Hanewald 1994). Second, equivalent ratings on self-reported arousal for the sexes assume that the response scale used by each sex is approximately identical, an assumption that lacks empirical verification. Third, although autonomic responses such as heart rate and pulse can be compared across sexes, and do indeed show similar patterns during arousal (Heiman 1977), there is no means of directly comparing magnitude of penile and vaginal responses. Finally, a subject selection bias occurs in laboratory investigations of sexual response. Women volunteers for such studies tend to be less sex role stereotyped than nonvolunteers, whereas men volunteers tend to be more sex role stereotyped (Wolchik, Braver & Jensen 1985).

Several recent studies have investigated the role of input from other sensory modalities, namely olfactory and tactile stimulation, on sexual arousal. Olfactory stimulation from a potential mate is essential to normal copulatory behavior in most mammalian species, including primates, but its role in human sexual arousal remains unclear (Vandenbergh 1988). In contrast, tactile stimulation of the genitalia is strongly associated with sexual arousal in both men and women. In laboratory studies using men, penile vibrotactile stimulation presented without visual stimulation appears to have little erotic value; however, when presented in conjunction with visual sexual stimulation, both self-reported and genital arousal are significantly enhanced compared with visual stimulation alone. This pattern is found even in men who have psychogenic erectile problems. It is also found in men who rate the vibrotactile stimulation low in "pleasantness" (Rowland & Slob 1992). Furthermore, loss of sensitivity in the genital region, as occurs from aging or disease, is associated with impaired sexual response, although a causal relationship has yet to be demonstrated (Rowland & Slob in press). In women, the role of genital sensory stimulation in sexual arousal has received little attention. One preliminary study (Slob, Bax, Hop, Rowland & van der Werff ten Bosch in preparation), investigating the effect of vibratory stimulation of the labial region, found that when women viewed an erotic videotape, the stimulation enhanced self-reported sexual arousal but not genital response.

A Role for Sexual Fantasy

Sexual fantasy and thoughts play an important role in arousal in both men and women. Laboratory studies have demonstrated that fantasy alone can be used to generate moderately high levels of subjective and genital arousal (Rowland & Heiman 1991; Whipple, Ogden & Komisaruk 1992). In fact, the use of sexual thoughts and fantasy provides a mechanism for partial voluntary control over a system that is largely viewed as involuntary. Indeed, training designed to increase the vividness of erotic fantasies can enhance both genital and subjective sexual arousal (Smith & Over 1990). Furthermore, fantasy can lower the threshold for orgasm during sexual stimulation and may even induce orgasm in the complete absence of physical stimulation.

Men with insufficient levels of testosterone as well as men and women with sexual dysfunctions exhibit diminished capacity to use fantasy to become sexually aroused. What may link these situations is the cognitive strategies used in generating and processing sexual information. In hypogonadal men, the absence of testosterone priming may render neural-cognitive circuits insensitive to the mechanisms that elicit spontaneous sexual fantasies. In men and women with psychogenic sexual dysfunction, cognitive fixation on various troublesome aspects of the sexual situation may interfere with the ability to attend to important erotic stimuli, including their own fantasies.

Effects of Repeated Stimulation

The effects of repeated exposure to erotica depend on a number of factors: the amount of repetition, time intervals between stimuli, the similarity of stimuli, and the likelihood of reinforcement through orgasm (O'Donohue & Geer 1985; Meuwissen & Over 1990). As might be anticipated, the more homogeneous the stimuli and the shorter the interstimulus interval are, the more likely it is that habituation will occur. The habituation effect requires that over a period of time, increasingly stronger stimuli must be used to evoke a response of equivalent magnitude.

In some instances, however, repeated exposure to erotica may sensitize the individual to the stimulation, that is, may lead to a stronger response. Several studies have demonstrated a priming effect on sexual arousal from exposure to a sexual stimulus (Mann, Berkowitz, Sidman, Starr & West 1974). Men and women who view two erotic films within several hours become more highly aroused during the second erotic film than those who view a neutral film followed by an erotic film (Rowland, Heiman, Hatch, Gladue, Doering & Weiler 1987; Heiman, Rowland, Hatch & Gladue 1991). Interestingly, in men this priming effect may be partially mediated through increased hormone output (e.g., LH or testosterone) resulting from sexual arousal during the initial film. Finally, when the presentation of erotica is reinforced with the opportunity for sexual gratification (Reifler, Howard, Lipton, Litzin & Widmann 1971), men and women may experience increased sexual arousal during subsequent presentations.

The Relationship between Subjective Sexual Arousal and Physiological Arousal

Inherent in most models of sexual response is the idea that physiological sexual arousal and the subjective experience of sexual arousal are inextricably linked. There are, however, clear situations where subjective and physiological arousal are disconnected. During rapid eye movement (REM) sleep, both men and women show genital activation in the absence of subjective arousal. The inverse situation is seen in men who suffer from psychogenic erectile dysfunction: they sometimes report high levels of subjective or "mental" arousal when there is little or no genital response (Rowland & Heiman 1991).

In sexually functional men, laboratory studies using continuous monitoring of both subjective arousal and genital response suggest correlations around .50 to .70 between these measures (Rosen & Beck 1988). These lower-than-expected correlations might well underestimate the true strength of the relationship because of measurement problems. For example, most studies have used circumferential measures to assess penile response, but these measure only a portion of penile changes during arousal, the latter stages of penile response being characterized more by increases in rigidity. Furthermore, the range of penile response differs from that of subjective response. That is, at low levels of stimulation, subjective arousal must first rise to a threshold before physiological systems become activated, and at high levels of stimulation, subjective arousal may continue to increase well after maximum erection has been attained (Sakheim, Barlow, Beck & Abrahamson 1984).

Aside from problems of measurement, there may be theoretical reason to expect only moderate correlations between subjective and physiological arousal. Information processing during sexual response may preclude an accurate assessment of the relationship between subjective and physical arousal. Other research suggests disruptions in information processing during sexual response; for example, the duration of intercourse is invariably overestimated. A similar phenomenon may be occurring with respect to judgments about physiological arousal. That is, strong attentiveness to genital response, which would presumably strengthen the correlation between subjective and physiological measures, may actually interfere with normal sexual response by preventing the processing of more relevant (i.e., erotic) sexual stimuli.

In women, the correspondence between subjective and physiological arousal is generally lower and more variable than that found in men, with typical correlations in the area of .40 (16 percent common variance). Two questions arise: Why are the correlations so low, and why are they lower than in men? Several explanations are worth considering. As with men, methodological problems stemming from the way in which genital response is assessed probably contributes to the problem (Hatch 1979). Specifically, pulse amplitude in the vagina (VPA), the most common measure used in these studies to assess genital response, is not well understood in terms of its overall relationship to the process of vasocongestion.

The role of sensory feedback from the genitals may also provide a basis for understanding why women show lower correlations between subjective-physiological measures than men. In men, increases in penile volume and hardness provide significant feedback. In contrast, there is little or no direct feedback from changes in vaginal pulse. Thus, there are at least two differences in the measures used to assess women's and men's genital responses. First, VPA measures physiological changes at a different stage and level of the arousal process than does penile circumference (perhaps comparable to measuring electrodermal response versus actual sweat). Whereas one measures subtle autonomic events, the other measures gross physical changes that result from the autonomic process. Second, unlike arterial pulse changes in the man, VPA does not eventually lead to gross changes that can be easily perceived through the sensory systems. Because strong sensory feedback from the genitals is lacking, women might rely more heavily on situational and other physiological (nongenital) cues than do men to determine their level of arousal (Laan 1994).

The Role of Emotional Response in Sexual Arousal

Emotional response is frequently associated with sexual response. First, both sexual and emotional arousal involve activation of the ANS. Some researchers have even posited that sexual arousal fits all the criteria of an emotion. Second, an individual's affective response to sexual stimuli is postulated to have a strong impact on the ensuing sexual response.

The role of affect in sexual response has, until recently, been presumed to be straightforward. Barlow (1986), for example, proposed that affective responses are determined by the contextual cues in which the sexual activity takes place. Positive affect increases attention to erotic cues, which in turn leads to autonomic and genital arousal. In some instances, the sexual situation may evoke negative affect, which then interferes with normal physiological sexual arousal. Unfortunately, this intuitively appealing model oversimplifies the roles of positive and negative affect in sexual response. Any impact of positive affect on arousal may be related more to the "arousal" component of the emotional state than to its "positive-negative" value. Consider the following findings. Simply increasing positive mood (but not arousal) through an experimental manipulation does not increase sexual arousal to erotic stimulation (Laan, Everaerd, van Berlo & Rijs 1994). Yet increasing general arousal by experimentally inducing a negative affective state can increase sexual arousal in both men and women (Beck, Barlow, Sakheim & Abrahamson 1987; Hoon, Wincze & Hoon 1977).

Why then do psychophysiological studies typically find positive correlations between sexual arousal and positive emotion? Perhaps the reason is that emotion comes into play at several points within the context of a sexual situation. Specifically, an individual's emotional state may be influenced by events or circumstances unrelated to the sexual situation, but this state may impinge upon the sexual situation. Yet as Barlow (1986) and Byrne (Byrne & Kelley 1986) point out, the contexts and stimuli of the sexual situation itself may evoke an emotional response. This emotional response is specific to the sexual situation and may guide cognitive processing such that sexual arousal is facilitated or inhibited. Finally, the specific acts or events of sexual arousal and sexual behavior, because of their typically rewarding nature, may themselves engender an emotional response. Research in this field has generally not made distinctions among these points of affective involvement. Thus, the role of emotion might be quite different at distinct points in the process of sexual arousal or in distinct sexual situations.

Consider stimuli that are emotionally arousing but not tied specifically to the sexual situation. Most studies indicate that any stimulus, either positive or negative, that induces a state of arousal has a fairly strong potential for increasing sexual arousal and response. On the other hand, affective responses that are derived specifically from the sexual context may have varied effects on sexual response. These effects may depend on a complex interplay of the arousal strength of the stimulus, the specific emotional state that is elicited (anger, fear, frustration, excitement, enjoyment, etc.), and the degree to which the feeling is tied to sexual performance and self-evaluation within the sexual situation. Typically, the positive feelings and expectations associated with sexual intercourse with a familiar partner might well facilitate sexual arousal. Yet a specific sexual situation that leads to worry and fear about one's sexual performance (sexual anxiety), as seen in persons with sexual dysfunctions, may induce negative feelings, which inhibit or disrupt sexual response (Rowland & Heiman 1991). In such situations, the positive-negative value of the emotion may have a critical impact on sexual performance.

In contrast, studies that measure affective state during sexual arousal itself indicate that arousal is consistently associated with high levels of positive affect. When affective state is measured as part of the sexual response, positive emotion clearly dominates, such that the higher the sexual arousal is, the greater is the positive emotional response. In fact, multivariate statistical procedures typically identify these two concepts as being part of the same dimension, at least in sexually functional men. Such findings imply that sexual arousal itself may represent a type of emotional state.

Theorists who view sexual arousal as an emotion typically subscribe to the cognitive arousal theory, which contends that the experience of an emotion depends on both physiological arousal and a cognitive interpretation of that arousal, an interpretation that relies heavily on contextual cues and past experiences (Schachter & Singer 1962). Everaerd (1988) argues that sexual arousal nicely fits this general model. In relation to a sexual context, appraisal of a situation as sexual elicits physiological arousal and primes a cognitive labeling process (Janssen & Everaerd 1993). The autonomic responses that follow may augment the subjective experience of the emotion.

Although the number of studies showing a common basis for emotion and sexual arousal are few, one recent study lends support to this idea. Everaerd and Kirst (1989) used prototypes (clusters of attributes or qualities that people use to describe that emotion) of various emotional states and compared these prototypes against one derived for sexual arousal. They found that the prototype for sexual arousal overlapped considerably with the emotional prototypes for "joy," "warm feeling," and "merry." Such a finding is consistent with related research suggesting that in sexually functional subjects, sexual arousal and positive affect might be viewed as part of the same dimension (Rowland & Slob in press).

The Role of Cognition in Sexual Arousal

The cognitive component of sexual arousal refers to the way in which information is processed and interpreted in a sexual situation. Unlike emotions, which can easily be categorized as either positive or negative, the thought processes that occur during sexual response can literally be infinite. Therefore, research on this component of sexual arousal has focused on particular strategies of information processing that might account for variability in sexual response (Cranston-Cuebas & Barlow 1990; Janssen & Everaerd 1993). Most research on sexual cognition has taken one of two tracks. One track is characterized by studies that determine the effect of introducing different cognitive sets or information in the experimental context and observing whether sexual response varies in relation to the cognitive set. The second track attempts to delineate the differing cognitive strategies of groups that show natural variability in sexual response—for example, sexually functional men versus men with erectile dysfunction.

The role of attention has occupied a prominent role in the search for cognitive factors that affect sexual arousal. Since no individual can process all information from the environment, selectivity is required. Within a sexual situation, attention typically focuses on cues relevant to generating sexual arousal. Not surprisingly, tasks that distract the individual from erotic cues diminish sexual response (see Cranston-Cuebas & Barlow 1990 for review). Tasks that focus the individual's attention on the end point of becoming sexually aroused, a situation analogous to performance demand (Heiman & Rowland 1983), generally increase sexual arousal. However, this pattern of responding to attentional cues appears to be quite different for men with psychogenic erectile problems. These men show lower response in situations where they feel increased demand to become sexually aroused (Beck, Barlow & Sakheim 1983; Abrahamson, Barlow & Abrahamson 1989). And in contrast, they may be helped by nonsexual distractions that redirect their focus away from certain kinds of nonarousing sexual cues. One explanation for this reversed pattern is that dysfunctional men are already highly focused on their genital response, and any demand to show stronger sexual response focuses their attention even more sharply on their genitals, to the point of interfering with the processing of more relevant and arousing sexual stimuli. Neutral distractors in dysfunctional individuals may enhance arousal because they distract the subject from focusing on stimuli that interfere with sexual response. However, as Janssen and Everaerd (1993) point out, determination of which stimuli are more relevant is always problematic.

Self-perceptions of physiological and affective responses also constitute an important part of information processing during sexual arousal. Sexually functional individuals of both sexes tend to be reasonably accurate at estimating their level of genital response in comparison with dysfunctional individuals. Dysfunctional subjects tend to underestimate their genital arousal and show somewhat lower correlations between subjective and physiological response. Why is there such a discrepancy between these measures in dysfunctional subjects? Is it a perceptive-cognitive distortion reflecting a lack of integration of physiological and psychological processes? Or might it be part of a strategy of setting low expectations so as to minimize the embarrassment of failure, or an underestimation simply resulting from low self-efficacy? There is no widely accepted explanation at this time, but some have attributed the respective tendencies in functional and dysfunctional subjects to perceived differences in the control over one's response in the sexual situation. Dysfunctional subjects feel less control (or self-efficacy) over their response than do their functional counterparts, therefore having lower expectations and consequently lower estimations of their arousal (Rowland & Heiman 1991). Alternatively, dysfunctional subjects, because they typically show less physical arousal, have fewer bodily cues to which they can attend, and therefore they may be more likely to draw conclusions about their level of arousal from other (nonphysical) cues (Palace & Gorzalka 1992).

The factors to which individuals attribute their sexual response can significantly affect their perception of sexual arousal. The cognitive processes underlying causal attribution are undoubtedly complex, but a number of researchers have addressed the issue by devising experiments that lead subjects to misattribute their perceived sexual arousal to external cues. The rationale behind misattribution studies can be understood by describing a recent study by Barlow and his colleagues (Cranston-Cuebas, Barlow, Mitchell & Athanasiou 1993). In this study, sexually functional subjects were led to misattribute part of their erectile response to a placebo pill that, they were informed, would inhibit their arousal and erection. Upon receiving the placebo, these subjects still, of course, became as aroused as they normally would. But believing that they should have experienced less arousal than usual (due to the presumed "arousal inhibitor"), they interpreted their normal response level as evidence that they must have been more highly aroused than usual. In other words, in order to achieve the level of arousal and erection that they did, while under the influence of an "arousal inhibitor," they had to perceive their level of arousal as being higher than usual. Interestingly, sexually functional men show this effect very clearly but men with erectile dysfunction show an opposite pattern: when given a placebo that purportedly diminishes erection, these subjects report diminished subjective and erectile response (Cranston-Cuebas et al. 1993). The rationale is that men who respond in accordance with the expected effect of the placebo (as do the dysfunctional men) are attending and responding to the information provided about the situation (claims made by the experimenter about the pill) and ignoring interoceptive information (i.e., arising from within the body). In contrast, men who respond with the perception of higher arousal than usual (functional men) are attending more to interoceptive cues to interpret their response than to situational cues (expectations induced by the experimenter).

Recently it has been suggested that responses to emotionally arousing stimuli may not require a controlled cognitive process but may reflect a type of automatic processing (Frijda 1986). Such processing implies a response that is elicited by the stimuli (i.e., inevitable from the nature of the stimuli), that is fast, and that requires minimal attention. This kind of processing might be distinguished from meditated, deliberate, controlled thought that characterizes other kinds of cognition, such as problem solving or synthesis. This distinction between modes of cognitive processing may be relevant to sexual arousal (Bancroft

1989; Janssen & Everaerd 1993). Highly controlled cognitive elaboration, as might occur in dysfunctional individuals who worry about sexual performance or achieving orgasm, might well interfere with the automatic processing required for the "effortless" response typical of functional men and women.

Theoretical approaches and experimental data enlist some support for the idea of automatic processing of sexual stimuli. Like emotional arousal, sexual arousal might involve inherent or highly conditioned response mechanisms (Rachman 1966) that require little, if any, deliberate cognitive processing. One line of research suggests that the use of sexual stimuli that are inherently arousing might be particularly effective in activating this automatic processing system. Direct genital stimulation induces a reflexive physical response in men and therefore may possess the characteristics needed to activate this automatic system. Indeed, penile vibrotactile stimulation has been found to be highly effective in enhancing sexual arousal in subjects who are viewing an erotic film (Rowland & Slob 1991). Even more interesting, men with psychogenic erectile dysfunction, who typically show much lower penile response to visual erotic stimulation than controls, do not differ from these controls when penile vibrotactile stimulation is added (Janssen, Everaerd, van Lunsen & Oerlemans 1994). In these dysfunctional men, the strong reflex response (inherent or conditioned) to genital tactile stimulation may assist in activating automatic cognitive mechanisms during sexual stimulation. When this happens, there may be a concomitant reduction in controlled cognitions that interfere with sexual arousal: cognitions focusing on sexual performance, self-evaluation, and feelings of lack of control.

VARIATIONS IN SEXUAL AROUSAL AND BEHAVIOR: CONCLUSIONS

Individuals vary considerably in the intensity and frequency of sexual arousal and behavior. These differences can be attributed to a host of physiological, psychological, and sociocultural factors. Specifically, physiological systems involved in sexual response can be altered by such conditions as disease, aging, pathophysiological agents, and pharmacological substances. For example, prolonged and heavy use of a pathophysiological agent such as nicotine, which diminishes vasomotor response, may have deleterious effects on erectile response in men; antidepressant drugs are known to inhibit ejaculation in men and produce anorgasmia in women. Some conditions may affect sexual response in one sex, while having minimal or no effect in the other. Diabetes, a condition known to produce peripheral neuropathy, often interferes with erectile ability in men but appears to have negligible effects on sexual arousal in women (Slob, Koster, Radder & van der Werff ten Bosch 1990). At the other end of the spectrum, some physiological agents may facilitate sexual arousal and response. Through the ages, reports abound on the use of putative aphrodisiacs (e.g., the bark of the yohimbine tree supposedly enhances arousal).

The importance of psychological factors to functional sexual response cannot be overemphasized. Numerous factors, ranging from the erotic value of the stimuli, expectations of the situation, and self-efficacy, on the one hand, to affective response, self-perceptions, and methods of cognitive processing, on the other, have been shown to have a significant impact on sexual arousal and may account for differential patterns of responding between sexually functional and dysfunctional individuals. Even when a sexual dysfunction has a strong somatic basis, psychological factors are implicated. Men and women who fail sexually, whether from somatic or psychogenic causes, are likely to react with worry and feelings of loss of control, which affects future sexual responses.

Beyond physiological and psychological influences, sociocultural factors play an important role in sexual arousal. In fact, once the study of sexuality moves from the laboratory to real-life situations, the impact of these factors is greatly enlarged. Among other things, the quality of the relationship between the sexual partners, the individual's personal priorities and values, and customs and expectations of one's culture play critical roles in defining any sexual situation and therefore have an impact on sexual arousal and behavior.

REFERENCES

Abrahamson, D. J., Barlow, D. H., & Abrahamson, L. S. (1989). Differential effects of performance demand and distraction on sexually functional and dysfunctional males. *Journal of Abnormal Psychology, 98,* 241–247.

Alzate, H., & Hoch, Z. (1986). The G-spot and female ejaculation: A current appraisal. *Journal of Sex and Marital Therapy, 11,* 211–220.

American Psychiatric Association. (1987). *Diagnostic and statistical manual of mental disorders* (3rd ed. rev.). Washington, DC: Author.

Bancroft, J. (1989). *Human sexuality and its problems.* Edinburgh: Churchill Livingston.

Barlow, D. H. (1986). Causes of sexual dysfunction: The role of anxiety and cognitive interference. *Journal of Consulting and Clinical Psychology, 54,* 140–148.

Batra, A. K., & Lue, T. F. (1990). Physiology and pathology of penile erection. In J. Bancroft, C. Davis & H. Ruppel, Jr. (Eds.), *Annual review of sex research* (Vol. 1, pp. 251–263). Mt. Vernon, IA: Society for the Scientific Study of Sex.

Baum, M. J. (1992). Neuroendocrinology of sexual behavior in the male. In J. Becker, S. M. Breedlove & D. Crews (Eds.), *Behavioral endocrinology* (pp. 97–130). Cambridge, MA: MIT Press.

Beck, J. G., Barlow, D. H., & Sakheim, D. K. (1993). The effects of attentional focus and partner arousal on sexual responding in functional and dysfunctional men. *Behavior Research and Therapy, 21,* 1–8.

Beck, J. G., Barlow, D. H., Sakheim, D. K., & Abrahamson, D. J. (1987). Shock threat and sexual arousal: The role of selective attention, thought content, and affective states. *Psychophysiology, 24,* 165–172.

Benson, G. S. (1988). Male sexual function: Erection, emission, and ejaculation. In E. Knobil & J. Neill (Eds.), *The physiology of reproduction* (pp. 1121–1139). New York: Raven Press.

Byrne, D., & Kelley, K. (Eds.), (1986). *Alternative approaches to the study of sexual behavior.* Hillsdale, NJ: Erlbaum.

Carmichael, M. S., Humbert, R., Dixen, J., Palmisano, G., Greenleaf, W., & Davidson, J. M. (1987). Oxytocin increase in human sexual response. *Journal of Clinical Endocrinology and Metabolism, 64,* 27–31.

Carter, C. S. (1992a). Neuroendocrinology of sexual behavior in the female. In J. Becker, S. M. Breedlove & D. Crews (Eds.), *Behavioral endocrinology* (pp. 71–95). Cambridge, MA: MIT Press.

Carter, C. S. (1992b). Hormonal influences on human sexual behavior. In J. Becker, S. M. Breedlove & D. Crews (Eds.), *Behavioral endocrinology* (pp. 131–142). Cambridge, MA: MIT Press.

Clark, A. S., Pfeifle, J. K., & Edwards, D. A. (1981). Ventromedial hypothalamic damage and sexual proceptivity in female rats. *Physiology and Behavior, 27,* 597–602.

Cranston-Cuebas, M., & Barlow, D. H. (1990). Cognitive and affective contributions to sexual functioning. In J. Bancroft, C. Davis & H. Ruppel, Jr. (Eds.), *Annual review of sex research* (Vol. 1, pp. 119–161). Mt. Vernon, IA: Society for the Scientific Study of Sex.

Cranston-Cuebas, M. A., Barlow, D. H., Mitchell, W., & Athanasiou, R. (1993). Differential effects of a misattribution on sexually functional and dysfunctional men. *Journal of Abnormal Psychology, 102,* 525–533.

Darling, C. A., Davidson, J. K., & Jennings, D. A. (1991). The female sexual response revisited: Understanding the multiorgasmic experience in women. *Archives of Sexual Behavior, 20,* 527–540.

Davidson, J. M. (1980). The psychobiology of sexual experience. In J. M. Davidson & R. J. Davidson (Eds.), *The psychobiology of consciousness* (pp. 271–332). New York: Plenum.

Davidson, J. M., & Myers, L. (1988). Endocrine factors in sexual psychophysiology. In R. Rosen & G. Beck (Eds.), *Patterns of sexual arousal: Psychophysiological processes and clinical applications* (pp. 158–186). New York: Guilford.

Dorries, K. M., Schmidt, H. J., Beauchamp, G. K., & Wysocki, C. J. (1989). Changes in sensitivity to the odor of androstenone during adolescence. *Developmental Psychobiology, 22,* 423–435.

Dunn, M. E., & Trost, J. E. (1989). Male multiple orgasms: A descriptive study. *Archives of Sexual Behavior, 18,* 377–388.

Everaerd, W. (1988). Commentary on sex research: Sex as an emotion. *Journal of Psychology and Human Sexuality, 2,* 3–15.

Everaerd, W., & Kirst, T. (1989). *Sexuele opwinding: een emotie?* Unpublished manuscript.

Frijda, N. H. (1986). *The emotions.* Cambridge: Cambridge University Press.

Garde, K., & Lunde, I. (1980). Female sexual behavior: A study in a random sample of 40 year old women. *Maturitas, 2,* 225–240.

Geer, J. H., & Broussard, D. B. (1990). Scaling sexual behavior and arousal: Consistency and sex differences. *Journal of Personality and Social Psychology, 58,* 664–671.

Hatch, J. P. (1979). Vaginal photoplethysmography: Methodological considerations. *Archives of Sexual Behavior, 8,* 357–374.

Heath, R. G. (1972). Pleasure and brain activity in man. *Journal of Nervous and Mental Disease, 154,* 3–18.

Heiman, J. R. (1977). A psychophysiological exploration of sexual arousal patterns in females and males. *Psychophysiology, 14,* 266–274.

Heiman, J. R., & Rowland, D. L. (1983). Affective and physiological response patterns:

The effects of instructions on sexually functional and dysfunctional men. *Journal of Psychosomatic Research, 27,* 105–116.

Heiman, J. R., Rowland, D. L., Hatch, J., & Gladue, B. (1991). Genital and psychological response following sexual arousal in women. *Archives of Sexual Behavior, 20,* 171–186.

Hoon, P. W., Wincze, J. P., & Hoon, E. (1977). A test of reciprocal inhibition: Are anxiety and sexual arousal in women mutually inhibitory? *Behavior Therapy, 8,* 694–702.

Janssen, E., & Everaerd, W. (1993). Male sexual arousal. In J. Bancroft, C. Davis & H. Ruppel, Jr. (Eds.), *Annual review of sex research* (Vol. 4, pp. 211–245). Mt. Vernon, IA: Society for the Scientific Study of Sex.

Janssen, E., Everaerd, W., van Lunsen, R. H. W., & Oerlemans, S. (in press). Visual stimulation facilitates penile responses to vibration in men with and without erectile disorder. *Journal of Consulting and Clinical Psychology.*

Kaplan, H. S. (1974). *The new sex therapy.* New York: Brunner/Mazel.

Kedia, K. (1983). *Ejaculation and emission: Normal physiology, dysfunction, and therapy.* In R. Krane, M. Siroky & I. Goldstein (Eds.), *Male sexual dysfunction* (pp. 37–54). Boston: Little, Brown.

Laan, E. (1994). *Determinants of sexual arousal in women: Genital and subjective components of sexual response.* Dissertation, University of Amsterdam.

Laan, E., Everaerd, W., van Bellen, G., & Hanewald, G. (1994). Women's sexual and emotional responses to male and female produced erotica. *Archives of Sexual Behavior, 23,* 153–170.

Laan, E., Everaerd, W., van Berlo, R., & Rijs, L. (in press). Mood and sexual arousal in women. *Behavior Research and Therapy.*

Levin, R. L. (1992) The mechanisms of human sexual female arousal. In J. Bancroft, C. Davis & H. Ruppel, Jr. (Eds.), *Annual review of sex research* (Vol. 3, pp. 1–48). Mt. Vernon, IA: Society for the Scientific Study of Sex.

McCoy, N. (1992). The menopause and sexuality. In R. Sitruk-Ware & W. Utian (Eds.), *The menopause and hormonal replacement therapy: Facts and controversies* (pp. 73–99). New York: Marcel Dekker.

McCoy, N. L., & Davidson, J. M. (1985). A longitudinal study of the effects of menopause on sexuality. *Maturitas, 7,* 203–210.

Mann, J., Berkowitz, L., Sidman, J., Starr, S., & West, S. (1974). Satiation of the transient stimulating effect of erotic films. *Journal of Personality and Social Psychology, 30,* 729–735.

Masters, W. H., & Johnson, V. E. (1966). *Human sexual response.* Boston: Little, Brown.

Meuwissen, I., & Over, R. (1990). Habituation and dishabituation of female sexual arousal. *Behavior Research and Therapy, 29,* 179–189.

Meuwissen, I., & Over, R. (1992). Sexual arousal across phases of the menstrual cycle. *Archives of Sexual Behavior, 21,* 101–120.

Michael, R. T., Gagnon, J. H., Laumann, E. O., & Kolata, G. (1994). *Sex in America: A definitive survey.* Boston: Little, Brown.

Mould, D. E. (1980). Neuromuscular aspects of women's orgasms. *Journal of Sex Research, 16,* 193–201.

O'Donohue, W. T., & Geer, J. H. (1985). The habituation of sexual arousal. *Archives of Sexual Behavior, 14,* 233–246.

Palace, E. M., & Gorzalka, B. B. (1992). Differential patterns of arousal in sexually functional and dysfunctional women: Physiological and subjective components of sexual response. *Archives of Sexual Behavior, 21,* 135–160.

Pfaff, D. W. (1982). Neurobiological mechanisms of sexual motivation. In D. W. Pfaff (Ed.), *The physiological mechanisms of motivation* (pp. 287–317). New York: Springer-Verlag.

Pfaff, D. W., & Schwartz-Giblin, S. (1988). Cellular mechanisms of female reproductive behaviors. In E. Knobil & J. Neill (Eds.), *The physiology of reproduction* (pp. 1487–1568). New York: Raven Press.

Rachman, S. (1966). Sexual fetishism: An experimental analogue. *Psychological Record, 16,* 25–27.

Reifler, C. B., Howard, J., Lipton, M. A., Liptzin, M. B., & Widmann, P. (1971). Pornography: An experimental study of effect. *American Journal of Psychiatry, 128,* 575–582.

Robinson, P. (1976). *The modernization of sex.* New York: Harper & Row.

Rosen, R. C., & Beck, J. G. (1988). *Patterns of sexual arousal: Psychophysiological processes and clinical applications.* New York: Guilford.

Rowland, D. L., Haensel, S., Blom, J., & Slob, A. K. (1993). Penile sensitivity in men with premature ejaculation and erectile dysfunction. *Journal of Sex and Marital Therapy, 19,* 189–197.

Rowland, D. L., & Heiman, J. (1991). Self-reported and genital arousal changes in sexually dysfunctional men following a sex therapy program. *Journal of Psychosomatic Research, 35,* 609–619.

Rowland, D. L., Heiman, J. R., Hatch, J., Gladue, B., Doering, C., & Weiler, S. (1987). Endocrinological, psychological, and genital response to sexual arousal in men. *Psychoneuroendocrinology, 12,* 149–158.

Rowland, D. L., den Ouden, A. H., & Slob, A. K. (in press). The use of vibrotactile stimulation for determining sexual potency in the laboratory in men with erectile problems: Methodological considerations. *International Journal of Impotence Research.*

Rowland, D. L., & Slob, A. K. (1992). Vibrotactile stimulation enhances sexual arousal in sexually functional men: A study using concomitant measures of erection. *Archives of Sexual Behavior, 21,* 387–400.

Rowland, D. L., & Slob, A. K. (in press). Understanding and diagnosing sexual dysfunction: Recent progress through psychophysiological and psychophysical methods. *Neuroscience and Biobehavioral Reviews.*

Sachs, B. D., & Meisel, R. L. (1988). The physiology of male sexual behavior. In E. Knobil & J. Neill (Eds.), *The physiology of reproduction* (pp. 1393–1486). New York: Raven Press.

Sakheim, D. K., Barlow, D. H., Beck, J. G., & Abrahamson, D. J. (1984). The effect of an increased awareness of erectile cues on sexual arousal. *Behavior Research and Therapy, 22,* 151–158.

Schachter, S., & Singer, J. (1962). Cognitive, social, and physiological determinants of emotional state. *Psychological Review, 69,* 379–399.

Sherwin, B. B. (1991). The psychoendocrinology of aging and female sexuality. In J. Bancroft, C. Davis & H. Ruppel, Jr. (Eds.), *Annual review of sex research* (Vol. 2, pp. 181–198). Mt. Vernon, IA: Society for the Scientific Study of Sex.

Sherwin, B. B., Gelfand, M. M., & Brender, W. (1985). Androgen enhances motivation of females: A prospective crossover study of sex steroid administration in the surgical menopause. *Psychosomatic Medicine, 47,* 339–351.

Siroky, M. B., & Krane, R. J. (1983). Neurophysiology of erection. In R. Krane, M. Siroky & I. Goldstein (Eds.), *Male sexual dysfunction* (pp. 9–20). Boston: Little, Brown.

Slob, A., Bax, C., Hop, C., Rowland, D., & van der Werff ten Bosch, J. J. (in preparation). *Sexual arousal, vibrotactile stimulation, and phase of the menstrual cycle in women.*

Slob, A. K., Koster, J., Radder, J. K., & van der Werff ten Bosch, J. J. (1990). Sexuality and psychophysiological functioning in women with diabetes mellitus. *Journal of Sex and Marital Therapy, 16,* 59–68.

Smith, D., & Over, R. (1990). Enhancement of fantasy-induced sexual arousal in men through training in sexual imagery. *Archives of Sexual Behavior, 19,* 477–490.

Steinman, D. L., Wincze, J. P., Sakheim, D. K., Barlow, D. H., & Mavissakaliam, M. (1981). A comparison of male and female patterns of sexual arousal. *Archives of Sexual Behavior, 10,* 529–547.

Tiefer, L. (1991). Historic, scientific, clinical and feminist criticisms of ''The Human Sexual Response Cycle'' model. In J. Bancroft, C. Davis & H. Ruppel, Jr. (Eds.), *Annual review of sex research* (Vol. 2, pp. 1–23). Mt. Vernon, IA: Society for the Scientific Study of Sex.

Vandenbergh, J. G. (1988). Pheromones and mammalian reproduction. In E. Knobil & J. Neill (Eds.), *The physiology of reproduction* (Vol. 2, pp. 1679–1698). New York: Raven.

Whipple, B., Ogden, G., & Komisaruk, B. (1992). Physiological correlates of imagery-induced orgasm in women. *Archives of Sexual Behavior, 21,* 121–134.

Wolchik, S. A., Braver, S. L., & Jensen, K. (1985). Volunteer bias in erotica research: Effect of intrusiveness of measure and sexual background. *Archives of Sexual Behavior, 14,* 93–107.

Part II

Theoretical Explanations of Sexual Orientation

3

Biological Aspects of Sexual Orientation and Identity

Milton Diamond

Among the most fundamental questions one can ask about sexual behavior are of the nature of attraction and arousal. Why is someone attracted to another? Why are some attracted to males, others to females, and yet others primarily to children? Why is obesity a "turn on" for Mary but not for Sally, and why are large breasts a "turn off" for Bill yet a stimulant for Bob? While such questions might be conscientiously asked, the meaningfulness of the answers is fleeting.

Fads may certainly be involved. At any particular time the relative value of each specific feature or trait varies. Looks, intellect, wealth, family, religion, sense of humor, independence, and fertility, just to name a few, have all had their time in the limelight as salient in partner selection. Among the matters that seem to be taken for granted, however, is sexual orientation: one's erotic attraction to those of the same or opposite sex, or both. Although there may be flexibility in some desires, only for a minority is there flexibility in sexual orientation. For most individuals it is a fundamental prerequisite in choosing a partner. In wanting an adult sexual encounter, an individual might act upon a concept like, "I want to bed someone five feet to five feet six inches, with blue eyes, blond hair, a long red dress, and high heels." Only rarely would this occur without an understanding that the individual would be a female or a male in drag. And this prime concern toward the sex of the intended partner is more than on the other features.

Where does this emphasis on sexual orientation come from? The simple answer is, "From an *interaction* of nature and nurture." Each of us has a biological predisposition to orient in a certain way—heterosexual, bisexual, or homosexual—and this bias, organized prior to birth, is then subsequently influenced by social and cultural forces.[1,2,3]

DEFINITIONS

To ensure the topic under discussion is clear, some definitions are in order. These are particularly important to provide a framework within which the evidence for biological influences can be evaluated. These definitions are concomitant with the proposition that five main levels of sexual expression must be appreciated to get a proper sexual profile of any individual: sexual identity, sexual orientation, gender patterns, mechanisms, and reproduction. The acronym PRIMO keeps all of these in mind (P = gender *P*atterns; R = *R*eproduction; I = sexual *I*dentity; M = sexual *M*echanisms; O = sexual *O*rientation; Diamond 1976).

Sexual orientation refers to the sex, male or female, of the erotic-love-affectional partners a person prefers. The terms *heterosexual, homosexual,* and *bisexual* should best be adjectives, not nouns, and best applied to behaviors, not people. Thus, a description might be, "Engages in homosexual activities." In casual usage, however, one often speaks of a person as a homosexual or a heterosexual; indeed people often refer to themselves the same way. Such usage does not direct itself to the frequency or motive for any particular behavior, only its focus. Use of such expressions as "Is a homosexual," often links together those whose regular sexual partners are of the same sex with those whose same-sex encounters are rare in comparison with heterosexual contacts. The term *homosexual* is best reserved for those whose sexual activities are exclusively or almost exclusively with members of the same sex, the term *heterosexual* for those whose erotic companions are always or almost always with the opposite sex, and the term *bisexual* or *ambisexual* for those with sexual activities with members of either sex (Diamond 1993a, 1993b, 1994a, 1994b). This is the way the terms will be used in this chapter.

Sexual identity speaks to the way one views one's self as male or female. Usually this inner conviction of identification coincides with society's and parental impressions and mirrors the outward physical appearance. It also typically follows with the gender role or behavior patterns society imposes or the individual prefers. But this is not always so. These distinctions are crucial, particularly in regard to transsexualism or other identity-gender pattern interactions. In the real world, the transsexual, as are others, is typically labeled in terms of his or her sexual anatomy. Initially reared as society views them, transsexuals eventually plot their own sex-reversed life course. The self-image of transsexuals is of the opposite sex, and their mirror images are in conflict with their mind's image (Benjamin 1966; Bolin 1987; Diamond 1992; Doctor 1988; Green & Money 1969). This aspect of life is separate from their sexual orientation since a transsexual may be homosexually or heterosexually inclined. In everyday terms, people may "identify" as homosexual or see their "identity" as heterosexual. This use of the term is in an affiliative sense. It is as if one might identify as an American Indian or a Unitarian. The term *core identity,* coined by Stoller (1968), is used by some to indicate the central nature of this conviction.[4]

One's *gender patterns, gender identity,* and *gender role* are different from, although related to, the concept of orientation and sexual identity. Gender refers to society's idea of how boys or girls or men and women are expected to behave and should be treated. A sex role is the acting out of one's biological predisposition, while a gender role is the acting out of social norms or expectations, whether or not they coincide with personal urges or preferences. Gender identity refers to how an individual sees himself or herself as fulfilling these societal expectations. The descriptive terms often used in this regard are relative to masculinity and femininity. Patterns of behavior are phenotypical expressions. The terms *boys* and *girls* and *men* and *women* are social terms; the terms *male* and *female* are biological terms. It is obvious that a male can act as a girl or woman and a female can act as a boy or man.[5]

Patterns, gender, and roles have everything to do with the society in which one lives and may or may not have much to do with biology (Gagnon & Simon 1973). Males, for instance, can live as women, and females can live as men; a male may be reared as a boy but grow to live as a woman. It is common but often misleading to use *sex* and *gender* as synonyms. One's sex is biological, and one's gender is socially taught, imposed, or chosen. True, sex and gender are most often in concert, but they are not necessarily so.[6]

Sexual mechanisms are inherent physiological differences between males and females that structure significant features of erotic life. In one of the most obvious distinctions, the counterpart to male penis erection as a feature of erotic arousal is female lubrication, not clitoral erection (Masters & Johnson 1966). Ejaculation is another obvious distinction; it is a common feature of male orgasm but not of female orgasm. Yet another well-known difference is the wide range of orgasmic types among females, ranging from the frequent finding of women for whom orgasm is rare or nonexistent to those for whom multiple orgasm is common. Among males either extreme is rare (Kinsey et al. 1948, 1953). These differences obviously pertain to copulation, but many other mechanisms exist that are less related to coitus but very much related to sexual expression and childbearing. Muscle mass, body and skeletal articulation, enzyme and endocrine production, and other physiological features and reflexes are additional distinctions. The endocrine system of males is relatively tonic in operation, while the female system is basically cyclic during the reproductive years (see Rowland, this volume).

Reproduction, the fifth level of analysis, is relatively evident. Males have testicles, produce sperm, and have a penis and associated organs for the delivery of their gametes. Females have ovaries, which produce ova, which can be fertilized; a uterus, within which an embryo can mature and be delivered through a vagina; and breasts, which can be stimulated by pregnancy to function. The neuroendocrine system of the male is tonic and programmed for the consistent production and delivery of these gametes, while the neuroendocrine system of the female is cyclic, paced so that ovulation is best timed to coincide with receptive uterine conditions.

For most people, all five levels of identity, orientation, gender patterns, mechanisms, and reproduction are in concert. The typical male sees himself as such, acts in a masculine manner—a combination of biologically and socially determined behaviors—is treated as a male by society, and prefers to have erotic interactions with females. The typical female sees herself as such, acts in a feminine manner—also a combination of biologically and socially determined behaviors—is treated as a female by society, and prefers to have erotic interactions with males. Variations are not uncommon: an individual can prefer erotic relations with one of the same sex (male or female homosexual), see himself as a female (male transsexual), see herself as a male (female transsexual), or prefer to adopt the clothing and lifestyle of the opposite gender while maintaining a heterosexual life (a transvestite) or a homosexual one (a drag queen). Knowing one's sexual orientation may allow predictions as to manifestations of other levels, but the permutations among the five levels are many.

Reproductive capacity and mechanisms are fixed, identity and orientation somewhat less so, and gender patterns most flexible. Thus, individuals can be heterosexual, ambisexual, or homosexual and yet be quite different in how their orientation is manifest to the outside world. Superimposed on all of this is one's personality, which often makes it seem impossible to unravel the mysteries of orientation and identity. I hold that those characters, orientation and identity, are central features of one's existence and thus structure manifestations of gender patterns more than vice versa; they determine how the individual will interact with the environment.

EVIDENCE: DIRECT

Before proceeding further, a comment about the nature of evidence is warranted. Each scholarly discipline has developed certain standards by which presented arguments or data are usually evaluated. These tests of validity might involve double-blind studies, the use of suitable controls, statistical analysis, peer review and critique, suitable comparison with available models, consistency with established theories within the particular field as well as other disciplines, and so on. Anecdotal findings are not evidence; they may, however, be presented.

In addition, the law of parsimony usually governs which of competing theories should reign; the explanation that best links the majority of findings and depends on the fewest assumptions is to be most credited. This chapter will attempt to hold to these standards in proving a biological predisposition for sexual orientation. Gladue (1993) uses a legal metaphor to suggest that perhaps instead of looking for "proof beyond a reasonable doubt," we accept "the preponderance of evidence."

Genetics

Twins and Families Reared Together

The strongest evidence that human sexual orientation has a biological bias comes from genetic studies of families and twins. The classical twin studies in this area were done in the 1950s by Franz J. Kallmann (Kallmann 1952a, 1952b, 1963). This researcher worked with monozygotic and dizygotic male twin pairs in which at least one of the co-twins at the onset of the study admitted to homosexual behavior. Among these twins Kallmann found that if one of the identical (monozygotic) twins was homosexually oriented, so was his brother. Among the nonidentical (dizygotic) brothers, on the other hand, the twins were not too different from the general male population relative to sexual preference. Kallmann also reported that if one member of a monozygotic twin pair of brothers rated a 5 or 6 on the Kinsey scale, the chance that his brother also rated 5 or 6 was better than 90 percent; if the brothers differed in rating, it was usually only within one or two points on the Kinsey scale.[7]

Kallmann's work was not easily accepted (e.g., Julian 1973). The mood of the 1950s through the 1970s preferred to have human behavior a matter of social construction or free will rather than biological predisposition. Further, the timing of Kallmann's work competed with that of Kinsey, who thought sexual orientation a product of upbringing or social situation.[8] The fact that Kallmann's numbers seemed to come out so cleanly also encouraged skepticism. A slew of studies soon followed that reported monozygotic twins not concordant for homosexuality (Davison, Brierley & Smith 1971; Friedman, Wollesen & Tendler 1976; Green & Stoller 1971; Heston & Shields 1968; Klintworth 1962; McConaghy & Blaszczynski 1980; Meskinoff et al. 1963; Parker 1964; Perkins 1973; Rainer et al. 1960; Wollesen & Tendler 1976; Zuger 1976). Thus, theories that held to a genetic component to homosexuality lost support. For twenty years (1955–1975) John Money argued that almost all aspects of orientation and identity were products of upbringing (Diamond 1995b), and Masters and Johnson (1979) also argued that homosexuality was of social rather than biologic origin.

This situation essentially held until the 1980s when newer studies emerged supporting a major biological component to sexual orientation. Richard Pillard and colleagues (Pillard, Poumadere & Carretta 1982; Pillard & Weinrich 1986) examined families in which at least one member was openly homosexual. As controls, a set of families from heterosexual "index" individuals were also studied. The investigators inquired of the sexual orientation of all siblings and found that if a family contained one son who was homosexual, 18 to 25 percent of his brothers would also be homosexual. If an index individual was heterosexual, the chance of other brothers being homosexual was only about 4 percent.

The former figure is significantly higher than expected by chance and the latter figure in the range to be expected (Diamond 1993b).

Michael Bailey and colleagues (Bailey & Bell 1993; Bailey & Benishay 1993; Bailey et al. 1993), as done for males, looked for familial factors in female homosexuality. Similar to the findings with males, female homosexuality appeared to be familial. Depending on how homosexuality was defined within the study, it was essentially found that 12 to 20 percent of the homosexual probands had homosexual siblings in comparison with some 2 to 5 percent for the heterosexual probands. From their data, Bailey and Bell (1993) noted that the strongest links to homosexual orientation were associated with genetic closeness rather than parental influences.

Recently, Blanchard and Sheridan (1992) and Blanchard, Zucker, Bradley, and Hume (1994) followed the early work of Lang (1940, 1960), Jensch (1941), Kallmann (1952a), Suarez and Przybek (1980), and others in comparing the sex, not the orientation, of siblings of a group of matched homosexual or effeminate (prehomosexual) boys with a control group of presumably heterosexual boys. The results of all these investigators are consistent: among siblings of such homosexual males, the sex ratio of brothers to sisters was significantly higher than the expected typical 106 males to 100 females. Among "homosexual families" the ratio was more like 126–131 brothers to 100 sisters (significantly more males than females). These high ratio differences were not seen among samples of homosexuals who were not feminine as boys (Zucker & Blanchard 1994). These data suggest an excess of brothers is seen more often among the most effeminate of homosexual males.

Blanchard and colleagues in these same and newer (Blanchard & Zucker 1994; Zucker & Blanchard 1994) studies looked at the loci of these probands in birth order. In keeping with the findings of Slater (1962) and Tsoi, Kock, and Long (1977), all studies found that males destined to be homosexual or who already were homosexual tended to be born significantly later than other siblings. Several theoretical hypotheses were postulated to link sex ratio and birth order effects biologically to homosexuality. One, put forth by MacCulloch and Waddington (1981) and reasserted by Ellis and Ames (1987), speculates that maternal immunization against male fetal tissues or products, specifically testosterone, brought about by previous pregnancies with males might reduce the mother's ability to carry male fetuses to term or the androgen's activity and ability to masculinize the fetal brain fully.[9] Another theory posited that stress to the mother during pregnancy might be involved (Dörner et al. 1980, 1983; Ellis & Ames 1987; Ellis et al. 1988).

Regardless of the mechanism involved in this sex ratio disparity, these findings essentially eliminate the theory that homosexuality results from the overabundance or presence of females (sisters) in families from which homosexuals originate, these sisters supposedly imparting feminine attributes and interests to their younger brothers (West 1977).

Family sibling studies and twin studies are significant in bolstering each other.

In recent investigations of twins, as with the most noted work of Kallmann and other earlier workers, the concordance for homosexuality is strong. Bailey and Pillard (1991) with a study of more than 100 twins found that 52 percent of identical brothers of self-identified homosexual men were also homosexual, compared with 22 percent of fraternal twins and 11 percent of unrelated (adoptive) brothers. Frederick Whitam and colleagues found even stronger concordances (Whitam, Diamond & Martin 1993): approximately 65 percent for identical male twins and 30 percent for fraternal twins. Among their small sample of females, they found that concordance for homosexuality was 75 percent for one-egg twins and 0 percent for male-female twins; among four male-female twin pairs the males all had Kinsey scores of 4, 5, or 6 while the females were exclusively heterosexual. Three sets of triplets also appeared in this sample. One set consisted of three females with a pair of monozygotic twins who are both lesbian and a third heterosexual sister. A second pair of triplets consisted of a monozygotic male pair, both homosexual, with a heterosexual sister. A third monozygotic male triplet set reported not only the same sexual orientation but similar lifestyle patterns.

Bailey et al. (1993) specifically looked for factors that influence sexual orientation in women. They found 48 percent concordance for homosexuality among monozygotic twins, 16 percent for dizygotic twins, and only 6 percent among adopted sisters. Probands also reported 14 percent of the nontwin biologic sisters to be homosexual.

Twins Reared Apart

Twins reared apart are especially useful for evaluating the relative roles of genetics and environment in behavior. In most modern societies, however, it is increasingly difficult to find such individuals. Elke Eckert and colleagues (Eckert, Bouchard, Bohlen & Heston 1986) reported findings from six pairs of monozygotic twins reared apart since infancy in which at least one member of each pair was homosexually active. Among the two male pairs, one pair was concordant for homosexuality, and one pair was partially concordant. Among the four female pairs, in contrast, none was concordant in sexual orientation. This, as in the other studies reported, implicates genetics as being a stronger factor in male than in female sexual orientation. Two such reared-apart male pairs appeared in the Whitam, Diamond, and Martin (1993) sample. Both pairs met only after they were adults. One set was concordant for homosexual orientation, and one was not.

Obviously simple genetics does not paint the total picture. An interesting factor exists that is not yet fully understood. Among both monozygotic and dizygotic twins, male and female, when the twins are discordant, the divergence is usually large. One might be a Kinsey 6 and the other a Kinsey 0. Why even identical twins who share the same set of genes and upbringing should differ so markedly is not yet understood. Unless some environmental feature acts as an on-off switch, which is certainly possible, more ambisexual siblings with a

Kinsey 2, 3, or 4 would be predicted.[10] Other interacting factors must be involved.

Chromosome Studies

A second most significant area of genetic evidence supporting a biological basis for sexual orientation comes from chromosome analysis and related types of pedigree studies.

At a basic level, it must be recognized that any behavior is dependent on some encoding within the nervous system. Since the work of Murry Barr (1966) it is known that mammalian neurons can be sexually distinguished by the presence or absence of so-called sex chromatin (Barr body). This is a special staining bit lodged on the inner surface of the nuclear membrane of nerve cells in females. It is the remnant of the second X chromosome in females; only one is typically functional. Not being females, neither male heterosexuals nor male homosexuals show such chromatin.

Recently the work of Dean Hamer and colleagues went further. Using family tree studies, they determined that not only did homosexuality seem to run in families, but it was more significantly influenced by the mother's lineage than the father's. Hamer and colleagues (Hamer et al. 1993; LaVay & Hamer 1994) found practically no homosexuals in paternal lines and "compared with randomly chosen families, rates of homosexuality in maternal uncles increased from 7 to 10 percent and in maternal cousins from 8 to 13 percent. This familial clustering, even in relatives outside the nuclear family, presents an additional argument for a genetic root to sexual orientation." Were a trait to be passed along on the X chromosome, which can only come from mothers (fathers contributing the Y), it would be preferentially manifest in brothers, maternal uncles, and maternal male cousins. This is precisely what was found.

Hamer and colleagues then sought physical evidence of such a trait that might be manifest by some chromosomal pattern. They found, in homosexual brothers, a remarkable and significantly similar marker pattern of genes on the Xq28 region of the X chromosome.[11] Of forty pairs of gay brothers investigated, thirty-three pairs shared the same marker. Among a randomly selected control group of brothers, Xq28 markers were randomly distributed. Although it is still curious that seven pairs of brothers did not show similarity in gene marking, the overall results are highly significant in indicating there is probably a gene or genes within this region that strongly influences sexual orientation.

Bolstering this conclusion is a new major study by William Turner (1995) investigating more than 200 families of homosexual male and female probands. Unlike the earlier studies, which looked at the sex ratio and heterosexual-homosexual composition of siblings, Turner compared the male-female parental sibling ratios in families. Instead of an anticipated 106 to 100, he found a very large unbalanced secondary sex ratio in the maternal generation of male, but not female, homosexuals, a highly significant ratio of twice (or more) as many aunts as uncles. The maternal uncle to aunt ratio for female homosexuals was about one to one. In his study, Turner also found 65 percent of the mothers of homosexuals had no or only one live-born brother. Fathers of homosexuals did not have sex ratio anomalies among their siblings. According to Turner's analysis, some 35 percent of the males conceived in the maternal generation were miscarried—a 50 percent excess of deaths of male concepti compared with female concepti. Other aspects of familiarity Turner found are multiple instances of infertility and suicides, almost exclusively among maternal rather than paternal relatives.

Turner did more: he compared these statistics with findings from other medical conditions with known genetic transmission rates, such as Addison's disease (adrenoleukodystrophy), color blindness, and hemophilia A. Male fetal wastage similar to that of offspring of fathers in families known to have male semilethal Xq28 disorders and children born to the mothers of these Xq28 problems show about the same ratio of those children born to mothers of homosexuals. Hemophilia A and color blindness were relatively rare in the control population. From his pedigree studies, Turner concludes that homosexuality is a semidominant genetic phenomenon, semilethal to males, with gene(s) in the pseudoautosomal region of Xq28.[12] Moreover, hypothesizes Turner, this region is very vulnerable to variable postmitotic cytosine methylation to produce the elongated trinucleotide repeats in the Xq28 region that Hamer et al. (1993) find a marker of homosexuality. All of these findings, regardless of rearing practices, support a genetic factor operating in sexual orientation.

Turner also contributes to this argument in another way. He cites numerous medical, biological, and social conditions in which monozygotic twins have been shown to differ although their parentage and environment are shared. But he makes the point that neither genetically nor environmentally does this mean their heritage is identical. While the environment may intuitively be accepted as variable between each member of a monozygotic twin set, it is also possible their genetics also differs. For instance, Kastern and Krypsin-Sorensen (1988) documented a set of monozygotic twins where one is male and the other female. They state: "While the role of chromosomal fragility in rearrangements is not certain, it is clear that somatic variations, such as translocations, deletions and so forth, in the genome are quite common. . . . The genome of mammals is a very plastic entity, capable of frequent changes and indicating subtle, but perhaps very important, differences from the genetic structure of the germ line." It has been estimated that approximately 1 in 20,000 males has two X chromosomes and no Y and about 1 in 20,000 females is XY (Kelly 1991).

Buhrich, Bailey, and Marlin (1991) studied twins specifically in an attempt to identify how much genetics or the environment might contribute to sexual preference. While they conservatively call their results tentative, they conclude "restrictive multivariate models yielded a significant genetic influence on sexual orientation."

Before leaving this section we must deal with the question: If sexual orientation is genetic, why don't all monozygotic twins behave similarly? Genetic transmission may follow patterns of other behaviors assumed to have a strong genetic component and yet not display 100 percent concordance in monozygotic pairs. Kaij (1960) found, for example, the rate of concordance for alcoholism to be 54 percent in monozygotic pairs and 24 percent for dizygotic pairs. Most significant, Nagylaki and Levy (1973) found monozygotic twins have more reversed asymmetries than dizygotic pairs; there is a larger proportion of discordance of handedness in monozygotic pairs. Also Bouchard and colleagues (1990), among the twins they studied, many reared apart since birth, found the traits most fixed by heredity were those intuitively thought to be most influenced by training. The closest links between twins were: 1) traditionalism or obedience to authority (the tendency to follow rules and authority, to endorse high moral standards and strict discipline), 2) harm avoidance (the tendency to shun the excitement of risk and danger), and 3) aggression (to be physically aggressive and vindictive). But even in these features, not all twins showed these traits equally. Even conjoined twins have often been seen to be quite disparate in temperament and interests.

It also must be appreciated that while monozygotic twins may share the same genetics, they might not share the same prenatal environment and only partially share the same postnatal one. Sexual orientation might be seen as biologically related to different *in utero* conditions. Melnick, Myrianthopolos, and Christian (1978), for example, have suggested that monochorionic twins are more alike than dichorionic twins. However, the shared blood circulation of the common chorion may be more unfavorable for one twin than the other. There often are, for instance, significant differences in birth weight between monozygotic twins. Sexual orientation may be biologically determined *in utero* by biochemical mechanisms that remain to be identified, but these influences must be recognized as under genetic influence.

Lastly, in considering genetics and homosexuality one must mention the work of Hall and Kimura (1994). These investigators detected that male heterosexuals and homosexuals differ significantly in the type of fingerprint pattern (leftward asymmetry) they possess. This biological feature is present before birth starting at about the seventh week post conception; about the same time sexual differentiation starts. Thus sexual orientation and dermatoglyphics must assort similarly or these two characteristics must be subject to the same prenatal processes.

Nervous System

It is true, but simplistic, to point out that males and females are anatomically significantly different in many more ways than in relation to genitals and the reproductive system. Mean height and weight differences and so forth are outward manifestations of other anatomical and physiological processes that differ over and above those mechanisms required for reproduction. Enzymatic processes of the brain and liver, workings of the kidney, and behavioral circadian rhythms, for instance, differ between men and women. Do these processes differ between heterosexuals and homosexuals? And what if they do? It is difficult for most laypeople and many scientists to see how physiological or biochemical differences could affect behavior even when they do.[13]

It is in the realm of the nervous system, however, that laypeople and scientists alike can accept that differences may have an influence on behavior. As the storehouse and mediator of instinct, reflex, and learning, the nervous system looks to be the ideal place to search for meaningful differences between males and females and those of different sexual orientations. In the past several years, this area of research has, like the classical sex chromatin work of Barr (1966), stimulated the imaginations of the general and gay public, as well as the scientific community.

Nervous System Structure

Research reports from the Netherlands were among the first to indicate that certain brain structures differ between males and females and heterosexuals and homosexuals. The Dutch researchers F. Swaab and M. A. Hofman (Swaab & Hofman 1990) found a brain region called the suprachiasmatic nucleus is much larger (approximately 1.7 times as large and containing 2.1 times as many cells) in homosexual males than in heterosexual males. Swaab and Fliers (1985), Swaab and Hofman (1988), and Swaab et al. (1993), found that the sexually dimorphic nucleus of the preoptic area (SDN-POA) of the human hypothalamus, as reported earlier for the rat by Gorski et al. (1978), also differed in size between men and women. Swaab and Hofman found the SDN-POA from brains of two male-to-female transsexuals fell within the female range, not the male range. Significantly, these researchers reported that this locus in the human, although first showing signs of development prenatally, seemed to be maximally differentiated between the ages of 2 and 4 years. Since this nucleus is involved in the regulation of sexual behavior in male and female rats and other species as well, this suggests human differences related to the organization and later activation of levels of human sexual activity may be more or less set from early on. Interestingly, Swaab and Hofman (1988) also found that the sex difference in this nucleus begins a sharp decline after the age of 50, about when the sex drive of men is said to diminish.

The comparison between heterosexual and homosexual brains was relatively new, but the findings of sex differences in the brain were not. Morel (1948) from France and Rabl (1958) from Germany had shown that the massa intermedia, a commissural fiber group linking thalamic lobes of the right and left, were different between the sexes. Newer studies in the United States by Allen and Gorski (1987) again found the massa intermedia 50 percent larger in females as in males and more often missing altogether in males (Allen & Gorski 1992). They found sex differences in the bed nucleus of the stria terminalis (Allen & Gorski 1990) and the anterior commissure. In animals the bed nucleus has been shown to be involved in sex-specific activities, aggression, sexual behavior, and neuroendocrine functioning. In all mammals, the anterior commissure is a major fiber bundle that links the right and left hemispheres.

These studies did not cause much of a stir until Simon LeVay, in the United States, found a region of the medial preoptic area of the hypothalamus (interstitial nucleus of the anterior hypothalamus, 3 or INAH3) smaller in homosexuals and women than in male heterosexuals (LeVay 1991). It is, on average, about two times larger in men than women and two to three times larger in heterosexual males than in homosexual males. And the INAH3 region of homosexuals is about the same size as that of the women's (LeVay 1993).[14] In some gay men the INAH3 was completely absent. The brains of lesbians have yet to be examined.

Others too reported that different areas of the human brain differ between males and females and that these differences are associated with nonreproductive as well as reproductive functions. But the work of LeVay, published in the widely read journal *Science,* stimulated review of and attention to brain differences that might be associated with sexual orientation. Allen et al. (1989), Allen and Gorski (1992), Hines et al. (1992), and Hines (1993) found that the anterior commissure is smallest in heterosexual males, larger in females, and largest in homosexual males. These differences held even after correction for overall brain size.

In 1982, de Lacoste-Utamsing and Holloway reported sexual dimorphism in the human corpus callosum. Demeter, Ringo, and Doty (1988) and Allen and Gorski (1992), while reporting some conflicting findings when looking at the corpus callosum (CC), the largest commissural body in the human brain, also report significant sex differences. After studying this structure, Hines reported (1993), "We have found that the size of the splenial [caudal] region of the corpus callosum, . . . reported to be larger in women than in men, may relate to sexual orientation in women. . . . Women with a history of some homosexual experience had significantly smaller midsagittal splenial areas than those whose sexual experience involved men only." Emory et al. (1991) looked for differences in the CC of transsexuals but found none; neither could they find sex differences. A recent study of the corpus callosum (Bosinski et al. 1994), however, reported the total size "relatively larger in females than in males and in female-to-male transsexuals. . . . Relative size of CC in FMT [female to male transsexuals] is different from ratios in their biological sex (female controls) and resembles that in males."

Most recently three new aspects of brain morphology were found to differ between homosexual and heterosexual males and between males and females. Scamvougeras et al. (1994) reported that the isthmus of the corpus callosum, associated with interhemispheric auditory transmissions, is on average 13 percent larger in gay men compared with straights, and Caillé and Lassonde (1994) reported these fibers differed between men and women. Also, patterns of neuronal density of cortical layers 2 and 6, the layers associated most with reception and distribution of intracortical information, were found to differ between males and females (Witelson, Glezer, & Kigar 1994). This finding is in keeping with many other sex differences reported by this investigator (see, e.g., Witelson 1991).

In addition to these findings from humans, much research on structural sex differences in the nervous system comes from animal experimentation studies. More than differences in the regions mentioned above, significant male-female differences have been found in the amygdala, an area associated with various emotions such as aggression and fear, and the spinal cord, associated with copulatory movements and functions (Clemens, Wagner & Ackerman 1993; for excellent reviews see Neumann & Steinbeck 1972 and Tobet & Fox 1992). Obviously, research in humans and animals focusing on brain differences between individuals with different sex, orientation, and identity is an area that will continue to receive a great deal of additional attention.

Nervous System Function

The functioning of the brain and nervous system has, since the 1950s and 1960s, been known to differ between men and women. Lansdell (1961, 1962) reported significant findings between men and women in their verbal ability and design preference, which reacts differentially to temporal lobe surgery. After surgery to the dominant lobe, women maintain their previous artistic judgment, while men lose theirs. This effect suggested to Lansdell that "judgment and verbal ability may overlap in the female brain, but are in opposite hemispheres [lateralized] in the male."[15] Lipsitt and Levy (1959) showed that at least some sex differences are set by 3 days of age; females have a lower threshold to electric shock stimulation than do males.

In more recent times the number of studies that show inherent sex differences in brain functioning has increased markedly (see Hampson & Kimura 1992 and Levy & Heller 1992 for review). These studies seldom fail to arouse consternation among those who feel that either this should not be or that such differences are the result of social conditioning or learning. One area of functioning in particular that has aroused critique is related to differences in mathematical and spatial reasoning between males and females.

A recent review by Camilla Benbow and David Lubinski (1993) shows that despite national testing agencies' continually trying to remove questions found to show the greatest gender disparities, males continue to outscore females in mathematical and spatial tasks at the highest levels. This holds even on tests, such as the SAT, where there is no sex difference in overall scores. The males score almost one-half standard deviation higher than do the females. And there is no evidence that these types of scoring differences have diminished among the highly gifted over the past decades.[16] Benbow and Lubinski document that this math ability is associated with enhanced right hemisphere brain functioning found in males and not females. Benbow (1988) suggests this difference is due to prenatal exposure to high levels of testosterone.

Wilmott and Brierley (1984) found that homosexual men scored lower on the

Wechsler Adult Intelligence Scale (WAIS) than did heterosexual men but comparable to heterosexual women. This IQ difference was thought related to significant differences in spatial ability. Such spatial ability differences were later specifically documented by Sanders and Ross-Field (1986) and confirmed by Gladue et al. (1990). Sanders and Ross-Field found that male homosexuals did less well than heterosexual males on two measures of spatial ability, the Vincent Mechanical Diagrams Test and the Water Level Task, a measure of horizontality. In 1993, Sanders and Wright reported that on performance tasks such as with targeted throwing and other manual dexterity tests, heterosexual men differed significantly from women and homosexual men. The heterosexual men were better at targeted throwing, while the women and homosexual men were better at pegboard tasks. Sanders (1994) recently also found the performance of homosexual men resembled that of heterosexual women more than heterosexual men in regard to different mechanical and visual tasks and cerebral lateralization less than heterosexual men. Others (Tkachuk & Zucker 1991; McCormick & Witelson 1991) also found similar differences related to sex and sexual orientation. This last team of investigators administered tests of verbal fluency. Here females typically show an advantage, and again the male homosexuals scored more like the high-scoring females than like the low-scoring heterosexual males. In essence, all of these studies show that heterosexual men were significantly better at tasks of spatial ability than were homosexual men or women and that male homosexuals either scored similarly to heterosexual women or intermediate to heterosexual men and women. Studies of the spatial ability or manual dexterity of lesbians have yet to be reported.[17] Animal research on the spatial ability of males and females shows strong sex differences and the organizational influences of gonadal steroids (Williams & Meck 1991, 1993).

Prenatal Influences

Although some of the sex differences noted may be directly linked to genetics, other crucial factors have to be considered. Any complete discussion of the etiology of anatomical and physiological differences between the sexes needs to deal with prenatal endocrine influences that intercede between the genetic influences and resulting sex-linked behaviors (Diamond 1965, 1968, 1979; Reinisch & Sanders 1992).

In mammals, genetic forces initiated by fertilization lead to gonadal processes—the maturation of testes or ovaries and release of their hormones, or absence thereof—that effect structural changes in genitalia and other structures and also organize the developing nervous system in gross and microscopic ways.[18, 19] This organization biases the individual toward male and or female behaviors. These influences are on reproductive and nonreproductive behaviors (Beatty 1979, 1992). This process is well documented for nonhuman mammalian species, and many reviews are available (Arnold & Gorski 1984; Diamond 1968, 1976; George & Wilson 1988; Gerall, Moltz & Ward 1992; Goy & McEwen

1980; Kelly 1992). By extension and evolutionary extrapolation, it is assumed that similar processes hold for humans, and indeed the references supply evidence for such. I have, for many years, proposed that organizational processes influence both sexual orientation and sexual identity (Diamond 1965, 1968, 1976, 1979, 1993a, 1994a, 1994b). Such has been adequately demonstrated in animal experimentation.

Starting in the late 1960s and into the 1980s much animal research, from many species, documented how hormones administered paranatally during critical periods could demasculinize and feminize male animals or masculinize and defeminize female ones.[20] Basically it was found that females exposed to testosterone during pregnancy or soon after birth, when adult, exhibit malelike copulatory behaviors and a lowered tendency to lordose, and males castrated or given antiandrogens during pregnancy or soon after birth, when adults, exhibit female copulatory behaviors and reduced male behaviors. The literature in this area is voluminous and has been well reviewed (Adler, Pfaff & Goy 1985; Arnold & Gorski 1984; Baum 1979; Döhler, Ganzemüller & Veit 1993; Gerall, Moltz & Ward 1992; Goy & McEwen 1980; Haug et al. 1993).

Work in the late 1980s and into the 1990s has greatly extended this area of research. Research, particularly in the Netherlands with the work of Slob and associates Bakker and Brand and in Sweden in the laboratories of Larsson and Vega-Matuszcyk (see References for the work of these authors), has shown that paranatal hormone manipulation during a critical period not only induces the changes noted but also significantly alters the development of sexual partner preference. Androgens given to a female rat during a critical period of neonatal or prenatal life induce her, when adult and treated with male hormones, to prefer a female sexual partner to a male. Conversely, neonatal castration or the administration of an antiandrogen to a male rat induces him, when adult, to prefer a male sexual partner when treated with female hormones.[21] Such behavior is not forthcoming from intact control animals. In essence, comparable influences are believed to intercede in human development.

Do these forces obtain for humans? Evidence is available to make it seem so. The strongest evidence comes from females that were subject to androgens prior to birth. This comes about from adrenal malfunctions of the fetus (congenital adrenal hyperplasia, CAH) or metabolic problems of the mother (e.g., adrenoblastoma). These individuals, depending on the amount of androgens to which they had been subjected and the timing of this exposure, vary in the demonstration of the effect. They might be only slightly affected or so affected they are misidentified as males at birth and reared accordingly. Overall, CAH females raised as women generally live and identify as women but show signs of defeminization and signs of physical and behavioral masculinization, and significantly, a higher-than-anticipated incidence of lesbianism (Ehrhardt, Epstein & Money 1968; Money, Schwartz & Lewis 1984). In one report by van Seters and Slob (1988) two CAH females not only adapted well to a crossed-sex assignment but married as men and, despite having only a micropenis (actually a hypertrophied clitoris) had "satisfactory" marital sexual relations with their wives.[22] (See Berenbaum 1990 for a review of CAH and intellectual and psychosexual functioning.)

On the opposite side of the coin are males who are somehow demasculinized and feminized. This is most dramatically seen in cases of androgen insensitivity. In such instances the XY individual is unable to utilize testosterone normally and thus retains the physical form of the female and the accompanying bias to female thinking patterns.[23] These persons are always raised as girls and seem to adapt well as women; albeit infertile ones. It might be argued that, raised as women, androgen-insensitive cases demonstrate the power of rearing. However, these individuals do not act as typical females but might be considered "hyperfemales." They almost invariably want to marry, have children, stay at home, and care for them. Few want to conquer the business world. Finally, consider that boys born to mothers subject to high dosages of estrogen during pregnancy showed extremely feminine behaviors despite normal male upbringing (Yalom, Green & Fisk 1973).

Significantly, it is not only endogenous hormones effects per se that might influence partner preference. Ward and coworkers (Ward 1972, 1977; Ward & Ward 1985; Ward & Weisz 1980, 1984) have shown that pregnant rats subject to extreme stress deliver male pups that, as adults, exhibit female lordosis patterns and fail to mate as males. This work was followed by others who showed that the stressors might include overcrowding (Dahlöf, Hård & Larsson 1977; Harvey & Chevins 1984) and malnutrition (Reese & Fleming 1981). The effect of stress has since been extended to other species and other behaviors (see Ward 1992 for review). Of particular interest is that the stressors can be of diverse types and affect brain and spinal cord sexual dimorphism.

Although the experimental work with animals is clear, the evidence for humans is still being gathered. Dörner et al. (1980), Ellis and Ames (1987), and Ellis et al. (1988) present data linking prenatal stress in human mothers to homosexuality in their sons. Dörner et al. looked at the effect of trauma from war, and Ellis looked at a set of thirty-one potentially stressful events in everyday life. This work follows from the animal literature but is controversial relative to the methods and criteria used for evaluating stress and the long retrospective period involved (Gandleman 1992). Also, the work of Bailey, Willerman, and Parks (1991) did not find the effect, but they report, "Mothers of effeminate children reported more stress-proneness than other mothers" and "Male homosexuality nevertheless was strongly familial." Further data are needed to substantiate or refute this thesis, but the door seems open to this influence.

It is also worthwhile mentioning the work of Reinisch and Karow (1977), who found significant personality differences among groups of children exposed prenatally to progestins or estrogens and their matched controls. Those exposed to progestins (with purported androgenic features) were "characterized as more independent, sensitive, self-assured, individualistic, and self-sufficient. In contrast, the subjects exposed to the estrogen regime were more group oriented and group dependent.'' These are differences usually associated with maleness and femaleness, respectively.

EVIDENCE: INDIRECT

Another line of thought seems to point to constitutional rather than environmental factors as directing sexual identity and orientation. These are instances where these vectors seem in conflict. Several types of studies are instructive here.

Upbringing and Culture

J. Imperato-McGinley (1983) and her colleagues (Imperato-McGinley et al. 1974, 1979; Imperato-McGinley & Peterson 1976) studied a group of indigenous persons in the Dominican Republic. These people were XY individuals who, due to a genetic quirk, were born without penises or a scrotum. During pregnancy these individuals had absent or reduced levels of 5a-reductase, which is needed to convert testosterone to dihydrotestosterone to differentiate the male genitals. Most subjects had separate urethral and vaginal openings within a urogenital sinus. Their parents thought these offspring to be girls and raised them accordingly. At puberty, however, the penis and scrotum developed.[24] Despite having been raised as females from birth, almost every one of these teenagers then switched to life as heterosexual males. Upbringing as girls destined to marry males had little influence on their adult orientation or sexual identity. Instead of being fixed in the sex of rearing from birth to puberty, these males readily adopted their sex-appropriate gender, orientation, and identity. Such cases, since they portray so little influence of upbringing, add grist to the argument that heterosexual orientation and masculine identity are more likely matters of genetic predisposition than social forces alone. Also reducing the factor of society is that similar findings were reported for indigenous populations in New Guinea, Turkey and among some Arabs in Israel. Here too, individuals reared as girls, on their own switched to living as males once past puberty.

Some argue (e.g., Gooren, Fliers & Courtney 1990) that the parents of these children knew in advance they would be switching their children's gender so these subjects do not constitute a true test of the nature-nurture issue. This is certainly true for the later cases studied, but it does not hold for the early cases, before the natives' association with modern medicine. Prior to contact, the children were reared as typical native girls until puberty and genital development, after which they switched to living as adolescent boys and married accordingly (Imperato-McGinley 1983). It also does not figure that if the parents knew the children would be boys after puberty, they would not raise them as boys from the start.

Work by Herdt (1981, 1984) and Stoller and Herdt (1985) offer examples where long-term exposure to childhood homosexual behaviors seems not to have induced postpubertal homosexual activity. These researchers document a New Guinea culture, the Sambia, where homosexual behavior is taught, encouraged, and institutionalized to transfer masculinity from adults to adolescents; the young boys are institutionalized to fellate the adult men to obtain their *mana* (spiritual power)-giving semen. Moreover, female bodies are presented as unattractive and poisonous, and to be avoided. Nevertheless, upon reaching adulthood, these boys choose females as regular sexual partners and are almost always heterosexual. Neither youths nor men report impulses to suck penises or engage in anal intercourse.

Schiefanhövel (1990) reports on a similar New Guinea culture, the Kaluli, who use anal intercourse to transmit the masculinity-inducing semen between older men and younger boys. He too stresses that heterosexual, not homosexual or bisexual, behavior is the preferred and exclusive outlet for these males when they mature. And this obtains despite a severe shortage of adult women due to female infanticide. Although adult-child same-sex activities are fostered in some societies, and this seems to have been part of the condition in ancient Greece (Cuillenain 1992), there is no known culture where adult-adult homosexual behavior is encouraged, is a preferred mode of behavior, or is a practice of other than a minority (Diamond 1993b; Ford & Beach 1951; Karlen 1971).

Sociologists Whitam and Mathy (1986) studied homosexuality in four different cultures: Brazil, Guatemala, the Philippines, and the United States. Across these quite diverse societies they found many similarities in how homosexual lifestyles were manifest—for example, preferences in occupational interests, involvement in entertainment and the arts, and cross-dressing. These researchers concluded that the similarities were not culturally instituted but were more likely the result of inherent biological tendencies manifest despite acceptance or rejection by the community. They conclude, "Sexual orientation is not highly subject to redefinition by any particular social structural arrangement" (p. 31).

There are societies in which homosexuality is not only illegal but subject to the death penalty (e.g., Iran) and societies in which the practice is tolerated or considered of little concern to the populace at large. And I have mentioned groups among which homosexual activities are encouraged as part of growing up. It is instructive to consider population figures to ascertain if the prevalence of homosexual activity is correlated with some environmental factor we might call social tolerance or intolerance. Intuitively it seems reasonable to assume that if homosexuality was a practice readily molded by culture, such behavior would be more prevalent in societies that tolerate it most or punish it least. This hypothesis is not supported by the data (Diamond 1993b), available from Britain, Denmark, France, Japan, the Netherlands, Palau, the Philippines, Thailand, and the United States. In the relatively nonhomophobic societies of Denmark, Palau, the Philippines, and Thailand, we find reported among the lowest rates of same-sex activity.[25]

Long-term longitudinal research studying the ontogenetic development of homosexuality is rare. Green (1987), in one of the few and perhaps best-known studies of this type, followed prepubertal boys with obvious effeminate behavior. These were matched with a control group of noneffeminate boys. Green's study lasted fifteen years, to see how the boys would develop. In U.S. culture being a "sissy" is socially difficult and stigmatized. Of the families involved with the "sissy" boys, many tried on their own as well as with professional help to discourage the effeminate behavior. A group of the parents even entered their sons into formal treatment programs to change their mannerisms. When interviewed as adults, "two-thirds of the original group of 'feminine' boys reveal that three-fourths of them developed as homosexual or bisexual. By contrast, only one of the two-thirds of the previously control boys was homosexually or bisexually oriented." The professional intervention did not alter the percentage of effeminate boys who, as adults, engaged in homosexual behavior.

Bell, Weinberg, and Hammersmith (1981) in the United States and Siegelman (1981a, 1981b) in Great Britain looked for features that might distinguish the family constellations and social backgrounds of adult heterosexuals, homosexuals, and bisexuals. Among other things, they were looking for evidence to support or refute hypotheses that associate homosexuality with a particular family constellation (e.g., close, binding and dominant mothers and weak, detached and rejecting fathers) as suggested by Bieber et al. (1962) and others. Their basic finding was that no common parameter of family or upbringing could be linked causally to sexual orientation, nor could any link be found between any aspect of an individual's childhood or adolescent experiences and homosexual or bisexual activities. Most homosexuals are reared as heterosexuals in apparently conventional households. Green (1987) said similarly about his group of effeminate boys.

Bell, Weinberg, and Hammersmith (1981) cautiously conclude: "Exclusive homosexuality seemed to be something that was firmly established by the end of adolescence and relatively impervious to change or modification by outside influences" (p. 211) and *"our findings are not inconsistent with what one would expect to find if, indeed, there were a biological basis for sexual preference"* (p. 216, emphasis in original).

Transsexuals

Transsexuals in many ways are the archetype to demonstrate that identity and orientation can be independent of rearing and environmental influences. Almost invariably these individuals are brought up in accordance with their bodily appearance. Then, against the wishes of their family and all social institutions, they refuse to continue in the life to which they feel they were wrongly born. If an XY individual is brought up as boy, the transsexual feels to be a girl and wishes to develop into a woman. If an XX individual is brought up as a girl, the opposite is true: this individual feels to be a boy and develop into a man (Benjamin 1966; Doctor 1988; Green & Money 1969). Often this occurs despite much evidence of success in the original gender (Diamond, 1995a).

This "fixedness" of heterosexuality, homosexuality, and transsexuality, despite accidental, family, or professional efforts to change these features, is noteworthy. Children brought up by transsexual parents do not develop as transsexuals, nor do those raised by homosexuals develop homosexually (Green 1978). Mandel, Hotvedt, and Green (1979) and Mandel and Hotvedt (1980) followed the development of boys raised in households where the parental influence was openly lesbian. They concluded, "Analysis of the children's data has not revealed any sexual identity conflict or homosexual interest. Relationships with fathers and other males do not differ significantly [from that of boys reared in heterosexually parented families]." There is "no evidence of gender conflict or poor peer relations" for samples of children reared by lesbian mothers (Hotvedt & Mandel 1982) and no significant differences between households run by lesbian or heterosexual mothers (Green et al. 1986). Similar work has been done studying boys growing up in households parented by openly gay males. These boys, when adult, like those brought up in lesbian households, also were heterosexually oriented without conflict or homosexual interest (Green 1978). Also, neither homosexuals nor heterosexuals perceived their parents' personalities differently (Newcomb 1985).

Cross-Sex Rearing

There are now known to me at least three instances, two sets of male twins and one singleton, in which an individual was reared as a female, with surgery and endocrine treatment to alter the biology to facilitate the transformation. The first case involved a set of twins extensively reported upon (Diamond 1982; Money & Ehrhardt 1972; Money & Tucker 1975). As a result of an accident during circumcision by cautery, one of the boys had his penis burned off. Believing that male identity requires a penis, it was decided to rear the individual as a female and augment the upbringing with surgical and endocrine treatment. The child was then subsequently reared as a girl. More than twenty years later, despite subsequent surgical orchiectomy, treatment with female hormones, rearing, and psychotherapy to facilitate a female psyche, this individual had never accepted the female status or role, despite earlier claims by Money and Ehrhardt (1972) and Money and Tucker (1975) (Diamond 1982, 1993a). From early on, the twin, without ever being told of his previous history, rebelled against the imposition of a female status. This individual, who was raised as a girl and given estrogen therapy, on his own elected to have a mastectomy and live as a male: he sought and had phalloplastic and scrotal reconstruction surgery. Now, as a mature adult, he lives as a married male. His adjustment is not without its difficulties but is preferable to imposed life as a female (Diamond & Sigmundson 1995).

The second set of identical twins involves two Samoan children who were brought to my attention when they were 6 years old. One was causing a great deal of disorder at school. The "female" of this twin set was acting rowdy and picking fights, not only with female classmates but also males. Case records revealed that ambiguous genitalia at birth had prompted the surgeons then in attendance to reassign him as a female. They convinced the parents to rear the child as a girl with appropriate castration and hormonal follow-up.

Despite the rearing as a female, even at this young age, the child rebelled against wearing girls' clothes and the parents' and teachers' admonitions to "act like a girl." His typical play patterns and demeanor were those of a 6-year-old rambunctious boy. In discussion with me, the brother often slipped into using the male pronoun when referring to his twin, for example, "*He,* I mean *she,* swims better than me." Asked to draw a child, the misassigned twin drew an ambiguous figure he identified as male. The child spontaneously expressed the desire to grow up as a boy.

The third case is similar. In 1990 I was called to review the behavior and condition of a 4-year-old child. Here again, the history revealed that due to the traumatic loss of a penis soon after birth, the decision was made to reassign the boy as a girl. The decision was followed with appropriate castration and therapy and the advice to rear the child as a girl. In consultation with Dr. Richard Green, then of UCLA, it became apparent that by the age of 4, this individual was exhibiting marked boyish behavior sufficient to disturb the parents and attending professionals; the child was not easily accepting the female role. The fixedness of behavior patterns along male lines, and aversion to the female role, was strong despite the contrary upbringing. This child, as far as is known, has not yet begun to show an erotic preference for males or females.

In these last two instances, the individuals were too young to express erotic interest in a sexual partner. I predict, as I did in regard to the first twin mentioned above (Diamond 1976, 1978, 1979), that despite being reared as girls, they will be gynophilic (heterosexual relative to biologic sex) (Diamond 1982). The post-natal removal of penis and testis in a human and imposition of a female rearing has never proved sufficient to overcome the inherent bias of the normally differentiated male nervous system.

A case I investigated with Dr. David Schnarch makes this point in a different way. A boy, at 3 years of age, was accidentally penectomized during a phimosis repair. The surgeons in residence wanted to "rectify" the situation by refashioning the genitals as a female and having the parents raise the child as a girl. It was determined, however, that the parents would not be sophisticated enough, motivated sufficiently, or otherwise capable of accepting and participating in this boy-to-girl transition. Also, experience with sex reassignment in a similar previous case had proved unsuccessful (Diamond 1982). The boy later had penile reconstruction, with favorable outcome. Now, at the age of 12, he has seemingly adjusted well, is socially accepted and identifies as a male. It is not known if he has had any sexual experiences.

In summary then, despite the supposed power of upbringing, role modeling, and learning, there is no known case anywhere in which an otherwise *normal* individual, even without suitable genitalia, has accepted rearing or life status in an imposed role of the sex opposite to that of his or her natural genetic and endocrine history or accepted an imposed homosexual sexual orientation. All cases of such supposedly happening have proved to be individuals genetically or endocrinologically influenced prior to birth.[26]

DISCUSSION AND CONCLUSIONS

This chapter started with a comment on evidence. One is also appropriate here: those who argue against a biological basis for sexual orientation often cite studies of negative findings that supposedly refute those of positive findings (e.g., Byne 1994; Byne & Parsons 1993). It is rare in biology or behavior to find all research to agree in every aspect of a long-running controversy. That is the nature of the controversy. If all evidence pointed in one direction, only the prejudiced would continue the debate. The behavioral and sexological sciences are not perfect. Argument by "objection" or "call for perfection" certainly might prompt additional research but will not yield solutions, nor do they really disprove a theory (Fearnside & Holther 1959). The opposition needs to do more: it needs to present strong alternative hypotheses with controlled research and data sufficient to substantiate them.

Any genetic patterning is complex because most parents of homosexuals are heterosexual and the input to any individual's development is numerous and both blunt and subtle. And there certainly are instances where one's manifestation of desired behaviors is modified by learning and social mores. Preferred innate behaviors of all types are avoided and nonpreferred ones adopted in order to comply with law or social pressures.

Looked at from another angle it can be asked, If sexual orientation is so easily modified by environmental forces, why don't we readily see its effect? Why is not therapy to change homosexual to heterosexual behavior readily successful even when started early and when parents and the individual are eager for such change (Green 1987)? If the basis for homosexual behavior is some set of environmental forces, why are these factors not only so difficult to identify but impossible to bolster with reliable and consistent findings? Those environmental forces most under suspicion have been looked for and found wanting. Certainly particular stages or critical periods in development seem more significant than others in organizing and activating these behaviors. Perhaps we have to be more sophisticated in selecting time periods to investigate or developing techniques of investigation.

Does this mean I think all features of the biological contribution to sexual orientation are understood? Hardly. We still have much to learn. Biology sets the predisposition, the bias to an orientation. The social experiences of the individual will determine how this bias is manifest and orientation evolves. One might have a constitution eminently suitable for swimming but never develop this skill without exposure to a pool; one can have great mathematical reasoning ability but never develop that skill without proper schooling. An individual may be mediocre in ability but excel as a result of certain experiences. The exposures, schooling, and experiences that are needed to release or mold the sexual orientation predisposition are yet to be documented. It is my guess, however, that the features needed to release these constitutional biases are quite plastic and the individual flexible in responding to opportunities. Free choice is also needed. The absent or weak father situation, when it seems associated with homosexuality, may be due to the child's being able to express himself or herself without excessive parental repression (Diamond 1979). (A model for how one's biological bias and predisposition might interact with the environment, via symbolism or learning or scripting, is offered in Diamond 1979.)

It must also be recognized that many individuals repeatedly manifest ambisexual and homosexual activities even when opportunities seem absent or against social dictates to the extent they put their social life, if not their actual physical life, in jeopardy. These behaviors, as with heterosexual ones, are often expressed as compulsive and self-generated and arising from within.

For some persons, the idea that sexual orientation is biologically biased toward heterosexuality or homosexuality and predisposed is threatening. They would like to think the choice is open and always fresh. This is more often a political stance than a scientific one. Others have expressed concern that if the developmental biological forces for sexual orientation are revealed, some nefarious agency might use the knowledge to force conformity to a dictated ideal or otherwise modify a potential homosexual outcome (DeCecco 1987; Gagnon 1987; Schmidt 1984; Sigusch et al. 1982; see also Dörner 1983). Believing it is social construction that leads to homosexual behavior is probably more destructive since even despots know it is easier to modify the social arena than the biological. And it has been shown by Ernulf, Innala, and Whitam (1989) that more people are tolerant of homosexual behavior if they think it is biological (see also Rosenberg, 1994). Regardless of such claims, I believe knowledge of the actual forces behind sexual orientation, whether they be biological or social, more than ignorance of these factors is increasingly likely to solve problems of social discord and foster a mutual respect for diversity.

NOTES

1. I first proposed and defended the interaction approach for humans in the 1960s. At this time it was generally believed that orientation and identity were solely products of the environment and upbringing (Diamond 1965, 1968, 1995b). Since then I have presented this view many times from different perspectives; see the References for details.

2. While this chapter assumes that most people accept that contemporary research holds that the expression of sexual orientation results from an interaction of biological and social forces, many persons still prefer to believe sexual orientation and partner preference are determined primarily or dominantly by social forces alone. See other chapters in this book for details.

3. The roots of bisexuality are similar to those for heterosexuality or homosexuality; for simplicity, however, discussion of bisexuality will be inferred from the basic overall discussion. A fuller exposition on bisexuality *per se* can be found in Diamond (1994b).

4. McConaghy and Armstrong (1983) cogently examine some aspects of the inter-relationship of orientation, identity, and gender and the way the terms are used. They went further: they found that subjects reporting a homosexual component were more consistent in their self-concept of identity than were those without homosexual components. This finding supports the ''hypothesis that subjects who are unaware of deviant sexual feelings [normal controls] may not have a strong, consistent sense of sexual identity'' dependent on standard environmental variables. Those whose characters are in question—homosexuals, transvestites, and transsexuals—may be more introspective about themselves and more consistent in their identity despite their usually typical rearing.

5. The distinctions of boy from man and girl from woman are typically those of age. In some cultures, however, they reflect parenthood, puberty, or accepted responsibility.

6. Since *gender* refers to human social views, it is confusing and obviously incorrect to use the term in regard to animals or when referring to biological differences.

7. The Kinsey scale is a seven-point ranking used as a shorthand measure of an individual's sexual orientation. Individuals whose sexual partners are all of the opposite sex are coded as $K = 0$; those whose partners are all of the same sex are coded as $K = 6$; those with half and half are coded as $K = 3$; and so on. This scale is used for both actual behavior and psychological desire or fantasy as well. Any individual might, for instance, be rated a 3 as a composite of a $K = 0$ in behavior with a $K = 6$ in fantasy.

8. The sexual behavior studies by Kinsey et al. (1948, 1953), in contrast to the personal view of Kinsey himself, hinted that the data they found pointed to biological factors as involved in sexual attraction.

9. Diamond and Young (1963) and Diamond, Westphal, and Rust (1969) showed that, in guinea pigs, there existed mechanisms that protect the mother during pregnancy from masculinization by androgens produced by male fetuses. These processes probably also occur in humans.

10. By no means do I think this would be a simple mechanism. Otherwise, it would certainly have been detected by now.

11. To systematize investigations of the human genome, all chromosome regions have been given identifying designations.

12. Why the loading of male offspring among male siblings of homosexuals but the loading in favor of females in the maternal generation is not clear.

13. Indeed, these biochemical differences may be quite important in engendering or signaling significant sex differences; they may even be more important than physical differences. However, their ''distance'' from any easy proximate behavior may shield them from easy discovery.

14. The range in size measured for this nucleus showed overlap in the sizes of the structure examined, so some females have nuclei larger than some males.

15. In concert with this finding, the size of the corpus callosum in women has been shown related positively to verbal fluency and negatively to language lateralization. See Hines et al. (1992), for an extended discussion of this cognitive functioning and brain differences.

16. There is a great sex difference in dispersion. Males are also overrepresented at the

lower end of the scoring as well. Meta-analytic reviews usually fail to consider these range differences but concentrate on means.

17. Studies of lesbians are relatively rare due to their small proportion in the general population (Diamond 1993a) and their comparatively more frequent reluctance to volunteer for such studies.

18. Fish and other nonmammalian vertebrate species are, in contrast, more definitely and dramatically influenced by environmental factors in their sexual development. See Diamond (1993a, 1994b) and Francis (1992).

19. *Organization* is a technical term used in embryology. It implies that the nervous system is programmed during pregnancy for activation later in life, usually starting at puberty.

20. Masculinization and feminization are not opposite ends of a continuum. They are two separate dimensions of gender patterns and mechanisms.

21. The mediation of these early endocrine influences is only briefly indicated here. The mode of action of different gonadal products, their metabolites or aromatized forms, in this process of sexual differentiation, development, or partner selection is noteworthy and should be appreciated. See, for example, Olsen (1993) and the other sources indicated in this section for an in-depth analysis.

22. It is true that these individuals, reared as males, as well as some of those from the earlier reports, can be said to be responding to environmental factors in "adopting" a homosexual orientation. However, the majority of such XX persons are not reared as males.

23. The inability to utilize testosterone is due to a genetically transmitted enzyme deficiency that prevents the body tissues from responding to the androgen.

24. The exact mechanism of this phenomenon is still being elucidated. It may be that at puberty the genital tissues become responsive to the circulating testosterone or levels of dihydrotestosterone increase. The full issue of *in utero* and pubertal sexual differentiation in these individuals is reviewed by Imperato-McGinley (1983).

25. Indeed, it may be because the incidence of homosexuality is so low in these societies that they are more tolerant of the practice. The chicken-and-egg question persists.

26. Unquestionably, fear of imprisonment or other severe punishment can induce an individual to avoid certain preferred behaviors or adopt nonpreferred ones. Here, however, we are considering instances where open choice is available and extreme conditions are not at issue.

REFERENCES

Adler, N., Pfaff, D., & Goy, R. W. (1985). *Handbook of behavioral neurobiology.* New York: Plenum Press.

Allen, L. S., & Gorski, R. A. (1987). Sex differences in the human massa intermedia. *Society of Neurosciences Abstracts, 13,* 46.

Allen, L. S., & Gorski, R. A. (1990). Sex differences in the bed nucleus of the stria terminalis of the human brain. *Journal of Comparative Neurology, 302,* 697–706.

Allen, L. S., & Gorski, R. A. (1991). Sexual dimorphism of the anterior commissure and massa intermedia of the human brain. *Journal of Comparative Neurology, 312,* 97–104.

Allen, L. S., & Gorski, R. A. (1992, August). Sexual orientation and the size of the anterior commissure in the human brain. *Proceedings of the National Academy of Sciences, 89,* 7199–7202.

Allen, L. S., Hines, M., Shryne, J. E., & Gorski, R. A. (1989). Two sexually dimorphic cell groups in the human brain. *Journal of Neuroscience, 9*(2), 497–506.

Arnold, A. P., & Gorski, R. A. (1984). Gonadal steroid induction of structural sex differences in the central nervous system. *Annual Review of Neuroscience, 7,* 413–442.

Bailey, J. M., & Bell, A. P. (1993). Familial aggregation of female sexual orientation. *Behavior Genetics, 23*(4), 312–322.

Bailey, J. M., & Benishay, D. S. (1993). Familial aggregation of female sexual orientation. *American Journal of Psychiatry, 150*(2), 272–277.

Bailey, J. M., Miller, J. S., & Wellerman, L. (1993). Maternally rated childhood gender nonconformity in homosexuals and heterosexuals. *Archives of Sexual Behavior, 22*(5), 461–469.

Bailey, J. M., & Pillard, R. C. (1991, December). A genetic study of male sexual orientation. *Archives of General Psychiatry, 48,* 1089–1096.

Bailey, J. M., Pillard, R. C., Neale, M. C., & Agyei, Y. (1993, March). Heritable factors influence sexual orientation in women. *Archives of General Psychiatry, 50,* 217–223.

Bailey, J. M., Willerman, L., & Parks, C. (1991). A test of the maternal stress theory of human male homosexuality. *Archives of Sexual Behavior, 20,* 277–293.

Bakker, J., Brand, T., Ophemert, J. van., & Slob, A. K. (1993). Hormonal regulation of adult partner preference behavior in neonatally ATD-treated male rats. *Behavioral Neuroscience, 107*(3), 480–487.

Bakker, J., Ophemert, J. v., Eijskoot, F., & Slob, A. K. (1994). A semiautomated test apparatus for studying partner preference behavior in the rat. *Physiology and Behavior, 56*(3), 597–601.

Bakker, J., Ophemert, J. v., & Slob, A. K. (1993). Organization of partner preference and sexual behavior and its nocturnal rhythmicity in male rats. *Behavioral Neuroscience, 107*(6), 1049–1058.

Bakker, J., Ophemert, J. v., & Slob, A. K. (1995). Postweaning housing conditions and partner preference and sexual behavior of neonatally ATD-treated male rats. *Psychoneuroendocrinology, 20*(3), 299–310.

Barr, M. L. (1966). The significance of the sex chromatin. *International Review of Cytology, 19,* 35–95.

Baum, M. J. (1979). Differentiation of coital behavior in mammals—A comparative analysis. *Neuroscience Biobehavior Review, 3,* 265–284.

Beatty, W. W. (1979). Gonadal hormones and sex differences in non reproductive behavior in rodents: Organizational and activational influences. *Hormones and Behavior, 12,* 112–163.

Beatty, W. W. (1992). Gonadal hormones and sex differences in nonreproductive behaviors. In A. A. Gerall, H. Moltz, & I. L. Ward (Eds.), *Sexual differentiation* (pp. 85–128). New York: Plenum Press.

Bell, A. P., Weinberg, M. S., & Hammersmith, S. K. (1981). *Sexual preference—Its development in men and women.* Bloomington: Alfred C. Kinsey Institute of Sex Research.

Benbow, C. P. (1988). Sex differences in mathematical reasoning ability in intellectually talented preadolescents: Their nature, effects, and possible causes. *Behavioral and Brain Science, 11,* 169–232.

Benbow, C. P., & Lubinski, D. (1993). Consequences of gender differences in mathematical reasoning ability and some biological linkages. In M. Haug, R. E. Whalen, C. Aron & K. L. Olsen (Eds.), *The development of sex differences and similarities in behavior.* Dordrecht: Kluwer Academic Publishers.

Benjamin, H. (1966). *The transsexual phenomenon.* New York: Julian Press.

Berenbaum, S. A. (1990). Congenital adrenal hyperplasia: Intellectual and psychosexual functioning. In C. S. Holmes (Ed.), *Psychoneuroendocrinology: Brain, behavior, and hormonal interactions* (pp. 227–260). New York: Springer-Verlag.

Bieber, I., Dain, H. J., Dince, P. R., Drellich, M. G., Grand, H. G., Grundlach, R. H., Kremer, M. W., Rifkin, A. H., Wilbur, C. B., & Bieber, T. B. (1962). *Homosexuality: A psychoanalytic study.* New York: Basic Books.

Blanchard, R., & Sheridan, P. M. (1992). Sibling size, sibling sex ratio, birth order, and parental age in homosexual and nonhomosexual gender dysphorics. *Journal of Nervous and Mental Diseases, 180*(1), 40–47.

Blanchard, R., & Zucker, K. J. (1994). Reanalysis of Bell, Weinberg, and Hammersmith's data on birth order, sibling sex ratio, and parental age in homosexual men. *American Journal of Psychiatry, 151*(9), 1375–1376.

Blanchard, R., Zucker, K. J., Bradley, S. J., & Hume, C. S. (1994). Birth order and sibling sex ratio in homosexual male adolescents and probably prehomosexual feminine boys. *Developmental Psychology, 31*(1), 22–30.

Bolin, A. (1987). *In search of Eve: Transsexual rites of passage.* South Hadley, MA: Bergin & Garvey.

Bosinski, H. A. G., Schubert, F., Willie, R., Heller, M., & Arndt, R. (1994). *MRI of corpus callosum and neurophysiological functions in female-to-male transsexuals.* Edinburgh: International Academy for Sex Research Conference.

Bouchard, T. J., Lykken, D. T., McGue, M., Segal, N. L., & Tellegen, A. (1990). Sources of human psychological differences: A Minnesota study of twins reared apart. *Science, 250,* 223–228.

Brand, T., Houtsmuller, E. J., & Slob, A. K. (1990). Androgens and the propensity for adult mounting behavior in the female Wistar rat. In J. Balthazart (Ed.), *Hormones, brain and behaviour in vertebrates. vol. 1. Sexual differentiation, neuroanatomical aspects, neurotransmitters and neuropeptides. Comparative physiology* (pp. 15–29). Basel: S. Karger.

Brand, T., Houtsmuller, E. J., & Slob, A. K. (1993). Neonatal programming of adult partner preference in male rats. In M. Haug, R. E. Whalen, C. Aron & K. L. Olsen (Eds.), *The development of sex differences and similarities in behaviour* (pp. 33–49). Dordrecht: Kluwer Academic Publishers.

Brand, T., & Slob, A. K. (1991a). Neonatal organization of adult partner preference behavior in male rats. *Physiology and Behavior, 49,* 107–111.

Brand, T., & Slob, A. K. (1991b). On the organization of partner preference behavior in female Wistar rats. *Physiology and Behavior, 49,* 549–555.

Buhrich, N., Bailey, J. M., & Martin, N. G. (1991). Sexual orientation, sexual identity, and sex dimorphic behaviors in male twins. *Behavior Genetics, 21,* 75–96.

Byne, W. (1994, May). The biological evidence challenged. *Scientific American,* 50–55.

Byne, W., & Parsons, B. (1993). Human sexual orientation: The biological theories reappraised. *Archives of General Psychiatry, 50,* 228–239.

Caillé, S., & Lassonde, M. (1994). Gender differences in sensory interhemispheric trans-
    mission times. *Abstracts: Society for Neuroscience,* 1425.
Clemens, L. G., Wagner, C. K., & Ackerman, A. E. (1993). A sexually dimorphic motor
    nucleus: Steroid sensitive afferents, sex differences and hormonal regulation. In
    M. Haug, R. E. Whalen, C. Aron & K. L. Olsen (Eds.), *The development of sex
    differences and similarities in behaviour* (pp. 19–31). Dordrecht: Kluwer Aca-
    demic Publishers.
Cuillenain, C. O. (1992). *Bisexuality in the ancient world.* New Haven, CT.: Yale Uni-
    versity Press.
Dahlöf, L.-G., Hård, E., & Larsson, K. (1977). Influence of maternal stress on the de-
    velopment of offspring sexual behaviour. *Animal Behaviour, 25,* 958–963.
Davison, K., Brierley, H., & Smith, C. (1971). A male monozygotic twinship discordant
    for homosexuality. *British Journal of Psychiatry, 118,* 675–682.
DeCecco, J. P. (1987). Homosexuality's brief recovery: Pertaining to sex research. *Jour-
    nal of Sex Research, 23*(1), 106–129.
de Lacoste-Utamsing, C., & Holloway, R. L. (1982). Sexual dimorphism in the human
    corpus callosum. *Science, 216,* 1431–1432.
Demeter, S., Ringo, J. L., & Doty, R. W. (1988). Morphometric analysis of the human
    corpus callosum and anterior commissure. *Human Neurobiology, 6,* 219–226.
Diamond, M. (1965). A critical evaluation of the ontogeny of human sexual behavior.
    Quarterly Review of Biology, 40, 147–175.
Diamond, M. (1968). Genetic-endocrine interaction and human psychosexuality. In
    M. Diamond (Ed.), *Perspectives in reproduction and sexual behavior* (pp. 417–
    443). Bloomington: Indiana University Press.
Diamond, M. (1976). Human sexual development: Biological foundation for social de-
    velopment. In F. A. Beach (Ed.), *Human sexuality in four perspectives* (pp. 22–
    61). Baltimore: Johns Hopkins Press.
Diamond, M. (1978 March–April). Sexual identity and sex roles. *Humanist,* 16–19.
Diamond, M. (1979). Sexual identity and sex roles. In V. Bullough (Ed.), *The frontiers
    of sex research* (pp. 33–56). Buffalo, NY: Prometheus.
Diamond, M. (1982). Sexual identity, monozygotic twins reared in discordant sex roles
    and a BBC follow-up. *Archives of Sexual Behavior, 11*(2), 181–185.
Diamond, M. (1992). *Sexwatching: Looking at the world of sexual behaviour* (2nd ed.).
    London: Prion Books.
Diamond, M. (1993a). Some genetic considerations in the development of sexual ori-
    entation. In M. Haug, R. E. Whalen, C. Aron & K. L. Olsen (Eds.), *The devel-
    opment of sex differences and similarities in behavior* (pp. 291–309). Dordrecht:
    Kluwer Academic Publishers.
Diamond, M. (1993b). Homosexuality and bisexuality in different populations. *Archives
    of Sexual Behavior, 22*(4), 291–311.
Diamond, M. (1994a). Sexuality: Orientation and identity. In R. J. Corsini (Ed.), *Ency-
    clopedia of psychology* (pp. 399–402). New York: John Wiley & Sons.
Diamond, M. (1994b). Bisexualitat aus biologischer Sicht (Bisexuality: Biological as-
    pects). In E. J. Haeberle & R. Gindorf (Eds.), *Bisexualitäten: Ideologie und Praxis
    des Sexualkontaktes mit beiden Geschlechtern* ([Bisexualities: Ideology and prac-
    tices of sexual contact with both sexes]) (pp. 41–68). Stuttgart: Gustav Fischer
    Verlag.
Diamond, M. (1995a). (In press). Self-testing: A check on sexual levels. In B. Bullough,

V. L. Bullough & J. Elias (Eds.), *Cross dressing and transgenderism*. Buffalo, New York: Prometheus.

Diamond, M. (1995b). (In press). Behavioral predisposition: Biased interaction. *Journal of Sex and Marital Therapy*.

Diamond, M., & Karlen, A. (1980). *Sexual decisions*. Boston: Little, Brown.

Diamond, M., Rust, N., & Westphal, U. (1969). High-affinity binding of progesterone, testosterone and cortisol in normal and androgen treated guinea pigs during various reproductive stages: Relationship to masculinization. *Endocrinology, 84*, 1143–1151.

Diamond, M., & Sigmundson, K. (1995). Sexual malassignment: Long term follow-up. In preparation.

Diamond, M., & Young, W. C. (1963). Differential responsiveness of pregnant and nonpregnant guinea pigs to the masculinizing action of testosterone propionate. *Endocrinology, 72*, 429–438.

Doctor, R. F. (1988). *Transvestites and transsexuals*. New York: Plenum Press.

Döhler, K. D., Ganzemüller, C., & Veit, C. (1993). The development of sex differences and similarities in brain anatomy, physiology and behavior is under complex hormonal control. In M. Haug, R. E. Whalen, C. Aron & K. L. Olsen (Eds.), *The development of sex differences and similarities in behaviour* (pp. 341–361). Dordrecht: Kluwer Academic Publishers.

Dörner, G. (1983). Letter to the editor. *Archives of Sexual Behavior, 12*(6), 577–582.

Dörner, G., Geier, T., Ahrens, L., Krell, L., Munx, G., Sieler, H., Kittner, E., & Muller, H. (1980). Prenatal stress as a possible etiological factor in homosexuality in human males. *Endokrinologie, 75*, 365–368.

Dörner, G., Schenk, B., Schmiedel, B., & Ahrens, L. (1983). Stressful events in prenatal life of bi- and homosexual men. *Experimental and Clinical Endocrinology, 81*, 83–87.

Eckert, E., Bouchard, T., Bohlen, J., & Heston, L. (1986). Homosexuality in monozygotic twins reared apart. *British Journal of Psychiatry, 148*, 421–425.

Ehrhardt, A., Epstein, R., & Money, J. (1968). Fetal androgens and female gender identity in the early-treated adrenogenital syndrome. *Johns Hopkins Medical Journal, 122*, 160–167.

Ellis, L., & Ames, M. A. (1987). Neurohormonal functioning and sexual orientation: A theory of homosexuality-heterosexuality. *Psychological Bulletin, 10*(2), 233–258.

Ellis, L., Ames, M. A., Peckham, W., & Burke, D. (1988). Sexual orientation of human offspring may be altered by severe maternal stress during pregnancy. *Journal of Sex Research, 25*(1), 152–157.

Emory, L. E., Williams, D. H., Collier, M. C., Amparo, E. G., & Meyer, W. J. (1991). Anatomic variation of the corpus callosum in persons with gender dysphoria. *Archives of Sexual Behavior, 20*(4), 409–417.

Ernulf, K., Innala, S., & Whitam, F. (1989). Biological explanation, psychological explanation, and tolerance of homosexuals: A cross-national analysis of beliefs and attitudes. *Psychological Reports, 65*, 1003–1010.

Fearnside, W. W., & Holther, W. B. (1959). *Fallacy: The counterfeit of argument*. Englewood Cliffs, NJ: Prentice-Hall.

Ford, C. S., & Beach, F. A. (1951). *Patterns of sexual behavior*. New York: Harper & Row.

Francis, R. C. (1992). Sexual liability in teleosts: Developmental factors. *Quarterly Review of Biology, 67*(1), 1–18.

Friedman, R. C., Wollesen, F., & Tendler, R. (1976). Psychological development and blood levels of sex steroids in male identical twins of divergent sexual orientation. *Journal of Nervous and Mental Diseases, 163,* 282–288.

Gagnon, J. H. (1987). Science and the politics of pathology. *Journal of Sex Research, 23*(1), 120–123.

Gagnon, J. H., & Simon, W. (1973). *Sexual conduct: The social origins of human sexuality.* Chicago: Aldine.

Gandelman, R. (1992). *The psychobiology of behavioral development.* New York: Oxford University Press.

George, F. W., & Wilson, J. D. (1988). Sex determination and differentiation. In E. Knobil & J. N. et al. (Eds.), *The physiology of reproduction* (pp. 3–26). New York: Raven Press.

Gerall, A. A., Moltz, H., & Ward, I. L. (1992). *Handbook of behavioral neurobiology.* New York: Plenum Press.

Gilson, M., Brown, E. C., & Daves, W. F. (1982). Sexual orientation as measured by perceptual dominance in binocular rivalry. *Personality and Social Psychology Bulletin, 8*(3), 494–500.

Gladue, B. (1993). The psychobiology of sexual orientation. In M. Haug, R. E. Whalen, C. Aron, & K. L. Olsen (Eds.), *The development of sex differences and similarities in behaviour* (pp. 437–455). Dordrecht: Kluwer Academic Publishers.

Gladue, B., Beatty, W. W., Larson, J., & Staton, R. D. (1990). Sexual orientation and spatial ability in men and women. *Psychobiology, 18,* 101–108.

Gooren, L., Fliers, E., & Courtney, K. (1990). Biological determinants of sexual orientation. In J. Bancroft (Ed.), *Annual review of sex research* (pp. 175–196). Lake Mills, IA: Society for the Scientific Study of Sex.

Gorski, R. A., Gordon, J. H., Shrayne, J. E., & Southam, A. M. (1978). Evidence for a morphological sex difference within the medial preoptic area of the rat brain. *Brain Research, 148,* 333–346.

Goy, R. W., & McEwen, B. S. (1980). *Sexual differentiation of the brain.* Cambridge, MA: MIT Press.

Green, R. (1978). Sexual identity of 37 children raised by homosexuals or transsexual parents. *Psychiatry, 135*(6), 692–697.

Green, R. (1987). *The "sissy boy syndrome" and the development of homosexuality.* New Haven: Yale University Press.

Green, R., Mandel, J. B., Hotvedt, M. E., Gray, J., & Smith, L. (1986). Lesbian mothers and their children: A comparison with solo parent heterosexual mothers and their children. *Archives of Sexual Behavior, 15*(2), 167–184.

Green, R., & Money, J. (1969). *Transsexualism and sex reassignment.* Baltimore, MD: Johns Hopkins Press.

Green, R., & Stoller, R. J. (1971). Two monozygotic (identical) twin pairs discordant for homosexuality. *Archives of Sexual Behavior, 1*(4), 321–327.

Hall, J. A. Y., & Kimura, D. (1994). Dermatoglyphic asymmetry and sexual orientation in men. *Behavioral Neuroscience, 108*(6), 1203–1206.

Hamer, D. H., Hu, S., Magnuson, V. L., Hu, N., & Pattatucci, A. M. L. (1993). A linkage between DNA markers on the X chromosome and male sexual orientation. *Science, 261,* 321–327.

Hampson, E., & Kimura, D. (1992). Sex differences and hormonal influences on cognitive function in humans. In J. B. Becker, S. M. Breedlove & D. Crews (Eds.), *Behavioral endocrinology* (pp. 357–358). Cambridge: MIT Press.

Harvey, P. W., & Chevins, P. F. D. (1984). Crowding or ACTH treatment of pregnant mice affects adult copulatory behavior of male offspring. *Hormones and Behavior, 18,* 101–110.

Haug, M., Whalen, R. E., Aron, C., & Olsen, K. (Eds.). (1993). *The development of sex differences and similarities in behavior.* Dordrecht: Kluwer Academic Publishers.

Herdt, G. H. (1981). *Guardians of the flute: Idioms of masculinity.* New York: McGraw-Hill.

Herdt, G. H. (1984). Semen transaction in Sambia culture. In G. H. Herdt (Ed.), *Ritualized homosexuality in Melanesia* (pp. 167–210). Berkeley: University of California Press.

Heston, L. L., & Shields, J. (1968). Homosexuality in twins: A family study and a registry study. *Archives of General Psychiatry, 18,* 149–160.

Hines, M. (1990). Gonadal hormones and human cognitive development. In J. Balthazart (Ed.), *Hormones, brain and behavior in Vertebrates. vol. 1. Sexual Differentiation, neuroanatomical aspects, neurotransmitters and neuropeptides* (pp. 51–63). Basel: Karger.

Hines, M. (1993). Hormonal and neural correlates of sex-type cognitive development in human beings. In M. Haug, R. E. Whalen, C. Aron & K. L. Olsen (Eds.), *The development of sex differences and similarities in behavior.* Dordrecht: Kluwer Academic Publishers.

Hines, M., Chiu, L., McAdams, L. A., & Bentler, P. (1992). Cognition and the corpus callosum: Verbal fluency, visuospatial ability, and language lateralization related to midsagittal surface areas of callosal subregions. *Behavioral Neurosciences, 106*(1), 3–14.

Hotvedt, M. E., & Mandel, J. B. (1982). Children of lesbian mothers. In W. Paul, J. D. Weinrich, J. C. Gonsiorek & M. E. Hotvedt (Eds.), *Homosexuality: Social, psychological and biological issues* (pp. 275–285). Beverly Hills: Sage.

Imperato-McGinley, J. (1983). Sexual differentiation: Normal and abnormal. In L. Martini & V. H. T. James (Eds.), *Current topics in experimental endocrinology: Fetal endocrinology and metabolism* (pp. 231–307). New York: Academic Press.

Imperato-McGinley, J., Geurrero, L., Gautier, T., & Peterson, R. E. (1974). Steroid 5a-reductase deficiency in man: An inherited form of pseudohermaphroditism. *Science, 186,* 1213–1215.

Imperato-McGinley, J., & Peterson, R. E. (1976). Male pseudohermaphroditism: The complexities of male phenotypic development. *American Journal of Medicine, 61,* 251–272.

Imperato-McGinley, J., Peterson, R. E., Gautier, T., & Sturia, E. (1979). Androgen and evolution of male-gender identity among male pseudohermaphrodites with 5a-reductase deficiency. *New England Journal of Medicine, 300,* 1233–1237.

Jensch, K. (1941). Weiter Betrag zur Genealogie der Homosexualitat. *Archives Psychiatrika Nervenkranken, 112,* 679–696.

Julian, J. (1973). *Social problems.* Englewood Cliffs, NJ: Prentice-Hall.

Kaij, L. (1960). *Alcoholism in twins.* Stockholm: Alqvist and Wiksell.

Kallmann, F. J. (1952a). Twin and sibship study of overt male homosexuality. *American Journal of Human Genetics, 4,* 136–146.

Kallmann, F. J. (1952b). Comparative twin study on the genetic aspects of male homosexuality. *Journal of Nervous and Mental Disease, 115,* 283–298.

Kallmann, F. J. (1963). Genetic aspects of sex determination and sexual maturation potentials in man. In G. Winokur (Ed.), *Determinants of human sexual behavior* (pp. 5–18). Springfield, IL: Charles C. Thomas.

Karlen, A. (1971). *Sexuality and homosexuality: A new view.* New York: W. W. Norton & Co.

Kastern, W., & Krypsin-Sorensen, I. (1988). Penetrance and low concordance in monozygotic twins in disease: Are they results of alteration in somatic genomes? *Molecular Reproductive Development, 1,* 63–75.

Kelly, D. D. (1991). Sexual differentiation of the nervous system. In E. R. Kandel, J. H. Schwartz & T. M. Jessell (Eds.), *Principles of neural science* (pp. 959–973). Norwalk, CT: Appleton & Lange.

Kinsey, A. C., Pomeroy, W. B., & Martin, C. E. (1948). *Sexual behavior in the human male.* Philadelphia: W. B. Saunders Company.

Kinsey, A. C., Pomeroy, W. B., Martin, C. E., & Gebhard, P. H. (1953). *Sexual behavior in the human female.* Philadelphia: W. B. Saunders Company.

Kirsch, J. A. W., & Rodman, J. E. (1982). Selection and sexuality: The Darwinian view of homosexuality. In J. D. W. William Paul, J. C. Gonsiorek & M. E. Hotvedt (Eds.), *Homosexuality: Social, psychological and biological issues* (pp. 183–196). Beverly Hills: Sage.

Klintworth, G. K. (1962). A pair of male monozygotic twins discordant for homosexuality. *Journal of Nervous and Mental Disease, 135,* 113–125.

Lang, T. (1940). Studies on the genetic determination of homosexuality. *Journal of Nervous and Mental Disease, 92,* 55–64.

Lang, T. (1960). Die Homosexualität als genetisches Problem. *Acta Genetica Medical Gemellol., 9,* 370–381.

Lansdell, H. (1961). The effect of neurosurgery on a test of proverbs. *American Psychologist, 16,* 418.

Lansdell, H. (1962). A sex difference in effect of temporal lobe neurosurgery on design preference. *Nature, 194,* 852–854.

LeVay, S. (1991, August 30). A difference in hypothalamic structure between heterosexual and homosexual men. *Science, 253,* 1034–1037.

LeVay, S. (1993). *The sexual brain.* Cambridge, MA: MIT Press.

LeVay, S., & Hamer, D. H. (1994, May). Evidence for a biological influence in male homosexuality. *Scientific American,* 44–49.

Levy, J., & Heller, W. (1992). Gender differences in neuropsychological function. In A. A. Gerall, H. Moltz & I. L. Ward (Eds.), *Sexual differentiation* (pp. 245–274). New York: Plenum Press

Lipsitt, I. P., & Levy, N. (1959). Electrotactile threshold in the neonate. *Child Development, 30,* 547–554.

McConaghy, N., & Armstrong, M. S. (1983). Sexual orientation and consistency of sexual identity. *Archives of Sexual Behavior, 12*(4), 317–327.

McConaghy, N., & Blaszeczynski, M. A. (1980). A pair of monozygotic twins discordant for homosexuality: Sex-dimorphic behavior and penile volume responses. *Archives of Sexual Behavior, 9*(2), 123–131.

McCormick, C. M., & Witelson, S. F. (1991). A cognitive profile of homosexual men compared to heterosexual men and women. *Psychoneuroendocrinology, 16,* 459–473.

MacCulloch, M. J., & Waddington, J. L. (1981). Neuroendocrine mechanisms and the aetiology of male and female homosexuality. *British Journal of Psychiatry, 139,* 341–345.

Mandel, J. B., & Hotvedt, M. E. (1980). Lesbians as parents. *Huisarts & Praktijk, 4,* 31–34.

Mandel, J. B., Hotvedt, M. E., & Green, R. (1979, September). *The lesbian parents: Comparison of heterosexual and homosexual mothers and their children.* Presented at Annual Meeting of the American Psychological Association.

Masters, W. H., & Johnson, V. (1966). *Human sexual response.* Boston: Little, Brown.

Masters, W. H., & Johnson, V. E. (1979). *Homosexuality in perspective.* Boston: Little, Brown.

Melnick, M., Myrianthopolos, N. C., & Christian, J. C. (1978). The effects of chorion on variation in I.Q. in the NCPP twin population. *American Journal of Human Genetics, 30,* 425–433.

Meskinoff, A. M., Rainer, J. D., Kolb, L. C., & Carr, A. C. (1963). Intrafamilial determinants of divergent sexual behavior in twins. *American Journal of Psychology, 119,* 732–738.

Money, J., & Ehrhardt, A. (1972). *Man and woman, boy and girl.* Baltimore: Johns Hopkins University Press.

Money, J., Schwartz, M., & Lewis, V. G. (1984). Adult erotosexual status and fetal hormonal masculinization and demasculinization: 46, XX congenital virilizing adrenal hyperplasia and 46, XY androgen-insensitivity syndrome compared. *Psychoneuroendocrinology, 9,* 405–414.

Money, J., & Tucker, P. (1975). *Sexual signatures: On being a man or woman.* Boston: Little, Brown.

Morel, F. (1948). La Massa intermedia ou commissure grise. *Acta Anatomica, 4,* 203–207.

Nagylaki, T., & Levy, J. (1973). "Sound of one paw clapping" isn't sound. *Behaviour Genetics, 3,* 279–292.

Neumann, F., & Steinbeck, H. (1972). Influence of sexual hormones on the differentiation of neural centers. *Archives of Sexual Behavior, 2*(2), 147–162.

Newcomb, M. D. (1985). The role of perceived relative parent personality in the development of heterosexuals, homosexuals, and transvestites. *Archives of Sexual Behavior, 14*(2), 147–164.

Olsen, K. L. (1992). Genetic influences on sexual behavior differentiation. In A. A. Gerall, H. Moltz & I. L. Ward (Eds.), *Sexual differentiation* (pp. 1–40). New York: Plenum Press.

Olsen, K. (1993). Sex and the mutant mouse: Strategies for understanding the sexual differentiation of the brain. In M. Haug, R. E. Whalen, C. Aron & K. L. Olsen (Eds.), *The development of sex differences and similarities in behavior* (pp. 255–278). Dordrecht: Kluwer Academic Publishers.

Parker, N. (1964). Homosexuality in twins: A report on three discordant pairs. *British Journal of Psychiatry, 110,* 489–495.

Perkins, A., & Fitzgerald, J. A. (1992). Luteinizing hormone and testosterone response of sexually active and inactive rams. *Journal of Animal Science, 70,* 2086–2093.

Perkins, M. W. (1973). Homosexuality in female monozygotic twins. *Behavior Genetics,* 3, 387–388.

Pillard, R., Poumadere, J., & Carretta, R. (1982). A family study of sexual orientation. *Archives of Sexual Behavior, 11*(6), 511–520.

Pillard, R., & Weinrich, J. (1986). Evidence of familial nature of male homosexuality. *Archives of General Psychiatry, 43,* 808–812.

Rabl, R. (1958). Strukturstudien an der Massa Intermedia des Thalamus opticus. *Journal Hirnforschung, 4,* 78–112.

Rainer, J. D., Mesnikoff, A., Kolb, L. C., & Carr, A. (1960). Homosexuality and heterosexuality in identical twins. *Psychosomatic Medicine, 22,* 251–259.

Reese, R. W., & Fleming, D. E. (1981). Effects of malnutrition, maternal stress or ACTH injection during pregnancy on sexual behavior of male offspring. *Physiology and Behavior, 27,* 879–882.

Reinisch, J. M., & Karow, W. G. (1977). Prenatal exposure to synthetic progestins and estrogens: Effects on human development. *Archives of Sexual Behavior, 6*(4), 257–288.

Reinisch, J. M., & Sanders, S. A. (1992). Prenatal hormonal contributions to sex differences in human cognitive and personality development. In A. A. Gerall, H. Moltz & I. L. Ward (Eds.), *Sexual differentiation* (pp. 221–243.). New York: Plenum Press.

Rosenberg, K. P. (1994). Biology and homosexuality. *Journal of Sex and Marital Therapy, 20*(2), 147–151.

Sanders, G. (1994). *Sexual orientation, cognitive abilities, and cerebral asymmetry: A replication.* International Academy for Sex Research, Edinburgh, Scotland: (Proceedings).

Sanders, G., & Ross-Field, L. (1986). Sexual orientation and visuospatial ability. *Brain and Cognition, 5,* 280–290.

Sanders, G., & Wright, M. (1993). *Sexual Orientation Differences in Targeted Throwing and Manual Dexterity Tasks.* International Academy for Sex Research, Conference. 27 June–1 July, Pacific Grove, California.

Scamvougeras, A., Witelson, S. F., Bronskill, M., Stanchev, P., Black, S., Cheung, G., Steiner, M., & Buck, B. (1994). Sexual orientation and anatomy of the corpus callosum. *Abstracts: Society for Neurosciences,* 1425.

Schiefenhövel, W. (1990). Ritualized adult-male/adolescent-male sexual behavior in Melanesia: An anthropological and ethological perspective. In J. R. Feierman (Ed.), *Pedophilia—Biosocial dimensions* (pp. 394–421). New York: Springer-Verlag.

Schmidt, G. (1984). Allies and persecutors: Science and medicine in the homosexuality issue. *Journal of Homosexuality, 10,* 127–140.

Siegelman, M. (1981a). Parental backgrounds of homosexual and heterosexual women: A cross-national replication. *Archives of Sexual Behavior, 10*(4), 371–378.

Siegelman, M. (1981b). Parental backgrounds of homosexual and heterosexual men: A cross national replication. *Archives of Sexual Behavior, 10*(6), 505–513.

Sigusch, V., Schorsch, E., Dannecker, M., & Schmidt, G. (1982, October). Guest editorial: Official statement by the German Society for Sex Research (Deutsche Gesellschaft fur Sexualforschung e.V.) on the research of Prof. Dr. Gunter Dörner on the subject of homosexuality. *Archives of Sexual Behavior, 11*(5), 445–449.

Slater, E. (1962). Birth order and maternal age of homosexuals. *Lancet, 1,* 69–71.

Stoller, R. J. (1968). *Sex and gender: On the development on masculinity and femininity.* New York: Science House.

Stoller, R., & Herdt, G. (1985). Theories of origins of male homosexuality. *Archives of General Psychiatry, 42*(4), 399–404.

Suarez, B. K., & Przybeck, T. R. (1980). Sibling sex ratio and male homosexuality. *Archives of Sexual Behavior, 9,* 1–12.

Swaab, D. F., & Fliers, E. (1985). A sexually dimorphic nucleus in the human brain. *Science, 228,* 1112–1115.

Swaab, D. F., & Hofman, M. A. (1988). Sexual differentiation of the human hypothalamus: Ontogeny of the sexually dimorphic nucleus of the preoptic area. *Developmental Brain Research, 44,* 314–318.

Swaab, D. F., & Hofman, M. A. (1990). An enlarged suprachiasmatic nucleus in homosexual men. *Brain Research, 537,* 141–148.

Swaab, D. F., Hofman, M. A., Lucasen, P. D., Purba, J. S., Raadsheer, F. L., & Van der Nas, J. A. P. (1993). Functional neuroanatomy and neuropathology of the human hypothalamus. *Anatomy and Embryology, 187,* 317–330.

Tkachuk, J., & Zucker, K. J. (1991). *The Relation among Sexual Orientation, Spatial Ability, Handidness and Recalled Childhood Gender Identity in Women and Men.* Conference Proceedings, International Academy for Sex Research, Barrie, Ontario, Canada.

Tobet, S. A., & Fox, T. O. (1992). Sex differences in neuronal morphology influenced hormonally throughout life. In A. A. Gerall, H. Moltz & I. L. Ward (Eds.), *Handbook of behavioral neurobiology* (pp. 41–83). New York: Plenum Press.

Tsoi, W. F., Kok, L. P., & Long, F. Y. (1977). Male transsexualism in Singapore: A description of 56 cases. *British Journal of Psychiatry, 131,* 405–409.

Turner, W. J. (1994). Comments on discordant monozygotic twinning in homosexuality. *Archives of Sexual Behavior, 23*(1), 115–119.

Turner, W. J. (1995). Homosexuality, type 1: An Xq28 phenomenon. *Archives of Sexual Behavior,* 24(2), 109–134.

van Seters, A. P., & Slob, A. K. (1988). Mutually gratifying heterosexual relationship with micropenis of husband. *Journal of Sex and Marital Therapy, 14*(2), 98–107.

Vega-Matuszczyk, J. (1993). *The differentiation of sexual behavior and partner preference of the male rat.* Experimental thesis, Göteborgs Universitet, Göteborgs, Sweden.

Vega-Matuszczyk, J., Fernandez-Guasti, A., & Larsson, K. (1988). Sexual orientation, proceptivity, and receptivity in the male rat as a function of neonatal hormonal manipulation. *Hormones and Behavior, 22,* 362–378.

Vega-Matuszczyk, J., Silverin, B., & Larsson, K. (1990). Influence of environmental events immediately after birth on postnatal testosterone secretion and adult sexual behavior in the male rat. *Hormones and Behavior, 24,* 450–458.

Ward, I. L. (1972). Prenatal stress feminizes and demasculinizes the behavior of males. *Science, 175,* 82–84.

Ward, I. L. (1977). Exogenous androgen activates female behavior in noncopulating, prenatally stressed male rats. *Journal of Comparative and Physiological Psychology 91,* 465–471.

Ward, I. L. (1992). Sexual behavior: The product of perinatal hormonal and prepubertal social forces. In A. A. Gerall, H. Moltz & I. L. Ward (Eds.), *Handbook of behavioral neurobiology: Sexual differentiation* (pp. 157–180). New York: Plenum.

Ward, I. L., & Ward, O. B. (1985). Sexual behavior differentiation: Effects of prenatal manipulations in rats. In N. Adler, D. Pfaff & R. W. Goy (Eds.), *Handbook of behavioral neurobiology* (pp. 77–97). New York: Plenum.

Ward, I. L., & Weisz, J. (1980). Maternal stress alters plasma testosterone in fetal males. *Science, 207,* 328–329.

Ward, I. L., & Weisz, J. (1984). Differential effects of maternal stress on circulating levels of corticosterone, progesterone, and testosterone in male and female rat fetuses and their mothers. *Endocrinology, 114,* 1635–1644.

Weinberg, M., & Williams, C. (1974). *Male homosexuals—Their problems and adaptations.* New York: Oxford University Press.

Weinrich, J. D. (1987). *Sexual landscapes: Why we are what we are, why we love whom we love.* New York: Charles Scribner's Sons.

West, D. J. (1977). *Homosexuality reexamined.* Minneapolis: University of Minnesota Press.

Whitam, F. L., & Mathy, R. M. (1986). *Male homosexuality in four societies: Brazil, Guatemala, the Philippines, and the United States.* New York: Praeger.

Whitam, F. L., Diamond, M., & Martin, J. (1993). Homosexual orientation in twins: A report on 61 pairs and three triplet sets. *Archives of Sexual Behavior, 22*(3), 187–206.

Williams, C. L., & Meck, W. H. (1991). The organizational effects of gonadal steroids on sexually dimorphic spatial ability. *Psychoneuroendocrinology, 16*(1–3), 155–176.

Williams, C. L., & Meck, W. H. (1993). Organizational effects of gonadal hormones induce qualitative differences in visuospatial navigation. In M. Haug, R. E. Whalen, C. Aron & K. L. Olsen (Eds.), *The development of sex differences and similarities in behavior* (pp. 175–189). Dordrecht: Kluwer Academic Publishers.

Wilmott, M., & Brierley, R. (1984). Cognitive characteristics and homosexuality. *Archives of Sexual Behavior, 13,* 311–319.

Wilson, E. O. (1975). *Sociobiology: The new synthesis.* Cambridge: Harvard University Press.

Witelson, S. F. (1991). Neural sexual mosaicism: Sexual differentiation of the human temporo-parietal region for functional asymmetry. *Psychoneuroendocrinology, 16*(1–3), 131–153.

Witelson, S. F., Glezer, I. I., & Kigar, D. L. (1994). Sex differences in numerical density of neurons in human auditory association cortex. *Abstracts: Society for Neurosciences,* page 1425.

Yalom, I. D., Green, R., & Fisk, N. (1973). Prenatal exposure to female hormones: Effect on psychosexual development in boys. *Archives of General Psychiatry, 28,* 554–561.

Zucker, K. J., & Blanchard, R. (1994). Reanalysis of Bieber et al.'s 1962 data on sibling sex ratio and birth order in male homosexuals. *Journal of Nervous and Mental Diseases, 182,* 528–530.

Zuger, B. (1976). Monozygotic twins discordant for homosexuality: Report on a pair and significance of the phenomenon. *Comparative Psychiatry, 17,* 661–669.

4

Sexual Orientation and Development: An Interactive Approach

Michael R. Kauth and Seth C. Kalichman

DEFINING SEXUAL ORIENTATION

It is difficult to imagine any other culture that has been as consumed by sexuality as modern Western society during the past century. Rather than a general interest in sexuality, the West has demonstrated an obsession with homosexuality and once-taboo practices such as masturbation and oral sex. Despite claims of scientific objectivism, most theories of sexual attraction are stereotypes about homosexual development cloaked in scientific jargon. Kuhn (1970) charged that scientific theories reflect the socially accepted assumptions of their day and therefore are bound by their sociological and historical context. When theoretic anomalies become numerous, a scientific revolution occurs. Current thought about sexual orientation is on the threshold of such a revolution as it struggles to incorporate data from DNA studies, family prevalence studies, and cross-cultural and transhistorical observations. This chapter shifts away from single-factor theories toward a more comprehensive interactive model of sexual orientation.

Many ancient writers mused on the nature of attraction to one gender or the other, or to both, without interference of social stigma or assignment of sexual identity (Boswell 1980, 1994). Although *sexual orientation* is a loaded Western concept, the term is still a useful one, if we avoid imposing Western thoughts and meanings associated with our language on non-Western, noncontemporary cultures.

Figure 4.1
Kinsey Scale of Sexual Orientation

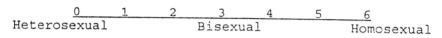

By sexual orientation, we mean the cumulative experience and interaction of erotic fantasy, romantic-emotional feelings, and sexual behavior directed toward one or both genders. These three somewhat independent and parallel dimensions are traditionally conceived as being overlaid on a plane of sexual orientation (Bell & Weinberg 1978; Weinberg, Williams & Pryor 1994; cf. Kinsey et al. 1948, 1953) (figure 4.1). Opposite-sex attraction is located on one end and same-sex attraction on the other. This model suggests that sexual orientation is not static and may vary throughout the course of a lifetime. Dimensional concordance for one gender (monosexuality) refers to exclusive homosexuality or heterosexuality. Gender divergence or dimensional concordance for both genders refers to bisexuality. Celibate individuals may identify as falling somewhere on this plane based on their feelings, fantasies, or political views. The cultural milieu determines the meaning of any given set of sexual feelings, fantasies, and behaviors. People who have sexual feelings or engage in stigmatized behaviors may proclaim or be assigned a social identity (Ross 1987). In repressive cultures, public sexual behavior may be inconsistent with personal attraction or identity, and socially unacceptable feelings may be suppressed or unrecognized for years.

Traditional theories of sexual orientation have often assumed default development of heterosexuality and presented a "sickness model" of homosexuality. Most theories have proposed single or few etiological factors, either constitutional or imposed, implying that humans somehow develop outside the influence of their biologic or social context. In addition, a great deal of current thinking about human sexual orientation comes from observations of nonhuman animal sexual development. Nonhuman sexual behavior is treated as homologous to human sexual orientation, although development between the two markedly differs, and reflexive nonhuman animal sexual behavior has little to do with human cognitive-affective experience.

While nonhuman animal observations raise many interesting questions about human experience, they answer few. To understand human behavior, we must study humans—and not only those with atypical or aberrant developmental histories. We must focus on what goes "right" with sexuality across a variety of populations. Anthropologist Ruth Benedict (1938) argued that the "facts of nature" are not "natural" for humans, for culture serves as nature's mediator. By comparing cultural influences on sexual experience at different historical periods, we can begin to map out a range of human sexual expressions and identify culture-constant regularities. A useful theory of sexual orientation will merge findings from the laboratory and the field into a transhistorical and interactive model.

What are the range and forms of gender attraction and sexual behavior across culture and time? Briefly, whether sanctioned or stigmatized or ignored, same-sex sexual behavior and thus for many, bisexuality, is not uncommon to most human societies. Heterosexual and homosexual behavior may occur concurrently or sequentially. Aristocratic men in ancient Japan and classical Athens practiced concurrent bisexuality (Bullough 1976), maintaining parallel sexual relationships with men and women. In Athens, male citizens were expected to marry and produce children, and as long as these social obligations were fulfilled, there was no stigma associated with simultaneous sexual relationships with men. In fact, in the *Symposium,* Plato proclaimed that profound love and intellectual intimacy are possible only with other men. Although the ideal affectional relationship was an older, married male with a younger, single male (Dover 1978), in noted cases the *erastes* (''lover'') and *eromenos* (''beloved'') were close in age (Achilles and Patroklos), the beloved was older (as was Socrates to Alcibiades), or the relationship continued past puberty (again, Socrates and Alcibiades; Boswell 1980). Furthermore, despite the custom of bisexuality, some men maintained only monosexual relationships and experienced not a small degree of harassment for their actions. While a few men may have been limited in their pool of sexual partners, it is curious that in a society that encouraged sexual activity with both genders, a minority of people had partners of only one. For ancient Greek women, same-sex sexual behavior has been documented, although it is unclear whether relationships were age structured or concurrent for both genders. Although there are many dissimilarities between the two cultures, men and women today in the United States who identify as bisexual often practice concurrent bisexuality and may or may not be in a heterosexual marriage (Weinberg, Williams & Pryor 1994).

Sequential bisexuality refers to alternating sexual relationships with one gender, then the other, but not both at the same time. An example of this type of sexual expression is present-day Melanesian societies and related cultures in the Pacific (Herdt 1984). At about age 9, Melanesian boys leave their families and reside exclusively with men until marriage or approximately 19 years of age. During this time, they acquire their manhood and sexual potency by regularly fellating to orgasm older males who are themselves married. A similar male fertility ritual among Sambians of New Guinea may last from age 7 to 30 years of age (Herdt 1981). Upon marrying, Melanesian and Sambian men maintain almost exclusive heterosexual relationships, with the exception that married men provide semen to young males. Observations often depict ritualized sexual behavior in these cultures as erotic and imply that emotional attachments between male pairs sometimes develop (Herdt 1981, 1984). In both Melanesian and Sambian cultures, women are perceived as inherently fertile. Therefore no procedure is necessary to acquire it, which is not to say that same-sex sexual behavior does not occur for other reasons among women in these cultures.

Nondevelopmental examples of sequential bisexuality include modern bisexual men and women who do not have concurrent relationships (Weinberg, Williams & Pryor 1994) and sexual behavior among men (and less often women) in same-sex living conditions such as military institutions (Berrube 1990; Shilts 1993). Among military personnel, neither party may identify as gay, and later each may engage in exclusive heterosexual behavior, although some do not. While most same-sex sexual activity among single-gender populations is viewed as situational and about sexual release, this explanation avoids the question of why celibacy or masturbation is not an option and ignores evidence of affectional relationships, some of which continue outside the restrictive environment.

A third expression of sexual orientation is *monosexuality,* meaning sexual feelings and interest in one gender. Heterosexual or homosexual relationships may be concurrent or sequential. Ideal heterosexual relationships involve marriage (and only one sexual partner), although most do not. Homosexuality as an identity is unique to the past century (Halperin 1990). In 1869, the term *homosexual* was first used to refer to men who love men and who enjoy receptive anal intercourse (Bullough 1976). The word was later applied to women who love women, and, finally, the terms *gay men* and *lesbians* were employed to represent same-sex attraction, as well as a political identity. Most modern societies influenced by the West have citizens who identify as gay or lesbian, including the United States, Great Britain, Canada, Australia, Germany, Denmark, and Norway. The last two countries recognize same-sex marriage. While at any given time a significant proportion of gay men and lesbians are in relationships (McWhirter & Mattison 1984; Peplau & Amaro 1982), a few may have more than one partner, and many may have no partner at all.

Simply because one form of sexuality (e.g., heterosexuality) is upheld as the ideal does not indicate that the ideal is typical or preferable or that other forms of behavior are uncommon. Variety in sexual expression, development, and social norms is one of the most striking features across different cultures. Keep this variety in mind while examining the following single-factor theories of sexual orientation and later two interactive approaches.

OVERVIEW OF SINGLE-FACTOR THEORIES OF SEXUAL ORIENTATION

Biologic Models: Homosexuals Are Born

Most biologic models of sexual orientation are founded on dichotomous categories (Ross 1987): masculine-feminine, active-passive, normal-abnormal, and heterosexual-homosexual. Biologic theories also assume that hormonalization, development, and sexual desires and behavior express (heterosexual) gender roles. *Gender role* may be defined as the public expression of what society considers maleness, femaleness, or ambivalence (Money 1988, 1991). (Although Money allowed for ambivalent identity and androgyny, these characteristics are either ignored or considered "cross-gendered" in his text). Biologic theory holds "normal" sexual development to be heterosexual. Androgens are thought to make "men," and the absence of androgen and/or presence of estrogen makes "women." Heterosexual gender role dictates that men act "masculine" and women act "feminine." Men are perceived as independent and active (the inserter) in the sexual role with women, while "women" are dependent and sexually passive (receptive) with men. All sexual dyads are conceived as expressions of heterosexual gender roles.

When the heterosexual gender role bias is applied to nonheterosexuals, it reads like this: Sexual attraction to men is what women do; therefore, men who like men are more like women ("feminine"). By contrast, attraction to women is what men do; therefore, women who like women are more like men ("masculine"). In a patriarchal society, men who are like women are less than "men," and women who are like men are a threat. This misogynist reasoning employs negative stereotypes about women to devalue gay men and lesbians. An interesting paradox within the heterosexual gender role bias is that gay men who perform in the active sexual role are viewed as more "masculine" and somehow less gay. Bisexuality is difficult, if not impossible, to explain within a gender-roled model.

Assuming for the moment that there are stark contrasts between (heterosexual) men and women, researchers reason that they may discover the source of these differences by examining sexual differentiation. Furthermore, if gay people are cross-gendered in sexual attraction, then gay men should have much in common with heterosexual women, and lesbians should be similar to heterosexual men. The following sections examine the degree to which data from hormonal, neuroanatomic, genetic, and twin-family studies confirm these presuppositions and support a biologic model of sexual orientation. (For a comprehensive review of biologic data, see Diamond in this volume or Byne & Parsons 1993.)

Hormonal Studies

Considerable research has produced evidence that sexually dimorphic reproductive behaviors are organized perinatally or prenatally by gonadal steroid hormones in laboratory animals. The premise behind hormonal studies is that human sexual orientation is determined by hormonalization and that all mammals develop similarly. Most hormonal studies focus on homosexual behavior in laboratory animals.

The prenatal hormonal hypothesis, based on studies with rats, purports that mammalian brain development is female and introduction of androgens by the male fetus differentiates the male brain. Unlike differentiation of external genitalia, loss of female characteristics and development of male characteristics in the brain is independent. In some species, testosterone has a direct effect on androgen receptors, while, among others, androgen must be converted to estrogen by aromatase enzymes in the brain. Presenting behavior, or lordosis, is displayed by female rats or by genetic males castrated perinatally and is dependent on gonadal hormones. Mounting and thrusting behavior is displayed by intact male rats or by genetic females exposed to androgens in early development. Thus, the prenatal theory holds that male heterosexuality and female homosexuality are products of prenatal exposure to androgens, while male homosexuality and female heterosexuality result from insensitivity to or lack of androgens. One would then predict that most gay men would evidence syndromes of androgen insensitivity or deficiency and lesbians would show signs of prenatal androgen exposure. However, extensive literature reviews by Meyer-Bahlburg (1984) and Byne and Parsons (1993) found no evidence of significant gonadal or hormonal dysfunction in gay men or lesbians. Although Meyer-Bahlburg cited three studies suggesting gay men had lower levels of testosterone, twenty studies found no differences.

There also was no evidence that progesterone-related compounds used during pregnancy to prevent miscarriage—which may have a demasculinizing effect on the brain—influence sexual orientation (Gooren 1990; Meyer-Bahlburg 1984; Ehrhardt, Meyer-Bahlburg, Feldman & Ince 1984; Beral & Colwell 1981; Kester, Green, Finch & Williams 1980; Hines 1982). Although one group of researchers (Ehrhardt et al. 1984) found an increase in bisexuality and homosexuality in women exposed to a potent progesterone, this finding is contrary to what is known about sexual differentiation of the brain, which is *not* mediated by estrogen. Another set of researchers (Dittmann, Kappes & Kappes 1992; Money, Schwartz & Lewis 1984) concluded that a genetic recessive condition in women, congenital virilizing adrenal hyperplasia (CVAH), which androgenizes development, increased the likelihood of homosexuality. However, the impact of having obviously masculinized genitals (an enlarged clitoris and shallow vagina) and knowledge about their condition were not assessed.

Support for prenatal hormonal theory has been sought in postnatal hormonal feedback mechanisms. In adult female rats, estrogen acts on the hypothalamus to exert positive and negative feedback on release of luteinizing hormone (LH) for regulation of ovulation. In normal adult male rats, estrogen has only a negative feedback on LH release, presumably because of early exposure to androgens. Therefore, the theory goes, if gay men were insufficiently androgenized prenatally, they should show a stronger positive feedback to estrogen than do heterosexual men. Although two groups of researchers reported that gay men do show a slight, positive feedback (Gladue, Green & Hellman 1984; Dorner, Rhode, Stall, Krell & Masius 1975), better-controlled studies demonstrated that the type of feedback response is determined by the hormonal status of the individual at the time of estrogen challenge rather than by genetic sex or sexual orientation (Gooren 1986a, 1986b). Among matched groups of homosexual and heterosexual men, no differences were found to estrogen challenge. Gooren suggested that previous supportive studies were influenced by differences in testicular function and that a true positive feedback response cannot be demonstrated in gonadally intact men (Gooren 1986b, 1990).

In sum, incomplete or disconfirming evidence has been found for a prenatal theory of human sexual orientation or, at least, homosexuality. There is no evidence that hormonalization and sexual development in rats is comparable to human development, and other data suggest that prenatal hormonalization differs in its process and effects across species (Money 1988, 1991). Consistent with the heterosexual gender role bias, laboratory observers viewed lordotic male rats and mounting females as homosexual, but male rats who mounted males were labeled heterosexual.

Neuroanatomic Studies

The idea behind neuroanatomic studies is that prenatal hormonalization results in sexually dimorphic brain structures or nuclei, which in turn affect sexual orientation and behavior. Recent attention has focused on a group of cells called the interstitial nuclei 2 through 4 of the anterior hypothalamus (INAH2, etc.). Two studies found differences in INAH3 (Allen, Hine, Shryne & Gorski 1989; LeVay 1991). Popular attention has been given to LeVay's study, which reported that INAH3 was smaller for gay men than for heterosexual men. LeVay speculated that INAH3 is comparable to the sexually dimorphic nucleus of the preoptic area (SDN-POA) in rats, which regulates sexual behavior and lordosis in male rats. In male rats, size of the SDN-POA is related to frequency of mounting. LeVay suggested that INAH3 operates similarly in gay men. Aside from conceptual problems and lack of supportive evidence from prenatal hormonal theory, LeVay's hypothesis fails to account for gay men who do not engage in receptive anal intercourse, for bisexuals, or for lesbians. Methodological concerns also render his conclusions premature and questionable. Sexual histories of subjects were incomplete, several subjects died of AIDS, and the size of INAH3 may depend on adult levels of testosterone that decrease during end-stage AIDS.

Other brain sites that have been purported to influence sexual orientation are the suprachiasmatic nucleus in the hypothalamus, the anterior commissure, and the corpus callosum. To date there is no indication how these structures influence sexual behavior. Anatomic correlates of sexual orientation do not in themselves denote a biologic origin. Experience is known to alter the physiology and structure of the brain in laboratory animals (Bhide & Bedi 1984; Turner & Greenough 1985; Kraemer, Ebert, Lake & McKinney 1984).

Twin and Family Studies

Despite weak data from hormonal and neuroanatomic studies, twin and family studies have produced supportive evidence for a biologic basis of sexual orientation. In a series of studies, Bailey and Pillard reported a significant correlation for homosexuality among monozygotic (MZ) and dizygotic twins (DZ). Among fifty-six MZ male twin probands and fifty-four DZ male twin probands, 52 percent of MZ co-twins and 22 percent of DZ co-twins were concordant for homosexuality (Bailey & Pillard 1991). Concordance for nontwin biologic brothers and unrelated adoptive brothers was 9.2 percent and 11.0 percent, respectively. Among seventy-one MZ female twin probands and thirty-seven DZ female twin probands, forty-eight percent of MZ co-twins and 16 percent of DZ co-twins were concordant for homosexuality, and 14 percent of nontwin biologic sisters and 6 percent of adoptive sisters of lesbians were also gay or bisexual (Bailey, Pillard, Neale & Agyei 1993). Significantly more women than men identified as bisexual. Bailey and colleagues concluded that there is strong support for a genetic, although independent, etiology for sexual orientation among gay men and lesbians. Although there were a large number of discordant MZ twins in these studies despite shared genes and similar environments, the authors questioned whether we can ever assume an equal environment for MZ twins.

Other studies have found that families with a homosexual member are more likely to have other homosexual relatives. Pillard and Weinrich (1986) reported that gay men were four times more likely than heterosexual men to have gay brothers, and Hamer and colleagues (1993) observed that their sample of seventy-six gay men were three to seven times more likely to have gay brothers. Hamer and associates also found a higher prevalence of homosexuality among maternal uncles (7.3 percent) and sons of maternal aunts (7.7 percent) and concluded that some forms of male homosexuality may be inherited via the mother's X chromosome. No hypothesis was proffered concerning a genetic mechanism for female homosexuality.

Genetic Studies

Hamer and colleagues (1993) compared twenty-two DNA markers on the X chromosome of forty gay sibling pairs using a polymerase chain reaction procedure to replicate genes quickly. Five consecutive markers on the long arm of Xq28 evidenced a .82 correlation. No matches were found outside this area. The authors speculated that recombination of adjacent repeated sequences, or between active and inactive sequences on the X and Y chromosomes, could produce a high rate of DNA sequence variants and could generate a trait that may reduce reproduction. It is not clear what mechanisms these markers may activate to influence sexual orientation. Although seven (18 percent) sibling pairs were not similar for all five genetic markers, Hamer and colleagues suggested that this discrepancy may be due to genetic variability or nongenetic variation in sexual orientation. Additional research is necessary to identify common DNA sequences between gay men and heterosexual brothers and between lesbians and heterosexual sisters before stronger conclusions can be drawn.

Summary of Biologic Data

A heterosexual gender role bias and reliance on nonhuman laboratory data have resulted in biologic theorists' drawing many premature conclusions; however, supportive data from twin and family studies argue for a reconception of biology's role. It may be that genetic or hormonal events form a predisposition that requires environmental events to shape and develop fully.

Psychoanalytic Models: Homosexuals Are Fixated and Perverse

A chronology of the development of psychoanalytic and psychodynamic theories of homosexuality is well described by Lewes later in this book. Briefly, Sigmund Freud's (1905, 1920) concept of a bisexual constitution was rejected after his death, and homosexuality was pathologized. "Normal" sexual orientation was declared to be heterosexual (Bergler 1947), and revised theories hypothesized that fixation during the early stages of psychosexual development predisposed or directly resulted in adult homosexuality and psychopathology. From case studies, theorists concluded that gay men fail to separate from their mothers in early childhood, fail to individualize fully (Socarides 1968; Socarides & Volkan 1990), and grow up in dysfunctional families (Bieber et al. 1962; Rado 1940; Wiedeman 1974). Yet empirical support for the notion that gay men or lesbians come from dysfunctional families or experience more psychopathology as adults is lacking. Hooker (1956) demonstrated that psychological functioning of well-adjusted homosexual men was indistinguishable from heterosexuals as assessed by the Rorschach. Consistent with this finding, Isay (1989) also reported that psychopathology was not prevalent among a sample of highly functional gay men.

Proponents of psychoanalytic theories of sexual orientation have offered circular stories, anecdotal evidence from case histories, or data from poorly controlled studies to support their (a priori) claims. No intrapsychic etiology of sexual orientation has been demonstrated. Unfortunately, homosexuality as a pathology has only recently been removed from the standards of psychiatric diagnosis and remains a part of psychoanalytic conceptual models, as well as biomedical models (Willerman & Cohen 1990).

Learning/Conditioning Models: Homosexuals Are Made

A history of learning theories of sexual orientation is presented later in this book. In short, radical behaviorists have claimed that accidental stimulation of infant genitals by the same-sex caregiver, punishment following genital stimulation by the opposite-sex parent, negative messages about heterosexual relations, attention from a same-sex person, lack of an opposite-sex partner when aroused, and poor heterosocial skills may promote adult homosexuality (Barlow & Agras 1973; Green 1985, 1987; Greenspoon & Lamal 1987). However, self-reported histories of gay men, lesbians, and heterosexuals have not shown these experiences to be predictive of later sexual orientation (Bell, Weinberg & Hammersmith 1981), and we know of no data that find that gay men and lesbians lack sufficient social skills for intimacy.

While acknowledging that they have not identified the relevant variables that contribute to and maintain homosexuality (Greenspoon & Lamal 1987), many behavioral clinicians in the 1960s and early 1970s proclaimed that gay men could be "cured" through reorientation or aversion therapies (Barlow & Agras

1973; Feldman & MacCulloch 1971; Marks & Gelder 1967). Despite claims of "success" (cf. Feldman & MacCulloch 1971; Masters & Johnson 1979), conversion therapies have demonstrated that heterosexual arousal does not make a "heterosexual," that many people are capable of bisexual responses, and that behavioral or physiological changes but not necessarily changes in erotic thoughts or desires that constitute sexual orientation may occur for highly motivated individuals and are not generally maintained outside the laboratory (Haldeman 1991).

Learning theorists evoke popular stereotypes when alluding to an older homosexual seducer, the lonely and desperate prehomosexual, the fragility of heterosexuality against which we must defend, and the highly reinforcing nature of same-sex sex (cf. Feldman & MacCulloch 1971; Greenspoon & Lamal 1987). Behaviorists sound curiously like psychoanalytic theorists when discussing the homosexual's fear and avoidance of heterosexual sex (cf. Bieber et al. 1962). However, several studies have reported that many gay men and lesbians have a great deal of heterosexual experience (Kinsey et al. 1948, 1953; Bell & Weinberg 1978), and bisexuals continue to do so (Weinberg, Williams & Pryor 1994).

The most obvious and damaging criticism of learning theorists with regard to sexual orientation is their lack of discussion about how society shapes sexuality. Westerners such as Americans grow up in an antihomosexual society and in families that do not encourage but rather explicitly and implicitly punish homosexual tendencies. Advertising, music, television, movies, and organized social functions remind us constantly that heterosexual behavior is rewarded, despite moral prohibitions against adolescent or premarital sexuality. At best, a few social messages about homosexuality may be ambiguous, although promotion of heterosexuality is loud, clear, and consistent. Within such a society, it seems unlikely that there should be more than occasional same-sex sexual behavior, and people who prefer such activities should be quite rare. Prevalence of gay men, lesbians, and bisexuals in Western societies suggests that same-sex sexual behavior is not uncommon. Furthermore, given the benefits of heterosexual behavior in the West, it is difficult to imagine why reorientation therapies have been so unsuccessful, if only conditioning principles were operative in the development of sexual orientation.

INTERACTIVE THEORIES OF SEXUAL ORIENTATION AND DEVELOPMENT

An interactive theory of sexual orientation must be able to account for all forms of gender attraction, explain cross-cultural variations in sexual behavior, and distinguish between development of an identity (heterosexual, bisexual, or gay) and sexual behavior (Ross 1987). An interactive theory also must be able to show how biologic mechanisms and environment influence each other to produce the spectrum of human sexual behavior. Bound less by hormone levels or cycles or seasons, people are aroused by a variety of sexual and nonsexual stimuli in the environment or through their imagination. Once aroused, unlike nonhumans, people may choose not to be sexual or may be sexual without emotional or erotic feelings. Finally, as cognitive beings in a complex social environment, people may identify with a certain sexuality without being sexually active. A practical theory of sexual orientation must account for all these elements.

A Neurohormonal/Stress-Diathesis Model

Pioneer sexologists Milton Diamond (1965; 1968; 1979) and John Money (1988, 1991) have presented the most accepted interactive theory of sexual orientation to date. For many years, Money's numerous and creative contributions have shaped and directed the field of sexology, and, consequently, many have been reluctant to examine his ideas critically. (For a writer who has been critical, see Diamond 1979, 1982).

Money (1988) claimed that sexuality exactly parallels native language development. A wealth of data suggests that humans are biologically predisposed, or hardwired, for language but dependent on a nurturing environment for development and expression. Of course, a predisposition for language does not specify which language or accent will be expressed; many forms of verbalization are viable. Money applied a similar relativism to the development of sexual orientation. It is surprising, then, and a little puzzling that he focused on only two "languages" (heterosexuality and homosexuality), giving little attention to the richness of bisexuality, and viewed heterosexuality as the "basal language" (Money & Russo 1979; Money 1988).

A biologic hardwiring or predisposition is hypothesized to be set by prenatal hormonalization. From data on sexual differentiation in laboratory animals and from his work with genetic and hormonal aberrations in humans, Money proposed that the male brain and genitalia are "masculinized" by fetal gonadal release of testosterone, while those same structures are "defeminized" by release of the müllerian inhibiting hormone. Testosterone is presumed to masculinize the brain by first being transformed to an estrogen-related substance. Only transformed estrogen can "masculinize" brain development. The female brain and genitalia are "feminized" by the presence or absence of estrogen, and those structures are "demasculinized" by the absence of androgen. Typical androgenic exposure in males is assumed to predispose attraction to females, while the absence of androgens in females is thought to favor an erotic interest in males, although how this is done is not discussed.

Sometimes something goes "wrong." Money (1988, 1991) postulated that biologic defects, certain prenatal events, or both may cause fetal males not to "masculinize," or "masculinization" and "feminization" may occur simultaneously, resulting in homosexuality. For example, high levels of maternal stress or indulgence in drugs or alcohol during critical or sensitive periods of development may dislodge prenatal hormonalization from its typical path. Money's stress-diathesis model of homosexuality predicts that mothers who are particularly stressed during pregnancy are more likely to produce gay male children. How or if this process differs for female children is unclear.

Only recently have we begun to be concerned about fetal effects of alcohol and drug use by expectant mothers and have begun to emphasize prenatal health care. If Money's maternal stress theory is correct, one would expect to find with the advent of better prenatal care a greater prevalence of adult heterosexuals and a marked decrease in the numbers of gay men and lesbians. Furthermore, children of poor and disadvantaged mothers, who probably experienced great stress and received inadequate health care during pregnancy, should be more likely to be gay or lesbian as adults. We know of no data to support this supposition.

Given that prenatal hormonalization may establish an inclination toward homosexuality, Money (1988) further proposed that expression of the disposition depends on environmental events. Like learning theorists, Money hypothesized that positive same-sex adult reactions to aroused infant genitalia may reinforce a predisposition toward homosexuality or set up an acquired disposition. In addition, adult interference with childhood (hetero) sexual play may alter sexual development. Money asserted that childhood (hetero) sexual play is necessary rehearsal for successful adult heterosexual identity and sexual behavior. Social or moral prohibitions against heterosexual play may result in inept heterosexuals or may unwittingly encourage homosexuality. Apparently childhood homosexual play does not produce healthy and happy gay people, because healthy homosexual development is never detailed by Money. Furthermore, no data are provided to support the claim that childhood heterosexual play is requisite for healthy adult heterosexuals, that childhood homosexual play interferes with adult heterosexuality, or that heterosexual play is more common than homosexual play among children. Money places a great deal of weight on adult reactions to infant genitals and on childhood sexual play in promoting homosexuality, while ignoring the larger influence of a heterosexist Western culture geared toward producing heterosexuals in thought, word, and deed.

What is more, Money's maternal stress-homosexuality hypothesis was tested by Bailey and colleagues (1991) and was not supported. Researchers recruited 116 gay men (and 83 of their mothers), 25 lesbians (19 mothers), 84 heterosexual men (60 mothers), and 72 heterosexual women (53 mothers). Mothers reported that their most common stressor during pregnancy was "moved residence." For males, mothers' level of stress while pregnant was not related to their sons' adult sexual orientation. However, a small but significant correlation for mother's stress and daughter's adult homosexuality was found. Specifically, reported stress during the first and second trimester of pregnancy was associated with daughter's lesbianism. This finding was not predicted by the maternal stress theory and remains difficult to explain.

Although Money has gone further than most others in explicating the interaction of biologic and environmental factors, his theory nevertheless fails to account for nondysfunctional human development. In addition, Money's heterosexual gender role bias contributes to conceptual problems of assigning culturally defined social roles to hormonalization. To assert that androgens "masculinize" is to imply that they make the organism "masculine" or a "man," and nothing else. What of the "man" who acts like a "woman"? Did "masculinization" occur, or is he a "woman"? Money's reliance on gender classification reinforces stereotypes about men and women. Note that prenatal hormonalization is a matter of degree, timing, and duration and androgens and estrogens are present in both genetic males and females, although in markedly different proportions. Hormonal exposure should predict a complex and rich set of outcomes rather than one or two. What is more, reliance on gender classification has another untoward effect: lack of parsimony. For example, to account for the abstruse phenomenon of gay male transsexuals, Money (1988) adopted a series of mind-numbing cross-gender transpositions that have little explanatory value.

Finally, Money's theory has a decidedly Western flavor. His maternal stress model of homosexuality and obstruction of childhood heterosexual play is an inadequate explanation for ritualized same-sex sexual behavior among men in Sambia, societal bisexuality among the privileged class in ancient Japan or ancient Greece, "mummy-baby" relationships (older-younger females) among women in the Basotho of southern Africa, or the existence of third-gender persons who engage in same-sex sexual activity, such as Indonesian *waria* or Indian *hijra*. An attempt to apply such an explanation imposes Western values translated into theoretical concepts on non-Western cultures.

An Epigenetic/Bisexual Potentiality Model

This section outlines our sociobiological interactionist model of sexual orientation. We think this perspective best incorporates research on sexual orientation and cross-culture observations of sexuality. The reasoning that led us to this model is highlighted below. The first four points represent conclusions from current research, and the remaining points and discussion that follow are extrapolations from the data.

1. Nonhuman sexual development and behavior is not homologous to human sexual development and behavior. Reflexive animal sexual behavior bears little resemblance to a cognitive-affective phenomena like human sexual orientation.
2. A biologic component of human sexual orientation, if it exists at all, is likely to be at the higher levels of brain functions. Owing to the variety of human sexual behavior, a sexual orientation "net" is more likely to be cortical than subcortical.
3. A biologic component of human sexual orientation is largely independent of sexual differentiation of the brain.
4. Hormonalization is a matter of degree, timing, and duration, allowing for an assortment of outcomes. The concept of brain genderization ("masculinization and defeminization" and "feminization and demasculinization") is oversimplistic. Hormones

Figure 4.2
Circle as Symbol for Sexual Orientation

Monosexual

Heterosexual   Homosexual

Bisexual

do not determine gender role behavior. Gender and gender roles are social constructions. Gender-typic social behaviors do not predict emotional attraction, erotic fantasies, or sexual behavior.

5. Homosexuality and heterosexuality are variants of human sexuality. Across cultures,
   bisexual behavior may be more common than either exclusive heterosexuality or
   homosexuality.

6. Human bisexuality may serve to facilitate and maintain a variety of social relationships with men and women, which may be advantageous to the individual and the
   species.

7. Prenatal and postnatal hormonalization does not affect sexual orientation directly.
   Hormones influence the perception and meaning of environmental stimuli and facilitate learned associations that canalize sexual feelings and behaviors.

8. Prenatal hormonalization produces a bisexual potentiality or range of sexual attraction. Behavior within that range depends on the social environment and individual
   reinforcement history. Those with a restricted range of attraction may have a more
   inflexible sexual orientation.

9. Plasticity of sexual attraction may decline over time and with consistent reinforcement of habitual behavior. However, plasticity is probably a function of the breadth
   of initial range of potentiality. People with a restricted range may have little flexibility; those with a wide range of attraction may retain considerable potentiality
   through adulthood.

10. Rather than a plane, sexual orientation may be better understood as a circle, with
    monosexuality at the top and bisexuality at the bottom (figure 4.2). Opposite-sex
    attraction may be placed on the left hemisphere of the circle, and same-sex attraction
    would fall on the right. The midpoint of the circle would represent asexuality. A
    circle symbolizes the range and fluidity of sexual orientation and suggests common
    elements of monosexual attraction.

Structure of the Model

Given the reasoning just presented, a single factor theory of sexual orientation
would be inadequate. However, in the past thirty years, a new wave of thinking

has begun to conceptualize human development in terms of a nature and nurture interaction. Within this construct, an organism's biologic makeup and environment interact in a reciprocally deterministic manner. An epigenetic developmental model (Gottlieb 1970; Lerner 1976) proposes that genetic structures set a reaction range (Gottesman 1963) or potentiality for expression of a given characteristic. The genetic range of responsiveness for a given characteristic may be narrow or broad. Depending on the range of responsiveness, expression of the characteristic may be relatively fixed, or flexible and open to influence.

Eye color is a characteristic with a narrow range of potentiality and is not known to vary much after birth. Height, however, has a wider range of biologic potentiality, although it is not without limits. Within genetic and physiological constraints, a given individual has a response range for the characteristic of height. Whether that individual eventually falls at the upper or lower end of the range depends upon many environmental factors, such as nutrition, health care, illness, physical injury, and other variables. Intelligence (as measured by standardized tests) appears to be a characteristic that for some people has a wide response range. Barring unusual genetic or hormonal limitations, environmental factors such as health, injury, and cognitive stimulation determine where in the range of potentiality an individual settles. Language is another characteristic with a wide response range, which warrants further examination since Money compared it to development of sexual orientation. Human children appear to have a predetermined period of biologic readiness or sensitivity for spoken language (cf. Bornstein 1989), during which time they are most able to make use of environmental input and feedback to comprehend and form words. While symbolic representations of objects and verbal skills evolve slowly from birth, children from ages 2 to 5 typically show dramatic and rapid development of language skills. During childhood, accents and verbal colloquialisms develop as supported by the child's social milieu, and verbal skills continue to improve into adulthood. Environmental stimulation prior to the period of readiness produces few noticeable effects, but if the period is missed, a child may be unable to develop spoken language fully beyond limited utterances.

Like language, sexual orientation may be a characteristic with a wide biologic range of potentiality. Individuals with a narrow range of potentiality may be able to respond only to men or to women as objects of emotional, romantic, or sexual interest. A monosexual orientation includes exclusive heterosexuality and homosexuality. While someone with a monosexual orientation may be able to perform sexually with a gender outside their range, that individual would probably find it awkward and unfulfilling. In a society that condemned heterosexuality and promoted homosexuality, a heterosexual woman would understand early that her feelings differed from those of peers and from what is socially approved. Although she may conform to society's rules by engaging in same-sex sexual behavior, it is likely that she would find sex far less rewarding than a casual conversation with a man she finds attractive.

People with a wide range of sexual attraction may be interested in both men and women. A bisexual potentiality may shift or set over time, depending on social pressure, personal reinforcement history, and motivation. Presumably an individual with flexibility in sexual responsiveness could adapt easily (and probably without conscious awareness of adaptation) to a society that prefers one form of gender attraction over another. However, a bisexual who is more attracted to one gender may find it difficult to fit into a society that disapproves of attraction to the nonpreferred gender. While plasticity in gender attraction may be repressed, diminished, or even extinguished over time through differential reinforcement, it seems likely that except in extreme cases, the ability to respond erotically to both genders would not be completely lost.

If biology determines our gender of attraction, why are more people not actively bisexual? Why do monosexuals not find everyone of their preferred gender attractive? How do we develop personal erotic and partner preferences? Here, learning theory is useful. Across cultures and time, the popularity or repulsion for particular sexual acts with particular genders—what we view as "normal" or "deviant"—is a product of social learning. From infants, members of a culture are indoctrinated (i.e., reinforced) to accept without question the rightness or wrongness of certain acts and ways of living. Those who can conform with little cost, such as bisexuals, do so. Similarly, eroticism toward certain physical or imaginal stimuli such as hair color, body shapes and sizes, ethnicity, clothing, mannerisms, smells, and sounds in our partner, as well as physical stimulation and fetishes, are most parsimoniously explained as learned associations within a cultural context. Of course, cultures evolve, and accepted practice changes. The recent history of masturbation and oral sex in the United States illustrates this point. Each has shifted from taboo to relatively accepted sexual practice. In essence, biology determines the gender of sexual attraction, and psychosocial factors shape its expression (Diamond 1979).

Biology also may influence which associations are learned. Here, observations of nonhuman animal behavior can provide an understanding of human behavior. Previous theorists have employed comparative laboratory data as homologues (similar in etiology and structure) rather than analogues (similar in function but not in origin) of human experience (Whalen 1991). Comparative observations may offer clues to the function or process of many human sexual behaviors. For example, some species appear to be predisposed to associate particular reinforcers with particular stimuli and, in turn, are resistant to punishment or extinction of those conditioned behaviors (Weinrich 1987, 1990). Pigeons will peck for a reward but not to avoid a shock; newly hatched chicks will not avoid a shock in an effort to be near their mother; rats readily make complex odor discriminations but do poorly with visual cues; and humans are much better at visual discriminations than with odors (Whalen 1991). Furthermore, Whalen has noted that among some animal species, circulating hormones and the presence of relevant environmental stimuli interact to evoke behavior, whereas hormones or external stimuli alone do not. In laboratory studies, a castrated male rat will display lordotic behavior only after injection of progesterone, *and* estrogen "priming," *and* exposure to male urine. Among rats, biologic events may create a context for behavior that depends on the presence of relevant environmental releasing stimuli. Stimuli are not equally evocative.

Whalen (1991) added that a biologic interpretation of events may account for individual preferences in sexual partners observed in dogs, cats, and primates. He suggested that hormones may function to make sense of environmental stimuli rather than to direct behavior and speculated that a similar process may occur for humans. Genetic structure and hormonal context may determine stimuli saliency and detectability and make certain erotic associations more likely. Once an association is well established, the production of behavior is guided by motivation and other factors.

Additional cross-species analogues of human sexual behavior include observations of homosexual and bisexual behavior in nearly all species of animals, both captive and in the wild (Beach 1949; Weinrich 1987). While same-sex activity is usually associated with social positioning or play among nonhuman animals (Gadpaille 1980), there are reports of apparently lifelong affectional bonds and, in some cases, what appears to be preferential same-sex sexual activity among dolphins, monkeys, baboons, rams and goats, rats, dogs, and several species of birds, such as mallards and Western gulls (Money, 1991). It is difficult to discount same-sex sexual activity among pair bonds as social play when opposite-sex partners are available and ignored or when same-sex pairs live as isolates and mount reciprocally.

With humans as with nonhumans, characteristics that exist and thrive must be adaptive and serve some function. Therefore, homosexuality and bisexuality, which exist and thrive, must be adaptive to humans, or these characteristics, being unstable, would have diminished or disappeared over time. Trivers (1972, 1974) hypothesized that if people with same-sex erotic interests acted altruistically, they would increase the reproductive success of relatives and make a case for a biologic predisposition of homosexuality. An example might be the third-gender people of Native American cultures: male Berdache who have sexual relationships with men and female Amazons who have relationships with women (Williams 1986). Berdache are able to perform heavier work than women for the household, provide additional resources to kin, and do not compete for wives or produce children like other men. Amazons do men's work, and both Berdache and Amazons perform unique spiritual duties for the service of the community. In a modern, less-kinship-oriented society, it may be more difficult to make this argument. However, gay people do not compete for heterosexual mates, produce fewer children, and have more time, money, and creative resources to invest in the community.

Bisexual potentiality in romantic feelings, fantasies, and sexual behavior may offer another evolutionary advantage to humans. Within small social bands, at least, the ability to have emotional and erotic feelings, or both, for both men and women could facilitate social bonding, increase cooperation, and decrease competition and community infighting. However, in large and impersonal societies, this would be difficult to maintain, and same-sex affection could be used for political advantage. Imagine a matriarchal society that views men as erotically (and emotionally) interesting but distrusts and subordinates them to maintain social power. The holding of political power by some women would not mean that all women are advantaged. Women on the low end of the economic and class spectrum may experience few benefits from the matriarchy. However, a social glue of homoerotic feelings, fantasies, symbols, and rituals could be directed to temper intergender competition and distrust among women. More than sexual, a homo-*eros* (Greek for ''love'') adhesive represents a deep desire to identify with, be in the company of, derive affection from, and care for other members of the same gender. In patriarchal Western societies, much has been written on the function of homoeroticism to unify and regulate male behavior in pre-Nazi Germany and Hitler's Nazi party (Oosterhuis & Kennedy 1991), warfare and military institutions (Dundes 1985; Kauth & Landis 1994), and competitive sports (Pronger 1990). Although it is not in the interests of a patriarchy for women to form strong social bonds, homoerotic rituals may be evident among women in southern U.S. families, churches, and some professions. Fear of female bonding may account for the negative reaction many men display toward feminists, lesbians, and strong women.

Up to this point, men and women of any sexual orientation have been discussed as though they express sexuality similarly. However, significant gender differences exist. For example, lesbians may perceive sexual orientation in terms of political views and affectional relationships, while gay men view orientation through erotic fantasy and sexual behavior (Golden 1990; Gonsiorek 1988). Feminist influences aside, differences between gay men and lesbians appear similar to Western gender roles in which women are socialized to be emotionally oriented and interested in forming relationships and men are reinforced to be sexual and nonmonogamous. Cross-cultural observations suggest that most characteristics associated with one or the other gender are social constructions (Mead 1935). Whether straight, gay, bisexual, or asexual, women may have more in common with other women than they have with men, and vice versa. A theory of biologic bisexual potentiality does not contradict and is consistent with observed social and sexual gender differences. However, the biologic mechanisms that produce a bisexual potential may differ for men and women and are as yet unclear.

CONCLUSIONS

Theories are products of their cultural environment and bound by its biases and assumptions. Previous theories of sexual orientation have espoused a heterosexual gender role bias and often focused only on homosexuality. A general theory of human sexual orientation requires examination of sexual attraction across cultures and history, comparison across theoretical paradigms, and conceptualization of development as an evolving and active interaction between biology and environment. A biologic bisexual potentiality model may best meet this goal.

Our intent was to propose a new way of conceptualizing sexual orientation and to open a dialogue on sexuality. It now will be up to our critics and future theorists to take us beyond this paradigm and into the next.

REFERENCES

Allen, L. S., Hines, M., Shryne, J. E., & Gorski, R. A. (1989). Two sexually dimorphic cell groups in the human brain. *Journal of Neuroscience, 9,* 497–506.

Bailey, M. J., & Pillard, R. D. (1991). A genetic study of male sexual orientation. *Archives of General Psychiatry, 48,* 1089–1096.

Bailey, M. J., Pillard, R. D., Neale, M. C., & Agyei, Y. (1993). Heritable factors influence sexual orientation in women. *Archives of General Psychiatry, 50,* 217–223.

Bailey, M. J., Willerman, L., & Parks, C. (1991). A test of the maternal stress theory of human male homosexuality. *Archives of Sexual Behavior, 20*(3), 277–293.

Barlow, D. H., & Agras, W. S. (1973). Fading to increase heterosexual responsiveness in homosexuals. *Journal of Applied Behavior Analysis, 6,* 355–366.

Beach, F. A. (1949). A cross-species survey of mammalian sexual behavior. In P. H. Hoch & J. Zubin (Eds.), *Psychosexual development in health and disease.* New York: Grune & Stratton.

Bell, A. P., & Weinberg, M. S. (1978). *Homosexuality: A study of diversity among men and women.* New York: Simon & Schuster.

Bell, A. P., Weinberg, M. S., & Hammersmith, S. K. (1981). *Sexual preference: Its development in men and women.* Bloomington: Indiana University Press.

Benedict, R. (1938). Continuities and discontinuities in cultural conditioning. *Psychiatry, 1,* 161–167.

Beral, V., & Colwell, L. (1981). Randomized trial of high doses of stilboestrol and norethisterone therapy in pregnancy: Longterm follow-up of the children. *Journal of Epidemiology and Community Health, 35,* 155–160.

Bergler, E. (1947). Differential diagnosis between spurious homosexuality and perversion homosexuality. *Psychiatric Quarterly, 31,* 399–409.

Berube, A. (1990). *Coming out under fire: The history of gay men and women in World War Two.* New York: Free Press.

Bhide, P. G., & Bedi, K. S. (1984). The effects of a lengthy period of environmental diversity on well-fed and previously undernourished rats, II: Synapse to neuron ratios. *Journal of Comparative Neurology, 227,* 305–310.

Bieber, I., Dain, H. J., Dince, P. R., Drellich, M. G., Grand, H. G., Gundlach, R. H., Kremer, M. W., Rifkin, A. H., Wilber, C. B., & Bieber, T. B. (1962). *Homosexuality: A psychoanalytic study of male homosexuals.* New York: Basic Books.

Bornstein, M. H. (1989). Sensitive periods in development: Structural characteristics and causal interpretations. *Psychological Bulletin, 105*(2), 179–197.

Boswell, J. (1980). *Christianity, social tolerance, and homosexuality.* Chicago: University of Chicago Press.

Boswell, J. (1994). *Same-sex unions in premodern Europe.* New York: Villard Books.

Bullough, V. L. (1976). *Sexual variance in society and history.* New York: Wiley.

Byne, W., & Parsons, B. (1993, March). Human sexual orientation: The biologic theories reappraised. *Archives of General Psychiatry, 50,* 228–239.

Diamond, M. (1965). A critical evaluation of the ontogeny of human sexual behavior. *Quarterly Review of Biology, 40,* 147–175.

Diamond, M. (1968). Genetic-endocrine interaction and human psychosexuality. In M. Diamond (Ed.), *Perspectives in reproduction and sexual behavior.* Bloomington: Indiana University Press.

Diamond, M. (1979). Sexual identity and sex roles. In V. Bullough (Ed.), *The frontiers of sex research* (pp. 35–56). Buffalo, NY: Prometheus.

Diamond, M. (1982). Sexual identity, monozygotic twins reared in discordant sex roles and a BBC follow-up. *Archives of Sexual Behavior, 11*(2), 181–186.

Dittman, R. W., Kappes, M. E., & Kappes, M. H. (1992). Sexual behavior in adolescent and adult females with congenital adrenal hyperplasia. *Psychoneuroendocrinology, 17,* 153–170.

Dorner, G., Rhode, W., Stahl, F., Krell, L., & Masius, W. G. (1975). A neuroendocrine predisposition for homosexuality in men. *Archives of Sexual Behavior, 4,* 1–8.

Dover, K. J. (1978). *Greek homosexuality.* Cambridge, MA: Harvard University Press.

Dundes, A. (1985). The American game of "smear the queer" and the homosexual component of male competitive sport and warfare. *Journal of Psychoanalytic Anthropology, 8*(3), 115–129.

Ehrhardt, A. A., Meyer-Bahlburg, H. F., Feldman, J. F., & Ince, S. E. (1984). Sex-dimorphic behavior in childhood subsequent to prenatal exposure to exogenous progestogens and estrogens. *Archives of Sexual Behavior, 13,* 457–477.

Feldman, M. P., & MacCulloch, M. J. (1971). *Homosexual behavior: Therapy and assessment.* Oxford: Pergamon Press.

Freud, S. (1905). Three essays on the theory of sexuality. In J. Strachey (Ed.), *The standard edition of the complete psychological works of Sigmund Freud* (Vol. 7, pp. 123–246). London: Hogarth, 1953.

Freud, S. (1920). The psychogenesis of a case of homosexuality in a woman. In J. Strachey (Ed.), *The standard edition of the complete psychological works of Sigmund Freud* (Vol. 18, pp. 155–172). London: Hogarth, 1955.

Friedman, R. C., & Downey, J. (1993). Psychoanalysis, psychobiology, and homosexuality. *Journal of the American Psychoanalytic Association, 41*(4), 1159–1198.

Gadpaille, W. J. (1980). Cross-species and cross-cultural contributions to understanding homosexual activity. *Archives of General Psychiatry, 37*(3), 349–356.

Gladue, B. A., Green, R., & Hellman, R. E. (1984). Neuroendocrine response to estrogen and sexual orientation. *Science, 225,* 1496–1499.

Golden, C. (1990, August). *Our politics and our choices: The feminist movement and sexual orientation.* Paper presented at the American Psychological Association, Boston.

Gonsiorek, J. C. (1988). Mental health issues of gay and lesbian adolescents. *Journal of Adolescent Health Care, 9,* 114–122.

Gooren, L. (1986a). The neuroendocrine response of luteinizing hormone to estrogen administration in heterosexual, homosexual and transsexual subjects. *Journal of Clinical Endocrinological Metabolism, 63,* 583–588.

Gooren, L. (1986b). The neuroendocrine response of luteinizing hormone to estrogen administration in the human is not sex specific but dependent on the hormonal environment. *Journal of Clinical Endocrinological Metabolism, 63,* 589–593.

Gooren, L. (1990). Biomedical theories of sexual orientation: A critical examination. In D. P. McWhirter, S. A. Sanders & J. M. Reinisch (Eds.), *Homosexuality/heterosexuality: Concepts of sexual orientation* (pp. 71–87). New York: Oxford University Press.

Gottesman, I. I. (1963). Genetic aspects of intelligent behavior. In N. Ellis (Ed.), *Handbook of mental deficiency: Psychological theory and research.* New York: McGraw-Hill.

Gottlieb, G. (1970). Conceptions of prenatal development. In L. R. Aronson, E. Tobach, D. S. Lehrman & J. S. Rosenblatt (Eds.), *Development and evolution of behavior: Essays in memory of T. C. Schneirla.* San Francisco: Freeman.

Green, R. (1985). Gender identity in childhood and later sexual orientation: Follow-up of seventy-eight males. *American Journal of Psychiatry, 142,* 339–341.

Green, R. (1987). *The "sissy boy syndrome" and the development of homosexuality.* New Haven, CT: Yale University Press.

Greenspoon, J., & Lamal, P. A. (1987). A behavioristic approach. In L. Diamant (Ed.), *Male and female homosexuality: Psychological approaches* (pp. 109–128). New York: Hemisphere Publishing Corporation.

Haldeman, D. C. (1991). Sexual orientation conversion therapy for gay men and lesbians: A scientific examination. In J. C. Gonsiorek and J. D. Weinrich (Eds.), *Homosexuality: Research implications for public policy* (pp. 149–160). Newbury Park, CA: Sage.

Halperin, D. M. (1990). *One hundred years of homosexuality and other essays on Greek love.* New York: Routledge.

Hamer, D. H., Hu, S., Magnuson, V. L., Hu, N., & Pattatucci, A. M. L. (1993, July 16). A linkage between DNA markers on the X chromosome and male sexual orientation. *Science, 261,* 321–327.

Herdt, G. H. (1981). *Guardians of the flutes: Idioms of masculinity.* New York: McGraw-Hill.

Herdt, G. H. (1984). *Ritualized homosexuality in Melanesia.* Berkeley: University of California Press.

Hines, M. (1982). Prenatal gonadal hormones and sex differences in human behavior. *Psychological Bulletin, 92,* 56–80.

Hooker, E. (1956). The adjustment of the male overt homosexual. In H. M. Ruittenbeck (Ed.), *The problem of homosexuality in modern America* (pp. 141–161). New York: Dutton.

Isay, R. (1989). *Being homosexual.* New York: Farrar, Straus & Giroux.

Kauth, M. R. & Landis, D. (1994, July). *The U.S. military's "Don't ask; Don't tell" personnel policy: Fear of the open homosexual.* Presented at Second International Congress on Prejudice, Discrimination and Conflict, Jerusalem, Israel.

Kester, P., Green, R., Finch, S. J., & Williams, K. (1980). Prenatal "female hormone" administration and psychosexual development in human males. *Psychoneuroendocrinology, 5,* 269–285.

Kinsey, A. C., Pomeroy, W. B., & Martin, C. E. (1948). *Sexual behavior in the human male.* Philadelphia: W. B. Saunders.

Kinsey, A. C., Pomeroy, W. B., Martin, C. E., & Gebhard, P. H. (1953). *Sexual behavior in the human female.* Philadelphia: W. B. Saunders.

Kraemer, G. W., Ebert, M. H., Lake, C. R., & McKinney, W. T. (1984). Hypersensitivity to d-amphetamine several years after early social deprivation in rhesus monkeys. *Psychopharmacology, 82,* 266–271.

Kuhn, T. S. (1970). *The structure of scientific revolutions* (2nd ed.). Chicago: University of Chicago Press.

Lerner, R. M. (1976). *Concepts and theories of human development.* Reading, MA: Addison-Wesley.

LeVay, S. (1991). A difference in hypothalamic structure between heterosexual and homosexual men. *Science, 253,* 1034–1037.

McWhirter, D. P., & Mattison, A. M. (1984). *The male couple: How relationships develop.* Englewood Cliffs, NJ: Prentice-Hall.

Marks, I. M., & Gelder, M. G. (1967). Transvestism and fetishism: Clinical and psychological changes during faradic aversion. *British Journal of Psychiatry, 113,* 711–729.

Masters, W. H., & Johnson, V. E. (1979). *Homosexuality in perspective.* Boston: Little, Brown.

Mead, M. (1935). *Sex and temperament in three primitive societies.* New York: William Morrow & Co.

Meyer-Bahlburg, H. F. (1984). Psychoendocrine research on sexual orientation: Current status and future options. *Progressive Brain Research, 61,* 375–398.

Money, J. (1988). *Gay, straight, and in-between: The sexology of erotic orientation.* New York: Oxford University Press.

Money, J. (1991). The development of sexuality and eroticism in humankind. In M. Haug, P. F. Brain & C. Aron (Eds.), *Heterotypical behaviour in man and animals* (pp. 127–166). London: Chapman and Hall.

Money, J., & Russo, A. J. (1979). Homosexual outcome of discordant gender activity role in childhood: Longitudinal follow-up. *Journal of Pediatric Psychology, 4,* 29–49.

Money, J., Schwartz, M., & Lewis, V. G. (1984). Adult erotosexual status and fetal hormonal masculinization and demasculinization: 46, XX congenital virilizing adrenal hyperplasia and 46, XY androgen-insensitivity syndrome compared. *Psychoneuroendocrinology, 9,* 405–414.

Oosterhuis, H., & Kennedy, H. (1991). *Homosexuality and male bonding in pre-Nazi Germany.* New York: Harrington Park Press.

Peplau, L. A., & Amaro, H. (1982). Understanding lesbian relationships. In W. Paul et al. (Eds.), *Homosexuality: Social, psychological and biological issues.* Beverly Hills, CA: Sage.

Pillard, R. C., & Weinrich, J. D. (1986). Evidence for a familial nature of male homosexuality. *Archives of General Psychiatry, 43,* 808–812.

Pronger, B. (1990). *The arena of masculinity: Sports, homosexuality, and the meaning of sex.* New York: St. Martin's Press.

Rado, S. (1940). A critical examination of the concept of bisexuality. *Psychosomatic Medicine, 2,* 459–467.

Ross, M. W. (1987). A theory of normal homosexuality. In L. Diamant (Ed.), *Male and female homosexuality: Psychological approaches* (pp. 237–259.) New York: Hemisphere Publishing Corporation.

Shilts, R. (1993). *Conduct unbecoming: Gays and Lesbians in the U.S. military.* New York: Fawcett Columbine.

Socarides, C. (1968). *The overt homosexual.* New York: Grune & Stratton.

Socarides, C., & Volkan, V. (1990). *The homosexualities: Reality, fantasy, and the arts.* Madison, CT: International University Press.

Trivers, R. L. (1972). Parental investment and sexual selection. In B. Campbell (Ed.), *Sexual selection and the descent of man, 1871–1971* (pp. 136–179). Chicago: Aldine.

Trivers, R. L. (1974). Parent-offspring conflict. *American Zoologist, 14,* 249–264.

Turner, A. M., & Greenough, W. T. (1985). Differential rearing effects on rat visual cortex synapses, I: Synaptic and neuronal density and synapses per neuron. *Brain Research, 329,* 195–203.

Weinberg, M. S., Williams, C. J., & Pryor, D. W. (1994). *Dual attractions: Understanding bisexuality.* New York: Oxford University Press.

Weinrich, J. D. (1987). *Sexual landscapes: Why we are what we are, why we love whom we love.* New York: Charles Scribner's Sons.

Weinrich, J. D. (1990). The Kinsey scale in biology, with a note on Kinsey as a biologist. In D. P. McWhirter, S. A. Sanders & J. M. Reinisch (Eds.), *Homosexuality/heterosexuality: Concepts of sexual orientation* (pp. 115–137). New York: Oxford University Press.

Whalen, R. E. (1991). Heterotypical behaviour in man and animals: Concepts and strategies. In M. Haug, P. F. Brain & C. Aron (Eds.), *Heterotypical behaviour in man and animals* (pp. 215–227). London: Chapman and Hall.

Wiedeman, G. H. (1974). Homosexuality: A survey. *Journal of American Psychoanalytic Association, 22,* 651–696.

Willerman, L., & Cohen, D. (1990). *Psychopathology.* New York: McGraw-Hill.

Williams, W. L. (1986). *The spirit and the flesh: Sexual diversity in American Indian culture.* Boston: Beacon Press.

5

Psychoanalysis and Male Homosexuality

Kenneth Lewes

The subject of homosexuality has occupied a central place in psychoanalytic thinking from the beginning. Although psychoanalysis has never absolutely decided what causes homosexuality—whether homosexuality is an emotional disturbance or even just what homosexuality really is—psychoanalytic theoreticians and clinicians have nevertheless made important contributions to such issues. The debates swirling around these complex questions continue to this day and have a history of their own, which, though long and convoluted, can be summarized in a few sentences. Freud never concluded whether homosexuality was a pathological condition or merely represented a variant of the many forms that mature adult sexuality might assume. But by the 1930s, psychoanalysts generally thought it was an emotional disturbance—either a perversion (classified with fetishism, sadism, pedophilia, and the like) or a stunting and blockage of a more "natural" heterosexuality. This view continued unchallenged until the 1970s, when analytically oriented clinicians again began to think of it as a variant. This is now the official position of psychiatrists and clinical psychologists, but some, perhaps many, psychoanalysts still adhere to the older, more conservative view of it as pathology (Lewes 1988). Recently, the most powerful argument for considering homosexuality an entirely "natural" condition comes from biologists, who argue for genetic, neurologic, or hormonal causes for that orientation. It is not yet clear how such arguments will ultimately affect psychoanalytic theories of homosexuality, but the relation between biological and psychoanalytic explanations today provides one of the liveliest debates in the behavioral sciences.[1]

FREUD'S THEORIES

The psychoanalytic theory of homosexuality began with Freud, who laid out the basic terms for the discourse in his "Three Essays on the Theory of Sexuality," which he kept revising for twenty years. From his knowledge of the varieties of sexual behavior in his patients and in literature and anthropology, he distinguished between the sexual drive itself (what he called libido) and the persons or things sought out for sex (the libidinal object), observing that one libidinal object could be substituted for another without essentially changing libido itself. How these substitutions occurred, what psychic forces required them to be made, and what effect they had on psychological functioning in general came to occupy him for almost his entire life (Freud 1905).

For Freud, sexuality was not a simple, natural aspect of human functioning and development, not even the usual, "normal" form, heterosexuality. Instead, all forms of adult sexuality were the end results of a complex set of inhibitions and transformations of libido and in this sense were all neurotic: that is, they were all shaped and determined by unconscious processes of anxiety and psychic defense. Thus, for Freud, the fact that homosexuality was neurotically determined by such processes did not distinguish it from the similarly determined heterosexuality. In fact, heterosexuality was as puzzling a phenomenon to Freud as homosexuality, and he thought that it required an explanation as much as homosexuality did (1905, note from 1915, pp. 145–146). The theory he evolved to account for homosexuality formed part of his larger project of describing the psychic processes that, in their complexity, determined all variations in adult sexual orientation and behavior (Freud 1924).

According to his developmental scheme, sexuality begins shortly after birth when infants are neither heterosexual nor homosexual but are stimulated and excited by any number of experiences, only a few of which can be considered sexual from an adult point of view. Infants are all, in his famous phrase, "polymorphously perverse" (Freud 1905, pp. 191, 234, 277). In the first months of life, the oral stage, the infant's sensual gratification inheres in nursing, and the preponderance of stimulation and excitement arises from the skin, the mucous membranes, and, most important, the mouth. Later, in the anal stage, the locus of excitement shifts to the anus, and gratification inheres in defecation. At about 4 years of age, another shift, the phallic stage, gradually occurs, this time to the genitals—the penis for boys and the clitoris for girls—as pleasure becomes unequivocally sexual for the first time.

Several ideas inhere in this developmental scheme, which is essentially a "natural" maturational process and involves no significant operation of anxiety and inhibition, and thus resembles what we might expect in the sexual development of higher but nonhuman animals. As libido, the drive itself and innate search for pleasure, undergoes development with the shift in locus of excitement from mouth to anus to genitals, certain libidinal objects are preferred over others only because of their ability to stimulate and give pleasure, not essentially because they are male or female. Children therefore are neither heterosexual nor homosexual but merely the recipients of pleasurable stimulation acting on their sensory organs.

With the onset of the phallic stage, however, new factors intervene, which henceforth transform sexual development from a "natural," animal maturational scheme into a "neurotic," human developmental sequence. The most important is that the child, with growing awareness of the world and a separate identity, makes the crucial recognition of sexual differences. For the 4-year-old boy, all people fall into two categories: those who have penises like his own and those who have mysteriously lost them. In addition, he now actively seeks out the figure who has since birth provided the preponderance of his sexual excitement and pleasure—most commonly, his mother—as he tries in some obscure way to act on her with his penis, the organ that provides him with his most vivid pleasures. But as he makes this active choice, he becomes aware that he has entered into competition with his father for possession of the mother, and he actively wishes to eliminate the father as rival, either by killing him off or by castrating him. In a parallel manner, another set of competitive fantasies develops, this time driven by the boy's passive yearnings for the father and his wishes to continue passively to receive excitement and pleasure from him and his intense rivalry with the mother for sole possession of the father. Both sets of wishes occur simultaneously, although one set will be stronger for some boys than for others. This complicated, fourfold set of relationships constitutes what Freud called the Oedipus complex (Freud 1923).

What makes the operation of the Oedipus complex so momentous for the boy's sexual development is that the strength of his sexual wishes to possess one or both parents is checked by an equally strong fear of retaliation from the rival parent. Specifically, the boy's recent recognition of sexual differences provides the basis for his terror: if one or both parents are desired for the pleasure they can provide to his penis, the fear checking him is his fantasy of losing that very organ. Thus, along with incestuous wishes for one parent comes the counterbalancing fear of castration by the other. This balance of desire and dread is the prototype of what Freud meant by psychic conflict and represents the central, crucial event of childhood. The way the boy resolves it determines what pathways he will take to the final form of his adult sexuality (Freud 1925).

Boys who grow up to be heterosexual resolve the conflict between desire and fear in favor of fear: the mother's penis-less, "castrated" state reminds them that it is possible to suffer that fate, and they imagine that the father, in angry rivalry, will castrate them. In response to this possibility, the boy relinquishes his claims on the now partly loathed mother and seeks to pacify the father by deferring to him and leaving him as sole possessor of the mother. This he does by internalizing the image of the father and becoming like him, and, in doing so, lays the foundation for his superego. He is thus transformed from a "natural," pleasure-seeking animal into a "neurotic" human being whose impulses are now internally controlled by his conscience, his superego (Freud 1923). Finally, he psychically leaves the arena of sexual rivalry as he enters the "latency" stage of development, and a kind of amnesia settles over the entire conflict. For the next half-dozen years or so, the boy directs his energies toward nonsexual goals as he learns to function in and adapt to the social world (Erikson 1950). His sexual strivings are renewed at puberty when he seeks an object that unconsciously resembles his mother, his now-forgotten oedipal object, but differs from her sufficiently for his old castration anxieties not to be reenergized. Nonetheless, throughout his adult life, he will continue to be nagged by such anxieties whenever his deeper sexual or aggressive nature is stirred (Freud 1923).

This scheme was the prototype for male resolution of the Oedipus complex, and later psychoanalysts came to consider it as the only "normal" and "natural" process (Feldman 1956; Kardiner 1954). For Freud, though, it was, despite its commonness, not the only one. It was also a neurotic development, and its result was lifelong anxiety and guilt (1908, pp. 186ff.). While by far the largest proportion of heterosexual men underwent basically the same resolution of the Oedipus complex, Freud recognized that different forms of homosexuality employed distinctly different oedipal schemes. He outlined four of them, which have one characteristic in common: unlike the heterosexual resolution of the Oedipus complex, wherein the boy surrenders his oedipal object out of fear of castration, all four homosexual resolutions seek to maintain erotic ties to the oedipal object while at the same time attempting to minimize the conscious experience of castration dread.

The first variation is the simplest. The boy attempts to preserve his libidinal tie to the mother unconsciously, but to do so he must find a way of diminishing the intensity of his castration fear. He therefore seeks unconscious assurance from his libidinal object that castration is not a possibility, that his mother has not been deprived of her penis, and that his father will not succeed in his terrible revenge. Hence he looks for a libidinal object that unites characteristics of the mother with the possession of a penis and finds it in a young, effeminate boy, who in his unconscious represents a woman with a penis. Homosexual men who employ this particular resolution of the Oedipus complex will seek out as their partners only young men and boys, but their ability to form rich and stable relationships with them is compromised by their lurking castration fear, and they typically harbor extreme feelings of loathing for women. In many ways, they resembled fetishists and exhibitionists, who, according to Freud, are also driven to seek out deep, unconscious assurance that women, despite appearances, really do possess a penis (Freud 1910, pp. 94ff.).

The second variation is rather more complicated, although it is motivated by the same wish. Rather than seeking to maintain the mother as unconscious object, homosexuals of the second variation try instead unconsciously to preserve the relationship that existed between them and their mothers. To accomplish this, they identify with their mothers and choose as their objects men who resemble an idealized image they maintain of themselves. They henceforth love them as they imagined they were once loved themselves or as they wish they had been loved. Because of their simultaneous identification with both their libidinal objects and their lost mother, such men are typically effeminate and maternal in their behavior and personality traits and characteristically seek out ideally beautiful and "perfect" men on whom to lavish affection and generosity (Freud 1910, pp. 99–100; 1905, note from 1910, p. 144).

The third variation is markedly different from the others in that it does not involve the mother as primary oedipal object but derives from the boy's longing to be the passive libidinal object of his father. According to Freud, all boys experience such wishes, and all adult men continue to harbor them unconsciously in varying degrees of intensity, but for some boys, the erotic longing for the father is constitutionally stronger than corresponding wishes for the mother. Other boys desire the mother more strongly than the father, but their Oedipus complex is so fraught with anxiety that they seek safety in the relatively less anxious tie to the father. Both groups of boys can become "fixated" at this "negative" or "inverted" aspect of the Oedipus complex, and for them, the most desirable libidinal objects are those that resemble the yearned-for father. Such homosexual men typically attach themselves to older men and establish quasi-pedagogical relationships with them. They idealize the penis of the partner and harbor fantasies—either conscious or unconscious—of bearing their children or of becoming idealized men themselves through incorporating their masculinity by swallowing semen (Freud 1923, pp. 33ff.).

The fourth and the last variation, like the first two, involves the mother as libidinal object but, unlike the first three, is initiated by the consequences not of erotic wishes but of aggressive ones. It posits a similar refusal to relinquish the erotic bond to the mother but focuses on the boy's rivalry with erotic competitors—his father or, in some cases, older brothers. This rivalry can become so intense and murderous that the boy fantasizes correspondingly murderous retribution from them. He masters the set wishes by a process Freud called "reaction formation." That is, the rivalrous feelings are preserved in all their intensity, but they are converted into their opposites, and where he once hated virile men as rivals, he now loves them as erotic objects. Such men typically are quite masculine in appearance, are sometimes bisexual in behavior, and are frequently characterized by highly developed, though sometimes unstable, feelings of esteem and admiration for other men (Freud 1922, pp. 231–232).

These are the four processes Freud outlined, although he acknowledged that there were very likely many more to be discovered. It is important to note several implicit ideas that Freud and his immediate followers espoused but later psychoanalysts until the 1970s either ignored or explicitly denied (Bergler 1947; Gershman 1957; Kestenberg 1971; Rado 1940). First, homosexuality does not represent a single, unitary phenomenon. Instead, it is more accurate to speak of "the homosexualities," since apart from the choice of same-sex objects, the four separate varieties have little in common among themselves. Second, these and other forms of homosexuality represent a wide range of psychological adaptation, which corresponds to the range from pathological to "normal" one finds among heterosexuals (Glover 1933, pp. 486, 495, 500). In other words, there is nothing in Freud's formulations to support the view that a homosexual orientation is inherently and necessarily psychopathological (Lewes 1988, pp. 82–84). Third, the instincts, drives, fantasies, and defense mechanisms that give rise to homosexuality are not specific to homosexuality but constitute part of a universal human psychic reservoir. Fourth, and most important for the contemporary debate, since homosexuality is not essentially different from heterosexuality apart from the fact that homosexual activity does not result in procreation, there is no apparent reason that psychoanalysis should attempt to "cure" that condition. Freud and his followers were explicit in condemning what at a later time would be called homophobia (e.g., Ferenczi 1916). If homosexuals suffered from society's judgment of them, the fault lay in society. Fifth, it is not only pointless to attempt to "cure" homosexuality but probably also impossible. A homosexual's orientation arises from so deep a stratum in his personality and is determined by so basic a configuration that, in Freud's words, "to undertake to convert a fully developed homosexual into a heterosexual is not much more promising than to do the reverse" (Freud 1920, p. 151). Finally, a homosexual orientation is not caused by learning or by imitating others, nor is it determined by seduction. Instead, it results from a complex set of unconscious psychic mechanisms that are complete by the age of 6.

Given these ideas, it is not surprising that the early psychoanalytic attitude toward homosexuality was either objective and neutral or quite positive. For early analysts, it represented merely a set of variations of a basic human sexuality. Although there were surely many troubled, unhappy, or disturbed homosexuals (and these, they recognized, were more typical of people encountered in psychoanalytic treatment), there were others who were happy, productive, and highly creative (Freud 1908, p. 180). Freud himself repeatedly called attention to the often striking correspondence of homosexuality with creative achievement (1910, 1914, 1951). In addition, all the early Freudians believed in the essential bisexuality of all human beings and used this idea to account for many of the achievements and failures of people who embraced a heterosexual orientation (Boehm 1920; Brill 1913). For the first two decades of the history of the psychoanalytic movement, then, psychoanalysts had evolved a discourse and theory that was quite friendly and positive to homosexuals and to the homosexual movement that was developing in Europe.

Later Analytic Views

This untroubled relationship did not continue for long. For the next forty years, most psychoanalysts took a progressively more critical view of homosexuality, seeing it increasingly as a pathological condition. During this period, homosexuals themselves did not change, but psychoanalysis did. Most basically, after Freud's initial discoveries, psychoanalysis began to direct its attention to psychic stages and developments earlier and more primitive than those that occupied Freud's attention (Fine 1979; Oberndorf 1953). This redirection of attention to prephallic stages led to important and profound insights about psychosexual development and allowed analysts to understand and treat mental conditions that had eluded Freud (Rosenfeld 1949). To that extent, this was an important and positive development. But insofar as the center of attention in psychoanalytic theory shifted to more disturbed and primitive mental conditions, the psychoanalytic understanding of homosexuality as a whole suffered, as the figure of the "typical" homosexual became more disturbed, primitive, and fragmented.

Recall that for Freud, the psychic birth of the human being occurred with the Oedipus complex. Almost all psychological problems were explained by using that construct, and psychoanalytic treatment, for the most part, consisted of analyzing and resolving conflicts that arose during its operations (Fenichel 1945). With analysts who came into prominence in the 1930s, however, the Oedipus complex, important as it was, represented merely the last of a series of developmental crises that extended back into the oral stage. For them, the very fact that an individual had arrived at the complex meant that he had already successfully negotiated more basic preceding crises (Klein 1932). Confronted by examples of mental disturbance that did not respond to traditional analysis of the Oedipus complex (and homosexuality was one condition that seemed not to be "cured" through psychoanalysis), these later analysts argued that such disturbance stemmed from disruptions of psychosexual development at stages earlier and more primitive than the phallic (Bergler 1949; Socarides 1968).

Oral theories of psychosexual development are extremely difficult to summarize, but they clearly differ from more classical theories in the emphasis they place on the earliest stages of development—oral and anal. In this early period, the infant is involved not in a triangular relationship with mother and father but a dyadic one with the mother alone. And while in the phallic stage, the primary project occupying the child is the winning of the oedipal object, in the oral stage it is the psychic differentiation of the self from the mother. In this struggle, the infant attempts to negotiate his relationship not with the mother's genitals but with her breast, and the drive he attempts to master is not pleasure-seeking libido but rage and aggression (Segal 1979, pp. 76–89, 113–124).

Although oral theories for the development of homosexuality emphasize one or another aspect, I can still outline a basic developmental scheme that most oral analysts would subscribe to. According to them, infants who will become homosexual never complete the process of psychic differentiation from the mother generally referred to as separation-individuation. Never having formed clear and reliable boundaries between themselves and their object, the mother's breast, they remain fixated at this point in their development, unable to enter the Oedipus complex. The psychological consequences of this fixation is that they remain identified with the mother at a primitive level and never achieve a stable male identity. In addition, this identification is quite unstable, as the homosexual vacillates between seeking to recapture a lost union with the mother and fleeing from the horror of engulfment that such a union would represent (Socarides 1968). This contradictory search for union and independence is played out in the homosexual's later erotic relationships as he seeks the lost breast of his mother in his partner's penis in a driven attempt to love libidinal objects and simultaneously to vent the rage that results from a frustrated struggle for self-differentiation (Bergler 1956). These men suffer under a seriously split ego, which is unable to unite disparate images and feelings into one stable whole. Hence they are prone to compulsive sexual behaviors, substance abuse, violent and unprovoked emotional storms, and an inability either to be alone or to experience true intimacy (Bychowski 1945). Because of their fractured identities, they have never really experienced the Oedipus complex or achieved its positive results, most notably a stable superego, which would allow them to contain and control their impulses or to obey basic social rules and conventions (Bergler 1959; Hendin 1978).

Even analysts who were not primarily interested in the oral phase of sexual development contributed to the view that homosexuality represented a disturbed and "unnatural" condition. Most important, after the death of Freud, who had insisted on the universality of bisexuality in all people, an important group of analysts denied that homosexual or bisexual trends existed in a healthy constitution (Rado 1940). Men, they claimed, were unqualifiedly masculine and should seek out only women as their passive sexual objects. That a man experienced any sexual desire for another man or entertained passive wishes was itself a sign of psychopathology, which had resulted from the blockage of more "natural" heterosexual strivings. In these terms, homosexuality represented a damaged, second-best attempt at object choice, an alternative that was psychically safer than heterosexual striving. For them, homosexuality could never be thought of as "natural" or "healthy" (Gershman 1966; Kardiner 1954).

This is, to be sure, an extremely dark portrayal of homosexual personality and behavior. Its saving feature is its ability to describe and account for certain extremely disturbed cases of what later would be called borderline personality disorders (Klein 1932). Such suffering occurs in both homosexual and heterosexual people, and there is nothing in this description that is really specific to homosexuality, but an extreme and hateful portrayal of the "typical homosexual" nevertheless characterized much psychoanalytic writing on homosexuality from the 1930s to the 1970s (Bergler 1959; Fried 1960; Kardiner 1954). The general air of hostility between psychoanalysis and homosexuals derives from this phase of psychoanalytic theory, which has been repudiated by most analysts, but traces of it are still to be found in some contemporary psychoanalytic opinion (Socarides 1979). In any case, it represents an extended shameful episode in the history of psychoanalysis, and it caused much cruel and unnecessary suffering.

The ideas I have been discussing represent the most extreme and lurid psychoanalytic theories of homosexuality, but during this period, other ideas came to be formulated; they are perhaps more recognizable and plausible, even though it can be argued that they represent the same narrowness of view. The most widely disseminated was proposed by Bieber and his colleagues in 1962, who undertook a survey of 106 homosexual men in psychoanalytic treatment (Bieber et al. 1962). Although the sample Bieber employed was psychologically quite disturbed and therefore not representative of the population of homosexuals as a whole, he proposed a model for the development of homosexuality that emphasized the childhood families of these men. They found a majority of "close-binding-intimate mothers," who were seductive toward their sons and inhibited their relationships with their father and with their peers, discouraging them from developing masculine personalities. Along with this, Bieber found that not one subject in his study recalled a warm and supportive relationship with his father, remembering him instead as detached, hostile, or rejecting. Thus, for Bieber, what primarily determined homosexuality in men was neither an individual's biological or psychological nature, nor intrapsychic processes of defense, but patterns of child rearing and particular kinds of families. He assumed that homosexuality was a damaged, pathological condition and that its cause was defective parents, especially mothers, of homosexuals. Implicit in this view was the hope that although homosexuality might not easily be "cured," it could be prevented by correcting faulty family dynamics.

Another approach to homosexuality was articulated by Ovesey and his "adaptational" school of analysis, which distinguished between true homosexuality, which was a disturbance of sexuality, and "pseudohomosexuality," which represented difficulties over issues of dependency and power (Ovesey 1969). For Ovesey, pseudohomosexuals were men who were deeply convinced of their inability to be competent in the social world and who acted under a series of unconscious equations: "I am a failure = I am castrated = I am not a man = I am a woman = I am a homosexual" (Ovesey 1954, p. 247). According to him, many forms of overt homosexuality were thus motivated by despair over competence, which led to a displacement of "normal" heterosexual function onto the "safer" arena of homosexual behavior. Therapy and "cure" for such men consisted of uncovering and analyzing their fear of competence and buttressing their weakened sense of masculinity.

By the 1970s, then, psychoanalytic ideas about homosexuality, which had begun so promisingly with Freud, had evolved into a discourse that for the most part was quite homophobic (Lewes 1988, pp. 140–172). With only a few exceptions, most analysts, although disagreeing on many subsidiary issues, agreed about several major ones. Homosexuality for them was a psychological disturbance, either a relatively benign oedipal disturbance or a more severe preoedipal one. It was not simply a question of a difference in the sex of the libidinal object but of serious disturbances in impulse control, ego functioning, and superego formation. Homosexuals, accordingly, were incapable of real intimacy, stable emotional ties to others, or genuine satisfaction and achievement in life. All suffered under a defective masculinity and were essentially handicapped in their ability to lead rich and rewarding lives (Fried 1960; Bergler 1956, 1959; Kardiner 1954). The only adequate therapeutic goal in the psychoanalytic treatment of such men was to "cure" them. Merely to attempt to make them less anxious and more content with their lot was to admit to a kind of therapeutic despair. Some analysts, especially those in Europe (e.g., Glover 1939), challenged this view, of course, but their objections were never really answered or adequately addressed.

Apart from the adequacy, fairness, or even basic humanity of these views, the analytic theory of homosexuality by the 1970s was also quite unstable and approaching a crisis. Most generally, even those most committed to these theoretical formulations admitted that the theory was conceptually unsatisfying. There were many cases of homosexuality that did not correspond to proposed developmental schemes, and many people whose history corresponded to these schemes turned out not to be homosexual. Despite many attempts, no one was able to propose a set of characteristics and psychosexual histories that applied to all or even most cases of homosexuality (Wiedemann 1962). And for those who were aware of such things, homosexuals in the real world did not correspond to the picture psychoanalysis had painted of the "sad, dark world of the homosexual." Finally and most telling, psychoanalysis, for all its subtle and complex ideas, could not claim that it was effective in achieving a cure. Although a few analysts claimed impressive rates (Bergler 1947; Socarides 1969), no coherent or systematic body of evidence supported these claims, and almost all homosexuals who undertook psychoanalysis in order to be "cured" were disappointed. The record of psychoanalysis in curing homosexuality thus remained much as it had appeared to Freud, who characterized it as "not very impressive" (1920 p. 151).

MODERN ANALYTIC IDEAS

By the 1970s, those outside the psychoanalytic establishment and many within it were dissatisfied with the theory of homosexuality as it had evolved since Freud. There were many important insights that had to be acknowledged, but the theory itself was inconsistent and powerful only in fragments. Even analytic advocates admitted that there simply was no coherent theory (Wiedemann 1974). Still, the striking turnabout that occurred in the psychoanalytic theory of homosexuality beginning in the 1970s was not really generated from within psychoanalysis itself but from larger intellectual and cultural developments. The first and most important group that successfully challenged traditional analytic ideas about homosexuality was, of course, homosexuals themselves, who no longer acquiesced in their portrayal as psychic cripples or sociopathic deviants but challenged it on the basis of accuracy, basic human decency, and justice. They made their claims by citing empirical data that contradicted psychoanalytic observations obtained in a casual, unsystematic manner (Ford & Beach 1951;

Hooker 1957; Saghir & Robins 1973). This group, though it had no representation inside psychoanalysis itself, was able to influence informed opinion in such related disciplines as psychiatry, clinical psychology, and psychiatric social work, so that by 1973, the three professional organizations officially rejected the idea that homosexuality is a mental disorder (Bayer 1981). Over the next twenty years, psychoanalytic organizations gradually and grudgingly followed suit.

The second group that helped shift psychoanalytic opinion was feminist critics of psychoanalytic ideas of sexuality and gender development, who faulted the theory for being unnecessarily male oriented and "phallocentric," and who pointed out how such an emphasis had limited conceptualizing the ways by which people could achieve a mature and healthy sexuality. Though focusing primarily on the psychoanalytic theory of femininity, they helped widen the discourse so that other theorists could, for the first time in fifty years, consider alternative dynamics and developmental schemes. In addition, their criticism of analytic norms of masculinity made it possible to maintain that homosexuality could be a perfectly adequate and undamaged form of masculinity (Benjamin 1988; Chodorow 1989).

The third group, biological researchers, not only occupied a position outside psychoanalysis but often claimed an antianalytic stance, denying the basic analytic project of deriving adult sexual orientation from infantile and childhood experience. They claimed, to the contrary, that the primary determinant of sexual orientation was biological in nature, although individual developmental patterns did play a part (LeVay & Hamer 1994). Population studies suggested that a homosexual orientation was a widespread and relatively common occurrence (Gebhard 1972), transcending all sorts of cultural differences that influence family organizations and patterns of child rearing (Ford & Beach 1951). In addition, homosexuality seemed to occur in some families more frequently than in others and often followed a maternal line of transmission (Bailey & Pillard 1991). All this suggested that homosexuality might be governed by genetic, not psychological, principles. Preliminary confirmation of this view followed with the identification of a particular spot on the X chromosome that was consistent with maternal patterns of inheritance (Hamer et al. 1993), and the discovery of brain structures that differed in size between homosexual and heterosexual men (LeVay 1991).

All of this work is quite preliminary, and most of it is fraught with methodological deficiencies and ambiguous results. Some of it has not proved replicable, and one finding frequently contradicts another (Byne 1994; Byne & Parsons 1993). In addition, the history of such research has been marked by what seemed to be conclusive results that proved in the end to be mistaken. As of 1995, no researcher has produced conclusive results that satisfy strict biological research norms. More important, no one has proposed a convincing way of conceptualizing a process that mediates between a biochemical event or structure and the complex observable set of behaviors that constitute a sexual orientation.

Still, the general trend of biological research has been toward the view that adult sexual orientation is determined primarily by biological, as opposed to psychological, factors (Friedman & Downey 1993).

In obvious ways such a view contradicts and denies psychoanalytic theory, but in other important ways, it is compatible with certain aspects of traditional analytic ideas. First, both points of view see a homosexual orientation as determined quite early in life. Although homosexual behavior may not appear until adolescence, its determinants are firmly in place by the end of the first six years. Thus, both camps reject the idea that homosexuality is "caused" by homosexual role models or by seduction in adolescence or adulthood. Second, both see individual psychological development as a process by which interpersonal and intrapsychic events transform a given biological constitution (Friedman 1988). While psychoanalysis emphasizes psychological factors and processes of anxiety and defense, it has always in the end accounted for why one individual embraces one set of dynamics and not another by referring to an individual's biological nature, his "constitution." And for Freud, at least, constitution was always prior to and more determinative of sexual orientation than individual dynamics (Freud 1920).

In these terms, one can see that recent biological findings, should they prove to be accurate, although they force a reconceptualization of some traditional analytic ideas, are quite compatible with the basic psychoanalytic project and can provide it with a new focus and mode of approach. Even if biology should demonstrate conclusively that a homosexual orientation is determined at birth and that it is therefore an entirely "normal" and "natural" condition, it still remains necessary for psychoanalysis to trace the exact ways such a biological potential develops and exfoliates. The task for psychoanalysis with respect to homosexuality thus resembles that facing Freud when he undertook to describe the ways psychosexual development occurred for all people. These new biological findings, then, may signal a new beginning for the psychoanalytic theory of homosexuality.

Consequently, the most recent work in psychoanalysis on homosexuality can be seen as a response to this new reconceptualization. What distinguishes it from more traditional analytic approaches is that, whether or not it subscribes to the modern biological trend, it assumes at the outset the complete equivalence of homosexuality with heterosexuality with respect to its "normalcy" and "naturalness." It deals, of course, with psychopathology but does not view it as intrinsic to a homosexual orientation and instead traces patterns of homosexual development much as it would the heterosexual equivalent. It no longer sees homosexuality as a defense against a previous anxiety-fraught heterosexual orientation. The striving for same-sex libidinal objects is merely given, much the way the search for cross-sex objects is. Theoretically, this means emphasizing the "negative" aspect of the Oedipus complex, wherein the young boy's primary libidinal attachment is to the father. But it reads this attachment back into the other mechanisms that psychoanalysis has uncovered using the mother as primary libidinal object. The father remains as the prototype for all later object choice and serves as the nucleus around which such defensive mechanisms as narcissistic identification operate (Corbett 1993). Thus, a boy may identify with his paternal oedipal object, retain a solidly masculine sexual identity, and still be stably homosexual in orientation. Other recent work focuses on the boy's shame and guilt as consequences of the father's rejection of his sexual strivings for him (Isay 1989, pp. 32–46). Implicit in this is the focus on homophobia, in both social and familial settings, as an important determinant of later homosexual neurotic inhibition (Isay 1989, pp. 67–81). In this work, there is no attempt to "cure" homosexuality or to convert it to heterosexuality through uncovering developmental dynamics. Instead, the goal becomes to lift neurotic inhibition and to encourage the full experience of intimacy and freedom from guilt and anxiety. Normative patterns of development and identity formation are more varied here than in traditional formulations, and they encompass a wide range of models of masculinity that include a complex interplay of sexual activity and passivity (Corbett 1993). As I have already suggested, it is not yet clear what stance psychoanalysis will take toward biological research: whether it will reject it as essentially antianalytic or assimilate it. It is important, however, to think carefully about what essential relation the two disciplines have to each other, at least with respect to the subject of homosexuality. Both seek to explain its origins, but each answers the question in ways that have radically different implications, ramifications, and significance. Biology attempts to explain through what biochemical mechanisms a homosexual orientation came to be. Psychoanalysis, on the other hand, attempts to understand the experience of being homosexual—what it means to be homosexual and how it affects other aspects of life. Its ultimate terms, then, are not physical processes but individual meanings (Schafer 1983). To this end, it can learn from and use scientific findings but it is not made obsolete by them.[2]

NOTES

1. This essay surveys only the psychoanalytic theory of male homosexuality, partly because the subject of female homosexuality has not occupied as prominent a place in psychoanalytic thinking as its male equivalent. Why this should be so, or why male homosexuality has been such an important subject, is an extremely interesting question, but it cannot be discussed here. Freud published an account of a lesbian patient (Freud 1920), but only a few analysts addressed the topic after him (e.g., Thompson 1947). So, in a certain sense, there has been no psychoanalytic theory of female homosexuality until recent times. What little attention psychoanalysis has devoted to lesbianism maintains that it is essentially a different condition or set of conditions from male homosexuality. It emphasizes the girl's preoedipal attachment to the mother and the later attempt to maintain a merged identity with the lesbian partner. Recently, lesbianism is beginning to receive the attention it deserves. Readers who wish to acquaint themselves with it might begin with O'Connor and Ryan (1993), Elise (1986), Burch (1993), and McDougall (1986).

2. I have indicated sources for ideas throughout, but those who wish to have an overview of the subject can try the following recommended readings. A detailed history of
psychoanalytic ideas about male homosexuality, along with a theoretical critique and
historical analysis, is provided in Lewes (1988). The story of the official deletion of
homosexuality from the list of mental disorders is well told by Bayer (1981). The classical theory of psychosexual development for heterosexuals and homosexuals was laid
out by Freud himself (1905), and an important and interesting elaboration of it was made
by Erikson (1950). The most important theorist of preoedipal development is Melanie
Klein, whose work is extremely difficult but interesting (1932). An overview of her ideas
is provided by Segal (1979). For a sampling of how this theory affected analytic views
of homosexuality, begin with Bychowski (1945), Bergler (1956), and Socarides (1968).
Relevant contemporary feminist developments are best represented by Benjamin (1988)
and Chodorow (1989). Recent biological research is quite technical. To understand and
evaluate it properly, one needs to be comfortable with statistical and genetic theory. Two
articles, however, summarize these projects and their conclusions. The first was written
by an analyst (Friedman & Downey 1993), the second by biological researchers (LeVay
& Hamer 1994). Their approach and conclusions, however, are challenged on serious
methodological and theoretical grounds by Byne and Parsons (1993) and Byne (1994).

REFERENCES

Bailey, J., & Pillard, R. (1991). A genetic study of male sexual orientation. *Archives of
General Psychiatry, 48,* 1089–1096.

Bayer, R. (1981). *Homosexuality and american psychiatry.* New York: Basic Books.

Benjamin, J. (1988). *The bonds of love: Psychoanalysis, feminism and the problem of
domination.* New York: Pantheon.

Bergler, E. (1947). Differential diagnosis between spurious homosexuality and perversion
homosexuality. *Psychiatric Quarterly, 21,* 399–409.

Bergler, E. (1949). *The basic neurosis.* New York: Harper and Brothers.

Bergler, E. (1956). *Homosexuality: Disease or way of life.* New York: Hill and Wang.

Bergler, E. (1959). *One thousand homosexuals: Conspiracy of silence or curing and
deglamorizing homosexuals?* Paterson, NJ: Pageant Books.

Bieber, I., et al. (1962). *Homosexuality: A psychoanalytic study of male homosexuals.*
New York: Basic Books.

Boehm, F. (1920). Beitraege zur Psychologie der Homosexualitaet I: Homosexualitaet
und Polygamie. *Internationale Zeitschrift fuer Psychoanalyse, 6,* 297–319.

Brill, A. (1913). The conception of homosexuality. *Journal of the American Medical
Association, 61,* 335–340.

Burch, B. (1993). Heterosexuality, bisexuality and lesbianism: Rethinking psychoanalytic
views of women's sexual object choice. *Psychoanalytic Review, 80,* 83–99.

Bychowski, G. (1945). The ego of homosexuals. *International Journal of Psychoanalysis,
26,* 114–127.

Byne, W. (1994). The biological evidence challenged. *Scientific American, 270,* 50–55.

Byne, W., & Parsons, B. (1993). Human sexual orientation: The biological theories reappraised. *Archives of General Psychiatry, 50,* 228–239.

Chodorow, N. (1989). *Feminism and psychoanalytic theory.* New Haven: Yale University
Press.

Corbett, K. (1993). The mystery of homosexuality. *Psychoanalytic Psychology, 10,* 345–357.

Elise, D. (1986). Lesbian couples: The implications of sex differences in separation-individuation. *Psychotherapy, 23,* 305–310.

Erikson, E. (1950). *Childhood and society.* New York: Norton.

Feldman, S. (1956). On homosexuality. In S. Lorand (Ed.), *Perversions, psychodynamics and therapy* (pp. 71–96). New York: Random House.

Fenichel, O. (1945). *The psychoanalytic theory of neurosis.* New York: Norton.

Ferenczi, S. (1916). The nosology of male homosexuality (homoerotism). In *Sex in psychoanalysis* (pp. 6–318). Boston: Gorham.

Fine, R. (1979). *A history of psychoanalysis.* New York: Columbia University Press.

Ford, C., & Beach, F. (1951). *Patterns of sexual behavior.* New York: Harper & Row.

Freud, S. (1905). Three essays on the theory of sexuality. In *The standard edition of the complete psychological works of Sigmund Freud* (Vol. 7, pp. 125–245). London: Hogarth Press.

Freud, S. (1908). "Civilized" sexual morality and modern nervous illness. In *The standard edition of the complete psychological works of Sigmund Freud* (Vol. 9, pp. 179–204). London: Hogarth Press.

Freud, S. (1910). Leonardo da Vinci and a memory of his childhood. In *The standard edition of the complete psychological works of Sigmund Freud* (Vol. 11, pp. 59–137). London: Hogarth Press.

Freud, S. (1914). The Moses of Michelangelo. In *The standard edition of the complete psychological works of Sigmund Freud* (Vol. 13, pp. 209–238). London: Hogarth Press.

Freud, S. (1920). The psychogenesis of a case of female homosexuality. In *The standard edition of the complete psychological works of Sigmund Freud* (Vol. 18, pp. 147–172). London: Hogarth Press.

Freud, S. (1922). Some neurotic mechanisms in jealousy, paranoia and homosexuality. In *The standard edition of the complete psychological works of Sigmund Freud* (Vol. 18, pp. 223–232). London: Hogarth Press.

Freud, S. (1923). The ego and the id. In *The standard edition of the complete psychological works of Sigmund Freud* (Vol. 19, pp. 1–66). London: Hogarth Press.

Freud, S. (1924). The dissolution of the Oedipus complex. In *The standard edition of the complete psychological works of Sigmund Freud* (Vol. 19, pp. 173–179). London: Hogarth Press.

Freud, S. (1925). Some psychical consequences of the anatomical distinction between the sexes. In *The standard edition of the complete psychological works of Sigmund Freud* (Vol. 19, pp. 243–258). London: Hogarth Press.

Freud, S. (1951). Letter to an American mother. *American Journal of Psychiatry, 107,* 786.

Fried, E. (1960). Homosexuality as a disturbance in human relationships. In *The ego in love and sexuality* (pp. 99–131). New York: Grune and Stratton.

Friedman, R. (1988). *Male homosexuality: A contemporary psychoanalytic perspective.* New Haven: Yale University Press.

Friedman, R., & Downey, J. (1993). Neurobiology and sexual orientation: Current relationships. *Journal of Neuropsychiatry and Clinical Neurosciences, 5,* 131–153.

Gebhard, R. (1972). Incidence of overt homosexuality in the United States and Western Europe. In J. Livingood (Ed.), *National Institute of Mental Health task force on homosexuality: Final report and background papers.* Washington, DC: US Department of Health, Education and Welfare.

Gershman, H. (1957). Psychopathology of compulsive homosexuality. *American Journal of Psychoanalysis, 17,* 58–77.

Gershman, H. (1966). Reflections on the nature of homosexuality. *American Journal of Psychoanalysis, 26,* 46–62.

Glover, E. (1933). The relation of perversion-formation to the development of reality sense. *International Journal of Psychoanalysis, 14,* 486–504.

Glover, E. (1939). *Psychoanalysis: A handbook for medical practitioners and students of comparative psychology.* London: Staples.

Hamer, D., et al. (1993). A linkage between DNA markers on the X chromosome and male sexual orientation. *Science, 261,* 321–327.

Hendin, H. (1978). Homosexuality: The psychosocial dimension. *Journal of the American Academy of Psychoanalysis, 6,* 479–496.

Hooker, E. (1957). The adjustment of the male overt homosexual. *Journal of Projective Techniques, 21,* 18–31.

Isay, R. (1989). *Being homosexual: Gay men and their development.* New York: Avon Books.

Kardiner, A. (1954). Flight from masculinity. In *Sex and morality* (pp. 160–192). Indianapolis: Bobbs-Merrill.

Kestenberg, J. (1971). A developmental approach to disturbances in sex-specific identity. *International Journal of Psychoanalysis, 52,* 99–102.

Klein, M. (1932). *The psychoanalysis of children.* London: Hogarth Press.

LeVay, S. (1991). A difference in hypothalamic structure between heterosexual and homosexual men. *Science, 253,* 1034–1037.

LeVay, S., & Hamer, D. (1994). Evidence for a biological influence in male homosexuality. *Scientific American, 270,* 44–49.

Lewes, K. (1988). *The psychoanalytic theory of male homosexuality.* New York: Simon and Schuster.

McDougall, J. (1986). Identification, neoneeds and neosexualities. *International Journal of Psychoanalysis, 67,* 19–31.

Oberndorf, C. (1953). *A history of psychoanalysis in America.* New York: Grune and Stratton.

O'Connor, N., & Ryan, J. (1993). *Wild desires and mistaken identities: Lesbianism and psychoanalysis.* New York: Columbia University Press.

Ovesey, L. (1954). The homosexual conflict: An adaptational analysis. *Psychiatry, 17,* 243–250.

Ovesey, L. (1969). *Homosexuality and pseudohomosexuality.* New York: Science House.

Rado, S. (1940). A critical examination of the concept of bisexuality. *Psychosomatic Medicine, 2,* 459–467.

Rosenfeld, H. (1949). Remarks on the relation of male homosexuality to paranoia, paranoid anxiety and narcissism. *International Journal of Psychoanalysis, 30,* 36–47.

Saghir, M., & Robins, E. (1973). *Male and female homosexuality: A comprehensive investigation.* Baltimore: Williams & Wilkins.

Schafer, R. (1983). *The analytic attitude.* New York: Basic Books.

Segal, H. (1979). *Melanie Klein.* New York: Viking.

Socarides, C. (1968). *The overt homosexual.* New York: Grune and Stratton.

Socarides, C. (1969). Psychoanalytic therapy of a male homosexual. *Psychoanalytic Quarterly, 38,* 173–190.

Socarides, C. (1979). The psychoanalytic theory of homosexuality with special reference to therapy. In I. Rosen (Ed.), *Sexual deviance* (pp. 243–277). Oxford: Oxford University Press.

Thompson, C. (1947). Changing concepts of homosexuality in psychoanalysis. *Psychiatry, 10,* 183–189.

Wiedemann, G. (1962). Survey of psychoanalytic literature on overt male homosexuality. *Journal of the American Psychoanalytic Association, 10,* 386–409.

Wiedemann, G. (1974). Homosexuality: A survey. *Journal of the American Psychoanalytic Association, 22,* 651–696.

6

Sexual Behavior and Orientation: Learning and Conditioning Principles

Geary S. Alford, Joseph J. Plaud, and Tavia L. McNair

Sexual behavior entails a multitude of complex and interactive components. Traditionally, in both animal studies and human research, these are divided into four behavioral clusters: sexual arousal pattern, courtship, mating, and, in humans at least, gender identity, as sometimes distinct from biological gender. This chapter focuses on the development of the first and most central of these, sexual arousal pattern. We consider it the primary and most fundamental of the components because regardless of actual or self-identified gender, or courtship and seduction behavioral repertoires, or even actual sexual mating acts desired or performed, it is the sexual arousal pattern that determines the nature and type of potential sexual objects toward which a person or organism's other sexually related behaviors are focused and directed.

Sexual arousal pattern is defined here as incorporating both stimulus events and psychophysical response events, including those of sexual-reproductive organs, associated autonomic and central nervous system reactions, and sensory-perceptual events of a sexual nature. The pattern of sexual arousal, then, refers to the parameters of stimulus properties of potentially sexual objects to which an organism responds with one or more patterns of sexual excitation. By identifying these "effective" stimulus characteristics (i.e., effective in eliciting psychophysiological sexual arousal), one can thereby identify and define sexual orientation and the core components of sexual arousal.

In spite of over a century of psychodynamic theorizing and several decades of empirical research, it is still not known how and why human beings develop their individual, sometimes strangely idiosyncratic sexual arousal patterns and sexual practices. Nevertheless, a growing body of evidence implicates and supports highly complex interactive processes that include genetic, anatomical, and biochemical-hormonal components interacting with environmental-learning factors involving psychological conditioning and social learning phenomena. This chapter focuses on the principles of behavioral acquisition and modification through which environmental experience affects and modifies organisms' sexual behaviors, albeit via sensory-perceptual stimulus-neuronal events' modification of the biological substrates.

Psychological learning and conditioning models of human sexual behavior do not postulate a singular, monolithic etiology. Instead, multiple etiological pathways involving both biological and environmental-experiential learning factors are recognized. The core dynamic of learning models applies well-established principles of conditioning and animal learning to analysis of experiences or sets of experiences through which sexual arousal is paired with sets of classes of stimuli that come to serve as the initial conditioned stimuli from which subsequent normative and/or deviant arousal and sexual behaviors subsequently develop. These conditioning-learning experiences may occur in a wide variety of ways, ranging from accidental or incidental pairing of certain kinds of stimuli with primary or direct sexual stimulation or arousal, to vicarious exposure, to sexually evocative models displaying normative or deviant sexual events, to deliberate sexual stimulation by another person involving conditionable stimulus elements. Before examining these and other forms and categories of sexual learning experiences from the behavioral learning perspective, let us first review some models and theories of conditioning and evidence for respective empirical support.

Because learning has traditionally been viewed as playing a central role in shaping individual patterns of sexual arousal and behavior, it becomes important to analyze the empirical support for this position. Plaud and Vogeltanz (1991) and O'Donohue and Plaud (1994) in their extensive reviews of the literature on the roles of conditioning in human sexuality have noted the importance of adequately evaluating conditioning phenomena in three particular areas: classical conditioning, operant conditioning, and the habituation of sexual arousal.

HABITUATION AND SENSITIZATION

Habituation and sensitization are hypothesized to be the most fundamental forms of learning (Domjan & Burkhard 1986). These processes are regarded as such because they involve a two-term relation between stimuli and responses (S-R) rather than a four-term relation found in classical conditioning (CS-US-UR-CR), or a three-term relation thought to be involved in operant conditioning (SD-R-Sr+). Habituation and sensitization are also thought to be simpler than classical and operant conditioning because these responses occur in organisms that are phylogenetically simple and are hypothesized to be a precondition for the occurrence of other conditioning processes. For example, emotional respond-ing of experimental animals to the experimental chamber must habituate before operant conditioning can take place (Skinner 1938).

There are five possible patterns of responding that can result from repeated presentations of a constant eliciting stimulus (O'Donohue & Plaud 1991):

1. Response magnitude can systematically decrease,
2. Response magnitude can systematically increase,
3. Response magnitude can remain constant,
4. Response magnitude can be unsystematic, or
5. Response magnitude can vary between these in any complex variation.

When a systematic decrease in response magnitude is not due to physiological fatigue or response adaptation, then habituation is said to occur. When response magnitude is systematically increased, sensitization is said to occur.

No direct studies of sensitization processes in sexual responding were found. Although several studies of the habituation of sexual arousal were located and although theorists have suggested a dual process theory of habituation in which sensitization processes are prominent in early trials of stimulus repetition (Thompson & Spencer 1966), these studies revealed almost no systematic evi-dence of any sensitization effects (a mild sensitization effect in one subject is described in O'Donohue & Plaud 1991). In the dual process model, habituation tends to predominate when the stimulus intensity is low, and sensitization pre-dominates when the stimulus intensity is high. Given problems associated with producing a high-intensity analogue erotic stimulus in sex research, it is expected that sensitization would be very difficult to demonstrate. However, future re-search might partially offset this problem by manipulating the degree of sexual deprivation, which has been shown to increase stimulus intensity (Domjan & Burkhard 1986).

O'Donohue and Geer (1985) reported a study demonstrating the short-term habituation of male sexual arousal. They found that both physiological and sub-jective arousal decreased significantly more in the constant stimulus condition than in the varied stimulus condition. However, contrary to the experimenters' hypothesis, high-intensity erotic stimuli (slides of heterosexual interactions) did not habituate at a slower rate than medium-intensity stimuli (slides of nude females). Moreover, the slides used generally produced low levels of arousal (on average approximately 0.5 centimeter of penile circumference change) and therefore limit the generalizability of these results to the natural environment.

O'Donohue and Plaud (1991) investigated the long-term habituation of male sexual arousal. Long-term habituation is said to occur when short-term (intras-ession) habituation occurs, habituated arousal spontaneously recovers, across habituation sessions the magnitude of spontaneous remission decreases, and the number of trials to habituation decreases across sessions. O'Donohue and Plaud replicated the earlier study in that a short-term habituation process was observed. Spontaneous recovery was demonstrated in all subjects who showed intrasession habituation. Finally, these subjects also generally met the other criteria for long-term habituation: all subjects showed systematic decreases in the magnitude of spontaneous recovery across weekly sessions, and the number of trials to habituation across sessions systematically decreased in three of the four subjects.

Smith and Over (1987) reported that fantasy-induced arousal in males failed to habituate in the short term, although several methodological confounds, such as lack of control over stimulus variability, question the findings. Koukounas and Over (1993), in contrast, did find short-term habituation of fantasy and film-induced sexual arousal, contradicting the results of the earlier study performed by Smith and Over. Meuwissen and Over (1990) investigated the habituation and dishabituation of subjective and physiological sexual arousal in females and found that subjective arousal and the average vaginal pulse amplitude, as measured by photoplethysmography, significantly decreased over trials in both the film and fantasy conditions. The results also indicated that consistent with dishabituation, arousal on the last two trials (with novel stimuli) was significantly greater than arousal to trials 16 to 18. This was found for both physiological and subjective arousal. The authors conclude that female sexual arousal to both fantasy and visual erotic stimuli can habituate and dishabituate.

CLASSICAL CONDITIONING

Like the studies in habituation (with one exception), studies of the classical conditioning of human sexual arousal pertain exclusively to the measurement of male sexual arousal. In the review of this area conducted by O'Donohue and Plaud (1994), studies of classical conditioning were evaluated using the following criteria:

1. Was the CS presented alone in order to test for familiarity with the CS?
2. Were any novel CSs used in order to test for the unconditioned effects of the CS?
3. Was the US presented alone to test for any prior sensitization or habituation to the US?
4. Was backward conditioning investigated (i.e., was the US presented prior to the CS) in order to test for any effects of temporal order?
5. Was a truly random control procedure utilized (i.e., presentation of CS, US, each programmed entirely independently) in order to test for all nonassociative effects?
6. Could other factors such as subject awareness of the experimental procedures account for the findings as plausibly as a conditioning explanation?

A potentially significant problem with demonstrating classical or operant conditioning of sexual arousal concerns the issue of voluntary control. Laws and Rubin (1969) provide evidence of the voluntary control of penile tumescence.

They found that four of seven male subjects developed full erections when exposed to erotic motion pictures. When the experimenters instructed the subjects to inhibit their erections when viewing the erotic films, every subject showed reduction in erection by at least half. This effect lasted as long as the instructions were in effect and ceased once the verbal instructions to inhibit responding were lifted. Furthermore, the researchers found that when asked to develop an erection in the absence of erotic stimuli, every subject was able to do so, each reaching a peak of approximately 30 percent of maximum. This study has been criticized on the grounds that subjects might have inhibited sexual responding by not attending to the erotic stimuli; therefore, instructions used could have had negligible direct effects.

Rachman (1966) conducted one of the earliest studies on the classical conditioning of sexual arousal and sexual fetishism by pairing a visual stimulus of a pair of black boots with visual stimuli of attractive, nude women. Rachman defined a conditioned response as five successive penile responses to the conditioned stimulus (black boots). However, Rachman did not define the minimum size of penile responding necessary for criterion-conditioned responding. Rachman also assessed stimulus generalization after criterion responding to the CS by presenting stimuli of other types of boots and shoes. He found that all three subjects showed criterion-conditioned responding, extinction of conditioned responding, and stimulus generalization. Consistent with behavioral accounts of sexual deviation, Rachman concluded that sexual arousal can be conditioned to previously neutral stimuli, providing a basis for arguing that sexual arousal can become conditioned to stimuli that may be described as deviant.

There are several problems with Rachman's findings, however. Although he did pretest for initial levels of sexual arousal to black boots and the stimuli of the other foot apparel, this study did not have a control for pseudoconditioning. In other words, it may have been the US itself that led to sexual responding to the supposed CS and similar stimuli. Rachman could have investigated this possibility by using novel stimuli in order to probe for any unconditioned effects of generalized sensitization associated with sexually oriented stimuli, but he did not perform these methodological control procedures. Rachman also disclosed the nature of the experiment to his colleagues prior to their participation, leading to the possibility that demand characteristics interfered with the experimental procedure.

Rachman and Hodgson (1968) attempted to replicate the earlier study and to rule out any pseudoconditioning confound. They also attempted to control for subject awareness by not informing the subjects about the nature of the study. The control condition consisted of a backward conditioning procedure (the CS was presented after the US). Rachman and Hodgson found the acquisition of a classically conditioned arousal response and failed to find conditioning in the control group, concluding that "apparently, it is possible to establish an experimental model of sexual fetishism" (p. 27). This study, however, suffers from several methodological problems. Although a backward conditioning was employed by Rachman and Hodgson, the sample size was small, no mention was made concerning any pretesting of the CS alone, no novel stimuli were used in either the forward or backward conditioning conditions to test for unconditioned effects of the CS, and although many different US were used, no random control procedure was administered.

McConaghy (1967) also used a classical conditioning procedure similar to that of the Rachman studies, employing motion picture visual stimuli rather than static slides. McConaghy used both homosexual and heterosexual subjects, displaying preferred and nonpreferred sexual partner stimuli (male/female) as the US. Green and red circles and triangles were used as the CS. McConaghy found that conditioned penile tumescence occurred to the CS paired with the preferred partner stimuli, while "negative" responding occurred to the CS paired with nonpreferred stimuli. A confound of this study, discussed by Langevin and Martin (1975), was that McConaghy did not allow for detumescence periods (i.e., intertrial intervals) to allow the subjects to return to baseline. The "negative" responding that McConaghy discovered might have been due to natural detumescence following a period of arousal and not to conditioned responses to stimuli paired with nonpreferred sex partners. Also McConaghy did not use novel stimuli as probes for unconditioned effects of the CS, no backward conditioning procedure was employed, and as with the Rachman studies, no random control procedure was utilized.

Langevin and Martin (1975) performed two classical conditioning experiments designed to control for prior methodological flaws. In the first experiment, slides taken from "men's magazines" (p. 351) served as the unconditioned stimuli. In addition, slides taken from other nonerotic material and pretested for sexual arousal were included as neutral stimuli. They found that penile tumescence occurred to the conditioned stimuli, that the conditioned response extinguished when the CS was presented alone for ten trials, and that tumescence was not affected by the intensity of the US. They also found that only changes in amplitude of arousal greater than 0.02 ml. (the smallest noticeable change) were significant, not the number of conditioned responses among the adaptation, conditioning, and extinction phases. Therefore, a consistent conditioning pattern over trials in terms of the increasing strength of CRs was not shown. Langevin and Martin pointed out that because stimulus intensity had no effect on changes in penile tumescence, erotic conditioning may be difficult to demonstrate. Given that 24 percent of the US trials elicited no UR, the visual stimuli used may not have had powerful eliciting properties themselves, thereby severely limiting the ability for CS to elicit conditioned responses. For example, in the Rescorla/Wagner model of classical conditioning, the associative strength of a CS is increased by a fraction of the difference between the total combined associative strength of all CSs present in a conditioning trial and the maximal associative strength that can be supported by the US (O'Donohue & Plaud 1994). Thus, weak USs are expected to produce weak conditioning effects. Moreover, Langevin and Martin used a trace conditioning procedure (in which the CS terminates before US onset), and trace conditioning tends to produce less conditioning than a delay procedure (in which the offset of the CS either overlaps the US or coincides with the US onset; Wasserman, Deich & Hunter 1977). It would seem beneficial to use the strongest conditioning procedure in initial attempts to demonstrate the possibility of classical conditioning of sexual arousal.

Another issue related to classical conditioning concerns the assertions made by Garcia and Koelling (1966) and Seligman (1970) that natural selection has favored the associations between certain kinds of stimuli and certain kinds of responses. For example, Gosselin and Wilson (1980) found that male fetishists evidenced sexual arousal mainly to stimuli that were pink, black, smooth, silky, and shiny. McConaghy (1987) argued that the characteristics just mentioned may be similar to properties of the female vulva, suggesting a dimension of biological preparedness. A notion such as biological preparedness can be used to explain plausibly why it is not common to find persons sexually aroused by pillows or ceilings: items commonly contingently paired with orgasm and other reinforcers in a bedroom. One explanation is that these items have not been prepared in evolution for association because they are recent artifacts and are not biologically significant or related to sexual behavior directly. In relation to these points, Langevin and Martin's (1975) choice of random geometrical patterns as CSs in the conditioning of sexual arousal might be insensitive or unresponsive to possible belongingness and preparedness.

Although there has been a progression in the methodological sophistication of the research investigating the classical conditioning of sexual arousal, arguably a crucial component of a learning-based theory of sexual problems, to date all studies directly investigating the basic parameters of classical conditioning have methodological confounds. Also, female sexuality remains a relatively unexplored phenomenon. While it is true that both sexual arousal and classical conditioning are complex phenomena, basic laboratory studies are needed that will allow learning theorists the ability to make unambiguous inferences about the relationship between the classical conditioning of sexual arousal and sexual behavior.

OPERANT CONDITIONING

Skinner (1969, 1988) argued that it is the influence and contingencies of survival and past and present contingencies of reinforcement that shape sexual behavior. By ''contingencies of survival'' Skinner is referring to the selective action of the environment on the species gene pools. In Skinner's behavioral account, sexual contact has come to function as a powerful primary reinforcer through the contingencies of survival. Skinner also argued that the ontogeny and phylogeny of sexual behavior are closely related.

According to Skinner, the contingencies of survival have played a role in shaping global behavioral patterns exhibited by different organisms. However, natural selection is also complemented in the lifetime of the organism through selection of behaviors by their consequences. Operant conditionability was an adaptive mutation because organisms responsive to immediate environmental consequences survived temporally unstable shifts in prevailing environmental features. This selection of behavior Skinner termed *operant conditioning,* and the behaviors selected through consequences are called *operants.*

While Skinner focused only on natural selection in the evolution of human sexuality, Darwin (1871) suggested that evolution operates through two selection mechanisms: natural selection and sexual selection. According to Darwin (1871), sexual selection involves male competition for females and female choice among males. Darwin thought that the "law of battle," or male competition for mates, accounted for the evolution of male aggressiveness, the male's greater size, and in some species the male's anatomical weapons for fighting. Furthermore, Darwin believed that females would choose males based on factors such as quality of their adornment, their courtship display, and the quality of the resources they control. Sexual selection is currently an area of intense interest among evolutionary biologists and behavioral geneticists and ought to be considered in any account of the phylogenetic heritage of an organism (O'Donohue & Plaud 1994).

A central question pertaining to operant studies of sexual arousal is whether operant rather than respondent (or classical conditioning) responses have been properly demonstrated. O'Donohue and Plaud (1994) used criteria developed by Millenson and Leslie (1979) in their evaluation of studies claiming to demonstrate the operant conditionability of sexual behavior. These criteria include the following:

1. Breaking of the contingency produces a short-term increase in responding (an "extinction burst") in operant but not classical conditioning.

2. Intermittent reinforcement produces greater resistance to extinction in operant conditioning but this effect is not seen in classical conditioning.

3. Complex skeletal behavior (striated muscle) is readily conditioned in operant but not classical conditioning.

4. Autonomic behavior is readily conditioned in classical but not operant conditioning.

5. The conditioned response is not usually a component of behavior elicited by the reinforcer in operant conditioning, in contrast to classical conditioning.

6. In operant but not classical conditioning, the experimenter usually specifies the nature of the conditioned response (within the often broad constraints of biological preparedness).

The data on operant conditioning, like classical conditioning, are scant considering the importance of basic studies to behavioral models of sexual behavior and problems. Quinn, Harbison, and McAllister (1970) studied operant conditioning of sexual arousal with one homosexual subject. They placed the subject on a water-deprivation schedule in which presentation of liquid (its delivery signaled by a light) was contingent on increases in penile tumescence to a slide of an adult female. The researchers found that in contrast to baseline tumescence recording, the subject emitted increased levels of tumescence when tumescence (operant response) to a slide of a female adult (discriminative stimulus) was explicitly reinforced by a cold lime juice concentration. Although this study found a direct contingent relationship between tumescence and reinforcing consequences, the researchers did not attempt to break the contingency in order to investigate whether any short-term increase in responding would occur (i.e., an extinction burst), and they did not investigate whether penile tumescence was sensitive to the effects of intermittent reinforcement. However, this study did address several of the classical/operant distinctiveness criteria: the researchers specified the operant response (a criterion increase in tumescence), and penile tumescence was not a component of behavior elicited by the reinforcer used (cold lime juice). Rosen and Kopel (1977) reported a case study in which a transvestic exhibitionist deliberately faked positive changes (although these authors only used self-report) in a biofeedback treatment study.

Using an aversive conditioning procedure, Rosen and Kopel (1977) scheduled a contingent relationship between penile tumescence and the amplitude of an alarm clock buzzer. As penile tumescence increased to video stimuli of the subject's initial sexual preference, the alarm sound also increased. They found a reduction in tumescence while this contingency was in effect. Different schedules of punishment were not used, and the potential physiological effects of fatigue or habituation were not ruled out.

Schaefer and Colgan (1977) studied whether sexual reinforcement increased penile responding. The researchers used sexually explicit scripts and neutral scripts, which the subjects read. They found that penile responding continued to increase over trials when the sexually explicit scripts were followed by sexual reinforcement. The control subjects demonstrated decreased responding over trials.

Perhaps the most sophisticated study of the operant conditionability of sexual arousal to date was conducted by Cliffe and Parry (1980), who utilized sexual stimuli to test the matching law, a mathematical statement of the law of effect (Plaud 1992). Originally formulated by Herrnstein (1970), the matching law predicts that when concurrent variable-interval schedules of reinforcement are in effect, there exists a one-to-one (or matching) relation between relative overall number of responses and the overall relative number of reinforcement presentations. A variable-interval schedule of reinforcement is one in which a reinforcer is presented for the first response that occurs after a variable amount of time has passed since the previous reinforcer presentation. Concurrent schedules exist when two (or more) schedules are in effect at the same time.

Cliffe and Parry studied the sexual behavior of a male pedophile who was on three concurrent variable-interval schedules: the first concurrent choice involved choosing (by pressing keys) to view slides of either women or men; the second condition, between slides of men or children; and the third, between slides of women or children. Results showed that the matching law accurately described the subject's behavior in the first two conditions and also accurately predicted performance in the third condition. Therefore, studies have found support for the operant conditioning of sexual arousal, but like classical conditioning, the database at present is limited by the limitations of the methodologies employed, and there exists a paucity of studies of female sexual arousal.

In addition to principles of behavioral acquisition that have been discovered and investigated within the domain of conditioning research and theory, evidence from ethological and comparative psychology research also implicates an even more interactive role between learning phenomena and biology. In his chapter in this book on biological aspects of sexual orientation, Diamond carefully reviews and elucidates the various underlying biological components that contribute to the patterns of sexual arousal and sexual behavioral expressions that ultimately emerge (see also Rowland, this volume). In this regard, there also exists a large body of empirically derived literature documenting the fact that many species of animals have inherent propensities to respond to specific types of stimuli with "courtship" and sexual approach–copulatory behaviors (see Hinde 1970). Although these biologically determined stimulus–sexual response patterns have not been identified in humans, the possibility of their contribution should not be ignored. Similarly, the role of animals' early life experiences on a wide range of adult behaviors, including sexual behaviors, has been well documented in both primates (Harlow & Harlow 1965) and many nonprimate species such as birds (Lorenz 1965). Lorenz, for example, observed that adult geese that as goslings had been imprinted to humans would frequently display courtship behavior toward and even attempt to mate with humans in preference over adult geese. Whether human beings experience some form of imprinting, particularly to initial sexual arousal experiences (especially orgasms), is not known, but three additional learning factors may exert at least an analogous impact. Certainly sexual arousal and associated stimuli constitute highly salient stimulus events. Together with saliency, the principle of primacy would indicate that initial and especially early sexual experiences might well have a disproportionate impact on subsequent, long-term sexual arousal and practices. Third, whatever stimulus events were present and associated with initial high-level sexual arousal and possibly orgasms would have a high probability of being also associated (paired) with immediately subsequent sexual experiences were a child, for example, to seek to repeat the behavioral experience, to self-stimulate, or even to review (rehearse) covertly the experience through imaginal recall with or without accompanying overt behavioral acts such as masturbation.

In still other ways, biological factors may indirectly contribute to the development of sexual arousal patterns. As Diamond has noted (see Diamond, this volume), brain anatomical and hormonal factors influence a variety of biobehavioral systems beyond sexuality per se. These behavioral classes include such diverse domains as social-physical aggressiveness in males, "tomboyishness" in females, differential motor and verbal skill abilities, and such subtle behaviors as mathematical and spatial-geometric reasoning. From these behavioral systems involved in stereotypic motor and social behaviors, it follows that specific individuals may well experience differential treatment from both their male and female peers. Such differential peer treatment, especially to the extent that it involved anxiety-inducing aversive elements versus positive bonding, social inclusion, peer acceptance, and positive reinforcement, might well exert an indirect influence on sexual arousal and attraction. Ethological studies have found that same-sex-only exposure or isolation-induced "fear" avoidance can inhibit courtship-copulatory behavior, which may be modified in a normative direction following a prolonged desensitizing exposure to the opposite sex (Hinde 1959; Fisher & Hale 1956; Harlow & Harlow 1965). In humans, aversive conditioning experiences with age-appropriate heterosexual peers might well contribute to an individual's finding himself or herself being or becoming more sexually aroused by and attracted to alternative sexual objects, such as, for example, children or fetishistic stimuli. It can be seen, then, that anatomical and hormonal factors may exert either direct or indirect effects in their interaction with environmental-learning events in their combined synergistic impact on the development of sexual arousal and behavioral expressions. Similarly, any biological propensity to respond to certain sexual stimulus characteristics that are subsequently reinforced and undergo further enhancement through classical conditioning would certainly be more likely instated as a principal sexual arousal–behavior pattern.

Two other basic principles of acquired behavior are thought to play a role in sexual behavior: stimulus generalization (emitting a similar response to stimuli that are potentially discriminably different but close in stimulus properties to the original or primary CS) and response generalization (emitting a response that is identifiably different but analogous to the original or primary response). These principles account for variations in the target sexual objects and for variation in actual overt sexual acts common to individuals, while at the same time defining the parameters of the properties and dimensions (e.g., generalization gradients) involved in sexual arousal patterns and their behavioral expression. However, in contrast to the usual and traditional findings regarding generalization, in humans at least, new and different stimulus properties that nevertheless fall within the "desired" parameters often evoke a stronger response than do particular and specific sexual stimuli to which an individual has had substantial exposure. Put simply, novelty within a class or dimension of effective sexual stimuli may evoke an enhanced responsivity. It is well known that humans often experience a heightened sexual arousal and responsivity when sexual activity takes place in different and novel settings. Similarly, many humans find sexual arousal significantly greater during courtship and copulation with novel partners in contrast to a sexual partner with whom they have engaged in long-term, frequent sexual activity. If there is a human psychological aphrodisiac, it is not moonlight, candles, raw oysters, or even champagne; it is novelty. Considering the nature of generalization gradients and the usually reinforcing effects of novelty, it can be seen how variations in reactivity and responsivity can contribute to individual differences in sexual behavior.

Learning principle–based therapeutic procedures also cast some light on these issues. Clinical research in behavioral psychotherapies has addressed both sexual dysfunction (principally inhibited sexual arousal and orgasm) and sexual deviations, including exhibitionism, telephone scatologia, and pedophilia.

Psychogenic sexual dysfunction of inhibited sexual arousal and orgasm has been successfully treated by employing procedures that systematically expose the patient to elected, desirable sexual stimuli in the absence of aversive or otherwise inhibitory stimuli, usually in a psychophysical state of tranquility and relaxation induced by progressive muscle relaxation exercises. The patient is exposed to sexual CSs in the absence of US and, by use of the competitory relaxation response, without or with diminished aversive, undesirable CRs. Thus, desirable sexual arousal CRs that may be present but inhibitorily masked by the aversive CRs may begin to emerge more strongly in reaction to appropriate "sexual" CSs. In addition, sexual responsivity may be enhanced by specifically pairing selected sexual stimuli with primary, usually direct physical sexual stimulation by masturbation (i.e., weak elicitory CSs paired with highly sexually stimulating US). These kinds of procedures have received extensive support in the literature (Brownell & Barlow 1980). In a variation of this classical extinction-reconditioning methodology, Alford (1979) applied "errorless discrimination learning" principles (Terrace 1965) in successfully treating vaginismus. In this clinical study, CSs were successively introduced in such a fashion as to make discrimination maximally difficult, thereby avoiding aversive vaginal spasms that served as both CRs and through their pain as aversive USs. (Ss were paired simultaneously with sexual arousal and, ultimately, with the "positive" US, orgasm.)

In contrast to learning-based procedures to reduce inhibitory aversive autonomic arousal and to enhance positive, desirable sexual responsivity, behavioral therapies have also utilized conditioning-learning methods to decrease undesirable sexual arousal. The most frequently used and most well researched of these is aversion therapy. In essence, aversion therapy is designed to decrease undesirable, deviant sexual arousal by pairing those sets or classes of "deviant sexual" stimuli (deviant CSs) to which the patient responds with significant sexual arousal with aversive stimuli (aversive USs). These procedures have variously employed aversive faradic (electric) stimuli (Rachman & Teasdale 1969), aversive olfactory stimuli (Earls & Castonguay 1989), or aversive covert imaginal stimuli (Alford, Webster & Sanders 1980) as the aversive USs. In most cases, significant diminution of deviant arousal has been both experimentally and clinically demonstrated; however, relapse and return of deviant arousal is a frequent problem (Marshall & Barbaree 1990).

A second procedure derived from conditioning principles that has shown promise in diminishing deviant sexual arousal is masturbatory satiation (Marshall 1979) and its close analogue, masturbatory extinction (Alford, Morin, Atkins & Schoen 1987). In these therapeutic procedures, the deviant CSs are repeatedly paired with the patient's attempt to induce sexual arousal through masturbatory behaviors immediately following the patient's having masturbated one or more times to orgasm. Therefore, the deviant CSs are presented in the absence of significant sexual arousal or orgasm (US), leading to extinction of the deviant conditioned sexual response.

While dysfunctionally inhibited as well as deviant sexual arousal has repeatedly been found to be clinically modifiable by therapeutic application of conditioning principles and methods, this does not in itself necessarily prove their role in the etiological acquisition of sexual problems. It does, however, demonstrate the powerful capacities of learning-conditioning phenomena to shape and modify sexual behavior.

Taken together, research on animal conditioning, ethological investigations, human experimentation, and experimental clinical studies provides strong empirical evidence indicating how basic principles of human and animal learning certainly play a crucial role in the development of the fundamental sexual arousal patterns and in the specific and diverse behavioral expressions of sexuality that individual humans ultimately exhibit.

REFERENCES

Alford, G. S. (1979). Tactile stimulus fading in treating vaginismus. *Behavior Modification, 3*, 273–283.

Alford, G. S., Webster, J. S., & Sanders, S. H. (1980). Covert aversion to two interrelated deviant sexual practices: Obscene phone calling and exhibitionism. *Behavior Therapy, 11*, 15–25.

Alford, G. S., Morin, C., Atkins, M., & Schoen, L. (1987). Masturbatory extinction of deviant sexual arousal: A case study. *Behavior Therapy, 18*, 265–271.

Brownell, K. D., & Barlow, D. H. (1980). The behavioral treatment of sexual deviation. In E. Foa, A. Goldstein & J. Wolpe (Eds.), *The handbook of behavioral interventions.* New York: Wiley.

Cliffe, M. J., & Parry, S. J. (1980). Matching to reinforcer value: Human concurrent variable-interval performance. *Quarterly Journal of Experimental Psychology [A] or [B], 32*, 557–570.

Darwin, C. (1871). *The descent of man and selection in relation to sex.* London: Murray.

Domjan, M., & Burkhard, B. (1986). *The principles of learning and behavior.* Belmont, CA: Brooks/Cole.

Earls, C. M., & Castonguay, L. G. (1989). The evaluation of olfactory aversion for a bisexual pedophile with a single-case multiple baseline design. *Behavior Therapy, 20*(1), 137–146.

Fisher, A. E., & Hale, E. B. (1956). Stimulus determinants of sexual and aggressive behavior in male domestic fowl. *Behavior, 10*, 309–323.

Garcia, J., & Koelling, R. (1966). Relation of cue to consequence in avoidance learning. *Psychonomic Science, 4*, 123–124.

Gosselin, C., & Wilson, G. (1980). *Sexual variations.* London: Faber & Faber.

Harlow, H. F., & Harlow, M. K. (1965). The affectional systems. In A. M. Schrier, H.

F. Harlow & F. Stollnitz (Eds.), *Behavior of nonhuman primates: Modern research trends* (pp. 287–334). New York: Academic Press.

Herrnstein, R. J. (1970). On the law of effect. *Journal of the Experimental Analysis of Behavior, 13,* 243–266.

Hinde, R. A. (1959). Some factors influencing sexual and aggressive behavior in male chaffinches. *Bird Study, 6,* 112–122.

Hinde, R. A. (1970). *Animal behavior: A synthesis of ethology and comparative psychology.* New York, McGraw-Hill.

Koukounas, E., & Over, R. (1993). Habituation and dishabituation of male sexual arousal. *Behavior Research and Therapy, 31,* 575–585.

Langevin, R., & Martin, M. (1975). Can erotic response be classically conditioned? *Behavior Therapy, 6,* 350–355.

Laws, D. R., & Marshall, W. L. (1990). A conditioning theory of the etiology and maintenance of deviant sexual preference and behavior. In W. L. Marshall, D. R. Laws & H. E. Barbaree (Eds.), *Handbook of sexual assault: Issues, theories, and treatment of the offender* (pp. 209–229). New York: Plenum.

Laws, D. R., & Rubin, H. B. (1969). Instructional control of an autonomic sexual response. *Journal of Applied Behavior Analysis, 2,* 93–99.

Lorenz, K. (1965). *Evolution and modification of behavior.* Chicago: University of Chicago Press.

McConaghy, N. (1967). Penile volume change to moving pictures of male and female nudes in heterosexual and homosexual males. *Behavior Research and Therapy, 5,* 43–48.

McConaghy, N. (1987). A learning approach. In J. Geer & W. O'Donohue (Eds.), *Theories of human sexuality* (pp. 287–334). New York: Plenum.

Marshall, W. L. (1979). Satiation therapy: A procedure for reducing deviant sexual arousal. *Journal of Applied Behavior Analysis, 12,* 377–389.

Marshall, W. L., & Barbaree, H. E. (1990). Outcome of comprehensive cognitive-behavioral treatment programs. In W. L. Marshall, D. R. Laws & H. E. Barbaree (Eds.), *Handbook of sexual assault: Issues, theories, and treatment of the offender* (pp. 363–385). New York: Plenum.

Meuwisen, I., & Over, R. (1990). Habituation and dishabituation of female sexual arousal. *Behavior Research and Therapy, 28,* 217–226.

Millenson, J. R., & Leslie, J. C. (1979). *Principles of behavioral analysis.* New York: Macmillan.

O'Donohue, W. T., & Geer, J. H. (1985). The habituation of sexual arousal. *Archives of Sexual Behavior, 14,* 233–246.

O'Donohue, W., & Plaud, J. J. (1991). The long-term habituation of human sexual arousal. *Journal of Behavior Therapy and Experimental Psychiatry, 22,* 87–96.

O'Donohue, W., & Plaud, J. J. (1994). The conditioning of human sexual arousal. *Archives of Sexual Behavior, 23,* 321–344.

Plaud, J. J. (1992). The prediction and control of behavior revisited: A review of the matching law. *Journal of Behavior Therapy and Experimental Psychiatry, 23,* 25–31.

Plaud, J. J., & Vogeltanz, N. (1991). Behavior therapy: Lost ties to animal research? *Behavior Therapist, 14,* 89–93, 115.

Quinn, J. T., Harbison, J. J., & McAllister, H. (1970). An attempt to shape human penile responses. *Behavior Research and Therapy, 8,* 213–216.

Rachman, S. (1966). Sexual fetishism: An experimental analogue. *Psychological Record, 16,* 293–296.

Rachman, S., & Hodgson, R. J. (1968). Experimentally-induced "sexual fetishism": Replication and development. *Psychological Record, 18,* 25–27.

Rachman, S., & Teasdale, J. (1969). *Aversion therapy and behavior disorders.* Coral Gables, FL: University of Miami.

Rosen, R. C., & Kopel, S. A. (1977). Penile plethysmography and bio-feedback in the treatment of a transvestite-exhibitionist. *Journal of Consulting and Clinical Psychology, 45,* 908–916.

Schaefer, H. H., & Colgan, A. H. (1977). The effect of pornography on penile tumescence as a function of reinforcement and novelty. *Behavior Therapy, 8,* 938–946.

Seligman, M. E. P. (1970). On the generality of the laws of learning. *Psychological Review, 77,* 406–418.

Skinner, B. F. (1938). *The behavior of organisms: An experimental analysis.* Englewood Cliffs, NJ: Prentice-Hall.

Skinner, B. F. (1969). *Contingencies of reinforcement: A theoretical analysis.* New York: Appleton-Century-Crofts.

Skinner, B. F. (1988). The phylogeny and ontogeny of behavior. In A. C. Catania & S. Harnad (Eds.), *The selection of behavior: The operant behaviorism of B. F. Skinner* (pp. 382–400). Cambridge: Cambridge University Press.

Smith, D., & Over, R. (1987). Does fantasy-induced sexual arousal habituate? *Behavior Research and Therapy, 25,* 477–485.

Terrace, H. S. (1965). Wavelength generalization after discrimination learning with and without errors. *Science, 144,* 78–80.

Thompson, R. F., & Spencer, W. A. (1966). Habituation: A model phenomenon for the study of neuronal substrates of behavior. *Psychological Review, 73,* 16–43.

Wasserman, E. A., Deich, J. D., Hunter, N. B., & Nagamatsu, L. S. (1977). Analyzing the random control procedure: Effects of paired and unpaired CSs and USs on autoshaping the chick's key peck with heat reinforcement. *Learning and Motivation, 8,* 467–487.

7

Sexual Orientation: What Have We Learned from Primate Research?

Karen Hambright

Because of the ideas of Alfred Russel Wallace and Charles Darwin regarding the continuity of species, humans look to nonhuman species to understand the biological basis of human sexual behavior. Animal models were used initially to address fundamental questions of how. Research focused on reproductive physiology, and the value of these animal models in biomedical research has been firmly established (Beach 1979a; Gooren 1990). Subsequently, the focus of research shifted to questions of why and there has been a disproportionate emphasis on explaining the causes and functions of nonreproductive sexual behavior (e.g., homosexual behavior) and associated phenomena such as sexual orientation.

This focus has been attributed to teleology inherent in the biomedical approach to sexual behavior wherein reproductive sexual behavior is viewed as a "natural" process shaped by a purpose and directed toward an end (Gooren 1990). Cause and function are simultaneously explained as procreation and then dismissed. In contrast, nonreproductive sexual behavior precludes procreation and is considered "unnatural" and thus demands explanation (Gooren 1990). Unfortunately, this view confuses causation and function. Whether or not the function of reproductive sexual behavior is the contribution of genes to future generations, the immediate causes and developmental influences also warrant investigation. Moreover, one cannot expect to understand nonreproductive sexual behavior fully until there is a sufficient understanding of the causal mechanisms for reproductive sexual behavior (Beach 1979a).

Attempts to develop a suitable animal model of human sexual orientation have involved a variety of nonhuman animals, including laboratory rats, guinea pigs, ferrets, domestic dogs, and rhesus monkeys (Adkins-Regan 1988). However, Frank Beach, the eminent comparative psychologist, expressed doubts that our understanding of human sexual behavior, including sexual orientation, would be significantly advanced using nonprimate animal models (1979a). Beach and others (Galt 1947; Hamilton 1914; Maple 1977) considered the use of primate species a more appropriate choice for an animal model of human sexual behavior, for a number of reasons. Nonhuman primates (hereafter referred to as primates) are our nearest phylogenetic relatives; thus, we have more in common with them than with other species. Similar physiology gives rise to similar behavior, and monkeys, apes, and humans share a certain degree of freedom from the strict endocrinological control of sexual behavior seen in nonprimate species. This freedom permits sexual behavior in both reproductive and nonreproductive social contexts, and the sexual behavior of nonhuman primates is readily observable in laboratory, semi-free-ranging, and free-ranging conditions. As a result, one can obtain information about physiological mechanisms as well as environmental determinants of sexual behavior. Primates are relatively altricial, and their lengthy development creates opportunities for experiential factors to influence the development of sexual behavior, as well as opportunities for students of behavior to examine the influences of ontogenetic factors. Furthermore, homosexual behavior (male-male or female-female sexual behavior) has been reported in a number of nonhuman primate species (Nadler 1990).

Thus, it should come as no surprise that for more than seventy years a major issue in primate research has been the biological basis of human homosexual behavior and sexual orientation (Nadler 1990; Nadler & Phoenix 1991). A primate model of sexual orientation has come to be the holy grail, and the search continues today. However, Beach (1976, 1979a, 1979b) cautioned against naive assumptions that a primate model will necessarily increase our understanding of human sexual orientation. Animal models are "seductively easy to fabricate" (Beach 1979b, p. 99), particularly those lacking adequate empirical foundations and constructed with little regard for the fundamentals of comparative methodology. The comparative approach requires description of the similarities in behavior of different species, yet the mere existence of similarities in the sexual behavior of two species has no explanatory value, and "surface similitude by itself does not justify theoretical inference" (Beach 1976, p. 469). For example, the fact that macaque males mount other macaque males in a copulatory fashion provides no insight as to why human males engage in anal intercourse with other human males.

Ideally, interspecific commonalities between species with close phyletic relationships reflect broad trends in biology (Nadler & Phoenix 1991), and ultimately a primate model might reveal such a trend. However, Beach (1979b) argued that in order for X to serve as a model for Z, there are three implications: (1) there are similarities between X and Z, (2) X is understood in terms of causation and function, and (3) application of the X model will increase understanding of Z.

Therein lies one of the fundamental problems regarding a primate model of human sexual orientation. Intraspecific analysis must precede interspecific generalizations, yet primatology is only beginning to describe sexual behavior in nonhuman species, and little is known of causal mechanisms and functional outcomes. Beach (1979a) argued that until sexual behavior in humans and other primates is examined using a common analytical procedure, interspecific comparisons will remain scientifically meaningless. Precise definition of terms should be followed by careful description and measurement of form, frequency, and social context of behavior patterns so that hypotheses may be constructed to test the applicability of our understanding of one species to that of another. Only then will a primate model increase our understanding of human sexual orientation.

DEFINITIONS

Interdisciplinary discourse is often fraught with the problem Beach (1979b) labeled "Humptydumptyism." This term refers to a statement by the Lewis Carroll character that words mean whatever one chooses them to mean. This problem arises when experts in different fields use the same words to mean different things yet assume mutual understanding. To avoid this problem and communicate effectively both within and across disciplines, it is necessary to begin any scientific endeavor by precisely defining terms. I begin with *sexual orientation.*

Kinsey, Pomeroy and Martin (1948) argued that sexual orientation should be conceptualized as a unidimensional continuum whose end points are labeled according to the sex of an individual's object choices or partners. Sexual orientation should describe behavior on the basis of the ratio of the frequency of an individual's heterosexual and homosexual behavioral interactions. In contrast, Money (1987) argued that an individual's sexual orientation (also referred to as sexual status) is not based on behavior but is entirely independent of behavior and is cognitive in origin. He defined sexual orientation in terms of an individual's potential to fall in love with another having the same or different external genital morphology. Money's definition of sexual orientation encompasses all cultural manifestations of heterosexuality, homosexuality, and bisexuality. He conceptualized its development in humans as a sequential process that begins prenatally and continues postnatally under the aegis of the senses, social communication, and learning.

The concepts of heterosexuality, homosexuality, and bisexuality are inherently problematic when applied to nonverbal species, because whatever sex is, sexuality seems to imply something more—an abstraction representing a theoretical framework (Katchadourian 1979). Beach (1974) argued that sexuality is an emergent property of sexual behavior and is applicable only to *Homo sapiens.*

Like Money, Beach felt that "the essence of homosexuality lies in its homophilic foundation and not in the overt behavior through which the homosexual attraction or love is expressed" (Beach 1976, p. 482). Yet nonhuman animal models are necessarily based on analysis of observable behavior. To include more than that would create difficult, if not insurmountable, problems of definition (Nadler 1990). Accordingly, sexual orientation of nonhuman primates is at best a hypothetical construct that may or may not enhance the understanding of sexual behavior in human and nonhuman species (although cf. Adkins-Regan 1988). The parsimonious approach is taken here, and discussion is limited to an analysis of observable sexual behavior in primates.

Sexual behavior was defined by Kinsey as behavior that leads to orgasm (Katchadourian 1979). Although empirically based, this definition is probably too restrictive. At the opposite extreme, Freudian and Reichian definitions are so overly inclusive and nonempirical as to be useless in scientific endeavors (Katchadourian 1979). Beach (1947) defined sexual behavior as "the overt acts comprising heterosexual copulation, . . . those contiguous reactions commonly designated as courtship or pre-coital play, and . . . a variety of noncopulatory sexual responses such as those involved in auto-erotic and homosexual activities" (p. 240). Note that each of these authors defined sexual behavior as inclusive of those behavior patterns where the probability of fertilization is near zero, that is, nonreproductive sexual behavior (Wundram 1979), although when behavior is removed from the context of reproduction, defining sexual behavior becomes quite difficult.

In all primate species observed to date, behavioral elements that appear in the context of fertile copulation between male and female also appear in other social contexts and are known as sociosexual behavior (Hanby 1976). Hanby distinguished between copulatory and affinitive categories of sociosexual behavior, and described the development of each in terms of form, onset, frequency, patterning, social context, and partner selection. In social species, sexual behavior cannot be clearly defined or understood in isolation from the social milieu (Beach 1976), and no behavior can be understood simply in terms of motor pattern. Both the casual observer and the serious investigator may easily misinterpret the sociosexual behavior of primates when little attention is given to the social context in which the behavior occurs. Kohler was among the first to note the difficulty in determining the motivation of behavior patterns that appear sexual in form "which can hardly be classed definitely under either the category of joyous and cordial welcome, or that of sexual intimacy" (Kohler 1925, p. 303). For example, dorsiventral mounting occurs in many species in the context of sexual arousal, in the contexts of play and reunions. Although she acknowledged that an individual's motivation cannot be known, Hanby would probably classify the mounting in the first case as copulatory sociosexual behavior and in the latter two cases as affinitive sociosexual behavior (Hanby 1976).

Although one cannot in any absolute sense demarcate copulatory behavior from sex-ritualized contacting (i.e., affinitive behavior patterns), certain types of evidence can be used to facilitate arbitrary distinctions (Fedigan 1982; Hanby 1976). For example, primatologists today restrict the label *sexual* to those behavior patterns with evident sexual arousal (Nadler 1990). Following Beach and Nadler, the term *sexual behavior* will be used here in reference to behavior patterns that are elements of heterosexual copulation, are either performed in association with heterosexual copulation or involve persistent (i.e., more than perfunctory) genital stimulation, and/or there is evidence of sexual arousal in at least one member of a pair of interacting individuals (Beach 1947; Nadler 1990). The descriptors *sexual* and *copulatory* will be used synonymously. Sociosexual behavior patterns that occur in contexts other than heterosexual copulation and are not associated with persistent genital stimulation or evidence of sexual arousal will be referred to as affinitive behavior.

Zuckerman (1932) maintained that in the primate literature, the use of the terms *heterosexual* and *homosexual* provides no more information than the sex of partners. Although the distinction between the two depends on the sex of the individuals involved, there are difficulties in defining homosexual behavior that extend from the problems involved in defining sexual behavior in general. Beach (1979a) said that homosexual behavior in nonhuman species typically has been determined on the basis of three variables: (1) the genetic sex of the two individuals, (2) the "sex" of the behavior patterns displayed by each individual, and (3) the "sex" of the stimulus pattern to which an individual responds. The sex of the behavior patterns, including the stimulus behavior patterns, refers to sexual dimorphism observed in the copulatory behavior in certain species (e.g., males typically mount and females show lordosis). Beach observed that the term *homosexual behavior* was often applied when males exhibited male-typical (i.e., homotypical) copulatory responses to other males and when females exhibited male-typical (heterotypical) copulatory responses to other females (Beach 1979a). However, Beach and others warned that it is a serious conceptual error to equate homosexuality or homosexual behavior with the capacity to perform heterotypical behavior, particularly in investigations in which individuals were exposed only to same-sex partners (Beach 1979a; Kinsey, Pomeroy & Martin 1948).

Defining homosexual behavior in primates is complicated further because their patterns of sexual behavior are not highly sex specific or dimorphic. Individuals of either sex may perform any pattern of sexual behavior (with the obvious exception of intromission and ejaculation by females), and many patterns may appear in a variety of social contexts (Hanby 1976; Lancaster 1979; Maslow 1936; Rosenblum 1990). Nadler (1990) suggested that homosexual behavior should be defined as behavioral interactions between same-sex individuals that include persistent genital stimulation and evidence of sexual arousal in at least one of the individuals involved. Unfortunately, in most cases, evidence of arousal is more discernible in males than females. For males sexual arousal may be inferred by erection accompanied by ejaculation. For males and females sexual arousal may be inferred by behavioral and physiological responses identified in the literature as species-typical patterns of reproductive behavior (Nadler, 1990). The definition of homosexual behavior used here is more conservative than Nadler's in that discussion is limited to interactions between postpubertal individuals.

DESCRIPTIVE DATA

This section provides a general overview of sexual behavior in the three superfamilies of anthropoid primates: Ceboidea—New World monkeys, Cercopithecoidea—Old World monkeys, and Hominoidea—apes. Descriptions of heterosexual behavior cover the breeding system, structural form of copulatory behavior including solicitations, duration of female receptivity, external signs of endocrine status, and evidence of seasonality. A brief description of data that have been reported as evidence of homosexual behavior follows, and an attempt is made to distinguish between reports that meet the criteria I have specified and others that do not.

Ceboidea

Heterosexual Behavior

New World species in the family Callithricidae, such as common marmosets (*Callithrix jacchus*) and cotton-top tamarins (*Saguinus oedipus*), are sexually monomorphic and are often described as monogamous, given that usually only a single male-female pair within a family group engages in complete, that is, ejaculatory, copulations (Michael & Zumpe 1971). Mounting is dorsiventral, and ejaculation is achieved with a single intromissive mount; complete copulations are not limited to estrus (Hershkovitz 1977). Females show no obvious physical changes that are reliably associated with ovulation, and both males and females perform many of the same courtship displays (e.g., mutual following, arched backs, piloerection, scent marking, lip smacking, tongue flicking, and tongue-to-tongue licking) (Michael & Zumpe 1971). No seasonality has been observed in the copulatory behavior of the common marmoset (Rothe 1975).

Another New World species belonging to the family Cebidae, the squirrel monkey (*Saimiri sciureus*), is sexually dimorphic and breeds in multimale, multifemale social groups (Hershkovitz 1977). According to Michael and Zumpe (1971), mounting is dorsiventral with foot clasp of the female hind limbs, males exhibit a series of intromissive mounts prior to ejaculation, and complete copulations occur only during a brief period of two hours to two days of estrus. Cyclic swelling of female external genitalia is minimal and/or unpredictable. Male courtship displays include ritualized jumping, chasing, genital inspection, and silent vocalization (an open mouth display with abdominal contractions). Female solicitations include displays of the erect clitoris and hindquarters presentation. Squirrel monkeys are seasonal breeders (Michael & Zumpe 1971; Hershkovitz 1977).

Homosexual Behavior

Rothe (1975) reported mounting with pelvic thrusting by captive juvenile and subadult male common marmosets living in family groups. These mounts primarily occurred in the context of social play. In most instances, the mountee was a juvenile and subordinate to the mounter, and in a number of cases the mountee attempted to dislodge the mounter. Information concerning occurrence of erection, intromission, or ejaculation was lacking (Rothe 1975). Given the immediate social context, the developmental stage of the participants, and no clear evidence of sexual arousal, it is likely that much of this behavior was affinitive (possibly mildly agonistic) and thus inappropriately labeled homosexual.

Ploog, Blitz, and Ploog (1963) described the sexual behavior of a captive group of squirrel monkeys and reported that copulation and genital displays were performed between males as well as females, although complete copulation rarely occurred. Copulation attempts were observed initially when newcomers were introduced to a group cage, and the animals made no distinction as to the sex of the mount partner. Ploog and colleagues noted that "steady sexual relationship(s)" were observed only between male and female partners and were distinct from sporadic copulatory behavior, which could occur between any two animals in the group. The implication is that males were not observed to engage in serial mounting with intromission and/or ejaculation with other males. Nadler (1990) concluded that no homosexual behavior has been observed in fully adult male squirrel monkeys. Ploog and colleagues also reported that females exhibited erections during genital displays toward other females, although these displays were not described in the context of persistent genital stimulation, serial mounting, or complete copulation. It is not clear that these female behavior patterns were appropriately described as homosexual.

In other investigations, however, female squirrel monkeys in laboratory caging (Talmadge-Riggs & Anschel 1973; Mendoza & Mason 1991) and in semi-free-ranging conditions (Dumond 1968) were reported to mount other females in a pattern closely resembling heterosexual copulation. Talmadge-Riggs and Anschel (1973) found that female-female mounting is more frequent in exclusively female groups, whereas Mendoza and Mason (1990) observed none prior to the introduction of a male to triads of females. Females that actively mounted others were ovulatory and were higher ranking than the females that received genital investigation and to which genital displays and mounts were directed (Mendoza & Mason, 1990). Talmadge-Riggs and Anschel (1973) noted that female-female mounting did not occur in the context of play and that the female that was soliciting another to mount emitted the vocalizations characteristic of females that were soliciting a male to mount. Although neither of these investigations stated whether mounting occurred in series, the social context, the endocrine status of the mounting females, the proceptive behavior, and mount postures, which may stimulate the clitoris of the mounter, suggest that mounting occurred in the context of sexual arousal. Thus, it is probably appropriate to label such female-female mounting in this species as homosexual.

Cercopithecoidea

Heterosexual Behavior

The source of the following descriptions unless noted otherwise is a review of primate sexual behavior by Hrdy and Whitten (1987). In the Cercopithecoid species in Africa and Asia, variability in sexual behavior (including breeding system) is the rule. Breeding systems include single-male groups within larger troops (e.g., hamadryas baboons: *Papio hamadryas*); multimale, multifemale groups with copulation occurring in the context of temporary exclusive consort relationships (e.g., Japanese macaques: *Macaca fuscata*); and the same without consortships (e.g., talapoin monkeys: *Myopithecus talapoin*). All Old World monkeys exhibit the dorsiventral mount pattern, yet some species require a series of mounts for ejaculation (e.g., rhesus macaques: *Macaca mulatta*), others ejaculate during a single intromissive mount (e.g., gelada baboons: *Theropithecus gelada*, and stumptail macaques: *M. arctoides*), and others display more variation in mounting style (e.g., crab-eating macaque: *M. fascicularis*). Females of some species display highly visible perineal swellings associated with ovulation (e.g., sooty mangabeys: *Cercocebus torquatus atys*), others show only reddening of the face and perineum (e.g., rhesus macaques), and others show no visible changes but may exhibit other sensory cues (e.g., Hanuman langurs: *Presbytis entellus*). Duration of receptivity varies from that of females that engage in complete copulations throughout the menstrual cycle (e.g., stumptail macaques) to those whose copulatory behavior is limited to a period of time around ovulation (e.g., gray cheeked mangabeys: *Cercocebus albigena*). Proceptive behavior of females includes a variety of species-specific patterns, such as grabbing the male's head, vocalization, inflating check pouches, head shakes, hand slaps, approaches, and hindquarters presentation. Male solicitations are also species specific and include simple approach, stereotyped prancing gaits, lip smacking and puckering, tongue flicking, hip touch, and genital inspection. Breeding in some species is distinctly seasonal (e.g., rhesus macaques), in others cyclicity is apparent in terms of birth peaks (e.g., pigtail macaques: *M. nemestrina*), and in others copulation is distributed evenly throughout the year (e.g., stumptail macaques) (Michael & Zumpe 1971).

Homosexual Behavior

Two of the earliest reports of "homosexual" behavior in Old World monkeys were provided by psychiatrists Hamilton (1914) and Kempf (1917). Hamilton described experimental observations involving various combinations of the members of a colony of twenty mixed macaques and baboons. He concluded that homosexual behavior occurs frequently among male monkeys even when opportunities for heterosexual copulation are available and that this tendency declines as males reach adulthood. Kempf observed a group of five mature male and one immature female rhesus macaques and reported high rates of male-male mounting, including an unspecified number of anal intromissions and ejaculations. Both Hamilton and Kempf stated that male-male mounting occurred in a variety of social contexts. Unfortunately, contextual distinctions were obscured by the labeling of all same-sex mounting as homosexual.

Carpenter (1942) described female-female mounting in semi-free-ranging rhesus macaques. Mounting between females occurred during the breeding season in the context of consort relationships and was temporally associated with and notably similar to heterosexual copulation (Carpenter 1942). Akers and Conaway (1979) observed similar behavior in a captive social group of eight adult female and two adult male rhesus macaques. Female-female mounting occurred during the breeding season and was related to female cycle stage; mounters were usually in the follicular stage and mountees in the ovulatory stage of the menstrual cycle. Each of these females copulated with the adult males, sometimes on the same day as with females. The female-female mounting was remarkably similar to heterosexual copulation. Females spent more time soliciting than actually mounting, mounts occurred in series, and females solicited with male-typical approach—hip touch and "kiss and run" display—as well as female-typical hindquarters presentation and following. Although dorsiventral mounting by rhesus females provides little direct stimulation of the genitalia, sometimes the mountee would reach back and stimulate the mounter's clitoris, and self-stimulation by the mounter (using her tail) was common. Several females exhibited a rigid pause in thrusting after a series of mounts that resembled the male ejaculatory pause (Akers & Conaway 1979). This female-female behavior clearly meets the criteria for homosexual behavior.

Carpenter (1942) also described male-male mounting in adolescent rhesus in peripheralized all-male groups on Cayo Santiago. Goy and Goldfoot (1975) discussed similar behavior between two young peripheralized males. Film of these two individuals documented a mount series with anal intromission, thrusting to ejaculation, as well as the mountee's masturbating to ejaculation during the mount (Goy & Goldfoot 1975). Clearly this example also qualifies as homosexual behavior.

Gordon and Bernstein (1973) provided a clear demonstration of the occurrence of male-to-male sexual behavior among captive rhesus. The members of an exclusively male group with visual access to a breeding group underwent seasonal changes in skin coloration and engaged in serial mounting with anal intromission and ejaculation. The pattern of copulation was frequently indistinguishable from that seen in male-female consortships. Copulation in both groups declined at the end of the breeding season, and in subsequent seasons the same males copulated with females but did not engage in mount series with other males (Gordon & Bernstein 1973).

Erwin and Maple (1976) described a more ambiguous example: mounting with anal intromission between two rhesus males reared in the laboratory in mother-only followed by single-peer-only social conditions. In the peer-only condition, these two males were housed together for about two years and were subsequently separated and reintroduced a number of times. In pair tests, each of these males copulated to ejaculation with females, yet when together in triad tests with a single estrous female, these males directed only agonistic behavior toward the female and were observed to mount each other instead. Ejaculations were suspected but never documented, and male-male mounts occurred singly and in series with pelvic thrusting. The authors suggest that this behavior was more affectional than sexual due to the history of social deprivation in these individuals (Erwin & Maple 1976). From the information provided, the classification of the same sex interactions is indeterminate.

Female-female mounting closely resembling male-female copulation was observed during the breeding season in Japanese macaques in the wild (Enomoto 1974), in semi-free-ranging social groups (Fedigan & Gouzoules 1978; Wolfe 1986), and in social groups in captivity (Hanby, Robertson & Phoenix 1971; Chapais & Mignault 1991). All females observed to mount with other females also copulated with males. In captivity all females engaged in same-sex mounting (Chapais & Mignault 1991), and in semi-free-ranging groups as many as 78 percent of females were observed to do so (Wolfe 1986). Females involved in same-sex mounting exhibited all the characteristics of estrous females and displayed all the behavioral components of heterosexual copulation except intromission and ejaculation. It seems clear that homosexual behavior is part of the total repertoire of sexual behavior for female Japanese macaques (Fedigan & Gouzoules 1978).

In contrast, male-male mounting in most cases did not resemble heterosexual copulation in Japanese macaques living in feral groups (Enomoto 1974) or in captive social groups (Hanby 1974). Most of the male-male mounting occurred outside the breeding season and consisted of single mounts. These mounts often occurred in the context of social play or general excitement from a nearby fight (Hanby 1974) and seem clearly affinitive. However, Hanby also observed male-male mount series during the breeding season; two of them terminated in ejaculation and thus meet the criteria for homosexual behavior. Yet all eight males involved in these mount series with other males were more sexually active with females than with males (Hanby 1974).

Although virtually nothing is known of their behavior in the wild (Bertrand 1969), captive stumptail macaques engage in a variety of mount patterns and genital contacts between opposite- and same-sex partners (Chevalier-Skolnikoff 1974). Females mounted other females dorsiventrally, sometimes with foot clasp, and sometimes with genital rubbing by the mounter on the back of the mountee. The duration of these mounts as well as the number of thrusts closely resembled male-female copulations. Both mounter and mountee exhibited positive affective expressions, and the female mounter sometimes displayed the frowning round mouth expression and vocalization typical of males during ejaculation. The author concluded that this behavior clearly involved sexual arousal to orgasm (Chevalier-Skolnikoff 1974). Goldfoot, Westerborn-van Loon, Groeneveld, and Slob (1980) gave further support to this conclusion by using telemetric devices to document orgasmic-like responses in female stumptails that were mounting other females. Whether there is definitive evidence of orgasm, female-female mounting in this species clearly involves sexual arousal and genital stimulation and is appropriately labeled as homosexual behavior.

The behavior of male stumptail macaques is more variable and includes extensive manual manipulation of genitalia, oral-genital contacts, anal intromission, and mounting with mutual oral-genital stimulation (Chevalier-Skolnikoff 1976). However, orgasmic responses and ejaculation have rarely been observed, even in pair tests with male-male contacts (Slob & Schenck 1986). For most of these behavior patterns, the social context is agonistic, and the function appears to be reconciliation, deference, and/or generalized affectional association (Chevalier-Skolnikoff 1976). Only cases with documented ejaculation would qualify as homosexual behavior.

Evidence of homosexual behavior reported for Hanuman langurs (*Presbytis entellus*) is ambiguous (Hrdy 1977). Female-female mounting that closely approximated male-female copulation was observed in free-ranging langurs. Pelvic thrusting occurred in a third of these mounts, the mounter was in estrus in about 45 percent of these mounts, and in three cases the female pair was harassed by adult females and juveniles, as is common for copulating male-female pairs (Hrdy 1977). Srivastava, Borries, and Sommer (1991) described similar female-female mounting; participants were frequently in the periovulatory stage of the female cycle. There was no visible indication of genital stimulation or orgasm in either mounter or mountee, and only a few mounts were harassed by group members. Some of the female-female mounts reported may have involved sexual arousal, yet many probably did not (Hrdy 1977; Srivastava, Borries & Sommer 1991).

Hrdy (1977) also reported male-male mounting in peripheralized exclusively male groups of langurs that had visual access to breeding groups and described those mounts as indistinguishable from heterosexual copulations. Hrdy's observations parallel those reported for rhesus (Carpenter 1942; Gordon & Bernstein 1973; Goy & Goldfoot 1975) and may qualify as homosexual behavior, although details such as the occurrence of ejaculation were not provided.

There are many reports of homosexual behavior for other species of Old World monkeys that are either insufficiently detailed to distinguish between affinitive and sexual behavior or that are clearly descriptions of affinitive sociosexual behavior patterns between same-sex partners and should not be labeled as homosexual behavior, including the following: bonnet macaque males, *M. radiata,* (Makwana 1980); pigtail macaques, *M. nemestrina* (Tokuda, Simons &

Jensen 1968); Celebes macaques, *M. nigra* (Dixson 1977); gelada baboons (Bernstein 1975); talapoins, (Dixson, Scruton & Herbert 1975); and proboscis monkeys, *Nasalis larvatus* (Yeager 1990).

Hominoidea

Heterosexual Behavior

Variability is also the rule among the apes. Breeding systems include monagamous pairs (e.g., lar gibbons: *Hylobates lar*), solitary individuals with overlapping ranges (orangutans: *Pongo pygmaeus*), single male groups of females (gorilla: *Gorilla gorilla* spp.), and large multimale, multifemale groups (common chimpanzees: *Pan troglodytes,* and bonobos: *Pan paniscus*) (Hrdy & Whitten 1987). Serial mounting to ejaculation has not been reported for any species of ape (Dewsbury & Pierce 1989). Copulatory posture varies. Adult common chimpanzees typically exhibit the dorsiventral pattern, although bonobos, gorillas, and orangutans copulate ventroventrally, dorsiventrally, and in variations of the two patterns (Nadler 1977). Female lar gibbons exhibit some reddening of the vulva, but the relationship to ovulation is unclear (Hrdy & Whitten 1987). Midcycle labial tumescence is characteristic of adult lowland gorillas but is virtually absent in orangutans (Graham 1981). In contrast, cyclic anogenital swelling in common chimpanzees and bonobos is highly conspicuous (Hrdy & Whitten 1987). Early reports of the duration of receptivity in female chimpanzees, orangutans and gorillas were confounded by conditions of captivity. Subsequent experimental and field observations revealed that females initiate copulation mainly during periods of maximum fertility, and males initiate copulation at other times, particularly when the female cannot escape (Nadler & Phoenix 1991). Female solicitations are species specific: female gorillas back into a male and rub their genitals on the male's, and orangutans and chimpanzees may crouch and present hindquarters to the male (Hrdy & Whitten 1987). Male proceptive behavior varies across species as well. Chimpanzees display an erect penis while swaggering bipedally, orangutans display an erection while reclining, and male gorillas show little or no solicitation other than contact following a female's approach (Nadler & Phoenix 1991). There is no evidence of seasonality in these species (Michael & Zumpe 1971).

Homosexual Behavior

Kohler (1925) was among the earliest to report same-sex mounting and genital stimulation in male and female chimpanzees, yet he realized the limitations of this information given that there were no fully mature males in his colony. Kohler noted the social context and emotional expressions of his chimpanzees and concluded that much behavior that seemed clearly sexual is probably more conservatively and accurately assessed as friendly greetings, reassurance, or consoling gestures. Yerkes (1939) observed mounting with thrusting, as well as genital-genital rubbing between mature and immature female chimpanzees in pair tests. Sexual arousal is suggested by the fact that the recipients of the mounts and the rubbing were usually females at maximal tumescence. Kollar, Beckwith, and Edgerton (1968) observed mounting and genital stimulation between same-sex members of a large colony of captive chimpanzees. Some descriptions clearly depicted sexual arousal and ejaculation, although many did not and should be labeled affinitive behavior. Kollar and colleagues concluded that all these behaviors were "perversions" and were most frequent in animals that had severely abnormal rearing environments and social experience. There are few reports of clearly homosexual behavior in free-ranging common chimpanzees (Nadler 1990).

Pygmy chimpanzees are notorious for high rates of "sexual" interactions. Both males and females engage in various types of genital stimulation and mounting of same-sex individuals in captivity and in the wild (de Waal 1990). The genitalia of pygmy chimpanzees are more ventrally directed than those of the common chimpanzees, and adult females engage in a species-specific behavior known as genito-genital (G-G) rubbing in which they embrace ventriventrally and laterally rub their vulvas together (Kuroda 1980). Other sociosexual patterns of behavior that have been reported between same-sex partners include ventriventral mounting with mutual penis rubbing, back-to-back genital rubbing (males and females), mouth-to-mouth kissing, manual genital massage, and fellatio (de Waal 1990). A number of authors (Dahl 1987; Enomoto 1990; Idani 1991; de Waal 1990) have suggested that these behavior patterns are not sexual in nature but instead serve in the regulation of social tension, for they occurred in social contexts such as that following a chase or during aggressive competition for food when they were often followed by food sharing. These sociosexual behavior patterns occurred between all possible age and sex combinations, did not result in male ejaculation, did not vary across the menstrual cycle, and appeared to result from interindividual tension (de Waal 1990). Thus, these behavior patterns are primarily affinitive and probably should not be labeled homosexual.

Same-sex mounting and genital stimulation have been reported in captive and wild gorillas (Nadler 1990). Reports have often described the interactions of immature and/or young adults (e.g., mountain gorilla: *G. g. berengei,* Harcourt, Stewart & Fossey, 1981; lowland gorilla: *G. g. gorilla,* Hess 1973), and these interactions occurred more frequently among females. Harcourt, Stewart, and Fossey (1981) concluded that female-female mounting between adults was clearly sexual in nature due to the close temporal association with heterosexual copulation, involvement of estrous females, and copulatory vocalizations given by at least one of the participants. Fischer and Nadler (1978) observed similar behavior in captive female mountain gorillas and noted that the occurrence was related to the female menstrual cycle. Male-male mounting outside the context of social play has been observed in agonistic contexts (Harcourt, Stewart & Fossey 1981; Harcourt 1988) and should not be labeled homosexual.

Very little evidence of homosexual behavior is available for orangutans (Nadler 1990). MacKinnon (1974) reported no observations of same-sex genital stimulation or mounting among feral orangutans in his field studies in Borneo and Sumatra. However, Rijksen (1978) observed a variety of interactions including fellatio and anal intromission with ejaculation in adolescents and subadult males that were in the process of rehabilitation to the wild after having lived in captivity. Most reports of homosexual behavior pertain to captive or formerly captive immature orangutans, yet sexual arousal is apparent in those cases involving ejaculation and thus qualifies as homosexual behavior (Nadler 1990). Maple (1977) suggested, however, that some fellatio occurring in captive orangutans may be motivated by nutritional deficiencies.

Edwards and Todd (1991) reported mounting between an adult male and a younger male (approximately 4 years old) lar gibbon living in a free-ranging family group. The mounts occurred in the form of ventriventral embracing, and the adult solicited the younger male by presenting his ventrum with legs spread revealing the genitalia. More than half of the mounts observed in entirety involved erection and pelvic thrusting, and sometimes they resulted in ejaculation. During the first year of observation, this behavior occurred during feeding or rest periods, and during the second year the context was social play. Although some unspecified number of ejaculations occurred during these mounts, there was no indication of which male ejaculated, and it is doubtful that the younger male was postpubertal. No heterosexual mounting was observed with the unreceptive lactating female; the authors implied that the male-male mounting could be facultative homosexual behavior but concluded that most was probably affinitive and provided reassurance to the younger male, who appeared to be socially dependent on the adults and may not have been completely weaned (Edwards & Todd 1991).

PROXIMATE CAUSATION

Proximate causation of sexual behavior in primates involves the interaction of complex neuromuscular and neuroendocrine mechanisms with the immediate social context (Beach 1947; Herbert 1977). In general, the proximate factors controlling homosexual behavior differ little if at all from those for heterosexual behavior (Beach, 1979a). Some discrete sensory motor components of the basic copulatory pattern are mediated at the level of the spinal cord in both males and females, yet these spinal reflexes are subject to facilitative and inhibitory control from neocortical input (Herbert 1977). Relative to other mammals, primates show increased size and complexity of cortical structures and increased encephalization of sensory motor functions involved in sexual behavior. This difference is assumed to account for the relative freedom or relaxation of endocrine control of sexual behavior seen in many primate species (Beach 1976). However, in monkeys and apes the degree of freedom is intermediate to that of nonprimate species and humans (Gadpaille 1980). Endocrine influence is evident in a number of primate species in that mountees are more often ovulatory females, and when the mounter is female, it is most often one who is in the follicular or ovulatory stage of the female cycle (Beach 1976).

The probability that an individual will engage in copulatory behavior is at least as dependent on immediate social context as on endocrine changes (Hanby 1974). Both males and females are more likely to mount an individual that presents the hindquarters or exhibits other species-specific solicitations than one that does not (Beach 1976; Hanby 1974). The behavioral cues that elicit copulatory behavior are referred to as appetitive or proceptive behavior (Beach 1976), and their function is to increase the attractiveness of individuals that display them, increase levels of arousal, and in general synchronize sexual behavior. Hanby (1974) stated that the availability of "willing" (i.e., cooperative) partners cannot be overemphasized, and she suggested consideration of the difference between a partner that crouches or cringes upon approach or contact and another that actively solicits copulation.

Partner compatibility is another determinant in the expression of sexual behavior in primates (Goy & Goldfoot 1975). Primates can discriminate between and recognize individuals (Cheney, Seyfarth & Smuts, 1987), and individuals of a number of species display idiosynchratic partner preferences in pair tests (Herbert 1977). Mate choice that appears to be based on the physical attributes of partners has also been observed (Hambright 1993). Physical attributes almost certainly interact with the behavior of an individual to affect attractivity.

Size and sex ratios of social groups are critical in terms of partner availability and choice, and unisex groups increase the probability of the occurrence of same-sex copulatory behavior over that of groups where individuals have other options (Nadler 1990; Wolfe 1986). The combination of physical proximity and lack of opportunity for escape from conspecifics increases the probability of sexual behavior in certain primate species (Nadler & Phoenix 1991; Wallen & Winston 1984). Maple (1977) stated that the varied conditions associated with captivity almost certainly account for the increase in frequency of both heterosexual and homosexual behavior compared to that observed in feral-group-living individuals.

ONTOGENY

General Development

As early as 1914, Hamilton suggested that the same-sex mounting observed in juvenile macaques and baboons might serve as practice for adult heterosexual copulation. Subsequently, Bingham (1928) observed that early social experience is required for the development of functionally effective patterns of copulatory behavior in adults. Much research was stimulated by these initial observations, and knowledge of experiential factors that influence the development of sexual behavior in primates has increased. (The general description that follows was derived from Hanby 1976 unless noted otherwise.)

The behavioral elements of mounting, thrusting, hindquarters presentation, and intromission seem to be integrated into definite patterns during infancy in monkeys and apes. Males and females begin receiving mounts around the same time that they begin mounting. By the end of the first year, both sexes display the complete mounting pattern, although males mount and thrust significantly more often than females. Partner choice is largely a function of group size and sex ratio, and infants mount available individuals with little regard to sex. The onset and frequency of intromission is difficult to determine and is indicated primarily by a change from shallow to deep pelvic thrusting of the mounter. Infant male monkeys and apes are incapable of ejaculation. Hindquarters presentation occurs more frequently and in more social contexts than mounting and is more variable in form; thus, its development is more difficult to document. In social groups, infants first present to adults, but the context rarely appears to be sexual.

In the juvenile stage of development of monkeys and apes, most elements of the adult copulatory pattern are integrated and are becoming more clearly associated with certain social situations and specific kinds of partners. Copulatory postures become more stereotyped, awkwardness declines, and the frequency of mature patterns increases. Overall frequency of mounting declines during the juvenile period for males. The copulatory behavior of juvenile females is seldom described and appears to occur infrequently.

Serial mounting and seasonal variation in mount patterns and partner choice first appear in juveniles of those species with distinct breeding seasons. Like infants, juvenile monkeys are still noted for their lack of discrimination in partner choice to the extent that Kempf (1917) concluded that homosexual behavior is a normal developmental antecedent to the development of heterosexual behavior in males.

During adolescence, copulatory patterns become more specialized, and formation of consortships and behavioral preference for ovulatory females appears. For female Old World monkeys and apes, adolescence is marked by the onset of regular menses, as well as a significant increase in mounting, receiving mounts, and the display of species-specific solicitations. The relationship between chronological age and onset of fertile copulatory behavior is highly variable across species. Fully adult males and females generally exhibit the full species-specific repertoire and patterning of copulatory behavior.

Altered Development

Rearing Conditions

Experimental manipulations in which the number and kinds of social companions available during infancy were restricted have revealed gross and often persistent distortions of sexual behavior (Hanby 1976; Harlow & Harlow 1969; Sackett, 1974). At risk are the onset of copulatory patterns, as well as their form, frequency, potential for insemination, and even partner choice. Restrictions in social experience appear to retard the development of the two distinct systems of sociosexual behavior (Hanby 1976).

Rhesus infants reared in total social isolation were completely sexually inadequate in adulthood (Harlow & Harlow 1969). The presence of peers seems to moderate the effects of social deprivation. However, low rates of proper mount orientation, idiosyncratic patterns such as nonintromissive ejaculation, and collapsing under a mount were typical (Erwin & Maple 1976; Goy & Goldfoot 1974; Harlow & Harlow 1969). Infants raised with mother but no peers made adequate heterosexual adjustments following repeated exposure to group-reared peers but remained wary of physical contact (Harlow & Harlow 1969). Hand rearing of infants by humans has varying effects, in that some individuals developed copulatory behavior and others did not. However, this technique is definitely superior to rearing in total social isolation (Hanby 1976).

Chimpanzees and gorillas showed similar deficiencies as result of early social deprivation (Rogers & Davenport 1969; Nadler 1975). Chimpanzees, however, showed greater improvement in sexual behavior than individuals of other species following experience with skilled partners during adulthood (Davenport & Rogers 1970; Kollar, Beckwith & Edgerton 1968).

Sex differences in the effects of restricted rearing are marked (Hanby 1976; Harlow & Harlow 1969). The behavior of males was much more adversely affected; their sexual behavior was grossly distorted, and they generally fail to modify their behavior even after years of postrearing experience (Sackett 1974). Females reared in restricted social conditions remained to some degree deficient in species-typical sociosexual behavior, although postrearing experience improved their copulatory behavior (Hanby 1976).

Hormonal Manipulations

Since the 1940s researchers have investigated the possibility that steroid hormones present early in development have organizational effects that are capable of influencing the pattern of sexual behavior displayed in adults (Goy & Goldfoot 1975; Money 1987). More specifically, it was hypothesized that during a restricted period in prenatal or early postnatal development, secretions from the XY gonad caused changes in the external genitalia and neural tissues mediating sexual behavior that facilitated sexual responses characteristic of genetic males and suppressed sexual responses characteristic of genetic females. Prenatal exposure to androgens has been shown to masculinize both the genitalia and copulatory behavior of genetic female rhesus monkeys; however, this manipulation fails to suppress homotypical behavior in adults, whose behavior differs from controls only in terms of frequency of solicitation of males (Nadler & Phoenix 1991).

Although much is known about how hormonal manipulations influence sexual differentiation in diencephalic nuclei and patterns of copulatory behavior in primates and other species (Adkins-Regan 1988), the occurrence of heterotypical motor patterns (e.g., increased frequency of mounting by females) does not qualify as homosexual behavior unless performed with a same-sex partner (Beach 1979a; Kinsey, Pomeroy & Martin 1948). Little is known of the interaction between hormonal manipulations and various rearing conditions, and there is little evidence that hormonal manipulations have anything to do with choice of sexual partners (Beach 1979a; Adkins-Regan 1988).

PROXIMATE FUNCTION

Early primatologists (Hamilton 1914; Galt 1947; Kohler 1925; Maslow 1936; Zuckerman 1932) suggested that sexual behavior in primates serves functions other than that of reproduction. Undoubtedly, these investigators were referring to the more inclusive behavioral category defined above as sociosexual behavior (i.e., affinitive and copulatory behavior). The apparent functions of affinitive sociosexual behavior are varied and include appeasement, reconciliation, polite greeting, reassurance, and social tension regulation (Fedigan 1982; Hanby 1974; de Waal 1990). In humans, heterosexual and homosexual behavior has many proximate functions, such as obtaining social goals, securing companionship, fulfillment of emotional needs, as well as providing sensual pleasure or gratification. Similarly there is some suggestion that behavior between same-sex primates that appears to be sexual may serve an affectional function in terms of a close socioemotional relationship (Chevalier-Skolnikoff 1976), particularly in socially deprived individuals reared in captivity (Erwin & Maple 1976). Given the available data in these two cases, the distinction between copulatory and affinitive behavior is obscured.

From an anthropomorphic view, the proximate functions of copulatory sociosexual behavior appear to be hedonic in that it may result in ejaculation or behavioral responses indicative of orgasm. However, the question of reinforcing properties or sexual reward requires additional study, and assumptions based on human experience are risky (Beach 1979b). The basic consummatory reflexes are identical, whether the stimulation is provided by a same- or opposite-sex partner (Beach 1979a).

Some cases of homosexual behavior in primates have been described as facultative or *faute de mieux* (Goy & Goldfoot 1975), for example, when opposite-sex partners are either unavailable (Gordon & Bernstein 1973; Wolfe 1986) or unresponsive (Akers & Conway 1979; Carpenter 1942). If so, the proximate function of homosexual behavior appears to be that of sexual reward, reinforcement, pleasure, or drive reduction, depending on one's theoretical perspective, and choice of partner is irrelevant in terms of sexual orientation (Nadler 1990).

ULTIMATE FUNCTION

Beach (1979b) and Lancaster (1979) suggested that we often ignore the fact that proximate mechanisms (both causes and functions) exist and are maintained because in the past they served some ultimate function, that is, they had some adaptive significance in terms of increasing reproductive success. The ultimate function of copulatory behavior between fertile males and periovulatory females is assumed to be apparent and is rarely questioned. Yet the ultimate function of nonreproductive sexual behavior in terms of adaptive significance is more obscure. Beach (1976) argued that deviations in sexual behavior that seriously reduce the occurrence or effectiveness of heterosexual mating could never have survived the process of natural selection. However, when searching for the ultimate function of specific behavior patterns, particularly nonreproductive behavior patterns, such as homosexual interactions, one should heed the words of the renowned primatologist Hans Kummer: "Discussions of adaptiveness sometimes leave us with the impression that every trait observed in a species must by definition be ideally adaptive, whereas all we can say with certainty is that it must be tolerable since it did not lead to extinction. Evolution, after all, is not sorcery" (Kummer 1968, p. 90).

CONCLUSIONS

It is clear from the literature reviewed here that adult primates living in social groups with access to members of both sexes are more likely to engage in copulatory behavior with opposite-sex individuals (Hanby 1974; Nadler 1990). Because few studies have specifically focused on the description and analysis of homosexual behavior, many reports are incidental to the original purpose of an investigation. Often they are vague and lacking in detailed information regarding the immediate social environment, evidence of sexual arousal, hormonal state of individuals, and form or pattern of behavior in terms of the degree of genital stimulation and the degree of similarity to heterosexual copulation. Without this information, the casual reader is easily misled, and much behavior has been mislabeled as homosexual solely on the basis of the sex of the partners and the involvement of motor patterns associated with heterosexual copulation.

Many reports may be disregarded as they almost certainly describe affinitive and not copulatory sociosexual behavior between same-sex individuals (Hanby 1974; Nadler 1990). For example, Nadler (1990) found this to be the case for more than 75 percent of the studies he examined. In this review, I have found that for 57 percent of the evidence examined, the authors either failed to distinguish between affinitive and copulatory behavior or clearly described only the former.

To summarize the information available, Nadler (1990) delineated eight variables that relate to homosexual behavior in primates:

1. *Species.* There are species differences in the incidence of homosexual behavior, partly due to actual variation and partly due to the extent to which a species has been investigated. There are a large number of primate species for which there are virtually no data concerning their sexual behavior, particularly in feral conditions.

2. *Sex.* In species for which there is information available, sex differences have been found in the occurrence of homosexual behavior.

3. *Development.* Stage of development is an important factor in the incidence of homosexual behavior. Immatures engage in various copulatory motor patterns with both same- and opposite-sex partners. By adulthood, most individuals primarily limit their sexual interactions to opposite-sex partners.

4. *Endocrine status.* Hormones influence homosexual as well as heterosexual behavior, and females involved in homosexual interactions are most often follicular or ovulatory in regard to menstrual cycle stage.

5. *Dominance.* Depending on the species, social dominance relationships may determine choice of partner and/or position in mounting.

6. *Experience.* Experiential factors, particularly the social environment during early rearing, profoundly influence the expression of sociosexual behavior in general, and of copulatory behavior specifically. The effects range from total dysfunction to well-integrated species-typical patterns of copulatory behavior.

7. *Environment.* In most species, homosexual behavior occurs at higher rates in captivity than in semi-free-ranging and free-ranging individuals living in social groups. Higher rates are also seen in unisex groups and during breeding seasons.

8. *Interaction.* The seven factors above are not independent, nor do they apply equally to all species. The probability of homosexual behavior in any primate species is a function of the interaction of some combination of these multiple influences.

Experts continue to argue whether it is even possible to develop an animal model for sexual orientation. Obviously there is none for the emergent properties of human sexual orientation that involve symbolic and emotional cognitive components. Although many experts agree that primates are the most appropriate potential model, comparative evidence neither supports nor refutes a biological basis for human sexual orientation per se (Beach 1979a). No conclusions regarding the human condition can be drawn from primate studies at present (Rosenblum 1990).

In this review I did not attempt to address the demonstration of sexual orientation as measured by behavioral partner choice because there is very little available information. Suggestive although not conclusive evidence of homosexual orientation in terms of choice of partners was seen in captive animals that endured extreme forms of social and environmental deprivation for prolonged periods during early development and displayed a variety of deficiencies in species-typical social behavior. However, such conditions either do not exist or would preclude survival in feral environments. Moreover, these causal factors are not evident in humans with homosexual orientation. In other cases, particularly macaque species, Nadler (1990) concluded that the copulatory behavior of captive and semi-free-ranging individuals appears to be ambisexual. In other words, the sex of the mounter seems irrelevant in terms of the hypothetical construct "primate sexual orientation," and the key factor to idiosyncratic choices in mount partners appears to be sexual responsiveness. Nonetheless, if it is possible clearly to demonstrate homosexual orientation in nonhuman species, investigations must be conducted that utilize choice paradigms (Adkins-Regan 1988).

One of the most important contributions of the search for an animal model for human sexual orientation is that the data have forced the realization that sexuality and sexual behavior are multidimensional in expression as well as in causation and function (Whalen, Geary & Johnson 1990). Money (1987) warned of the dangers of "venerable dichotomies," and others (Sanders et al. 1990; Whalen, Geary & Johnson 1990) agree that it is overly simplistic and foolish to frame questions regarding the causes of sexual orientation in terms of nature versus nurture arguments. Those who would seek to fulfill political agendas with arguments for the naturalness of homosexual behavior by touting similarities as evidence of genetically transmitted behavior are no more justified than others who argue for the unnaturalness of human homosexual behavior using socio-cultural premises or the absence of an accepted animal model. Interactionist approaches that give full consideration to both biological and socioenvironmental factors are considerably more productive (Money 1987; Saunders et al. 1990).

Valid models increase our understanding, but as long as we know little of the causes and functions of primate sexual behavior, we will have only invalid models of human sexual orientation (Beach 1979a, 1979b). Our failure to understand homosexual behavior in humans may stem from our lack of understanding of the sexual behavior of nonhuman species (Adkins-Regan 1988). There is a tremendous need for additional intraspecific analysis into causal mechanisms, particularly development influences, as well as functional outcomes, and this information is critical to interspecific generalization (Beach 1979a, 1979b; Nadler, 1990; Saunders et al. 1990). However, great caution should be used whenever generalizing across species, and conclusions must never exceed the data. Invalid models are not only scientifically meaningless, but as Beach (1979a) warned, they may also have undesirable social consequences.

ACKNOWLEDGMENTS

I am extremely grateful to Dr. Irwin Bernstein, Teresa Lindquist, and Richard Simpson for suggesting improvements of an earlier draft of this chapter, and to librarian Pat Bork of Macon College and the staff of the Primate Information Center of the University of Washington for their essential contributions to this review.

REFERENCES

Adkins-Regan, E. (1988). Sex hormones and sexual orientation in animals. *Psychobiology, 16*(4), 335–347.

Akers, J. S., & Conaway, C. H. (1979). Female homosexual behavior in *Macaca mulatta. Archives of Sexual Behavior, 8*(1), 63–80.

Beach, F. A. (1947). A review of physiological and psychological studies of sexual behavior in mammals. *Physiological Review, 27,* 240–307.

Beach, F. A. (1976). Cross-species comparisons and the human heritage. *Archives of Sexual Behavior, 5*(5), 469–485.

Beach, F. A. (1979a). Animal models for human sexuality. *Sex, Hormones and Behavior, 62,* n.s., 113–132.

Beach, F. A. (1979b). Animal models and psychological inference. In H. A. Katchadourian (Ed.), *Human sexuality: A comparative and developmental perspective* (pp. 98–112). Berkeley: University of California Press.

Bernstein, I. S. (1975). Activity patterns in a gelada monkey group. *Folia Primatologica, 23,* 50–71.

Bertrand, M. (1969). The behavioural repertoire of the stumptail macaque. *Contributions to Primatology, 11,* 1–273.

Bingham, H. C. (1928). Sex development in apes. *Comparative Psychology Monographs, 5,* 1–65.

Blaffer-Hrdy, S. (1977). *The langurs of Abu: Female and male strategies of reproduction.* Cambridge, MA: Harvard University Press.

Carpenter, C. R. (1942). Sexual behavior of free ranging rhesus monkeys (*Macaca mulatta*). II. Periodicity of estrus, homosexual, auto-erotic and non-conformist behavior. *Journal of Comparative Psychology, 33,* 143–162.

Chapais, B., & Mignault, C. (1991). Homosexual incest avoidance among females in captive Japanese macaques. *American Journal of Primatolgy, 23*(3), 171–183.

Cheney, D. L., Seyfarth, R., & Smuts, B. B. (1986). The evolution of social cognition in nonhuman primates. *Science, 243,* 1361–1366.

Chevalier-Skolnikoff, S. (1974). Male-female, female-female, and male-male sexual behavior in the stumptail monkey, with special attention to the female orgasm. *Archives of Sexual Behavior, 3*(2), 95–116.

Chevalier-Skolnikoff, S. (1976). Homosexual behavior in a laboratory group of stumptail monkeys (*Macaca arctoides*): Forms, contexts, and possible social functions. *Archives of Sexual Behavior, 5,* 511–527.

Dahl, J. F. (1987). Sexual initiation in a captive group of pygmy chimpanzees (*Pan paniscus*). *Primate Report, 16,* 43–53.

Davenport, R. K., & Rogers, C. M. (1970). Differential rearing of the chimpanzee: A project survey. *Chimpanzee, 3,* 337–360.

Dewsbury, D. A., & Pierce, J. D. (1989). Copulatory patterns of primates as viewed in broad mammalian perspective. *American Journal of Primatology, 17,* 51–72.

Dixson, A. F. (1977). Observations on the displays, menstrual cycles and sexual behavior of the "black ape" of Celebes (*Macaca nigra*). *Journal of Zoology, 182,* 53–84.

Dixson, A. F., Scrutton, D. M. & Herbert, J. (1975). Behavior of the talapoin monkey (*Miopithecus talapoin*) studied in groups, in the laboratory. *Journal of Zoology, 176,* 177–210.

Dumond, F. V. (1968). The squirrel monkey in a seminatural environment. In L. A. Rosenblum & R. W. Cooper (Eds.), *The squirrel monkey* (pp. 87–145). New York: Academic Press.

Edwards, A. A. R., & Todd, J. D. (1991). Homosexual behaviour in wild white-handed gibbons (*Hylobates lar*). *Primates, 32*(2), 231–235.

Enomoto, T. (1974). The sexual behavior of Japanese monkeys. *Journal of Human Evolution, 3,* 351–372.

Enomoto, T. (1990). Social play and sexual behavior of the bonobo (*Pan paniscus*) with special reference to flexibility. *Primates, 31*(4), 469–480.

Erwin, J., & Maple, T. (1976). Ambisexual behavior with male-male anal penetration in male rhesus monkeys. *Archives of Sexual Behavior, 5*(1), 9–14.

Fedigan, L. M. (1982). *Primate paradigms: Sex roles and social bonds.* Montreal: Eden Press.

Fedigan, L. M. & Gouzoules, H. (1978). The consort relationship in a troop of Japanese monkeys. In D. J. Chivers & J. Herbert (Eds.), *Recent advances in primatology, Vol. 1: Behaviour* (pp. 493–495). New York: Academic Press.

Fischer, R. B., & Nadler, R. D. (1978). Affiliative, playful, and homosexual interactions of adult female lowland gorillas. *Primates, 19*(4), 657–664.

Gadpaille, W. J. (1980). Cross-species and cross-cultural contributions to understanding homosexual activity. *Archives of General Psychiatry, 37,* 349–357.

Galt, W. E. (1947). Sex behavior in primates. *Annals of the New York Academy of Sciences, 47,* 617–630.

Goldfoot, D. A., Westerborn-van Loon, H., Groeneveld, W., & Slob, A. K. (1980). Behavioral and physiological evidence of sexual climax in the female stump-tailed macaque (*Macaca arctoides*). *Science, 208,* 1477–1479.

Gooren, L. (1990). Biomedical theories of sexual orientation: A critical examination. In D. P. McWhirter, S. A. Sanders & J. M. Reinisch (Eds.), *Homosexuality/heterosexuality: Concepts of sexual orientation* (pp. 71–87). New York: Oxford University Press.

Gordon, T. P., & Bernstein, I. S. (1973). Seasonal variation in sexual behavior of all-male rhesus troops. *American Journal of Physical Anthropology, 38,* 221–226.

Goy, R. W., & Goldfoot, D. A. (1974). Experiential and hormonal factors influencing development of sexual behavior in the male rhesus monkey. In F. O. Schmitt & F. G. Worden (Eds.), *Neurosciences* (pp. 571–581). Cambridge, MA: MIT Press.

Goy, R. W., & Goldfoot, D. A. (1975). Neuroendocrinology: Animal models and problems of human sexuality. *Archives of Sexual Behavior, 4*(4), 405–420.

Graham, C. E. (1981). Menstrual cycle of the great apes. In C. E. Graham (Ed.), *Reproductive biology of the great apes* (pp. 1–43). New York: Academic Press.

Hambright, M. K. (1993). *Females, familiarity and mate choice in rhesus macaques (Macaca mulatta).* Unpublished doctoral dissertation, University of Georgia, Athens.

Hamilton, G. V. (1914). A study of sexual tendencies in monkeys and baboons. *Journal of Animal Behavior, 4,* 295–318.

Hanby, J. P. (1974). Male-male mounting in Japanese monkeys (*Macaca fuscata*). *Animal Behaviour, 22,* 836–849.

Hanby, J. P. (1976). Socio-sexual development in primates. In P. P. G. Bateson & P. H. Klopfer (Eds.), *Perspectives in ethology* (pp. 1–67). New York: Plenum Press.

Hanby, J. P., Robertson, L. T., & Phoenix, C. H. (1971). The sexual behavior of a confined troop of Japanese macaques. *Folia Primatologica, 16,* 123–143.

Harcourt, A. H. (1988). Bachelor groups of gorillas in captivity: The situation in the wild. *Dodo, 25,* 54–61.

Harcourt, A. H., Stewart, K. J., & Fossey, D. (1981). Gorilla reproduction in the wild. In C. E. Graham (Ed.), *Reproductive biology of the great apes: Comparative and biomedical perspectives* (pp. 265–279). New York: Academic Press.

Harlow, H. F., & Harlow, M. K. (1969). Age-mate or peer affectional system. *Advanced Study Behavior, 2,* 333–383.

Herbert, J. (1977). The neuroendocrine basis of sexual behavior in primates. In J. Money & H. Musaph (Eds.), *Handbook of Sexology* (pp. 449–459). New York: Elsevier.

Hershkovitz, P. (1977). *Living New World monkeys (Platyrrhini), with an introduction to primates* (Vol 1). Chicago: University of Chicago Press.

Hess, J. P. (1973). Some observations on the sexual behaviour of captive lowland gorillas, *Gorilla gorilla* (Savage and Wyman). In R. P. Michael & J. P. Cook (Eds.), *Comparative ecology and behaviour of primates* (pp. 507–581). London: Academic Press.

Hrdy, S. B. (1977). *The langurs of Abu.* Cambridge: Harvard University Press.

Hrdy, S. B., & Whitten, P. L. (1987). Patterning of sexual activity. In B. B. Smuts, D. L. Cheney, R. M. Seyfarth, R. W. Wrangham & T. T. Struhsaker (Eds.), *Primate societies* (pp. 370–384). Chicago: University of Chicago Press.

Idani, G. (1991). Social relationships between immigrant and resident bonobo (*Pan paniscus* females at Wamba. *Folia Primatologica, 57,* 83–95.

Katchadourian, H. A. (1979). The terminology of sex and gender. In H. A. Katchadourian (Ed.), *Human sexuality: A comparative and developmental perspective* (pp. 8–34). Berkeley: University of California Press.

Kempf, E. J. (1917). The social and sexual behavior of infra-human primates with some comparable effects in human behavior. *Psychoanalytical Review, 4,* 127–153.

Kinsey, A. C., Pomeroy, W. B., & Martin, C. E. (1948). *Sexual behavior in the human male.* Philadelphia: W. B. Saunders.

Kohler, W. (1925). *The mentality of apes.* London: Routledge & Kegan Paul.

Kollar, E. J., Beckwith, W. C., & Edgerton, R. B. (1968). Sexual behavior of the ARL colony chimpanzees. *Journal of Nervous and Mental Disease, 147*(5), 444–459.

Kummer, H. (1968). *Social organization of hamadryas baboons.* Chicago: University of Chicago Press.

Kuroda, S. (1980). Social behavior of the pygmy chimpanzees. *Primates, 21,* 181–197.

Lancaster, J. B. (1979). Sex and gender in evolutionary perspective. In H. A. Katchadourian (Ed.), *Human sexuality: A comparative and developmental perspective* (pp. 51–80). Berkeley: University of California Press.

MacKinnon, J. K. (1974). The behavior and ecology of wild orang-utans (*Pongo pygmaeus*). *Animal Behaviour, 22,* 3–74.

Makwana, S. C. (1980). Observations on population and behaviour of the bonnet monkey *(Macaca radiata). Comparative Physiology and Ecology, 5*(1), 9–12.

Maple, T. (1977). Unusual sexual behavior of nonhuman primates. In J. Money & H. Musaph (Eds.), *Handbook of Sexology* (pp. 1167–1186). New York: Elsevier.

Maslow, A. H. (1936). The role of dominance in the social and sexual behavior of infra-human primates: III. A theory of sexual behavior of infra-human primates. *Journal of Genetic Psychology, 48,* 310–338.

Mendoza, S. P., & Mason, W. A. (1991). Breeding readiness in squirrel monkeys: Female-primed females are triggered by males. *Physiology and Behavior, 49,* 471–479.

Michael, R. P., & Zumpe, D. (1971). Patterns of reproductive behavior. In E. S. E. Hafez (Ed.), *Comparative reproduction of nonhuman primates* (pp. 205–242). Springfield, IL: Charles C. Thomas.

Money, J. (1987). Sin, sickness, or status? Homosexual gender identity and psychoneuroendocrinology. *American Psychologist, 42,* 384–399.

Nadler, R. D. (1975). Determinants in variability in reproductive behavior of captive gorillas. *Symposium of the 5th Congress of the International Primatology Society.* Tokyo: Japan Science Press.

Nadler, R. D. (1977). Sexual behavior of the chimpanzee in relation to the gorilla and orangutan. In G. H. Bourne (Ed.), *Progress in ape research* (pp. 191–206). New York: Academic Press.

Nadler, R. D. (1990). Homosexual behavior in non-human primates. In D. P. McWhirter, S. A. Sanders & J. M. Reinisch (Eds.), *Homosexuality/heterosexuality: Concepts of sexual orientation* (pp. 138–171). New York: Oxford University Press.

Nadler, R. D., & Phoenix, C. H. (1991). Male sexual behavior: Monkeys, men, and apes. In J. D. Loy & C. B. Peters (Eds.) *Understanding behavior: What primate studies tell us about human behavior* (pp. 152–189). New York: Oxford University Press.

Ploog, D. W., Blitz, J., & Ploog, F. (1963). Studies on social and sexual behavior of the squirrel monkey *(Saimiri sciureus). Folia Primatologica, 1,* 29–66.

Rijksen, H. D. (1978). *A field study on Sumatran orang utans (Pongo pygmaeus abelii, Lesson 1827): Ecology, behaviour and conservation.* Wageningen, The Netherlands: H. Veenman & Zonen B. V.

Rogers, C. M., & Davenport, R. K. (1969). Sexual behavior of differentially-reared chimpanzees. *Proceedings of the Second International Congress of Primatologists* (Vol. 1). Basel: Karger.

Rosenblum, L. A. (1990). Primates, *Homo sapiens,* and homosexuality. In D. P. McWhirter, S. A. Sanders & J. M. Reinisch (Eds.), *Homosexuality/heterosexuality: Concepts of sexual orientation* (pp. 172–174). New York: Oxford University Press.

Rothe, H. (1975). Some aspects of sexuality and reproduction in groups of captive marmosets *(Callithrix jacchus). Zeitschrift für Tierpsychologie, 37,* 255–273.

Sackett, G. P. (1974). Sex differences in rhesus monkeys following varied rearing experiences. In R. C. Friedman, R. M. Richart & R. L. van de Wiele (Eds.), *Sex differences in behavior* (pp. 99–122). New York: John Wiley and Sons.

Sanders, S. A., Reinisch, J. M. & McWhirter, D. P. (1990). Homosexuality/heterosexuality: An overview. In D. P. McWhirter, S. A. Sanders, & J. M. Reinisch (Eds.), *Homosexuality/Heterosexuality: Concepts of sexual orientation* (pp. xix–xxvii). New York: Oxford University Press.

Slob, A. K., & Schenck, P. E. (1986). Heterosexual experience and isosexual behavior in laboratory-housed male stumptailed macaques *(M. arctoides). Archives of Sexual Behavior, 15*(3), 261–268.

Srivastava, A., Borries, C., & Sommer, V. (1991). Homosexual mounting in free-ranging female Hanuman langurs *(Presbytis entellus). Archives of Sexual Behavior, 20*(5), 467–512.

Talmage-Riggs, A., & Anschel, S. (1973). Homosexual behavior and dominance hierarchy in a group of captive female squirrel monkeys (*Saimiri sciureus*). *Folia Primatologica, 19,* 61–72.

Tinbergen, N. (1963). On aims and methods of ethology. *Zeitschrift für Tierpsychologie, 20,* 410–433.

Tokuda, K., Simons, R. C., & Jensen, G. D. (1968). Sexual behavior in a captive group of pigtailed monkeys (*Macaca nemestrina*). *Primates, 9,* 283–294.

de Waal, F. B. M. (1990). Sociosexual behavior used for tension regulation in all age and sex combinations among bonobos. In F. R. Feierman (Ed.), *Pedophilia: Biosocial dimensions* (pp. 378–393). New York: Springer-Verlag.

Wallen, K., & Winston, L. A. (1984). Social complexity and hormonal influences on sexual behavior in rhesus monkeys (*Macaca mulatta*). *Physiology and Behavior, 32,* 629–637.

Whalen, R. E., Geary, D. C. & Johnson, F. (1990). Models of sexuality. In D. P. McWhirter, S. A. Sanders & J. M. Reinisch (Eds.), *Homosexuality/heterosexuality: Concepts of sexual orientation* (pp. 61–70). New York: Oxford University Press.

Wolfe, L. D. (1986). Sexual strategies of female Japanese macaques (*Macaca fuscata*). *Human Evolution, 1*(3), 267–275.

Wundram, I. J. (1979). Nonreproductive sexual behavior: Ethological and cultural consideration. *American Anthropologist, 81,* 99–103.

Yeager, C. P. (1990). Notes on the sexual behavior of the proboscis monkey (*Nasalis larvatus*). *American Journal of Primatology, 21,* 223–227.

Yerkes, R. M. (1939). Social dominance and sexual status in the chimpanzee. *Quarterly Review of Biology, 14,* 115–136.

Zuckerman, S. (1932). *The social life of monkeys and apes.* London: Kegan Paul.

Part III

Sexual Dysfunctions in Nonclinical Populations

8

Sexual Dysfunction among Heterosexual Adults: Description, Epidemiology, Assessment, and Treatment

Michael P. Carey and Christopher M. Gordon

At least two factors conspire to limit our knowledge about sexual function and dysfunction among heterosexual adults. First, most men and women, young and old alike, are reluctant to seek help for sexual difficulties. In an interesting nonclinical field study conducted with middle-class couples, Frank, Anderson, and Rubinstein (1978) found that 40 percent of the men had experienced an erectile or ejaculatory difficulty, and a similar proportion of women had experienced a desire or orgasmic difficulty; however, only 12 percent had participated in any kind of therapy. Further, 83 percent of both husbands and wives rated their marriage as "happy" or "very happy," and the vast majority of couples did not cite sexual dissatisfaction as a complaint about their marriage. Even when clients do seek help, they are embarrassed about their difficulties. Whether due to conservative sexual attitudes, religious values, or simply a desire to keep their intimate lives private, many people prefer not to share information about their sexuality. They come to therapists as a last resort, when all self-help strategies have failed.

Second, social and cultural influences limit the sexual expression of many older adults, who believe that sex belongs to the young; many older men and women expect their sexual lives to end as they reach their 50s or 60s. Comfort (1980) speaks eloquently to this issue: "In our culture . . . many features of aging as observed are examples not of natural change, but of role-playing, based on a combination of folklore and prejudice" (p. 885). Several studies confirm these attitudes in older adults, despite our knowledge that satisfying sexual relationships often occur in later years. Cameron (1970) found that persons 65 years and older viewed themselves, compared to younger generations, to be the least sexually knowledgeable, desirous, and skilled. In another study, older adults reported that young people hold the least favorable attitudes toward sex among older adults (Bond & Tramer 1983). Thus, there appears to be an unfavorable atmosphere for older adults to be forthcoming about their sexual functioning.

Although our knowledge of sexual function and dysfunction in adult heterosexual men and women must be considered incomplete, sexuality scholars and clinicians have begun to collect pieces of this puzzle. This chapter examines the commonly recognized sexual dysfunctions, reviews evidence regarding their prevalence and etiology, and presents basic information about the assessment and treatment of these problems.

THE SEXUAL DYSFUNCTIONS

Current conceptualization of the sexual dysfunctions is based on the sexual response cycle first described by Masters and Johnson (1966) and later modified by several theorists, including Kaplan (1974). Masters and Johnson completed laboratory research with healthy adult volunteers and provided a physiological model of sexual functioning that documented the genital and other physical changes that usually occur at each stage. The sexual response cycle was thought to proceed through excitement, plateau, orgasm, and resolution. Kaplan (1974), drawing on clinical experience, proposed that there was a part of the sexual process that should be added to earlier conceptualizations, prior to excitement or arousal. This stage, subsequently labeled desire, has been broadly defined as a person's cognitive and affective readiness for, and interest in, sexual activity. Today, most models of healthy sexual functioning include desire, arousal, and orgasm.

Definitions and classification of sexual dysfunction have evolved from laboratory observation, clinical practice, and empirical research to include impairments or disturbance in one of these three stages. In the following section, each sexual dysfunction is introduced, along with available information regarding prevalence and etiology. Diagnostic criteria are drawn from the fourth edition of the *Diagnostic and Statistical Manual of Mental Disorders* (DSM-IV) (American Psychiatric Association 1994).

In general, the categories of sexual dysfunction closely reflect the stage-oriented model, with disorders grouped in terms of desire, arousal, and orgasm, as well as sexual pain. Each disorder can be further characterized as lifelong versus acquired, generalized (occurs in all situations with all partners) versus specific, and due to psychological factors versus due to combined psychological factors and a general medical condition. In addition, we believe that the disorders are best appraised in the light of several caveats. First, by design, sexual dysfunctions in the DSM-IV are defined as either present or not, when sexual health (and mental health, as well) is more accurately placed along a continuum. Second, although the disorders provide useful heuristics for diagnosis and communication, in clinical practice the treatment plan must often account for the biopsychosocial complexities of sexual functioning. For example, difficulties at one stage can impinge upon the functioning of a later stage (and vice versa). In a study of 374 men with sexual disorders, Segraves and Segraves (1990) found that 20 percent of the men with erectile disorder had an additional desire disorder. Interpersonal-dyadic factors can also play important roles in the development and maintenance of a sexual dysfunction.

Two diagnostic criteria apply to all of the disorders. First is that the sexual problem "does not occur during the course of another Axis I disorder," such as a major depressive disorder and is not substance induced (e.g., through the use of cannabis). Second, the clinician must determine that the sexual dysfunction "causes marked distress or interpersonal difficulty." This second criterion, new to the fourth edition of the DSM, will likely have a marked effect on the diagnosis and prevalence of the sexual dysfunctions; individuals who previously would have been classified as experiencing a disorder based solely on physical symptoms (such as persistent absence of orgasm) will not be diagnosed if the individual and/or dyad copes reasonably well with the difficulty.

DESIRE DISORDERS

It is commonly held that "healthy" individuals will experience sexual desire regularly and, moreover, that they will take advantage of appropriate opportunities for sexual expression when they arise. In contrast, individuals who are persistently and recurrently disinterested in sexual expression, who report the absence of sexual fantasies, or who are fearful and phobic of sexual contact are said to be experiencing a desire disorder.

Hypoactive Sexual Desire Disorder

A person with hypoactive sexual desire has low levels of sexual activity and fantasies. Clinicians must make this judgment based on factors that may affect desire and activity levels, such as gender and the context of the person's life. Although the definition is succinct, hypoactive sexual desire disorder can be challenging to diagnose because the construct of desire is not yet well understood or defined and is subject to many interpretations. Due to a wide variability in what individuals perceive as "normal" sexual drive, it is usually a change in desire that leads to help seeking.

The interplay of behavior, cognitions, and affect is important in diagnosing this disorder. Clinicians have the latitude to make this diagnosis in different scenarios—when a person lacks desire and fantasies about sex but has intercourse regularly in response to a partner's advances, or when a person in his or her 20s has no regular partner, is distressed by a perception of a significant lack of interest in sex, and has little interest in masturbation, but does experience infrequent fantasies of sexual activity. The trade-off for this diagnostic flexibility is a potential sacrifice in interclinician reliability.

Prevalence

Few frequency estimates of hypoactive sexual desire are available from community samples, which attempt to determine prevalence data for the general population. Two studies conducted in the 1970s suggested that low desire occurred in about 34 percent of females and 16 percent of males (Frank, Anderson & Rubinstein 1978). However, these were not clinicians' diagnoses; rather, small samples of respondents endorsed items such as being "disinterested in sex." The best information currently available about the frequency of desire disorders comes from clinic-based studies. Research indicates that desire disorders are the reason for about one-half to two-thirds of persons presenting at sexual health clinics (Segraves & Segraves 1991); this represents an increase from the 1970s when female patients with this difficulty outnumbered males. Males may now be as likely as females to present with low desire; however, differences in sampling methodologies make precise estimates for each gender difficult. For example, data presented by Segraves and Segraves were from a multisite pharmaceutical treatment study, which suggests individually centered treatment. Women made up 81 percent of those with hypoactive sexual desire disorders, whereas 78 percent of males presented with erectile disorder.

Etiology

Clinicians have suggested an assortment of causal agents for low sexual desire, including individual factors, relationship factors, and biological influences. Regarding individual factors, LoPiccolo and Friedman (1988) cite aging-related concerns, fear of loss of control over sexual urges, gender identity conflict, poor psychological adjustment, and fear of pregnancy or sexually transmitted disease. Hypothesized relationship causes have included a lack of attraction to partner, dyadic differences regarding optimal closeness, and marital conflict. Pituitary and gonadal hormone levels and several pharmacological agents may also influence desire.

Researchers have only recently begun to study these potential causes of hypoactive sexual desire. Typically, investigators have compared persons seeking treatment for a desire disorder and a control group without a desire problem (sometimes matched on age, relationship status, or other factors) on biological factors, psychological adjustment, and interpersonal functioning. These studies use correlational designs, and, thus, causality cannot be inferred; factors are suggested that may be associated with low desire.

Schiavi, Schreiner-Engel, White, and Mandelli (1988) examined the possible influence of hormone levels on sexual desire. Compared to a control group of men without desire disorder, men with hypoactive sexual desire disorder had lower plasma testosterone; however, it was not clear whether the observed hormonal difference was strong enough to lead to clinically significant desire differences. Segraves (1988) listed several families of prescription drugs that have been associated with hypoactive desire; antihypertensives, psychiatric medications, and anticonvulsants. Regarding psychological adjustment, Schreiner-Engel and Schiavi (1986) reported that clients with desire disorder were twice as likely as control subjects to have previously experienced an affective disturbance. Donahey and Carrol (1993) compared the case presentations of forty-seven men and twenty-two women they had treated for low desire and reported that women were likely to report greater stress and distress levels and more relationship dissatisfaction than were men. Also at the dyadic level, Stuart, Hammond, and Pett (1987) studied women with desire disorder and control subjects on a set of variables including marital adjustment, psychological health, and sexual functioning. They concluded that the poor quality of the marital relationship was most important in the development of the disorder.

Sexual Aversion Disorder

Sexual aversion disorder, though diagnostically distinct from hypoactive desire disorder, may be understood as an extreme form of low sexual desire. The two disorders have been categorized as distinct clinical diagnoses primarily due to differences in clinical presentation: those with sexual aversion disorder fear and avoid sexual contact. There has been little systematic research of sexual aversion disorder, so it remains to be seen whether common etiologies underlie the two desire disorders. According to the DSM-IV, an individual with this disorder experiences persistent or recurrent extreme aversion to, and avoidance of all, or almost all, genital sexual contact with a sexual partner.

Prevalence

The recent introduction of this disorder and methodological limitations in epidemiological and clinical studies prevent differentiation between rates of sexual aversion disorder and hypoactive desire disorder. Typically, these disorders were lumped together in reports of "low desire" difficulties.

Etiology

Although sexual aversion disorder is understudied, victims of sexual traumas such as rape may be more vulnerable to the development of this extreme fear and avoidance of sex. Several studies provide preliminary support for this hypothesis. Chapman (1989) determined the frequency of sexual dysfunction in women who had experienced sexual or physical assault (thirty rape victims and thirty-five abuse victims). Between two and four years after their victimization, over 60 percent of these women experienced some sexual dysfunction. Katz, Gipson, and Turner (1992) developed the Sexual Aversion Scale (SAS) to assess thoughts, feelings, and behaviors consistent with the diagnostic criteria (e.g., "I have avoided sexual relations recently because of my sexual fears"). Although this scale has not been used to establish diagnoses, responses from high school students, college students, and sexual assault victims suggest a positive relationship among a history of sexual victimization, generalized anxiety, and an elevated SAS score.

AROUSAL DISORDERS

Sexual arousal includes all of the changes that were originally thought to accompany the excitement phase of the sexual arousal, including the narrowing of attention to immediate sexual stimuli, a subjective sense of sexual arousal, and the bodily changes that prepare men and women for sexual activity. The physiological changes, especially in the genital region, are the most obvious, and the lack of these changes most often leads to a person's awareness of sexual difficulty. As a result, a lack of vaginal lubrication for women and difficulty getting or maintaining an erection for men have come to define the arousal disorders. However, cognitive and affective features can have important implications for appropriate treatment planning and should also be assessed carefully.

Male Erectile Disorder

Men should be diagnosed with this disorder if persistently or recurrently unable to attain or maintain an erection until completion of sexual activity. The DSM-IV criteria no longer include the subjective lack of arousal as sufficient for diagnosis.

Prevalence

Prevalence estimates come from two main sources, large-scale community surveys and clinic-based studies. Erection problems account for 36 to 53 percent of men presenting at specialty clinics (Bancroft & Coles 1976; Hawton 1982; Renshaw 1988). Yet these data gathered at clinics miss clients who seek help from private practitioners, urologists, and other health care providers. Spector and Carey (1990) estimated that 4 to 9 percent of adult males in the community experience this disorder. Solstad and Hertoft (1993) provided a higher estimate: roughly 20 percent. Two methodological considerations may have influenced these findings. First, men who completed a self-report questionnaire about erectile dysfunction and were also interviewed regarding the same information reported different information; that is, 26 percent reported at least occasional erectile difficulties during the interview versus 11 percent on the survey. This finding highlights the importance of careful questioning in establishing diagnoses. Second, the men were all 51 years old. Although it does not appear that age per se explains increased incidence of erectile dysfunction (but rather, concomitants of aging, such as vascular disease), only 5 percent of men thought that their erectile functioning was "abnormal for their age." This tendency for respondents to normalize their difficulties underscores the point made earlier—

that age-related misperceptions may be a significant barrier to help-seeking behavior, as well as an obstacle to researchers who are not mindful of this issue.

Etiology

Male erectile disorder has by far been the most studied of the sexual dysfunctions. Because adequate blood flow and enervation are key requisites for erections, vascular and neurologic compromise are prominent physical causes of erectile disorder (Meisler, Carey, Lantinga & Krauss 1989). Insufficient blood flow to the penis may result from arteriosclerosis or vascular disease that affects the fine arteries of the penis. Malfunctioning valves in the penile blood vessels can lead to venous leakage, when blood leaves the penis too quickly, causing a rapid loss of erection. Long-term cigarette smoking has been associated with a greater risk of erection problems, probably through compromise of the fine penile arteries (Shabsign, Fishman, Schum & Dunn 1991). Neurologic dysfunction has been linked to diseases of the spinal cord and peripheral nervous system. Among the several chronic illnesses that can cause erectile dysfunction is diabetes.

In the psychological domain, negative affect, particularly anxiety, has often been proffered as a causal factor. Barlow (1986) conducted a series of studies delineating two main components apparent in men with erectile dysfunction. First, these men tend to experience more cognitive interference during sexual activity, primarily negative thoughts, which create performance anxiety, and are more likely to focus on their erectile response, usually underestimating the degree of erection. Second, men with erectile problems often experience a cycle of negative affect related to their erectile dysfunction.

Although in a few cases a clearly identifiable physical cause figures prominently in the erectile problem, most instances involve a complex interplay of biological, psychological, and interpersonal factors.

Female Sexual Arousal Disorder

Female sexual arousal disorder refers to a lack of responsiveness to sexual stimulation—specifically, a persistent or recurrent inability to attain or maintain the lubrication-swelling response of sexual excitement until completion of sexual activity.

Prevalence

Evidence for the prevalence of female sexual arousal disorder is scant and should be regarded with caution. In clinical studies conducted in the 1970s, arousal disorders in women were poorly defined. Frank, Anderson, and Kupfer (1976) reported that 57 percent of females seeking therapy experienced arousal disorders. Estimates from community studies vary, with prevalence rates from 11 percent (Levine & Yost 1976) to 48 percent (Frank, Anderson & Rubinstein 1978).

Etiology

Relatively little research has explored the etiology of arousal disorders in women. However, like male genital arousal, we know that the female lubrication-swelling response also relies on intact vascular and neurologic functioning. Therefore, we may deduce that pelvic vascular disease, and neuropathy among women with diabetes or multiple sclerosis, may lead to decreased vaginal vasocongestion (Spector, Leiblum, Carey & Rosen 1993). Decreases in estrogen can also lead to vaginal dryness.

Relationship factors are important in the development of female arousal disorder. Partners may not provide adequate stimulation; because of poor communication, the problem may be unresolved. A woman may experience a lack of attraction toward a partner despite a wish or desire to engage in sexual activity. These scenarios, though highlighting interpersonal factors, may lead to the use of a readily available solution, such as a vaginal lubricant. This type of problem solving may be one reason that dyadic factors, and female arousal disorders in general, have received little research attention.

ORGASM DISORDERS

Male and female orgasmic disorder refers to a delay or lack of orgasm, whereas premature ejaculation refers to orgasm in males before they desire it. It appears that men perceive a window of time when orgasm is deemed "appropriate." Orgasm may also be the arena in which there is the most misinformation and subjectivity. The absence of orgasm during intercourse is not a dysfunction, but if this pattern persists in all sexual activity and stimulation, the problem may be diagnosable. Male orgasmic disorder is the least frequent of the male disorders, but female orgasmic disorder may be the most common complaint among women. Some sexologists suggest that premature ejaculation usually should not be considered a dysfunction except in extreme circumstances (Wincze & Carey 1991).

Female Orgasmic Disorder

This disorder, formerly referred to as inhibited female orgasm, refers to the persistent or recurrent delay in, or absence of, orgasm following a normal sexual excitement phase. The criteria allow that women exhibit a wide variability in the type and intensity of stimulation for orgasm; the clinician must make a judgment regarding orgasmic capacity based on the woman's age, sexual experience, and adequacy of stimulation.

Prevalence

In community and clinical studies, a wide range of frequency of female orgasmic disorder has been reported—from 5 percent (Levine & Yost 1976) to

15 or 20 percent (Ard 1977; Hunt 1974) in community samples. Clinicians report that 18 to 76 percent of women at sex therapy clinics report lack of orgasm as their primary complaint.

Etiology

Masters and Johnson (1966) observed that the female orgasm is frequently accompanied by rhythmic contractions of the walls of the outer third of the vagina. As a result, it was speculated that weakness of the pubococcygeus muscle would be related to anorgasmia. In general, this and other physiological causes (such as hormonal levels) have not been supported by research. Derogatis and Meyer (1979) suggested that women with orgasmic disorder may have poorer psychological adjustment, including feelings of inferiority and negative body image. However, interpersonal and sexual technique factors may be more pivotal in the onset of this difficulty. Women with this disorder, compared to control subjects who experience orgasm consistently, are more often dissatisfied with their relationship and the type and range of sexual activity, and their partners were less informed of the woman's sexual preferences (Kilmann, Mills, Caid, Bella, Davidson & Wanlass 1984).

Male Orgasmic Disorder

The male orgasmic disorder refers to the persistent or recurrent delay or absence of orgasm, during sexual stimulation that is judged to be adequate in focus, intensity, and duration (DSM-IV).

Prevalence

In clinical practice, this difficulty is infrequently observed. Spector and Carey (1990) reviewed community studies that indicated this as the least common of disorders for men, occurring among 4 to 10 percent of the general population. These could even be overestimates because the "delay" in orgasm and the length of time considered normal before ejaculation have not been well defined.

Etiology

We know quite a bit about healthy orgasm for men: how it occurs, physiological changes that accompany orgasm, and so on. We do not know much about why orgasm may not occur, perhaps because it is a relatively rare condition. For the most part, research reports consist of case studies, with individual explanations ranging from fear of castration and previous sexual trauma to anorgasmia as a side effect to a host of medications (Munjack & Kanno 1979). These issues await further research.

Premature Ejaculation

What is considered a "normal" length of sexual contact before orgasm? This question leads to challenging diagnoses for practitioners and is subject to all sorts of misconceptions among clinic clients. Although some men and women may have unrealistic expectations regarding time until orgasm, and clinicians may disagree about the precise definition of premature, there are many cases in which ejaculation before intercourse (when intercourse is desired), or immediately after penetration, causes significant personal and interpersonal distress.

The DSM-IV definition of premature ejaculation is imprecise: ejaculation with minimal sexual stimulation, before, upon, or shortly after penetration and "before the person wishes it." Thus, a lack of control and mistiming are involved.

Prevalence

Most authors agree that this dysfunction, as defined, is the most prevalent one among males. Spector and Carey (1990), in a review of empirical evidence, concluded that 36 to 38 percent of men in the general population may experience this difficulty. Social and cultural factors may be influencing a decrease in incidence rates in clinical samples; two studies found that premature ejaculation was the primary problem for about 20 percent of men at their clinics (Hawton 1982; Renshaw 1988). Perhaps an increase of information in the media (e.g., about average length of intercourse) or a deemphasis on coitus as the epitome of sexual activity has caused men to be less preoccupied with "rapid" ejaculation as a dysfunction. It has been reported that most healthy men usually ejaculate within seven to ten minutes of intromission (Schover & Jensen 1988).

Etiology

In a review of theoretical causes of premature ejaculation, St. Lawrence and Madakasira (1992) identified several physiological and behavioral etiologic models; they also speculated about interpersonal factors but concluded that these are understudied. Physically, it appears that some men may have a predisposition of heightened sensitivity to penile stimulation. Spiess, Geer, and O'Donohue (1984) found that premature ejaculators ejaculated at a lower level of arousal. However, as a single cause for the problem, this explanation accounts for only a small percentage of cases. A conditioned response may also be involved; in early sexual experiences, it may have been adaptive for sexual activity to end quickly (e.g., to avoid being discovered). Such sexual settings may also have been anxiety provoking. Within a diathesis-stress framework, physical hypersensitivity, learned responses, and dyadic overemphasis and overreaction to a rapid ejaculation may each contribute to the development and maintenance of the difficulty.

SEXUAL PAIN DISORDERS

Dyspareunia is defined by the presence of pain itself, and vaginismus is marked by involuntary spasms of the musculature of the outer third of the vagina, which essentially blocks intercourse and may cause pain if intercourse is still attempted. Dyspareunia during or after intercourse may occur for men but is extremely infrequently (1 percent of men presenting for sexual difficulties). This section focuses on pain disorders in women.

Dyspareunia

The DSM-IV criterion for dyspareunia is persistent or recurrent genital pain associated with sexual intercourse (in either a male or female) that is not caused exclusively by the lack of lubrication or vaginismus and is not due to a general medical condition. As with all of the other sexual dysfunctions, the DSM-IV adds the criterion that the problem causes marked distress or interpersonal difficulty.

Prevalence

It appears that when dyspareunia is present, women rarely seek help at sex therapy clinics. Although community surveys suggest that as many as 33 percent of women experience ongoing sexual pain (Glatt, Zinner & McCormack 1990) only about 3 to 5 percent of clients in sex therapy clinics complain of dyspareunia (Hawton 1982; Renshaw 1988). Perhaps many women interpret this difficulty as a medical problem; indeed, recent information concerning the prevalence and etiology of dyspareunia comes from gynecological practices. Bachman, Leiblum, and Grill (1989) used a questionnaire and direct inquiry to screen for sexual complaints among 887 consecutive gynecological outpatients. Only 3 percent offered sexual complaints on the survey; however, during inquiry, an additional 16 percent reported sexual difficulties. The most common complaint was dyspareunia, occurring in about 9 percent of the entire sample, representing 48 percent of the total complaints. It appeared that women did not consider dyspareunia as a sexual problem or the difficulty was not causing enough distress to report.

Etiology

Dyspareunia may be caused, in part, by postoperative tenderness from vaginal surgery, endometriosis, pelvic inflammation, vulvar vestibulitis, and others (Sandberg & Quevillion 1987). If it is determined that one of these medical conditions is solely responsible for the sexual pain, then the appropriate diagnosis would be sexual dysfunction due to a general medical condition. If the dyspareunia is not exclusively due to physiological effects, then a diagnosis of dyspareunia due to combined factors should be made. Psychosocial factors such as fear, depressed affect, low self-esteem, distrust, anger, and inadequate communication may be implicated but are less commonly seen.

Vaginismus

Vaginismus refers to recurrent or persistent involuntary spasms of the musculature of the outer third of the vagina that interferes with coitus. Lamont

(1978) reports that when couples attempt intercourse, the sensation is that the penis "hits a 'brick wall' about one inch inside the vagina" (p. 633). The repercussions of this difficulty can be significant. Due to the importance that many couples place on intercourse, the man may feel that the woman is resisting his intimacy. The woman, despite the involuntary nature of the spasms, may blame herself for the problem, and anticipation of future occurrences can cause the spasms to occur prior to intercourse attempts (Wincze & Carey 1991).

Prevalence

Vaginismus may be the least talked about of the common sexual dysfunctions, due to the extreme embarrassment that is experienced. No prevalence estimates from the general population are available but vaginismus has been documented in 5 to 42 percent of women presenting for sex therapy. Social and cultural influences may moderate its prevalence; the highest estimates are reported among Irish women.

Etiology

Despite the paucity of empirical research on vaginismus, several plausible causes have been advanced through clinical case studies and supported by preliminary evidence. Regarding physical factors, several authors suggest that painful hymenal tags, a rigid hymen, pelvic tumors, and obstruction from previous vaginal surgery should be evaluated as potential causes (Lamont 1978).

Working from a clinical perspective, Silverstein (1989) reviewed the case histories of twenty-two women she had treated for psychogenic vaginismus after organic factors had been ruled out. In these cases, nearly all of the women had domineering, aggressive fathers. In Silverstein's view, vaginismus (with the current sexual partner) was a symptom that served to protect the self against intercourse, which was perceived as a violation or invasion. Interestingly, in the Irish culture, where some of the highest rates of vaginismus have been reported, several authors have also found that women with vaginismus often come from a family where the father is a threatening figure (Barnes 1986; O'Sullivan 1979). Negative sexual conditioning involving religious themes was also more common. Based upon clinical observation, it has also been suggested that prior sexual trauma or assault may lead to vaginismus. This causal factor fits into a learned response (and self-protective) model of the development of this disorder. Dyspareunia during assault or early intercourse attempts are thought to cause the involuntary tightening of vaginal muscles upon subsequent vaginal penetration. Although research on this issue is inconclusive, clients presenting with either of the sexual pain dysfunctions should be screened for prior sexual trauma.

ASSESSMENT

We have made several assumptions to streamline the assessment of the sexual dysfunctions in heterosexual adults. We assume that the sex therapist is the primary treatment provider, that the clients are involved in a relatively stable relationship (we also treat single clients, but working with a couple is optimal), and that the clients have had a complete and thorough medical evaluation to determine that biological factors are not the exclusive or primary cause of the sexual compliant. This medical evaluation should rule out other serious conditions (e.g., cancer, diabetes) that might be causing the dysfunction and assess the presence and likely influence of various neurologic, vascular, and hormonal conditions on sexual health. Consultation with medical experts regarding the effects of prescription medications is also warranted, especially for male erectile disorder. Finally, we assume that a careful psychological evaluation has been done to rule out other conditions (e.g., major depression or other serious psychopathology) that might be producing sexual concerns or might have a higher priority.

Comprehensive and accurate assessment is crucial to formulating a helpful treatment program, yet therapists must rely basically upon often unreliable self-report information. Clients may find it difficult to express their concerns due to embarrassment, misunderstandings of sexual anatomy or terminology, limitations of memory, and more complex psychodynamic influences.

Next, we provide information on the use of interviewing, questionnaires, and psychophysiological procedures. The assessment should allow the therapist to describe the problem, formulate its etiology, identify therapeutic goals, provide feedback to the client, and establish baseline functioning from which to evaluate the efficacy of treatment.

Interviewing

Process Issues

An effective sexual health interview involves more than just asking the technically correct questions. The process of interviewing is critical because most clients are uncomfortable discussing their sexual behaviors and may feel judged if their therapist is not sensitive. One way to increase trust is to tailor word choice to match the client's vocabulary. When we are contacted by a prospective client to set up an appointment, we encourage the client to bring his or her partner to the first session.

Interviews start by providing an appropriate introduction to sexual health services (we prefer this broader label, which is more descriptive than "sex therapy"), presenting information about the clinical setting (e.g., specialty clinic, private practice) as well as professional credentials. We indicate that sexual health concerns are common and natural and that the setting is one where problems are handled in a nonjudgmental manner. We emphasize that overcoming sexual difficulties requires the cooperative efforts of both partners. We make this explicit because people often blame one person for the problem and believe that the therapist will cure the "sick" one.

Typically, we plan three sessions for the assessment. First, we interview the presenting partner; at this time, the partner completes paper-and-pencil questionnaires. We believe that it is important to interview each person separately to gather accurate information that is unencumbered by the partner's presence. For many individuals, there may be sensitive material, such as a history of affairs or bisexual experiences, that would never be revealed in the presence of their partner, and this information is vital for developing a case formulation and planning the therapy program. This plan is reversed for the second session. Finally, we assess the interaction of the couple together, present an initial case formulation, and provide an outline of the therapy plan.

During all sessions, we attend to the couple's interactions, problems, and strengths in communication; how caring, or hostile, or honest the couple appears to be; and how much trust each partner has in the other. We try to do this by comparing the amount of self-disclosure that occurs during the couple session with the earlier individual sessions, and we invite the couple to raise questions.

A psychosocial history is taken, including a thorough review of other life concerns and current stressors. Sex therapy may or may not be appropriate for the client or couple at this time, and there are no specific guidelines for making this determination. The therapist should determine on a case-by-case basis whether working on a sexual problem will benefit the client or couple. Certainly if either partner is depressed or overly anxious, or if there is a great deal of conflict, it is more appropriate to address nonsexual issues first. In some cases, sexual reparation may be secondary to solving other problems. Effective assessment and therapy usually require a collaborative attitude among both partners and the therapist, which may be undermined by the presence of such hostility. Similarly, there may be very dysfunctional communication between a couple, which must be addressed before sexual issues can be effectively addressed.

Interview Content

The interview should reflect the needs of the client. Frequently crisis issues must be addressed first, or a client may need to digress if this contributes to a better understanding of the client or the client's problem. Nevertheless, there may be an order that might be a useful beginning or "default" structure to use. Start by asking the client to explain the sexual problem that brings him or her in, or even to ask why he or she decided to come to therapy. (The latter may reveal hidden agendas of partners.) Notice how freely and comfortably the client discusses sexual matters, and his or her particular difficulty. Use probes and directive comments to keep the client's report on target. Once the therapist has a general impression of the sexual problem, taking the history is the next step.

The following topics may seem like a formidable amount of material to cover in one or two sessions; consider it as a menu of issues that potentially may be important. With experience, therapists often obtain more details in one of the areas that may be more relevant to a particular type of presenting problem. Here we present one road map for a brief psychosexual and psychosocial history.

Ask about the family structure and experiences, social status, abuse or neglect, first sexual experience, parents' relationship, and early messages about sex. Adolescence can also be an influential time, so inquire about relationships with peers, body image, dating, sexual experiences, menarche, school experiences, substance use, and any other information that emerges as potentially relevant. We sometimes find that it is more important in the early sessions to get a general impression of the client's sexual history rather than all the details, which may emerge later, when we have established a trusting relationship.

We spend most of our time asking about significant relationships and events in adulthood; we try to address self-esteem, marriage and other relationship history, sexual experiences, and we inquire about any unusual sexual experiences, psychiatric history, or treatment. We focus on current sexual functioning and acquire details regarding sexual and nonsexual experiences in the current relationship, recent changes in sexual functioning and/or satisfaction, flexibility in sexual attitudes and behaviors, extramarital affairs, strengths and weaknesses of partner, likes and dislikes of partner's sexual behavior, and so on.

The therapist will find it useful to obtain a brief medical history, including information about significant diseases, surgery, medical care, congenital disorders, secondary sex changes, and similar other topics. Pay particular attention to the medical history after age 20, asking about any significant diseases, surgery, or medical care. Ask if the client has had medical care, is currently taking medications, or is being treated for any medical problems. For women, inquire about menstrual difficulties, and, if appropriate, ask about the menopause.

Throughout the assessment process, the therapist needs to be sensitive to potential covert issues. Are there any issues that a client does not want discussed in front of his or her partner? We believe strongly in creating an interview environment in which each partner can be assured of confidentiality. Without separate confidential interviews, there may be crucial information that might remain hidden. Finally, we provide the client with a second opportunity to reveal anything he or she thinks may be relevant. LoPiccolo and Heiman (1978) recommend ending the questioning by asking: ''Is there anything else that you would like to tell me about your background that you feel bears on your sexual life?''

During the second interview, with the partner, we ask if anything has changed since the first interview and if the partner discussed the first interview. The answers may yield information about the couple's openness in communication and ability to schedule time for important issues. We also ask the partner if there are any questions he or she would like addressed. This approach allows the discussion of process issues (such as a client's doubt about a therapist's qualifications) as well as important personal issues that may have an impact on the therapy (e.g., a client's affair, recent death in the family).

The third interview includes both partners except when one individual's needs are so overwhelming that individual therapy was indicated. The interview should again begin in an open-ended manner to determine what changes and conversations may have occurred since the previous session. A couple's response to this approach is important because it gives the therapist an understanding of how they approach and discuss problematic topics. The remainder of the third session should be spent providing the formulation, identifying treatment goals (sexual and nonsexual), outlining therapy plans, and explaining details regarding the initial stages of therapy. To facilitate rapport, the therapist should ask each partner how each feels about the plan and what problems each foresees in it.

For many clients, further assessment information will be needed, such as psychological testing or psychophysiological assessment. If this is the case, therapy may have to be postponed until the assessment picture is complete. The therapist should explain the importance of further assessment so the client does not get discouraged.

Self-Administered Questionnaires

Self-administered questionnaires are standardized measures that can be filled out by clients in a short period of time, that can be easily administered, and that provide information about the client's condition over a period of many administrations. These questionnaires may allow clients to organize their thoughts in a reflective way that is not always possible during an interview, and they permit clients to disclose sensitive information that they might not reveal during a "live" interaction. Questionnaires also allow the therapist to compare the current client to other individuals (with the help of established norms) and, thus, in difficult cases, provide a metric against which to make judgments. These instruments may provide information to help guide the interview and can be used to assess a client's progress over time. Despite their many potential advantages, however, self-report questionnaires have not been widely used in sexuality assessments.

Obtaining good questionnaires has been difficult in the past. Many research-oriented journals that provided psychometric information on new measures did not publish the actual questionnaires. Clinical sources that devised the items often did not provide psychometric characteristics. As a result, many practitioners have resorted to homemade instruments that are of dubious quality. Fortunately, it is now easier to learn about, and obtain, self-report questionnaires for clinical use.

Several journals make questionnaires available to other users (e.g., *Psychological Assessment*). There are also several books devoted to the use of self-report questionnaires. For general clinical measures, we have found Fisher and Corcoran's (1994) book, *Measures for Clinical Practice: A Sourcebook,* useful. For measures of sexual functioning, Davis, Yarber, and Davis's (1988) book, *Sexuality-Related Measures: A Compendium,* warrants attention. We also recommend a good medical history screening questionnaire (these are often available from local health maintenance organizations).

Although we encourage therapists to use carefully selected self-report questionnaires in their work, we also wish to be clear about their limitations. Such measures should never be used blindly or without a careful interview. Moreover, we wish to be clear about traditional psychological measures such as the Minnesota Multiphasic Personality Inventory or the Rorschach Inkblot Test. These measures have not been found useful for diagnosing the presence of sexual dysfunction or for delineating its etiology (Conte 1986).

Psychophysiological Assessment

Direct measurement of sexual arousal can be helpful in the assessment process, especially for male erectile disorder. This objective approach tends to be less susceptible to the distortions and biases that can occur with interviews and questionnaires. In addition, psychophysiological measures sometimes allow one to understand the physiological underpinnings of the disorder better. However, two considerations have limited the use of psychophysiological methods. First, these methods require technical skill that many practitioners have not acquired. Second, psychophysiological recording apparatus and supplies are expensive. An assessment laboratory can cost $10,000.

When applied, psychophysiology methods tend to be used primarily with men. According to Hoon (1979), their infrequent use with women reflects sexist biases among sex researchers and clinicians, a culture-wide failure to recognize how widespread sexual problems are, and a lack of technology for assessing sexual problems of women. Since Hoon's review article, some progress has been made (Rosen & Beck 1988), and additional progress is anticipated, although little clinically relevant work with women is being done now.

When working with men, two approaches are noteworthy. The first general approach is the physiological recording of nocturnal penile tumescence (NPT) (Meisler & Carey 1990). Briefly, the rationale for this procedure is as follows: If a man can obtain an erection during sleep (which most men do on two to four occasions per night) but cannot obtain an erection during partner stimulation, it is assumed that the source of the erectile disorder is primarily psychosocial. In contrast, if a man cannot obtain an erection at night, it has been assumed that his disorder is a product of primarily biological factors. NPT evaluations are usually done in a sleep laboratory in a medical center. This setting yields important data related to the quality of sleep and sleep disorders (e.g., apnea). The disadvantages of the sleep laboratory are cost, inconvenience, and availability. As a result of these disadvantages, two less expensive and more convenient procedures have been developed: home-based NPT recording and NPT recording during morning naps.

In home-based NPT recording, the client wears a portable monitor during sleep at home. Although these monitors may be useful screening tools for the presence or absence of erections, no information is obtained about sleep architecture. For example, if the recording indicates that no erections occurred, it is not known whether the client experienced rapid eye movement (REM) sleep (the sleep stage most strongly associated with sleep erections), had significant REM disturbances, or slept at all. Morning nap assessment, however, yields data similar to the overnight assessment and can be conducted during a 150 to 180 minute outpatient session (Gordon & Carey, 1993, 1994). We have found that healthy, sexually functional men often experience erections during morning naps, after shortening their sleep the previous night. Although the nap procedure needs to be replicated and extended to men with erectile dysfunction, it holds promise as an efficient (and reliable) means of assessment, which is critical in the light of ongoing health care initiatives.

The second general approach is the assessment of erectile capacity while the client is awake, specifically in response to erotic stimulation; it is the lack of such a response that is often reported as the problem in erectile disorder. Such daytime arousal studies or visual sexual stimulation studies, as they have been called, have proven valuable in the assessment process. We have found that some dysfunctional men who view erotic stimulation experienced full erection responses even though those men reported an inability to obtain an erection. Such data can be critically helpful in formulating a case.

Case Formulation

One of the goals of the assessment is to develop a coherent case formulation—a working hypothesis of the etiology of the problem. This formulation should integrate all aspects of the client's complaints to one another and explain why the individual developed these difficulties (Carey et al. 1984). One purpose of this formulation is to aid in the development of a treatment plan. A second purpose is to communicate to clients that their problem is an understandable one, given their physiology, medical history, and life experiences; there is reason for hope and optimism; and the therapist has a rationale for therapy. Finally, developing a case formulation allows the therapist to check with the client to see if he or she has obtained the necessary and correct information.

It is challenging to integrate multiple levels of influence (biological, psychological, dyadic, cultural) into the case formulation, but this is an important task. A client is more likely to try a psychosocial approach if the therapist recognizes that biological causes are not irrelevant but they might be overridden or compensated for. A client is also more likely to agree to try a psychosocial approach if the therapist inquires about and recognizes specific dyadic, social, and cultural influences. Therapists should be sensitive to rituals and traditions that a couple has established, as well as ethnic, cultural, and religious issues. The case formulation should include biological, psychological, and social areas even if one area does not currently contribute to the problem. This comprehensive approach to case formulation will give the client confidence that all possibilities have been considered. The clients should also think about the problem within a biopsychosocial framework.

Although assessment is a distinct phase, it cannot and should not be seen as completely separate from therapy. During the assessment process, client attitudes are often challenged, new information is learned, and misunderstandings are corrected. The clients learn to view the sexual problem as a state rather than as an unchangeable trait, a conceptualization that is important to restore optimism. Assessment solicits information from each partner and thus helps redirect blame and guilt and focuses the couple's energies on solving problems. Assessment also facilitates the breakdown of barriers to communication. The therapist models effective communication by discussing sexual matters in an open and non-threatening manner and encourages couples to discuss sexual matters in a constructive, rather than a destructive or avoidant, manner.

TREATMENT

Although the treatment of sexual dysfunction is often referred to as "sex therapy," this label may belie the complexity of many client difficulties. "Sex therapy" may be an apt descriptor for clients whose problems are relatively straightforward and not complicated by intrapsychic problems or dyadic problems extending beyond the sexual domain. However, many clients present with a variety of complex concerns that require therapeutic strategies from outside the traditional sex therapy domain. Sex therapists have been recognizing for over a decade that the excellent success rate of sex therapy in the 1970s and early 1980s has been replaced with outcomes more common to the general practice of psychotherapy (Hawton 1992).

The primary goal should not be to increase erections, choreograph simultaneous orgasms, or discover G-spots. Clients who seek therapy have been influenced by misleading stories in the popular media of sexual prowess and new erotic experiences; many seek quick fixes to longstanding problems. The therapist must not reinforce goals that increase performance anxiety. For example, goals such as "increasing erections, "producing orgasm," or "controlling ejaculation" may exacerbate the problem, especially if performance anxiety already inhibits sexual satisfaction.

Instead, therapists must help clients reframe their goals and develop new ones. We encourage clients to restore mutual sexual comfort and satisfaction. We emphasize the importance of becoming comfortable with one's sexuality, of taking more time for sexual expression, and eliminating performance pressures that can block the sexual response and impair enjoyment. We strive to help the couple to understand the psychological as well as the mechanical and technical factors that contribute to sexual satisfaction and enjoyment. These therapeutic goals must be developed together with the couple in such a way that the couple understands that, in order to reach advanced goals (e.g., heightened sexual pleasure), they must first work on preliminary goals (e.g., improved communication).

Moreover, it is important for the couple to understand that achieving these preliminary goals may be slower than the "cure" they were expecting. We encourage clients to conceptualize these preliminary goals as stepping stones toward more advanced goals.

We have found that it is rarely effective to work on sexual problems when there is an ongoing alcohol or drug use problem. The substance use problem should be treated first before an effective program for sexual dysfunction can be established.

Scheduling

We use a weekly schedule for most dysfunctions. We may see clients at a more accelerated pace during the initial assessment, but weekly sessions allow for homework practice without losing continuity. The spacing of sessions should be reevaluated regularly to determine if a different schedule will better serve the couple, for whatever reason, without disrupting the flow of therapy. Once a couple or individual has demonstrated that they can follow therapy instructions, then spacing sessions every several weeks may be worthwhile, especially after progress has been established. When sessions are spaced out, instructions should be given that allow frequent telephone contact if appropriate.

Components of Sex Therapy

Four components tend to be useful for most dysfunctions: education, sexual skills training, cognitive therapy, and communication training. Treatment for each of the sexual dysfunctions incorporates one or more of these components, tailored to the specific context of the problem. For example, therapy for female orgasmic disorder may include education about the female sexual response, sensate focus, and training to help the couple become more comfortable expressing their sexual preferences. Even when we describe a specific method, such as the squeeze technique for premature ejaculation, we highlight the importance of a multicomponent approach to treatment planning.

Education

Providing information to clients may be the most common component of sex therapy. Accurate information can correct misunderstandings that impair sexual functioning or satisfaction. Zilbergeld (1992) and others have reminded us over the years that, as a culture, we unwittingly subscribe to an unhealthy, performance-based model of sexuality. In this model, men and women measure themselves against an unwritten but widely accepted set of standards that are inappropriate for most or all of us. Zilbergeld argues that we think that we are sexually liberated and sophisticated, but our behavior suggests the contrary. He identifies myths that many of us subscribe to, for example: "We're liberated folks who are very comfortable with sex," "A real man isn't into sissy stuff like feelings and communicating," "All touching is sexual or should lead to sex," "Sex equals intercourse," and "Good sex requires orgasm."

The educational aspects of sex therapy can involve challenging some or all of these myths, sometimes by presenting new information or offering alternative views. Clients should always be encouraged to ask questions during therapy about things they "know" to be true about sex. This will not always be easy. Many clients are eager to learn and may request reading suggestions. For men, we like Zilbergeld's (1993) book, *The New Male Sexuality: A Guide to Sexual Fulfillment;* for women, we recommend Heiman and LoPiccolo's (1988) *Becoming Orgasmic: A Sexual and Personal Growth Program for Women.* There are many other fine books (including many college-level human sexuality textbooks), and we encourage therapists to develop lists of favorites.

Erotica can be used to foster more tolerant attitudes, teach partners how to eroticize safer sexual practices, encourage experimentation, and introduce partners to novel behaviors. Erotica can also be used when a couple's sexual repertoire has become stale or rigid. Elsewhere, we have suggested that low desire in an otherwise happy couple may reflect a kind of sexual habituation (Wincze & Carey 1991); couples who are in stable, long-term relationships but always approach sex in the same fashion may become bored. However, erotic materials should be used only after a thorough discussion between the therapist and client. Objections to pornography, particularly the objectification and degradation of women, should be addressed so there are no barriers to accepting and experiencing nondegrading but erotic materials.

Because tastes differ, therapists should develop a library of materials that they have previewed so that they can make knowledgeable recommendations to clients. We also encourage clients to browse in video rental stores or to subscribe to catalogs produced by reputable sexual supply vendors. The need for safer sex materials has increased the social acceptance of such vendors, which may allow these often marginal companies to survive in a competitive marketplace. One such company that we recommend is the Good Vibrations mail order house (938 Howard Street, San Francisco, CA 94103).

Sexual Skills Training

Sensate focus. This approach and its procedures were initially described by Masters and Johnson (1970). The term *sensate focus* refers to a set of procedures designed to help a couple to develop a heightened awareness of, and focusing on, sensations rather than performance. One goal of this approach is to reduce client anxiety by seeking something that is immediately achievable (e.g., pleasurable touching) rather than striving toward a goal. Working for a larger erection or simultaneous orgasm that may not be achievable increases the risk of "failure" and embarrassment.

Sensate focus involves explicit instructions for intimacy; if these instructions are followed, the couple will gradually regain confidence in themselves and in their relationship. Sensate focus is flexible in that it can be accommodated to any couple's unique circumstances. In general, sensate focus is designed to bring about change gradually. It is anticipated that change will take time, and there is no effort to rush. One example is that clients are often advised to discontinue intercourse early in therapy so that they can relearn the basics of being affectionate, receiving pleasure, and so forth. The gradual approach can be disappointing to some clients because it can seem slow, so special care is needed in explaining the importance of this approach to clients.

Sensate focus home-based exercises need to be conducted in a shared and nonthreatening environment. The therapist should encourage the couple to "practice" in a physically and psychologically comfortable and private space; awkward circumstances are not conducive to relaxed enjoyable sexual relations. Couples sometimes need to be told to minimize interfering circumstances. Even simple suggestions such as arranging for a baby-sitter, cleaning up the bedroom, or putting on relaxing music can be helpful. Many partners ensconced in a relationship do not attend to courtship or romantic rituals and sometimes need to be reminded of the efforts they made during courtship to set the mood. We often encourage clients to schedule a time for sex, and to plan for it with as much effort as they might for any other special event in their lives. We remind them that anticipation fuels desire.

The procedures of sensate focus involve encouraging intimacy through gradual, nonthreatening "sexercises." The procedure involves homework, which encourages the couple to engage in sexually related exercises, and ongoing therapy sessions, which are used to discuss the exercises, emotions triggered, problems, and similar other issues.

Homework involves explicit instructions to the client; these instructions require practice of some exercise outside the therapeutic sessions. Both therapist and client understand that the homework will be reviewed and modified (as necessary) at each session. The homework exercises can be broken down into four steps, typically followed in a sequential fashion (but there are no absolutes here). Whether each step should be included and the amount of time devoted to each are clinical judgments.

The first step of sensate focus typically is nongenital touching (i.e., pleasuring) while both partners are dressed in comfortable clothing. Variations in the amount of clothing worn, the length of sessions, who initiates, the types of behaviors participated in, and the frequency of sessions should all be discussed in the therapy sessions before a couple goes home to practice. The couple should begin their physical involvement at a level that is acceptable to both participants.

Because many couples will find this step to be indirect, the therapist must emphasize that they are going through a necessary process in order to address their long-term goal but that the short-term goal is to focus on sensations and not performance. Discuss with the couple the mechanics of the approach, including structured versus unstructured, frequency, potentially interfering factors, and anticipation of any problems. Even if the therapist gives a clear explanation, some clients will misunderstand, so we tell them, "The next time you have a therapy session, I will *not* ask you about erections or orgasms. What I will ask you about is your ability to concentrate on receiving and giving pleasure, and on your ability to enjoy what you are doing.'' We repeat this message because most couples are performance oriented (they focus on erection and orgasm), and, unless the therapist challenges this notion, they will retain performance criteria during the sensate focus exercises. The therapist might also discuss with the client or couple the concepts of performance anxiety and other factors that interfere with enjoyable sex.

The second step typically will involve genital pleasuring. Partners are encouraged to extend gentle touching to the genital and breast regions and to caress each other in a way that is pleasurable. As before, the couple should be discouraged from focusing on performance-related goals (e.g., orgasm). Once a couple becomes comfortable with genital touching and is ready to resume intercourse, we emphasize that intercourse can be broken down into several behaviors. Thus, we encourage some couples to engage in "containment without thrusting." That is, the woman permits penetration and controls all aspects of this exercise (e.g., the depth of penetration and the amount of time spent on penetration). Again, we encourage flexibility and variation in order to remove pressure associated with a couple's tendency to think in all-or-none terms.

A common problem with this stage of sensate focus is that therapists rigidly adhere to the proscription on intercourse (Lipsius 1987). If employed mechanically, proscription of intercourse can lead to loss of erotic feelings and spontaneity, unnecessary frustration, and resistance. We discuss with the couple the potential benefits of proscription and point out that the couple is building for the future. In our view, a proscriptive approach may help a couple resume physical contact under certain circumstances. Three circumstances come to mind: when a couple is very stressed by sexual performance, there are interfering performance-oriented thoughts, or the couple has avoided all physical contact. On the other hand, couples who have not approached sexual relations so rigidly or with such intense emotional reactions may benefit from a general understanding of the purpose of sensate focus but with a more relaxed attitude toward proscription.

The final step of sensate focus proper includes thrusting and intercourse. Again, it is usually a good idea to encourage the receptive partner to initiate slow and gradual movements. The couple is encouraged to focus on the sensations associated with intercourse and to experiment with different intercourse positions.

These are the procedures that generally constitute what is commonly referred to as sensate focus. At this point, we want to identify a few potential problems that a therapist may encounter. Sensate focus can be misapplied and misunderstood by both therapist and client. It is not unusual for couples to enter therapy and report that they had previously tried to "abstain from sex" and this did not work. For example, a new couple explained that they had participated in sex therapy before and had tried sensate focus. From their perspective, the approach used was "not to have sex." The couple had no understanding of the purpose of the procedure and, as a result, left their previous therapy dissatisfied.

McCarthy (1985) encourages therapists to engage the couple in the decision-making process and to avoid placing performance demands on the couple. Another difficulty can occur when therapy moves into the arena of homework procedures. Here a conflict could occur between being natural and unstructured and being mechanistic and structured. Most couples and individuals express a preference to approach homework assignments in a natural, unstructured manner. With this approach, the therapist describes the procedures and the principles behind the procedures but leaves it up to the couple to schedule other details, such as frequency. Although this may intuitively be the preferred strategy, the therapist can expect couples to return to therapy without having carried out the assignment. The reason is that all too often there is a strong history of avoidance; thus, the couple cannot get started without raising anxiety levels.

To avert these outcomes, we explain the pluses and minuses of structured versus unstructured strategies before providing homework. The client can then choose a strategy and be aware of the potential for noncompliance. At times, a client may try out a certain strategy and later adopt a different approach. In addition to exploring structured versus unstructured practice, the therapist should explore other potential obstacles in the face of carrying out therapy procedures, such as relatives living in the house, work, medical concerns, and travel plans. Once these potential obstacles are identified and solutions generated, then the rationale and details of homework can begin.

There are many benefits that may result from the sensate focus procedure. New behaviors may be learned along with new approaches to sexual interactions. We have dealt with couples who have had very narrow approaches to sex. It is not unusual, for example, for a couple to report that they engage in no touching behavior at all. They may kiss once and then have intercourse. We have even encountered couples who view foreplay as "something that kids do." For such a couple, sensate focus offers a structured opportunity to challenge established habits that may be restricting pleasure and causing sex problems.

Sensate focus can also be quite diagnostic. Difficulties that emerge often carry important information about other problems that a couple is having but often cannot be addressed through sensate focus itself. Sensate focus may also help to change a person's perception of his or her partner. A common problem we run into is with men who approach sexual intimacy with intercourse as the only goal. In a heterosexual couple, the female partner may begin to see herself as an object of her partner's pleasure and not as a companion who is loved. The sensate focus procedure can help a couple to focus on each other with mutual affection rather than as objects of arousal.

Progressive dilation for Vaginismus and Dyspareunia. The most common psychological etiologic explanation of vaginismus and dyspareunia is founded in prior sexual trauma and negative sexual messages. Overcoming these problems often involves the complex task of reviewing and processing negative sexual experiences and attitudes. In contrast, clients who have not had extreme sexual trauma often profit from an in vivo desensitization procedure involving gradual insertion of a finger or dilator into the vaginal opening. Some clinicians advise the use of a graduated set of dilators (available from a medical supply house) to desensitize a woman to vaginal insertion. The woman should be instructed to practice in privacy using the dilators; penetration depth can be varied and practiced, and only when a woman is comfortable with inserting a dilator should she move on to the next size. A lubricant can be advised.

It is often more convenient for women to practice insertion using their own fingers. Again, the strategy should be thoroughly discussed and reviewed before actually suggesting it. It may be helpful to approach the topic by saying, "Some women who have difficulty with penetration have found by practicing insertion very gradually they can overcome the problem. How would you feel about the technique of practicing insertion while you are alone and in the complete privacy of your home?" Once a woman has agreed to try, the therapist should explain that she is in complete control of the procedures. It should be emphasized that the depth of penetration and length of time of penetration can be controlled and varied by the client. The client should approach this while bathing or while relaxed on the bed and should start with inserting her little finger. Over a number of sessions, she should work up to inserting two fingers for a few minutes. Because many women will have strong objections to touching their genitals or masturbating, this exercise has to be put into perspective and distinguished from masturbation.

As a woman becomes more comfortable with insertion, her partner can be included. It should be emphasized that the woman must be in complete control of the procedure and that she can stop at any time. Moreover, the insertion process should be approached gradually with partial penetration and withdrawal. This process is usually started with digital penetration; over a number of sessions, the couple moves toward penile insertion. Again, the use of vaginal lubricants may be a useful addition to the insertion procedures.

Masturbation Training. Although traditionally viewed as a sign of psychopathology, masturbation is now increasingly used in sex therapy. The two most common applications are with women who are anorgasmic and with men who experience premature ejaculation. The book *Becoming Orgasmic* by Heiman and LoPiccolo (1988) provides the rationale for masturbation training in women. Specifically, it is argued that, the easiest, most intense, and most reliable orgasms for most women occur during masturbation. For women who have not yet experienced orgasm, masturbation is encouraged as a sure-fire way to allow them this pleasure. Heiman and LoPiccolo outline a program for helping women to use masturbation as a vehicle for self-exploration and liberation. Over time, women include their partners, who are taught how to touch and pleasure the woman.

With men who are concerned about premature ejaculation, masturbation can also be used to raise the men's awareness of arousal and orgasm stimulation.

Masturbation is used in conjunction with the penile squeeze method or the stop-start technique and should be approached in a similar fashion to erotica. Negative attitudes are explored first, and then attention is paid to maximizing a positive sexual experience. The therapist should not assume that the client knows how to masturbate. For example, we had a client who reported to us a lack of success in attempting to masturbate. When he was asked how he masturbated, he reported that he masturbated with his hand open so that his palm rubbed against the underside of his penis. In addition, he reported putting honey on his penis as a lubricant. He thought he had read somewhere that honey was a good lubricant. Specific instructions with pictures helped this client to learn how to masturbate successfully. Carefully prepared and sensitive educational videotapes are also available from Focus International and Good Vibrations. Masturbation training helps some clients to become more sensitive to the necessary conditions for a positive sexual experience. For clients who lack desire or confidence, masturbation training can lead to positive experiences that build desire and confidence.

Squeeze technique. The squeeze technique, used in the treatment of premature ejaculation, involves instructing the male to masturbate to a point just before ejaculation. He should pause at this point and squeeze the head of his penis by placing his forefinger and middle finger on one side of his penis and his thumb on the other side. The squeeze should be firm and last about 10 seconds. By repeating this process several times before ejaculation and by practicing this procedure, the man will learn to control his ejaculation.

Although this technique can be an effective, therapists should be cautioned not to endorse this technique if there are other relationship problems. Premature ejaculation can sometimes be a smokescreen for relationship problems. Therefore, in many cases of premature ejaculation, we direct our initial discussion to the question: ''Why do you have sex?'' After some thought, a number of reasons are suggested by clients. ''To have pleasure or because it feels good'' may be the most common response. We point out that couples have sex for a variety of reasons, including pleasure, to express love and affection, to make up after an argument, to have children, to make oneself feel better, and to please a partner. Moreover, the reason changes from occasion to occasion. The goal of this general discussion is to impress on our clients that pleasure, or pleasuring, and all of the other reasons we have sex, are not dependent on the length of time between intromission and orgasm. Furthermore, the length of time a man ''lasts'' should be looked upon as but one small part of the whole sexual exchange. Indeed, we encourage the couple to focus on general pleasuring rather than orgasm and to continue being intimate even after ejaculation. This takes the pressure off ejaculation and properly puts the emphasis on the total sexual relationship. This approach usually results in a couple's reporting a more satisfying relationship. Interestingly, even though we do not focus on the length of time between intromission and ejaculation, this time interval usually increases.

A second question that we ask clients and their partners is: "What do you believe is causing the problem?" In some cases of premature ejaculation, the female partner might express anger because her sexual needs are going unmet. Similarly, some women may believe that their men are able to control ejaculation more than is truly the case; they might interpret their partner's haste as the man's way of being thoughtless or inconsiderate. Certainly there are insensitive lovers, but it is rare that a client can control his ejaculation in order to hurt his partner's feelings. To the contrary, most men who seek treatment for premature ejaculation want desperately to please their partners. They tend to be embarrassed and confused about their difficulty.

Communication Training

Couples' counseling, including communication training, is critical to sex therapy. In a sense, this should not be seen as a separate component, but we do so here to emphasize its importance. Throughout assessment and therapy, the therapist should serve as a model of good communication by active listening, display of empathy, asking clients to express themselves clearly, and other such social and communication skills. In addition, the therapist should continually look for improvement in communication skills and point these out to a couple when they occur. It is helpful to inform the couple throughout the therapy that communication skills are important and will be addressed routinely. By stating this at the outset, an individual will not feel picked on when a communication issue is raised.

A common difficulty involves partners with different levels of desire. Initially this difference might be masked because one partner (usually the less desirous) accommodates to the other. Over time, however, some resentment develops, and the problem surfaces. In such couples, it is common for the less desirous partner to be labeled the client. As it turns out, however, there is simply a discrepancy between a relatively low-desire partner and a relatively high-desire partner. In such couples, the therapist can expect communication and problem-solving skills to be poor; these will require attention before the couple can begin to negotiate a sexual pattern that is mutually acceptable and satisfying.

Supplementing Sex Therapy with Cognitive Therapy

Sexual dysfunction is often associated with negative thoughts and feelings toward sex (in general), oneself, or one's partner. With some clients, we have also encountered fears regarding fainting, losing control, or increased vulnerability. In order to use a sexual skill-building procedure (e.g., masturbation training), the therapist should first explore in detail whether negative cognitions are present. It would be a strategic blunder to outline masturbation training without first assessing the couple's beliefs about the nature of the problem and the acceptability of masturbation.

Specific dysfunctions are also commonly accompanied by maladaptive thoughts. For example, many males who experience erectile disorder become very upset with themselves and fear ridicule from their partner. In heterosexual males, fears of homosexuality may emerge; that is, heterosexual men often interpret difficulty in obtaining or maintaining an erection as a sign that they are gay. Regardless of the precipitating factors, most cases of erectile disorder are maintained by interfering thoughts that may precede and occur during sexual relations. These interfering thoughts are not erotic thoughts, and they decrease arousal. In nondysfunctional men, thoughts preceding and occurring during sexual relations usually focus on their partner's or their own body parts, seductive behaviors, and anticipation of arousal and pleasure. In contrast, the dysfunctional male may be preoccupied with worries regarding the firmness of his erection, images of one's partner being disappointed or angry, and feelings of anxiety and depression.

The therapist must address interfering thoughts when they occur by helping the client to restructure her or his thoughts, that is, to focus on sexually facilitating thoughts rather than on sexually inhibiting ones. One way to help clients to refocus their thinking is to have them recall their thought content during past satisfying sexual experiences. This usually sensitizes clients to the types of positive thoughts they should concentrate on. If they have difficulty remembering positive sexual thoughts, the therapist should suggest typical helpful thoughts. Once clients are readily able to identify the positive sexual thinking process, treatment may advance to the next step, for example, sensate focus. The goal during sensate focus can now be positive sexual thinking (rather than achieving or maintaining an erection). Although the client may return to negative thinking, the therapist can help by encouraging him or her to return focus onto erotic thoughts and images. With practice, disruptive thoughts and images should gradually become less intrusive.

When a partner is involved in treatment, it is important also to consider that partner's cognitions around the dysfunction. Just as the man with erectile disorder harbors negative associations around this problem, so too the partner can be expected to have negative cognitions. A partner may fear that she is no longer attractive, that the man does not love her anymore, or that the partner is having an affair. We usually ask the partner what she thinks is the cause of the erectile problem. It is very important to help to clear up possible misunderstandings before proceeding to an intervention, such as sensate focus exercises. If misunderstandings are not addressed, it is likely they will arise again and sabotage treatment progress.

SUMMARY AND FUTURE DIRECTIONS

The understanding of sexual dysfunctions has advanced considerably since the pioneering work of Masters and Johnson. Drawing upon these advances, we have presented basic information about the prevalence and etiology of these difficulties as well as provided a basic guide for their assessment and treatment. Our progress should not deceive us, however, for there is still much that we need to know about the prevalence, etiology, assessment, and treatment of the sexual dysfunctions.

Many areas warrant further investigation, but we wish to call attention to four. First, we need to know more about all of the sexual dysfunctions that occur in women. Relatively few investigations have explored the etiology of sexual impairment in women. Second, we need to know more about comorbidity, that is, how commonly do sexual dysfunctions occur in the context of another Axis I or Axis II disorder, and what special considerations are required in such cases. Third, we need to explore the efficacy of combining medical and psychological treatments. Unidimensional treatments focusing on only one part of the person are likely to be less effective than are multimodal interventions. Finally, we need high-quality treatment outcome research documenting the strength and weaknesses of sex therapy. Investment in research will increase the value and efficacy of sex therapy and ensure the continuation of this specialty into the next century.

ACKNOWLEDGMENTS

Preparation of this chapter was supported by a Scientist Development Award to Michael P. Carey from the National Institute of Mental Health and a National Research Service Award to Christopher M. Gordon from the National Institute on Alcohol Abuse and Alcoholism.

REFERENCES

American Psychiatric Association. (1994). *Diagnostic and statistical manual of mental disorders* (4th ed.). Washington, DC: Author.

Ard, B. N. (1977). Sex in lasting marriages: A longitudinal study. *Journal of Sex Research, 13,* 274–285.

Bachman, G. A., Leiblum, S. R., & Grill, J. (1989). Brief sexual inquiry in gynecological practice. *Obstetrics and Gynecology, 73,* 425–427.

Bancroft, J., & Coles, L. (1976). Three years' experience in a sexual problems clinic. *British Medical Journal, 1,* 1575–1577.

Barlow, D. H. (1986). Causes of sexual dysfunction: The role of anxiety and cognitive interference. *Journal of Consulting and Clinical Psychology, 54,* 140–148.

Barnes, J. (1986). Primary vaginismus (Part 2): Aetiological factors. *Irish Medical Journal, 79,* 62–65.

Bond, J. B., & Tramer, R. R. (1983). Older adult perceptions of attitudes toward sex among the elderly. *Canadian Journal on Aging, 2,* 63–70.

Cameron, P. (1970). The generation gap: Beliefs about sexuality and self-reported sexuality. *Developmental Psychology, 3,* 272.

Carey, M. P., Flasher, L. V., Maisto, S. A., & Turkat, I. D. (1984). The a priori approach to psychological assessment. *Professional Psychology: Research and Practice, 15,* 515–527.

Chapman, J. D. (1989). A longitudinal study of sexuality and gynecological health in abused women. *Journal of the American Osteopathic Association, 89,* 619–624.

Comfort, A. (1980). Sexuality in later life. In J. E. Birren & R. B. Sloane (Eds.), *Handbook of mental health and aging.* Englewood Cliffs, NJ: Prentice-Hall.

Conte, H. R. (1986). Multivariate assessment of sexual dysfunction. *Journal of Consulting and Clinical Psychology, 5,* 149–157.

Davis, C. M., Yarber, W. L., & Davis, S. L. (Eds.). (1988). *Sexuality-related measures: A compendium.* Lake Mills, IA: Graphic Publishing Company.

Derogatis, L. R., & Meyer, J. K. (1979). A psychological profile of the sexual dysfunctions. *Archives of Sexual Behavior, 8,* 201–223.

Donahey, K. M., & Carroll, R. A. (1993). Gender differences in factors associated with hypoactive sexual desire. *Journal of Sex and Marital Therapy, 19,* 25–40.

Fisher, J., & Corcoran, K. (1994). *Measures for clinical practice: A sourcebook* (2nd ed.). New York: Free Press.

Frank, E., Anderson, C., & Kupfer, D. J. (1976). Profiles of couples seeking sex therapy and marital therapy. *American Journal of Psychiatry, 133,* 559–562.

Frank, E., Anderson, C., & Rubinstein, D. (1978). Frequency of sexual dysfunction in "normal" couples. *New England Journal of Medicine, 299,* 111–115.

Glatt, A. E., Zinner, S. H., & McCormack, W. M. (1990). The prevalence of dyspareunia. *Obstetrics and Gynecology, 75,* 433–436.

Gordon, C. M., & Carey, M. P. (1993). Penile tumescence monitoring during morning naps: A pilot investigation of a cost-effective alternative to full night sleep studies in the assessment of male erectile disorder. *Behaviour Research and Therapy, 31,* 503–506.

Gordon, C. M., & Carey, M. P. (1994). Penile tumescence monitoring during morning naps to assess male erectile functioning: An initial study of healthy men of varied ages. *Archives of Sexual Behavior,* in press.

Hawton, K. (1982). The behavioural treatment of sexual dysfunction. *British Journal of Psychiatry, 140,* 94–101.

Hawton, K. (1985). *Sex therapy: A practical guide.* Northvale, NJ: Aronson.

Hawton, K. (1992). Sex therapy research: Has it withered on the vine? *Annual Review of Sex Research, 3,* 49–72.

Heiman, J. R., & LoPiccolo, J. (1988). *Becoming orgasmic: A sexual and personal growth program for women* (rev. exp. ed.). New York: Prentice-Hall.

Hoon, P. W. (1979). The assessment of sexual arousal in women. *Progress in Behavior Modification, 7,* 1–61.

Hunt, M. (1974). *Sexual behavior in the 1970's.* Chicago: Playboy.

Kaplan, H. S. (1974). *The new sex therapy.* New York: Brunner/Mazel.

Katz, R. C., Gipson, M., & Turner, S. (1992). Brief report: Recent findings on the Sexual Aversion Scale. *Journal of Sex and Marital Therapy, 18,* 141–146.

Kilmann, P. R., Mills, K. H., Caid, C., Bella, B., Davidson, E., & Wanlass, R. (1984). The sexual interaction of women with secondary orgasmic dysfunction and their partners. *Archives of Sexual Behavior, 13,* 41–49.

Lamont, J. A. (1978). Vaginismus. *American Journal of Obstetrics and Gynecology, 131,* 632–636.

Levine, S. B., & Yost, M. A. (1976). Frequency of sexual dysfunction in a general gynecological clinic: An epidemiological approach. *Archives of Sexual Behavior, 5,* 229–238.

Lipsius, S. H. (1987). Prescribing sensate focus therapy without proscribing intercourse. *Journal of Sex and Marital Therapy, 11,* 185–191.

LoPiccolo, J., & Friedman, J. M. (1988). Broad-spectrum treatment of low sexual desire: Integration of cognitive, behavioral, and systemic therapy. In S. R. Leiblum & R. C. Rosen (Eds.), *Sexual desire disorders* (pp. 107–144). New York: Guilford.

LoPiccolo, J., & Heiman, J. R. (1978). Sexual assessment and history interview. In J. LoPiccolo & L. LoPiccolo (Eds.), *Handbook of sex therapy* (pp. 103–112). New York: Plenum.

McCarthy, B. W. (1985). Uses and misuses of behavioral homework exercises in sex therapy. *Journal of Sex and Marital Therapy, 11,* 185–191.

Masters, W. H., & Johnson, V. E. (1966). *Human sexual response.* Boston: Little, Brown.

Masters, W. H. & Johnson, V. E. (1970). *Human sexual inadequacy.* Boston: Little, Brown.

Meisler, A. W., & Carey, M. P. (1990). A critical reevaluation of nocturnal penile tumescence monitoring in the diagnosis of erectile dysfunction. *Journal of Nervous and Mental Disease, 178,* 78–89.

Meisler, A. W., Carey, M. P., Lantinga, L. J., & Krauss, D. J. (1989). Erectile dysfunction in diabetes mellitus: A biopsychosocial approach to etiology and assessment. *Annals of Behavioral Medicine, 11,* 18–27.

Munjack, D. J., & Kanno, P. H. (1979). Retarded ejaculation: A review. *Archives of Sexual Behavior, 8,* 139–150.

O'Sullivan, K. (1979). Observation on vaginismus in Irish women. *Archives of General Psychiatry, 36,* 824–826.

Renshaw, D. C. (1988). Profile of 2376 patients treated at Loyola Sex Clinic between 1972 and 1987. *Sexual and Marital Therapy, 3,* 111–117.

Rosen, R. C., & Beck, J. G. (1988). *Patterns of sexual arousal: Psychophysiological processes and clinical applications.* New York: Guilford.

Sandberg, G., & Quevillon, R. P. (1987). Dyspareunia: An integrated approach to assessment and diagnosis. *Journal of Family Practice, 24,* 66–69.

Schiavi, R. C., Schreiner-Engel, P., White, D., & Mandeli, J. (1988). Pituitary-gonadal function during sleep in men with hypoactive sexual desire and in normal controls. *Psychosomatic Medicine, 50,* 304–318.

Schover, L. R., & Jensen, S. B. (1988). *Sexuality and chronic illness: A comprehensive approach.* New York: Guilford.

Schreiner-Engel, P., & Schiavi, R. C. (1986). Life psychopathology in individuals with low sexual desire. *Journal of Nervous and Mental Disease, 174,* 646–651.

Segraves, R. T. (1988). Drugs and desire. In S. R. Leiblum & R. C. Rosen (Eds.), *Sexual desire disorders* (pp. 313–347). New York: Guilford.

Segraves, R. T., & Segraves, K. B. (1990). Categorical and multi-axial diagnosis of male erectile disorder. *Journal of Sex and Marital Therapy, 16,* 208–213.

Segraves, R. T., & Segraves, K. B. (1991). Hypoactive sexual desire disorder: Prevalence and comorbidity in 906 subjects. *Journal of Sex and Marital Therapy, 17,* 55–58.

Shabsign, R., Fishman, I. J., Schum, C., & Dunn, J. K. (1991). Cigarette smoking and other vascular risk factors in vasculogenic impotence. *Urology, 38,* 227–231.

Silverstein, J. L. (1989). Origins of psychogenic vaginismus. *Psychotherapy and Psychosomatics, 52,* 197–204.

Solstad, K., & Hertoft, P. (1993). Frequency of sexual problems and sexual dysfunction in middle aged Danish men. *Archives of Sexual Behavior, 22,* 51–58.

Spector, I. P., & Carey, M. P. (1990). Incidence and prevalence of the sexual dysfunctions: A critical review of the literature. *Archives of Sexual Behavior, 19,* 389–408.

Spector, I. P., Leiblum, S. R, Carey, M. P., & Rosen, R. C. (1993). Diabetes and female sexual function: A critical review. *Annals of Behavioral Medicine, 15,* 257–264.

Spiess, W. F., Geer, J. H., & O'Donohue, W. T. (1984). Premature ejaculation: Investigation of factors in ejaculatory latency. *Journal of Abnormal Psychology, 93,* 242–245.

St. Lawrence, J. S., & Madakasira, S. (1992). Evaluation and treatment of premature ejaculation: A critical review. *Clinical Psychology Review, 22,* 77–97.

Stuart, F. M., Hammond, D. C., & Pett, M. A. (1987). Inhibited sexual desire in women. *Archives of Sexual Behavior, 16,* 91–106.

Wincze, J. P., & Carey, M. P. (1991). *Sexual dysfunction: Guide for assessment and treatment.* New York: Guilford.

Zilbergeld, B. (1992). *The new male sexuality.* New York: Bantam Books.

9

Overcome: Repositioning Lesbian Sexualities

Ruth E. Fassinger and Susan L. Morrow

Lesbians face unique issues as they attempt to live as sexual beings in a society that ignores or condemns their sexuality. We begin this chapter with a discussion of the difficulties in naming and defining lesbian sexuality, review some specific sexual problems, and conclude with a brief discussion of the importance of understanding lesbian sexuality. Our perspectives here are informed primarily by the social and clinical conceptualizations that have characterized lesbians in the United States and Europe over the past fifty years. We take the stance that lesbian sexuality is a positive, affirmative option for women and that lesbian sexualities are constantly changing and emerging in the midst of challenges from within and outside lesbian communities and as a consequence of the enormous psychological creativity necessary to being lesbian in a society characterized by compulsory heterosexuality (Rich 1980).

LESBIAN SEXUALITY AND THE POLITICS OF DEFINITION

Early in the women's movement, Elsa Gidlow (1975) affirmed lesbian sexuality and foreshadowed some of the definitional problems that face lesbians today: "What needs to be understood is that erotic love between women is not a deviation from some presumed 'normal.' The Lesbian, to use a designation with an honorable history, is not a spoiled, failed or diverted so-called heterosexual woman. . . . Nature needs the Lesbian as she is. She needs me as I am" (p. 5). In addition to being described as a perversion or variation of the heterosexual female, the lesbian has also been seen frequently as homosexual (a female version of the gay male) or even as a woman trying to be like a man (Lamos 1994; Rich 1980). These definitional problems have led to the virtual invisibility of lesbian sexuality in research and writing, even in the area of female sexuality. When lesbian sexuality has been addressed, it typically has been focused on only differences from heterosexual women.

The pioneering work of Masters and Johnson (1965) shed light on the formerly dark continent of female sexuality; however, in their models for human sexual response, both the structure and function of women's (hetero)sexuality were seen as parallel to that of men; the clitoris, although finally acknowledged as critical to all orgasms in women, was viewed as a tiny penis and the sole source of sexual stimulation. Only many years later were women introduced to a different anatomical model, when the Federation of Feminist Women's Health Centers (1981) described the clitoral structure, a network of highly charged nerves infusing the vulvar area and culminating in the clitoris.

Lesbians were at the forefront of women's exploration and redefinition of their sexuality. For example, the Nomadic Sisters (1976) published "a sex manual by, for and about women" (p. 7). Heterosexual techniques were omitted intentionally because the authors wished to dedicate all of their energies and focus "to the uniqueness of women and their sexual pleasures" (p. 7). Perhaps even more important than redefining female anatomy and technique, however, was JoAnn Loulan's (1984) introduction, in her groundbreaking book *Lesbian Sex,* of willingness into the sexual response cycle. Instead of the phased linear model suggested by Masters and Johnson, consisting of excitement, plateau, orgasm, and resolution—which, following a phallocentric model, was incomplete in the absence of orgasm—Loulan suggested a complex, circular model consisting of loops, choices, and possibilities. The response cycle was described as beginning with willingness, leading through desire, emotional and physical excitement responses, orgasm, and return to a resting state. Most important, pleasure (or shutdown) was postulated as a possible outcome at any step of the process, not just at orgasm.

The importance of these lesbian pioneers to the understanding of female sexuality cannot be overstated. It has been said that a lesbian is "woman squared," that is, a woman whose sexuality need not function as a complement to or compromise with that of a man. However, until recently, women have not had a role in the construction of their own sexual paradigms; existing paradigms are therefore ignorant of women's interior reality, needs, and desires (Daniluk 1993). Many have noted that sexuality is culturally constructed (Blumstein & Schwartz 1990; Greenberg 1988; Vance 1992), with preferences and practices "elicited and shaped by the systems of meaning offered for conduct in a culture" (Gagnon 1990, p. 194), and inextricably linked to gender (Butler 1993) and class (Greenberg 1988). As a social construction, sexuality also is political and has been used as a tool of oppression of women, particularly lesbians (Rich 1980). D'Emilio and Freedman (1988) note that the signal achievement of this first generation of self-conscious lesbian feminists was to put in bold relief the part that sexuality played in the subordination of women. . . . To challenge the inevitability or naturalness of heterosexuality was to open new realms of freedom for females. As such, acceptance of lesbianism could serve as a benchmark for the whole panopoly of sexual questions that the second wave of feminism raised. Whether the issue was reproductive control, rape, sexual harassment, medical authority, prostitutes' rights, or lesbianism, feminists sought an authentic autonomy in sexual matters and an end to the gender inequality that prevented its achievement. (p. 318)

As a cultural construction, sexuality is subject to interpretation by a scientific community enmeshed in and constrained by that culture. In the past, the typical research study investigating sex or sexual relations failed to capture the uniqueness, diversity, and complexity of lesbian experiences and definitions of sex. Most research about women's sexuality has focused traditionally on orgasmic response (typically during heterosexual coitus) and ignores the emotional and relational components of the sexual experience (Koppelman 1988). This focus has led, in turn, to problems in defining lesbian sexuality and relationships by the absence or presence of genital sex, which an abundance of evidence (Blumstein & Schwartz 1983; Loulan 1984, 1987; Peplau & Cochran 1990) suggests may not be particularly important to many lesbians. Frye (1992), in a critique of Blumstein and Schwartz's (1983) oft-cited finding of low sexual frequency in lesbian (as compared to heterosexual) couples, argues that what is being counted as sex by heterosexual couples probably is focused on male orgasm in an act that takes about eight minutes to complete and does not rely on female orgasm or pleasure for its accomplishment. She wryly notes of lesbians:

What we do . . . considerably less frequently, takes on the average, considerably more than 8 minutes to do. Maybe about 30 minutes at the least. Sometimes maybe about an hour. And it is not uncommon that among these relatively uncommon occurrences, an entire afternoon or evening is given over to activities organized around doing it. The suspicion arises that what 85% of heterosexual married couples are doing more than once a month, and what 47% of lesbian couples are doing less than once a month is not the same thing. (p. 110)

Confusion exists not only in the research but also in lesbian communities, where "lacking the social institutions that define and structure heterosexual courtship in America, homosexuals may emphasize the occurrence of sexual behavior as a key to labeling their own same-sex relationships" (Peplau & Cochran 1990, p. 325). Heterosexual couples, defined by the institution of legalized marriage, are assumed to be in a relationship until death or divorce, even if they are living apart, having no sex, or having sex with others. Lesbian couples, by contrast, are considered couples if they are having (genital) sex (Rothblum in press). Expectations of genitally defined sex and sexually defined relationships may pressure lesbians to begin or continue sex in order to define and protect the relationship or to ignore or devalue other ways of relating with an intimate partner. Rothblum (in press) points out that our language has no terminology for sexual crushes that girls have on older women, for passionate feelings between adult women friends, for the closeness of lesbians with their ex-lovers, or for any other romantic friendships (Faderman 1981) or other non-genital love relationships. This lack of articulation about the complexity of lesbian sexual and emotional experience keeps it invisible and misunderstood by lesbians and nonlesbians alike.

What does it mean to current conceptions of sexuality to make lesbian experience central to our understanding? Brown (1988) observed, "Simply being lesbian or gay has been something we've had to invent for ourselves, since whatever roadmaps offered to us by the dominant culture have been full of wrong terms and uncharted territories" (p. 11). This "normative creativity" has encouraged a movement toward a "deeper and more complex understanding" of lesbian relationships and sexuality (p. 14). For example, there is a long history of lesbian committed relationships that are physically asexual (Faderman 1981, 1991; Rothblum & Brehony 1991). However, heterosexually derived models for sex in relationships have influenced lesbians, their therapists, and sex researchers to problematize this asexuality, reducing passion to the erotic and minimizing the legitimacy of romantic, committed expression that does not include genital sexual activity. A lesbocentric model, on the other hand, would be more psychologically true for lesbians, in that it would describe and ascribe value to sexual patterns perhaps unique to their experience. Fortunately, a growing body of scholarly work has sought to determine what sexual issues lesbians face from their points of view (Frye 1992; Loulan 1984, 1987, 1990; Rothblum in press).

A social constructionist perspective necessarily leads to difficult questions as we try to understand lesbian sexuality. Is lack of sexual desire or genital activity a "problem" in a loving and romantic woman-to-woman relationship? From whose point of view? Would the women in the relationship perceive it as a problem if not for the expectations of heterosexual society and lesbian culture? Who determines what is sexually normative for lesbians? If lesbians are seen as "just as normal, just as healthy, and just as valuable members of a pluralistic society" (Kitzinger 1987, p. 8) as are heterosexual women, what unique aspects of their political, social, and cultural locations are being implicitly erased? Such questions are not answered easily. As Vance (1992) pointed out, "To the extent social construction theory strives for uncertainty through questioning assumptions rather than seeking closure, we need to tolerate ambiguity and fluidity. . . . All movements of sexual liberation, including lesbian and gay, are built on imagining: imagining that things could be different, other, better than they are" (p. 144). It is with this imagination that it becomes possible to examine lesbian sexuality from a fresh perspective.

A vital aspect of the social construction of lesbian sexuality is the impact of feminism on lesbian definitions of what constitutes truly "woman-identified" sex. Nichols (1987) wrote in jest, "Lesbians clearly spend more time discussing the political correctness of sex than they spend doing sex" (p. 100). Controversy among both feminists and nonfeminists surrounds issues of sex therapy, sado-masochism (SM), butch-femme roles, monogamy, bisexuality, erotica, pornography, and other aspects of lesbian sexualities. Like Nichols, some maintain that, short of sexuality that is coercive or self-destructive, "anything that lesbians do sexually really is lesbian sexuality" and that "all our sexuality [is] politically correct sex" (p. 124). Grosz (1994) points out that to begin truly to explore lesbian sexuality is to accept nothing at face value. This endeavor demands a complex, multidimensional commitment to abandoning polarizations, being open to self-criticism, avoiding a moral high ground, and challenging the privileging of genitality over other forms of sexuality. A first step in this process is to explore the range of activities that characterize lesbian sex.

WHAT DO LESBIANS DO?

Lesbian sexuality is female sensuality blended into a collage of eyes, lips, legs, arms, hair, breasts, bellies and buttocks. It is fingers seeking, toes tensing, tongues searching, nipples blossoming, ear lobes tingling, bodies rubbing, juices flowing, backs arching, thighs questing, clitorises rising and cunts yawning. (Martin & Lyon, 1975, p. 62)

In order to determine what is normative or problematic in lesbian sexuality, we first need to know what it is lesbians actually do sexually. Most people, including lesbians themselves, really do not know. The sexual practices of lesbians have been mystified and stereotyped for many reasons, not the least of which is lesbians' attractiveness to those in the pornography industry. From the turn-of-the-century image of lesbian as "dildo-wielding butch" (Lamos 1994, p. 91) to modern-day portrayals of lipstick lesbians found in *Playboy* magazine, lesbians have been depicted in impossible erotic positions that bear little resemblance to what the majority of lesbians "do" sexually.

According to pioneering research on 1,566 lesbians (Loulan, 1987), 62 percent were in couple relationships, 26 percent were single, 12 percent were casually involved in sexual relationships, and 3 percent engaged in sex with men. The most common sexual activities among lesbians were hugging (96 percent), snuggling (92 percent), and kissing (91 percent). Other sexual activities engaged in by over 80 percent were touching and kissing breasts, holding body to body, masturbating, being naked with a partner, putting fingers in the partner's vagina, and holding hands in private (hand holding dropped to 27 percent in public, illustrating the powerful effect of homophobia and lesbian oppression in the culture at large). Over 50 percent of lesbians engaged in french kissing, licking breasts, petting, necking, oral sex, putting the tongue in the partner's vagina, masturbating the partner, and kissing all over the body. Other frequently chosen activities included sharing baths and massages and being naked with others. Less frequent sexual activities included using a vibrator; putting hands or dildos in the partner's vagina or fingers, hands, or dildos in the anus; using fantasy or erotic or pornographic stimuli; practicing bondage, or sadomasochism; and participating in group sex.

It is notable that, contrary to societal opinions about lesbian preferences for dildos or lesbian cultural beliefs that oral sex is the predominant mode of sexual relating, other forms of sexual expression actually took precedence over these stereotypic activities. Perhaps even more unexpected in a population frequently defined by its sexuality is the finding that hugging, snuggling, and kissing were seen by lesbians as sexual activities—indeed, those in which lesbians most frequently engaged. Frye (1992) points out that both lesbians and the culture at large have internalized heterosexual images of sexuality. She urges lesbians, instead of "trying to mold our loving and passionate carnal intercourse into explosive 8-minute events" (p. 116), to create a language that is as broad and varied as the activities and expressions that lesbians experience as sexual:

Let it be an open, generous, commodious concept encompassing all the acts and activities by which we generate with each other thrills, tenderness and ecstasy, passages of passionate carnality of whatever duration or profundity. Everything from vanilla to licorice, from puce to tangerine, from velvet to ice, from cuddles to cunts, from chortles to tears. Starting from there, we can let our experiences generate a finer-tuned descriptive vocabulary that maps and expresses the differences and distinctions among the things we do, the kinds of pleasures we get, the stages and styles of our acts and activities, the parts of our bodies centrally engaged in the different kinds of "doing it," and so on. (pp. 117–118)

SEXUAL ISSUES OF LESBIANS

Context

In understanding lesbian sexuality and relationship issues, it is important to consider the sociocultural context in which lesbians learn about themselves and behave as women, as sexual beings, as partners and lovers, and as members of families and communities. The first contextual reality is the well-documented process of female gender socialization and the kinds of roles and behaviors sanctioned or discouraged in women. Most relevant to discussions of sexuality and relationships are expectations of passive, dependent, and nurturant roles; denial and repression of women's sexuality; and body image pressures and concerns. Lesbians are in an interesting paradoxical position having declared themselves as sexual beings by the mere act of coming out, yet this declaration flies in the face of societal expectations that women are not sexual beings, creating confusion and conflict about the expression of sexuality in any form. Expectations of female passivity create further conflict as lesbians grapple with who will initiate sexual actitivity. Additional pressures to meet strict, unrealistic, unattainable images of female attractiveness and body image (Rothblum in press) are likely to add to sexual and relationship anxieties. Seeing oneself as nonsexual, passive, nurturant, physically imperfect, or unattractive results in difficulties in knowing or asking for what one wants in a sexual relationship with another woman. Lesbians, like their nonlesbian sisters, are likely to be uninformed, ashamed, or embarrassed about their bodily appearance and sexual functioning; to feel unworthy of pleasure; to engage in unwanted sexual activity to meet nonsexual (e.g., security) needs; and to put others' needs above their own, to the extent of being involved in insensitive or abusive sexual encounters (Califia 1988; Daniluk 1993; Koppelman 1988; Wyatt & Riederle in press). When two women with similar socialization patterns attempt to create sexual intimacy between them, the likelihood is doubled that any of these factors will affect the relationship.

A second contextual reality that defines the lives of lesbians is the existing "rape culture"—that is, pervasive acceptance and promotion of sexual objectification, denigration, abuse, harassment, and violent assault of women, even in their most intimate relationships. Indeed, Rothblum (in press) comments that "sex and violence are so linked in woman's experiences and emotions that we have yet to invent a sexuality . . . that has no history of violence against women" (p. 5). Traditionally, women's sexuality has been controlled by their reproductive roles and the needs of men. Lesbians, most (over 90 percent) of whom have had sex with men and many (approximately 33 percent) of whom have been married to men, are not immune from these influences (Nichols 1987). In addition, there has been reluctant admission in lesbian communities that physical, sexual, and emotional violence characterizes some lesbian relationships as well (Lobel 1986). Loulan (1987) found that 37 percent of her sample had been sexually abused as children (the same percentage for women in general), and most had experienced various forms of harassment and violence as adults: verbal harassment (49 percent), physical harassment (26 percent), rape (16 percent, much lower than the overall prevalence among women), and beating (9 percent). Again, pairings between women double the probability of negative past sexual experiences, and it is virtually certain that both will have experienced fear and caution regarding sexual behavior and personal safety:

Women—socialized by mothers to keep their dresses down, their pants up, and their bodies away from strangers—come to experience their own sexual impulses as dangerous. Self-control and watchfulness become necessary female virtues. As a result, female desire is suspect from its first tingle, questionable until proven safe, and frequently too expensive when evaluated within the larger cultural framework which poses the question, Is it really worth it? (Vance, 1984, p. 4)

The third contextual reality facing lesbians in their attempts to live out their sexuality and form intimate relationships is a pervasive social climate of compulsory heterosexuality, stigmatization, heterosexism, and homophobia, resulting in closeted individual identities and relationships. Energy is wasted on passing as heterosexual or struggling to disclose an invisible identity. Loss or lack of

family and other environmental supports, barriers to the formation and maintenance of partnerships and families (including custody of children), and internalized shame, anger, fear, and self-hatred negatively affect the identity
development process (see Fassinger 1991 for a more comprehensive discussion).
Since social sanction is a critical factor in relationship longevity (Blumstein &
Schwartz 1983) and the boundaries of lesbian relationships are repeatedly ignored or attacked in a heterosexist and homophobic society (Krestan & Bebko
1980), it is clear that these relationships face formidable challenges while "operating in a field of centrifugal force" (Krestan & Bebko 1980, p. 279) and that
their mere existence is an extraordinary accomplishment of courage and perse-
verance on the part of lesbians.

Some additional realities that may face lesbians include economic disadvantage (due to women's persistently poor earning potential), responsibility and care
for children, and the existence of lesbian communities. The lesbian community
is a source of support for individuals and couples who may not experience any
other validation for their lives. It is also a powerful source of norms and expectations regarding behavior, some of which may present difficulties in terms
of sexuality and relationships. It is an interesting paradox that while the lesbian
community has worked very hard over the years to decenter relationships and
honor celibacy and singlehood as well as multiple sexual liaisons and nonmonogamous connections among women, it is also true that coupled relationships
remain central to a great many lesbians (Loulan 1984), who live in communities
where there may be an implicit and pervasive insistence upon coupling. Since
it is in the context of intimate connection with another person that sexual issues
often arise, our discussion here includes much about lesbian relationships. However, our intention is not to present a couplist point of view, and we begin the
following section with a focus on the individual.

Self-Loving

In a population subject to some of the negative influences we have noted,
self-loving—both psychological and physical—assumes a position of considerable importance in the development of healthy sexuality. Loulan (1987) makes
very clear that sexual energy can be experienced in many ways and does not
necessarily have to involve genitals, orgasms, or partners. There appears to be
wide agreement in the sex therapy literature that, for women, learning to pleasure
oneself in the form of genital masturbation and other sensual activities is important for healthy sexual functioning. Through masturbation, women can learn
about and come to value their own bodies and responses and can develop a
sense of control over their sexuality and pleasure (Califia 1988). It is widely
known at this point in studies of female sexuality that masturbation (presumably
because of direct clitoral stimulation) is the most reliable way for many women
to achieve orgasm (Koppelman 1988); in fact, 86 percent of the lesbians in
Loulan's (1987) study achieved orgasm through a variety of forms of mastur-

bation, including using hands (58 percent), vibrators (24 percent), tribadism (8 percent), and other activities (6 percent). Women who masturbate are also more likely to climax with a partner than women who do not (Califia 1988), and it is clear that, among lesbians at least, masturbation is not merely a substitute for a partner. In Loulan's (1987) study, 92 percent of lesbians who were single, 92 percent of those casually involved, and 88 percent of those in couples reported masturbating, and most of these women (75 percent) reported frequencies of two to twenty times per month.

Celibacy (with or without masturbation) also may be a preferred lifestyle for many women. In Loulan's (1987) study, the majority of lesbians (78 percent) had been celibate at some point, with 38 percent celibate for periods from one to five years and 8 percent celibate for six years or more; 84 percent of these described their celibacy as self-chosen to some degree. Celibacy, like masturbation, can be an opportunity for tremendous personal growth and self-awareness, particularly for women healing from addictions, prior negative experiences, or extremely constricted socialization (Califia 1988; Loulan 1987) or those for whom lesbianism is a political choice and for whom sex may be of little importance (Faderman 1984). In addition to individual celibacy, lesbian couples may become celibate. In Loulan's (1987) study, four percent of lesbians self-identified as celibate were in a relationship, a number that does not include those in relationships who were not having sex but did not identify themselves as celibate. Because the issue of celibacy in a couple is more complex than as an individual choice, we discuss asexuality in couples in a later section.

Characteristics of Lesbian Couples

Because lesbians are so seriously underresearched, we know less about lesbian couples than any other kind of pairing (Nichols 1990). However, many (Frye 1992; Loulan 1984, 1987; Nichols 1987, 1990; Rothblum in press) have observed that relationships between women (because of women's relational capacities) contain a unique potential for levels of connection, caring, and equality that are unparalleled in heterosexual or gay male couples. While lesbian relationships may exhibit similarities to other kinds of relationships in terms of levels of love, satisfaction, adjustment, cohesion, relationship dynamics and processes, and the importance of psychological femininity in preserving stability and security (Garnets & Kimmel 1991; Kurdek 1994; Peplau & Cochran 1990), they also differ in some important ways. The existing literature suggests that lesbian relationships (Berger 1990; Blumstein & Schwartz 1983; Garnets & Kimmel 1991; Kurdek 1994; Lewis et al. 1992; Nichols 1990; Peplau & Cochran 1990):

- Exhibit flexibility in roles, an absence of sex role stereotyping, and egalitarianism.

- Emphasize power balance in the couple, with power imbalance a factor in breakups.

- Receive less emotional support from family than friends, may experience a general lack of social support, and are less likely to experience psychological distress when levels of support are high.

- Experience fewer barriers to relationship dissolution than heterosexual couples.

- Are more likely to exhibit satisfaction when some outside disclosure of lesbian identity has occurred and when both partners are strongly and equally committed to the relationship.

- Exhibit concern with boundary maintenance in the relationship and find variations in attachment and autonomy to influence the relationship.

- Report very high levels of relationship satisfaction and liking for the partner, intrinsic motivation for being in the relationship, trust, and shared decision making.

For lesbians, love and sex are closely linked, and sexual intimacy is characterized by partner choices focused on affection and caring rather than on physical attributes (Garnets & Kimmel 1991; Nichols 1990; Peplau & Cochran 1990). Overall, lesbians appear to have no pervasive sexual problems (Nichols, 1990); they do not exhibit significant rates of orgasmic dysfunction, and dyspareunia and vaginismus are almost unheard of in this population (Nichols 1990). Lesbians do exhibit low frequencies of sex in long-term committed relationships but appear to be more responsive and more satisfied with the sex they do have than are heterosexual women (Nichols 1990; Peplau & Cochran 1990). In Loulan's (1987) study, for example, 81 percent reported experiencing orgasm during partner sex, and 87 percent reported that they loved sex.

Stages of Lesbian Relationships

Lesbian couples, like other couples, go through stages in the establishment and maintenance of their relationships. However, the process in lesbian couples is complicated by the contextual issues already noted. Clunis and Green (1988) outlined six relationship stages characterizing lesbian couples. They note that their stage model is only a "rough map" (p. 9) of the process of relationship formation in lesbians and that much variation and recycling will occur. They caution that individual difference factors such as age, cohort, class, race and ethnicity, religion, geographic location, stage of lesbian identity, (dis)ability, and access to the lesbian community will have profound impact on coupling processes, dynamics, and emergent problems.

The first, prerelationship, stage, often called dating by lesbians, is characterized by the couple's getting to know one another. In this stage, choices are made about sexual and emotional intimacy, and expectations regarding the relationship are negotiated. Like heterosexual couples, the dating behavior of lesbians and gay men is guided by cultural scripts, which proscribe socially normative expectations and actions regarding courtship and sexual behavior in these communities (Klinkenberg & Rose 1992). While dating scripts and behaviors of gay men and lesbians differ from those of heterosexual couples in their greater independence of rigid gender roles, lesbians also differ from gay men in that their scripts and behaviors tend to be less sexually oriented and more focused on intimacy, as well as including greater attention to the partner in the dating situation (Klinkenberg & Rose 1992). This focus on forming a deep and caring connection with the partner often leads the couple very quickly, sometimes prematurely (Nichols 1987, 1990), to later stages of the relationship. Nichols (1987) notes how clearly female socialization affects lesbian sexuality, in that lesbians value relationships over being single and tend to express sexual feelings only in the context of a relationship, which results in the rapid relationship formation that tends to characterize lesbian dating patterns.

The second, romance (often termed "limerance"), stage is characterized by merger and fusion, as the couple experiences a feeling of harmony and acceptance of one another, shared fantasies and dreams, and complete focus on one another. There is often a great deal of sexual activity during this stage, and Clunis and Green (1988) note that the "gift" (p. 15) of this stage is the vision of what might be in the future as two women (both socialized for intense intimacy) create a oneness of their separate lives. Differences between the two individuals in the couple tend to be glossed over or ignored during this stage, and for lesbians involved in various kinds of cross-cultural relationships, partner differences may heighten the sense of romance and eroticism common to this stage. The sexual and emotional exhilaration of this stage does not last indefinitely. However, some couples cling to the feeling of perfect togetherness in this stage for prolonged periods, which may result in the merger or fusion of the couple. Indeed, Hall (1984) observed that only one-third of the lesbians in the Blumstein and Schwartz (1983) study pursued activities independent of their partners and that lesbians in other studies have indicated a desire for personal independence as a factor leading to problems in committed relationships.

The third, conflict, stage of the relationship is characterized by the emergence of differences (ignored, suppressed, or irrelevant in the previous stages) between the members of the couple in temperament, goals, needs, values, beliefs, and desires. When conflict erupts as a result of these differences, the task is to establish ground rules and communication patterns for the relationship. For lesbians in cross-cultural relationships, differences may be particularly unexpected and troubling, as each struggles to understand not only her partner's world but also the profound effects of growing up in her own world and finding that "the person closest can also be the enemy" who inflicts insult and hurt (Garcia et al. 1987, p. 143). In addition, lesbians in cross-cultural relationships must negotiate differences in cultural defenses that each has learned and privilege that each may experience as a result of racial, ethnic, religious, class, age or (dis)ability status, as well as confront the prejudices of their particular communities. Finally, since sex is often inextricably bound with emotional intimacy in lesbian couples, the conflicts of this stage are likely to be played out in the sexual arena (Clunis & Green 1988; Nichols 1987).

The fourth, acceptance, stage is described by Clunis and Green (1988) as "the calm after the storm" (p. 20), in which a sense of stability and contentment is achieved in the relationship. The members of the couple come to appreciate themselves as two different people, each with her own history, and begin to recognize patterns in problems and conflict, thereby speeding up the process of resolving issues when they arise. Deep affection and appreciation of each other often occur at this stage, and, for many, stability in sexual intimacy patterns is achieved as well. However, for some couples, a dramatic decline in sexual activity may begin during this stage. Such decline may be acceptable to both partners, one partner, or neither partner, but the issue is seldom discussed (Nichols 1987, 1990). Thus, a long-term asexual relationship may evolve, with or without outside affairs leading to the breakup of the relationship.

In the fifth, commitment, stage, the members of the couple make choices about the priority of the relationship and take responsibility for them. There is an acceptance of the partner as trustworthy and the relationship as enduring, so that differences and changes are not threatening. Particularly important in this stage are the negotiation and acceptance of the balance between separateness and togetherness, and the development of strategies to meet individual as well as relationship needs. In the sexual arena, achieving such balances in interdependence and personal power may lead the couple to explore areas such as nonmonogamy, butch-femme roles, and SM sexual behavior.

Finally, the last, collaboration, stage of the relationship involves the direction of energy of the couple into some project beyond themselves and the relationship: volunteer work in the community, having a child (see Loulan 1984 for discussion), opening a business, or the creation of some other entity beyond the relationship itself. Clunis and Green (1988) note that the completion of the final stage may cause the couple to recycle through some of the earlier stages as they act upon their dream together. Presumably sexual issues will (re)surface as conflicts and intimacy wax and wane, and earlier unresolved issues are likely to reappear.

Sex in Lesbian Relationships

In examining the sexual dynamics in lesbian relationships, it seems apparent—problems of genitally based definitions of sex and sex-based definitions of relationships notwithstanding—that some lesbian individuals and couples do experience as problems low eroticism or discrepancy in sexual initiation or desire between partners (Clunis & Green 1988; Hall 1987; Loulan 1987; Nichols 1987; Roth 1985). Research generally suggests that lesbians are less likely to engage in (presumably genital) sex than heterosexual or gay male couples. In the Blumstein and Schwartz (1983) sample, 76 percent of lesbian couples (compared to 83 percent of married heterosexuals) were having sex once or more per week during the first two years of the relationship, while after two years, only 37 percent of the lesbian couples (compared to 73 percent of the heterosexuals) were having sex once or more per week; in addition, 47 percent of lesbian couples in relationships for more than five years (versus 15 percent of heterosexual couples) were having sex once a month or less. Loulan (1987) reported that in her sample, 12 percent of lesbians in couples never had partner sex, while others reported ranges per month of once or less (19 percent), two to five times (35 percent), six to ten times (20 percent), and eleven or more (14 percent); overall, then, 31 percent of lesbians were having sex once per month or less. Blumstein and Schwartz (1983) reported that half of the lesbians in couples with low sexual frequency in their sample expressed relationship dissatisfaction. In Loulan's (1987) sample, only 16 percent of lesbians in couples expressed sexual dissatisfaction, while the remainder indicated that they were somewhat to completely satisfied with sex.

Several scholars (Faderman 1981, 1991; Rothblum in press; Rothblum & Brehony 1991) have written extensively of the asexuality that characterizes many long-term lesbian relationships, both historically and at present. Rothblum and Brehony (1991) reclaimed the turn-of-the-century term *Boston marriage* to describe these relationships in their modern form:

There are women in our lesbian communities who live together and share long histories together. They may have been sexual in the past, or they may never have had genital sex. They are "lovers" in every sense of the word except the absence of current genital sexual activity. They are usually viewed as couples by the lesbian community, which may in fact idealize the couples for the longevity and romantic nature of their relationship. Often, in marked contrast to Boston marriages in previous times, these lesbians keep their *asexuality* hidden from the community. (Rothblum in press, p. 13)

Rothblum and Brehony (1991) also note the many different motivations for and forms of asexuality in modern-day Boston marriages, which may range from monogamous celibacy on the part of both partners, to a kind of celibate non-monogamy in which asexual romantic pairings outside the primary relationship are permitted, to accepted sexual relationships on the part of one or both partners outside the primary relationship. These authors also point to the difficulties in defining and maintaining such couples in the context of prevailing sexual definitions of relationships. For example, members of a couple may have different perceptions of what constitutes sex, whether they are, indeed, "having sex," or even whether they are in a "real" relationship; it is also likely that they rarely discuss the lack of sexual activity in their relationship. In addition, the lesbian community may explicitly or implicitly deny that they are a couple if they are not having genital sex, particularly if one or both are having relationships outside the primary couple.

There are myriad reasons discussed in the literature for patterns of low sexual activity in some long-term lesbian couples, many of them related to the contextual factors. Nichols (1987) argues, for example, that most of the sexual "problems" observed in lesbians are linked inextricably with the sexual repression of women; therefore, lesbian relationships are bound to exhibit less sexual activity than couples that include men. Due to socialization, lesbians are less likely to seek out, request, or initiate sex or to pressure a reluctant partner (Clunis & Green 1988; Nichols 1987). Because of socialized links between sex and love, lesbians may be especially vulnerable to the personalization of sexual refusal. If, as Blumstein and Schwartz (1990) suggest, eroticization between women is more often a consequence of their emotional attraction than a catalyst for involvement, then sexual refusal is likely to be interpreted as a rejection of the person instead of the sexual act itself (Roth 1985). Similarly, the linking of love and sex by lesbians creates "the last of the modern-day romantics" (Nichols 1987, p. 104), rendering sexual desire extremely vulnerable to interference from conflicts or boredom in the relationship (Clunis & Green 1988; Hall 1984; Loulan 1987; Nichols 1987; Smalley 1987). Sexual or relationship dissatisfaction may be dealt with by falling in love (the only acceptable path to sexuality for a "romantic") with someone new, leading to the termination of the relationship (Nichols 1987). Repressive sexual socialization also leads to the expression of arousal through emotional or intellectual channels not recognized as "sexual," by either the woman experiencing them or her partner (Loulan 1984; Nichols 1987). Other factors implicated in infrequent sex in long-term lesbian couples include psychological defenses adopted to cope with internalized or environmental homophobia; the political rejection of "looksism" as dampening lesbians' own responses to beauty and physical attractiveness; learned shame about bodies and sexuality; and earlier negative or insensitive experiences with men (Clunis & Green 1988; Hall 1984; Loulan 1984; Nichols 1987; Roth 1985).

One area that has garnered considerable blame in the literature for sexual inactivity in lesbian couples concerns the tasks of the second stage described by Clunis and Green (1988): merger and fusion in lesbian relationships. Hall (1987) notes that the observation of extreme, prolonged (sometimes dysfunctional) merger and fusion in lesbian couples has been noted by many but that the explanations for this merger are the subject of much debate. According to psychodynamic interpretations, permeable boundaries in women result from the primary mother-daughter bond, and the lack of sex observed in merger relationships occurs because "partners fear they will be reduced to the state of a powerless infant, subject to the whims of an engulfing mother" (Hall 1987, p. 139). Sociological explanations postulate that fusion arises from gender role socialization, in which the notion of ego boundaries is irrelevant in the face of the supportive, self-sacrificing, passive roles proscribed for women and that such roles create much caring and connection but little eroticism in relationships. Physiological explanations view such relationships as needing "a good skirmish" (Hall 1987, p. 139) or some outside threat to increase adrenaline and catalyze eroticism in the couple, for whom the relationship has become too comfortable and protected.

Probably most plausible (particularly in combination with socialization interpretations) is a systems-oriented social analysis (Krestan & Bebko 1980; Pearlman 1989), which postulates that existence in a hostile, homophobic society leads to multiple and continuous disruptions of couple bonding, preventing or delaying the formation of a stable internal image of the relationship. Pearlman (1989) wryly observes that while heterosexual couples go out to be together, lesbian couples go out to separate. These presses, in turn, lead lesbian couples to adopt an "us-against-the-world stance" (Hall 1987, p. 140) in order to protect the boundaries of the relationship from outside threat. In order to preserve and project a unified front, individual differences must be suppressed or ignored, a relatively easy task for women, who have been socialized for self-denial. Thus, merger, rather than characterizing a stage in the relationship, comes to characterize the couple permanently, as individual boundaries become increasingly blurred and the relationship forms a closed system as an adaptive response to societal negation "in the interests of its own survival" (Krestan & Bebko 1980, p. 284). Thus, "one function of prolonged merger is to create some sense of enduring relationship connection and security" (Pearlman 1989, p. 83). If, as some postulate (Hall 1987; Nichols 1987), eroticism requires difference to maintain the distance, mystery, and unpredictability necessary to spark desire, then fusion is likely to lead to decreased desire. Sex, which often serves a bridging function in relationships to connect two separate people more intimately, thus becomes redundant and unnecessary in fused couples.

The issue of merger in lesbian relationships raises unsettling questions about the meanings we give intimacy and autonomy in our current conceptions of sexuality. While it is probable that some lesbian couples suffer from difficulties in negotiating individual and relationship boundaries, it is also critical to remember that the autonomy and independence promoted in modern developmental and relationship frameworks reflect heterosexist and androcentric notions of what is healthy and comfortable for "normal" adults in relationships. The possibility of different pathways to intimacy and autonomy for women is well documented, and the intense connection of lesbian relationships offers a glimpse of what is possible when women define for themselves the scope and range of their loving.

Other Sexually Related Issues

A number of issues are currently public and controversial in lesbian communities and may have considerable impact on the sexuality of both individuals and couples. The first issue is monogamy. Blumstein and Schwartz (1990) claimed that, on average, lesbians have about the same rate of nonmonogamy as heterosexuals (28 percent report at least one outside relationship) but far less than that of gay men, for whom nonmonogamy seems to be normative. In Loulan's (1987) study, 88 percent of lesbians described themselves as monogamous. Nonmonogamy in lesbians appears to be uncommon (15 percent) during the first two years of a relationship, but in couples together ten years or more, 43 percent report at least one instance of nonmonogamy (Blumstein & Schwartz 1990). In

addition, lesbians who are nonmonogamous are more likely to report dissatisfaction in their primary relationship (Blumstein & Schwartz 1990). Finally, lesbian couples handle their relationships in ways qualitatively different from
heterosexuals and gay men (Nichols 1987). Unlike their gay male counterparts,
the relationships lesbians have outside their primary relationships are usually
built on love and friendship and are thus more like heterosexual affairs than the
purely sexual "tricking" common to gay male relationships. However, unlike
their heterosexual counterparts (and similar to their gay male brothers), lesbians
are generally open with their primary partners about their liaisons outside the
relationship. Thus, outside relationships for lesbians tend to the serious affairs,
known to the primary partner, and may coincide with unhappiness in the primary
couple.

Lesbian nonmonogamy developed in the mid-1970s out of a political rhetoric
that labeled monogamy as patriarchal and ownership oriented and celebrated
nonjealous sex as a natural extension of all loving relationships and therefore
not threatening to the primary relationship (Nichols 1987). Potential benefits to
the development of the individual or the couple include providing a relational
structure for gaining personal power and meeting unmet needs, resolving conflicted and immature boundaries, affirming the primary bond, allowing the transition out of the relationship, or serving a symbolic function whose mere
possibility serves as an "individuating boundary" (Kassoff 1989, p. 168). Nichols (1987) argues, however, that most lesbians, given their propensity to fuse
sex and love, are incapable of engaging in prolonged sexual and emotional
affairs without damaging the primary relationship. Since lesbians tend to reject
casual sex, Nichols maintains that it is unlikely that lesbian relationships will
successfully weather nonmonogamy unless lesbians develop alternative modes
of conceptualizing relationships. She suggests that this involves the psychological separation of infatuation or romance from committed love and allows for
the awareness of limitations, in both the primary relationship (which makes
outside relationships necessary to meet individual needs) or the outside relationship (which must be accepted as fleeting and circumscribed). It is also important for couples not to view nonmonogamy as a sign of dissatisfaction with
the relationship and to reach agreement about how it will be integrated into the
primary relationship (Pelau & Cochran 1990).

Another controversial issue in the lesbian community is butch-femme roles
(Lamos 1994; Loulan 1990; Nestle 1992). Some see such roles as a regression
to monstrous butch-femme images of the 1950s and earlier (Lamos 1994) or an
unthinking imitation of heterosexist norms and rigid role playing that limits
women's potentialities. Others argue that the reemergence of butch-femme roles
is a liberation from the monotonous lesbian "clone" (Nichols 1987, p. 114)
that the lesbian feminist community created in its attempt to throw off male-
defined standards of beauty and define lesbian desire not by traditional gender
differences (as captured in butch-femme roles) but by gender identification—
the woman-identified-woman of the 1970s (Lamos, 1994). Still others argue that

butch-femme roles are attractive to many because of the eroticism inherent in personal differences (indeed opposites) in appearance, tastes, responses, and needs (Nichols 1987). Interestingly, Loulan (1990), in a study of butch-femme roles and attitudes among lesbians, found that 95 percent of her respondents were familiar with such roles and "rated" themselves and others; however, she also found that the same percentage of lesbians reported that these roles were not important in their lives. Such results suggest that "butch-femme may be a widely recognized set of conventions within lesbian culture, but it must not be assumed to be a constitutive or obligatory identification" (Lamos 1994, p. 101).

Nichols (1987) maintains that ambivalence about gender roles has consistently characterized the lesbian community: "On the one hand, the greatest criticism one could make of another woman is that she is male-identified. On the other hand, we despise the traditionally feminine as male-defined. This has left us very little room to maneuver, and has surely been one of the factors constraining our sexual selves" (p. 116). Some (Lamos 1994; Nichols 1987) argue that the butch-femme position can ultimately help us transcend gender roles by breaking the link between traits or behaviors and gender, redefining characteristics as neither male nor female but rather as "human idiosyncratic differences" that are "fluid, changeable, and multifaceted" (Nichols 1987, pp. 116–117). However, Lamos (1994) cautions: "Although . . . 'new' butches and femmes take an ironic, campy stance toward the gender roles they imitate, butch/femme always runs the risk of becoming naturalized, either by being reduced to male/female heterosexual norms, or by being adopted as the psychological, inner truth of a person" (p. 98).

A third controversial issue in the lesbian community is SM practices (Nichols 1987, 1990; Samois 1981). Opponents view SM behaviors, a "form of eroticism based on a consensual exchange of power" (Samois 1981, p. 3), as heterosexist and patriarchal, rooted in the domination and humiliation that characterize the rape culture and therefore oppressive of women no matter how they are practiced. Arguments against SM also point to the addictive aspects of SM, which are said to develop as individuals become tolerant of ever-increasing levels of pain or discomfort. In addition, opponents decry the violence in other aspects of the relationship to which SM may lead, particularly as SM practices may attract those who experienced violent or abusive experiences in childhood. Finally, opponents criticize the cultlike aspects of the SM movement, particularly as it has arisen in some segments of lesbian communities.

Proponents of SM practices focus on the consensual nature of SM relationships and the power of the masochist in the sexual encounter. They argue that SM is sexually enhancing and freeing in that it allows partners to exchange power and transcend the limiting gender roles and conditioning promulgated in a sexist, misogynist culture. It has been pointed out that public attention has been given to the excesses of SM rather than its normative practices and that, among lesbians, there are "probably more silk scarves, mild spankings, and fantasy being used than whips and chains, probably more talk than action"

(Nichols 1987, p. 110). Finally, Nichols (1987) argues that the larger issue of the repression of female sexuality is far more critical than the issue of whether some areas of sexuality have been "contaminated by patriarchal modes" (p. 111). In this view, SM practices and other activities promoted by lesbian sex radicals serve to free lesbian sexuality and open up erotic potential in the entire lesbian community (Nichols 1987, 1990).

The final area we briefly examine is sexual health care. According to the National Lesbian Health Care Survey (Ryan & Bradford 1987), which surveyed almost 2,000 women nationally and represents the first large-scale study of lesbian health care needs and concerns, one out of ten lesbians were not receiving any care for general health problems, and 36 percent of these reported not doing so because of negative experiences or inability to pay for care. About 10 percent of the respondents felt that the quality of their health care had been compromised because of their lesbianism, and 27 percent reported that their physicians believed them to be heterosexual. Almost one-fourth (23 percent) of the respondents were treating themselves for gynecological problems, and few reported that they worried about getting sexually transmitted diseases (less than 25 percent) or AIDS (10 percent). It should be noted that this sample represents the experiences of a group of women who were relatively young (81 percent were under age 44) and well educated (almost 70 percent had graduated from college); given the widely documented difficulty for the old, poor, and uneducated of obtaining health care, these figures may represent a considerable underestimation of health care problems for lesbians.

Although the unique health care issues related to aging and disability in sexuality and sexual orientation are covered elsewhere in this book, our awareness of the pervasive invisibility of lesbians (indeed, of women) in most existing aging and disability literature leads us to mention briefly some of these issues here as well. Older lesbians and lesbians with disabilities are more likely than men or heterosexual women to face ignorance regarding their needs and concerns. Lesbians confront many of the same issues as their heterosexual counterparts, such as: coping with stigmatization; developing and maintaining support systems; dealing with pain or deteriorating physical functioning and attractiveness; accommodating to increasingly restricted activities; and coping with helplessness, loss, lack of control, and despair. However, older lesbians and lesbians with disabilities face additional stresses as well. For example, the pervasive societal heterosexism that denies hospital visitation rights, legitimacy of participation in health care decisions, and financial and legal protection can be especially devastating to those in couples or close relationships. For lesbians, who typically value equality in relationships, the power imbalances or increasing dependency of one of the partners also may create conflict and stress. In addition, the isolation and homophobia in traditional nursing homes and other care facilities, combined with economic disadvantage, make such options unavailable to many lesbians. For some, the disclosure of identity forced by the illness of oneself or one's partner or the need to get one's legal affairs in order may be difficult, particularly for lesbians who "came out" at a time when attitudes were much more oppressive and who subsequently have led very closeted lives (Clunis & Green 1988). Finally, most lesbians who are coping with disability and aging at this point in historical time are inventing the resources, roles, and rules as they go along—there are no role models to emulate, resources to seek out, or normative standards by which to judge their experiences.

On the positive side, lesbians coping with disability, chronic illness, or aging are advantaged in ways their heterosexual and gay male counterparts are not. Lesbians as a group exhibit more flexible gender roles and better coping, as well as fewer "looksist" attitudes, so that the physical changes associated with disability and age may affect lesbians less negatively than others (Rothblum 1992). In addition, lesbian communities have been in the forefront of ensuring accessibility to women with a variety of disabling conditions. Some of the physical changes associated with menopause (such as vaginal dryness) are less disruptive to women not engaged in heterosexual intercourse, and lesbians' focus on the affective rather than performance aspects of sex may lead to less anxiety about bodily functioning (Cole & Rothblum 1991). Indeed, research suggests that older lesbians are leading healthy, satisfying sexual lives. Loulan (1987) found that lesbians over age 60 were both masturbating and having partner sex two to five times per month (more than any other age group), while Cole and Rothblum (1991) found that the majority of their sample of forty-one postmenopausal women reported that their sex lives were as good as or better than ever.

It should be clear from the discussion that feminist models of women's sexual health that attend to the unique experiences of lesbians are much needed. New woman-defined models of sexuality and sexual health have recently been proposed (Daniluk 1993; Koppelman 1988), which suggest that some combination of positive body image and comfort, autonomy and assertiveness in sexual expression, sense of self-worth beyond one's reproductive capacities, and participation in egalitarian intimate relationships are markers that help to define sexual health for women. Such models thoroughly displace concepts of sexual dysfunction, because they suggest complex levels of sexual and relationship functioning that rely on individual women's own definitions of what is pleasurable and healthy. Sexual frequency, means of stimulation, augmentation of excitement, and orgasmic focus are all defined by the woman herself, and her sexual choices and responses are "problems" only if she sees them as such (Koppelman 1988).

CONCLUSION

Lesbians are "sexual explorers" (Kassoff 1991, p. 181), charting new experiential and conceptual territory. Undergirding these adventurous capacities, as Rothblum (1989) points out, is "not just the absence of psychopathology but *increased* mental health for women" (p. 6), including such protective factors as freedom from health risks of contraception, relative protection from sexually transmitted diseases, freedom from marriage (a documented mental health risk for women), self-reliance and financial independence in relationships, full-time employment, flexible roles and coping skills, and the presence of lesbian communities for support. Smalley (1987) notes that lesbians, forced to engage in intensive self-examination in order to achieve integrated identities, usually are more self-aware; have more friendships; attend more to personal health, nutrition, and balance in their lives; have fewer "shoulds"; and are more oriented toward expanded models for relationships than are other people.

Although it would be foolhardy to suggest that there is a "natural" woman—untainted by the influence of patriarchy, female socialization, and the repression of her sexuality—lesbians demonstrate the pioneering creativity that can emerge from their positioning on the margins of society and sexuality. It might be that frequencies of sex viewed as "normal" in heterosexual couples are merely artifacts of male initiation behavior and female acquiescence and that lesbian sexual patterns represent the beginnings of divergence from a heteropatriarchal model of sexual expression. Rothblum (in press) argues that lesbians can serve as models for sexual activity free from reproduction and independent of genital activity, their sexuality therefore including all aspects of their bodies, passions, spiritualities, and love. Indeed, women's relationships offer unique views of what intimacy can be, "forging possibilities of extraordinary connectedness, compatibility, and happiness in a disconnected and alienating world" (Pearlman 1989, p. 87).

The normative creativity of lesbians in relation to their sexuality provides awareness and knowledge that can inform our understanding of human sexualities in general and women's sexualities in particular. Lesbian sexualities both excite and frighten. What is truly exciting, and perhaps a bit frightening, is that we may have to rethink everything we believe we know about human sexuality if we pay attention to lesbian experience.

REFERENCES

Berger, R. M. (1990). Passing: Impact of the quality of same-sex couple relationships. *Social Work, 35,* 328–332.

Blumstein, P., & Schwartz, P. (1983). *American couples.* New York: William Morrow.

Blumstein, P., & Schwartz, P. (1990). Intimate relationships and the creation of sexuality. In D. P. McWhirter, S. A. Sanders & J. M. Reinisch (Eds.), *Homosexuality/heterosexuality: Concepts of sexual orientation* (pp. 307–320). Oxford: Oxford University Press.

Brown, L. S. (1988, August). *New voices and visions: Toward a lesbian/gay paradigm for psychology.* Paper presented at the annual convention of the American Psychological Association, Atlanta, GA.

Butler, J. (1993). *Bodies that matter: On the discursive limits of "sex."* New York: Routledge.

Califia, P. (1988). *Sapphistry: The book of lesbian sexuality* (3rd ed.). Tallahassee, FL: Naiad Press.

Clunis, D. M., & Green, G. D. (1988). *Lesbian couples.* Seattle: Seal Press.

Cole, E., & Rothblum, E. D. (1991). Lesbian sex at menopause: As good or better than ever. In B. Sang, J. Warshow & A. J. Smith (Eds.), *Lesbians at midlife: The creative transition* (pp. 184–193). San Francisco: Spinsters Book Co.

Daniluk, J. C. (1993). The meaning and experience of female sexuality: A phenomenological analysis. *Psychology of Women Quarterly, 17,* 53–69.

D'Emilio, J., & Freedman, E. (1988). *Intimate matters: A history of sexuality in America.* New York: Harper & Row.

Faderman, L. (1981). *Surpassing the love of men: Romantic friendship and love between women from the Renaissance to the present.* New York: William Morrow & Co.

Faderman, L. (1984). The ''new gay'' lesbians. *Journal of Homosexuality, 10,* 85–89.

Faderman, L. (1991). *Odd girls and twilight lovers: A history of lesbian life in 20th century America.* New York: Columbia University Press.

Fassinger, R. E. (1991). The hidden minority: Issues and challenges in working with lesbian women and gay men. *Counseling Psychologist, 19,* 157–176.

Federation of Feminist Women's Health Centers. (1981). *A new view of a woman's body.* New York: Simon & Schuster.

Frye, M. (1992). *Willful virgin.* Freedom, CA: Crossing Press.

Gagnon, J. H. (1990). Gender preference in erotic relations: The Kinsey Scale and sexual scripts. In D. P. McWhirter, S. A. Sanders & J. M. Reinisch (Eds.), *Homosexuality/heterosexuality: Concepts of sexual orientation* (pp. 177–207). Oxford: Oxford University Press.

Garcia, N., Kennedy, C., Pearlman, S. F., & Perez, J. (1987). The impact of race and culture differences: Challenges to intimacy in lesbian relationships. In Boston Lesbian Psychologies Collective (Ed.), *Lesbian psychologies: Explorations and challenges* (pp. 142–160). Urbana, IL: University of Illinois Press.

Garnets, L., & Kimmel, D. (1991). Lesbian and gay male dimensions in the psychological study of human diversity. In J. D. Goodchilds (Ed.), *Psychological perspectives on human diversity in America* (pp. 137–189). Washington, DC: American Psychological Association.

Gidlow, E. (1975). *Ask no man pardon: The philosophical significance of being lesbian.* Mill Valley, CA: Druid Heights Books.

Greenberg, D. F. (1988). *The construction of homosexuality.* Chicago: University of Chicago Press.

Grosz, E. (1994). Refiguring lesbian desire. In L. Doan (Ed.), *The lesbian postmodern* (pp. 67–84). New York: Columbia University Press.

Hall, M. (1984). Lesbians, limerance, and longterm relationships. In J. Loulan (Ed.), *Lesbian sex* (pp. 141–150). San Francisco: Spinsters/Aunt Lute.

Hall, M. (1987). Sex therapy with lesbian couples: A four stage approach. *Journal of Homosexuality, 14,* 137–156.

Kassoff, E. (1989). Nonmonogamy in the lesbian community. In E. D. Rothblum & E. Cole (Eds.), *Loving boldly: Issues facing lesbians* (pp. 167–182). New York: Harrington Park Press.

Kitzinger, C. (1987). *The social construction of lesbianism.* London: Sage.

Klinkenberg, D., & Rose, S. (1992, August). *Dating scripts of gay men and lesbians.* Paper presented at the annual meeting of the American Psychological Association, Washington, DC.

Koppelman, A. S. (1988). *A feminist model of women's sexual health*. Unpublished manuscript, Wright State University.

Krestan, J., & Bebko, C. S. (1980). The problem of fusion in the lesbian relationship. *Family Process, 19,* 277–291.

Kurdek, L. A. (1994). The nature and correlates of relationship quality in gay, lesbian, and heterosexual cohabiting couples: A test of the individual differences, interdependence, and discrepancy models. In B. Greene & G. M. Herek (Eds.), *Lesbian and gay psychology: Theory, research, and clinical applications* (pp. 133–155). Thousand Oaks, CA: Sage Publications.

Lamos, C. (1994). The postmodern lesbian position: *On Our Backs.* In L. Doan (Ed.), *The lesbian postmodern* (pp. 85–103). New York: Columbia University Press.

Lewis, R. A.. Kozac, E. B., Milardo, R. M., & Grosnick, W. A. (1992). Commitment in same-sex love relationships. In W. R. Dynes & S. Donalson (Eds.), *Homosexuality and psychology, psychiatry, and counseling* (pp. 174–194). New York: Garland Publishing.

Lobel, K. (Ed.), (1986). *Naming the violence: Speaking out about lesbian battering.* Seattle: Seal Press.

Loulan, J. (1984). *Lesbian sex.* San Francisco: Spinsters Ink.

Loulan, J. (1987). *Lesbian passion: Loving ourselves and each other.* San Francisco: Spinsters/Aunt Lute.

Loulan, J. (1990). *The lesbian erotic dance: Butch, femme, androgyny, and other rhythms.* San Francisco: Spinsters Book Co.

Martin, D., & Lyon, P. (1975). Womanlove. *Amazon Quarterly, 3*(2), 62.

Masters, W. H., & Johnson, V. E. (1965). The sexual response cycle of the human female: II. The clitoris: Anatomic and clinical considerations. In J. Money (Ed.), *Sex research—New developments* (pp. 90–112). New York: Holt, Rinehart & Winston.

Nestle, J. (Ed.). (1992). *The persistent desire: A femme-butch reader.* Boston: Alyson.

Nichols, M. (1987). Lesbian sexuality: Issues and developing theory. In Boston Lesbian Psychologies Collective (Ed.), *Lesbian psychologies: Explorations and challenges* (pp. 97–125). Urbana, IL: University of Illinois Press.

Nichols, M. (1990). Lesbian relationships: Implications for the study of sexuality and gender. In D. P. McWhirter, S. A. Sanders & J. M. Reinisch (Eds.), *Homosexuality/heterosexuality: Concepts of sexual orientation* (pp. 350–364). Oxford: Oxford University Press.

Nomadic Sisters (1976). *Loving women.* Sonora, CA: Author.

Pearlman, S. F. (1989). Distancing and connectedness: Impact on couple formation in lesbian relationships. In E. D. Rothblum & E. Cole (Eds.), *Loving boldly: Issues facing lesbians* (pp. 77–88). New York: Harrington Park Press.

Peplau, L. A., & Cochran, S. D. (1990). A relationship perspective on homosexuality. In D. P. McWhirter, S. A. Sanders & J. M. Reinisch (Eds.), *Homosexuality/heterosexuality: Concepts of sexual orientation* (pp. 322–349). Oxford: Oxford University Press.

Rich, A. (1980). Compulsory heterosexuality and lesbian experience. *Signs, 5,* 631–660.

Roth, S. (1985). Psychotherapy with lesbian couples: Individual issues, female socialization, and the social context. *Journal of Marital and Family Therapy, 11,* 273–286.

Rothblum, E. D. (1989). Introduction: Lesbianism as a model of a positive lifestyle for women. *Women and Therapy, 8,* 1–12.

Rothblum, E. D. (1992, August). *Lesbian and gay health agenda beyond HIV/AIDS: What can psychology offer?* Paper presented at the annual meeting of the American Psychological Association, Washington, DC.

Rothblum, E. D. (in press). Transforming lesbian sexuality. *Psychology of Women Quarterly.*

Rothblum, E. D., & Brehony, K. A. (1991). The Boston marriage today: Romantic but asexual relationships among lesbians. In C. Silverstein (Ed.), *Gays, lesbians, and their therapists: Studies in psychotherapy* (pp. 210–226). New York: Norton.

Ryan, C., & Bradford, J. (1987). *The national lesbian health care survey: An overview.* Washington, DC: National Gay and Lesbian Health Foundation.

Samois Organization (1981). *Coming to power.* Boston: Alyson Press.

Schneider, M. S. (1986). The relationships of cohabiting lesbian and heterosexual couples: A comparison. *Psychology of Women Quarterly, 10,* 234–239.

Smalley, S. (1987). Dependency in lesbian relationships. *Journal of Homosexuality, 14,* 125–135.

Vance, C. S. (1984). *Pleasure and danger: Exploring female sexuality.* London: Routledge & Kegan Paul.

Vance, C. S. (1992). Social construction theory: Problems in the history of sexuality. In H. Crowley & S. Himmelweit (Eds.), *Knowing women: Feminism and knowledge* (pp. 132–145). London: Polity Press.

Wyatt, G. E., & Riederle, M. H. (in press). Reconceptualizing issues that affect women's sexual decision-making and sexual functioning. *Psychology of Women Quarterly.*

10

Sex Therapy for Gay and Bisexual Men

Andrew E. Behrendt and Kenneth D. George

Although there has been considerable literature on sex therapy for treatment of sexual dysfunctions (Kaplan 1974; Leiblum & Rosen 1989; Masters & Johnson 1970), little has been written about sex therapy with gay and bisexual men. This chapter describes four specific therapeutic issues that cause stress for gay and bisexual men and may cause or contribute to a sexual dysfunction: stereotypic male gender roles, stereotypic male sexual roles, homophobia, and HIV/AIDS-related issues. The specific male sexual dysfunctions are then discussed and suggestions for treatment are given.

SPECIFIC ISSUES FOR GAY AND BISEXUAL MEN IN THERAPY

The discussion will be limited to treatment that is specific to gay and bisexual men, for there exists a wealth of generalized material about sexual dysfunctions and their treatment (Kaplan 1974; Leiblum & Rosen 1989; Masters & Johnson 1970). Four specific issues need to be examined with gay and bisexual men who seek treatment. These issues cause stress and anxiety, which can reduce sexual pleasure and relationship intimacy. Alone or in combination they can cause or contribute to any of the sexual dysfunctions.

Stereotypic Male Gender Roles

The adoption of and adherence to the stereotypic male gender role affects gay and bisexual men's sexual functioning (George & Behrendt 1987). The stereotypic male gender role in our society is to be competitive. Boys are given toys symbolic of power and achievement (e.g., guns and erector sets), and they are socialized toward competitive activities where winning is everything (e.g., football). Boys are taught that males should be successful, unemotional, the best, in control, strong, tough, capable, and independent (Berzon 1988; Zilbergeld 1978, 1992). Boys are taught this is how to behave and how to feel (and how not to feel) in order to gain status, to achieve and to be "appropriate" men. They are also taught not to have "feminine" traits (Herek 1986). Being loved depends on these rules. Boys learn that it would make them feminine if they were tender or caring or if they acknowledged their weaknesses and needs and asked for what they want rather than demanded it (Zilbergeld 1978, 1992). Boys should not be "sissies" in their appearance or in their behaviors.

Many men have been socialized to separate sex from affection (Berzon 1988). Males are socialized that sex can be casual, anonymous, and/or bought. Their partners are objects, commodities, and/or property. Sex is genitally oriented and has orgasm as its goal. Frequent "conquests" are watched by other male peers, and there is a competition among males to ascertain who can "score" the most. When it comes to sex, males are taught to be the initiators and the executors of the game plan; they should orchestrate the whole procedure from the onset, defining and designing the attainment of an orgasm.

Additionally, sensual and sexual sensations are tender feelings; many men have been taught not to have tender feelings, and consequently they are literally out of touch with their bodies. Being trained to be genitally focused, many men do not know what other parts of their bodies feel good when stimulated. Men are taught to be in control. They may demand certain sexual activities, but it may not even occur to them to ask a partner for a particular type of stimulation. A man who has adopted and acts on these stereotypic male gender role messages of what a man should be will have stresses and may have difficulty in sexual functioning.

Gay and bisexual men were socialized as children by these rules. They, as well as nongay men, have learned that manhood is conditional, something to be achieved by mastering certain behaviors, including not being "feminine" and not being homosexual (Herek 1986). The same rules and behaviors when applied to their sexual lives can then adversely affect their sexual functioning. How can both men be the initiators? What does it mean if one man lets the other initiate? Who orchestrates the sex? Who decides what behaviors are "safer" than other behaviors in preventing HIV infection? Who ensures that they both have orgasms? What kind of sexual relationship can exist if both men vie to be in control?

Most gay and bisexual men prefer a variety of sexual positions and activities. They usually do what feels good and gives them pleasure. While many have specific preferences, many do not. Unfortunately many people, including some gay and bisexual men, equate specific sexual acts with masculinity and others with femininity. For instance, the person who is sexually "active," the inserter, is often considered the more masculine sex partner, and the sexually "passive" person, the insertee, is often considered the more feminine sex partner. There are exceptions to this dictum. It could be the one who is controlling the pleasure of his partner who is perceived as the more masculine one. Regardless, problems can occur when the partners get limited and restricted by the stereotypic male gender roles. The complaint that is often voiced in sex therapy is not about the sexual activity and position but rather on the perception of what is occurring regarding the stereotypic male sex role. Hence, one man may enjoy being the insertee in anal intercourse but may resent being called the more feminine one by his partner.

Stereotypic Male Sexual Roles

The second issue for gay and bisexual men is stereotypic sexual roles—that men in American society should be sexually active, experienced, ready, and able to perform at any time or any circumstance. Zilbergeld (1978, 1992) identifies "The Fantasy Model of Sex," which he initially labeled, "It's Two Feet Long, Hard As Steel, and Can Go All Night" (1978), and then modified to, "It's Two Feet Long, Hard as Steel, Always Ready and Will Knock Your Socks Off" (1992). The American culture supports this fantasy model of sex in which there are two components: the equipment and the partner. This fantasy model aptly applies to gay and bisexual men. The effects are exacerbated when both components of the model are male.

Gay male erotic videotapes usually show young, attractive, and well-built men. Male erotica magazines catering to the gay male market depict rugged hunks, "real men." Gay and bisexual men learn that in order to be sexually desirable, they must be young, attractive, and well built. They demand the same characteristics of their partner. These videotapes are designed to emphasize massive penis size: the bigger, fatter, and longer, the better. As is standard in this genre, the climax scene is craftily edited in order to create the delusion of a continuous flood of copious ejaculatory fluid. With video splicing, several different sexual scenes may be reduced to a final ten-minute sequence creating an illusion that these men maintain their erections after ejaculating and that they ejaculate more than once every time they have sex. These videotapes are carefully fabricated to show the men in perpetual sexual high performance. Gay and bisexual men expect as much for themselves and for their partner.

In gay male fictional stories in some of the popular magazines, there is a common recurrent theme centering around a heretofore exclusively heterosexual man being swept into the arms of homosexuality by another man and being so overjoyed with the sensation that he yields to the seduction and experiences the most explosive orgasm of his life.

Gay and bisexual men are exposed to these cultural messages of hypermaleness, hypermasculinity, and hypersexual activity, and they internalize this script of who they should be, how they should act, and how they should react. Most gay and bisexual men, however, are not built those ways, do not behave in those ways, and do not respond in those ways. Nevertheless, the fantasy model of sex is believed by many gay and bisexual men, who then feel inadequate about themselves as men because they cannot measure up to this model. Even though they may know better intellectually, they are still influenced by this model. The surge in eating disorders such as bulimia found among young gay and bisexual men in their 20s and 30s, and the daily ritual of working out at the gym obsessively-compulsively, are a partial result of this fantasy model.

When gay and bisexual men use the script of the fantasy model in forming relationships, they find them short-lived and superficial. They enter therapy wondering why their relationships do not seem to last long or develop far. They need to learn that common interests and values, and interpersonal interactions that allow for trust, openness, honesty, and growth, are better predictors of satisfying and intimate love relationships.

Homophobia

In addition to the normal stresses in our society, gay and bisexual men are subjected to the internal and external stresses due to homophobia, the irrational fear or intolerance of homosexuality or homosexual persons (Herek 1986). Our society has traditionally held a negative view of homosexuality. In the Judaic-Christian religions, homosexuality has been considered a sin. Sodomy laws have made many homosexual (and heterosexual) sexual acts illegal. Until recently homosexuality was defined as a mental illness by the medical profession, until a vote changed its diagnostic classification. Most gay and bisexual men grew up hearing derogatory putdowns, such as "queer," "fag," and "faggot." Most gay and bisexual men cannot escape internalizing into their own self-concepts these negative homophobic societal messages, and it takes great effort to free oneself from these messages.

Many gay and bisexual men have internalized homophobic misconceptions about homosexuality (Vining 1986). The first of these homophobic misconceptions is that sex between two men is unnatural and immoral. If the gay or bisexual man believes this, he will experience severe conflict in his sexual interactions with other men. The second misconception is that a primary relationship between two men is immoral and unnatural. If the gay or bisexual man views male relationships in this way, he will have a conflict in thinking of his own relationship in healthy, constructive, and intimate terms. The third misconception is that same-gender relationships are short-lived and that two men cannot sustain continued, long-term relationships. If the gay or bisexual man adheres to this belief, this can became a self-fulfilling prophecy that prevents him from forming and maintaining a loving relationship with another man. The fourth misconception is that gay and bisexual men have sex with many different partners. If the gay and bisexual man accepts this message, he may act on this belief and have many unwanted sexual partners. Or he may feel trapped in a relationship that does not allow him to have many partners. Acting on this belief has caused sexual and relational problems for many gay and bisexual men.

Homophobia is present in most people. What many therapists do not realize is that internalized homophobia is also present among many gay and bisexual men. Homophobia is a crucial factor to explore in therapy. The therapist must examine the gay or bisexual man's own internalized homophobia. Homophobia puts extra stress on gay and bisexual men; internalized, it influences identity formation and self-esteem. However, the therapist working with gay and bisexual men must also examine his or her own views on homosexuality. If homophobic messages are believed by the therapist, regardless of his or her sexual orientation, then the gay or bisexual man should be referred to another therapist, who is not homophobic.

Steinem (1992/1993) has elevated the coming-out process as a protocol and model to be emulated for other personal issues. In the coming-out process, a gay or bisexual man examines his own conflicts about being gay or bisexual and living as a gay or bisexual man and in the process deals with some of the homophobic messages. There are several models that describe the coming-out process (Coleman 1981/1982; Dank 1971), and there are several books that men have found useful (Eichberg 1990, Muchmore & Hanson 1982). Most of the literature describes three phases to the coming-out process.

The first stage is the acknowledgment of one's own self as a gay or bisexual man. This realization is often traumatic, especially if the man has not challenged some of the societal attitudes about homosexuality. The gay or bisexual man must privately admit his own gayness or bisexuality, or he will not be able to accept and maintain a sexual and loving relationship with another man. A healthy gay or bisexual identity needs to be established before a man can successfully navigate Erikson's (1950) ego developmental stage of intimacy (Malyon 1982).

The second stage is acknowledging his gayness or bisexuality to other gay or bisexual people and building a support system consisting of other gay or bisexual people. Unless he enters this stage of coming out, it will be difficult for the gay or bisexual man to meet other men for sexual and/or loving relationships.

The third stage, which not all gay or bisexual men aspire to or attain, is that of sharing the knowledge of one's gayness or bisexuality with relatives, heterosexual friends, coworkers, and employers. Often the third stage creates conflicts. It may be that by coming out to others, the gay or bisexual man suffers rejection and abuse. Yet by not coming out, there is the stress of not being true to oneself and having to live a double life, putting on a mask to the world and pretending to be heterosexual. The need to be true to oneself is important for growth as a person. Each gay or bisexual man has to decide for himself with whom he shares his sexual identity. This is a difficult decision. Because of societal homophobia and because of the internalized homophobia, the coming-out process may be a lifelong, arduous, and exhausting effort.

While there are bona-fide bisexuals, many gays and nongays do not accept that bisexuals exist. Bisexuality is often seen as not being "straight" by nongay persons, as a developmental phase on the way to total homosexuality, or as a homophobic response to being gay. Our society does not readily adapt to concepts that do not fit in either-or categories, and there is a generalized biphobia (Udis-Kessler 1991) that the bisexual man must work through. Bisexual men and their partners often greatly benefit from community support groups and reading about bisexuality (Hill 1987; Klein 1978; Klein & Wolf 1985).

When the individuals in a couple are at different stages of the coming-out process, stresses can arise in the relationship. The therapist should be aware of the amount of disclosure and the stage of coming out of each of the partners. Even if they are at the same stage, there may be problems due to the amount of psychic energy devoted to this process. The stage of coming out frequently predicts the psychological healthiness of the individual and the relationship. The more comfortable that the members of a couple are about their gay or bisexual identity, the more adjusted the individuals and the relationship tend to be.

Gay and bisexual men who have only recently admitted and acted on their gayness or bisexuality may not be ready to enter into a one-to-one relationship. Instead they may need to go through a period of exploration. The majority of men have learned to date as adolescents. At that time boys are given certain guidelines by their parents and peers—rules on how to behave on a date. Coincidentally, this is the time that many gay and bisexual male adolescents start the first stage of the coming-out process. They may feel different yet date girls because of peer pressure.

When the gay or bisexual man enters the second stage of the coming-out process, when he meets other men with whom he can share his gayness, it is as if a child has entered a candy store. All of the feelings he has denied expression previously are ready to explode in his sharing with others, and his feelings of isolation begin to disappear. For the first time he will begin to date someone to whom he is erotically attracted. This is a period of exploration. However, unlike during the adolescent years, there are no guidelines and no parents to help with certain decisions. Some men in this period act as if they are compensating for lost time, and just like a child in a candy store, they may want to sample each of the different "goodies."

Many of these men enter the candy store but do not take the time to go through a dating stage. Later when they meet someone, they form a relationship too quickly. This male couple then exchange rings, sign a lease on an apartment, and adopt a kitten from the animal shelter, all within a short period of time. A couple of months later, they enter therapy as a couple, wanting the relationship to work but concerned because one or both of them are not as sexually responsive as when they first met. (This also commonly also occurs when one or both have formed a relationship too soon after leaving a heterosexual marriage.) Their being seen and treated as a male couple by the therapist is especially significant in this situation. Generally it is recommended that gay or bisexual men experience the exploratory phase of dating prior to forming a one-to-one relationship.

This might include the "candy store." Regardless of age or previous relationship history with women, the gay or bisexual man in this stage needs to date over a period of time, perhaps with different people. This is a time when the gay or bisexual man can experience and reflect in order to determine his needs in a relationship with another man.

HIV/AIDS-Related Issues

Issues about HIV infection and AIDS have created stresses for gay and bisexual men, even men in relationships, and these issues must be dealt with in therapy. A gay or bisexual man may remember times when he did not engage in safer sex acts, and this memory may cause anxiety. Am I infected now because of something I did in my past? Should I be tested? What can I now do sexually and still be safe? Is my partner infected? Is he being truthful with me about this? Has my lover remained monogamous? In newer relationships, the question arises of when the couple will no longer need to practice safer sex, especially if they are in a monogamous relationship. In open relationships, safer sex must be practiced with all the partners. Men may stay in unhealthy relationships out a fear of not having a sexual partner if they ended this relationship.

There are some gay and bisexual men who have associated being sexual with dying and death. Lovers, friends, and acquaintances have become ill and died from AIDS. Death is seen as a consequence of acts of sex. These gay and bisexual men need to challenge their conditioned reaction that sex equals death and will need to talk about their losses due to AIDS. Many wonder why they are not infected when those around them are infected, a "guilt of the survivor" phenomenon. Many are anxious and fatalistic: they are convinced that they will be infected eventually.

Recent evidence in urban areas with a high gay male population suggests that some men are not practicing safer sex. Some possible explanations include alleviating the guilt of not being infected when others are, relieving the anxiety of not knowing when they will be infected, and enacting the ultimate in romantic fantasies—of preparing to die with one's love. Many already know that AIDS is caused by specific high-risk behaviors, but the therapist must still give this message again because many have only partial information or misinformation. They also need to be reminded that being sexual is a normal physiological experience (Masters & Johnson 1966), and having a satisfying and healthy sexuality is their right as a human being.

Safer sex health guidelines recommend the use of latex condoms with nonnoxynol-9 during activities that involve penetration, including oral and anal intercourse. Some men have reported that the use of latex condoms affects their sexual performance. The two most common complaints are loss of erection while applying the condom to the penis or before penetration and decreased sensation, which can also lead to loss of erection during intercourse or taking "too long" to ejaculate. This "failure" is remembered at the next sexual encountered, add-

ing more stress and anxiety and leading men consciously to observe their performance (''spectatoring'') rather than abandoning themselves to sensation.
Educating men to eroticize putting on a condom, incorporating the condom into
the sexual activity, is an important part of sex therapy. Some men also report
that applying a water-soluble lubricant on the penis before unrolling the condom,
so that there is lubrication on both the inside and outside of the condom, increases sensation and pleasure.

All of these concerns and fears about AIDS and the stresses that gay and
bisexual men have experienced with regard to HIV infection and safer sex have
led to an increase in sexual dysfunctions among gay and bisexual men. These
men may seek professional help. They will often come into therapy for other
reasons, not initially identifying HIV infection or AIDS as a problem. While
taking a sex history it is important to ask about HIV status, specific sexual acts,
condom use, and about who in their lives are infected with HIV and how this
has affected them.

SEXUAL DYSFUNCTIONS AND TREATMENT

General Treatment Issues

Gay or bisexual men do experience sexual dysfunctions and the associated
problems of those dysfunctions, and they will seek professional assistance in
order to improve their sexual functioning, as either an individual or part of a
couple. The presenting problem when entering therapy may be about an issue
other than sexual functioning; concerns about sexual functioning may be only
voiced after a few sessions (George & Behrendt 1987). Evaluation, diagnosis,
and treatment follow the protocols of sex therapy regardless of the distressed
person's sexual orientation (Masters & Johnson 1979). Sex therapy usually includes individual and relationship therapy to foster self-actualization and to resolve conflicts that affect sexual functioning. Reading about issues for gay and
bisexual men and about male couples (Berzon, 1988; Blumenfeld & Raymond
1993; Eichberg 1990; Isensee 1990; Marcus 1988; McWhirter & Mattison 1984;
Mendola 1980; Muchmore & Hanson 1982; Silverstein 1981) is a useful adjunct
to therapy.

Some gay and bisexual men may enter therapy for help in being able to
perform certain sexual behaviors, such as being able to be an ''expert'' recipient
during oral or anal intercourse. Not all gay and bisexual men engage in these
behaviors, but there are some who want to do so and have difficulty. A common
complaint is not being able to take the partner's erect penis all the way down
the throat or gagging while attempting to do so. Another common complaint is
not being able to receive anally the partner's penis, or there is too much pain
when attempting this act. The result is that these men feel inadequate as a lover
and as a gay or bisexual man. This may actually add another stress to the sexual

relationship. The therapist will need to review specific sexual techniques that can alleviate these problems.

Probably all men at some point in their lives do not function sexually in the ways that they would like: having difficulty getting or maintaining an erection (inhibited sexual excitement or erectile dysfunction); having difficulty in controlling when they ejaculate, either ejaculating "too soon" (premature ejaculation) or taking "too long" (inhibited male orgasm or retarded ejaculation); or having limited sexual desire while their partner wants sex (inhibited sexual desire). The typology of sexual dysfunctions has been identified and described in an earlier chapter in this book (Carey & Gordon, this volume).

This discussion will be limited to treatment that is specific to gay and bisexual men, for there already exists a wealth of generalized material about sexual dysfunctions and their treatment (Kaplan 1974; Leiblum & Rosen 1989; Masters & Johnson 1970). Often the basis for therapeutic success is education. There are also a number of good sexual manuals specifically for gay men (Freedman & Mayes 1976; Morin, 1986; Silverstein & White 1986; Walker 1985), which can be used in conjunction with sex therapy.

It is important during sex therapy that the gay and bisexual man learns that he does not have to have sex if he chooses not to, ejaculate during the sexual activity, assume the responsibility for how the sexual activity goes, or do any sexual act unless he chooses to do so. The therapist may need to give him permission to be sensual, to ask for what he wants, and to receive as well as give pleasure. The gay or bisexual man should never be made to believe that his particular sexual activity is "abnormal," "sick," or dysfunctional because it does not meet with an arbitrary standard of "normality."

It is important for the therapist to take a sexual history and to ask questions about sexual functioning. Many gay and bisexual men and male couples who have been in therapy have reported that a previous therapist never took a sex history, asked them to discuss the sexual part of their lives, or explored the possibility of a sexual dysfunction (George & Behrendt 1987). A possible explanation is that some therapists are uncomfortable discussing sex between two men, or these therapists may have an abhorrence of and aversion to specific sexual acts between two men, for example, anal intercourse. Some therapists may believe that gay and bisexual men do not have problems with sexual functioning because the labels commonly affixed to these men, "homosexual" and "bisexual," have the word *sexual* in them, and therefore it is assumed they must be sexual without any type of problem. The studies indicate, however, that gay and bisexual men do on occasion have problems in sexual functioning (Bahr & Weeks 1989; George & Behrendt 1987; Masters & Johnson 1979; McWhirter and Mattison, 1978), whether or not they are in therapy for treatment.

In doing sex therapy it is useful to help gay and bisexual men to identify the stresses in their lives that may be causing a sexual dysfunction. The issues previously identified are particularly pertinent to gay and bisexual men. Each of these issues, alone and in combination with each other, affects sexual function-

Table 10.1

The Erotic Stimulus Pathway Model[1]: Implications for Sexual Function and Dysfunction with Specific Issues for Gay and Bisexual Men

Phases	Sexual Functions	Specific Issue for Gay and Bisexual Men	Sexual Dysfunctions
Seduction	Desire to be with Partner	Homophobia & St. Sexual Role[2]	Inhibited Sexual Desire
	Physical Appeal	St. Gender Role	Erectile Dysfunction
	Sexual Awareness	St. Sexual Role	
	Sexual Readiness	St. Sexual Role	
	Seducing Self to be with a Man	Homophobia	
	Seducing Another Man	Homophobia	
Sensation	Touch	St. Gender Role	Erectile Dysfunction
	Emoting	St. Gender Role	All Dysfunctions
	Taste	HIV/AIDS-related	Inhibited Sexual Desire
	Smell		
	Hearing		
	Seeing		
Surrender	Orgasm	St. Male Role	Inhibited Male Orgasm
			Inhibited Sexual Excitement
Reflection	Emoting	St. Gender Role	Inhibited Sexual Desire
	Intimacy	Homophobia	Relationship Problems

1. Adapted from Reed (as cited in Stayton 1989).
2. St. Sexual Role = Stereotypical sexual role.

ing, particularly among gay and bisexual men, and can cause or contribute to any of the sexual dysfunctions.

Many models of sexual functioning and the human response cycles describe physiological responses (Kaplan 1974, 1979; Leiblum & Rosen 1989; Masters & Johnson 1966, 1970) and then discuss treatment at each of the phases: desire, excitement, plateau, orgasmic phase, and resolution. Reed (cited in Stayton, 1989) offers a valuable perspective of the human sexual response cycle based on a theory of psychosexual development he calls the erotic stimulus pathway (ESP). In the ESP there are four stages for sexual functioning: seduction, sensation, surrender, and reflection. The acronym itself underscores the need for men to be more aware of and responsive to their intuition. ESP is a powerful concept especially when applied to relationships involving two men (table 10.1)

Seduction, the first stage, which corresponds to the desire and the beginning of the excitement phase in other models, includes the anticipation of being with someone and behaviors designed to attract another and to be found attractive by another. Often men forget the excitement of the lure and how this can be developed into an art, with intrinsic meaning of its own.

The next stage in the ESP model is sensation. Our senses (sight, touch, smell, taste, and hearing) are necessary to maintain sexual arousal and pleasure, and hence are important for sexual functioning. The therapist who is helping gay and bisexual men get in touch with their senses will also help them to get in touch with their feelings.

The third stage, surrender, is perhaps the most important part of doing sex therapy with gay and bisexual men. Since many men have issues of being goal oriented, orgasm becomes the goal for sex. Many men have an issue around control. In order to have an orgasm and in order to enjoy it, men need to let go and give up control. In applying the concept of surrender to replace orgasm as the goal for sex, men can experience more pleasure in their activities and have more intimacy with their partners. If two men can give up control with each other, they can give up the male stereotypic gender and sexual roles. They can give up competition and spectatoring. They can relax with each other and enjoy sex without the pressures of focusing on an orgasm or their penises and evaluating what they are doing with each other. Particularly men who have been taught all their lives to be competitive, to win, and to be in control need to learn how to surrender. Male couples involved in power struggles will have trouble surrendering. Sexual dysfunctions exist with men who cannot or do not surrender.

The last stage in the ESP model is reflection. In order to reflect, a man must feel. The feelings that follow the sexual experience are necessary to help identify what has been enjoyable and what has not been enjoyable. Desire for the next sexual experience is increased if the reflection has been pleasurable. Reflection is very important for sex therapy—it clarifies what is meaningful for gay and bisexual men in a loving and sexual relationship. It helps these men develop intimacy.

Sexual Dysfunctions

While the following discussion addresses the sexual dysfunctions that may occur among gay and bisexual men, anecdotal evidence (Fisher 1972) and research (Masters & Johnson 1979) indicate that same-gender couples report the highest degree of sexual satisfaction among all couples, presumably because they have a better understanding of their partner's anatomy and physiology and can therefore be more sensitive and responsive to particular sexual stimulation.

Men regardless of their sexual orientation often experience sex as a chore or burden (Zilbergeld 1978, 1992). When surveyed, even nonclinical samples of both gay men and nongay men report a significant amount of sexual dissatisfaction, including specific sexual dysfunctions and sexual difficulties (Bahr & Weeks 1989; Frank, Anderson & Rubinstein 1978). Bahr and Weeks (1989) report that there are some gay men not in therapy who have a sexual dysfunction yet do not cite this as a problem. Often sexual dysfunctions are not reported as the initial presenting problem but will be discovered in the course of the first several sessions if the therapist asks questions about sexual functioning.

There is no agreement on the relative frequencies of the sexual dysfunctions in gay or bisexual men. George and Behrendt (1987) found inhibited sexual desire to be the most common sexual dysfunction, then inhibited male orgasm (retarded or ejaculatory incompetence), inhibited sexual excitement (impotence or erectile dysfunction), and premature ejaculation; inhibited sexual excitement was the most frequent dysfunction of the gay men seen by Masters and Johnson (1979) and by McWhirter and Mattison (1978). These discrepancies in relative frequencies may be due to the fact that there has been no systematic random sampling of gay and bisexual men seeking therapy for sexual functioning. Additionally, it is not uncommon for excitement and orgasmic dysfunctions to transform into inhibited sexual desire, which would be psychologically useful in alleviating the negative affect and stress associated with the original dysfunction. Not desiring or not having sex removes the original problem and, unless a partner complains, eliminates the problem; however, it creates another sexual dysfunction if the partner complains.

Inhibited Sexual Desire

People rarely complain about inhibited sexual desire in themselves. It is more common that a partner identifies the problem. A male couple may enter therapy with one complaining that his partner does not want to have sex with him. The partner may counter that he does not need sex, does not want it, and does not enjoy it.

Among gay and bisexual men, the stress of homophobia may cause inhibited sexual desire. In working with gay and bisexual men and male couples, the therapist needs to explore with each partner the homophobic messages he has learned. How does he feel about his homosexuality or bisexuality? How do his parents view his homosexuality or bisexuality? Does his family now accept his partner? What were his childhood religious convictions? Did anything traumatic happen early in his life to cause him to be anxious about his sexuality and his homosexuality or bisexuality? Frequently, reading gay-supportive books (Berzon 1988; Blumenfeld & Raymond 1993) helps him work through his internalized homophobia.

For other gay and bisexual men who report a lack of sexual desire, one of the sources of stress is frequently a traumatic experience early in life arising out of religious, social, or family taboos against homosexuality. Consequently, the therapist should examine his views about homosexuality. The gay and bisexual man with inhibited sexual desire usually has integrated many of the negative societal messages about homosexuality, causing him to be homophobic, which manifests itself as inhibited sexual desire.

Inhibited sexual desire also occurs when gay and bisexual men adhere to the fantasy model of sex (Zilbergeld 1978, 1992). They form relationships based on how the partner looks and how the partner performs sexually. After a couple of years, the initial attraction and passion decline, and so does sex. This male couple comes into therapy complaining that they are not as sexual as they were at the beginning and that their sex is not as wild or passionate as it once was. They want to stay together, and they want this relationship to include sex. The ESP stages of seduction, sensation, and reflection are helpful here.

For couples experiencing inhibited sexual excitement but who want to stay together, seduction is an important part of sex therapy. They may need help initially identifying enjoying both being seduced, which may seem antithetical to the stereotypic sexual and gender roles, and being the seducer. A part of the sexual history may identify how each of the men likes to be seduced. This history will also identify how each likes to seduce the other. They may need to be given permission to come in touch with their sexual fantasies, some of which they probably will want to keep in the fantasy realm but others of which may later be enacted with their partner.

Initially it is useful to concentrate on sensation and the pleasure of sensual touch without the requirement of sexual arousal or orgasm—a variation of Master and Johnson's sensate focus. These men usually respond well to receiving permission to experiment with different places and times for sexual activities, different positions, and different activities. Reflection is important for these men to increase self-awareness of their likes, dislikes, and desires, and when shared with a partner may improve communication and their sexual experience.

There is another group of men who avoid sex due not to lack of desire but to a phobic aversion to sex. These men are different from those who lack desire. These men are not overly homophobic. In these men with a phobic reaction to sex, the therapist needs to explore their fear of AIDS. The stress associated with a fear of HIV infection and AIDS may cause a phobic reaction to sex. Some men recently diagnosed as infected with HIV may have a phobic reaction to sex. The therapist needs to explore what this man feels and believes about HIV infection, and any confusion about being sexual should be clarified. Frequently education can help this aversion.

Another stress for the therapist to examine with gay and bisexual men who have a phobic aversion to sex is their feelings about men. Many men have an unconscious anger and resentment against men in general, often a result of an unresolved issue with their fathers. This presents especially for men who are attracted to other men. A phobic aversion to getting close to, loving, and having sex with another man is experienced. They avoid sex and relationships until one day they meet someone special. They then come into therapy because they want to maintain a sexual relationship with this special person.

Inhibited Male Orgasm

A gay or bisexual man or a male couple may enter therapy with a complaint that one of them is not able to ejaculate with oral or anal sex, regardless of whether he is the inserter or the insertee. Often he may be able to ejaculate through masturbation when he is alone. Usually these are controlled men, often with a degree of religiosity in their childhoods, even if they are no longer religious.

There are two stresses common to many gay and bisexual men experiencing inhibited male orgasm. The first stress is an internal conflict regarding homosexuality. They are homophobic; they believe that homosexuality is wrong and they should not be having sex with a man, and thus they have difficulty getting close to and intimate with another man. The therapist must explore and process any internalized homophobia. The second stress is due to their sexual fantasies. These sexual fantasies, of aggression, cause these men to have fears that they might try to enact their sexual fantasies with another man. Because they need to be in control, enacting their fantasies would be unacceptable, for they would then be out of control. As in any other therapy, the meaning of those fantasies needs to be explored.

These gay and bisexual men are usually very controlled in their lives, and this control frequently surfaces as inhibited male orgasm. Again the concept of surrender identified in the ESP model is quite helpful. The therapist can encourage them to play and to relax and have them do "fun" things like carrying a stuffed teddy bear to work, taking a bubble bath, or getting a relaxing massage. These men need to surrender and to give up control.

Inhibited Sexual Excitement

A common scenario is a male couple entering therapy in which one man cannot maintain an erection. It is often revealed in his sexual history that he has had many different sexual partners and that he rarely could maintain an erection with any of them. The excuse he frequently has given is that he has had too much to drink. Forming a relationship with someone he would like to stay with and have sex with usually brings him into therapy.

The major stress is that gay and bisexual men with inhibited sexual excitement usually believe the stereotypic views of masculinity and male sexuality. They have adopted a role and thus experience performance anxiety. How am I doing? How do I compare with his previous partners? What does he think of my sexual activity? Will he tell others I am not very good? Such men are performance oriented. They are a spectator rather than a participant in the sexual activity, are constantly grading themselves or believe that they are being graded by their partner on how well they are doing sexually, and very rarely abandon themselves in a sexual act. There is little pleasurable involvement. These gay and bisexual men also need to learn to play and have fun. They need to learn to surrender.

Premature Ejaculation

Some gay and bisexual men start therapy either individually or as part of a male couple for a relationship problem, and during an early session one states, "I come too quickly to enjoy having sex." These men report the same stresses as other men, and the treatment for gay and bisexual men is similar to that of other men. In some studies, premature ejaculation is the least reported of the sexual dysfunctions among gay and bisexual men (George & Behrendt 1987). Perhaps when two men are sexually involved, the goal is orgasm; therefore, they do not as often complain of being "premature." Alternatively, by the time they have entered therapy, the original problem of being "premature" has generated sufficient anxiety to transform to an erectile dysfunction or inhibited sexual desire.

SUMMARY

GWM, 29, 5'8", 155 lbs, br/bl, in shape, ISO . . . playmate, 25–45, taller and in shape. I'm willing to submit to the right man. Masc., attr., down to earth GWM MD, top, . . . yng 42, 5'10", 154 lbs, good shape. Dominant, safe, fit, hung GWM, 42 seeks shy, submissive boy, 18–30's. GBM, attract. bottom ISO top GB or bi B. Muscular gym body. Athletic and masculine. Straight acting. WM, in shape, str. acting, clean cut, masc. ISO guys for massage and safe sex. Hairy guys a +. HIV+ seeking same. I'm straight acting. No fats, fems. Bi WM (26 y.o.) muscular & masculine ISO athletic and masculine str/bi WMs 18–30. Straight acting/appearing.

These personal ads illustrate some of the specific issues involved in working with gay and bisexual men in sex therapy. They include the stereotypic male sexual roles: a top man willing to submit to the right man; a bottom, looking for sexual objects, (playmate, guys for safe sex). They include as well stereotypic male gender roles—physically in shape, tall, muscular gym body, athletic, masculine, hung, hairy—as well as personality and status qualities—dominant, a doctor. They contain messages relating to homophobia: straight acting, straight appearing, no fems. And the constant issue of AIDS: some infected with HIV seeking the same. These four factors influence the way gay and bisexual men see themselves and others, and they affect sexuality. Sometimes gay and bisexual men enter therapy specifically to deal with a sexual dysfunction. At other times gay and bisexual men enter therapy, and the sexual dysfunction is mentioned only after many visits. In either case, successful sexual therapy must address these issues, which are specific to gay and bisexual men.

REFERENCES

Bahr, J. M., & Weeks, G. R. (1989). Sexual functioning in a nonclinical sample of male couples. *American Journal of Family Therapy, 17*(2), 110–127.

Berzon, B. (1988). *Permanent partners: Building gay and lesbian relationships that last.* New York: E. P. Dutton.

Blumenfeld, W. J., & Raymond, D. (1993). *Looking at gay and lesbian life.* (Updated and exp. ed.). Boston: Beacon Press.

Carey, M. P., & Gordon, C. (1996). Sexual dysfunctions in heterosexual couples. In L. Diamant & R. McAnulty (Eds.) *The psychology of sexual orientation, behavior, and identity: A handbook.* Westport, CT: Greenwood Publishing Group.

Coleman, E. (1981/1982). Developmental stages of the coming out process. *Journal of Homosexuality, 7*(2/3), 31–43.

Dank, B. M. (1971). Coming out in the gay world. *Psychiatry, 34,* 189–197.

Eichberg, R. (1990). *Coming out: An act of love.* New York: Dutton/Penguin Books.

Erikson, E. (1950). *Childhood and society.* New York: W. W. Norton.

Fisher, P. (1972). *The gay mystique: The myth and reality of male homosexuality.* New York: Stein & Day.

Frank, E., Anderson, C., & Rubinstein, D. (1978). Frequency of sexual dysfunction in "normal" couples. *New England Journal of Medicine, 299*(3), 111–115.

Freedman, M., & Mayes, H. (1976). *Loving man: A photographic guide to gay male lovemaking.* New York: Hark Publishing Company.

George, K. D., & Behrendt, A. E. (1987). Therapy for male couples experiencing relationship problems and sexual problems. *Journal of Homosexuality, 14*(1/2), 77–88.

Herek, G. M. (1986). On heterosexual masculinity: Some psychical consequences of the social construction of gender and sexuality. *American Behavioral Scientist, 29*(5), 563–577.

Hill, I. (1987). *The bisexual spouse: Different dimensions in human sexuality.* McLean, VA: Barlina Books.

Isensee, R. (1990). *Love between men: Enhancing intimacy and keeping your relationship alive.* New York: Prentice-Hall.

Kaplan, H. S. (1974). *The new sex therapy: Active treatment of sexual dysfunction.* New York: Brunner/Mazel.

Kaplan, H. S. (1979). *Disorders of sexual desire.* New York: Brunner/Mazel.

Klein, F. (1978). *The bisexual option: A concept of one hundred percent intimacy.* New York: Priam Books/Arbor House.

Klein, F., & Wolf, T. J. (1985). *Two lives to lead: Bisexuality in men and women.* New York: Harrington Press.

Leiblum, S., & Rosen, R. (1989). *Principles and practices of sex therapy* (2nd ed.). New York: Guilford.

Malyon, A. K. 1982. Psychotherapeutic implications of internalized homophobia in gay men. *Journal of Homosexuality, 7,* 59–69.

Marcus, E. (1988). *The Male couple's guide to living together: What gay men should know about living together and coping in a straight world.* New York: Harper & Row.

McWhirter, D. P., & Mattison, A. M. (1978). The treatment of sexual dysfunction in gay male couples. *Journal of Sex and Marital Therapy, 4,* 213–218.

McWhirter, D. P., & Mattison, A. M. (1984). *The male couple.* Englewood Cliffs, NJ: Prentice-Hall.

Masters, W. H., & Johnson, V. E. (1966). *Human sexual response.* Boston: Little, Brown.

Masters, W. H., & Johnson, V. E. (1970). *Human sexual inadequacy.* Boston: Little, Brown.

Masters, W. H., & Johnson, V. E. (1979). *Homosexuality in perspective.* Boston: Little, Brown.

Mendola, M. (1980). *The Mendola report: A new look at gay couples.* New York: Crown Books.

Morin, J. (1986). *Anal pleasure and health: A guide for men and women.* Burlingame, CA: Down There Press.

Muchmore, W., & Hanson, W. (1982). *Coming out night: A handbook for the gay male.* Boston: Alyson Publications.

Silverstein, C. (1981). *Man to man: Gay couples in America.* New York: William Morrow.

Silverstein, C., & White, E. (1986). *The joy of gay sex: An intimate guide for gay men to the pleasures of a gay lifestyle.* New York: Pocket Books.

Stayton, W. R. (1989). A theology of sexual pleasure. *American Baptist Quarterly, 8*(2), 94–108.

Steinem, G. (1992/1993). *Revolution from within: A book of self-esteem.* Boston: Little, Brown.

Udis-Kessler, A. (1991). *Present tense: Biphobia as a crisis of meaning.* In L. Hutchins & L. Kaahumanu, *Bi any other name: Bisexual people speak out* (pp. 350–358). Boston: Alyson Publications.

Vining, D. (1986). *Myths about gay men that even gay men believe.* In E. E. Rofes, *Gay life, leisure, love, and loving for the contemporary gay male* (pp. 251–255). Garden City, NY: Doubleday.

Walker, M. (1985). *Men loving men: A gay sex guide and consciousness book.* San Francisco: Gay Sunshine Press.

Zilbergeld, B. (1978). *Male sexuality.* Boston: Little, Brown.

Zilbergeld, B. (1992). *The new male sexuality: The truth about me, sex, and pleasure.* New York: Bantam Books.

Part IV

Clinical Disorders of Sexual Behavior and Identity

11

The Paraphilias: Classification and Theory

Richard D. McAnulty

Defining sexual deviance is a difficult task. The erotic fantasies and behaviors that presumably constitute sexual deviance are relative since they vary over time within a given culture as well as across cultures. Sexual behavior is considered deviant or pathological when a large or influential segment of society disapproves of it because it violates explicit or implicit social norms about "normal" sexuality. Thus, with rare exceptions (such as sexual homicide), no sexual behavior is deviant in an absolute sense.

As Wakefield (1992) persuasively noted, all diagnostic labels entail value judgments: The observer chooses to attend to some phenomena while disregarding others. Wakefield proposed a formulation of disorders as "harmful dysfunctions." To qualify as a disorder, the condition in question must represent a dysfunction and must be viewed as harmful or undesirable by society. According to Wakefield, "a disorder exists when the failure of a person's internal mechanisms to perform their functions as designed by nature impinges harmfully on the person's well-being as defined by social values and meanings" (p. 373). In the case of homosexuality, no dysfunction has been identified, but the history of psychiatric classifications is replete with attempts to categorize homosexuality as harmful (as a sexual deviation).

BACKGROUND

The changing sociopolitical views of homosexuality have been paralleled by changes in the psychiatric nomenclature, as illustrated by the removal of the diagnostic category from the third edition of the *Diagnostic and Statistical Manual of Mental Disorders* (DSM-III) (American Psychiatric Association 1980). Over the past forty years, sexual fantasies and acts that were formerly considered deviant or harmful were reclassified as acceptable, whereas other patterns of fantasy and behavior were labeled maladaptive. Changes in official terminology parallel the evolution in sociocultural attitudes toward normal and abnormal sexual proclivities.

Historically, psychoanalytic writers have favored the term *perversions* (Freud 1953; Stolle 1978), but this term has been relegated to the vernacular in recent years. The term *paraphilia* (from the Greek *para-*, or "altered," "abnormal," and *philia-*, or "love") was first used systematically by Karpman (1954) and gained official status in DSM-III (APA 1980) when it replaced the "sexual deviation" label. Specific types of sexual deviation (e.g, fetishism, exhibitionism, and homosexuality) were introduced in DSM-II (APA 1967) where they were subsumed under the heading, "Personality Disorders and Certain Other Non-Psychotic Mental Disorders."

According to DSM-IV, the defining features of the paraphilias entail "recurrent, intense sexually arousing fantasies, sexual urges, or behaviors involving 1) nonhuman objects, 2) the suffering or humiliation of oneself or one's partner, or 3) children or other nonconsenting persons, that occur over a period of at least 6 months" (APA 1994, pp. 522–523). In addition, the fantasies or behaviors must generate "clinically significant distress" or impairments in one or more important areas of functioning. By implication, sexual urges and activities per se do not qualify as paraphilic. For instance, if an individual experiences intense sexual arousal to women's footwear but does not experience subjective distress or any associated impairments in functioning, then a diagnosis of fetishism is not warranted.

The newly revised diagnostic criteria of paraphilia represent a departure from previous systems. In DSM-III, it was specified that the paraphilic fantasies and acts must be preferred or necessary for sexual excitement: "Since paraphiliac imagery is necessary for erotic arousal, it must be included in masturbatory or coital fantasies, if not actually acted out alone or with a partner and support cast or paraphernalia. In the absence of paraphiliac imagery there is no relief from nonerotic tension, and sexual excitement or orgasm is not attained" (APA 1980, p. 267). The specification that the individual's paraphilia must be preferred or necessary was an attempt to preclude the application of the label in instances of an isolated act rather than a repetitive pattern in sexual fantasy or behavior.

The paraphilia criteria in DSM-III-R required the person to have acted on the urges or be distressed by them. These modified criteria reflected dissatisfaction with the DSM-III paraphilia-as-preference requirement. As clarified in the revised edition, "Some people with paraphilias did not actually prefer the object or behavior but, in fact, suffered considerably from having to engage in the paraphilia. Furthermore, the paraphilia was often not the exclusive means of

Table 11.1
DSM-IV Paraphilias

Disorder	Sexual fantasies, urges, and/or activities
Exhibitionism	exposing to an unsuspecting stranger
Fetishism	use of a nonliving object (not limited to cross-dressing)
Frotteurism	touching and rubbing against a nonconsenting person
Pedophilia	sexual activity with a prepubescent child
Sexual Masochism	being humiliated, beaten, bound, or otherwise made to suffer
Sexual Sadism	inflicting psychological or physical suffering
Transvestic Fetishism	cross-dressing
Voyeurism	observing an unsuspecting person who is disrobing or having sex

Paraphilia Not Otherwise Specified:

Telephone Scatologia	making obscene phone calls
Necrophilia	sexual activity with corpses
Partialism	exclusive sexual focus on part of the body
Zoophilia	bestiality or sex with animals
Coprophilia	sexual arousal to feces
Klismaphilia	sexual arousal to enemas
Urophilia	arousal to urine

sexual excitement: people might engage in other paraphilias or in more ordinary sexual behavior as well'' (APA 1987, p. 481).

A final consideration pertains to the comprehensiveness of the DSM categories for paraphilias. The classification includes eight major types and one generic category (''Paraphilias Not Otherwise Specified''), which lists seven other types (table 11.1). A number of questions are raised by the inclusion of some types and exclusion of others. For example, frotteurism was elevated to a full-fledged paraphilia in DSM-III-R, having previously been classified as a ''Paraphilia Not Otherwise Specified.'' The reasons for this change are unclear. It is accepted among experts that the DSM paraphilias represent only a sample of existing types, probably the most common and visible. Money (1984, 1986) has identified over thirty types, the majority of which are not represented in DSM-IV.

The regular revisions in the essential features of paraphilias illustrate the lack of consensus among mental health professionals on what is truly deviant with respect to sexual behavior and fantasy. The problem is exacerbated by the relative absence of information on "normal" sexual behavior and fantasy. One recent survey suggested that sexual practices that are considered deviant (e.g., fetishism and bondage/domination) are reported by over 10 percent of the population (Janus & Janus 1993). Epidemiological studies of the paraphilias are very uncommon for several reasons. First, the socially reprehensible and often criminal nature of the sexual activities requires secretiveness. Most paraphiliacs do not divulge the nature of their sexual proclivities. Second, the paraphilias have historically been viewed as uncommon or rare (APA 1980), hence the term *sexual deviations.* Finally, changing social attitudes toward sexual behavior render survey results obsolete in relatively short periods of time. The few existing survey results should be considered tentative since they are usually derived from volunteers, often college student populations, and are subject to the usual response biases. Further, none would qualify as representative of the population as a whole (Templeman & Stinnett 1991). (For more detail on the historical changes in definitions of sexual deviance, readers are referred to Money and Lamacz (1989) and Bullough (1976).

DIAGNOSTIC CONSIDERATIONS

An essential feature of paraphilic arousal is the extent to which it is disturbing to the individual—either subjectively distressing or causing interference in important areas of functioning, such as occupation and interpersonal adjustment. If discovered, paraphilic interests often precipitate interpersonal and marital conflict and may lead to criminal prosecution, which frequently results in a host of other difficulties, such as social alienation and job loss. As noted in DSM-IV, paraphilias commonly interfere with the capacity for affectionate relationships. Thus, some degree of clinical judgment is required in gauging the extent to which the paraphilia causes problems in living. Some individuals are incapable of performing sexually without the preferred sexual stimulus, and, in this sense, it is necessary for sexual fulfillment. For others, the erotic preference generates guilt, shame, and other negative emotions. Accurate diagnosis is complicated by the denial and efforts to make positive impressions, which are common among sexual offenders (Grossman & Cavanaugh 1990; Laws & Holmen 1978).

Paraphilic fantasies and acts are regularly observed in individuals afflicted with other mental disorders, such as schizophrenia, bipolar disorder, and organic conditions such as dementia and mental retardation. In these instances, however, the sexual interests occur only in the context of the specified disorder and are isolated acts rather than marked sexual preferences or necessities. Therefore, deviant sexuality that is symptomatic of another condition does not qualify as a paraphilia in DSM-IV.

Further, some activities may appear sexually deviant on the surface, although they do not represent sexually motivated or sexually preferred behaviors. For instance, public urination is viewed as socially unacceptable and illegal in the United States. However, it is not equivalent to exhibitionism since it is not sexually motivated (although some exhibitionists offer public urination as an excuse to avoid criminal prosecution).

An association between the paraphilias and personality disorders is recognized in DSM-IV, following a long tradition in psychiatry. Krafft-Ebing (1931) proposed biological causes (inherited constitutional abnormalities) for most paraphilias, although he provided that a psychopathic personality may be a factor in some instances. In DSM-I, sexual deviation was construed as a symptom of a sociopathic personality disturbance (APA 1952). Karpman (1954) favored a formulation of paraphiliac neurosis, reserving the term *sexual psychopath* for the few cases characterized by compulsive sexual urges, extreme aggressiveness, and absence of remorse. Personality disorders are identified in a sizable minority of cases, but the degree of comorbidity is not higher than that observed in other diagnostic groups.

A particularly difficult diagnostic decision ensues from the revised criteria for sexual sadism and sexual masochism (see Lohr & Adams, this volume). In DSM-III, sexual masochism could be diagnosed if a person preferred being humiliated as a means of becoming sexually aroused. Fantasies alone were not sufficient: the person had to have acted on them. In DSM-IV, masochistic fantasies justify the diagnosis if they have occurred for at least six months and cause subjective distress or impairments in functioning. Enacting these fantasies is no longer necessary for a diagnosis. However, it is emphasized that the fantasies and acts must involve real, not simulated, humiliation, bondage, or suffering. Thus, sexual sadism and masochism diagnoses require that the sexual interest be disturbing or disruptive and involve actual humiliation or suffering, not merely role playing.

One condition omitted from DSM-IV is rape. Unless there is evidence of sadistic fantasies and behaviors as determinants of a rape, a case would not qualify as a paraphilia in DSM-IV nomenclature. Abel and Rouleau (1990) criticized the exclusion of rape from DSM because they believe that rapists display "recurrent, repetitive, and compulsive urges and fantasies to commit rapes" (p. 18). The authors of the DSM-IV diagnostic criteria for paraphilias apparently avoided introducing paraphilic rape out of concern that it might be used in court as a defense against prosecution. Curiously, the same line of reasoning was not applied to pedophilia.

As noted in DSM-IV, the paraphilias occur almost exclusively in males. Females represent less than 1 percent of all cases of reported sexual offenders (McConaghy 1993). In many instances of sexual offenses by women, the women were allegedly coerced or enticed into acting as accomplices of men perpetrating a sexual offense (Travin, Cullen & Protter 1990). Sexual masochism is the most common paraphilia reported in women (Levitt, Moser & Jamison 1994). Any comprehensive theory of paraphilia must consider the gender disparity in the prevalence of these disorders.

ISSUES IN CLASSIFICATION

The science of classifying diseases has contributed to major advances in medicine. Classifications of phenomena allow more precise communication, stimulate research, and ultimately allow users of the system to reduce a potentially overwhelming amount of information into a more manageable quantity (Adams & Cassidy 1993). Most important, valid classifications of disorders "provide clues for research into etiology" and ultimately may facilitate the development of effective treatment procedures (Bard et al. 1987, p. 219). Thus, classification is one of the most basic processes in science.

A preliminary step in developing a categorical classification of diseases entails the description of symptoms or signs and the organization of clusters of related symptoms into "syndromes." Once discrete syndromes, or disorders, are identified, they can be grouped with other syndromes on the basis of similarity. The similarity may be based on the nature of the symptoms, the presumed etiology (such as bacterial versus viral diseases), or the prognosis. A fundamental assumption is that disorders within a category share core features that distinguish them from disorders classified in other categories. For example, in psychiatry, the anxiety disorders are grouped on the basis of the common symptom of anxiety, and they are distinguished from other categories in which the core problem is not anxiety.

The DSM-IV nosology adheres to the principles of scientific classification: it is intended (1) to be comprehensive but parsimonious and (2) to include homogeneous categories, and (3) the units of classification (symptoms) are simple and measurable, at least in theory (Adams & Cassidy 1993). Thus, DSM-IV was developed with the goal of offering complete descriptions of the sexual deviations. This assumption has been challenged by several researchers, including Money (1984, 1986), who coined his own terms, such as *apotemnophilia* (fantasies of self-amputation) and *symphorophilia* (sexual arousal to accidents or catastrophes), to classify idiosyncratic erotic fantasies and practices.

There is ongoing controversy over the co-occurrence of paraphilias in an individual. According to DSM-IV, it is not uncommon for individuals to have multiple paraphilias, and if an individual meets criteria, then all of the appropriate diagnostic codes may be applied. In contrast, Money (1984) argued that it is rare "for a person to have more than one paraphilia, or to change from one to another" (p. 166). Based on clinical experience, McConaghy (1993) also concluded that most paraphiliacs have a single preferred deviation, although they may occasionally experiment with others. Other researchers believe that multiple deviations are quite common (Abel et al. 1987; Freund, Scher & Hucker 1983;

Langevin 1983). Abel, Becker, Cunningham-Rathner, Mittelman, and Rouleau (1988) reported that 80 percent of nonfamilial pedophiles and 70 percent of incest offenders admitted to at least one other paraphilia. In contrast, Marshall, Barbaree, and Eccles (1991) obtained much lower rates of co-occurring paraphilias in their sample: only 14 percent of pedophiles who had molested girls and 8 percent of incest perpetrators admitted to other paraphilias. Such discrepant findings require additional investigation. The sample of Abel et al. (1988) may have been more deviant or, alternatively, more candid. Another possibility involves differences in diagnosing paraphilias: an isolated instance of deviant behavior or fantasy does not qualify as a paraphilia in DSM-IV. However, researchers may not always adhere rigidly to diagnostic criteria when classifying subjects.

The specification of types of paraphilias in DSM-IV is based on the premise that they differ on the variables of interest, symptomatology. An alternative basis for classification could be etiology, but we have not reached the level of sophistication necessary for a classification of psychological disorders on the basis of etiology, as has been done in medicine. In order to advance our understanding of paraphilias, and ultimately to elucidate their etiologies, researchers have studied groups of individuals who allegedly suffer from deviant sexual fantasies and behaviors. Variables that have been studied in this context include personality, coexisting psychopathology, background, marital and social competence, and criminal history. Unfortunately, the findings of these studies have limited usefulness.

Results of studies of exhibitionists provide a good illustration of the typical findings from descriptive studies of paraphiliacs. Intelligence, education level, and vocational interests of exhibitionists do not appear different from the general population (Blair & Lanyon 1981). Karpman (1954) reported that exposers perceived themselves as inferior, were generally timid and unassertive, and experienced problems expressing hostility. Several researchers have found exposers to be narcissistic or antisocial (Lang, Langevin, Checkley & Pugh 1987; Langevin 1983); others have failed to find definitive character types or evidence of comorbid pathology in these individuals (Langevin et al. 1979; Smukler & Schiebel 1975). Therefore, despite much speculation and theory, descriptive studies of exhibitionists have yielded equivocal findings.

The most consistent finding from these descriptive studies is that sexual offenders constitute a heterogeneous group (Adams & McAnulty 1993; Knight, Rosenberg & Schneider 1985). The same conclusion may be drawn from studies of specific types of paraphilias (Bradford, Bloomberg & Bourget 1988; Okami & Goldberg 1992). One possible reason for these findings is that types of paraphilias do not actually differ significantly beyond the nature of their fantasies, urges, and behaviors. If this were accurate, then the DSM-I system of having but one generic category would be appropriate. However, the continuing inclusion of types of paraphilias attests to the general belief that there are important distinctions among them.

A number of methodological problems may account for the heterogeneity within types of paraphilias. Sampling biases are evident, since most studies have relied on incarcerated subjects (Gebhard, Gagnon, Pomeroy & Christenson 1965), who may not be representative of the larger population of paraphiliacs. Another common practice has been to administer psychometric tests to large groups of "sex offenders" and report the resulting average or modal profile as being characteristic of the group (Armentrout & Hauer 1978; Panton 1979). Such a practice perpetuates the illusion of homogeneity and fosters stereotypic descriptions of the sample under study. Several studies of pedophiles reveal that less than 15 percent of subjects conform to the modal profile on the Minnesota Multiphasic Personality Inventory, one of the most widely used measures of psychopathology (Erickson, Luxenberg, Walbek & Seely 1987; McAnulty, Adams & Wright 1994). Similar findings have been obtained when assessing erotic preferences of pedophiles using the penile plethysmograph (Barbaree & Marshall 1989). To date, no consistent personality features have been identified among sexual offenders (Okami & Goldberg 1992).

Another methodological problem involves group assignment. For example, Hall, Maiuro, Vitaliano, and Proctor (1986) included subjects who had molested children up to age 18 in their study of child molesters. In other studies, these same subjects would be classified as rapists. Finally, it has been suggested that incarcerated sexual offenders may not be representative of the population of paraphiliacs (McConaghy, 1993). Therefore, methodological problems have impeded the search for commonalities in paraphiliacs.

Recent controlled studies have confirmed that paraphiliacs form a heterogeneous group. As Earls and Quinsey (1986) commented, "While it may be parsimonious to hypothesize common factors among sexual offenders, it is undoubtedly naive to expect that the etiologies of all sexually deviant behaviors are necessarily identical" (p. 382). Consequently, researchers have developed typologies of subtypes of paraphilias in order to form homogeneous subgroups. One early attempt to identify subtypes of sexual offenders was the classification of rapists and pedophiles by Cohen, Seghorn, and Calmas (1969). They proposed three types of pedophiles—fixated, regressed, and aggressive—on the basis of their social adjustment as measured by sociometric ratings. A similar scheme was offered by Lanyon (1986). Using multivariate clustering techniques, Knight and Prentky (1990; Knight, Rosenberg & Schneider 1985) have developed taxonomies of child molesters and rapists. For example, their classification of rapists involves four primary motives (opportunistic, pervasively angry, sexual, and vindictive). These categories, excluding the pervasively angry type, are subdivided on the basis of social competence, yielding a total of nine types of rapists. This promising classification system has been extended to other sexual offender samples, and with some success (Barbaree, Seto, Serin, Amos & Preston 1994; Knight & Prentky 1993).

There are several noteworthy features to these new developments in classifying paraphilias. First, it is increasingly clear that categorizing subjects solely of the basis of their erotic fantasies, urges, and behaviors, as is done in DSM-IV, is inadequate. The resulting groups are extremely heterogeneous; in many instances, the only commonality among individuals in a diagnostic category is their pattern of sexual arousal, or criminal charges in the case of forensic samples. Second, the recent taxonomies incorporate variables that may be relevant to theory, treatment, and prognosis. Such variables as social competence, background, and motives for committing sexual aggression have long been considered pertinent to understanding several sexual deviations (Bard et al. 1987; Gebhard et al. 1965; Knight, Rosenberg & Schneider 1985). Finally, the commitment to empirically derived classification systems represents a major advance over previous approaches, which relied on case studies and small, heterogeneous groups of sexual offenders.

THEORIES

Theory initially directs the choice of variables to be used in classification. The selection of variables for classifying disorders is guided by hypotheses about the significance of these variables to understanding the disorders (Adams & Cassidy 1993). To illustrate, in DSM-I the sexual deviations were classified as "reactions" to a "Sociopathic Personality Disturbance," as were alcoholism and the "antisocial reaction." The personality disorders were divided into four groups on the "basis of the dynamics of personality development. The Personality pattern disturbances are considered deep seated disturbances, with little room for regression" (APA 1952, p. 34). This nosology was based on the prevailing psychodynamic theory of psychopathology. A major revision that occurred in DSM-III (1980) was the adoption of a descriptive and atheoretical approach to classification. The rationale for this shift included the fact that etiologies for most disorders remained unknown and that clinicians had higher rates of agreement for symptoms than etiologies. As noted, "Because DSM-III is generally atheoretical with regard to etiology, it attempts to describe comprehensively what the manifestations of the mental disorders are, and only rarely attempts to account for *how* the disturbances come about, unless the mechanism is included in the definition of the disorder" (APA, 1980, p. 7). This atheoretical descriptive approach to classification is still in effect in DSM-IV (APA 1994).

Devising a classification system ideally requires alternating between theoretical postulates and empirical tests of their validity (Skinner 1981). An initial classification scheme is developed using variables believed to be characteristic of the disorders. This system is subsequently subjected to empirical tests and revised on the basis of the findings.

Theories of paraphilia may be categorized as single factor or multifactorial theories. The single factor theories postulate that the factor in question is necessary and sufficient for the development of sexually aberrant fantasies, urges, and behaviors. Early conditioning and psychoanalytic and biological theories fall under this rubric.

Early behavioral theorists suggested that paraphilic behavior was the result of one-trial learning from crucial, possibly incidental, sexual experiences that later served as a fantasy for masturbation (McGuire, Carlisle & Young 1965). For example, these authors cited an example of an exhibitionist who was observed by a female while he was urinating in a public place. By later incorporating this experience into a masturbatory fantasy, and thus pairing the exposure with orgasm, the individual conditioned an association between exposing his genitals and sexual satisfaction. Thus, the exposing fantasies became conditioned stimuli for conditioned arousal. Other behavioral theories of paraphilia stressed the importance of early conditioning, direct reinforcement, or modeling experiences (see Alford, Plaud & McNair, this volume; O'Donohue & Plaud 1994, for reviews).

Recent investigations have explored possible biological factors that may be associated with sexually deviant behavior. Neuropsychological studies of sexually deviant populations have emerged from a convergence of literature on animal sexual behavior with neurologic case studies. In both animal and human research, brain damage and dysfunction resulting from accidents, surgery, epilepsy, and toxic substances have been correlated with changes in personality or behavior. More specifically, changes in sexual behavior, including the appearance of sexually deviant behaviors such as fetishism, exhibitionism, and pedophilia, have been reported subsequent to disruptions in brain function (Cummings 1985; Epstein 1961; see Langevin 1990 for review).

Mitchell, Falconer, and Hill (1954) described an epileptic subject who exhibited a fetish for safety pins. In fact, fetishism appears to be the most common paraphilia associated with epilepsy, especially temporal lobe epilepsy. In other cases, pedophilic behavior has been reported in epileptic patients (Regenstein & Reich 1978). Langevin's (1990) review of these findings led to the hypothesis of an association between paraphilias and neurologic anomalies. Hendricks et al. (1988) reported reduced regional cerebral blood flow in a sample of pedophiles. Despite these postulations, largely derived from case studies, support for this view has been mixed in controlled studies that use modern imaging technologies (Hucker et al. 1985; Langevin, Wortzman, Wright & Handy 1989). Although cerebral deficits may correlate with behavioral disinhibition, they do not explain the presence of deviant fantasies and urges. Further, the majority of cases with neurologic impairment, including epilepsy, do not exhibit paraphilic behavior.

Perhaps the most popular single-factor theory of pedophilia is the "abused-abuser hypothesis," which postulates that individuals who were sexually abused in childhood are predisposed to developing pedophilia (Finkelhor et al. 1986; Lanyon 1986). As Garland and Dougher (1990) commented, despite the popularity of this view, there is surprisingly little empirical support. There are at least three theoretical problems with this hypothesis: (1) although most victims of child sexual abuse are females, the vast majority of pedophiles are males; (2) a majority of pedophiles deny any personal history of sexual victimization by an adult in childhood (see Garland & Dougher 1990 for review); and (3) some pedophiles apparently allege having been sexually abused in childhood as a ploy to reduce their perceived responsibility for their sexual offenses (Freund, Watson & Dickey 1990). Thus, it appears that the majority of individuals who were sexually molested as children do not develop pedophilia (Hanson & Slater 1988).

There are several limitations with singular theories of paraphilia such as the abused-abuser hypothesis of pedophilia. The specificity problem (Fowles 1994) refers to the fact that the same precipitant, such as sexual victimization, may lead to a variety of disorders (e.g., Beitchman et al. 1992; Kendall-Tackett, Williams & Finkelhor 1993). In such cases, the identified stressor is a nonspecific factor. Such nonspecific risk factors appear to defy investigation because they are not necessary and sufficient for explaining the etiology of a disorder. Further, if one accepts the findings of Finkelhor, Hotaling, Lewis, and Smith (1990) that 16 percent of males and 27 percent of females have been sexually victimized, one would predict that the same percentage of all males and females would develop pedophilia. Because this is not the case, other factors must be invoked, and, accordingly single factor theories of paraphilia have proven inadequate.

Only recently have multifactorial theories of paraphilia been proposed, and they have not been subjected to sufficient empirical tests. Finkelhor and Araji (1986) concluded that existing single-factor theories of pedophilia rely on one of four factors: emotional congruence, sexual arousal, disinhibition, or blockage (see Long, this volume). They proposed that a theory combining these four factors is more useful in explaining the heterogeneity of pedophilia. These interactive factors are combined to estimate an individual's risk for developing pedophilia. For example, a male who is emotionally and sexually attracted to children may not act on his urges if he has adequate inhibitions (e.g., impulse control) and has alternative socially acceptable outlets for his social, emotional, and sexual needs. At this stage, the four-factor model may have heuristic value, but empirical tests are needed.

One of the newest and most elaborate multifactorial theories of paraphilia was proposed by Marshall and colleagues (Marshall 1989; Marshall & Barbaree 1990; Marshall, Hudson & Hodkinson 1993). In this formulation, a lack of intimacy in adulthood and the resulting experience of loneliness predispose some individuals to sexually aggressive behavior. This deficiency in adult intimacy may interact with sociocultural influences, precocious sexualization, conditioning events, and biological factors in the development and maintenance of deviant sexuality (Marshall & Eccles 1993). These authors suggest that the developmental history of sex offenders renders them vulnerable to various influences and events; this proposed developmental vulnerability is attributed to inadequate parent-child attachment early in life. Consequently, the child lacks the skills and self-confidence necessary for mastering the challenges in the transition to adolescence. The vulnerable male experiences pubertal development and emerging sexual urges while feeling socially inept, especially with female peers. Thus, the individual is believed to be especially susceptible to nondemanding and non-threatening sexual scripts (Marshall & Eccles 1993). Examples of nonthreatening scripts for a socially incompetent male might include child molestation, voyeurism, and fetishism. For a male who fears intimacy, nonconsenting sexual activity, including rape, may be less threatening. These individuals may also be attracted to cultural messages perpetuating gender role stereotypes, such as the view that males are naturally aggressive and women are inherently passive (see Hardy, this volume, for review). It is further postulated that if the individual incorporates these nonthreatening and distorted fantasies into masturbation practices, this may strengthen the conditioning process (McGuire, Carlisle & Young 1965). The presence of any disinhibiting influences, including drug abuse and brain damage, may contribute to the risk of enacting any existing deviant urges.

The fact that paraphilias occur almost exclusively in males must be considered in any theory of sexual deviance. According to Marshall and Eccles (1993), Western culture shapes males into developing an overly sexualized view of the world. Additionally, males more than females are conditioned to perceive sexual aggression as acceptable. Cross-cultural differences in the prevalence of paraphilias, such as the virtual absence of exhibitionism in some cultures (Rooth 1973), highlight the role of sociocultural factors in shaping sexual behavior and attitudes.

The multifaceted theory of sexual aggression provides a useful illustration of recent attempts to overcome the limitations of single factor theories of paraphilia. The theory postulates that family, sociocultural, and biological factors interactively influence the development and maintenance of deviant sexual fantasies and behavior. It proposes that some of these experiences are unique to sex offenders, while others may be observed in other disturbed samples, such as delinquent adolescents. Thus, some testable predictions are offered that make the theory falsifiable and therefore scientifically useful. For example, Marshall, Hudson, and Hodkinson (1993) hypothesized that adolescent sex offenders should display more social skills deficits, less self-confidence, and more fragile masculinity than other adolescent delinquents and nondelinquents.

CONCLUSIONS

Perhaps no other single category of "psychological disorders" has elicited more controversy, curiosity, and outrage than the paraphilias. Naturally, such controversy is also reflected in both the past and recent classifications of these conditions. Over the course of the history of psychiatric nosologies, there has been significant disagreement over the etiologies, descriptions, and types of paraphilias, illustrated by seemingly arbitrary decisions to exclude some "disorders" while including others. These decisions are often dictated by sociocultural influences rather than empirical findings. As a consequence, the current classification system clusters such widely disparate conditions as fetishism and pedophilia in the same category. Not surprisingly, we find the category of paraphilias to be extremely heterogeneous.

Notable advances in the study of paraphilias include attempts to delineate empirically derived subtypes. Further, methodological improvements have helped dispel many myths about these conditions. These refinements have been paralleled by a shift from single factor to multifactorial theories of paraphilias. Continued progress in describing, classifying, and explaining these disorders is contingent on empirical tests of these developments in the study of the paraphilias.

REFERENCES

Abel, G. G., Becker, J. V., Cunningham-Rathner, J., Mittelman, M., Rouleau, J. L., & Murphy, W. D. (1988). Multiple paraphilic diagnoses among sex offenders. *Bulletin of the American Academy of Psychiatry and the Law, 16,* 153–168.

Abel, G. G., Becker, J. V., Mittelman, M., Cunningham-Rathner, J., Rouleau, J. L., & Murphy, W. D. (1987). Self-reported sex crimes of nonincarcerated paraphiliacs. *Journal of Interpersonal Violence, 2,* 3–25.

Abel, G. G., & Rouleau, J. L. (1990). The nature and extent of sexual assault. In W. L. Marshall, D. R. Laws & H. E. Barbaree (Eds.), *Handbook of sexual assault: Issues, theories, and treatment of the offender* (pp. 9–21). New York: Plenum.

Adams, H. E., & Cassidy, J. F. (1993). The classification of abnormal behavior: An overview. In P. B. Sutker & H. E. Adams (Eds.), *Comprehensive handbook of psychopathology* (2nd ed.) (pp. 3–25). New York: Plenum.

Adams, H. E., & McAnulty, R. D. (1993). Sexual disorders: The paraphilias. In P. B. Sutker & H. E. Adams (Eds.), *Comprehensive handbook of psychopathology* (2nd ed.) (pp. 563–579). New York: Plenum.

American Psychiatric Association. (1952). *Diagnostic and statistical manual of mental disorders.* Washington, DC.: Author.

American Psychiatric Association. (1968). *Diagnostic and statistical manual of mental disorders* (2nd ed.). Washington, DC: Author.

American Psychiatric Association. (1980). *Diagnostic and statistical manual of mental disorders* (3rd ed.). Washington, DC: Author.

American Psychiatric Association. (1987). *Diagnostic and statistical manual of mental disorders* (3rd ed. rev.). Washington, DC: Author.

American Psychiatric Association. (1994). *Diagnostic and statistical manual of mental disorders* (4th ed.). Washington, DC: Author.

Armentrout, J. A., & Hauer, A. L. (1978). MMPI's of rapists of children and non-rapist sex offenders. *Journal of Clinical Psychology, 34,* 330–332.

Barbaree, H. E., Hudson, S. M., & Seto, M. C. (1993). Sexual assault in society: The role of the juvenile offender. In H. E. Barbaree, W. L. Marshall & S. M. Hudson (Eds.), *The juvenile sex offender* (pp. 1–24). New York: Guilford.

Barbaree, H. E., & Marshall, W. L. (1989). Erectile responses among heterosexual child molesters, father-daughter incest offenders, and matched nonoffenders: Five distinct age preference profiles. *Canadian Journal of Behavioral Sciences, 21,* 70–82.

Barbaree, H. E., Seto, M. C., Serin, R. C., Amos, N. L., & Preston, D. L. (1994). Comparisons between sexual and nonsexual rapist subtypes. *Criminal Justice and Behavior, 21*, 95–114.

Bard, L. A., Carter, D. L., Cerce, D. D., Knight, R. A., Rosenberg, R., & Schneider, B. (1987). A descriptive study of rapists and child molesters: Developmental, clinical, and criminal statistics. *Behavioural Sciences and the Law, 5*, 203–220.

Beitchman, J. H., Zucker, K. J., Hood, J. E., daCosta, G. A., Akman, D., & Cassavia, E. (1992). A review of the long-term effects of child sexual abuse. *Child Abuse and Neglect, 16*, 101–118.

Blair, C. D., & Lanyon, R. I. (1981). Exhibitionism: Etiology and treatment. *Psychological Bulletin, 89*, 439–463.

Bradford, J. M. W., Bloomberg, D., & Bourget, D. (1988). The heterogeneity/homogeneity of pedophilia. *Psychiatric Journal of the University of Ottawa, 13*, 217–226.

Bullough, V. L. (1976). *Sexual variance in society and history.* New York: Wiley.

Cohen, M. L., Seghorn, T., & Calmas, W. (1969). Sociometric study of sex offenders. *Journal of Abnormal Psychology, 74*, 249–255.

Cummings, J. L. (1985). *Clinical neuropsychiatry.* New York: Grune & Stratton.

Earls, C. M., & Quinsey, V. L. (1986). What is to be done? Future research on the assessment and behavioral treatment of sex offenders. *Behavioral Sciences and the Law, 3*, 377–390.

Epstein, A. W. (1961). Relationship of fetishism and transvestism to brain and particularly to temporal lobe dysfunction. *Journal of Nervous and Mental Disease, 133*, 247–253.

Erikson, W. D., Luxenberg, M. G., Walbek, N. G., & Seely, R. K. (1987). Frequency of MMPI two-point code types among sex offenders. *Journal of Consulting and Clinical Psychology, 55*, 566–570.

Finkelhor, D., & Araji, S. (1986). Explanations of pedophilia: A four factor model. *Journal of Sex Research, 22*, 145–161.

Finkelhor, D., Hotaling, G., Lewis, I. A., & Smith, C. (1990). Sexual abuse in a national survey of adult men and women: Prevalence, characteristics, and risk factors. *Child Abuse and Neglect, 14*, 19–28.

Fowles, D. C. (1994). Biological variables in psychopathology: A psychobiological perspective. In P. B. Sutker & H. E. Adams (Eds.), *Comprehensive handbook of psychopathology* (2nd ed.) (pp. 57–82). New York: Plenum.

Freud, S. (1953). Three essays on the theory of sexuality. In J. Strachey (Ed. and Trans.), *The standard edition of the complete psychological works of Sigmund Freud* (Vol. 7, pp. 123–246). London: Hogarth. (original work published 1905)

Freund, K., Scher, H., & Hucker, S. (1983). The courtship disorders. *Archives of Sexual Behavior, 12*, 369–379.

Freund, K., Watson, R., & Dickey, R. (1990). Does sexual abuse in childhood cause pedophilia: An exploratory study. *Archives of Sexual Behavior, 19*, 557–568.

Garland, R. J., & Dougher, M. J. (1990). The abused/abuser hypothesis of child sexual abuse: A critical review of theory and research. In J. R. Feierman (Ed.), *Pedophilia: Biosocial dimensions* (pp. 488–509). New York: Springer-Verlag.

Gebhard, P. H., Gagnon, J. H., Pomeroy, W. B., & Christenson, C. V. (1965). *Sex offenders.* New York: Harper & Row.

Grossman, L. S., & Cavanaugh, J. L. (1990). Psychopathology and denial in alleged sex offenders. *Journal of Nervous and Mental Disease, 178,* 739–744.

Hall, G. C. N., Maiuro, R. D., Vitaliano, P. P., & Proctor, W. C. (1986). The utility of the MMPI with men who have sexually assaulted children. *Journal of Consulting and Clinical Psychology, 54,* 493–496.

Hanson, R. K., & Slater, S. (1988). Sexual victimization in the history of sexual abusers: A review. *Annals of Sex Research, 1,* 485–499.

Hendricks, S. E., Fitzpatrick, D. F., Hartmann, K., Quaife, M. A., Stratbucker, R. A., & Graber, B. (1988). Brain structure and function in sexual molesters of children and adolescents. *Journal of Clinical Psychiatry, 133,* 694–696.

Hucker, S., Langevin, R., Wortzman, G., Bain, J., Handy, L., Chambers, J., & Wright, S. (1985). Neuropsychological impairment in pedophiles. *Canadian Journal of Behavioral Science, 18,* 440–448.

Janus, S. S., & Janus, C. L. (1993). *The Janus report on sexual behavior.* New York: Wiley.

Karpman, B. (1954). *The sexual offender and his offenses.* New York: Julian.

Kendall-Tackett, K. A., Williams, L. M., & Finkelhor, D. (1993). Impact of sexual abuse on children: A review and synthesis of recent empirical studies. *Psychological Bulletin, 113,* 164–180.

Knight, R. A., & Prentky, R. A. (1990). Classifying sexual offenders: The development and corroboration of taxonomic models. In W. L. Marshall, D. R. Laws & H. E. Barbaree (Eds.), *Handbook of sexual assault: Issues, theories, and treatment of the offender* (pp. 23–52). New York: Plenum.

Knight, R. A., & Prentky, R. A. (1993). Exploring characteristics for classifying juvenile sex offenders. In H. E. Barbaree, W. L. Marshall & S. M. Hudson (Eds.), *The juvenile sex offender* (pp. 45–83). New York: Guilford.

Knight, R. A., Rosenberg, R., & Schneider, B. A. (1985). Classification of sexual offenders: Perspectives, methods, and validation. In A. W. Burgess (Ed.), *Rape and sexual assault: A research handbook* (pp. 222–293). New York: Garland.

Krafft-Ebing, R. von. (1931). *Psychopathia sexualis with especial reference to the antipathic sexual instinct: A medico-forensic study.* Chicago: Login Brothers.

Lang, R. A., Langevin, R., Checkley, K. L., & Pugh, G. (1987). Genital exhibitionism: Courtship disorder or narcissism? *Canadian Journal of Behavioral Science, 19,* 216–232.

Langevin, R. (1983). *Sexual strands: Understanding and treating sexual anomalies in men.* Hillsdale, NJ: Lawrence Erlbaum Associates.

Langevin, R. (1990). Sexual anomalies and the brain. In W. L. Marshall, D. R. Laws & H. E. Barbaree (Eds.), *Handbook of sexual assault: Issues, theories, and treatment of the offender* (pp. 103–113). New York: Plenum.

Langevin, R., & Lang, R. A. (1987). The courtship disorders. In G. D. Wilson (Ed.), *Variant sexuality: Research and theory* (pp. 202–228). Baltimore: Johns Hopkins University Press.

Langevin, R., Paitich, D., Ramsay, G., Anderson, C., Kamrad, J., Pope, S., Geller, G., Pearl, L., & Newman, S. (1979). Experimental studies of the etiology of genital exhibitionism. *Archives of Sexual Behavior, 8,* 307–331.

Langevin, R., Wortzman, G., Wright, P., & Handy, L. (1989). Studies of brain damage and dysfunction in sex offenders. *Annals of Sex Research, 2,* 163–179.

Lanyon, R. I. (1986). Theory and treatment in child molestation. *Journal of Consulting and Clinical Psychology, 54,* 176–182.

Laws, D. R., & Holmen, M. L. (1978). Sexual response faking by pedophiles. *Criminal Justice and Behavior, 5,* 343–356.

Levitt, E. E., Moser, C., & Jamison, K. V. (1994). The prevalence and some attributes of females in the sadomasochistic subculture: A second report. *Archives of Sexual Behavior, 32,* 465–473.

McAnulty, R. D., Adams, H. E., & Wright, L. (1994). Relationship between MMPI and penile plethysmograph in accused child molesters. *Journal of Sex Research, 31,* 179–184.

McConaghy, N. (1993). *Sexual behavior: Problems and management.* New York: Plenum.

McGuire, R. J., Carlisle, J. M., & Young, B. G. (1965). Sexual deviations as conditioned behavior: A hypothesis. *Behavior Research and Therapy, 2,* 185–190.

Marshall, W. L. (1989). Intimacy, loneliness, and sexual offenders. *Behaviour Research and Therapy, 27,* 491–503.

Marshall, W. L., & Barbaree, H. E. (1990). An integrated theory of the etiology of sexual offending. In W. L. Marshall, D. R. Laws & H. E. Barbaree (Eds.), *Handbook of sexual assault: Issues, theories, and treatment of the offender* (pp. 257–275). New York: Plenum.

Marshall, W. L., Barbaree, H. E., & Eccles, A. (1991). Early onset and deviant sexuality in child molesters. *Journal of Interpersonal Violence, 6,* 323–336.

Marshall, W. L., & Eccles, A. (1993). Pavlovian conditioning processes in adolescent sex offenders. In H. E. Barbaree, W. L. Marshall & S. M. Hudson (Eds.), *The juvenile sex offender* (pp. 118–142). New York: Guilford.

Marshall, W. L., Hudson, S. M., & Hodkinson, S. (1993). The importance of attachment bonds in the development of juvenile sex offending. In H. E. Barbaree, W. L. Marshall & S. M. Hudson (Eds.), *The juvenile sex offender* (pp. 164–181). New York: Guilford.

Mitchell, W., Falconer, M. A., & Hill, D. (1954). Epilepsy with fetishism relieved by temporal lobectomy. *Lancet, 2,* 626–630.

Money, J. (1984). Paraphilias: Phenomenology and classification. *American Journal of Psychotherapy, 38,* 164–179.

Money, J. (1986). *Lovemaps: Clinical concepts of sexual/erotic health and pathology, paraphilia, and gender transposition in childhood, adolescence, and maturity.* New York: Irvington.

Money, J., & Lamacz, M. (1989). *Vandalized lovemaps.* Buffalo, NY: Prometheus.

O'Donohue, W., & Plaud, J. J. (1994). The conditioning of human sexual arousal. *Archives of Sexual Behavior, 23,* 321–344.

Okami, P., & Goldberg, A. (1992). Personality correlates of pedophilia: Are they reliable indicators? *Journal of Sex Research, 29,* 297–328.

Panton, J. H. (1979). MMPI profile configurations associated with incestuous and non-incestuous child molesting. *Psychological Reports, 45,* 335–338.

Regenstein, Q. R., & Reich, P. (1978). Pedophilia occurring after onset of cognitive impairment. *Journal of Nervous and Mental Disease, 166,* 794–798.

Rooth, G. (1973). Exhibitionism—outside Europe and America. *Archives of Sexual Behavior, 2,* 351–362.

Skinner, H. A. (1981). Toward the integration of classification theory and methods. *Journal of Abnormal Psychology, 90,* 68–87.

Smukler, A. J., & Schiebel, D. (1975). Personality characteristics of exhibitionists. *Diseases of the Nervous System, 36,* 600–603.

Stoller, R. J. (1975). *Perversion: The erotic form of hatred.* New York: Pantheon Books.

Templeman, T. L., & Stinnett, R. D. (1991). Patterns of sexual arousal and history in a "normal" sample of young men. *Archives of Sexual Behavior, 20,* 137–150.

Travin, S., Cullen, K., & Protter, B. (1990). Female sex offenders: Severe victims and victimizers. *Journal of Forensic Sciences, 35,* 140–150.

Wakefield, J. C. (1992). The concept of mental disorder: On the boundary between biological facts and social values. *American Psychologist, 47,* 373–388.

12

Sexual Sadism and Masochism

Bethany Lohr and Henry E. Adams

A thirty-five-year-old married writer entered into therapy because of distressing impulses of a sadistic nature. He has been married for fifteen years and has sex with his wife about once a week. The individual's fantasy life is predominantly heterosexual, although he has felt sexually attracted to males since childhood, but resisted acting on these impulses until mid-adulthood. Before that, he felt sexually aroused by homosexual pornography, particularly that with sadistic content. Although also aroused by sexually explicit videos of heterosexual interactions, he was never excited by heterosexual activity with sadistic content.

The patient married in hopes of diminishing his homosexual sadistic fantasies, but his sadistic impulses continued, and fantasies during masturbation were of binding and whipping another man. About eight years ago, the patient went to a gay bar with an associate from his office who was aggressive, demanding, and openly homosexual. The associate indicated that the bar was often frequented by "the leather crowd who like S&M." The patient had a brief homosexual encounter with someone he picked up in the bar in hopes of satisfying and squelching his sadistic impulses. Several weeks later, the patient could not resist going back to the S&M bar; his sadistic urges had escalated. At the bar, he met a man who was sexually aroused by being beaten, and the patient engaged in pleas-

urable sadistic activity with the understanding that the severity of the beating and administration with a belt was under the control of his masochistic partner. This was the first of a series of encounters, eventually bringing the man to therapy. Once or twice a week the patient would dress in a leather jacket and leather cap and frequent homosexual sadomasochistic bars. The activities he engaged in included binding his partner with ropes, whipping him, threatening to burn him with cigarettes, forcing him to drink urine, and begging. The patient would experience orgasm during these activities, usually by forcing his partner to engage in fellatio.

During the year before consultation, the patient's wife had become dissatisfied with their marriage. She was unaware of his homosexual or sadistic tendencies but reported that he seemed uninterested whenever they engaged in sexual intercourse. The patient realized that he still wanted the relationship with his wife but did not feel able to deal with her sexual dissatisfactions. He avoided communication with her about the situation and resisted attending any of the S&M bars in anticipation that his sadistic impulses would subside. Unfortunately, mounting stressors at work and at home only increased his desires for sadomasochistic activity. Alarmed that his lack of control over these urges would ultimately end his marriage, he presented for a psychological consultation. (adapted from APA 1994, pp. 217–219)

Sexual sadism and sexual masochism are generally construed as an association between sexual arousal and physical and/or psychological pain. The term *sadism* is derived from the practices of marquis de Sade (1740–1814), who attained sexual gratification from fantasizing or inflicting punishment and cruelty on his sexual partners, and he recorded these activities in his novels. Masochism is named after an Australian storyteller named Leopold von Sacher-Masoch (1835–1895) who wrote stories of males who attained sexual satisfaction from having a female partner inflict pain on them by flagellation. Scientific and clinical concern with sadism and masochism dates back to the publication of Krafft-Ebing's *Psychopathia Sexualis* in 1886. More recently, the fourth edition of the *Diagnostic and Statistical Manual of Mental Disorders* (DSM-IV) (APA 1994) describes sexual sadism as consisting of recurrent urges, fantasies, and behavior that center on physical or psychological suffering or humiliation of a victim and are sexually exciting to the person. Sexual masochism is defined by repeated urges and behavior involving being subjected to physical or psychological suffering or humiliation. In both cases, the fantasies or acts must be real (not simulated) and must cause subjective distress to the individual or significant impairment in daily functioning. Although DSM-IV categorizes sexual sadism and masochism as discrete disorders that must be perceived as distressing or handicapping to be considered paraphilic, in many cases, sadistic and masochistic sexual acts are consensually performed in conjunction with one another and give pleasure, not distress, to both partners involved and may not cause impairment (Stoller 1991). Thus, many individuals exhibiting these behaviors do not meet criteria for a clinical diagnosis and are subclinical examples of this disorder. In fact, a sadomasochistic subculture comprising individuals who practice S&M in regular sexual encounters has recently been identified and studied (Levitt, Moser & Jamison 1994; Moser 1988; Weinberg 1987).

SADOMASOCHISM

A diagnosis is only the start of the definitional and classification problems with these "disorders." For example, a person may experience sexual arousal to giving physical or psychological pain (sadism), receiving pain (masochism), or both (sadomasochism). It is not clear whether there are two or three types of these disorders, although the concept of comorbidity is one way to approach sadomasochism. The term *sadomasochism* is misleading since it may describe only a percentage of these cases. In Krafft-Ebing's (1886) early description of sadomasochistic behavior, the wide range of performed behaviors proposed also caused definitional difficulties. Physical pain was described as ranging from biting, scratching, and other similar courtship activities to behavior that produced lesions or drew blood. Similarly, psychological pain ranged from verbal abuse to bondage or being forced to do various sexual and nonsexual acts such as licking the shoes of a sex partner or being urinated or defecated upon. Moser (1979) discussed other problems in defining sadomasochism, including the facts that the pain experienced is altered during sexual arousal, ranging from pain to sexual pleasure; not all pain is arousing to sadomasochists (most have very specific preferences for the type of pain or humiliation they seek); and some S&M experiences (e.g., bondage or restraint) are not painful.

Consistent with the popularized subculture, sadomasochistic literature and research indicates that typical sadistic behavior requires that it be received masochistically in a cooperative, pleasurable sexual exchange. In fact, the same person may exhibit sadistic behavior on one occasion and masochistic in another instance (McConaghy 1993). Whether the person is sexually aroused by both forms of behavior or simply being accommodating for a sexual partner is seldom clarified. Gosselin (1987) describes the "sadomasochistic contract," which governs the sexual behavior of sadistic and masochistic partners. It is these consensual "exchanges involving eroticized mental, emotional, or physical pain" (Scott 1991, p. ix) that have been studied. For example, Gosselin and Wilson (1984) found that most sadists do not derive pleasure from inflicting more pain than is enjoyed or at least tolerated by their partner. Furthermore, most sadomasochists seek only partners who are also sexually excited by practices involving physical and psychological suffering or humiliation (McConaghy 1993). Thus, sadists and masochists in consensual relationships are rarely sufficiently distressed by their urges or behavior to present for treatment or meet criteria for a diagnosis.

Recent surveys aimed at identifying prevalence rates of sadomasochistic behavior have found that approximately 3 to 4 percent of university students report having been bound or sexually degraded during sexual interactions, and 1 percent of these students report having recently whipped, spanked, or beaten a consenting sexual partner (Person et al. 1989). Janus and Janus (1993) reported that 11 to 14 percent of their sample endorsed the use of sadomasochism in sexual activity. Thus this S&M subculture is not as rare as once thought (Weinberg 1987).

Many studies investigating individuals involved in sadistic or masochistic behavior have utilized magazines or clubs aimed at facilitating the selection of appropriate partners for this subculture. In earlier studies, most subjects were male and either bisexual or homosexual (Spengler 1979). Later investigations unveiled that sadists and masochists may be of heterosexual, homosexual, or bisexual orientation. Until the landmark study by Breslow, Evans, and Langley (1985), it was assumed that women involved in sadomasochistic activity were rare and were primarily involved in prostitution. More recent investigations have found that 20 to 30 percent of sadomasochists are female (Breslow, Evans & Langley 1985; Moser & Levitt 1987), few of whom report to be prostitutes. As summarized by McConaghy (1993), studies indicated that male and female sadomasochists typically play both sadistic and masochistic sexual roles, and more than 50 percent of men and 21 percent of women were aware of their sadomasochistic interest by age 14. Contrary to early belief, most men are reportedly heterosexual, whereas the majority of women claim bisexual orientation. A significant minority of respondents report self-bondage and pain infliction during masturbation. Subjects of both genders typically are of above-average intelligence and social status, and most wish to continue engaging in sadomasochistic activity. Levitt, Moser, and Jamison (1994) found similar results in a sample of forty-five women sadomasochists, with the exception that most designated themselves as heterosexual. Additionally, a majority of the sample considered themselves submissive in the S&M role, although most reported playing both roles on some occasions. Thus, masochism purports to be the most common paraphilia in women. This is consistent with Person, Terestman, Myers, Goldberg, and Salvadori's (1989) findings that although more males have fantasies with a sadistic content, females report primarily masochistic fantasies. Despite these results, sadomasochistics of both genders indicated that their fantasies did not support the stereotype that male sexuality is aggressive and sadistic and that the female role is passive and masochistic.

Most sadomasochists have very specific preferences for the types of pain or suffering they seek to give or receive. According to McConaghy's (1993) summary of the literature, the most common practices appear to be beating (spanking), fetishism, and bondage. Stoller (1991) commented that "no sadomasochists like all kinds of pain. The distinctions, though fine, are precise" (p. 16). For example, some sadomasochists require physical and pain-inflicting activities for sexual excitation, while others prefer mental techniques. Stoller (1991) described variables that were typically specific in the S&M individuals he studied. He noted that roles (e.g., dominant, submissive), sex of partner, erotic versus non-erotic scenarios, physical or mental activity, and overt versus covert practices emerged as extremely important to the players involved in sadomasochistic practices. He described some sadists who "are not directly excited by the lash of a whip . . . but are profoundly turned on by the idea that being whipped puts them in to a special, high-intensity contact with another person. They hate pain; they love to play at subjugation" (p. 9). In fact, sadomasochistic activities often involve role playing in which there is a prominent imbalance of power (e.g., dominatrix and slave). Stoller also provides an extensive list of sadomasochistic practices and instruments (pp. 10–14).

Gosselin (1987) described three characteristic aspects of sadomasochism:

1. Beatings, which varied in both intensity and duration and included use of such instruments as hands, paddles, whips, canes, and chains.

2. Bondage, which was described as often ritualistic, done in conjunction with beatings. Common forms of bondage include blindfolds, handcuffs, and rope or leather restraints. Binding may also be designed to cause partial asphyxiation.

3. Humiliation, which ranged from boot licking and crawling to the employment of degrading activities such as those involving urine, feces, and enemas.

HYPOXYPHILIA

Few sadomasochists report engaging in dangerous activities (McConaghy 1993). In fact, S&M organizations stress and teach safety, and serious injury is rare (Moser 1988). One dangerous practice that is discussed in DSM-IV is commonly known as hypoxyphilia: sexual excitation by oxygen deprivation, which may be accomplished by means of chest compression, noose, plastic bag use, or chemicals. Although reportedly rare, hypoxyphilia is often publicized after equipment malfunction or other errors cause accidental death by self-strangulation (Resnik 1972). The inclusion of hypoxyphilia under DSM-IV's description of masochism is questionable, since it is not clear whether this behavior occurs because of its masochistic aspects or whether it is merely a way of intensifying a sexual orgasm by physiologic means. In other words, it may be performed to attain a more intense orgasm, not because it is painful or humiliating.

Most of the knowledge about sexual hypoxyphilia has been obtained from the study of accidental fatalities. Evidence of autoerotic activity such as erotic magazines, exposure of genitals, pain-producing devices such as nipple clamps, and cross-dressing has been found (Byard, Hucker & Hazelwood 1990), particularly with male victims. Oxygen-depriving activities may be exhibited by an individual or with a partner. It is estimated that sexual asphyxia results in 500 to 1,000 deaths per year in the United States alone. As suggested in DSM-IV, dangerous practices such as hypoxyphilia demonstrate the tendency for sadists and masochists to increase the severity of their acts over time. Despite these concerns, Lee (1979) did not find any nonaccidental instances where S&M activities escalated to a dangerous level in his search of the medical and psychiatric literature.

SADISM: THE ISSUE OF RAPE

According to Stoller (1991), the most important issue to sadomasochists is the difference between consensual and nonconsensual activity. Most of the literature has focused on subclinical cases and individuals involved in mutually pleasurable activity, which may have little overlap with clinical cases. Rare exceptions involve sadistic rapists and sadistic murderers who seek nonconsenting victims. In the DSM-IV, these cases meet criteria for sexual sadism and may be associated with antisocial personality disorder. Some rapists may be considered sexual sadists, although only an estimated 10 percent of sex offenders charged with rape meet diagnostic criteria for this paraphilia (APA 1987). However, a pilot study of sexual aggressives by Langevin et al. (1985) found that 45 percent of their sample of twenty incarcerated rapists met criteria for sadism. Results comparing the sadists with nonsadistic rapists indicated that sadists reported using more aggression in the sexual acts, which resulted in their incarceration than nonsadists; sadists tended to have a more feminine gender identity or show ambivalence; sadists reported more acts of toucherism, frottage, exhibiting, and cross-dressing than nonsadists; and right temporal abnormalities were evidenced in sadistic rapists. Langevin et al. concluded that sadism is a separate sexual anomaly from rape, although rape is not delineated from sadism in DSM-IV.

There are several proposed types of rape: stranger rape, acquaintance or date rape, marital rape, and gang rape. It is estimated that the victim knows the assailant in as many as four out of five rapes (Gibbs 1991) Furthermore, research indicates that rapes, particularly acquaintance and marital rapes, are highly underreported. Epidemiologic surveys suggest that as many as 50 percent of women have been subjected to some degree of sexual assault (Koss & Oros 1982; Koss, Gidycz & Wisniewski 1987) and from 15 to 25 percent of male college students report engaging in sexual aggression (Malamuth, Sockloskie, Koss & Tanaka 1991). Sexually assaultive behaviors vary in degree of force and include verbal coercion, threat of physical violence, actual physical force, and the use of deadly violence (Benson, Charlton & Goodhart, 1992; Berkowitz 1992). Although FBI statistics indicate there are approximately forty-one reported rapes for every 100,000 inhabitants in this country (U.S. Department of Justice, Federal Bureau of Investigation 1990), rape is not included as a distinct category of paraphilia in DSM-IV. Hypotheses to explain its omission include the belief that rape is an aggressive and not a sexual act and the concern that if rape were considered a paraphilia, it would be used as a legal defense to exonerate offenders. The latter argument is weak, as pedophiles and other paraphilics are consistently prosecuted. The major point is that if hostile, aggressive acts are sexually arousing for the individual, then the criteria for a diagnosis of sexual sadism are met.

Specific categorization systems have been developed in an attempt to facilitate appropriate classification of rape and sexual assault. For example, Blader and Marshall (1989) describe a distinction between sadistic and nonsadistic rape, with indications that sadistic rapists display a marked preference for nonconsenting and aggressive sexual fantasies and activities. Although some researchers have concluded that there is not sufficient evidence to substantiate a categorical delineation between sadistic and nonsadistic rape, there has been an attempt to subdivide rapists on both categorical and dimensional levels. Knight and Prentky (1990) identified four general categories of rapists and further specified these typologies on the basis of motivation for rape, degrees of social competence, and lifestyle impulsivity. The four general categories are as follows:

1. Opportunistic rapists, who display an impulsive, predatory lifestyle marked by antisocial behavior patterns, one of which may be sexual aggression.

2. Pervasively angry rapists, who evidence undifferentiated anger and tend to be generally aggressive toward a number of target groups.

3. Sexual rapists, who have prominent sexually sadistic fantasies and urges, which motivate sexual aggression.

4. Vindictive rapists, who suffer from hostility specifically aimed toward women. Rape in this case is intended to degrade and punish the victim.

Other researchers have criticized Knight and Prentky's (1990) classification system as having limited utility for diagnosis and treatment of "less pathological sexually aggressive populations" (Hall & Hirschman 1991, p. 663). Hall and Hirshman (1991) developed a quadripartite model of sexual aggression that classifies subtypes of rape according to motivational precursors. The first subtype is characterized by physiological sexual arousal to aggressive contextual cues, which is modulated by deviant sexual fantasies. This is consistent with the DSM-IV diagnostic criteria for sexual sadism. It is hypothesized that this type of sexual aggressor is likely to have committed more than one act of sexual coercion with numerous victims (Abel, Becker, Mittleman, Cunningham-Rathner, Rouleau & Murphy 1987). Other characteristics that may differentiate this subtype from normal men is that aggressive cues may not inhibit sexual arousal (Marshall & Barbaree 1984). Evidence to support Marshall and Barbaree's inhibition theory of rape has been found with date rapists, whose sexual arousal was not inhibited when force was introduced into sexually explicit scenarios (Lohr, Adams & Davis 1994). A second subtype is characterized by a cognitive motivation for sexual aggression. In this case, cognitive distortions or justifications would determine the amount of physical violence exerted toward the victim, which would typically be low. Acquaintance rape has been hypothesized to be a common type of sexual aggression for this subtype (Koss 1985). Although the level of physical aggression in date rape is generally low, it may be facilitated by the aggressor's need for dominance in the sexual situation (Ellis 1989; Malamuth 1986). This view is consistent with the feminist perspective that hostility toward women and a need for dominance are prime motivators for sexually aggressive behavior (Brownmiller 1975). A third subtype of sexual aggression is marked by episodic affective dyscontrol (Knight & Prentky 1990). Unlike the deliberate, controlled aggression in the cognitive subtype, this category is characterized by opportunistic, unplanned, violent sexual and nonsexual aggression. A fourth subtype of sexual aggressor is characterized by a developmentally related personality problem or disorder as the motivational precursor (Hall & Proctor 1987). Chronic problems such as intellectual impairment, delinquency, family problems, poor social skills, poor adult adjustment, substance abuse, and general antisocial components would be characteristic of this subtype.

Characteristics of sexually assaultive males include antisocial personality traits such as impulsivity and irresponsibility (Lisak & Roth 1988; Rapaport & Burkhart 1984) and dominance over and hostility toward women (Malamuth 1986). Men who have sexually assaulted women and/or report a higher probability of doing so are more likely to accept myths and stereotypes about rape, are more tolerant of rape, and have more conservative attitudes about sex and sex roles (Koss, Leonard, Beezley & Oros 1985; Muehlenhard & Linton 1987). Developmental factors such as incidence of sexual abuse and deviation within the family of origin (Prentky, Knight & Rosenberg 1988) and earlier sexual experiences and greater promiscuity during adolescence (Koss & Dinero 1988) may be predisposing factors in sexual coercion and rape (Berkowitz 1992).

The term *rape* or *sexual assault* has typically been restricted to sexual encounters in which a male coerces a female to participate in undesired sexual activity under threat of physical violence (Sarrel & Masters 1982). Other than the cases of homosexual assault reported by men in prison, almost all reported victims are women who have been assaulted by men. Recently, a small body of research has accumulated that suggests that nonincarcerated men experience unwanted sexual contact from male and female acquaintances and strangers by means that range from verbal persuasion to physical force (Struckman-Johnson 1991). Research shows that approximately 10 percent of reported rape victims are men (Forman 1982; Gordon & Snyder 1988), although this estimate is considered conservative because most cases of male assault are not reported (Myers 1989). In a recent study of predominantly heterosexual college men, approximately one-third reported that they had experienced an episode of pressured or forced sex since the age of 16 (Struckman-Johnson & Struckman-Johnson 1994). Twenty-four percent indicated that a sexually coercive experience had occurred with women and 4 percent with men, and 6 percent reported that they had been coerced by both sexes. Although the majority of incidents involved verbal pressure, intoxication, and emotional manipulation, 12 percent of the instances could be described as forced sexual contact involving physical restraint or threat of harm. Most of these incidents involved female acquaintances or girlfriends. Sarrel and Masters (1982) presented a classification of typical cases of male sexual victims: (1) forced assault, where physical restraints or believable threats of physical violence are used, (2) "baby-sitter" abuse, in which a young boy is seduced by an older female, (3) incestuous abuse of a male minor by a female relative, and (4) dominant woman abuse, where a female aggressively approaches an adult male without direct physical force.

Despite the research supporting dimensional and/or categorical classification systems of rape, unless there is evidence of sadistic fantasy and behavior as determinants of the crime, rape by either sex would not qualify as a paraphilia in DSM-IV nomenclature. Sexual assaults when the suffering inflicted on the victim is far in excess of that necessary for compliance and is sexually arousing for the assailant are considered to be a severe form of sexual sadism. Yet in DSM-III-R (1987), it was estimated that only 10 percent of rapists met diagnostic criteria for sadism. Abel and Rouleau (1990) criticized the exclusion of rape from DSM and suggested that "the weight of scientific evidence supports rape of adults as a specific category of paraphilia" (p. 19). They argued that rapists and sadists exhibit significant differences in sexual arousal. For example, rapists are aroused to both consenting and nonconsenting sexual scenarios, whereas sadists typically are not excited by depictions of mutually consensual activity. Furthermore, depictions of nonsexual physical assault are sexually arousing for sadists but not for rapists (Abel, Becker, Blanchard & Flanagan 1981). In most cases, it appears that rapists' sexual arousal was not initiated by the psychological or physical suffering of their victims but was not impaired by this suffering either. This is consistent with Marshall and Barbaree's (1984) inhibition theory of rape motivation, which has accumulated empirical support with acquaintance rapists (Lohr, Adams & Davis 1994). As noted by McConaghy (1993), a delineation between sexually coercive behavior and sadism would seem to be a valid addition to the DSM classification. Opponents to this suggestion argue that a distinct diagnostic category of rape would become an excuse for sexually coercive acts and subsequently provide offenders a means of escape from the criminal justice system. Thus, political and legal motivations have precluded any changes in the classification system.

SADISTIC MURDER

Another condition that has been ignored by DSM-IV is sexual or sadistic homicide (Ressler, Burgess & Douglas 1988). Violent acts such as rape, mutilation, and murder are often associated with sadists, although they appear to be performed by this population rarely (McConaghy 1993). The rarity of sadistic murders is masked by widespread media attention that they receive. In a study by Swigert, Farrell, and Yoels (1976), of 444 cases of homicide, only 5 qualified as sexual homicides, and only 3 were considered congruent with severe sexual sadism.

Several studies have examined characteristics of these rare offenders (Dietz, Hazelwood & Warren 1990; Revitch 1980). Findings from these investigations indicate that the typical sexually sadistic murderer is a socially isolated male with flat affect who carefully plans and executes his killings. Crimes often involved careful selection of victims, approaching the victim under a pretext, restraining and beating victims, anal rape, forced fellatio, vaginal rape, foreign object penetration, and keeping personal items of the victims. Ejaculation may or may not accompany the aggressive acts. Characteristics of antisocial personality disorder often typify sadistic murderers. For example, one study found that 43 percent of their sample had prior arrests for nonsexual or nonsadistic sexual offenses, 50 percent reported abuse of drugs other than alcohol, and 100 percent had engaged in an extensive pattern of antisocial behavior in adulthood (Deitz, Hazelwood & Warren 1990). Furthermore, approximately 20 percent of sexually sadistic murders exhibited evidence of other paraphilic behavior, such as exhibitionism, voyeurism, and telephone scatologia.

Recently another classification problem has emerged with the definitional revisions present in DSM-IV. In DSM-III -R (APA 1987), sexually arousing urges or fantasies involving psychological or physical suffering were sufficient for a diagnosis of sadism or masochism. According to DSM-IV, these urges and fantasies must be accompanied by actual behavior (that is, real, not simulated). This poses a problem in classification of individuals who do not use a partner but want to practice alone through fantasy (Stoller 1991). Thus, simulated suffering would no longer be categorized as sadistic or masochistic behavior. As a matter of fact, the use of the term *simulated* is confusing. How can an urge or fantasy be real, not simulated? How do you simulate a fantasy or urge?

ISSUES FOR FUTURE RESEARCH AND
CLINICAL ACTIVITY

Contrary to prior belief, the sadomasochistic subculture does not comprise a limited number of male homosexuals whose behavior often escalates to dangerous and violent acts. Research has shown that sadomasochism typically involves mutually consenting homosexual and heterosexual males and females who engage in activity that is safe and pleasurable for both partners.

Our current DSM-IV classification system does not appear to cover the breadth of sadistic and masochistic practices and cases of "sadism" that are evidenced in the literature. First, perhaps the frequently studied subculture of sadomasochists are not sadists or masochists but comprise a third and quite different group of individuals. Second, rape continues to be a categorizational problem in DSM-IV. Rapists constitute a manifestly heterogeneous group of sexual offenders (Knight & Prentky 1990) who may or may not possess the sadistic characteristics required for a diagnosis. Currently, only sadistic rapists could be appropriately classified, although empirical research would suggest other delineations as valid. Furthermore, sadistic murder appears to have been ignored by our current classification system. Finally, DSM-IV requires real (not simulated) sadistic or masochistic acts, which may preclude accurate diagnosis and treatment of distressed individuals who prefer simulation or fantasy.

Future research endeavors should continue to identify characteristics of individuals who engage in activities of a sadistic or masochistic nature. More specifically, delineations of types of sadists, masochists, and a perhaps subclinical subculture of sadomasochists need to be made for correct classification and subsequent study of these individuals. By improving our ability to classify individuals into specific subgroups (such as sexually coercive women, subtypes of rapists, sexually sadistic murderers), appropriate assessment, prevention, and intervention will be possible.

REFERENCES

Abel, G. G., Becker, J. V., & Flanagan, B. (1981). The behavioral assessment of rapists. In J. Hays, T. Roberts & K. Solway (Eds.), *Violence and the violent individual.* Holliswood, NY: Spectrum Publications.

Abel, G. G., Becker, J. V., Mittleman, M., Cunningham-Rathner, J., Rouleau, J. L., & Murphy, W. D. (1987). Self-reported sex crimes of nonincarcerated paraphiliacs. *Journal of Interpersonal Violence, 2,* 3–25.

Abel, G. G., & Rouleau, J. L. (1990). The nature and extent of sexual assault. In W. L. Marshall, D. R. Laws & H. E. Barbaree (Eds.), *Handbook of sexual assault: Issues, theories, and treatment of the offender* (pp. 23–52). New York: Plenum.

American Psychiatric Association. (1987). *Diagnostic and statistical manual of mental disorders* (3rd ed. rev.). Washington, DC: Author.

American Psychiatric Association. (1994). *Diagnostic and statistical manual of mental disorders* (4th ed.). Washington, DC: Author.

American Psychiatric Association. (1994). *DSM-IV casebook* (3rd ed. rev.). Washington, DC: Author.

Benson, D., Charlton, C., & Goodhart, F. (1992). Acquaintance rape on campus: A literature review. *Journal of American College Health, 40,* 157–165.

Berkowitz, A. (1992). College men as perpetrators of acquaintance rape and sexual assault: A review of recent research. *Journal of American College Health, 40,* 175–181.

Blader, J. C., & Marshall, W. L. (1989). Is assessment of sexual arousal in rapists worthwhile? A critique of current methods and the development of a response compatibility approach. *Clinical Psychology Review, 9,* 569–587.

Breslow, N., Evans, L., & Langley, J. (1985). On the prevalence and roles of females in the sadomasochistic subculture: Report of an empirical study. *Archives of Sexual Behavior, 14,* 303–317.

Brownmiller, S. (1975). *Against our will: Men, women and rape.* New York: Simon & Schuster.

Byard, R. W., Hucker, S. J., & Hazelwood, R. R. (1990). A comparison of typical death scene features in cases of fatal male and female autoerotic asphyxia with a review of the literature. *Forensic Science International, 48,* 113–121.

Dietz, P. E., Hazelwood, R. R., & Warren, J. (1990). The sexually sadistic criminal and his offenses. *Bulletin of the American Academy of Psychiatry and Law, 18,* 163–176.

Ellis, L. (1989). *Theories of rape.* New York: Hemisphere.

Forman, B. D. (1982). Reported male rape. *International Journal of Victimology, 7,* 235–236.

Gibbs, N. (1991, June 3). When is it rape? *Time,* pp. 48–54.

Gordon, S., & Snyder, C. W. (1988). *Personal issues in human sexuality.* Boston: Allyn & Bacon.

Gosselin, C. C. (1987). The sadomasochistic contract. In G. D. Wilson, *Variant sexuality: Research and theory* (pp. 229–257). Baltimore: Johns Hopkins University Press.

Gosselin, C. C., & Wilson, G. (1984). Fetishism, sadomasochism and related behaviors. In K. Howells (Ed.), *The psychology of sexual diversity* (pp. 89–110). Oxford: Basil Blackwell.

Hall, G. C. N., & Hirschman, R. (1991). Toward a theory of sexual aggression: A quadripartite model. *Journal of Consulting and Clinical Psychology, 59,* 662–669.

Hall, G. C. N., & Proctor, W. C. (1987). Criminological predictors of recidivism in a sexual offender population. *Journal of Consulting and Clinical Psychology, 55,* 111–112.

Janus, S. S., & Janus, C. L. (1993). *The Janus report on sexual behavior.* New York: Wiley.

Knight, R. A., & Prentky, R. A. (1990). Classifying sexual offenders: The development and corroboration of taxonomic models. In W. L. Marshall, D. R. Laws & H. E. Barbaree (Eds.), *Handbook of sexual assault: Issues, theories, and treatment of the offender* (pp. 23–52). New York: Plenum.

Koss, M. P. (1985). The hidden rape victim: Personality attitudes and situational characteristics. *Psychology of Women Quarterly, 9,* 193–212.

Koss, M. P., & Dinero, T. E. (1988). Predictors of sexual aggression among a national sample of male college students. In R. A. Prentky & V. L. Quinsey (Eds.), *Human sexual aggression: Current perspectives* (pp. 133–147). New York: New York Academy of Sciences.

Koss, M. P., Gidycz, C. A., & Wisniewski, N. (1987). The scope of rape: Incidence and prevalence of sexual aggression and victimization in a national sample of higher education students. *Journal of Counseling and Clinical Psychology, 55,* 162–170.

Koss, M. P., Leonard, K. E., Beezley, D. A., & Oros, C. J. (1985). Nonstranger sexual aggression: A discriminant analysis of psychological dimensions. *Sex Roles, 12,* 981–992.

Koss, M. P., & Oros, C. J. (1982). Sexual Experiences Survey: A research instrument investigating sexual aggression and victimization. *Journal of Consulting and Clinical Psychology, 50,* 455–457.

Krafft-Ebing, R. von. (1886). *Psychopathia sexualis with especial reference to the antipathic sexual instinct: A medico-forensic study.* Chicago: Login Brothers.

Langevin, R., Ben-Aron, M. H., Couthard, R., Heasman, R., Purins, J. E., Handy, L. C., Hucker, S. J., Russon, A. R., Day, D., Roper, V., Bain, J., Wortzman, G., & Webster, C. D. (1985). Sexual aggression: Constructing a predictive equation. A controlled pilot study. In R. Langevin (Ed.), *Erotic preference, gender identity, and aggression in men: New research studies* (pp. 39–76). Hillsdale, NJ: Erlbaum.

Lee, J. (1979). The social organization of sexual risk. *Alternative Lifestyles, 2,* 69–100.

Levitt, E. E., Moser, C., & Jamison, K. V. (1994). The prevalence and some attributes of females in the sadomasochistic subculture: A second report. *Archives of Sexual Behavior, 23,* 465–473.

Lisak, D., & Roth, S. (1988). Motivational factors in nonincarcerated sexually aggressive men. *Journal of Personality and Social Psychology, 55,* 795–802.

Lohr, B., Adams, H. E., & Davis, J. M. (1994). *Date rape: Sexual arousal to erotic stimuli depicting various levels of force among college perpetrators.* Manuscript submitted for publication.

McConaghy, N. (1993). *Sexual behavior: Problems and management.* New York: Plenum.

Malamuth, N. M. (1986). Predictors of naturalistic sexual aggression. *Journal of Personality and Social Psychology, 50,* 953–962.

Marshall, W. L., & Barbaree, H. E. (1984). A behavioral view of rape. Special issue: Empirical approaches to law and psychiatry. *International Journal of Law and Psychiatry, 7,* 51–77.

Moser, C. A. (1979). *An exploratory-descriptive study of a self-defined S/M sample.* Unpublished doctoral dissertation, Institute for the Advanced Study of Human Sexuality, San Francisco.

Moser, C. (1988). Sadomasochism. *Journal of Social Work and Human Sexuality, 7,* 43–56.

Moser, C., & Levitt, E. E. (1987). An exploratory-descriptive study of a sadomasochistically oriented sample. *Journal of Sex Research, 23,* 322–337.

Muehlenhard, C. L., & Linton, M. A. (1987). Date rape and sexual aggression in dating situations: Incidence and risk factors. *Journal of Counseling Psychology, 34,* 186–196.

Myers, M. G. (1989). Men sexually assaulted as adults and sexually abused as boys. *Archives of Sexual Behavior, 18,* 203–215.

Person, E. S., Terstman, N., Myers, W. A., Goldberg, E. L., & Salvadori, C. (1989). Gender differences in sexual behavior and fantasies in a college population. *Journal of Sex and Marital Therapy, 15,* 197–198.

Prentky, R. A., Knight, R. A., & Rosenberg, R. (1988). Validation analyses on MTC taxonomy for rapists: Disconfirmation and reconceptualization. In R. A. Prentky & V. Quinsey (Eds.), *Human sexual aggression: Current perspectives* (Vol. 528, pp. 21–40). New York: New York Academy of Sciences.

Rapaport, K., & Burkhart, B. (1984). Personality and attitudinal characteristics of sexually coercive college males. *Journal of Abnormal Psychology, 93,* 216–221.

Resnik, H. L. P. (1972). Eroticized repeated hanging: A form of self-destructive behavior. *American Journal of Psychotherapy, 26,* 4–21.

Ressler, R. K., Burgess, A. W., & Douglas, J. E. (1988). *Sexual homicide: Patterns and motives.* Lexington, MA: Lexington Books

Revitch, E. (1980). Gyocide and unprovoked attacks on women. *Correctional and Social Psychiatry, 26,* 6–11.

Sarrel, P., & Masters, W. (1982). Sexual molestation of men by women. *Archives of Sexual Behavior, 11,* 117–131.

Scott, G. G. (1991). *Erotic power: An exploration of dominance and submission.* New York: Citadel Press.

Spengler, A. (1979). Manifest sadomasochism of males: Results of an empirical study. *Archives of Sexual Behavior, 6,* 441–456.

Stoller, R. J. (1991). *Pain and passion: A psychoanalyst explores the world of S&M.* New York: Plenum.

Struckman-Johnson, C. (1991). Male victims of acquaintance rape. In A. Parrot & L. Bechhofer (Eds.), *Acquaintance rape: The hidden crime* (pp. 192–214). New York: John Wiley.

Struckman-Johnson, C., & Struckman-Johnson, D. (1994). Men pressured and forced into sexual experience. *Archives of Sexual Behavior, 23,* 93–114.

Swigert, V. L., Farrell, R. A., & Yoels, W. C. (1976). Sexual homicide: Social, psychological, and legal aspects. *Archives of Sexual Behavior, 5,* 391–401.

U.S. Department of Justice, Federal Bureau of Investigation. (1990). *Uniform Crime Reports. Rape statistics.* Washington, DC: U.S. Government Printing Office.

Weinberg, T. S. (1987). Sadomasochism in the United States: A review of recent sociological literature. *Journal of Sex Research, 23,* 50–69.

Wilson, G. D., & Gosselin, C. (1980). Personality characteristics of fetishists, transvestites, and sadomasochists. *Personality and Individual Differences, 1,* 289–295.

13

Pedophilia

Gene G. Abel and Candice Osborn

Pedophilia, according to the fourth edition of *Diagnostic and Statistical Manual of Mental Disorders* (DSM-IV) (American Psychiatric Association 1994), is a psychiatric diagnosis that identifies individuals who have recurrent, intense sexual urges and sexually arousing fantasies involving sexual activity with a prepubescent child (13 years of age or younger) that persist for at least six months. The pedophile must have acted on these urges or be markedly distressed by them. The pedophile must be at least 16 years of age and at least five years older than the children to whom he is attracted. The pedophile may target an individual of the same sex, the opposite sex, or both and is identified as either limited to incest or to nonincest or both, is either exclusive in type (attracted only to children) or nonexclusive (attracted to both children and adults).

Pedophilia is multifactorial in etiology. A review of the psychological literature (Abel & Blanchard 1974) indicates that there is surprising agreement on how pedophilic interests develop. The developing young child is surrounded by a variety of stimuli, including the people, activities and clothing, and objects surrounding him. As the child begins to experience his own body, bodily touching (including genital touching) becomes paired or associated with these objects, people, or activities. Development continues with differentiation of sexual arousal affected by the experiences of the child and his activities with others. As the child's body reacts to increasing levels of testosterone, he experiences a heightened sexual drive and incorporates the attitudes and beliefs of his culture.

Genital and nongenital touching, masturbation, and orgasm occur at an increasing frequency. In most Western cultures, talking about one's personal sexual interests is discouraged, so the child does not discuss his sexual interests and behavior with others, and, thus, they become idiosyncratic. Some personal sexual experiences are less interesting to the individual and are recalled less frequently or not at all. These images are then infrequently associated with the physical pleasures of touch, masturbation, or sexual interaction with a partner and, as a consequence, become nonerotic. Conversely, some of these unique images, sensations, and experiences are remembered more often and are used repetitively during sexual fantasizing so that events that may have occurred only once are paired hundreds or thousands of times with the pleasures of physical touching and/or orgasm.

When this process includes sexual fantasies of young children, the potential pedophile arrives at adolescence with a relatively well-established sexual interest toward children.

ETHOLOGIC FACTORS CONTRIBUTING TO PEDOPHILIA

The function of sex from an ethological point of view, as proposed by Feierman (1990), is to get one's genes in the gene pool. To accomplish this, the sexual preference pattern of the species has had to evolve so that the male chooses a partner who has a high probability of becoming impregnated during sexual intercourse. Adolescent boys initially find themselves attracted to older females (where intercourse would more probably lead to impregnation than with female peers). As the adolescent matures, there is a general shifting of the male's arousal to female peers, and as he becomes older still, to females younger than he. This gradual shifting of the male's arousal preference maximizes the probability of impregnation of his sexual partner. (See figure 13.1)

By adulthood, the average male is therefore attracted to young adult females, but nature is not perfect. Some males are not "average" and are attracted to partners who are not young adult females. The male sexual arousal pattern is actually a bell-shaped curve, with the average male being attracted to so-called nubile females. As the arms of the bell-shaped curve trail downward, some males are attracted to individuals possessing fewer feminine secondary sex characteristics than nubile females who are younger (adolescents) or considerably younger (children), or to individuals older with less robust feminine secondary sex characteristics (older females), that is, females older than they. At the bottom of the arms of the bell-shaped curve are individuals not attracted to feminine characteristics (homosexuals).

This ethological theory of the development of sexual preference indicates that, due to the imperfections of stimulus acquisition, there will always be pedophiles and ephebophiles (individuals attracted to adolescents 14 to 17 years of age).

Figure 13.1
Relationship of Gynephilic (Attracted to Female Targets) and Androphilic (Attracted to Male Targets) Pedophiles and Ephebophiles to the Normal Curve of Adult Males' Sexual Attraction.

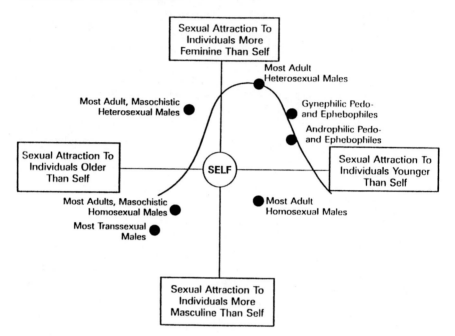

Source: Adapted from Feierman (1990).

THE IMPACT OF CULTURALIZATION

An individual's sexual preference is further modified by cultural and societal expectations. The adolescent whose development has led to a heterosexual arousal pattern fits in easily with a culture endorsing heterosexual interactions between adults. The adolescent with exclusive or nonexclusive pedophilic arousal, however, finds himself with an entrenched arousal pattern that conflicts with his culture's norms and laws. This adolescent pedophile's predicament is complicated by the taboo nature of talking about personal sexual arousal and the lack of information regarding pedophilic arousal and how to deal with it. Many adolescent pedophiles initially do not appreciate the intensity of their attraction to children and proceed with attempts to meet the cultural standard: heterosexual dating and heterosexual sexual interactions. This can be exceedingly difficult for the exclusive pedophile who has no sexual arousal to peers or adults and yet attempts to initiate and sustain such sexual interactions. It becomes apparent to the adolescent that, whereas his peers sustain arousal and sexual interactions with same-age partners, his arousal remains attached to younger children.

The resolution of the pedophile's quandary can take several routes. First, the impact of the cultural norms may be so great, and the anticipated negative consequences of acting on one's pedophilic interest so powerful, that the pedophile is able to suppress his pedophilic behavior, incorporate societal norms, and carry out a heterosexual sexual role with adults, while sometimes fantasizing about pedophilic experiences. Second, cultural factors may be only partially effective at suppressing or inhibiting pedophilic interest. In this case the pedophile is able to control his pedophilic interests and behavior except under circumstances that increase his sexual drive or decrease his control. The easy accessibility of sexual access to a vulnerable child, the blocking of access to an adult sexual partner, the increased stress of divorce, drug and alcohol misuse, or central nervous system damage may be contributors. Third, the pedophile (especially the exclusive type) may modify his lifestyle so as to have ready access to children by marrying a woman who already has children, moving to a culture in which sexual interactions between adults and children are accepted, joining groups or organizations that interact predominantly with children, or in a few cases engaging in sexual aggression upon children who are strangers to him.

MISCONCEPTIONS REGARDING PEDOPHILIA

Americans have become increasingly concerned about violence, especially sexual violence. The response has been an increased incidence of incarceration and a tougher criminal justice response to crime. Society's response to pedophilia is, in part, based on a number of misconceptions about pedophilia. These include the following myths:

Myth 1: Sexual activities between older males and younger females are abnormal. Most of American society believes that pedophiles are basically evil individuals who prey upon children because they are easy to victimize. We find it impossible to imagine how an individual could be sexually attracted to a child. In reality, most adult males are sexually attracted to individuals younger, smaller, and weaker than themselves. Furthermore, most males consider the neediness and/or helplessness of their sexual partners as sexually arousing. Attraction to children is, in actuality, an exaggeration of these normal proclivities.

Anthropological data (Okami & Goldberg 1992) suggest that the average age of marriage, cross-culturally, is between females 12 to 15 years of age and males 19 to 21 years of age. Adult males' sexual attraction to female adolescents is considered normal, and preferable, in many societies. Sociological and psychological studies indicate that both males and females tend to prefer heterosexual pairings where the male is stronger, larger, and older than the female. These findings suggest that our society needs to reexamine what constitutes "normal" sexual and marital pairings.

Myth 2: The term pedophile is interchangeable with child molester, sex offender, perpetrator, abuser, rapist, victimizer, and others. As Americans have become more alarmed with the reports of sexual behavior between adults and children and as more cases have led to criminal action, the term *pedophile* has frequently been misused to label any individual who carries out inappropriate sexual interaction with a child. Pedophilia is a psychiatric diagnosis describing the sexual preference of the patient; the term *child molester* describes an individual who carries out a sexual interaction with a child, regardless of the reason. Thus, not all child molesters are pedophiles because some individuals molest children for reasons other than having recurrent, intense sexual urges and/or fantasies involving sexual activity with children. Conversely, not all pedophiles act upon their urges, and therefore these pedophiles cannot correctly be labeled as child molesters.

The term *sex offender* applies to all individuals who carry out any type of sexual offense, including rape, exhibitionism, and voyeurism, as well as child molestation. *Rapist* refers to individuals who use force to accomplish a sexual interaction with an adult, nonconsenting partner. The terms *perpetrator, abuser,* and *victimizer* identify the individual who initiates the inappropriate sexual act and may be applied to all types of sex offenders.

This labeling problem is compounded in the media and the criminal justice system, where these terms are used indiscriminately and interchangeably without reference to the specific behavior being discussed. Legal terminology defining various forms of illegal sexual interaction varies tremendously from one state to another and is not consistent with the psychiatric terminology. For example, in the criminal justice system, sexual behavior between an adult and a child that would meet DSM-IV criteria for pedophilia may be labeled child rape, since, in many states, the legal terminology for sex with a partner who cannot consent is rape. Legally, the distinction between pedophilia and child molestation is irrelevant because the motive for the adult-child sexual interaction is not included in the legal definition of the offense. There are different degrees of murder based on the cause of the act (e.g., self-defense, accident, negligence) and whether the act was premeditated; however, with sex crimes, degree is based on the type of behaviors carried out (fondling, oral contact, penetration, etc.) and the viciousness of the act (use of force, a weapon, etc). In some states, acts between two children under 13 years of age are defined as sex crimes, with the older child being identified as the perpetrator, even if the younger child initiated the sexual act. This interaction would not be defined as pedophilia according to the DSM-IV criteria, nor would sexual interaction between adults and adolescents 14 to 17 years of age, although it is considered a sex crime in some states.

Unfortunately, these terms are also frequently misused within the professional literature, so it is extremely difficult to compare findings from different studies since the exact behavior being evaluated is unclear (Okami & Goldberg 1992).

Myth 3: Sexual molestation of children involves more female than male victims. Treatment programs for victims of sexual molestation serve predominantly female victims, which suggests that females are more frequently victimized than are males. Information collected from child molesters reveals contradictory data. When all types of sexual interactions between adults and children are examined, the majority of victims are indeed girls. This occurs because over 95 percent of sex crimes involve nontouching of the victim (e.g., exposing to or window peeping on children) and primarily target young girls. Excluding this category of victimization and examining sexual interactions that include actual touching of the victim indicates that 62 percent of all victims are boys (Abel 1989). Thus, there is a significant difference in rates of victimization between boys and girls depending on the type of behavior involved (touching or nontouching).

It is also probable that the referral pattern of victims of child molestation to treatment agencies favors girls. Boys are less likely to report being molested because if the perpetrator is a male, boys may fear that their being molested will be labeled as a homosexual experience. If the perpetrator is a female, boys may fear that they will not be believed or may be embarrassed that they could not "defend" themselves from a female.

Myth 4: Incest is the most common type of child molestation. Data from centers that provide treatment for victims of child molestation suggest that incestuous child molestation is exceedingly common when compared to nonincestuous child molestation. Studies of child molesters reveal quite the contrary; less than 1 percent of all victims of sexual molestation are primary family members, and only 20 percent of molestations involve incestuous victims (Abel 1989). This apparent discrepancy occurs because incestuous interactions are more likely to involve repetitious acts with the same victim than are nonincestuous interactions. Repetitious molestation is likely to produce significant physical and emotional consequences to the child, subsequent referral to a therapist for treatment, and easier identification of the perpetrator for legal action. These consequences result in a skewed referral pattern for incest victims as opposed to nonincest victims and a subsequent overrepresentation of such victims in clinical populations known to therapists and the criminal justice system. This overrepresentation of victims of incest should not be confused with the actual prevalence of incestuous versus nonincestuous victims.

Myth 5: Sexual victimization of a child causes the child to become a pedophile as an adult. As society has become more aware of the prevalence of child molestation, it has become increasingly anxious to identify the etiology of pedophilia. When children are molested at an early age, they frequently act out sexual behavior inconsistent with their agemates and may also become involved in sexual behavior with peers similar to the behavior they participated in when victimized. This has led some to conclude that most child molestation results from the perpetrator's own prior sexual abuse as a child (Schwartz & Brasted 1985). If this were the case, however, 25 percent of all females and 10 percent of all males should be pedophiles (since most studies suggest that at least 25 percent of all females and 10 percent of all males under 18 years of age have been sexually molested). Data collected by Peters, Wyatt, and Finkelhor (1986) found significantly lower percentages of pedophiles in both male and female populations.

The assumption that pedophilia results from having been victimized as a child appears to have emanated from studies investigating the prevalence of childhood and adolescent histories of sexual behavior with adults among adjudicated and incarcerated sex offenders of children and adolescents. Subsequent studies involving not only incarcerated sex offenders but incarcerated nonsex offenders found no statistical difference between these two populations in terms of prior victimization (Condy, Templer, Brown & Veaco 1987; Gebhard, Gagnon, Pomeroy & Christianson 1965). Being molested as a child does, however, appear to have some influence on the gender selection of victims by pedophiles. The authors' data indicate that only 24 percent of those who molest girls report prior victimization, while 40 percent of those who molest boys report prior victimization, a finding significant at the .05 level (Abel & Rouleau 1990). However, a critical review of the abused-abuser hypothesis of child sexual abuse concluded that "sexual contact with an adult during childhood or adolescence is neither a necessary nor a sufficient cause of adult sexual interest in children or adolescents" (Garland & Dougher 1990, pp. 505–506).

Myth 6: Incarcerated or clinical populations are representative of the general population of child molesters. The majority of the scientific literature in the area of pedophilia involves incarcerated child molesters. Data from incarcerated perpetrators are skewed due to a number of factors:

1. Individuals who molest more children or whose acts are more aggressive are more likely to be incarcerated.
2. Socioeconomic factors can contribute to a child molester's successful defense, since higher socioeconomic status and higher intellectual functioning make it more likely that the perpetrator will be able to hire a more effective defense lawyer.
3. Individuals who carry out oral, rectal, or vaginal penetration represent only a small percentage of all child molesters; the vast majority of child molesters limit their sexual interactions with children to fondling. Perpetrators who primarily carry out fondling, however, are less likely to be incarcerated, so the incarcerated population is not representative of the general population of child molesters.
4. Repetition of pedophilic behavior with the same victim, especially a victim known to the perpetrator, is more likely to lead to identification of the perpetrator than acts involving perpetrators who are strangers to the child. As noted, incestuous crimes are more likely to be discovered and thus are over-represented in reports and convictions of sexual crimes.

Myth 7: Treatment for child molesters (including pedophiles) is nonexistent, ineffective, and too costly. Treatment for child molesters, when accompanied by appropriate supervision of the perpetrator, produces at least a 20 percent reduction in recidivism compared to incarceration without treatment (Marshall & Barbaree 1990). The cost of bringing an accused child molester through the criminal justice system, including one year of incarceration without treatment, amounts to approximately $185,000 in the United States. One year of specialized cognitive-behavioral treatment in a group setting costs approximately $4,000. The cost savings of treatment, as opposed to incarceration, are immense.

A large number of child molesters are motivated for treatment or can become motivated for treatment once they become aware that effective treatment exists. Individuals dealing with child molesters within the criminal justice context see the perpetrator at his worst (usually denying the offense itself, denying responsibility for the offense, or minimizing the severity or significance of the offense). In the therapeutic setting, when the individual has had the opportunity to become involved in sex offender treatment, he generally is able to admit his offense, learn to accept responsibility for his actions, and eventually learn to appreciate the consequences of his action for the victim. By actively participating in treatment, the majority of child molesters are able to learn the necessary skills to prevent recurrence of their inappropriate sexual acts.

CONSENT INVOLVING SEXUAL INTERACTIONS
BETWEEN CHILDREN AND ADULTS

The issue of consent appears to be consistently confused by child molesters (Abel, Becker & Cunningham-Rathner 1984). Most child molesters take a rather simplistic view of the ability of children to give consent for sexual activities with an adult. The child molester assumes that if the child does what he says, the child is, in essence, giving consent. And if the child does not physically resist, does not report the activity to adults, participates a second, third, or fourth time in such activity, accepts rides, gifts, or favors from the perpetrator, or appears to enjoy the sexual interaction, the child molester assumes the child has given consent.

To add to the confusion, the child victim, and unfortunately sometimes friends or family members of the child, may question whether the child consented to the sexual interaction with the perpetrator. The child may feel that since he or she did not say "no" or did not physically resist, he or she consented to the interaction. Like the perpetrator who dismisses his sexual involvement with the child as consensual, the child may also perceive his or her behavior as consensual. In both instances, each side concludes it is right without understanding the actual requirements for informed consent.

First, before consent can be given, the participant has to know to what he or she is giving consent. To consent to a nephrectomy, for example, the individual must know what the term means and must understand the procedure. When adults agree to participate with other adults in sexual activity, they generally understand the nature of the acts involved, and thus consent is possible. Most children are uninformed regarding sexual activity between adults and children, and child molesters do not explain to their potential child participant what activity is expected. Therefore, it is impossible for the child to give consent.

Second, in order to give consent to an activity, the individual needs to know the potential consequences of the activity to which he or she is consenting. An individual may be aware of the elements of the proposed activity but unaware of the consequences of participating in that activity. If someone consents, for example, to using an experimental drug, he or she might be knowledgeable about what is involved in taking the drug but if not informed about the potential side effects of taking the drug, the person is not fully informed and therefore cannot give consent. Adults planning to involve themselves with a child do not outline for the child the negative consequences that may result from others learning of the activity, the likelihood of their being interrogated by victim counselors and the police should the event become known to others, the disruption in the family that could result from family members' becoming aware of the act, the ostracism or stigmatization of the child that may occur should he or she be viewed as having consented to the activity, the shame and guilt felt by many children, or the resultant financial, legal, and emotional consequences on family members. Since the child is not made aware of these factors, informed consent cannot be given.

Third, consent cannot be given unless the individual is able to deny consent without fear of possible consequences. This can occur only when both individuals are on an equal power basis. Adults are larger, stronger, and in positions of authority over children and therefore have a higher power base. As a result, it is not possible for a child to consent to sexual interaction with an adult.

Finally, an individual being asked to participate in a sexual interaction must know the available alternatives, that is, the alternatives to participating in the interaction. These alternatives are virtually never provided to a child by the adult making such requests, and, as a consequence, informed consent cannot be given.

It would be helpful if the criteria for giving informed consent were made known to both adults and children. This issue is generally never discussed, either because the activity is concealed or, once the activity becomes public knowledge, society takes the position that since adult-child sexual interaction is morally wrong, there is no need to clarify the issue of consent. Unfortunately, adults involved in such activities then retain the belief that adult-child sexual activities are perfectly acceptable as long as the child directly or indirectly appears to agree to the participation. However, informed consent is not a simple yes or no issue.

SOCIETY'S RESPONSE TO ADULT-CHILD SEXUAL INTERACTIONS

Society's response to adult-child sexual interaction is frequently sizable but surprisingly ineffective at reducing adult-child sexual interactions. The National Organization for Women, the grass-roots support group for victims of sexual assault, should be given credit for identifying child abuse and the sexual assault of adults as a public health problem. The outcome of this heightened public awareness has been the improvement and expansion of health services for the victim under the assumption that better support services for the victim will significantly reduce such child molestation. The problem with such a focus is that an individual has to be victimized before these services are provided. Furthermore, given the high frequency of such victimizations, it is exceedingly unlikely that sufficient therapists or monies can be made available to provide therapy for all victims of sexual abuse. In fact, many communities have long waiting lists for these services.

The criminal justice system's response to sex crimes is to increase and toughen the laws against sex crimes under the assumption that fear of legal consequences and incarceration will serve as a sufficient deterrent to sex crimes. However, there is generally a gap of several years between a sex offender's perpetration of his first sex crime and his first arrest. During this lag time, many further victimizations occur. Furthermore, the majority of pedophiles develop their pedophilic interests prior to age 18 and, as a consequence, have been involved in a variety of victimizations of younger children long before they generally come of age for incarceration (Abel, Osborn & Twigg 1993). Equally problematic is that when incarcerated, child molesters who generally are free of other antisocial behaviors, spend time with more experienced, chronic offenders and thereby become hardened and more prone to participate in antisocial acts once released.

Finally, when child molesters are incarcerated, many of them rely on their fantasies for developing sexual arousal and gratification. They repeatedly use those fantasies familiar to them, pedophilic fantasies, and there is even further pairing and association between pedophilic fantasy and the pleasure of genital touching and orgasm.

Religious approaches, like other approaches, have never condoned child molestation, but the moralistic approach to the problem of child molestation has proven ineffective. A religious approach views the molestation of children as immoral but at the same time is a strong advocate of forgiveness as being a solution to this problem. As reviewed in various books recounting the problems that churches have had in dealing with child molesters within their organizations, forgiveness is frequently a camouflage that perpetrators of adult-child sexual interaction use to admit the inappropriateness of their behavior and to ask for and receive forgiveness while at the same time maintaining their pedophilic preferences (Berry 1992).

Psychiatry and psychology, until the last few decades, have also stumbled in their attempts to deal with this major public health problem via intrapsychic therapies. Psychoanalytic and twelve-step addiction programs have yet to demonstrate, in controlled outcome studies, their effectiveness at treating child molesters. By contrast, cognitive-behavioral treatment and hormonal therapies have demonstrated potential success. The key aspect of psychological and psychiatric treatment, however, appears to be a thorough, unified, cooperative effort to monitor the pedophile (and other child molesters) in his environment so as to ensure awareness of his potential for molestation and the need to reduce those factors that increase the risk of molesting a child. Such an approach (Abel & Osborn in press; Abel & Rouleau 1990; Marques, Day, Nelson & Miner 1989; Pithers 1990; Pithers, Marques, Gibat & Marlatt 1983) requires not only therapies to reduce the pedophile's sexual preference for children but also therapies to increase normative skills so as to allow greater comfort in interacting with potential adult sexual partners, as well as the combined efforts of family, friends, work associates, and especially probation or parole officers' involvement in monitoring the child molester's behavior from the criminal justice vantage point (Abel & Rouleau 1990). Such efforts demand cooperation across disciplines that have traditionally been quite territorial in their approach to this problem. Pivotal to this cooperative effort, however, is the attitude of society toward this public health problem.

Our culture appears to be so inflamed and angered by child molestation that it has difficulty separating its emotional response to perpetrators from the issue of which approach is most successful at reducing the public health problem of child molestation. Society's response to those with illnesses such as tuberculosis, AIDS, and drug addiction has typically been to label the affected individuals and attempt to separate them from society, without understanding the source or etiology of the problem, or how to treat and monitor individuals with these illnesses so as to prevent further victimizations. Society's response to child molestation has followed the same pattern. The more recent cognitive-behavioral therapies and hormonal therapies, incorporated with an organized monitoring system as described in the relapse prevention model, appear to be the most effective approach for reducing the victimization of children by pedophiles and other child molesters. The next step is to enjoin society to participate in a combined effort to implement treatment for child molesters in order to accomplish our ultimate goal: prevention of the victimization of children.

REFERENCES

Abel, G. G. (1989). Behavioral treatment of child molesters. In A. J. Stunkard & A. Baum (Eds.), *Perspectives on behavioral medicine* (pp. 223–242). Hillsdale, NJ: Lawrence Erlbaum Associates.

Abel, G. G., Becker, J. V., & Cunningham-Rathner, J. (1984). Complications, consent and cognitions in sex between children and adults. *International Journal of Law and Psychiatry, 7*(1), 89–103.

Abel, G. G., & Blanchard, E. B. (1974). The role of fantasy in the treatment of sexual deviation. *Archives of General Psychiatry, 30*(6), 467–475.

Abel, G. G., & Osborn, C. A. (in press). Behavioral therapy treatment for sex offenders. In I. Rosen (Ed.), *Sexual deviation* (3rd ed.). London: Oxford University Press.

Abel, G. G., Osborn, C. A., & Twigg, D. A. (1993). Sexual assault through the life span: Adult offenders with juvenile histories. In H. E. Barbaree, W. L. Marshall & D. R. Laws (Eds.), *The juvenile sexual offender* (pp. 104–117). New York: Guilford Publications.

Abel, G. G., & Rouleau, J.-L. (1990). Male sex offenders. In M. E. Thase, B. A. Edelstein & M. Hersen (Eds.), *Handbook of outpatient treatment of adults* (pp. 271–290). New York: Plenum Press.

American Psychiatric Association. (1994). *Diagnostic and statistical manual of mental disorders* (4th ed.). Washington, DC: Author.

Berry, J. (1992). *Lead us not into temptation: Catholic priests and the sexual abuse of children.* Garden City, NY: Doubleday.

Condy, S. R., Templer, D. I., Brown, R., & Veaco, L. (1987). Parameters of sexual contact of boys with women. *Archives of Sexual Behavior, 16,* 379–394.

Feierman, J. R. (1990). A biosocial overview of adult human sexual behavior with children and adolescents. In J. R. Feierman (Ed.), *Pedophilia: Biosocial dimensions* (pp. 8–68). New York: Springer-Verlag.

Garland, R. J., & Dougher, M. J. (1990). The abused/abuser hypothesis of child sexual abuse: A critical review of theory and research. In J. R. Feierman (Ed.), *Pedophilia: Biosocial dimensions* (pp. 488–509). New York: Springer-Verlag.

Gebhard, P. H., Gagnon, J. H., Pomeroy, W. B., & Christianson, C. V. (1965). *Sex offenders: An analysis of types.* New York: Harper & Row.

Marques, J. K., Day, D. M., Nelson, C., & Miner, M. H. (1989). The sex offender treatment and evaluation project: California's relapse prevention program. In D. R. Laws (Ed.), *Relapse prevention with sex offenders* (pp. 247–267). New York: Guilford Press.

Marshall, W. L., & Barbaree, H. E. (1990). Outcome of comprehensive cognitive-behavioral treatment programs. In W. L. Marshall, D. R. Laws & H. E. Barbaree (Eds.), *Handbook of sexual assault: Issues, theories and treatment of the offender* (pp. 363–385). New York: Plenum Press.

Okami, P., & Goldberg, A. (1992). Personality correlates of pedophilia: Are they reliable indicators? *Journal of Sex Research, 29,* 297–328.

Peters, S., Wyatt, G., & Finkelhor, D. (1986). Prevalence. In D. Finkelhor, S. Araji, L. Baron, A. Browne, S. Peters & G. Wyatt (Eds.), *A sourcebook on child sexual abuse* (pp. 15–59). Beverly Hills, CA: Sage.

Pithers, W. D. (1990). Relapse prevention with sexual aggressors. In W. L. Marshall, D. R. Laws & H. E. Barbaree (Eds.), *Handbook of sexual assault: Issues, theories, and treatment of the offender* (pp. 343–361). New York: Plenum Press.

Pithers, W. D., Marques, J. K., Gibat, C. C., & Marlatt, G. A. (1983). Relapse prevention with sexual aggressives: A self-control model of treatment and maintenance of change. In J. G. Greer & I. R. Stuart (Eds.), *The sexual aggressor: Current perspectives of treatment* (pp. 214–239). New York: Van Nostrand Reinhold.

Schwartz, M., & Brasted, W. (1985). Sexual addiction. *Medical Aspects of Human Sexuality, 19,* 103–107.

14

Perpetrators of Incest

Patricia J. Long

Incest can be defined as any sexual contact, or behavior intended to be sexually stimulating, between persons who are biologically or legally related. This contact may include behaviors where no actual contact occurs (e.g., solicitations to engage in sexual activities, erotic material shown to a child) as well as all behaviors that do include sexual contact (e.g., fondling of the breasts and genitals, intercourse, and oral or anal sex). Recently, incest and childhood sexual abuse in general have gained recognition as problems of significant proportions.

Reviews of the literature on childhood sexual abuse indicate prevalence estimates ranging between 6 percent and 62 percent for females and from 3 percent to 31 percent for males (Peters, Wyatt & Finkelhor 1986; Salter 1992). Further, members of the extended and nuclear family are frequently found to be the perpetrators of these victimizations. For example, Finkelhor (1979) found family members to be the perpetrators of 43 percent of the female victims in his sample and of 17 percent of the male victims. Other researchers typically find family members to be perpetrators in 20 percent to 30 percent of the sexual abuse cases studied (Haugaard, cited in Haugaard & Reppucci 1988; Russell 1983).

Studies typically suggest that sibling sexual abuse is the most common form of incestuous behavior (Finkelhor 1980; Lindzey 1967). Abuse by fathers, stepfathers, and other father figures, although not as common as sibling incest, appears to account for approximately 24 percent of intrafamilial abuse cases (Russell 1983). Abuse by mothers has been thought to occur much more rarely (Finkelhor & Russell 1984).

While abuse by fathers and father figures is not the most frequent form of incest, abuse by these individuals comprises over 75 percent of reported incest cases and predominates in reports from the child welfare system (Finkelhor 1987; Kempe & Kempe 1984). Given this, and the findings that father-daughter/stepdaughter incest is one of the most common types of sexual abuse requiring mental health services and is among the most psychologically damaging to the victim (Harter, Alexander & Neimeyer 1988; Kendall-Tackett 1987; Russell 1983), father-daughter incest has become the most widely researched form of incest.

Despite the increasing research attention given to incest perpetrators, much is still to be learned about this group of sexual offenders. To date, no single taxonomy of incest perpetrators or of the etiology of incest has been developed. This perhaps is not surprising given that literature suggests that incest offenders tend to be a complex, heterogeneous group (Groth 1983; McIvor & Duthie 1986).

Researchers have investigated a number of factors in attempts to understand the phenomenon of incest and the incest perpetrator. Efforts to conceptualize the perpetrator have resulted in theoretically based classification systems, typologies based on personality characteristics, models of family dynamics, investigations of sexual arousal, and studies of single index behaviors thought to distinguish incest offenders from others. In addition, the behavior of incest offenders has been conceptualized within a multifactor theory.

Research within the area of incest is limited, however, by a number of methodological difficulties. Many theories about the incest perpetrator are based primarily on clinical cases. When these cases have been investigated, findings have often been limited by the uncontrolled nature of the studies. For example, frequently conclusions have been made based on studies with very small samples, using subjective measures, or lacking appropriate control groups. Control groups have also been used in an inconsistent manner across studies, thereby limiting conclusions. Within a topic area, studies may be available that compare incest offenders with nonoffenders, nonsexual offenders committing other crimes, pedophiles, or paraphiliacs. When looking at this body of literature as a whole, a systematic study of the factors of interest has rarely been conducted. Therefore, much of the evidence for the theories regarding incest should be viewed as preliminary.

This chapter provides an overview of the theories of incest and research on incest perpetrators. Given that father-daughter/stepdaughter incest has been the most commonly studied form of incest, this chapter will focus primarily on theories and findings with this group. Relative strengths and weaknesses of the research methodology employed and the strength of conclusions that can be drawn from the studies will be discussed within each area. Sibling incest and mother-child incest are addressed briefly at the end of the chapter.

THE FATHER-DAUGHTER INCEST PERPETRATOR

Fixated versus Regressed Offenders

Historically, sexual offenders were frequently classified into one of two types: fixated or regressed (Groth & Birnbaum 1978; Groth, Hobson & Gary 1982). According to this model, the fixated molester has an exclusive sexual orientation toward children, beginning in adolescence, which is the result of an arrestment in sociosexual maturation. Fixated offenders are thought to be sexually attracted to children based on identification with children and their desires to remain childlike, and no precipitation factors are typically associated with the onset of the orientation. Male children are most often abused by fixated offenders.

The regressed offender's sexual involvement with children, on the other hand, is thought to be a departure from a more characteristic attraction to adults. This change in orientation is thought to be brought about by a precipitating stressor and may vary in response to the level of stress experienced. Regressed offenders tend to select female victims, and frequently the victims are related to the offender.

Although this model was quite popular for a time, it is based primarily on anecdotal data and clinical descriptions of molesters. No empirical evidence exists for the accuracy of this classification system, and it appears that the majority of offenders may have characteristics of both the fixated and regressed type (Simon, Sales, Kaszniak & Kahn 1992).

Incest versus Paraphilia

A second classification system employed by researchers of sexual offenders classifies perpetrators into incestuous versus nonincestuous types. Traditionally incest perpetrators have been portrayed as a homogeneous, and unique, group of sexual offenders different from nonincestuous offenders (i.e., pedophiles). Some researchers now believe that this distinction is not useful in understanding the offender. With the exception that incest also involves complex family dynamics, it has been suggested that incest offenders may not be much different from pedophiles.

Pedophilia, as defined by the *Diagnostic and Statistical Manual of Mental Disorders* (DSM-III-R and DSM-IV: American Psychiatric Association 1987, 1994), involves recurrent, intense sexual urges and sexually arousing fantasies of at least six months' duration involving sexual activity with a prepubescent child. Pedophiles may be attracted solely to children (exclusive type) or to both children and adults (nonexclusive type). (For an overview of pedophilia see Abel and Osborne, this volume.)

It has been noted that although an individual may meet diagnostic criteria for pedophilia, some professionals believe that the incest offender should not receive a pedophilia diagnosis (Conte 1986, 1990, 1991). Conte indicated that many professionals believe incest is not a sexual disorder but merely a family problem. He indicated further that this belief rests on the assumptions that incestuous fathers and stepfathers act out sexually only in the home and that incest is the sexual expression of nonsexual needs. While family dynamics are important in the occurrence of incest, recent data bring into question the premise that incest offenders victimize only children in their own homes.

In two studies examining nonincarcerated paraphiliacs, Abel and his colleagues (Abel, Becker, Cunningham-Rathner, Mittelman & Rouleau 1988; Abel, Becker, Mittelman, Cunningham-Rathner, Rouleau & Murphy 1987) found that multiple paraphilias were very common in both male- and female-targeted incest pedophiliacs and that incest offenders averaged 1.8 victims. Of the subjects who reported female-targeted incest, 49 percent also engaged in female nonincestuous pedophilia, 12 percent in male nonincestuous pedophilia, and 12 percent in male incestuous pedophilia. Half or more of the incest offenders had molested outside their family, and over 70 percent had engaged in another paraphilia.

Additional findings are also reported by Marshall, Barbaree, and Eccles (1991). Using different subject selection and interviewing techniques from Abel and his colleagues, Marshall and colleagues found that incest offenders abused an average of 1.4 victims. This is similar to that reported by Abel et al (1988). However, only 7.9 percent of incest offenders were found to have more than one paraphilia in this study, as compared to greater than 70 percent in the Abel et al. (1988) study.

Chaffin (1994) noted that several methodological differences help to explain the differences found by these two groups of researchers. First, Abel et al. (1988) required that subjects meet diagnostic criteria for a paraphilia to be included in their study (subjects were not included because they had simply engaged in a particular behavior once but had to demonstrate repetitive urges to engage in this behavior, as required by DSM criteria). Marshall, Barbaree, and Eccles, on the other hand, included men simply on the basis of previous behavior, without requiring that they meet diagnostic criteria.

Second, Chaffin pointed out that the data management strategies of Abel et al. result in overrepresentation of multiple paraphilias, as secondary paraphilias diagnoses were made on the basis of single behaviors and subjects with more than one paraphilia are represented more than once in the data set. Third, it has been suggested that subjects in the Abel et al. study may have been more open to disclosing a variety of paraphilias as they were interviewed in a research setting (compared to the clinical patients studied by Marshall, Barbaree, and Eccles).

Although findings from these two studies are discrepant, each study suggests that there is a subgroup of incest offenders for whom perpetration is not limited to family members. Although the findings of Abel and his colleagues should be replicated, they do raise suspicion about the premise that incest perpetrators are somehow unique or different from other pedophiles.

Sexual Arousal

Another classification used for sex offenders focuses on the role of physiological sexual arousal. DSM-III-R and DSM-IV require such arousal for the diagnosis of pedophilia; however, many writers have suggested that incest is the sexual expression of primarily nonsexual needs, such as affection, love, depression, and poor self-esteem (Conte 1986, 1991). Furthermore, not all molesters always achieve physical arousal with abuse, thus limiting the importance of the role of arousal for at least some offenders (Lanyon 1986). These contradictory viewpoints have led researchers to investigate the actual arousal experienced by incest offenders. Study results, however, have been contradictory and limited by methodological difficulties.

In phallometric studies, pedophiles are expected to reveal greater or equal sexual arousal to children as compared to adults, but results from several studies examining this premise with incest offenders have not supported the hypothesis. Murphy, Haynes, Stalgaitis, and Flanagan (1986) and Quinsey, Chaplin, and Carrigan (1979) have found that incest perpetrators demonstrate somewhat "normal" age preferences (i.e., greater responding to adults than to children). In contrast, extrafamilial pedophiles show greater responding to children as compared to adults.

Other studies suggest, however, that incest perpetrators may be sexually aroused to children (Barbaree & Marshall 1989). Results of the Barbaree and Marshall study suggest that incest offenders can be divided equally among adult and nondiscriminating responders (those whose responses are characterized by substantial erectile response to adult slides and those whose responses are characterized by moderate arousal throughout the range of target ages, including arousal to children).

Not only have incest offenders' relative age preferences been studied, but their patterns of arousal to children have been compared to other child molesters. Quinsey, Chaplin, and Carrigan (1979), using slides of target subjects, compared the arousal of incest offenders and matched extrafamilial child molesters and found that daughter-incest offenders demonstrate more appropriate age preferences (less response to children) than extrafamilial pedophiles. Findings by Grossman, Cavanaugh, and Haywood (1992), Murphy et al. (1986), and Marshall, Barbaree, and Christophe (1986), all also using slides as stimuli, support this difference in responding between incest and extrafamilial perpetrators.

Some debate has arisen over this finding, however, as other results have not supported these differences between incest offenders and extrafamilial pedophiles in erectile responses. For example, Abel, Becker, Murphy, and Flanagan (1981) examined arousal patterns and found extrafamilial and incest offenders to be equally aroused to children. This finding, which was established using audiotaped descriptions of sexual interactions as stimuli, has been replicated by Murphy et al. (1986), who also demonstrated that when slides are used as stimuli, incest offenders show more responding to adult stimuli than to child stimuli.

To explain these findings, it has been suggested that since audio cues only describe a child verbally, the incest offender may be able to imagine his own daughter in the scene, therefore increasing his arousal. Slides that depict a specific child may minimize this opportunity and may be less arousing for this reason (Murphy et al. 1986).

Sexual responses of incest offenders have also been compared to groups of nonoffenders. Four studies suggest that incest offenders as a group respond to child stimuli in the same way as do normals or matched nonoffender controls (Barbaree & Marshall 1989; Grossman, Cavanaugh, and Haywood 1992; Marshall et al. 1986; Quinsey, Chaplin & Carrigan 1979). Three of these same studies further suggest, however, that incest offenders display less arousal to adult women as compared to normals (Barbaree & Marshall 1989; Grossman, Cavanaugh & Haywood 1992; Marshall et al. 1986). In contrast, Frenzel and Lang (1989) found that incest perpetrators responded more to adolescent cues than did controls.

These study results suggest that incest cases may be more similar to normals in their sexual responding to children than extrafamilial pedophiles. However, conclusions regarding the role of sexual arousal in incest offenders would not be meaningful at this time. Studies investigating this issue are few and provide contradictory findings. Some studies suggest that incest perpetrators demonstrate age-appropriate sexual responding, while others do not. Some studies suggest that incest offenders respond differently than extrafamilial offenders do, while others suggest that they respond similarly. Clearly additional research is needed that employs adequate control groups to resolve these issues.

Personality and Psychopathology

Many of the early conceptualizations regarding incest perpetrators suggested that they were mentally or emotionally disturbed (Meiselman 1978). While it is generally believed now that most incest offenders do not experience significant pathology (other than their sexual offenses), research on personality features is common.

The Minnesota Multiphasic Personality Inventory (MMPI) is widely employed in clinical practice with sexual offenders and has been the subject of some research investigations. Researchers have attempted to identify an MMPI profile type associated with incest; however, these attempts have been largely unsuccessful. Support from numerous studies indicates that the MMPI profiles for intrafamilial perpetrators are essentially normal (subscale T-scores below clinical levels; Chaffin 1992; Hall 1989; Hall, Maiuro, Vitaliano & Proctor 1986; Scott & Stone 1986) and do not distinguish incest offenders and matched controls (Scott & Stone 1986).

A few studies have identified more specific MMPI patterns in incest populations. Erickson, Luxenberg, Walbek, and Seely (1987) have noted that 4-3/3-4 code types are frequent among incestuous biological fathers (12.9 percent of the fathers demonstrated these code types, which are thought to describe chronic anger, overcontrolled hostility, marital discord, and a passive-aggressive personality style). Incestuous stepfathers were noted to demonstrate 4-7/7-4 code types most often (11.1 percent of the stepfathers demonstrated these code types) which are associated with insensitivity to others, acting out, and alcoholism. Erickson and colleagues have, however, cautioned that their findings "do not support descriptions of any MMPI profile type as typical of any sort of sex offender" (p. 569). Few of the incest perpetrators actually displayed these code types, though they were the most common, and all subjects were assigned to a code type regardless of the clinical elevation of their profile.

Significant elevations on the Depression, Psychasthenia, Hypomania, and Schizophrenia subscales of the MMPI have also been noted from reviews of forensic and clinical files of incest perpetrators (Kirkland & Bauer 1982; Langevin, Paitich, Freeman, Mann & Handy 1978). Overall, findings with this instrument suggest that incest offenders are as varied as all other populations, and no one feature distinguishes this group from nonoffenders.

Poor self-esteem, lack of empathy, narcissism, and self-centeredness are additional personality traits that have been hypothesized to be related to incest offending (Gilgun 1988; Steele 1982). However, support for these characteristics comes primarily from clinical descriptions, and most empirical studies examining these traits find either no differences in personality characteristics between incest offenders and control subjects or no significant difficulties compared to normative information (Dadds, Smith, Webber & Robinson 1991; Langevin & Watson 1991).

Some data suggest that incest offenders as a group are generally shy and introverted (Gebhard, Gagnon, Pomeroy & Christenson 1965; Langevin 1983). A study by Milner and Robertson (1990) suggested that intrafamilial abusers display elevated levels of personal distress, unhappiness, loneliness, and rigidity. Poor social skills have also been noted in this group of men (Ballard, Blair, Devereaux, Valentine, Horton & Johnson 1990). Overall, however, incest offenders do not appear to share a common personality characteristic.

Alcohol is another factor hypothesized to play a role in the occurrence of incest. Reviews of the literature on this topic have suggested that incest offenders are the most likely of all pedophiles to be involved with alcohol (Aarens, Cameron, Roizen, Room, Schrerberk & Wingard 1978; Morgan 1982). Incest offenders also appear more likely to be both chronic alcohol users and to be drinking at the time of the offense, as compared to extrafamilial abusers (Avery-Clark, O'Neil & Laws 1981; Crewdson 1988; Erickson, Walbek & Seely 1987; Gebhard et al. 1965; Langevin & Lang 1990).

Araji and Finkelhor (1985) have speculated that alcohol may act as a disinhibitor to committing sexual abuse and may have some social meaning that allows a perpetrator to ignore cultural sanctions against sexual offenses. Alternatively, Cole (1992) has suggested that alcohol use by incest perpetrators may simply be an example of a more general pattern of poor impulse control. While it appears that alcohol is a common behavior problem among this group of offenders, studies are not available that investigate whether alcohol is a more frequent problem for incest offenders than for nonoffenders. This issue needs further investigation.

Other Individual Characteristics

Intelligence is another aspect of the incest offender that has been questioned. Results to date, however, do not suggest that this group of offenders differs from the general population (Hall 1989). Similarly, testosterone, follicle-stimulating hormone, luteinizing hormone levels, mental retardation, senility, and other brain pathology have not been shown to be related to sexual abuse (Lang, Flor-Henry & Frenzel 1990; Mohr, Turner & Jerry 1964; Regestein & Reich 1978), and computerized tomography scans have not distinguished incest offenders from offenders committing nonsexual crimes (Langevin, Wortzman, Dickey, Wright & Handy 1988).

It has been speculated that incest offenders may have distorted cognitions about children, which may help maintain their offending. Abel, Becker, and Cunningham-Rathner (1984) have developed an instrument to identify perpetrators' beliefs and have suggested that several distortions can be found among child molesters. These include the beliefs that children who do not resist want the sexual activity, that having sex with a child is educational for the child, that children who do not disclose the abuse wish the sexual activities to continue, and that children who ask questions about sex want to engage in sexual activities with adults.

Lang and Frenzel (1988) have further noted that incest offenders often either pretend or believe the child victim enjoyed the sexual activity with them and have exhibited stereotypic thinking about sex with children (e.g., seeing children as sexy and seductive, believing children initiate the sexual activity). Other researchers have also described distorted beliefs in child molesters about children and children's sexuality (Ballard et al. 1990; Gilgun & Connor 1989; Gore 1988; Gudjonsson 1990; Howells 1978; Pollock & Hashmall 1991). Empirical research in this area is relatively recent and has been criticized on methodological grounds (Langevin 1991). In addition, much of the research in this area has examined child sexual molesters as a group and has not examined the beliefs of incest perpetrators specifically. Additional research is needed to determine the role of cognitions in incest perpetrators' behavior.

Abuse History and Family of Origin Issues

Currently a popular belief is that childhood sexual abuse experiences may contribute to later sexual offending in perpetrators. This theory is based on social learning tenets and suggests that perpetrators learn sexual attraction to children through the processes of modeling and conditioning. It has also been suggested that the former victim takes on the perpetrator role later in life to resolve sexual trauma through identification with the more powerful perpetrator (Groth, Hobson & Gary 1982).

A number of studies are available to support the hypothesis that incest offenders were once physically or sexually abused themselves (Ballard et al. 1990; Erickson, Walbek & Seely 1987; Faller 1989; Langevin 1983; Parker & Parker 1986). Researchers have cautioned against hasty conclusions about the role of previous victimization in later perpetration, however (Murphy & Peters 1992). Many of the studies described here did not use control groups to examine the prevalence of childhood abuse. Thus, it is unknown if perpetrators in these samples are reporting abuse at levels higher than nonoffenders would. It has also been noted that the prevalence of sexual abuse for males ranges between 3 percent and 31 percent (Peters, Wyatt & Finkelhor 1986), but not all of these males later sexually offend. Therefore, assuming that early victimization will lead to later life perpetration appears too simplistic a model. Instead, such a history in combination with many other factors probably results in later offending.

An additional factor that clouds research on the role of childhood victimization comes from a study by Hindman (1988), who assessed a group of offenders before and after a lie detector procedure was introduced in her clinic. Perpetrators were asked about their previous histories of abuse at both assessments; results indicated that prior to the introduction of the lie detector, 67 percent of the offenders reported having been abused, as compared to only 21 percent of these same perpetrators after the lie detector was introduced. These findings call into serious question the validity of perpetrators' reports of childhood sexual victimization.

In addition to suggestions of prior victimization, researchers have also suggested that perpetrators are more likely to have been reared in dysfunctional families. Such families have been described clinically as unstable (Ballard et al. 1990), dysfunctional, and chaotic (Hanson, Lipovsky & Saunders 1994; Langevin, Wright & Handy 1989).

Retrospective reports have also found incestuous fathers to have experienced greater parental maltreatment than fathers committing other crimes (Parker & Parker 1986). Neglect and emotional abandonment by parents are also commonly reported by incest perpetrators (Justice & Justice 1979; Meiselman 1978; Will 1983).

Given the retrospective nature of these findings, and the fact that perpetrators are describing their families after they themselves have been identified as offenders, conclusions regarding the role of the families of origin of perpetrators would be inappropriate at this time. Nevertheless, results of this kind have led some to speculate that it may be the subtle characteristics within the family of origin, in combination with previous victimization, that lead an individual to offend sexually later in life (Hanson, Lipovsky & Saunders, 1994).

THE INCEST FAMILY

Family systems theories and concepts have long been considered the primary explanations of incest. However, this approach has come under increasing criticism in the past decade (Conte 1982; Finkelhor 1986a). Criticisms of these models are based on their limited scope and treatment implications (that incest is the fault of child, mother, and father). In addition, little empirical evidence exists to support many of the premises of these models. Nonetheless, systems theories continue to play a substantial role in the treatment of offenders and their families.

Family Dynamics

It is a popular belief that incest is a response to dysfunctional family dynamics. Systems theorists describe incest as being characterized by a pathological triangle comprising three persons: the adult perpetrator, the child victim, and the colluding, nonparticipating other adult (typically the mother; Rist 1979). According to this model, which has been described by Gelinas (1988), several characteristics, including bilateral marital estrangement, parentification of the child, and relationship imbalances among family members, play an important role in the occurrence of incest.

Gelinas has speculated that bilateral estrangement occurs with stress, often with the arrival of the first child. The mother in the incestuous family is thought to be ambivalent about the birth of the child but nevertheless shifts her attention toward the child and away from the husband. Over time, the wife is thought increasingly to avoid the husband, who then makes greater demands for her attention, affection, and nurturance. Gelinas postulates that the mother induces the victimized child gradually to assume caretaking responsibilities for the family by the mother. As the mother experiences more and more stress, the parentified child steps in to assist the mother in completing household tasks. With the mother's emotional estrangement and relational avoidance and the daughter's parentification, the father's attempts to meet his emotional needs through his daughter are thought to lead to incest. The mother is seen as encouraging the incest by consciously or unconsciously pushing the daughter toward the father and distancing herself from the daughter. This process, while potentially damaging, serves to stabilize the marital situation and allows members to avoid family dissolution.

Consistent with this model, others have suggested that the father-daughter incestuous family is a closed system with limited interactions outside the family and frequent social isolation (Alexander 1985; Gutheil & Avery 1977; Will 1983). The incestuous family has been further described as enmeshed and as having blurred family roles and high levels of internal disorganization (Will 1983).

Despite the fact that there is much speculation about these family dynamics, little evidence exists to support these specific patterns beyond simple clinical descriptions. For example, some researchers have found evidence of mother-daughter role reversal (Herman & Hirschman 1981), while others have not (Conte 1985). Weinberg (1955) has noted that incestuous fathers have been emotionally dominant in the family, while mothers have been indifferent to their daughters' situations. Role disorganization has also been reported. However, these findings are based solely on interviews with family members.

Using direct observations and questionnaires, Olson (1982) has found denial, inappropriate coalitions between father and daughter, and vague boundaries in incest families. Serrano, Zuelzer, Howe, and Reposa (1979) have also found support for maternal and paternal realignment patterns suggested by the systems model; incestuous families have reported a higher degree of involvement between fathers and daughters and less involvement between mothers and daughters. However, no study has used control groups, making comparisons to nonabused families difficult. On the other hand, Madonna, Van Scoyk, and Jones (1991) have found incest families to have rigid family beliefs, dysfunctional coalitions, emotional unavailability of parents, and little nurturance of autonomy in children, as compared to a clinical control population. More indirect support for this model comes from research on the mothers of incest victims. Several studies have noted that many women married to incest perpetrators were themselves sexually abused as children (Faller 1989; Goodwin, McCarty & Divasto 1982; Mayer 1983). It is thought that this history contributes to intergenerational abuse. Mothers have also been found to have high rates of physical and mental problems and to be emotionally distant (Finkelhor 1979; Herman 1981).

Other studies examining the family of incest victims focus not on specific dynamics but rather investigate the general environment of the family. These studies also examine this issue from the victims' perspective, typically in retrospective studies. Although conclusions from these studies are somewhat limited given the retrospective nature of the data, they are often stronger than other available studies because they employ standardized measures of family constructs and control groups.

Overall results of these studies suggest that incest families are somewhat pathological. Dadds et al. (1991) have noted that, as reported by mothers on the Family Environment Scale, incest families had higher levels of conflict and greater organization, and lower levels of cohesion, expressiveness, and active recreation, than did a matched comparison group. Alexander and Lupfer (1987) indicate that incest victims describe their families as having more traditional male-female and parent-child relationships than extrafamilial sexual abuse victims or nonvictims. Extending these findings, Harter, Alexander, and Neimeyer (1988) found that intrafamilial abuse victims described their families as less cohesive and less adaptable. Also reported was greater perception of social isolation.

Intrafamilial victims have described their families as less cohesive, more controlling, and less concerned with family members' personal growth (Jackson,

Calhoun, Amick, Maddever & Habif 1990). Having a stepfather, the absence of the mother, and mother disability have been associated with increased risk for the occurrence of incest and extrafamilial sexual abuse (Finkelhor 1979). Affective responsivity and affective involvement of family members have also distinguished intrafamilial and extrafamilial abuse victims' families (Hoagwood & Stewart 1989).

Results of the studies conducted thus far appear to suggest that family characteristics do distinguish the incestuous family from the nonincestuous family. However, these differences alone do not appear adequate to explain the occurrence of incest in all cases, and it is likely that other factors contribute to the perpetrators' behavior.

Marital Relationships

Impaired marital relationships may also contribute to the occurrence of incest. Control imbalances (Summit & Kryso 1987), ineffective communication patterns (Swanson & Biuggio 1985), unclear role expectations (Sgroi 1982), and sexual dissatisfaction (Pawlak, Boulet & Bradford 1991; Saunders, McClure & Murphy 1986) have been described between spouses in incest families. Lang, Langevin, Van Santen, Billingsley, and Wright (1990), in a study of incest perpetrators, have also reported that these mens' relationships were characterized by marital disharmony (especially distrustfulness), lack of time spent together, and emotional instability in both partners. Incest offenders reported confiding less in their spouses, being less cooperative in disagreements with spouses, and feeling more lonely in their marriage as compared to control subjects. Others (Parker & Parker 1986) have found few differences in marital functioning between incest offenders and other individuals. Additional controlled studies are needed to determine the role of marital relationships in offending.

Stern and Meyer (1980) have hypothesized that there are three patterns of interactions between incest perpetrators and their wives. First is the dominant father who controls a passive wife and is thought to believe that he should be able to control his daughter and that it is his right to exploit her sexually. Second is the dependent father who has strong feelings of inadequacy, is dominated by a controlling wife, and is thought to gain a sense of power through exploiting and sexually abusing the daughter. And third, it is postulated that two dependent individuals come together who both have unmeetable needs: a wife who, when overwhelmed with excessive demands from the husband, withdraws emotionally, leaving the husband to turn to daughters to meet his needs for nurturance. No empirical studies have established these patterns of behavior.

FEMINIST EXPLANATIONS OF INCEST

Feminist explanations for incest and other forms of sexual abuse are based on the premise that the patriarchal social system perpetuates inequality between the sexes (Haugaard & Reppucci 1988). According to this model, men are taught that their rights are superior to women's, and women and children are seen as private sexual property (Brownmiller 1975). The feminist perspective further suggests that the social system reinforces this belief. Family members therefore must work to meet the father's needs.

Feminist writers have also pointed to the role of economic factors in the perpetuation of abuse (Haugaard & Reppucci 1988). Mothers and children tend to be economically dependent on fathers in patriarchal societies, so for economic survival, the family is required to conform to the father's wishes. Given these two factors, when the father turns to his daughter for sex, he will often feel justified. The child and mother may be unable to confront him and stop the incest because of their dependency on him and also because of the social beliefs they have learned.

Currently, many feminist ideas remain only theoretical conceptualizations. Some clinical writings support these premises, but few empirical studies are available that test this model. (For a more complete discussion of this position see Vander Mey 1992 and Adams, Trachtenberg & Fisher 1992.)

FINKELHOR'S MULTIFACTOR THEORY

While many of the ideas regarding the etiology of incest rely on single factors or classification schemes, simplistic approaches will likely be unsuccessful in explaining the behavior of all incest perpetrators. It is more likely that both sexual and nonsexual factors will need to be combined in one theory to describe the occurrence of incest. One such conceptualization, the four preconditions model of sexual abuse, has been put forth by Finkelhor (1984, 1986a, 1986b). Currently, this is the one widely accepted multifactor theory that has been proposed to account for the occurrence of incest.

The preconditions model incorporates a number of the single factors already reviewed into a more complex and comprehensive conceptualization of perpetration. While the four preconditions model was developed to explain all types of sexual abuse, intrafamilial and extrafamilial, Finkelhor (1986b) has reported its specific application to incest. Finkelhor has proposed that four preconditions must be met before sexual abuse will occur: (1) the potential offender must have some motivation to abuse a child sexually; (2) the potential offender must overcome internal inhibitions acting against that motivation; (3) the potential offender has to overcome external obstacles to acting on the motivation to abuse; and (4) the potential offender, or some other factor, must overcome the child's resistance. Finkelhor has proposed that the four preconditions are met in a sequential order, with the possibility that abuse will be averted at each step.

Precondition 1: Motivation

Finkelhor puts forth three components that may contribute to a potential offender's motivation to abuse: emotional congruence, sexual arousal, and blockage. Not all three components will necessarily be evident in every abuser, but it is thought that many offenders will experience all three and that all offenders will experience some combination of these factors.

Emotional congruence suggests that relating sexually to a child is motivated by a need, such as the desire to feel powerful or the need to resolve feelings from prior sexual abuse. Such concepts as low self-esteem, anxiety, feelings of inadequacy, and narcissism have been tied to this factor. It has frequently been hypothesized by family system theorists that incest serves as a way for the father to meet his sexual and emotional needs.

The second component of motivation is *sexual arousal*. A number of studies lend support to the idea that perpetrators find children sexually arousing. Previous abuse may contribute to this arousal through the processes of modeling and conditioning.

Blockage is the third component of motivation and refers to the fact that, for many abusers, alternate sources of sexual satisfaction are unavailable. This unavailability may be related to internal conflicts or lack of a suitable partner. Research suggesting the presence of marital discord, introversion, and social skills deficits in incest perpetrators is relevant to blockage.

Precondition 2: Disinhibition

The second precondition necessary for sexual abuse to occur is that the potential offender must overcome internal inhibitions. Finkelhor has suggested that such factors as alcohol use, stress, cognitive distortions, and personality disturbances may explain how inhibitions are overcome.

Precondition 3: Overcoming External Obstacles

Even if a potential perpetrator is motivated to abuse and has overcome his own internal inhibitions, external impediments frequently prevent abuse within a child's environment, and many individuals who may be motivated do not actually abuse because of environmental restraints. Conditions such as poor parental supervision, social isolation, and maternal absence or unavailability may contribute to the occurrence of abuse. In the case of incest, external obstacles may be limited as the mother may be alienated from the daughter or emotionally unavailable, or she may collude with the father to allow abuse to occur.

Precondition 4: Overcoming the Child's Resistance

Finally, a potential offender must overcome a child's resistance in order to abuse sexually. Such factors as emotional insecurity, lack of sexual knowledge, trust in the offender, and coercion are thought to increase a child's vulnerability to abuse. On the other hand, Finkelhor (1986b) has suggested that some children may be more able to deter abuse through fighting back, running away, or simply indicating to the perpetrator that they are unlikely to be fooled or manipulated into abuse.

The four preconditions model incorporates many of the features of family systems models and single factor models to create a more comprehensive explanation for incest. However, this model retains the focus of study on the perpetrator. While additional elements, such as maternal behavior, are incorporated, the responsibility for incest remains with the offenders (Finkelhor 1986b). External elements are relevant only in steps 3 and 4. Only the offender himself is involved in the initially required conditions. As Finkelhor (1986b) has noted, external agents "are only germane to the situation after a potential offender has taken some giant strides toward committing the offense" (p. 63). If the offender lacked motivation and had not overcome internal inhibitions, then external agents would play no role in the occurrence of victimization.

Although this model, as a single theory, has not been tested fully, many of the factors incorporated within it have been subjected to empirical study. In fact, the preconditions model in many ways can be seen as a method of summarizing each of the current theories of the etiology of incest into one larger model. This focus on multiple factors will likely improve our understanding of incest.

CONCLUSIONS REGARDING FATHER-DAUGHTER INCEST

A number of factors are said to play a role in the etiology of father-daughter incest. Each factor, however, has mixed support, and no single factor explains all cases of incest. It appears that the search for a single-factor explanation for the cause of incest may not be productive or necessary (Haugaard & Reppucci 1988). Instead, it is likely that incest can be attributed to multiple factors that vary by perpetrator, as illustrated in the four preconditions model proposed by Finkelhor (1984, 1986a, 1986b).

MOTHER-CHILD INCEST

Until recently, mother-child incest was believed to be extremely rare. Now, however, this premise, and the belief that women in general are rarely sexual offenders, is being examined more closely. Recent studies suggest that maternal abuse may not be uncommon. For example, the Dallas Incest Treatment Program, a child protective service of the Texas Department of Human Resources, found that 4 percent of the offender population consisted of mothers or mother figures (McCarty 1986). Other studies with incest populations, however, suggest much lower rates of maternal incest. For example, Russell (1986) found only 1 victim in 930 who reported sexual abuse by a mother.

Differences of opinions on the prevalence of female perpetration have led to discussion of factors that may prevent recognition of female-perpetrated child sexual abuse (Allen 1990). Allen has proposed three barriers that may minimize recognition of such abuse: (1) overestimation of the strength of the incest taboo for women, (2) an overextension of feminist beliefs, and (3) overgeneralization of the observation that female child abuse is rare (Allen notes that even if such abuse is rare, there may still be a significant number of females who abuse children).

Wakefield and Underwager (1991) in their review of female perpetrators have information suggesting that female offenses may less often be recognized. Women may disguise inappropriate contact though normal caretaking activities such as dressing and bathing, and children who experience incest may be unwilling to disclose such abuse because of their dependence on the mother. Boys may often be the victims and may be less willing to offer disclosures than girls, and the types of sexual activities in which mothers engage are less likely to be reported (e.g., sleeping with a son, fondling, exposing her body to a son) (Banning 1989; Groth 1979; Justice & Justice 1979). Others (Finkelhor & Russell 1984) have criticized these views from a feminist point of view, indicating that they underemphasize the importance of the male role in victimization.

Despite the controversy regarding the actual prevalence of maternal incest, new research is investigating factors that may motivate women to be sexually abusive. Conclusions must be made cautiously, however, since much of the available information comes from case descriptions or from studies with small samples. Wakefield and Underwager (1991), based on their review of the literature of female offenders, conclude that female sexual abusers are less likely than men to fit the psychiatric definition of pedophilia, that different circumstances may lead women to abuse as compared to men, and that women who abuse can be characterized as loners, socially isolated, alienated, likely to have had abusive childhoods, and likely to have emotional difficulties but not psychosis. Many of these conclusions are based on samples containing intrafamilial and extrafamilial female perpetrators because studies examining only mother-child incest are relatively rare.

SIBLING INCEST

While current research in the area of incest focuses predominantly on father-daughter incest, there is general agreement that the most frequent type of incestuous behavior occurs between siblings (Finkelhor 1980; Lindzey 1967). In a survey of college students, Finkelhor found that 15 percent of the females and 10 percent of the males reported some type of sexual experience with a sibling. Other studies find that sibling abuse occurs in 6 percent (Pierce & Pierce 1985) to 33 percent (Thomas & Rogers 1983) of the cases studied. Despite this high prevalence rate, sexual experiences between siblings have often been disregarded as "sex play" (O'Brien 1991), and therefore this form of sexual abuse has been relatively neglected.

This type of offense deserves serious attention. Research with adult sex offenders has noted that many of the men began offending in their adolescence

(Groth & Loredo 1981; Longo & Groth 1983) and that adolescents who commit minor crimes early in life often go on to commit more serious offenses later (Stenson & Anderson 1987). Thus, sibling incest may be a precursor to adult pedophilia and serious adult offending.

Despite the possible implications of this type of abuse, few studies are available that have examined this population. Becker, Kaplan, Cunningham-Rathner, and Kavoussi (1986) studied twenty-two adolescent males charged with sexual crimes against siblings and found that these individuals had committed a number of sexual crimes in addition to the one charged, reported a very early onset of sexual behavior, had additional DSM-III psychiatric disorders (conduct disorder is the most frequent), and reported previous sexual victimization.

O'Brien (1991) also studied a sample of 170 adolescent males referred for evaluation or treatment. He found that incest offenders had committed on average 18 separate sexual offenses against their siblings, that 45 percent of the sibling offenders had durations of abuse extending beyond one year in length, and that incest offenders were more likely to have engaged in sexual intercourse with their victims, as compared to nonincest offenders. Moreover, sibling incest offenders were more likely than extrafamilial child molesters to have two or more victims, and the majority of incest offenders molested children under the age of 9. With regard to etiological factors, O'Brien reported that sibling incest offenders were more likely than other offender groups to have been sexually abused by their fathers, had relatively higher rates of other sexual and physical abuse in their families of origin, and were more likely to have mothers who were victims of sexual abuse. Family dysfunction was found to be common. Incest offenders also had relatively low rates of prior sexual intercourse and demonstrated serious deficits in social skills as compared to nonclinical teens.

Meiselman (1978) has also noted family dysfunction, describing lack of parental supervision to be common among eight sibling incest cases she studied. Similarly, Smith and Israel (1987) have noted distant, inaccessible parents, an excessively sexual climate in the home, and the presence of frequent family secrets in the homes of twenty-five families with a sibling incest offender.

Pierce and Pierce (1990) studied a group of forty-three sibling incest offenders and found that 81 percent of the offenders were male, multiple offenses were common, fondling was the most common type of offense, and offenses were typically perpetrated against people who were younger. The majority of these offenders were described as aggressive toward their family, had been involved in delinquent acts, and had academic problems. Many of the perpetrators had been sexually and physically abused themselves, and the majority came from families in which the parents were judged to be mentally ill.

While the literature on sibling incest is still relatively brief, some general patterns do appear. Results from studies suggest that sibling offenders commit a number of sexual crimes with multiple victims, these victims tend to be younger than the offender, and the offenses typically start when the perpetrators are relatively young themselves. Further, family dysfunction and previous sexual and physical abuse of the perpetrator may also contribute to the tendency to offend. Clearly, additional research on this group of perpetrators in needed, however, before any firm conclusions about the etiological factors involved in sibling incest can be delineated.

CONCLUSIONS

Incest is a complex problem that occurs for a variety of reasons. However, the current state of the literature on incest prohibits conclusions regarding the etiology of this problem. Findings of studies are often contradictory and vary depending on the methodology employed, and many factors have only been described clinically and have yet to be tested empirically.

Continued work with incest offenders, examining the many issues reviewed in this chapter with improved methodology, will move the field closer to an understanding of the incest perpetrator and the etiology of incest. For example, investigations of the role of marital relationships, family dynamics, sexual arousal, and history of previous abuse would be greatly strengthened if both extrafamilial offender and nonoffender control groups were employed. Use of standardized measures in such areas as the investigation of family relationships and personality dimensions would be beneficial.

In addition, studies that examine multiple facets of offenders' behavior are needed. Research thus far suggests that an adequate explanation of incest will likely require consideration of more than single factors because incest offenders appear to be a heterogeneous group. The preconditions model Finkelhor (1984, 1986a, 1986b) proposed provides a good example of how multiple factors can be integrated. Researchers should move toward designing multivariate studies to understand the etiology of incest more fully.

ACKNOWLEDGMENTS

Special thanks are due to Maureen Sullivan, Ph.D., for comments on earlier versions of this chapter. Please address correspondence to the author at the Department of Psychology, 215 North Murray, Oklahoma State University, Stillwater, OK 74078-0250.

REFERENCES

Aarens, M., Cameron, T., Roizen, J., Room, R., Schrerberk, D., & Wingard, D. (1978). *Alcohol casualties and crime.* Berkeley: Social Research Group.

Abel, G. G., Becker, J. V., & Cunningham-Rathner, J. (1984). Complications, consent and cognitions in sex between children and adults. *International Journal of Law and Psychiatry, 7,* 89–103.

Abel, G. G., Becker, J. V., Cunningham-Rathner, J., Mittelman, M., & Rouleau, J. L.

(1988). Multiple paraphilic diagnoses among sex offenders. *Bulletin of the American Academy of Psychiatry and the Law, 16,* 153–168.

Abel, G. G., Becker, J. V., Mittelman, M., Cunningham-Rathner, J., Rouleau, J. L., & Murphy, W. (1987). Self-reported sex crimes of nonincarcerated paraphiliacs. *Journal of Interpersonal Violence, 2,* 3–25.

Abel, G. G., Becker, J. V., Murphy, W. D., & Flanagan, B. (1981). Identifying dangerous child molesters. In R. B. Stuart (Ed.), *Violent behavior: Social learning approaches to prediction, management, and treatment* (pp. 116–137). New York: Brunner/Mazel.

Adams, J. H., Trachtenberg, S., & Fisher, S. (1992). Feminist views of child sexual abuse. In W. O'Donohue & J. H. Greer (Eds.), *The sexual abuse of children: Theory and research* (Vol. 1, pp. 359–396). Hillsdale, NJ: Lawrence Erlbaum Associates.

Alexander, P. C. (1985). A systems theory conceptualization of incest. *Family Process, 24,* 79–87.

Alexander, P. C., & Lupfer, S. L. (1987). Family characteristics and long-term consequences associated with sexual abuse. *Archives of Sexual Behavior, 16,* 235–245.

Allen, C. M. (1990). Women as perpetrators of child sexual abuse: Recognition barriers. In A. L. Horton, B. L. Johnson, L. M. Roundy & D. Williams (Eds.), *The incest perpetrator: A family member no one wants to treat* (pp. 108–125). Newbury Park, CA: Sage.

American Psychiatric Association. (1987). *Diagnostic and statistical manual of mental disorders* (3rd ed. rev.). Washington, DC: Author.

American Psychiatric Association. (1994). *Diagnostic and statistical manual of mental disorders* (4th ed.). Washington, DC: Author.

Araji, S., & Finkelhor, D. (1985). Explanations of pedophilia: Review of empirical research. *Bulletin of the American Academy of Psychiatry and the Law, 13,* 17–37.

Avery-Clark, C., O'Neil, J. A., & Laws, D. R. (1981). A comparison of intra-familial sexual and physical child abuse. In M. Cook & K. Howells (Eds.), *Adult sexual interest in children* (pp. 3–39). Toronto: Academic Press.

Ballard, D. T., Blair, G. D., Devereaux, S., Valentine, L. K., Horton, A. L., & Johnson, B. L. (1990). A comparative profile of the incest perpetrator: Background characteristics, abuse history, and use of social skills. In A. L. Horton, B. L. Johnson, L. M. Roundy & D. Williams (Eds.), *The incest perpetrator: A family member no one wants to treat* (pp. 43–64). Newbury Park, CA: Sage.

Banning, A. (1989). Mother-son incest: Confronting a prejudice. *Child Abuse and Neglect, 13,* 563–570.

Barbaree, H. E., & Marshall, W. L. (1989). Deviant responses among heterosexual child molesters, father-daughter incest offenders, and matched non-offenders: Five distinct age preference profiles. *Canadian Journal of Behavioural Science, 21,* 70–82.

Becker, J. V., Kaplan, M. S., Cunningham-Rathner, J. C., & Kavoussi, R. (1986). Characteristics of adolescent incest sexual perpetrators: Preliminary findings. *Journal of Family Violence, 1,* 85–97.

Brownmiller, S. (1975). *Against our will: Men, women and rape.* New York: Simon & Schuster.

Chaffin, M. (1992). Factors associated with treatment completion and progress among intrafamilial sexual abusers. *Child Abuse and Neglect, 16,* 251–264.

Chaffin, M. (1994). Research in action: Assessment and treatment of child sexual abusers. *Journal of Interpersonal Violence, 9,* 224–237.

Cole, W. (1992). Incest perpetrators: Their assessment and treatment. *Clinical Forensic Psychiatry, 15,* 689–701.

Conte, J. (1982, May). *Sexual abuse and the family: Unraveling the myths.* Paper delivered at the Second National Conference on the Sexual Victimization of Children, Washington, DC.

Conte, J. R. (1985). Clinical dimensions of adult sexual abuse of children. *Behavioral Sciences and the Law, 3,* 341–354.

Conte, J. R. (1986). Child sexual abuse and the family: A critical analysis. *Journal of Psychotherapy and the Family, 2,* 113–126.

Conte, J. R. (1990). The incest offender: An overview and introduction. In A. L. Horton, B. L. Johnson, L. M. Roundy & D. Williams (Eds.), *The incest perpetrator: A family member no one wants to treat* (pp. 19–40). Newbury Park, CA: Sage.

Conte, J. R. (1991). Child sexual abuse: Looking backward and forward. In M. Q. Patton (Ed.), *Family sexual abuse: Frontline research and evaluation* (pp. 3–22). Newbury Park, CA: Sage.

Crewdson, J. (1988). *By silence betrayed.* Boston: Little, Brown.

Dadds, M., Smith, M., Webber, Y., & Robinson, A. (1991). An exploration of family and individual profiles following father-daughter incest. *Child Abuse and Neglect, 15,* 575–586.

Erickson, W. D., Luxenberg, M. G., Walbek, N. H., & Seely, R. K. (1987). Frequency of MMPI two-point code types among sex offenders. *Journal of Consulting and Clinical Psychology, 55,* 566–570.

Erickson, W. D., Walbek, N. H., & Seely, R. K. (1987). The life histories and psychological profiles of 59 incestuous stepfathers. *Bulletin of the American Academy of Psychiatry and the Law, 15,* 349–357.

Faller, K. C. (1989). Why sexual abuse? An exploration of the intergenerational hypothesis. *Child Abuse and Neglect, 13,* 543–548.

Finkelhor, D. (1979). *Sexually victimized children.* New York: Free Press.

Finkelhor, D. (1980). Sex among siblings: A survey on prevalence, variety, and effects. *Archives of Sexual Behavior, 9,* 171–194.

Finkelhor, D. (1984). *Child sexual abuse: New theory and research.* New York: Free Press.

Finkelhor, D. (1986a). *A sourcebook on child sexual abuse.* Beverly Hills, CA: Sage.

Finkelhor, D. (1986b). Sexual abuse: Beyond the family systems approach. *Journal of Psychotherapy and the Family, 2,* 53–65.

Finkelhor, D. (1987). The sexual abuse of children: Current research reviewed. *Psychiatric Annals, 17,* 233–241.

Finkelhor, D., & Russell, D. E. H. (1984). Women as perpetrators: Review of the evidence. In D. Finkelhor (Ed.), *Child sexual abuse: New research and theory* (pp. 171–187). New York: Free Press.

Frenzel, R. R., & Lang, R. A. (1989). Identifying sexual preferences in intrafamilial and extrafamilial child sexual abusers. *Annals of Sex Research, 2,* 255–275.

Gebhard, P., Gagnon, J., Pomeroy, W., & Christenson, C. (1965). *Sex offenders.* New York: Harper & Row.

Gelinas, D. J. (1988). Family therapy: Characteristic family constellation and basic therapeutic stance. In S. M. Sgroi (Ed.), *Vulnerable populations: Evaluation and treatment of sexually abused children and adult survivors* (Vol. 1, pp. 25–49). Lexington, MA: Lexington Books.

Gilgun, J. F. (1988). Self-centeredness and the adult male perpetrator of child sexual abuse. *Contemporary Family Therapy, 10,* 216–234.

Gilgun, J. F., & Connor, T. M. (1989). How perpetrators view child sexual abuse. *Social Work, 34,* 249–251.

Goodwin, J., McCarty, T., & Divasto, P. (1982). Physical and sexual abuse of children of adult incest victims. In J. Goodwin (Ed.), *Sexual abuse: Incest victims and their families.* Boston: John Wright PSG.

Gore, D. K. (1988). *Cognitive distortions of child molesters and the cognition scale: Reliability, validity, treatment effects, and prediction of recidivism.* Unpublished doctoral dissertation, Georgia State University, Atlanta.

Grossman, L. S., Cavanaugh, J. L., & Haywood, T. W. (1992). Deviant sexual responsiveness on penile plethysmography using visual stimuli: Alleged child molesters vs. normal control subjects. *Journal of Nervous and Mental Disease, 180,* 207–208.

Groth, A. N. (1979). *Men who rape: The psychology of the offender.* New York: Plenum Press.

Groth, A. N. (1983). Treatment of the sexual offender in a correctional institution. In J. G. Greer & I. R. Stuart (Eds.), *The sexual aggressor: Current perspectives on treatment.* New York: Van Nostrand Reinhold.

Groth, A. N., & Birnbaum, H. J. (1978). Adult sexual orientation and attraction to underage persons. *Archives of Sexual Behavior, 7,* 175–181.

Groth, A. N., Hobson, W. F., & Gary, T. S. (1982). The child molester: Clinical observations. *Journal of Social Work and Human Sexuality, 1,* 129–144.

Groth, A. N., & Loredo, C. M. (1981). Juvenile sexual offenders: Guidelines for assessment. *International Journal of Offender Therapy and Comparative Criminology, 25,* 31–39.

Gudjonsson, G. H. (1990). Cognitive distortions and blame attributions among paedophiles. *Sexual and Marital Therapy, 5,* 183–185.

Gutheil, T. G., & Avery, N. C. (1977). Multiple overt incest as a defense against loss. *Family Process, 16,* 105–116.

Hall, G. C. (1989). WAIS-R and MMPI profiles of men who have sexually assaulted children: Evidence of limited utility. *Journal of Personality Assessment, 53,* 404–412.

Hall, G. C., Maiuro, R. D., Vitaliano, P. P., & Proctor, W. C. (1986). The utility of the MMPI with men who have sexually assaulted children. *Journal of Consulting and Clinical Psychology, 54,* 493–496.

Hanson, R. F., Lipovsky, J. A., & Saunders, B. E. (1994). Characteristics of fathers in incest families. *Journal of Interpersonal Violence, 9,* 155–169.

Harter, S., Alexander, P. C., & Neimeyer, R. A. (1988). Long-term effects of incestuous child abuse in college women: Social adjustment, social cognition, and family characteristics. *Journal of Consulting and Clinical Psychology, 56,* 5–8.

Haugaard, J. J., & Reppucci, N. D. (1988). *The sexual abuse of children: A comprehensive guide to current knowledge and intervention strategies.* San Francisco: Jossey-Bass.

Herman, J. (1981). *Father-daughter incest.* Cambridge: Harvard University Press.

Herman, F., & Hirschman, L. (1981). Families at risk for father-daughter incest. *American Journal of Psychiatry, 138,* 967–970.

Hindman, J. (1988). Research disputes assumptions about child molesters. *NDAA Bulletin, 7,* 1–3.

Hoagwood, K., & Stewart, J. M. (1989). Sexually abused children's perceptions of family functioning. *Child and Adolescent Social Work, 6,* 139–149.

Howells, K. (1978). Some meanings of children for pedophiles. In M. Cook & G. Wilson (Eds.), *Love and attraction* (pp. 57–82). Elmsford, NY: Pergamon.

Jackson, J., Calhoun, K., Amick, A., Maddever, H., and Habif, V. (1990). Young adult women who report childhood intrafamilial sexual abuse: Subsequent adjustment. *Archives of Sexual Behavior, 19,* 211–221.

Justice, B., & Justice, R. (1979). *The broken taboo.* New York: Human Science Press.

Kempe, R. S., & Kempe, C. H. (1984). *The common secret: Sexual abuse of children and adolescents.* New York: W. H. Freeman and Co.

Kendall-Tackett, K. A. (1987). Perpetrators and their acts: Data from 365 adults molested as children. *Child Abuse and Neglect, 11,* 237–245.

Kirkland, K. D., & Bauer, C. A. (1982). MMPI traits of incestuous fathers. *Journal of Clinical Psychology, 38,* 645–649.

Lang, R. A., Flor-Henry, P., & Frenzel, R. R. (1990). Sex hormone profiles in pedophilic and incestuous men. *Annals of Sex Research, 3,* 59–74.

Lang, R. A., & Frenzel, R. R. (1988). How sex offenders lure children. *Annals of Sex Research, 1,* 303–317.

Lang, R. A., Langevin, R., Van Santen, V., Billingsley, D., & Wright, P. (1990). Marital relations in incest offenders. *Journal of Sex and Marital Therapy, 16,* 214–229.

Langevin, R. (1983). *Sexual strands: Understanding and treating sexual anomalies in men.* Hillsdale, NJ: Erlbaum.

Langevin, R. (1991). A note on the problem of response set in measuring cognitive distortions. *Annals of Sex Research, 4,* 287–292.

Langevin, R., & Lang, R. A. (1990). Substance abuse among sex offenders. *Annals of Sex Research, 3,* 397–424.

Langevin, R., Paitich, D., Freeman, R., Mann, K., & Handy, L. (1978). Personality characteristics and sexual anomalies in males. *Canadian Journal of Behavioral Sciences, 10,* 222–238.

Langevin, R., & Watson, R. (1991). A comparison of incestuous biological and stepfathers. *Annals of Sex Research, 4,* 141–150.

Langevin, R., Wortzman, G., Dickey, R., Wright, P., & Handy, L. (1988). Neuropsychological impairment in incest offenders. *Annals of Sex Research, 1,* 401–415.

Langevin, R., Wright, P., & Handy, L. (1989). Characteristics of sex offenders who were sexually victimized as children. *Annals of Sex Research, 2,* 227–253.

Lanyon, R. I. (1986). Theory and treatment in child molestation. *Journal of Consulting and Clinical Psychology, 54,* 176–182.

Lindzey, G. (1967). Some remarks concerning incest, the incest taboo, and psychoanalytic theory. *American Psychologist, 22,* 1051–1059.

Longo, R. E., & Groth, A. N. (1983). Juvenile sexual offenders in the histories of adult rapists and child molesters. *International Journal of Offender Therapy and Comparative Criminology, 27,* 150–155.

McCarty, L. M. (1986). Mother-child incest: Characteristics of the offender. *Child Welfare, 65,* 447–458.

McIvor, D. L., & Duthie, B. (1986). MMPI profiles of incest offenders: Men who molest younger children and men who molest older children. *Criminal Justice and Behavior, 13,* 450–452.

Madonna, P. G., Van Scoyk, S., & Jones, D. (1991). Family interactions within incest and nonincest families. *American Journal of Psychiatry, 148,* 46–49.

Marshall, W. L., Barbaree, H. E., & Christophe, D. (1986). Sexual offenders against female children: Sexual preferences for age of victim and type of behavior, and their relationship to intelligence and offense history. *Canadian Journal of Behavioral Science, 18,* 424–439.

Marshall, W. L., Barbaree, H. E., & Eccles, A. (1991). Early onset and deviant sexuality in child molesters. *Journal of Interpersonal Violence, 6,* 323–335.

Mayer, A. (1983). *Incest: A treatment manual for victims, spouses, and offenders.* Holmes Beach, FL: Learning Press.

Meiselman, K. C. (1978). *Incest: A psychological study of causes and effects with treatment recommendations.* San Francisco: Jossey-Bass.

Milner, J. S., & Robertson, K. R. (1990). Comparison of physical child abusers, intrafamilial sexual child abusers, and child neglecters. *Journal of Interpersonal Violence, 5,* 37–48.

Mohr, J. W., Turner, R. W., & Jerry, M. B. (1964). *Pedophilia and exhibitionism.* Toronto: University of Toronto Press.

Morgan, P. (1982). Alcohol and family violence: A review of the literature. In National Institute on Alcoholism and Alcohol Abuse, *Alcohol consumption and related problems* (Alcohol and Health Monograph 1, pp. 223–259). Washington, DC: Department of Health and Human Services.

Murphy, W. D., Haynes, M. R., Stalgaitis, S. J., & Flanagan, B. (1986). Differential sexual responding among four groups of sexual offenders against children. *Journal of Psychopathology and Behavioral Assessment, 8,* 339–353.

Murphy, W. D., & Peters, J. M. (1992). Profiling child sexual abusers: Psychological considerations. *Criminal Justice and Behavior, 19,* 24–37.

O'Brien, M. J. (1991). Taking sibling incest seriously. In M. Q. Patton (Ed.), *Family sexual abuse: Frontline research and evaluation* (pp. 75–92). Newbury Park, CA: Sage.

Olson, V. A. (1982). An exploratory study of incest family interactions. *Dissertation Abstracts International, 43,* 1995B–1996B.

Parker, H., & Parker, S. (1986). Father-daughter sexual abuse: An emerging perspective. *American Journal of Orthopsychiatry, 56,* 531–549.

Pawlak, A. E., Boulet, J. R., & Bradford, J. M. W. (1991). Discriminant analysis of a sexual-functioning inventory with intrafamilial and extrafamilial child molesters. *Archives of Sexual Behavior, 20,* 27–34.

Peters, S. D., Wyatt, G. E., & Finkelhor, D. (1986). Prevalence. In D. Finkelhor, S. Araji, L. Baron, A. Browne, S. D. Peters & G. E. Wyatt (Eds.), *A sourcebook on child sexual abuse* (pp. 15–59). Newbury Park, CA: Sage.

Pierce, L. H., & Pierce, R. L. (1990). Adolescent/sibling incest perpetrators. In A. L. Horton, B. L. Johnson, L. M. Roundy & D. Williams (Eds.), *The incest perpetrator: A family member no one wants to treat* (pp. 99–107). Newbury Park, CA: Sage.

Pierce, R., & Pierce, L. (1985). Analysis of sexual abuse hotline reports. *Child Abuse and Neglect, 9,* 37–45.

Pollock, N. L., & Hashmall, J. M. (1991). The excuses of child molesters. *Behavioral Sciences and the Law, 9,* 53–59.

Quinsey, V. L., Chaplin, T. C., & Carrigan, W. F. (1979). Sexual preferences among incestuous and non-incestuous child molesters. *Behavior Therapy, 10,* 562–565.

Regestein, Q. R., & Reich, P. (1978). Pedophilia occurring after the onset of cognitive impairment. *Journal of Nervous and Mental Disease, 166,* 794–798.

Rist, K. (1979). Incest: Theoretical and clinical views. *American Journal of Orthopsychiatry, 49,* 680–691.

Russell, D. E. H. (1983). The incidence and prevalence of intrafamilial and extrafamilial sexual abuse of female children. *Child Abuse and Neglect, 7,* 133–146.

Russell, D. E. H. (1986). *The secret trauma: Incest in the lives of girls and women.* New York: Basic Books.

Salter, A. C. (1992). Epidemiology of child sexual abuse. In W. O'Donohue & J. H. Greer (Eds.), *The sexual abuse of children: Theory and research* (Vol. 1, pp. 108–138). Hillsdale, NJ: Lawrence Erlbaum Associates.

Saunders, B., McClure, S., & Murphy, S. (1986). *Final report: Profile of incest perpetrators indicating treatability.* Charleston, SC: Crime Victims Research and Treatment Centre.

Scott, R. L., & Stone, D. A. (1986). MMPI profile constellations in incest families. *Journal of Consulting and Clinical Psychology, 54,* 364–368.

Serrano, A. C., Zuelzer, M. B., Howe, D. D., & Reposa, R. E. (1979). Ecology of abusive and nonabusive families. *Journal of Child Psychiatry, 75,* 175–179.

Sgroi, S. M. (1982). Family treatment. In S. M. Sgroi (Ed.), *Handbook of clinical interventions in child sexual abuse* (pp. 241–267). Lexington, MA: Lexington Books.

Simon, L. M. J., Sales, B., Kaszniak, A., & Kahn, M. (1992). Characteristics of child molesters: Implications for the fixated-regressed dichotomy. *Journal of Interpersonal Violence, 7,* 211–225.

Smith, H., & Israel, E. (1987). Sibling incest: A study of the dynamics of 25 cases. *Child Abuse and Neglect, 11,* 101–108.

Steele, B. (1982). Abusive fathers. In S. Cath, A. Gurwitt & J. Ross (Eds.), *Father and child* (pp. 481–490). Boston: Little, Brown.

Stenson, P., & Anderson, C. (1987). Treating juvenile sex offenders and preventing the cycle of abuse. *Journal of Child Care, 3,* 91–102.

Stern, M. J., & Meyer, L. (1980). Family and couple interactional patterns in cases of father/daughter incest. In B. Jones, L. Jenstrom & K. McFarlane (Eds.), *Sexual abuse of children* (pp. 83–86). Washington, DC: US Government Printing Office.

Summit, R., & Kryso, J. (1987). Sexual abuse of children: A clinical spectrum. *American Journal of Orthopsychiatry, 48,* 237–251.

Swanson, L., & Biuggio, M. K. (1985). Therapeutic perspectives on father-daughter incest. *American Journal of Psychiatry, 142,* 667–674.

Thomas, J., & Rogers, C. (1983). A treatment program for intrafamily juvenile sexual offenders. In J. Greer & I. Stuart (Eds.), *The sexual aggressor: Current perspectives on treatment* (pp. 127–143). New York: Van Nostrand Reinhold.

Vander Mey, B. J. (1992). Theories of incest. In W. O'Donohue & J. H. Greer (Eds.),

The sexual abuse of children: Theory and research (Vol. 1, pp. 204–260). Hillsdale, NJ: Lawrence Erlbaum Associates.

Wakefield, H., & Underwager, R. (1991). Female child sexual abusers: A critical review of the literature. *American Journal of Forensic Psychology, 9,* 43–69.

Weinberg, S. K. (1955). *Incest behavior.* New York: Citadel Press.

Will, D. (1983). Approaching the incestuous and sexually abusive family. *Journal of Adolescence, 6,* 229–246.

15

Hypersexuality and Impulsive Sexual Behaviors

Victor J. Malatesta and Matthew S. Robinson

The diagnosis of sexual addiction seemed ridiculous and almost laughable to this 41-year-old, married, successful businessman who actually enjoyed, and to some extent, took pride in, his long history of multiple sexual partners, extramarital affairs, and periodic frequenting of "high-class" prostitutes and "gentlemen's" clubs. He agreed to see a professional only after he was confronted again by his justifiably angry and exasperated wife, who threatened divorce if he did not see someone. Informed of his diagnosis after a clinical interview with a therapist who specialized in addictions, he was told that his initial treatment plan recommended (1) a period of complete sexual abstinence, including marital intercourse, masturbation, and bottom-line forms of sexual acting out, (2) weekly individual psychotherapy, and (3) involvement in a twelve-step, AA-oriented self-help group, SLAA (Sex and Love Addicts Anonymous). After reluctantly attending his first SLAA meeting and hearing the painful personal stories of men and women alike (who, surprisingly, were struggling with different, but in many respects similar, sexual activities and resultant negative feelings), he finally realized that since early adolescence, he had been "addicted to love and sex." (from the authors' case files)

The characterization of sexual disorders is continually reshaped by powerful sociocultural and medical-political influences. When the 1960s ushered in an era of increased sexual freedom, experimentation, and relaxed inhibitions, people who came to view themselves as deficient in this area and were distressed by their "inhibitions" found help eventually in a mental health system that identified and later recognized officially a disorder called "inhibited sexual desire" (Kaplan 1977; Lief 1977; APA 1980). Therapists struggled with issues of treatment, theoretical controversy was stimulated, and a range of clinical and empirical challenges was unleashed (Kaplan 1979; Schover & LoPiccolo 1982).

Considerable good came from these developments. A plethora of research studies was generated, sexual assessment and treatment were advanced (Leiblum & Rosen 1988), and we came to appreciate—both clinically and theoretically—the importance of individual variations in sexual interest and activity. On the other hand, while therapeutic approaches became broader and more inclusive, a blurring of sex therapy occurred, which tended to reinforce more nonempirical approaches to treatment (Malatesta & Adams 1993).

Decades later, society has shifted its attention to the other end of the sexual continuum. Confronted by the growing reality of sexual abuse, the tragedy of AIDS and other sexually transmitted diseases, and other threats to an emerging traditionalism in long-term relationships, society has come to focus on those individuals whose sexual behavior is "excessive." Variants of sexual activity—rather than enhancing pleasure and intimacy and affirming one's self-esteem—are instead resulting in emotional and physical pain, shame and embarrassment, violation of other individuals, and the breakdown of important personal values. What once may have been regarded as liberated is now viewed as "addictive" or "compulsive." Again, clinicians are struggling with treatment issues, healthy theoretical controversy has been stimulated (Coleman 1986), and it has forced us to look more closely at the range of deviant sexual behaviors, including the paraphilias—all representing erotic activities that have both intrigued and repulsed society.

We are now in the very early stages of development in understanding and conceptualizing sexual behavior that has been labeled variously as compulsive, addictive, or impulsive in nature. Very few empirical data exist, yet treatment has proliferated to a point where there are now specialists in sexual addiction, specialized inpatient units for treatment of sexual dependencies, and several self-help groups devoted to the "disease" of sexual addiction (e.g., Sex and Love Addicts Anonymous, Sexaholics Anonymous). Although sincere, well intentioned, and addressing a previously unidentified group of individuals troubled by their sexual behavior (but who have not sought help), these treatment approaches have tended to reify the condition of sexual addiction. Conceptual curiosity, empirical developments, and even thoughtful assessment and treatment have been stymied, and the field has become mired in confusion and controversy regarding description, classification, diagnosis, and treatment.

This chapter sets out to address the nature of hypersexuality, trace the development and confusion associated with characterizing sexual activity that appears compulsive, impulsive, or addictive in nature, and review important issues and directions in description, classification, etiology, and treatment of these disorders.

THE NATURE OF HYPERSEXUALITY

Problems in Terminology and Labeling

Men and women who display high levels of sexual desire and engage in frequent and varied sexual activities have always been viewed by society with either fascination and admiration, or fear and degradation. Ambivalence about such behavior is reflected in society's exploitation of the power of sex and in its pathological or pejorative labeling of these activities.

In general, such individuals have been considered "hypersexual" (Masters, Johnson & Kolodny 1986). More pejoratively, individual labeling is demonstrated by use of the sexist term *nymphomania,* which, incidentally, has had greater popularity and has experienced a longer and more detailed psychiatric history than its male counterpart, *satyriasis* (Levine 1982). Societal ambivalence about "excessive" sexual drive and behavior has helped to generate a lexicon of various terms, which are unclear, ambiguous, and ultimately destructive. Table 15.1 provides a listing of terms that have been used historically to label variants of hypersexual behavior.

Not surprisingly, the use of terms to label the sexual activities of men and women has functioned to censor and to control individual sexual behavior. This pattern is at odds with the tenets of scientific psychopathology, even though it is impossible always to separate politics from science. A good example is the "depathologizing" of homosexuality by the American Psychiatric Association in 1974. After a heated and lengthy debate, the organization voted to remove the term from the official psychiatric nomenclature in the second edition of the *Diagnostic and Statistical Manual of Mental Disorders* (DSM-II: APA 1968). However, by the time the next edition was published (DSM-III: APA 1980), a compromise term was included: *ego-dystonic homosexuality.*

Classification of Hypersexuality

A more basic question is whether "hypersexual" individuals suffer from a disorder or illness or are just more endowed sexually. The question reflects the age-old problem of defining sexual normality and has been addressed by numerous authors.

The range and variation of human sexual activity make it impossible arbitrarily to define an individual's sexual behavior as abnormal or pathological based on inclination or frequency alone. Despite data from statistical surveys and diverse observations, the normal parameters of human sexual behavior have

Table 15.1
Terms Used Historically to Label Variants of Hypersexuality

Name of Historical Term	Origin and Description of Term
Satyriasis	Derived from the satyrs of Greek mythology. The satyrs were part-man, part-animal and were symbols of the sexually active male. The term commonly refers to an acute onset of: 1) marked increase in sex drive, 2) extremely frequent sexual behavior, and 3) numerous sexual partners. In addition, satyriasis often involves abnormal duration of the sex act. The use of the term is restricted to males.
Nymphomania	Derived from the nymphs of Greek mythology. Although the nymphs were less single-minded in their sexual pursuits than the satyrs, some nymphs behaved much as the satyrs did. The term commonly refers to an acute onset of the same 3 symptoms as are listed above. The use of the term is restricted to females.
Don Juanism	Derived from numerous literary portrayals of the fictional character Don Juan. The first portrayal of the profligate lover is attributed to the playwright Gabriel Tellez in 1630. Men who use sex as a weapon of conquest or punishment, successively seducing and abandoning their many lovers.
Hyperlibido	Originates from psychoanalytic theory and is used predominantly within the psychodynamic orientation. The term commonly refers to an acute increase in sex drive that is symptomatic of an underlying psychiatric disorder.
Primary Hyperactive Sexual Desire	Used by Kaplan (1979) to describe rare cases in which excessive sexual desire is the patient's primary complaint. A similar phenomena is labeled in the ICD-10 as Excessive Sexual Drive (Diagnostic Code F52.7).

yet to be established (Lazarus 1988). Even the most recent survey of nonclinical human sexual behavior sheds little light upon what is normal, only reinforcing the reality of human diversity and individual differences in sexual activity and inclination (Laumann, Gagnon, Michael & Michaels 1994).

A major difficulty in the classification of abnormal sexual behavior is reflected in the basic level of scientific development in sexual psychopathology. For example, despite advances in the conceptualization and treatment of sexual dysfunctions, we still rely on a binary classification system to diagnose presence or absence of a disorder, although the binary system has serious limitations. It implies that there is a discrete class of sexually dysfunctional individuals and a discrete class of sexually functional individuals; neither permits an analysis of the degree of a sexual problem or attends to the fact that people with sexual problems do not necessarily display a sexual dysfunction (see Apfelbaum 1977 for an expansion of this argument).

Paraphilias may be on somewhat firmer ground regarding classification. Instead of a multivariate or quantitative approach (which implies that all behavior occurs in degrees and can thus be placed on a continuum), it can be argued that the paraphilias may be best classified from a binary, class, or qualitative difference model, which assumes that some psychopathological disorders do not occur in the normal population. Money's (1986) outstanding work on paraphilia is a good example of effective utilization of this model.

While paraphilias may be best classified from a class or qualitative perspective, the same classification scheme does not apply to hypersexuality. Hypersexuality in and of itself cannot be regarded as a disorder per se, since it conforms more closely to the quantitative or multivariate model, which assumes a continuum. Moreover, before calling a behavioral pattern a disorder, it is also necessary to address other principles of classification. For instance, the criterion of labeled deviance addresses the extent to which a behavioral pattern is clinically significant, causing objective or subjective distress to the individual, and/or violates social norms. Similarly, the criterion of adjustment involves the degree to which a behavioral pattern exerts a negative biological or psychological effect on individual functioning (see Adams & Cassidy 1993 regarding the topic of abnormal classification).

Sexual Desire and Hypersexuality

As a starting point, therefore, clinical scientists have emphasized from a theoretical perspective that problems of sexual desire can be conceptualized as lying on a continuum ranging from hypoactive to hyperactive degrees of intensity. Using this quantitative or multivariate model, "normal" degrees of sexual desire would be placed somewhere in the middle of the distribution, and problems in desire would lie at either extreme. This framework addresses the range of human sexual desire and highlights the fact that "normal" desire and interest is just one point along a continuum. It also suggests that discrepancies in desire between two partners may represent a primary reason for distress and dissatisfaction within a relationship (Zilbergeld & Ellison 1980) and may be an important precursor to related problems in hypersexual behavior.

Hypersexuality and Other Factors

Sexual desire is only one part of the picture. Consistent with this multivariate perspective, it is likely that a continuum of sexual activity exists that is at least partially independent of sexual desire. Clinically, we may elaborate by using the example regarding partner discrepancies in desire. For example, it is a commonly reported pattern that one partner with a relatively lower level of sexual desire may engage—at least temporarily—in more frequent and varied sexual activity in order to avoid conflict and/or to satisfy a demanding partner who exhibits a relatively higher level of sexual desire. There is also the commonly reported scenario of the insecure male's engaging in frequent sexual intercourse with multiple partners—not because of high levels of sexual desire but as a way of self-validation and shoring up a fragile self-esteem. Finally, some individuals may engage in frequent sex primarily as a way to relieve tension or cope with loneliness.

These examples point to the fact that people may engage in higher levels of sexual activity as a function of factors other than sexual desire per se, and they may help to explain why the concept of hypersexuality remains a clinical enigma and one of the most controversial topics in clinical science. Moreover, this is why Kaplan (1979), Leiblum and Rosen (1988), and Lazarus (1988) have all viewed hyperactive sexual desire as a relatively rare disorder: "Basically, very few individuals experience an excessive or constant desire for sex per se; most who are viewed as sexually hyperactive tend to rely on sexual outlets to relieve discomfort (be it tension, insecurity, anxiety, or any other negative states of mind)" (Lazarus 1988, pp. 146–147). Similarly, Kaplan (1979) has stated, "In my experience, excessive sexual desire is so rare as to constitute a clinical curiosity when it is a primary symptom" (p. 76). In this regard, she distinguishes primary hyperactive sexual desire from those situations where high levels of sexual activity are a result of mood disorder (e.g., manic or hypomanic states), marked anxiety and tension, and obsessions centered on fears of inadequate sexual performance.

Finally, the paraphilias, discussed elsewhere in this book, represent another area where hyperactive sexual desire may operate in conjunction with sexual arousal to deviant thoughts, images, and behaviors. It is unclear, however, if individuals suffering from paraphilias characteristically exhibit a relatively higher level of sexual desire (Rosen & Beck 1988). Similarly, the paraphiliac may engage in high levels of deviant sexual activity not only because of hypersexual desire but also to satisfy a host of functions, ranging from self-punishment to issues of control and power (Money 1986).

Conceptually, therefore, hypersexuality may be regarded as a multiply determined set of behaviors, cognitions, and emotions that is a function of at least three factors: (1) level of sexual desire and pleasure seeking, (2) negative mood states and their avoidance or alleviation through sexual activities, and (3) concurrent or comorbid psychopathology. We will return to this later.

HYPERSEXUALITY: CONFUSION AND CONTROVERSY

Behavioral Pattern: Description

Independent clinicians (Carnes 1983; Coleman 1986; Quadland 1985; Schwartz & Brasted 1985) have described a similar pattern of hypersexual behavior:

- A preoccupation with idiosyncratic sexual activities that in many respects function to relieve negative mood states and/or produce pleasure and other positive emotions.

- A strong urge to engage in these activities in a repetitive or stereotyped manner and over which the individual experiences a perceived lack of control.
- Involvement in such activities to a point where it is self-injurious, interferes with, and undermines normal intimacy, relationships, and other life demands (e.g., career, parenting).
- A behavioral aftermath characterized by lowered self-esteem, feelings of shame, and increasing isolation, all of which function to prepare the individual to repeat the same or similar sequence of maladaptive sexual behavior.

Perceived lack of control represents a central feature of this behavioral pattern and is viewed typically as a chronic syndrome with no clear onset. It is distinguished from developmental periods where heightened sexual activities are to be expected (e.g., adolescence). However, according to Coleman (1992), some adolescents may begin to use sexual espression "to deal with the stress of adolescence, loneliness, or feelings of inadequacy" (p. 323). Authors have also reported that impulsive behaviors (e.g., gambling) and chemical dependencies (e.g., alcohol, cocaine) are often co-occurring, in both a chronic and acute manner.

The following description by one of our patients illustrates this behavioral pattern:

As a child, I can remember masturbating at night in my bed so I wouldn't hear my parents arguing and fighting. It seemed to be one of the few things I learned to do for myself to calm or sooth me. Masturbation got really out of hand in high school and college. I had a lot of social fears and I felt like I didn't measure up to my peers. I could always masturbate. It got to a point where I'd get brush burns on my penis from masturbating. Most days, I'd do it before I got up, four or five times during the day, and four or five times at night before falling asleep. There were days I chose to masturbate, smoke pot, and get into pornography, instead of trying to get on with a woman. Afterwards, sometimes I'd feel like shit—really horrible and down on myself, like really guilty and ashamed. Other times I'd just go on about my business.

This case example highlights the habitual and self-injurious nature of this behavioral pattern. It also reflects issues of comorbidity (e.g., social phobia, substance abuse). Finally, because the habitual masturbation appeared to result in both positive and negative reinforcement, it raises questions that have fueled a controversy about conceptualization of this behavioral pattern.

Although the case involved a circumscribed sexual activity, clinical impression is that any range of activities might be observed (Coleman 1992; Quadland 1985): frequent sexual encounters with multiple partners, habitual use of pornographic materials, habitual frequenting of X-rated theaters and bookstores, and anonymous sex in public places (e.g., rest rooms, bathhouses). Authors have also described a similar behavioral pattern within the context of a paraphilia (Schwartz & Brasted 1985). In fact, Coleman (1992) has divided compulsive sexual behaviors into two types, paraphilic and nonparaphilic. Finally, clinical impression suggests that the behavioral pattern may reflect heterosexual, homosexual, or bisexual activities.

Unlike more traditional descriptions of hypersexual behavior, which are more gender specific (e.g., nymphomania), clinical impressions suggest that a similar pattern of behavior may occur in women (e.g., much like the frequent one-night stands of the woman depicted in the book and movie, *Looking for Mr. Goodbar*). In other cases, the behavioral pattern for women may include preoccupation with a destructive relationship (Carnes 1983; Schwartz & Brasted 1985). Reported negative consequences of this sexual behavior have included unwanted pregnancies, exposure to HIV infection, contraction of sexually transmitted diseases, physical injury, legal problems including arrest, emotional difficulties, marital and relationship stress, and job loss (Coleman 1992).

Finally, it is important to note that, with few exceptions (Quadland 1985), there are minimal empirical data to support the clinical impressions regarding this pattern of hypersexual behavior.

Growing Clinical Interest and a Debate

Despite these complexities and the absence of empirical data, the area of hypersexuality has attracted considerable clinical and media attention in recent years (Goleman 1984; Dolan 1990). Popularly referred to as sexual addiction (Carnes 1983; Goodman 1992), sexual compulsivity (Coleman 1986; Quadland 1985), or sexual dependence (Orford 1978), the observed behavioral pattern has become a major treatment focus of practitioners and self-help groups espousing a disease model of addiction. Twelve-step programs, modeled after the twelve steps of Alcoholics Anonymous (AA), have proliferated, and AA-oriented therapies have become well established in treating "the disease of sexual addiction" (e.g., the new journal *Sexual Addiction and Compulsivity*).

Despite its popular appeal, the sexual addiction model has also become the center of intense criticism and controversy. Coleman (1986, 1990) argues that application of the addiction concept is fraught with difficulties, including (1) inadequate empirical support for the addiction theory—particularly as it is applied to nonpharmacologic substances (e.g., food) and mood-altering activities (e.g., gambling, sex); (2) the tendency of the addiction model to oversimplify complex phenomena and to deemphasize concurrent conditions (e.g., mood disorder); and (3) its consequent adherence to a binary, lifelong classification that fails to appreciate the reality of individual differences and variations in human sexual behavior:

The term "addiction" refers to a fundamental state that is invariable and somehow immutable. Once labeled, an individual is an "addict" for life. This is a dichotomous view, immersed in the traditional medical addiction model (i.e., addict-nonaddict). . . . One can be in "recovery" but never "recovered." (Coleman 1990, p. 11)

Money (1986), while noting that paraphilic behaviors appear "addictive," is also critical of the addiction model, particularly with regard to the assumption of disease-related progression, that is, the inherent escalation or progression from one form of sexual behavior to a more deviant and dangerous type. "This doctrine of progression is a recrudescence of degeneracy theory—a leftover from antisexualism of the last century. It is just plain wrong" (Money, 1986 p. 37).

In its place, Coleman (1990) describes an obsessive-compulsive (OCD) model, which views pathological hypersexuality as a "symptom of an underlying obsessive compulsive disorder in which the anxiety-driven behavior happens to be sexual in nature" (p. 12). Coleman notes that at first glance, this model may be criticized because in classic OCD, the obsessions and compulsions center around an unpleasant or unpleasurable activity in which the individual feels compelled to engage in order to decrease anxiety. However, he contends that "individuals with Compulsive Sexual Behavior rarely report pleasure in their obsessions or compulsive behavior" (p. 12). This is at odds with our clinical experience and that of writers who have noted that impulsive sexual activities are at least sometimes associated with pleasure or positive reinforcement for some people (Barth & Kinder 1987).

Notwithstanding, Coleman argues that the OCD model leads to a clearer understanding of this disorder, is sensitive to a continuum of severity, and suggests a range of potentially effective treatments, including pharmacotherapy. Recent pharmacologic work seems to support his claims (Kafka & Prentky 1992; Zohar, Kaplan & Benjamin 1994).

Despite this seeming improvement in conceptualization, the compulsivity model, along with the addiction model, has also been criticized. Levine and Troiden (1988), arguing from a social interactionist perspective, suggest that the definitions of sexual addiction (SA) and sexual compulsivity (SC) are both conceptually flawed and that the criteria for these "conditions" are subjective and value laden. They conclude that there is no evidence to suggest that the disorder exists.

Noting the absence of empirical findings, Barth and Kinder (1987) go even further and argue that the various labels applied—SA, SC, and hypersexuality— are inaccurate descriptions of this disorder and do not reflect the true nature of the condition. In addition to arguments made earlier, they cite the DSM-III in arguing that the identified sexual behavior is not a true compulsion:

Some activities, such as eating, sexual behavior, gambling, or drinking, when engaged in excessively may be referred to as "compulsive." However, these activities are not true compulsions, because the individual receives pleasure from the participation. (APA 1980, p. 235)

The DSM-IV (APA 1994) goes on to state:

However, these activities are not considered to be compulsions as defined in this manual because the person usually derives pleasure from the activity and may wish to resist it only because of its deleterious consequences. (p. 422)

As such, Barth and Kinder conclude that the condition is best construed—at least from the perspective of accepted psychiatric nosology—as an atypical impulse control disorder.

Finally, Moser (1993), in his criticism of the addiction model, emphasizes the importance of comorbid or concurrent psychopathology: "In my clinical practice, patients often contend that they are sexual addicts. I rarely concur with their diagnosis, but usually find significant depression, paraphilias, and conflict with societal expectations" (p. 222).

Minimal empirical data are available to address these important issues and points of controversy. Beyond the scope of this chapter, readers interested in addiction models are referred to Fowles (1988), Milkman and Sunderwirth (1987), and Peele (1985). Similarly, recent conceptualizations regarding OCD and related disorders are provided by Jenike (1989).

Finally, data relevant to this pattern of sexual behavior consist primarily of clinical impressions, case vignettes, and survey-type findings derived from patients already involved in treatment from an addiction perspective (Carnes, 1991). One exception is an empirical study reported by Quadland (1985).

Quadland's Study

A major purpose of Quadland's study was to determine how a group of thirty homosexual and bisexual men, who presented for group therapy of sexually compulsive behavior (SCB), differed from a matched control group (age, gender, sexual preference, therapy seeking) on measures of neurotic symptoms and frequency and type of sexual activities.

Using the Derogatis Brief Symptom Inventory and unpublished questionnaires, he found that the two groups did not differ on neurotic tendencies. However, the SCB group was found to have had significantly fewer long-term relationships (six months or longer), significantly more estimated sexual partners per month over three time periods (past five years, previous six months, and most sexually active year of their lives), and more reported sexual encounters occurring in public settings and under the influence of alcohol and/or other drugs. Further, the SCB group experienced significantly fewer positive feelings of love and relaxation prior to sex. The two groups did not differ significantly with respect to measures of negative feelings prior to sex (e.g., anxiety, frustration, loneliness). Similarly, they did not differ in reported desired number of sexual partners, desired frequency of sexual activity, or amount of group sex.

Because Quadland's study employed only homosexual and bisexual men as subjects, findings may have limited generalizability. Similarly, the study can be criticized for several methodological inadequacies, including lack of subject diagnoses using reliable measures and the unreliability of instruments assessing type and frequency of sexual activity.

Nevertheless, study findings provide some support for the existence of this disorder in showing that two matched groups of homosexual and bisexual men, who did not differ in neurotic tendencies or desired number of sexual partners, were self-identified as sexually compulsive, based on frequency and type of sexual behavior, including actual number of sexual partners. This latter finding is consistent with the idea that sexually compulsive activity is due to a lack of control, not elevated sexual desire.

Similarly, the finding that the SCB group had significantly fewer long-term relationships is consistent with a pattern of isolation and withdrawal associated with the behavior, and/or reflects preexisting interpersonal skill deficits—a finding that has been observed in the paraphilias. Finally, the finding that the SCB group reported significantly fewer positive feelings prior to sex is consistent with the idea that this group may be engaging in habitual sexual activities for other reasons. However, it must be recalled that the two groups did not differ significantly on measures of negative feelings prior to sex, which is contrary to the obsessive-compulsive model.

Accurate Diagnosis

Diagnosing the hypersexual behavior pattern as an addiction raises a host of complex problems. First, use of the term *addiction,* so closely associated with the disease model, is biased theoretically and implies a treatment approach based on that theory. This bias may cause the clinician to diagnose and treat prematurely, thus increasing the possibility that underlying conditions and comorbid disorders will go undetected. This is why the DSM-IV, like previous editions, avoids use of the term *addiction* and instead utilizes the less theoretically biased term *dependence* in describing disorders involving alcohol and other pharmacologic substances. Second, in contrast to chemical dependencies, upon which the term *addiction* is based, the status of behavioral dependencies is less clearly understood (Marks 1990). For this reason, the DSM-IV, like its recent predecessors, continues to classify pathological gambling, which is sometimes referred to as a behavioral dependency, within the category of "Impulse Control Disorder, Not Elsewhere Classified."

The diagnosis of compulsive sexual behavior, while less theoretically biased, also raises questions regarding the definition of compulsion as being associated typically with an unpleasant activity and not with behaviors that are intrinsically enjoyable and pleasurable. As discussed, use of the term in this way is inconsistent with that of accepted psychiatric nosology.

Although additional research may uncover various subtypes of hypersexual disorder, Barth and Kinder (1987) note that because of the early degree of empirical and conceptual development in this area, the identified behavioral pattern does not warrant a new diagnostic category. Instead, it may be best classified as an "Impulse Control Disorder, Not Elsewhere Classified," according to DSM-IV. Besides emphasizing an atheoretical approach, use of the impulse control disorder category remains consistent with classification of other behavioral dependencies (e.g., pathological gambling). It is important to note,

Table 15.2

DSM-IV Classification for Impulsive Sexual Behavior (Disorders and Symptoms)

DSM-IV Diagnosis	Description of sexual behavior
Disorder	
Sexual Disorder - Not Otherwise Specified	Distress about a pattern of repeated sexual relationships involving a succession of lovers who are experienced by the individual only as things to be used.
Impulse Control Disorder - Not Otherwise Specified	This category is for disorders of impulse control that do not meet the criteria for any specific Impulse-Control Disorder or for another mental disorder having features involving impulse control described elsewhere in the manual.
Symptom of Disorder	
Manic or Hypomanic Episode	1. Increase in goal-directed activity (either socially, at work or school, or *sexually*) or psychomotor agitation. 2. Excessive involvement in pleasurable activities that have a high potential for painful consequences (e.g., engaging in unrestrained buying sprees, *sexual indiscretions*, or foolish business investments).
Borderline Personality Disorder	Impulsivity in at least two areas that are potentially self-damaging (e.g., spending, *sex*, substance abuse, reckless driving, binge eating).
Alcohol Intoxication	Clinically significant maladaptive behavioral or psychological changes (e.g. *inappropriate sexual or aggressive behavior*, mood lability, impaired judgement, impaired social or occupational functioning) that developed during, or shortly after, alcohol ingestion.
Sedative, Hypnotic, or Anxiolytic Intoxication	Clinically significant maladaptive behavioral or psychological changes (e.g. *inappropriate sexual or aggressive behavior*, mood lability, impaired judgement, impaired social or occupational functioning) that developed during, or shortly after, sedative, hypnotic, or anxiolytic use.

however, that in general the category of "Impulse Control Disorders, Not Elsewhere Classified" has not been adequately studied. Recent work suggests that the various types of impulse control disorder are related to one another and to mood, anxiety, and psychoactive substance use disorders (McElroy, Hudson, Pope, Keck & Aizley 1992).

Indeed, there are various data, mostly correlational and impressionistic, indicating that hypersexual behavior may be a component of other diagnoses, including organic conditions (e.g., brain lesions, drug use), and other psychopathology. Table 15.2 provides a listing of DSM-IV diagnoses where impulsive sexual behavior represents either a discrete category or a feature of another

Table 15.3
Selective Listing of Sources Relevant to Neurological Disorder and Hypersexual Behavior

Disorder or Disease	Source
Brain injury	Lehne (1986) Miller et al. (1986) Zencius et al. (1990)

Brain lesions associated with:
  Bilateral temporal lobectomy
  (Kluver-Bucy Syndrome)
	Anson & Kuhlman (1993)

Multiple Sclerosis	Huws, Shubsachs, & Taylor (1991)
Ventriculoperitoneal shunts for hydrocephalus	Gorman & Cummings (1992)
Dementia associated with AIDS	Potocnik (1992)
Klein-Levin Syndrome	Cawthron (1990)

disorder. Seemingly underemphasized in the literature, this is the area to which we now turn.

ETIOLOGY AND TREATMENT DIRECTIONS

Biological Causes

From an ethical perspective, clinicians working in the area of sexual impulsivity, as in any other area of human sexuality, have a responsibility to be well informed regarding biological causes and concomitants. With few exceptions, cases of impulsive sexual behavior remain outside the domain of the mental health professional until biomedical factors have been addressed. As such, biomedical assessment represents a necessary prerequisite for formal psychological assessment and treatment planning. (Beyond the scope of this chapter, the reader is referred to Malatesta & Adams 1986, 1993 for guidelines regarding biomedical assessment of sexual disorders.)

Neurologic Factors

Table 15.3 shows that a range of neurologic conditions has been associated with hypersexuality. Although not a frequent occurrence, various types of brain lesions can result in impulsive and heightened sexual activities. Earlier studies suggested a common localization in the temporal lobes (Blumer 1970). More recent work has also implicated the frontal lobes (Huws, Shubsachs & Taylor 1991), the septal nuclei (Gorman & Cummings 1992), and the limbic system, the last of which has also been associated with alterations in sexual preference (Miller et al. 1986).

Pharmacologic Influences

Although well-controlled cause-effect studies are few, consistent correlational and case study data reveal that an array of drugs is capable of interfering with any phase of sexual response (Abel 1985). With regard to hypersexual activity, two drug classes have been implicated: the anti-Parkinson medications (Harvey 1988) and the antiseizure medication carbamazepine (Tegretol; Myers & Carrera 1989).

Alcohol and other drugs have also been implicated in hypersexuality and impulsive sexual behavior. Well-designed studies have shown a relationship between learned associations about alcohol's effects and disinhibition of deviant and nondeviant sexual behavior in men (see George & Norris 1991 for a review). Representing a complicated area involving neurophysiological factors, learned expectancies, and sociocultural variables, recent emphasis has addressed the "stigmatization" of the alcoholic woman; that is, in contrast to the alcoholic male, this stereotype includes a culturally ingrained expectation of hypersexuality and sexual promiscuity in the alcoholic woman. This myth is not supported by research (Blume 1991). Finally, study and debate continue concerning the sexually enhancing properties of cocaine and marijuana (Mieczkowski 1990; Webber 1991; Weller & Halikas 1984).

The Role of Psychopathology

Psychopathology traditionally has been associated with sexual problems. To date, however, a direct cause-effect relationship has not been established between psychopathology and hypersexual behavior disorders. Relevant research data must be viewed with caution because of a general lack of control groups and numerous confounds with psychopathology (e.g., medication, premorbid sex levels, partner response, heterosocial skill deficits). Nevertheless, available clinical and correlational data suggest that psychopathology may be a cause, a consequence, or a concomitant of sexually impulsive behavior.

Mood Disorder

One example is the frequently reported association between manic episodes of bipolar disorder and impulsive sexual behavior (Tsuang 1975). In this case, it is unclear whether mania is exerting its influence on sexual behavior via biochemical substrates of sexual desire, increased self-esteem, enhanced pleasure, and sensual awareness or whether there are other undisclosed variables (Goldberg 1987).

It is also reported anecdotally that there may be an increase in sexual activity associated with mild to moderate depression (Munjack & Oziel 1980). Typically, this heightened sexual behavior is not related to increased sexual desire per se but instead seems to be function of anxiety relief, self-esteem enhancement, and/ or desire for closeness.

Personality Disorder

Goldberg (1987) has remarked that hypersexual behavior is not an uncommon symptom among patients with certain personality disorders. While the DSM-IV notes that a feature of borderline personality disorder may be impulsive sexual behavior, Goldberg also includes sociopathic, histrionic, and narcissistic personality disorder in his clinical experience. Coleman (1992) reports that certain types of nonparaphilic compulsive sexual behavior (e.g., compulsive masturbation) may be comorbid with schizoid and avoidant personality disorders. Similarly, he suggests that "compulsive multiple love relationships" may be comorbid with narcissistic and dependent personality disorder. Data are impressionistic, and there is no clear evidence to suggest that enhanced sexual desire is a relevant factor. Rather, other types of need satisfaction seem to predominate (e.g., control and manipulation, attention seeking, self-defeating tendencies, and/ or coping with severe loneliness and emptiness).

Psychosocial Causes

The presence of childhood sexual abuse is a consistent finding in the clinical literature on hypersexuality and impulsive sexual behavior. Although correlational and retrospective, study findings indicate childhood incest or other childhood sexual trauma may be a precursor for hypersexual behavior disorders in adult men (Anderson & Coleman 1991) and women (Charmoli & Athelstan 1988; Craine, Henson, Colliver & MacLean 1988).

There are also data that suggest that a childhood characterized by highly restricted environments regarding sexuality and negative attitudes about sex and intimacy may be associated with impulsive sexual behavior in men (Anderson & Coleman 1991; Coleman 1992). We have also been impressed with the number of patients with patterns of impulsive sexual behavior who present with concomitant confusion and distress regarding their sexual orientation (Carnes 1983; Schwartz & Brasted 1985).

Although findings are purely anecdotal, it is often reported that relationship difficulties may represent an important maintaining cause for impulsive sexual behavior (Goldberg 1987). We have seen several cases in our practice where patterns of impulsive sexual behavior (e.g., prostitute seeking, cross-dressing) were maintained and/or triggered by marital conflict and difficulties in expressing anger assertively toward one's spouse. Partner discrepancies in sexual desire have also been reported as a maintaining factor to impulsive sexual activity. In this regard, Goldberg (1987) has noted that for couples with hypersexual desire discrepancies, "the sexual interaction quickly becomes an arena for playing out the struggle for power and control" (p. 210).

Treatment Directions

Consistent with the "medicalization" of sex therapy, pharmacologic treatments of hypersexual disorders, including related conditions (e.g., sexual aggression), have undergone significant development. Coleman's (1992) model of compulsive sexual behavior has served as an impetus for biologically oriented work in the field. Consistent with the growing body of information regarding biological substrates of OCD, recent pharmacological studies have described the effectiveness of two serotonin selective reuptake inhibitors (SSRIs: fluoxetine and fluvoxamine) in treating "nonparaphilic sexual addictions" and "compulsive exhibitionism" (Kafka & Prentky 1992; Zohar, Kaplan & Benjamin 1994).

Relatedly, it should be noted that the most significant organic treatment of the more violent sexual offender is the use of hormonal compounds (e.g., medroxyprogesterone) and antiandrogen medications (e.g., cyproterone acetate). Money's (1970) pioneering work with the therapeutic use of an androgen-depleting hormone is an early example. More recent work is summarized by Bradford (1989).

Psychosocial treatments, although discussed frequently, are at an early stage of development. Group therapy methods have been cited frequently (Carnes 1991; Quadland 1985; Turner 1990), while others have emphasized the importance of individual therapy approaches (Coleman 1992). In many cases, there is a need for basic skill building across domains (Malatesta & Adams 1993; Malatesta & Turner 1991; Schwartz & Brasted 1985). Similarly, Goldberg (1987) emphasizes the importance of couples therapy in managing hypersexual disorders. Finally, despite problems associated with the addiction model, twelve-step-oriented self-help groups may have an important role in helping certain individuals who have been devastated by their patterns of sexual behavior.

CONCLUSION

The study and treatment of pathological hypersexuality and impulsive sexual behavior should represent an important funding priority for our society. In addition to addressing issues of sexual abuse and sexual violence, supported work in this area would have direct implications for management of unwanted pregnancies and sexually transmitted diseases—not to mention the undocumented costs to individuals, their families, and society at large. The paraphilias may represent a good starting place since the field is blessed with many gifted clinical scientists and because a research methodology already exists.

Finally, we emphasize that clinicians have a professional and ethical responsibility to maintain, first, a firm knowledge of basic psychopathology and then a broad understanding of basic and applied research in human sexuality. Therapists with these credentials will ensure advancement of the field.

REFERENCES

Abel, E. L. (1985). *Psychoactive drugs and sex*. New York: Plenum.

Adams, H. E., & Cassidy, J. F. (1993). The classification of abnormal behavior: An overview. In S. P. Sutker & H. E. Adams (Eds.), *Comprehensive handbook of psychopathology* (2nd ed., pp. 3–25). New York: Plenum.

American Psychiatric Association. (1968). *Diagnostic and statistical manual of mental disorders* (2nd ed.). Washington, DC: Author.

American Psychiatric Association. (1980). *Diagnostic and statistical manual of mental disorders* (3rd ed.). Washington, DC: Author.

American Psychiatric Association. (1987). *Diagnostic and statistical manual of mental disorders* (3rd ed., rev.). Washington, DC: Author.

American Psychiatric Association. (1994). *Diagnostic and statistical manual of mental disorders* (4th ed.). Washington, DC: Author.

Anderson, N. B., & Coleman, E. (1991). Childhood abuse and family sexual attitudes in sexually-compulsive males: A comparison of three clinical groups. *American Journal of Preventive Psychiatry and Neurology, 3*, 8–15.

Anson, J. A., & Kuhlman, D. T. (1993). Post-ictal Kluver-Bucy syndrome after temporal lobectomy. *Journal of Neurology, Neurosurgery and Psychiatry, 56*, 311–313.

Apfelbaum, B. (1977). On the etiology of sexual dysfunction. *Journal of Sex and Marital Therapy, 3*, 50–62.

Barth, R. J., & Kinder, B. N. (1987). The mislabeling of sexual impulsivity. *Journal of Sex and Marital Therapy, 13*, 15–23.

Blume, S. B. (1991). Sexuality and stigma: The alcoholic woman. Special issue: Alcohol and sexuality. *Alcohol Health and Research World, 15*, 139–146.

Blumer, D. (1970). Hypersexual episodes in temporal lobe epilepsy. *American Journal of Psychiatry, 126*, 83–90.

Bradford, J. (1989). The organic treatment of violent sexual offenders. In A. J. Stunkard & A. Baum (Eds.), *Eating, sleeping, and sex* (pp. 203–221). Hillsdale, NJ: Erlbaum.

Carnes, P. (1983). *Out of the shadows: Understanding sexual addiction*. Minneapolis: CompCare.

Carnes, P. (1991). *Don't call it love: Recovery from sexual addiction*. New York: Bantam.

Cawthron, P. (1990). A disorder unique to adolescence? The Kleine-Levin syndrome. *Journal of Adolescence, 13*, 401–406.

Charmoli, M. C., & Athelstan, G. T. (1988). Incest as related to sexual problems in women. *Journal of Psychology and Human Sexual Behavior, 1*, 53–66.

Coleman, E. (1986). Sexual compulsion vs. sexual addiction: The debate continues. *SIECUS Report, 14*, 7–10.

Coleman, E. (1990). The obsessive-compulsive model for describing compulsive sexual behavior. *American Journal of Preventive Psychiatry and Neurology, 2*, 9–14.

Coleman, E. (1992). Is your patient suffering from compulsive sexual behavior? *Psychiatric Annals, 22*, 320–325.

Craine, L. S., Henson, C. E., Colliver, J. A., & MacLean, D. G. (1988). Prevalence of a history of sexual abuse among female psychiatric patients in a state hospital system. *Hospital and Community Psychiatry, 39*, 300–304.

Dolan, B. (1990, June 4). Do people get hooked on sex? *Time Magazine,* p. 72.

Fowles, D. C. (Ed). (1988). Special issue: Models of addiction. *Journal of Abnormal Psychology, 97,* 115–245.

George, W. H., & Norris, J. (1991). Alcohol, disinhibition, sexual arousal and deviant sexual behavior. *Alcohol Health and Research World, 15,* 133–138.

Goldberg, M. (1987). Understanding hypersexuality in men and women. In G. R. Weeks & L. Hof (Eds.), *Integrating sex and marital therapy* (pp. 202–220). New York: Brunner/Mazel.

Goleman, D. (1984, October, 16). Some sexual behavior viewed as an addiction. *New York Times,* pp. C1, C9.

Goodman, A. (1992). Sexual addiction: Designation and treatment. *Journal of Sex and Marital Therapy, 18,* 303–314.

Gorman, D. G., & Cummings, J. L. (1992). Hypersexuality following septal injury. *Archives of Neurology, 49,* 308–310.

Harvey, N. S. (1988). Serial cognitive profiles in levodopa-induced hypersexuality. *British Journal of Psychiatry, 153,* 833–836.

Huws, R., Shubsachs, A. P., & Taylor, P. J. (1991). Hypersexuality, fetishism and multiple sclerosis. *British Journal of Psychiatry, 158,* 280–281.

Jenike, M. A. (1989). Obsessive-compulsive and related disorders. *New England Journal of Medicine, 321,* 539–541.

Kafka, M. P., & Prentky, R. (1992). Fluoxetine treatment of nonparaphilic sexual addictions and paraphilias in men. *Journal of Clinical Psychiatry, 53,* 351–358.

Kaplan, H. S. (1977). Hyposexual sexual desire. *Journal of Sex and Marital Therapy, 3,* 3–9.

Kaplan, H. S. (1979). *Disorders of sexual desire.* New York: Brunner/Mazel.

Laumann, E. O., Gagnon, J. H., Michael, R. T., & Michaels, S. (1994). *The social organization of sexuality.* Chicago: University of Chicago Press.

Lazarus, A. A. (1988). A multimodal perspective on problems of sexual desire. In S. R. Leiblum & R. C. Rosen (Eds.), *Sexual desire disorders* (pp. 145–167). New York: Guilford Press.

Lehne, G. K. (1986). Brain damage and paraphilia: Treated with medroxyprogesterone acetate. *Sexuality and Disability, 7,* 145–158.

Leiblum, S. R., & Rosen, R. C. (Eds.). (1988). *Sexual desire disorders.* New York: Guilford.

Levine, M. P., & Troiden, R. R. (1988). The myth of sexual compulsivity. *Journal of Sex Research, 25,* 347–363.

Levine, S. B. (1982). A modern perspective on nymphomania. *Journal of Sex and Marital Therapy, 8,* 316–324.

Lief, H. I. (1977). Inhibited sexual desire. *Medical Aspects of Human Sexuality, 7,* 94–95.

McElroy, S. L., Hudson, J. I., Pope, H. G., Keck, P. E., & Aizley, H. G. (1992). The DSM-III-R Impulse Control Disorders Not Elsewhere Classified: Clinical characteristics and relationship to other psychiatric disorders. *American Journal of Psychiatry, 149,* 318–327.

Malatesta, V. J., & Adams, H. E. (1986). Assessment of sexual behavior. In A. R. Ciminero, K. S. Calhoun & H. E. Adams (Eds.), *Handbook of behavioral assessment* (2nd ed.) (pp. 496–525). New York: Wiley.

Malatesta, V. J., & Adams, H. E. (1993). The sexual dysfunctions. In P. B. Sutker & H.

E. Adams (Eds.), *Comprehensive handbook of psychopathology* (2nd ed.) (pp. 581–615). New York: Plenum.

Malatesta, V. J., & Turner, M. (1991). Self-nurturing activities in recovering sex addicts: Effects on depression, anxiety, and anger level. *American Journal of Preventive Psychiatry and Neurology, 3,* 6–7.

Marks, I. (1990). Behavioral (non-chemical) addictions. *British Journal of Addiction, 85,* 1389–1394.

Masters, W. H., Johnson, V. E., & Kolodny, R. C. (1986). *Masters and Johnson on sex and human loving.* Boston: Little, Brown.

Mieczkowski, T. (1990). The operational styles of crack houses in Detroit. *NIDA Research Monograph Series, 103,* 60–91.

Milkman, H., & Sunderwirth, S. (1987). *Craving for ecstasy: The consciousness and chemistry of escape.* Lexington, MA: Lexington Books.

Miller, B. L., Cummings, J. L., McIntyre, H., & Ebers, G. (1986). Hypersexuality or altered sexual preference following brain injury. *Journal of Neurology, Neurosurgery and Psychiatry, 49,* 867–873.

Money, J. (1970). Use of an androgen depleting hormone in the treatment of male sex offenders. *Journal of Sex Research, 6,* 165–172.

Money, J. (1986). *Lovemaps.* New York: Irvington.

Moser, C. (1993). A response to Aviel Goodman's "Sexual addiction: Designation and treatment." *Journal of Sex and Marital Therapy, 19,* 220–224.

Munjack, D. J., & Oziel, L. J. (1980). *Sexual medicine and counseling in office practice.* Boston: Little, Brown.

Myers, W. C., & Carrera, F. (1989). Carbamazepine-induced mania with hypersexuality in a 9-year-old boy. *American Journal of Psychiatry, 146,* 400.

Orford, J. (1978). Hypersexuality: Implications for a theory of dependence. *British Journal of Addiction, 73,* 299–310.

Peele, S. (1985). *The meaning of addiction: Compulsive experience and its interpretation.* Lexington, MA: D. C. Heath.

Potocnik, F. (1992). Successful treatment of hypersexuality in AIDS [letter to the editor]. *South African Medical Journal, 81,* 433–434.

Quadland, M. C. (1985). Compulsive sexual behavior: Definition of a problem and an approach to treatment. *Journal of Sex and Marital Therapy, 11,* 121–132.

Rosen, R. C., & Beck, J. G. (1988). *Patterns of sexual arousal: Psychophysiological processes and clinical application.* New York: Guilford.

Schover, L. R., & LoPiccolo, J. (1982). Treatment effectiveness for dysfunctions of sexual desire. *Journal of Sex and Marital Therapy, 8,* 179–197.

Schwartz, M. F., & Brasted, W. S. (1985). Sexual addiction. *Medical Aspects of Human Sexuality, 19,* 103–107.

Tsuang, M. T. (1975). Hypersexuality in manic patients. *Medical Aspects of Human Sexuality, 9,* 83–89.

Turner, M. (1990). Long-term outpatient group psychotherapy as a modality for treating sexual addiction. *American Journal of Preventive Psychiatry and Neurology, 2,* 23–26.

Webber, R. (1991). Cocaine dependency and sexual compulsion. *American Journal of Preventive Psychiatry and Neurology, 3,* 50–53.

Weller, R. A., & Halikas, J. A. (1984). Marijuana use and sexual behavior. *Journal of Sex Research, 20,* 186–193.

Zencius, A., Wesolowski, M. D., Burke, W. H., & Hough, S. (1990). Managing hyper-
    sexual disorders in brain-injured clients. *Brain Injury, 4,* 175–181.
Zilbergeld, B., & Ellison, C. R. (1980). Desire discrepancies and arousal problems in
    sex therapy. In S. R. Leiblum & A. Pervin (Eds.), *Principles and practice of sex
    therapy* (pp. 65–101). New York: Guilford.
Zohar, J., Kaplan, Z., & Benjamin, J. (1994). Compulsive exhibitionism successfully
    treated with fluvoxamine: A controlled case study. *Journal of Clinical Psychiatry,
    55,* 86–88.

16

Gender Identity Disorders: A Developmental Perspective

Kenneth J. Zucker

The topics of sex and gender grab headlines. In a humorous vein, Tiefer (1994) remarked that it has become quite tedious for academics to keep up with the compulsive task of filing away newspaper clippings about sex and gender because there are so many pieces being written about them in the popular press. But this was not always the case. When Kinsey, Pomeroy, and Martin (1948) published their landmark work, *Sexual Behavior in the Human Male,* the topic was considered almost lurid. Further back in the history of sexology, the major texts (Ellis 1936; Krafft-Ebing 1886) were deemed appropriate only for the eyes of physicians.

At a more scientific level, one needs to remember that our understanding of aspects of biological sex is rather new. For example, the karyotyping of the sex chromosomes in humans was a technique developed only in the 1950s (Moore & Barr 1955). The development of taxonomies to describe aspects of psychosexual differentiation remains an ongoing endeavor. Money (1955), for example, coined the term *gender role* forty years ago, and the term *gender identity* was introduced even later (Stoller 1964a).

It is not surprising, therefore, that it has been only in the past two or three decades that terms to describe disorders of psychosexual differentiation have reached a formal status in the psychiatric nomenclature. Transsexualism, a diagnosis reserved for postpubertal youth and adults, and the gender identity disorder of childhood, a diagnosis reserved for children, appeared for the first time in the publication of the third edition of the *Diagnostic and Statistical Manual of Mental Disorders* (DSM-III) (American Psychiatric Association 1980). Of course, these formal or institutionalized developments do not mean that these disorders appeared de novo in modern times. Indeed, the historical record amply documents that people from diverse backgrounds and cultures had phenomenological experiences akin to what we now consider to be disorders of gender identity (Bullough & Bullough 1993; Dekker & van de Pol 1989).

In this chapter, four aspects of gender identity disorder in children will be covered: phenomenology, diagnostic issues, a selected etiological review, and a summary of therapeutic interventions and techniques. Where appropriate, this chapter will emphasize developmental issues, since diagnosis and treatment considerations are affected by age-related matters and because etiological models are also necessarily developmental in nature.

PHENOMENOLOGY

The behavioral signs of gender identity disorder most typically appear for the first time during the toddler and preschool years (Green 1976, 1987), the years in which more conventional patterns of sex-typed behavior can first be observed. In extreme cases, parents will recall that behaviors such as cross-dressing began prior to the second birthday. The central clinical-diagnostic issue concerns the degree to which a pattern of behavioral signs is present, since this pattern is the basis for inference on the extent to which a child is cross-gender identified.

In boys, the clinical picture, in its full form, includes at least eight characteristics:

1. An occasional or frequently stated desire to be a girl or an insistence that he is a girl.
2. Verbal or behavioral expressions of anatomic dysphoria (e.g., saying that he does not like his penis and would prefer a vagina or vulva; urinating in the seated position to enhance the fantasy of having female genitalia).
3. Frequent cross-dressing in girls' or women's clothing or use of other apparel (e.g., towels) to simulate feminine attire.
4. A preference for female roles and an avoidance of male roles in fantasy play.
5. A preference for stereotypical feminine toys and activities and an avoidance of stereotypical masculine toys and activities.
6. Recurrent display of stereotypical feminine or effeminate mannerisms.
7. A preference for girls as playmates and an avoidance or dislike of boys as playmates.
8. An avoidance of rough-and-tumble play and/or participation in group sports with males.

In girls, the clinical picture is similar. It includes:

1. An occasional or frequently stated desire to be a boy or an insistence that she is a boy.

2. Verbal or behavioral expressions of anatomic dysphoria (e.g., stating a desire to have a penis; urinating in the standing position in order to enhance the fantasy of having male genitalia).

3. An intense aversion to wearing stereotypical feminine clothing and an insistence on wearing stereotypical masculine clothing.

4. A preference for male roles and an avoidance of female roles in fantasy play.

5. A preference for stereotypical masculine toys and activities and an avoidance of stereotypical feminine toys and activities.

6. Recurrent display of stereotypical masculine mannerisms.

7. A preference for boys as playmates and an avoidance or dislike of girls as playmates.

8. A strong interest in rough-and-tumble play and participation in group sports with boys.

Two clinical vignettes illustrate these behavioral patterns:

Larry, a 6-year-old boy with an IQ of 106, was referred at the request of his mother, who had spoken informally with a friend who was a therapist. He lived with his mother, who had a lower middle-class socioeconomic background. He was the product of a casual, almost anonymous, sexual encounter. As a consequence, Larry's biological father was unknown to him, although he often asked his mother to marry and thus provide him with a dad.

Larry's mother stated that he was happy in every way except for one thing: "He desperately wants to be a girl and to cut off his penis." Of particular concern to his mother was that of late Larry would sing himself to sleep with a sad song: "My dreams will never come true." Larry's mother had noted signs of cross-gender behavior since he was under 2 years of age. At that time, he began compulsively to cross-dress, using items such as towels and aprons.

At the time of assessment, Larry preferred girls as playmates but complained that some of them would tease him because he acted like a girl. He was also teased quite intensely by other boys because of his cross-gender behavior. Larry's favorite toys were Barbie dolls, of which he had dozens, and he would spend hours enacting nurturant, benevolent female roles, such as Snow White, Sleeping Beauty, and Cinderella.

During the clinical assessment, Larry's capacity to flip into female roles was striking. It was as if Larry had become another person. In fact, Larry had brought to the assessment some of his feminine dress-up apparel. He removed all of his outer clothing and put these on, commenting somewhat sadly that he hoped that if he was "good enough" that we might be able to give him an "operation" that day. Larry's mother reported that he had no interest in athletics or rough-and-tumble play and that they were both very "frightened" by a boy they had known who had intense temper tantrums.

Lana, a 10-year-old girl with an IQ of 100, was referred at the suggestion of a social worker at her new school. She lived with her mother, who had a lower-middle-class socioeconomic background. Her parents never lived together, as her father was uninterested in committing to a family at the time that she was conceived. Over the years, Lana had had only periodic contact with her father.

Lana's mother reported that her daughter had heard of sex-reassignment surgery about two years prior to the assessment and had expressed a very strong interest in it. Currently,

Lana's choice of clothing style and her shortly cropped hair resulted in her peer group and adult strangers' believing that she was in fact a boy. Over the months prior to the assessment, Lana had even "dated" a couple of girls who simply assumed that she was a boy.

Since the age of 3, Lana had refused to wear culturally stereotypic feminine clothing, preferred boys as playmates, enjoyed playing with masculine toys (e.g., guns and swords), and always role-played male figures. She joined boys in hockey games and could be quite rough. At the time of the assessment, Lana had been passing for four months at her new school as a boy. She refused to use the girls' washroom at school. The pressure of passing as a boy was causing her a lot of psychological distress, and she reported some suicidal ideation and one parasuicidal attempt.

DIAGNOSTIC ISSUES

Placement in the Nomenclature

In the DSM, the section placement of the gender identity disorder of child-hood has had an interesting history. It had somewhat of an outlaw status in the DSM-III, inasmuch it was the only disorder for children not located in the section entitled "Disorders Usually First Evident in Infancy, Childhood, or Adolescence." Instead, it was included in the section entitled "Psychosexual Disorders," along with other new sexological diagnoses, such as transsexualism. In the DSM-III-R (American Psychiatric Association 1987), the gender identity disorder of childhood and transsexualism were both moved to the child section of the manual. For better or worse, the situation changed yet again in the DSM-IV (American Psychiatric Association, 1994). Because the largely adult diagnosis of transsexualism (and its variants, such as gender identity disorder of adolescence or adulthood, nontranssexual type) had also been moved to the child section in the DSM-III-R (the section "Psychosexual Disorders" was eliminated and replaced with "Sexual Disorders"), clinicians working with adults were not particularly pleased with this state of affairs (Bradley et al. 1991; Pauly 1992). In addition, the DSM-IV Subcommittee on Gender Identity Disorders took the position that the gender identity disorder of childhood, transsexualism, and gender identity disorder of adolescence or adulthood, nontranssexual type were not qualitatively distinct disorders but reflected differences in both developmental and severity parameters. As a result, the subcommittee recommended one overarching diagnosis, gender identity disorder, that could be used, with appropriate variations in criteria, across the life cycle (Bradley et al. 1991). Accordingly, it was suggested that gender identity disorders be assigned a distinct section that would have the same status as, for example, "Anxiety Disorders" and "Mood Disorders." The framers of DSM-IV eventually settled on a section that was termed "Sexual and Gender Identity Disorders," which is, perhaps, a more descriptively accurate heading than the original DSM-III section title, "Psychosexual Disorders."

DSM-IV Diagnostic Criteria

Table 16.1 shows the DSM-IV criteria for gender identity disorder. Three criteria (points A, B, and D) are required for the diagnosis, and point C is an exclusion criterion. For comparative purposes, the DSM-III-R criteria for gender identity disorder of childhood are shown in table 16.2.

Compared to the DSM-III and DSM-III-R, there were five main changes in the criteria for use with children:

1. The point A criterion reflects the child's cross-gender identification, indexed by five behavioral characteristics, of which at least four must be manifested. Previously these characteristics were listed in either the point A or point B criteria in the DSM-III-R. In addition, they are more distinct in the DSM-IV.

2. The point B criterion reflects the child's rejection of his or her own anatomic status and/or rejection of same-sex stereotypical activities. In the DSM-III-R, the point B criterion had also included some of the behavioral signs of cross-gender identification, which are now restricted to the point A criteria.

3. The criteria for boys and girls are more similar than they were in the DSM-III-R. For example, in the DSM-III-R, girls had to have a "stated" desire to be a boy, whereas boys had to have an "intense" desire to be a girl. Zucker (1992) had noted that the basis for this distinction was unclear and was particularly confusing inasmuch as the phraseology had been identical for the two sexes in the DSM-III: "strongly and persistently *stated* desire to be a boy [girl]" (emphasis added). Moreover, the passage for girls in the DSM-III-R contained no reference to intensity or chronicity. In the DSM-IV, both boys and girls must manifest a "repeatedly" stated desire to be of the other sex. In addition, the other behavioral characteristics required for the diagnosis are more similar for boys and girls than they were in the DSM-III-R.

4. In the DSM-III-R, a girl's desire to be of the other sex could not be due "merely . . . for any perceived cultural advantages from being a boy," whereas this proviso was not included for boys. In the DSM-IV, this proviso applies to both boys and girls.

5. In the DSM-III-R, the point A criterion specified that a child must show a "persistent and intense distress" about being a boy or a girl. This phrase had not appeared in the DSM-III criteria, and in the DSM-III-R it was not specified how one should assess such distress or in what ways it might be distinct from other operationalized components in the criteria. This phrase has been deleted in the DSM-IV point A criteria, but the presence of distress must be inferred via impairment in "social, occupational, or other important areas of functioning" (point C).

Appraisal of the DSM-IV Criteria

Reliability and Validity

Can the DSM-IV diagnosis of gender identity disorder be made reliably? Because the criteria have changed and because no field trials were conducted, this question cannot yet be answered. We conducted one study pertaining to the

Table 16.1
DSM-IV Diagnostic Criteria for Gender Identity Disorder

A. A strong and persistent cross-gender identification (not merely a desire for any perceived cultural advantages of being the other sex).

   In children, the disturbance is manifested by at least four (or more) of the following:

   1. repeatedly stated desire to be, or insistence that he or she is, the other sex
   2. in boys, preference for cross-dressing or simulating female attire; in girls, insistence on wearing only stereotypical masculine clothing
   3. strong and persistent preferences for cross-sex roles in make-believe play or persistent fantasies of being the other sex
   4. intense desire to participate in the stereotypical games and pastimes of the other sex
   5. strong preference for playmates of the other sex

   In adolescents and adults, the disturbance is manifested by symptoms such as a stated desire to be the other sex, frequent passing as the other sex, desire to live or be treated as the other sex, or the conviction that he or she has the typical feelings and reactions of the other sex.

B. Persistent discomfort with his or her sex or sense of inappropriateness in the gender role of that sex.

   In children, the disturbance is manifested by any of the following: in boys, assertion that his penis or testes are disgusting or will disappear or assertion that it would be better not to have a penis, or aversion toward rough-and-tumble play and rejection of male stereotypical toys, games, and activities; in girls, rejection of urinating in a sitting position, assertion that she has or will grow a penis, or assertion that she does not want to grow breasts or menstruate, or marked aversion toward normative feminine clothing.

   In adolescents and adults, the disturbance is manifested by symptoms such as preoccupation with getting rid of primary and secondary sex characteristics (e.g., request for hormones, surgery, or other procedures to physically alter sexual characteristics to simulate the other sex) or belief that he or she was born the wrong sex.

C. The disturbance is not concurrent with a physical intersex condition.

D. The disturbance causes clinically significant distress or impairment in social, occupational, or other important areas of functioning.

Table 16.2
DSM-III-R Diagnostic Criteria for Gender Identity Disorder of Childhood

For females:

A. Persistent and intense distress about being a girl, and a stated desire to be a boy (not merely a desire for any perceived cultural advantages from being a boy), or insistence that she is a boy.

B. Either (1) or (2):

    (1) persistent marked aversion to normative feminine clothing and insistence on wearing stereotypical masculine clothing, e.g., boys' underwear and other accessories
    (2) persistent repudiation of female anatomic structures, as evidenced by at least one of the following:
        (a) an assertion that she has, or will grow, a penis
        (b) rejection of urinating in a sitting position
        (c) assertion that she does not want to grow breasts or menstruate

C. The girl has not yet reached puberty.

For males:

A. Persistent and intense distress about being a boy and an intense desire to be a girl or, more rarely, insistence that he is a girl.

B. Either (1) or (2):

    (1) preoccupation with female stereotypical activities, as shown by a preference for either cross-dressing or simulating female attire, or by an intense desire to participate in the games and pastimes of girls and rejection of male stereotypical toys, games, and activities

    (2) persistent repudiation of male anatomic structures, as indicated by at least one of the following repeated assertions:
        (a) that he will grow up to become a woman (not merely in role)
        (b) that his penis or testes are disgusting or will disappear
        (c) that it would be better not to have a penis or testes

C. The boy has not yet reached puberty.

reliability of the earlier DSM-III criteria (Zucker, Finegan, Doering & Bradley 1984), which involved thirty-six consecutive referrals to our clinic. Kappas of .89 and .80 were obtained for the point A and point B criteria, respectively (both $ps < .001$).

In the Zucker et al. (1984) study, the validity of the DSM-III criteria was also assessed by comparing the children who met the complete criteria with those children who did not meet the complete criteria on a number of demographic variables and sex-typed behaviors. By and large the children who did not meet the complete DSM-III criteria showed at least some characteristics of cross-gender identification and were not necessarily inappropriate referrals.

Elsewhere, we have provided an update of these initial analyses based on a considerably larger sample size (Zucker & Bradley in press). These analyses showed that the children who met the complete criteria for gender identity disorder were significantly younger, of a higher social class background, and more likely to come from an intact, two-parent family than the children who did not meet the complete criteria. The two subgroups did not differ significantly with regard to sex and IQ. Correlational analyses indicated that the variables of age, IQ, and social class and marital status of the parents were all significantly correlated with one another. Sex of child was unrelated to any of the other demographic variables.

To test which variables, if any, contributed to the correct classification of the subjects in the two diagnostic groups, a discriminant function analysis was performed. Age, sex, IQ, and marital status contributed to the discriminant function, with age showing the greatest power. In the DSM-III group, 82.6 percent were correctly classified, and in the non-DSM-III group, 68.8 percent were correctly classified.

We also compared the two diagnostic subgroups on several measures of sex-typed behavior (Zucker & Bradley in press). T-tests were performed, with age, social class, and marital status covaried. The DSM-III subgroup showed significantly more cross-gender behavior or less same-gender behavior than the non-DSM-III subgroup on eleven of seventeen measures. Thus, there seemed to be at least some behavioral differences between the two diagnostic subgroups in the degree of same-sex-typed or cross-sex-typed behavior, even after controlling for the demographic variables that also differed between the two subgroups.

Empirical Analyses

Initially, the DSM-IV subcommittee had recommended that the DSM-III-R point A and point B criteria for children be collapsed into one criterion set. In part, this was because the two criteria appeared conceptually and empirically related (Bentler, Rekers, & Rosen 1979; Rosen, Rekers & Friar 1977). Moreover, research utilizing the DSM-III and DSM-III-R criteria found that younger children (*M* age, 6.4 years, $N = 54$) were significantly more likely to receive the diagnosis than were older children (*M* age, 9.0 years, $N = 54$) (Zucker 1992; Zucker et al. 1984). This seemed mainly due to the fact that older children did not meet the point A criterion. Despite marked clinical evidence of cross-gender identification, these children did not frequently voice the desire to be of the opposite sex. In part, this seemed a function of social desirability and fear of stigma.

If, in fact, the stated desire to be of the opposite sex is simply one of a series of behavioral markers suggestive of gender identity disorder, then a factor analysis of these markers should yield one common factor. The DSM-IV subcommittee tested this hypothesis in a reanalysis of parent report and clinician ratings of cross-gender behavior in Green's (1987) sample of feminine and controls boys (Zucker et al. in press). A principal axis factor analysis with varimax rotation yielded one strong factor, accounting for 51.2 percent of the variance. The variable "son states wish to be a girl" was one of fifteen cross-gender behaviors that loaded on this factor (all factor loadings ≥ .40). Thus, there was some empirical support for the hypothesis.

Clinical experience and some research data (Bates, Skilbeck, Smith & Bentler 1974; Zucker et al. 1984) suggested that the wish to change sex is negatively related to age, that is, older children may be less likely to voice this wish, perhaps because of social desirability factors. Green's (1987) data were reanalyzed to explore the relation between age and the wish to be of the opposite sex. Given the age effects suggested by other analyses (Zucker 1992), Green's data were analyzed by comparing children between 3–9 and 9–12 years. The results showed that the wish to be of the opposite sex was more common in the younger age group but was not associated with several other demographic variables (Zucker et al. in press).

Given the changes in the point A criterion, Zucker et al. (in press) then reexamined the symptom ratings from parent interview data regarding a cohort of fifty-four children who did not meet the DSM-III criteria for gender identity disorder (Zucker 1992). In this analysis, we assessed whether children would meet the proposed DSM-IV point A criterion for gender identity disorder. Because these children did not repeatedly state the desire to be of the opposite sex, we coded as present or absent four remaining traits: cross-dressing, cross-sex roles in fantasy play, cross-sex activity/toy interests, and cross-sex peer preference. If all four traits were present, these children would meet the proposed cutoff for the point A criterion. (We chose not to reanalyze the data on the fifty-four other children who met the DSM-III criteria for gender identity disorder, since it was our impression that there would not be any substantive change, given that these children had already verbalized the wish to be of the opposite sex and had displayed marked cross-gender role behaviors.) Of the fifty-four children, the mean number of symptoms rated as present was 2.36 (SD = 1.33; range, 0–4). Only seven children did not have any symptoms rated as present. Of the fifty-four children, sixteen (29.6 percent) had all four symptoms, thus meeting the criterion for point A.

The subgroup that met the point A criterion was also compared to the subgroup that did not with regard to the demographic variables of age, IQ, and parent's social class and marital status. There was a trend for the children who met the point A criterion to be younger than the children who did not (8.0 versus 9.4 years; $t(52)$ = 1.74; p = .087, two-tailed). Thus, age continued to be a correlate of diagnostic status, but the correlation appeared to be weaker than that found in our earlier research (Zucker et al. 1984). None of the other demographic variables distinguished the two subgroups. These reanalyses suggest that the revisions to the diagnostic criteria may result in a modest increase in the number of cases that will meet the complete criteria.

Since these reanalyses were completed, the DSM-IV subcommittee, with feedback from the DSM-IV main office, developed the point B criterion (see table 16.1), which should, if anything, make the diagnosis even harder to meet. Unfortunately, the reanalyses just described did not explicitly focus on this criterion, so this conjecture will require additional empirical analysis.

Cultural Influences

In the DSM-IV, the simple perception of cultural advantage of being the other sex is deemed inadequate for the point A criterion. Unlike DSM-III or DSM-III-R, this exclusion requirement no longer applies only for girls.

Interestingly, the DSM-IV subcommittee had initially recommended that this proviso be deleted, since it was argued that although the motivational basis for the desire to be the other sex may have relevance for such parameters as natural history and response to treatment, it was not clear why it should be used diagnostically (Bradley et al. 1991). For example, it could be argued that boys who wish to be girls perceive similar, albeit inverted, cultural advantages (e.g., "girls can wear dresses *and* pants," "girls don't have to play rough; boys do"). It appears that there was a compromise in the deliberations between the DSM-IV subcommittee and the DSM-IV task force on this matter. Empirical research will have to resolve the question of whether including this proviso has any clinical utility or validity.

Judgments of Persistence

Judgments of behavioral persistence are required in both the point A and point B criteria. For example, the point A criterion requires a clinical judgment in determining what qualifies as a "repeatedly stated desire to be . . . the other sex." What criteria should clinicians utilize in deciding whether the desire to change sex is persistent? To some extent, the answer to this question hinges on what is known about the prevalence and intensity of cross-sex wishes in the general population. Given what is known about the prevalence of marked cross-gender behavior in the general population (for review, see Zucker 1985a; Zucker & Bradley in press), it is likely that the persistent desire to change sex is relatively uncommon, but there is really no gold standard for the clinician to use, and the DSM-IV does not provide explicit guidelines for these matters.

Differential Diagnosis

At least four differential diagnostic issues need to be considered in evaluating children (Bradley & Zucker 1990; Zucker & Bradley in press). Although not described formally in the literature, youngsters are occasionally encountered who display an acute onset of symptoms of gender identity disorder but that usually prove to be transient. In our experience, such onsets can usually be understood as a stress response to a specific life event. For example, some youngsters with a newborn sibling of the opposite sex may display delimited cross-gender behaviors (e.g., cross-dressing, "penis envy" in girls), which can be understood as related to feelings of displacement or jealousy. Such behaviors can be easily distinguished from the chronic feelings of jealousy that are sometimes observed among children with the full-blown disorder. Transient symptoms may also be manifested by youngsters who after having experienced temporary setbacks in same-sex peer groups may, for example, voice unhappiness about their status as boys or girls. Once the stress has been removed or the focal conflict reduced, the symptoms rapidly dissipate.

In the clinical psychoanalytic literature of toddlers and preschool children, it is not uncommon to encounter case reports of youngsters who show signs of gender dysphoria (e.g., "penis envy" in girls) that are understood to arise in the context of specific developmental crises (e.g., becoming more aware of the anatomic differences between the sexes). Our reading of this literature suggests that these symptoms are not pervasive and remit over time without much in the way of formal intervention (Roiphe & Galenson 1981; Roiphe & Spira 1991).

A second differential diagnostic issue involves a type of cross-dressing in boys that appears to be qualitatively different from the type of cross-dressing that characterizes gender identity disorder. In the latter, cross-dressing typically involves outerwear (e.g., dresses, shoes, and jewelry) that helps enhance the fantasy of being like the opposite sex. In the former, cross-dressing involves the use of undergarments, such as panties and nylons (Scharfman 1976; Stoller 1985). Clinical data show that such cross-dressing is not accompanied by other signs of cross-gender identification; in fact, the appearance and behavior of boys who engage in it are conventionally masculine (Zucker 1990a; Zucker & Bradley in press). Clinical experience also suggests that this type of cross-dressing is associated with self-soothing or reduction of anxiety. Many male adolescents and adults who display transvestic fetishism (American Psychiatric Association 1994) recall having engaged in this type of cross-dressing during childhood (Bradley & Zucker 1990; Zucker & Bradley in press). It should be noted, however, that prospective study has not verified the assumption that such cross-dressing is fully contiguous with later transvestism.

When all the clinical signs of gender identity disorder are present, it is not difficult to make the diagnosis. But the clinician who accepts the notion that there is a spectrum of cross-gender identification must be prepared to identify what Meyer-Bahlburg (1985) described as the "zone of transition between clinically significant cross-gender behavior and mere statistical deviations from the gender norm" (p. 682). Clinical experience suggests that boys who fall into this ambiguous zone do poorly in male peer groups, avoid rough-and-tumble play, are disinclined toward athletics and other conventionally masculine activities, and feel somewhat uncomfortable about being male; however, these boys do not wish to be girls and do not show an intense preoccupation with femininity. Friedman (1988) coined the term *juvenile unmasculinity* to describe such boys, who, he argued, suffer from a "persistent, profound feeling of masculine inadequacy which leads to negative valuing of the self" (p. 199). (Although not discussed by Friedman or well studied clinically, one might speculate that an analogous phenomenon, "juvenile unfemininity," is manifested among girls.) It is not clear, however, whether this putative behavior pattern constitutes a distinct syndrome or is simply below the clinical threshold for gender identity disorder; in any case, the residual diagnosis gender identity disorder not otherwise specified (American Psychiatric Association 1994) could be employed in such cases.

In girls, the primary differential diagnostic issue concerns the distinction between gender identity disorder and "tomboyism." The study of a community sample of tomboys by Green, Williams, and Goodman (1982) showed that these girls shared a number of the cross-gender traits observed in clinic-referred gender-disturbed girls (Zucker 1982). In part, the DSM-III-R criteria for gender identity disorder in girls were modified in the hope of better differentiating these two groups of girls (Zucker 1992). At least three characteristics may be most useful in making the differential diagnosis:

1. By definition, girls with gender identity disorder indicate an intense unhappiness with their status as females, whereas this should not be the case for tomboys.
2. Girls with gender identity disorder display an intense aversion to the wearing of culturally defined feminine clothing under any circumstances, whereas tomboys do not manifest this reaction with the same intensity, though they may prefer to wear casual clothing, such as jeans.
3. Girls with gender identity disorder, unlike tomboys, manifest a verbalized or acted-out discomfort with sexual anatomy.

The final differential diagnostic issue concerns children with physical intersex (hermaphroditic) conditions. In the DSM-III (American Psychiatric Association 1980), an intersex condition was an exclusion criterion for the adult diagnosis of transsexualism; however, it was not an exclusion criterion for the gender identity disorder of childhood, although the DSM-III noted that "physical abnormalities of the sex organs are rarely associated with gender identity disorder" (American Psychiatric Association 1980, p. 256). In the DSM-III-R (American Psychiatric Association 1987), this exclusion criterion was eliminated for transsexualism.

Given that some children with intersex conditions have been observed to experience severe gender identity conflict, the DSM-IV subcommittee considered the relevant diagnostic issues. As noted by Meyer-Bahlburg (1994), neither the DSM-III nor the DSM-III-R contained substantive information regarding the conceptual issues. The DSM-III-R did not explicitly address the question of whether children who displayed significant cross-gender identification and had an intersex condition should be given the diagnosis of gender identity disorder.

Meyer-Bahlburg (1994) pointed out that the intersex case report literature has rarely attempted to utilize DSM criteria in describing patients with gender identity and gender role conflicts. Thus, it is not possible to specify what percentage of intersex patients with gender identity problems would meet the formal criteria for gender identity disorder. Meyer-Bahlburg (1994) also argued that it is unclear whether the phenomenology surrounding gender identity concerns is the same as that observed in nonintersex persons with gender identity problems (see also Bradley et al. 1991); however, the DSM-IV subcommittee did not reach a consensus on this issue.

Even if the phenomenology of intersex and nonintersex youngsters is similar, there appear to be substantial differences between them in other variables, including associated features, prevalence, sex ratio, and age of onset (Meyer-Bahlburg 1994), which suggests at least a somewhat different etiology from that involved in nonintersex youngsters with gender identity disorder. For example, gender dysphoria seems to be experienced more frequently by intersex youngsters assigned to the female sex than by intersex youngsters assigned to the male sex, which is the opposite of what is observed among nonintersex youngsters with gender identity disorder (at least as inferred from referral rates).

The very real possibility of distinct etiological influences in intersex youngsters raises the question of whether there may be a risk in applying the same diagnosis to them that is applied to physically normal children (e.g., offering the same type of therapeutic intervention that is used with the latter). On the other hand, the risk is reduced if it is recognized that a particular diagnosis does not dictate identical treatment across cases. From an etiological standpoint, the use of Axis III for physical disorders or conditions would be important in noting the role of the physical anomaly, but this would not preclude using the gender identity disorder diagnosis if clinically justified (for further discussion, see Bradley et al. 1991; Meyer-Bahlburg 1994).

Following additional consultation with the DSM-IV task force, it was decided to allow inclusion of intersex persons with gender identity conflicts under the residual diagnosis, gender identity disorder not otherwise specified.

ETIOLOGY

Sexologists in the biological and social sciences have devoted considerable attention to identifying the determinants of psychosexual differentiation. There are those who argue that these determinants are predominantly biological, psychological, or sociological. Others advocate integrative or interactionist analyses, although most researchers tend to test rather specific hypotheses—pieces, so to speak, of the etiological puzzle. For heuristic purposes, this work can be divided into two main categories: biological and psychosocial. Because gender identity disorder in children is associated, albeit imperfectly, with gender identity disorder in adults or with a homosexual sexual orientation (Bailey & Zucker in press; Green 1987), the origins of one of these parent conditions might provide clues about the origins of the child condition.

Recent Biological Research on Sexual Orientation

It might be fair to state that we are in the midst of a renaissance of biological research on the origins of sexual orientation. Table 16.3 summarizes several domains of biological research that have been investigated, with selective references provided.

Recent work in behavior genetics has produced two findings: in both men and women, there is evidence that homosexuality runs in families, including siblings and in maternal or paternal siblings; and there is greater concordance for homosexuality in monozygotic than in dizygotic twins. This line of research is consistent with, although not proof of, a genetic influence on sexual orientation. In one molecular genetic study of forty pairs of homosexual brothers, a DNA marker was identified on the X chromosome that was shared by thirty-three of the forty pairs. Thus, considerable excitement has been given to the possibility of eventually identifying a gene or series of genes associated with sexual orientation.

Research on prenatal hormonal influences on sexual orientation has yielded decidedly mixed results, and this line of inquiry has been hampered by both conceptual and methodological limitations. It is of interest to note that even among populations with atypical levels of prenatal hormonal exposure, such as in women with congenital adrenal hyperplasia or in women whose mothers received diethylstilbestrol during the pregnancy, the majority of women have a heterosexual sexual orientation.

In humans without intersex conditions, the possibility remains that more subtle variations in prenatal hormone levels are related to sexual orientation, in which brain differentiation, but not genital differentiation, is affected (for an animal model, see Goy, Bercovitch & McBrair 1988). One line of research that has explored this possibility, albeit indirectly, has examined the relation between prenatal maternal stress and sexual orientation. The results have been mixed, and some of the studies have been methodologically suspect (for review, see Zucker & Green 1992).

Neuropsychological correlates of sexual orientation have been examined with regard to several putative behavioral markers of functional cerebral asymmetry, including handedness, dichotic listening tests, and spatial ability. This research has borrowed heavily from the normative literature on sex differences, with the basic hypothesis being that homosexual men and women will show patterns of behavior more typical of the opposite sex. Although positive findings have been reported in each of these three behavioral domains, there are also strong negative findings. Coupled with methodological issues, as yet unresolved, the empirical status of this work is far from clear.

Finally, there have been several postmortem neuroanatomic studies that have identified sexual orientation differences in men. The relevance of these studies to the more classical prenatal hormonal theory of psychosexual differentiation has been discussed in detail elsewhere, as have methodological issues (Byne &

Table 16.3

Selected Summary of Recent Biological Research on Sexual Orientation

Content Area	Selected References	Comment
Behavior Genetics		
Concordance rates in nontwin same-sex siblings	Bailey & Bell (1993); Bailey & Benishay (1993); Pillard & Weinrich (1986)	Studied both males and females.
Concordances rates in monozygotic and dizygotic twins	Bailey & Pillard (1991); Bailey et al. (1993); Whitam et al. (1993)	Studied both males and females.
Molecular Genetics	Hamer et al. (1993)	Studied males. As of yet, no independent replication.
Prenatal Sex Hormones		
Atypical exposure to cross-sex hormones	Dittmann et al. (1992); Ehrhardt et al. (1968, 1985); Money et al. (1984)	Studies pertain to females with certain intersex conditions or exogenous steroids; generalizability to unaffected people not clear.
Positive estrogen feed-back effect	Dorner et al. (1975); Dorner et al. (1986); Gladue et al. (1984)	Studied homosexual males. Studied homosexual transsexual males and females. Studied homosexual males. Gooren (1986) failed to replicate the feedback effect in homosexual males and homosexual transsexual males. Empirical findings, if valid, not necessarily explained by prenatal hormonal factors (for discussion, see Meyer-Bahlburg [1993] and Zucker & Bradley [in press]).
Prenatal Maternal Stress	Dorner et al. (1980); Dorner et al. (1983); Ellis et al. (1988)	Studied males. Studied males. Studied males and females. Major nonreplication by Bailey et al. (1991).
Neuropsychological Markers		
Handedness	Becker et al. (1992); Gotestam et al. (1992); McCormick et al. (1990)	Nonreplications reported in several studies: Blanchard & Bogaert (1994); Gladue & Bailey (in press); Marchant-Haycox et al. (1991); Satz et al. (1991). For a critical review, see Zucker & Bradley (in press).
Spatial Ability	Gladue et al. (1990); Sanders & Ross-Field (1986a, 1986b)	Major nonreplication by Gladue & Bailey (in press).
Neuroanatomy		
INAH	LeVay (1991)	Studied males. As of yet, no independent replication.
Anterior Commissure	Allen & Gorski (1992)	Studied males. As of yet, no independent replication.
Suprachiasmatic Nucleus	Swaab & Hofman (1990)	Studied males. As of yet, no independent replication.

Note. References are selective. An overview of this research can be found elsewhere (Zucker & Bradley, in press).

Parsons 1993; Friedman & Downey 1993; Meyer-Bahlburg 1993). All of these authors have noted the importance of independent replications before the validity of these findings can be more fully appraised.

Biological Research and Gender Identity Disorder in Children

Very little research has been conducted on biological correlates of gender identity disorder in children. For example, molecular genetics, prenatal sex hormones, and neuroanatomic structures have not been investigated at all in children with gender identity disorder, for both practical and ethical reasons. To date, there is little evidence of familiarity of gender identity disorder, which diverges from the evidence on sexual orientation. Indirect evidence for prenatal hormonal influences might be inferred from clinical and empirical observations that boys with gender identity disorder avoid rough-and-tumble play and have a low activity level, whereas the converse is observed in girls with gender identity disorder (Green 1987; Zucker & Green 1993). Apart from the inferential leap required to implicate a biological influence, it should also be recognized that such behaviors can be affected by the social environment. A second line of research suggests that boys with gender identity disorder have a relative deficit in spatial ability (Zucker & Bradley in press), but again the potential biological basis of this finding remains unclear. A third line of research, which is quite new, has shown that boys with gender identity disorder come from sibships with a disproportionate number of brothers and are later born (Blanchard, Zucker, Bradley & Hume in press). An excess of brothers and a later birth order have also been found in homosexual transsexual men (Blanchard & Sheridan 1992; Blanchard, Zucker, Cohen-Kettenis, Gooren & Bailey 1994), suggesting some continuity between gender identity disorder in childhood and adulthood. In contrast, an excess of brothers has not been found in samples of homosexual men without gender identity disorder; however, homosexual men have been shown to be later born (Blanchard & Bogaert 1994; Blanchard & Zucker 1994; Zucker & Blanchard 1994). Thus, there is partial convergence between gender identity disorder and homosexuality with regard to these two biodemographic variables. Unfortunately, we do not yet have a good understanding of the etiological relevance of these observations (for further discussion, see Blanchard & Sheridan 1992; Blanchard et al. in press; Blanchard et al. 1994).

In summary, recent research on the biology of sexual orientation has opened up several lines of inquiry. The consistency of the empirical returns has varied across the domains of study. The precise relevance of this work for gender identity disorder is unclear, but the notion that there is some biological predisposition that places children at risk has been entertained by several clinicians and researchers (Coates & Wolfe in press; Green 1987).

Psychosocial Research on Gender Identity Disorder in Children

Considerably more etiological or quasi-etiological psychosocial research has been conducted on children with gender identity disorder, particularly boys. Table 16.4 summarizes several domains of research, with selective references provided.

Among young children with physical intersex conditions, it was shown that ambiguity or uncertainty about sex assignment and rearing could lead to a conflicted gender identity (Money, Hampson & Hampson 1957; Stoller 1964b). There is, however, little evidence that uncertainty about sex assignment at birth is an important factor in explaining conflicted gender identity in physically normal children.

Along somewhat similar lines, it has been proposed that parental ambivalence about the child's sex may play a role in producing gender identity conflict. Thus, one line of empirical research explored whether parents of children with gender identity disorder disproportionately had preferred prenatally a child of the opposite sex. There was no evidence that this occurred. However, Zucker and Bradley (in press) have noted that among mothers of boys with gender identity disorder who had desired daughters, there appears to be a small subgroup who experience what might be termed pathological gender mourning (Zucker, Bradley & Ipp 1993). The wish for a daughter is acted out (e.g., by cross-dressing the boy) or expressed in other ways. Severe depression often occurs among these mothers, which is lifted only when the boy begins to act in a certain feminine manner. This clinical observation will have to be examined in much greater detail, including understanding how the wish for a child of the opposite sex is resolved in the majority of cases.

There is some consensus that a common psychosocial pathway involved in gender identity disorder concerns parental tolerance or encouragement of cross-gender behavior. Regardless of variations in parental motivation, such tolerance is observed clinically in the majority of cases and has been documented in two empirical studies. This line of research converges reasonably well with normative studies that have examined the role of parental encouragement of sex-dimorphic behavior in boys and girls (Fagot & Leinbach 1989; Lytton & Romney 1991).

Parents of children with gender identity disorder appear, on average, to show higher rates of psychiatric disorder and emotional impairment than do parents of nonclinical control children but as much as do parents of clinical controls. (A similar finding regarding psychopathology has also been observed in children with gender identity disorder, but this line of research is beyond the scope of this chapter. (For review, see Zucker & Bradley in press.) The role of parental psychopathology in explaining the gender identity disorder itself has been explored from several perspectives. One possibility is that such impairment prevents the parents from being able to mobilize themselves to set limits on the

Table 16.4
Selected Summary of Recent Psychosocial Research on Gender Identity Disorder in Boys

Content Area	Selected References	Comment
Prenatal Sex Preference	Zucker et al. (1994); Zuger (1974)	No effects.
Reinforcement of Cross-Gender Behavior	Green (1987); Mitchell (1991)	see also Roberts et al. (1987)
Rates of Father-Absence	Zucker & Bradley (in press)	Little evidence that rates of father absence are disproportionately elevated in families of boys with gender identity disorder.
Father-Son Shared Time	Green (1987)	see also Roberts et al. (1987)
Mother-Son Shared Time	Green (1987)	see also Roberts et al. (1987). Mothers of feminine boys recalled spending _less_ time with their sons than mothers of control boys.
Maternal Psychosexual Development	Green (1987); Mitchell (1991)	Little evidence that mothers of boys with gender identity disorder had had gender identity conflicts or marked cross-gender behavior during childhood.
Paternal Psychosexual Development	Green (1987)	Little evidence that fathers of boys with gender identity disorder had had gender identity conflicts or marked cross-gender behavior during childhood.
Maternal Psychiatric/Emotional Disorder	Marantz & Coates (1991); Zucker & Bradley (in press)	Higher in mothers of boys with gender identity disorder than in mothers of normal controls. Evidence is suggestive of nonspecificity, i.e., equivalent to mothers of clinical control boys.

Note. References are selective. An overview of this research can be found elsewhere (Zucker & Bradley, in press).

cross-gender behavior. Another possibility is that it contributes to the child's sense of insecurity, such that the child begins to question whether he or she is valued as a boy or as a girl. If the child suspects that he or she is responded to in a more favorable manner when engaging in cross-gender behavior, then this may inadvertently contribute to the beginnings of gender identity conflict. Several theorists have emphasized that such factors must be present during the putative sensitive period for gender identity formation early in development—between 2 and 4 years of age. Unfortunately, the database on which these speculations have been based is small. Moreover, one must grapple with the problem of specificity, since many parents with psychiatric impairment do not have children with gender identity conflicts. Thus, complex models are required, involving the sensitive period, factors in the child, and factors in the family (Coates 1990).

Another line of research has tried to examine both quantitative and qualitative aspects of the child's relationships with both parents. There is, for example, some evidence that boys with gender identity disorder have had less contact with their fathers than control boys, despite equal rates of parental separation or divorce. In girls with gender identity disorder, clinical observation has suggested that early severe maternal depression is common, which may result in a relative lack of identification with the mother (Zucker & Bradley in press).

In summary, psychosocial research on gender identity disorder has yielded both positive and negative findings. Ambiguity about sex assignment or an elevated prenatal preference for a child of the opposite sex has been negative. Positive findings have emerged with regard to unusual reactions to bearing a child of the nonpreferred sex, tolerance of cross-gender behavior, and the contributory role of parental emotional distress or psychiatric impairment. However, much of this work is preliminary and needs to be strengthened by replications and the testing of multifactor models of causation.

THERAPEUTIC INTERVENTIONS

There is considerable evidence that treatment with cross-sex hormones and physical surgery (e.g., in women, mastectomy, and, in some cases, creation of a neophallus; in men, removal of the genitals and creation of a neovagina) of adults with gender identity disorder reduces psychological distress and impaired psychosocial functioning (Blanchard 1985; Blanchard & Sheridan 1990). But what about psychological treatments for gender dysphoria? Here the dictum that transsexualism "resists psychiatric treatment" (Hertz, Tillinger & Westman 1961) is as true today as it was over thirty years ago. Although the occasional report on successful psychological treatments has appeared in the literature (Barlow, Abel & Blanchard 1979; Barlow, Reynolds & Agras 1973), including an apparent exorcism (Barlow, Abel & Blanchard 1977), I would argue that the prognosis for such interventions is rather bleak, along the same lines that I did several years ago (Zucker 1985b), in partial response to what struck me as an overly optimistic therapeutic claim provided by Lothstein (1983). A summary of clinical management strategies for adults with gender dysphoria can be found elsewhere (Blanchard & Steiner 1990).

Adolescents with gender dysphoria pose a considerable dilemma for the clinician. On the one hand, like adults with gender dysphoria, there is little in the treatment literature that would leave one optimistic that psychological interventions are very effective in resolving the gender dysphoria (Dulcan & Lee 1984; Newman 1970). On the other hand, it is ethically more dubious to institute irreversible hormonal and surgical treatments with adolescents, in part because some youngsters resolve their gender dysphoria without treatment. In our experience, about one-third of adolescents assessed for gender dysphoria relinquished the desire to change sex over time regardless of whether they had treatment (Zucker & Bradley in press). Thus, the adolescent with gender dysphoria presents the clinician with very complex treatment dilemmas.

Treatment of children with gender identity disorder has been approached from diverse conceptual orientations but primarily that of behavior therapy, psychoanalytic psychotherapy, and parent counseling. Proponents of behavior therapy (Rekers 1977) have focused largely on the development of techniques to modify specific sex-typed behaviors, such as cross-dressing and exclusive play with opposite-sex toys, whereas psychodynamically oriented clinicians have a greater preference to view gender identity disorder in the context of family pathology and associated personality psychopathology in the child (Meyer & Dupkin 1985) and to place as much emphasis on treating these problems as the gender identity symptomatology itself.

Empirical evaluation of treatment efficacy for children with gender identity disorder is weak. Comparative studies of different types of treatment approaches are unavailable; thus, any claim of superiority, particularly with regard to long-term effects, is unwarranted. There is virtually no systematic research concerning treatment in childhood and its effect on postpubertal outcome, including gender identity and sexual orientation. The only long-term effect of treatment was reported on by Green (1987), who noted that the rate of bisexuality or homosexuality was similar in the boys who had received treatment in childhood compared to those who had not received treatment; however, Green's study was not primarily a treatment investigation, so this outcome should be viewed with caution.

Three general comments about treatment of gender identity disorder during childhood will be made. First, clinical experience suggests that intervention can more readily reduce gender identity conflict during childhood than during adolescence. Accordingly, the earlier that treatment begins, the better.

Second, the importance of working with the parents of children with gender identity disorder has been much discussed in the literature (Newman 1976; Wolfe 1994). When there is a great deal of marital discord and parental psychopathology, treatment of these problems will greatly facilitate more specific work on gender identity issues. Management of the child's gender behavior in his or her daily environment requires that the parents have clear goals and a forum in which to discuss difficulties. Because parental dynamics and parental ambivalence about treatment may contribute to the perpetuation of gender identity disorder (Newman 1976), it is important for the therapist to have an appropriate relationship with the parents in order to address and work through these issues.

Finally, the therapist needs to consider closely the goals of treatment (for a detailed consideration, see Green 1987; Zucker & Bradley in press). In part, this issue will be conceptualized within the therapist's theoretical framework, but it will also be a function of the parents' concerns and, to some extent, of the child's concerns. Two short-term goals have been discussed in the clinical literature: the reduction or elimination of social ostracism and conflict and the alleviation of underlying or associated psychopathology. Longer-term goals have focused on the prevention of transsexualism and homosexuality. Little disagreement about the advisability of preventing gender dysphoria in adolescence or adulthood has been expressed in the clinical literature. Contemporary and secular-minded clinicians are, however, sensitive to the importance of helping people integrate a homosexual orientation into their sense of identity (Friedman 1988). Not surprisingly, however, the development of a heterosexual orientation is probably preferred by most parents of children with gender identity disorder. It is therefore important that clinicians point out to such parents that, as yet, there is no strong evidence that treatment affects later sexual orientation (Zucker 1990b). Many experienced clinicians in the field have preferred to emphasize the merit of reducing childhood gender identity conflict per se and to orient the parents of children with gender identity disorder to the short-term goals of intervention.

Behavior Therapy

Rekers (1977) has summarized the use of different types of behavioral techniques to treat gender identity disorder, such as differential social attention or reinforcement, token economy, and self-regulation. There is evidence that specific sex-typed behaviors can be either reduced or increased in their frequency. The techniques have been subject to two main limitations: stimulus specificity and response specificity. The first term refers to the phenomenon of a behavior's reappearing (e.g., cross-dressing) in the absence of the stimulus condition under which it was modified (e.g., parental negative sanctions, new environment). The second term means that the treatment did not generalize or influence untreated behaviors, although they appear to be of the same type as the treated behavior; thus, a procedure might modify cross-dressing but not generalize to play with Barbie dolls, a behavior that was not specifically subject to formal treatment techniques (for a review, see Zucker 1985a).

Despite these limitations, an overall analysis of the behavior therapy case report literature suggests some impact on the presenting problem and apparently an impact on the child's overall sense of gender identity. Rekers, Kilgus, and Rosen (1990) presented the results of behavior therapy of twenty-nine boys. At a mean follow-up of fifty-one months after treatment, it was found that "completion" of treatment accounted for 20 percent of the variance in change scores, as defined by a reduction in ratings of cross-gender identification. Unfortunately, no published longer-term follow-ups on this sample, in which their adolescent gender identity and sexual orientation were assessed, are available.

Psychotherapy

The English-language psychotherapy literature consists of a couple of dozen case reports (summarized in Zucker 1985a and Zucker & Bradley in press). Unlike the use of quantitative data in the behavior therapy case report literature, the psychotherapy literature is much more descriptive and qualitative in nature. Schultz's (1979) doctoral dissertation, a detailed account of the psychotherapy of one boy with gender identity disorder, provides an unusual glimpse of the process of therapeutic intervention. Although difficult to quantify, the impression one gets from studying this literature is that many of the children had made gains by the end of their therapy. Because many of the parents of these children were in therapy and in some instances the child received additional, concurrent treatments (e.g., as an inpatient), the precise mechanisms of change become even more difficult to identify. No systematic follow-up data on adolescent gender identity and sexual orientation are available from the psychotherapy case report literature.

Elsewhere, I have identified discernable themes in the psychotherapy case report literature (Zucker 1985a; Zucker & Bradley in press). These include an emphasis on the significance of the emergence of cross-gender behavior during the preoedipal years, with concomitant attention to early object relations, general ego functioning, evidence for developmental arrests, and the influence of temperamental traits (see, e.g., Coates, Wolfe & Friedman 1991). Attention is given to understanding the impact of the mother-child and father-child relationship on the formation of the gender symptomatology and the parental psychodynamics that putatively underlie their tolerance for the cross-gender behavior.

Although the treatment literature on children with gender identity disorder remains exceedingly thin in documenting its effectiveness, I can only conclude from my own experience, along with discussions with colleagues, that the overall prospects for reducing gender identity conflict should leave one optimistic, not nihilistic. Consolidation of a cross-gender identity is far from complete during the childhood years and certainly less so than what one observes in adolescents and adults. This is not to say that for some children resolution of marked gender dysphoria is easy, but in others it clearly is. Helping children and their parents work on the best possible resolution to the conflict in gender identity requires a great deal of effort, but in many cases the distress can be alleviated, resulting in a more comfortable psychosexual and psychosocial adaptation.

REFERENCES

Allen, L. S., & Gorski, R. A. (1992). Sexual orientation and the size of the anterior commissure in the human brain. *Proceedings of the National Academy of Sciences, 89,* 7199–7202.

American Psychiatric Association. (1980). *Diagnostic and statistical manual of mental disorders* (3rd ed.). Washington, DC: Author.

American Psychiatric Association. (1987). *Diagnostic and statistical manual of mental disorders* (3rd ed., rev.). Washington, DC: Author.

American Psychiatric Association. (1994). *Diagnostic and statistical manual of mental disorders* (4th ed.). Washington, DC: Author.

Bailey, J. M., & Bell, A. P. (1993). Familiality of female and male homosexuality. *Behavior Genetics, 23,* 313–322.

Bailey, J. M., & Benishay, D. S. (1993). Familial aggregation of female sexual orientation. *American Journal of Psychiatry, 150,* 272–277.

Bailey, J. M., & Pillard, R. C. (1991). A genetic study of male sexual orientation. *Archives of General Psychiatry, 48,* 1089–1096.

Bailey, J. M., Pillard, R. C., Neale, M. C., & Agyei, Y. (1993). Heritable factors influence sexual orientation in women. *Archives of General Psychiatry, 50,* 217–223.

Bailey, J. M., Willerman, L., & Parks, C. (1991). A test of the maternal stress theory of human male homosexuality. *Archives of Sexual Behavior, 20,* 277–293.

Bailey, J. M., & Zucker, K. J. (in press). Childhood sex-typed behavior and sexual orientation: A conceptual analysis and quantitative review. *Developmental Psychology.*

Barlow, D. H., Abel, G. G., & Blanchard, E. B. (1977). Gender identity change in a transsexual: An exorcism. *Archives of Sexual Behavior, 6,* 387–395.

Barlow, D. H., Abel, G. G., & Blanchard, E. B. (1979). Gender identity change in transsexuals: Follow-up and replications. *Archives of General Psychiatry, 36,* 1001–1007.

Barlow, D. H., Reynolds, J. E., & Agras, W. S. (1973). Gender identity change in a transsexual. *Archives of General Psychiatry, 28,* 569–576.

Bates, J. E., Skilbeck, W. M., Smith, K. V. R., & Bentler, P. M. (1974). Gender role abnormalities in boys: An analysis of clinical ratings. *Journal of Abnormal Child Psychology, 2,* 1–16.

Becker, J. T., Bass, S. M., Dew, M. A., Kingsley, L., Selnes, O. A., & Sheridan, K. (1992). Hand preference, immune system disorder and cognitive function among gay/bisexual men: The multicenter AIDS cohort study (MACS). *Neuropsychologia, 30,* 229–235.

Bentler, P. M., Rekers, G. A., & Rosen, A. C. (1979). Congruence of childhood sex-role identity and behavior disturbances. *Child: Care, Health and Development, 5,* 267–283.

Blanchard, R. (1985). Gender dysphoria and gender reorientation. In B. W. Steiner (Ed.), *Gender dysphoria: Development, research, management* (pp. 365–392). New York: Plenum Press.

Blanchard, R., & Bogaert, A. F. (1994). *Biodemographic comparisons of homosexual and heterosexual men in the Kinsey interview data.* Manuscript submitted for publication, Clarke Institute of Psychiatry, Toronto, Ontario.

Blanchard, R., & Sheridan, P. M. (1990). Gender reorientation and psychosocial adjustment. In R. Blanchard & B. W. Steiner (Eds.), *Clinical management of gender identity disorders in children and adults* (pp. 161–189). Washington, DC: American Psychiatric Press.

Blanchard, R., & Sheridan, P. M. (1992). Sibship size, sibling sex ratio, birth order, and parental age in homosexual and nonhomosexual gender dysphorics. *Journal of Nervous and Mental Disease, 180,* 40–47.

Blanchard, R., & Steiner, B. W. (Eds.). (1990). *Clinical management of gender identity disorders in children and adults.* Washington, DC: American Psychiatric Press.

Blanchard, R., & Zucker, K. J. (1994). Reanalysis of Bell, Weinberg, and Hammersmith's data on birth order, sibling sex ratio, and parental age in homosexual men. *American Journal of Psychiatry, 151,* 1375–1376.

Blanchard, R., Zucker, K. J., Bradley, S. J., & Hume, C. S. (in press). Birth order and sibling sex ratio in homosexual male adolescents and probably prehomosexual feminine boys. *Developmental Psychology.*

Blanchard, R., Zucker, K. J., Cohen-Kettenis, P. T., Gooren, L. J. G., & Bailey, J. M. (1994). *Birth order and sibling sex ratio in two samples of Dutch gender-dysphoric homosexual males.* Manuscript submitted for publication.

Bogaert, A. F., & Blanchard, R. (1994). *Handedness in homosexual and heterosexual men in the Kinsey Interview data.* Unpublished manuscript, Clarke Institute of Psychiatry, Toronto, Ontario, Canada.

Bradley, S. J., Blanchard, R., Coates, S., Green, R., Levine, S. B., Meyer-Bahlburg, H. F. L., Pauly, I. B., & Zucker, K. J. (1991). Interim report of the DSM-IV Subcommittee for Gender Identity Disorders. *Archives of Sexual Behavior, 20,* 333–343.

Bradley, S. J., & Zucker, K. J. (1990). Gender identity disorder and psychosexual problems in children and adolescents. *Canadian Journal of Psychiatry, 35,* 477–486.

Bullough, V. L., & Bullough, B. (1993). *Cross dressing, sex, and gender.* Philadelphia: University of Pennsylvania Press.

Byne, W., & Parsons, B. (1993). Human sexual orientation: The biologic theories reappraised. *Archives of General Psychiatry, 50,* 228–239.

Coates, S. (1990). Ontogenesis of boyhood gender identity disorder. *Journal of the American Academy of Psychoanalysis, 18,* 414–438.

Coates, S., Friedman, R. C., & Wolfe, S. (1991). The etiology of boyhood gender identity disorder: A model for integrating temperament, development, and psychodynamics. *Psychoanalytic Dialogues, 1,* 341–383.

Coates, S., & Wolfe, S. (in press). Gender identity disorder in boys: The interface of constitution and early experience. *Psychoanalytic Inquiry.*

Dekker, R. M., & van de Pol, L. C. (1989). *The tradition of female transvestism in early modern Europe.* New York: St. Martin's Press.

Dittmann, R. W., Kappes, M. E., & Kappes, M. H. (1992). Sexual behavior in adolescent and adult females with congenital adrenal hyperplasia. *Psychoneuroendocrinology, 17,* 153–170.

Dörner, G., Geier, T., Ahrens, L., Krell, L., Munx, G., Sieler, H., Kittner, E., & Muller, H. (1980). Prenatal stress as possible aetiogenic factor of homosexuality in human males. *Endokrinologie, 75,* 365–368.

Dörner, G., Rohde, W., Seidel, K., Haas, W., & Schott, G. (1976). On the evocability of a positive oestrogen feedback action on LH secretion in transsexual men and women. *Endokrinologie, 67,* 20–25.

Dörner, G., Rohde, W., Stahl, F., Krell, L., & Masius, W. G. (1975). A neuroendocrine predisposition for homosexuality in men. *Archives of Sexual Behavior, 4,* 1–8.

Dörner, G., Schenk, B., Schmiedel, B., & Ahrens, L. (1983). Stressful events in prenatal life of bi- and homosexual men. *Experimental Clinical Endocrinology, 81,* 83–87.

Dulcan, M. K., & Lee, P. A. (1984). Transsexualism in the adolescent girl. *Journal of the American Academy of Child Psychiatry, 23,* 354–361.

Ehrhardt, A. A., Evers, K., & Money, J. (1968). Influence of androgen and some aspects of sexually dimorphic behavior in women with the late-treated adrenogenital syndrome. *Johns Hopkins Medical Journal, 123,* 115–122.

Ehrhardt, A. A., Meyer-Bahlburg, H. F. L., Rosen, L. R., Feldman, J. R., Veridiano, N. P., Zimmerman, I., & McEwen, B. S. (1985). Sexual orientation after prenatal exposure to exogenous estrogen. *Archives of Sexual Behavior, 14,* 57–75.

Ellis, H. (1936). *Studies in the psychology of sex* (Vol. 2). New York: Random House. (Originally published 1910)

Fagot, B. I., & Leinbach, M. D. (1989). The young child's gender schema: Environmental input, internal organization. *Child Development, 60,* 663–672.

Friedman, R. C. (1988). *Male homosexuality: A contemporary psychoanalytic perspective.* New Haven, CT: Yale University Press.

Friedman, R. C., & Downey, J. (1993). Neurobiology and sexual orientation: Current relationships. *Journal of Neuropsychiatry and Clinical Neurosciences, 5,* 131–153.

Gladue, B. A., & Bailey, J. M. (in press). Spatial ability, handedness, and sexual orientation. *Psychoneuroendocrinology.*

Gladue, B. A., Beatty, W. W., Larson, J., & Staton, R. D. (1990). Sexual orientation and spatial ability in men and women. *Psychobiology, 18,* 101–108.

Gladue, B. A., Green, R., & Hellman, R. E. (1984). Neuroendocrine response to estrogen and sexual orientation. *Science, 225,* 1496–1499.

Gooren, L. (1986). The neuroendocrine response of luteinizing hormone to estrogen administration in heterosexual, homosexual, and transsexual subjects. *Journal of Clinical Endocrinology and Metabolism, 63,* 583–588.

Goy, R. W., Bercovitch, F. B., & McBrair, M. C. (1988). Behavioral masculinization is independent of genital masculinization in prenatally androgenized female rhesus macaques. *Hormones and Behavior, 22,* 552–571.

Green, R. (1974). *Sexual identity conflict in children and adults.* New York: Basic Books.

Green, R. (1976). One-hundred ten feminine and masculine boys: Behavioral contrasts and demographic similarities. *Archives of Sexual Behavior, 5,* 425–446.

Green, R. (1987). *The "sissy boy syndrome" and the development of homosexuality.* New Haven, CT: Yale University Press.

Green, R., Williams, K., & Goodman, M. (1982). Ninety-nine "tomboys" and "nontomboys": Behavioral contrasts and demographic similarities. *Archives of Sexual Behavior, 11,* 247–266.

Hamer, D. H., Hu, S., Magnuson, V. L., Hu, N., & Pattatucci, A. M. L. (1993). A linkage between DNA markers on the X chromosome and male sexual orientation. *Science, 261,* 321–327.

Hertz, J., Tillinger, K., & Westman, A. (1961). Transvestitism: Report on five hormonally and surgically treated cases. *Acta Psychiatrica Scandinavica, 37,* 283–294.

Kinsey, A. C., Pomeroy, W. B., & Martin, C. E. (1948). *Sexual behavior in the human male.* Philadelphia: W. B. Saunders.

Krafft-Ebing, R. V. (1886). *Psychopathia sexualis.* Stuttgart: Ferdinand Enke.

LeVay, S. (1991). A difference in hypothalamic structure between heterosexual and homosexual men. *Science, 253,* 1034–1037.

Lothstein, L. M. (1983). *Female-to-male transsexualism: Historical, clinical, and theoretical issues.* Boston: Routledge & Kegan Paul.

Lytton, H., & Romney, D. M. (1991). Parents' differential socialization of boys and girls: A meta-analysis. *Psychological Bulletin, 109,* 267–296.

McCormick, C. M., Witelson, S. F., & Kingstone, E. (1990). Left-handedness in homosexual men and women: Neuroendocrine implications. *Psychoneuroendocrinology, 15,* 69–76.

Marantz, S., & Coates, S. (1991). Mothers of boys with gender identity disorder: A comparison of matched controls. *Journal of the American Academy of Child and Adolescent Psychiatry, 30,* 310–315.

Marchant-Haycox, S. E., McManus, I. C., & Wilson, G. D. (1991). Left-handedness, homosexuality, HIV infection and AIDS. *Cortex, 27,* 49–56.

Meyer, J. K., & Dupkin, C. (1985). Gender disturbance in children: An interim clinical report. *Bulletin of the Menninger Clinic, 49,* 236–269.

Meyer-Bahlburg, H. F. L. (1985). Gender identity disorder of childhood: Introduction. *Journal of the American Academy of Child Psychiatry, 24,* 681–683.

Meyer-Bahlburg, H. F. L. (1993). Psychobiologic research on homosexuality. *Child and Adolescent Psychiatric Clinics of North America, 2,* 489–500.

Meyer-Bahlburg, H. F. L. (1994). Intersexuality and the diagnosis of gender identity disorder. *Archives of Sexual Behavior, 23,* 21–40.

Mitchell, J. N. (1991). *Maternal influences on gender identity disorder in boys: Searching for specificity.* Unpublished doctoral dissertation, York University, Downsview, Ontario.

Money, J. (1955). Hermaphroditism, gender and precocity in hyperadrenocorticism: Psychologic findings. *Bulletin of the Johns Hopkins Hospital, 96,* 253–264.

Money, J., Hampson, J. G., & Hampson, J. L. (1957). Imprinting and the establishment of gender role. *Archives of Neurology and Psychiatry, 77,* 333–336.

Money, J., Schwartz, M., & Lewis, V. G. (1984). Adult erotosexual status and fetal hormonal masculinization and demasculinization: 46, XX congenital virilizing adrenal hyperplasia and 46, XY androgen-insensitivity syndrome compared. *Psychoneuroendocrinology, 9,* 405–414.

Moore, K. L., & Barr, M. L. (1955). Smears from the oral mucosa in the detection of chromosomal sex. *Lancet, 2,* 57–58.

Newman, L. E. (1970). Transsexualism in adolescence: Problems in evaluation and treatment. *Archives of General Psychiatry, 23,* 112–121.

Newman, L. E. (1976). Treatment for the parents of feminine boys. *American Journal of Psychiatry, 133,* 683–687.

Pauly, I. B. (1992). Terminology and classification of gender identity disorders. *Journal of Psychology and Human Sexuality, 5,* 1–14.

Pillard, R. C., & Weinrich, J. D. (1986). Evidence of familial nature of male homosexuality. *Archives of General Psychiatry, 43,* 808–812.

Rekers, G. A. (1977). Assessment and treatment of childhood gender problems. In B. B. Lahey & A. E. Kazdin (Eds.), *Advances in clinical child psychology* (Vol. 1, pp. 267–306). New York: Plenum Press.

Rekers, G. A., Kilgus, M., & Rosen, A. C. (1990). Long-term effects of treatment for gender identity disorder of childhood. *Journal of Psychology and Human Sexuality, 3,* 121–153.

Roiphe, H., & Galenson, E. (1981). *Infantile origins of sexual identity.* New York: International Universities Press.

Roiphe, H., & Spira, N. (1991). Object loss, aggression, and gender identity. *Psychoanalytic Study of the Child, 46,* 37–50.

Rosen, A. C., Rekers, G. A., & Friar, L. R. (1977). Theoretical and diagnostic issues in child gender disturbances. *Journal of Sex Research, 13,* 89–103.

Sanders, G., & Ross-Field, L. (1986a). Sexual orientation and visuo-spatial ability. *Brain and Cognition, 5,* 280–290.

Sanders, G., & Ross-Field, L. (1986b). Sexual orientation, cognitive abilities and cerebral asymmetry: A review and a hypothesis tested. *Italian Journal of Zoology, 20,* 459–470.

Satz, P., Miller, E. N., Selnes, O., Van Gorp, W., D'Elia, L. F., & Visscher, B. (1991). Hand preference in homosexual men. *Cortex, 27,* 295–306.

Scharfman, M. A. (1976). Perverse development in a young boy. *Journal of the American Psychoanalytic Association, 24,* 499–524.

Schultz, N. M. (1979). *Severe gender identity confusion in an eight-year-old boy.* Unpublished doctoral dissertation, Yeshiva University.

Stoller, R. J. (1964a). The hermaphroditic identity of hermaphrodites. *Journal of Nervous and Mental Disease, 139,* 453–457.

Stoller, R. J. (1964b). A contribution to the study of gender identity. *International Journal of Psychoanalysis, 45,* 220–226.

Stoller, R. J. (1985). Maternal influences in the precocious emergence of fetishism in a two-year-old boy. In E. J. Anthony & G. H. Pollock (Eds.), *Parental influences in health and disease* (pp. 427–475). Boston: Little, Brown.

Swaab, D. F., & Hofman, M. A. (1990). An enlarged suprachiasmatic nucleus in homosexual men. *Brain Research, 537,* 141–148.

Tiefer, L. (1994). Three crises facing sexology. *Archives of Sexual Behavior, 23,* 361–374.

Whitam, F. L., Diamond, M., & Martin, J. (1993). Homosexual orientation in twins: A report on 61 pairs and three triplet sets. *Archives of Sexual Behavior, 22,* 187–206.

Wolfe, S. (1994, October). Case illustration of intervention strategies for boys with gender identity disorder and their families. In S. J. Bradley (Chair), *Gender identity disorder: Recent research and approaches to treatment.* Institute presented at the meeting of the American Academy of Child and Adolescent Psychiatry, New York.

Zucker, K. J. (1982). Childhood gender disturbance: Diagnostic issues. *Journal of the American Academy of Child Psychiatry, 21,* 274–280.

Zucker, K. J. (1985a). Cross-gender-identified children. In B. W. Steiner (Ed.), *Gender dysphoria: Development, research, management* (pp. 75–174). New York: Plenum Press.

Zucker, K. J. (1985b). [Review of *Female-to-male transsexualism: Historical, clinical, and theoretical issues*]. *Archives of Sexual Behavior, 14,* 377–381.

Zucker, K. J. (1990a). Gender identity disorders in children: Clinical descriptions and natural history. In R. Blanchard & B. W. Steiner (Eds.), *Clinical management of gender identity disorders in children and adults* (pp. 1–23). Washington, DC: American Psychiatric Press.

Zucker, K. J. (1990b). Treatment of gender identity disorders in children. In R. Blanchard & B. W. Steiner (Eds.), *Clinical management of gender identity disorders in children and adults* (pp. 25–47). Washington, DC: American Psychiatric Press.

Zucker, K. J. (1992). Gender identity disorder. In S. R. Hooper, G. W. Hynd, & R. E. Mattison (Eds.), *Child psychopathology: Diagnostic criteria and clinical assessment* (pp. 305–342). Hillsdale, NJ: Erlbaum.

Zucker, K. J., & Blanchard, R. (1994). Re-analysis of Bieber et al.'s 1962 data on sibling sex ratio and birth order in male homosexuals. *Journal of Nervous and Mental Disease, 182,* 528–530.

Zucker, K. J., & Bradley, S. J. (in press). *Gender identity disorder and psychosexual problems in children and adolescents.* New York: Guilford Press.

Zucker, K. J., Bradley, S. J., & Ipp, M. (1993). Delayed naming of a newborn boy: Relationship to the mother's wish for a girl and subsequent cross-gender identity in the child by the age of two. *Journal of Psychology and Human Sexuality, 6,* 57–68.

Zucker, K. J., Finegan, J. K., Doering, R. W., & Bradley, S. J. (1984). Two subgroups of gender-problem children. *Archives of Sexual Behavior, 13,* 27–39.

Zucker, K. J., & Green, R. (1992). Psychosexual disorders in children and adolescents. *Journal of Child Psychology and Psychiatry, 33,* 107–151.

Zucker, K. J., & Green, R. (1993). Psychological and familial aspects of gender identity disorder. *Child and Adolescent Psychiatric Clinics of North America, 2,* 513–542.

Zucker, K. J., Green, R., Bradley, S. J., Williams, K., Rebach, H. M., & Hood, J. E. (in press). Gender identity disorder of childhood: Diagnostic issues. In T. A. Widiger, A. F. Frances, H. A. Pincus, M. B. First & W. W. Davis (Eds.), *DSM-IV sourcebook.* Washington, DC: American Psychiatric Association.

Zucker, K. J., Green, R., Garofano, C., Bradley, S. J., Williams, K., Rebach, H. M., & Lowry Sullivan, C. B. (1994). Prenatal gender preference of mothers of feminine and masculine boys: Relation to sibling sex composition and birth order. *Journal of Abnormal Child Psychology, 22,* 1–13.

Zuger, B. (1974). Effeminate behavior in boys: Parental age and other factors. *Archives of General Psychiatry, 30,* 173–177.

Part V

Sexual Orientation and Social Issues

17

Sexual Reorientation Therapy for Pedophiles: Practices and Controversies

Howard E. Barbaree, Anthony F. Bogaert, and Michael C. Seto

This chapter reviews the changes in pedophilia as a sexual orientation that have been achieved and describes how therapeutic changes in the sexual responses of pedophiles have been integrated into a comprehensive cognitive-behavioral treatment involving relapse prevention. Before we begin, it will be helpful to define some terms here and to provide a disclaimer. In 1973, the American Psychiatric Association removed homosexuality from its *Diagnostic and Statistical Manual of Mental Disorders* (DSM-II: American Psychiatric Association 1973), thereby conveying its disagreement with the illness model of homosexuality. Since then there has been widespread rejection of the illness model, reflected in a 1975 resolution of the American Psychological Association encouraging its members to provide leadership in counteracting the stigma attached to homosexuality. As a consequence, there have been strong ethical objections raised about attempts to convert homosexuals to heterosexuality (Haldeman 1994). The ethical arguments are twofold. First, it is unethical to attempt to cure a condition that is not judged to be an illness. Second, attempts to "cure" homosexual orientation reinforce the prejudicial and unjustified devaluation of homosexuals (Haldeman 1994). This chapter supports the anti-illness view of homosexuality, and the methods described here for achieving change in sexual orientation are not presented in any way as a promotion of attempts to change homosexual orientation. Nevertheless, attempts to change homosexuality have historical interest since later attempts to change pedophilia and other paraphilias were based on earlier work with homosexuals.

Adams and Sturgis (1977) critically reviewed thirty-seven published studies of behavioral reorientation of homosexuality published from 1960 to 1976. Not all studies reported positive outcomes, and positive results were inversely related to the adequacy of methodological controls that were used. As well, very few of these studies involved follow-up periods greater than eighteen months, limiting their ability to evaluate the permanence of any changes achieved. Overall, modest changes were found in the desired direction: increased heterosexual arousal and decreased homosexual arousal. However, these changes could not be attributed to any single learning or other psychological process.

We use the term *sexual orientation* in this chapter as if it were synonymous with similar terms used elsewhere in the literature such as *sexual preference, erotic preference,* and *erotic orientation.* Sexual orientation is defined by (1) the ability of a certain class of stimuli to evoke sexual arousal and desire in the individual, (2) the persons or objects toward which sexual behavior and activity are directed by the individual, and (3) the persons or objects depicted in sexual fantasies and cognitions.

PEDOPHILIA

The individual and social costs of child molestation have received increasing recognition in the past two decades. A recent large-scale national survey in the United States suggests that approximately 27 percent of females and 16 percent of males have experienced sexual abuse as children (Finkelhor, Hotaling, Lewis & Smith 1990). The negative consequences for the victims of childhood sexual abuse are often serious and long-lasting, including substance abuse, sexual acting out, and suicidal behavior (Briere 1988; Conte 1988). Moreover, child molesters underreport the number of children they have victimized, and many of these cases go undetected (Abel et al. 1987; Kaplan, Abel, Cunningham-Rathner & Mittleman 1990). Even after being identified as a child molester and after involvement in the criminal justice system, child molesters are likely to reoffend. Hanson, Steffy, and Gauthier (1993) found that 42 percent of the total sample of 197 child molesters released between 1958 and 1974 committed a new sexual or violent offense during an average follow-up period of nineteen years. Consequently, treatment of child molesters is considered to be of paramount importance.

Many of the men who sexually molest children are thought to be motivated by a sexual orientation toward children and would therefore be identified as pedophiles in the latest version of the *Diagnostic and Statistical Manual of Mental Disorders* (DSM-IV: American Psychiatric Association 1994). Pedophilia is one form of paraphilia and is characterized by persistent sexual fantasies, urges, and arousal in response to children. Consequently, measuring sexual interest in children is an important part of the comprehensive clinical assessment of child molesters (Barbaree 1990; Freund & Blanchard 1981). Self-report data from questionnaires or interviews can be helpful but are limited by the problem of dissimulation, particularly with men facing legal sanctions. In response to this problem, more objective measures of sexual interest have received a great deal of attention.

The measurement of changes in penile erection is considered to be a reliable and valid physiological measure of male sexual arousal (Zuckerman 1971). In the assessment of child molesters, the typical test procedure is to measure circumferential or volumetric changes in penile erection while the subject is presented with sexual stimuli of nude or seminude persons varying in age or sex (see Earls & Marshall 1983; Laws & Osborn 1983 for reviews). The stimuli are usually still photographs in the form of slides projected onto a screen in front of the subject. Target age is systematically varied by presenting persons differing in age-related physical attributes such as size, maturity of facial features, and secondary sexual characteristics (e.g., the presence or absence of pubic, facial, and body hair and variation in breast size). Erectile responses are often quantified as the largest (peak) erectile response during a stimulus presentation. A pedophilic index, conventionally defined as the average erectile response to stimuli depicting children divided by the average erectile response to stimuli depicting adults, can be used to summarize the individual's responding. Subjects with an index of 1.0 or greater are identified as pedophiles (Freund & Blanchard 1989). According to some authorities, a sexual preference for children is relatively stable and is probably determined at an early stage of psychosexual development (Freund 1967, 1981; Freund & Blanchard 1989).

A distinction can be made between incest offenders and nonfamilial child molesters. The incest offender is defined as a child molester who has assaulted children who live in his own home: his own biological children, his stepchildren, or the children of the woman with whom he lives. In contrast, the extrafamilial child molester has assaulted children with whom he has no familial or legal relationship. A man is usually considered to be an extrafamilial child molester once he has assaulted a child outside a familial relationship, even though he may have also assaulted a child with whom he lives.

Freund (1967) conducted the pioneering work in the phallometric assessment of child molesters. In some of the studies that subsequently have been reported (Freund 1981; Freund, McKnight, Langevin & Cibiri 1972; Quinsey, Chaplin & Carrigan 1979; Quinsey, Steinman, Bergersen & Holmes 1975), the target stimuli have been divided into broad age categories, such as children, adolescents, and adults, and these studies have compared the strength of sexual responses across categories. Other studies have divided the stimuli into finer age groupings and have plotted the strength of sexual arousal over the age-of-target distribution, resulting in an age-preference profile (Baxter, Marshall, Barbaree, Davidson & Malcolm 1984; Marshall, Barbaree & Butt 1988; Marshall, Barbaree & Christophe 1986; Murphy, Haynes, Stalgaitis & Flanagan 1986).

Studies examining age preferences have found consistent results. Heterosexual nonoffenders show strong arousal to adult females and a sharp decrease in arousal to adolescent and child targets. Compared to matched nonoffenders, men who have molested nonfamilial female children show greater relative arousal to prepubescent girls, although they also respond quite strongly to adult women. Similarly, men who have molested nonfamilial male children show greater relative arousal to boys, although again this group shows at least moderate arousal to adult men and women.

Incest offenders as a group do not show strong responses to children, but their responses to adults are also relatively weak when compared to the responses of nonoffenders. Some authors have suggested different underlying psychological processes in incest versus extrafamilial child molestation (Williams & Finkelhor 1990). While a preference for children as sexual partners may play an important role in extrafamilial child molestation, it has been hypothesized that incest is more likely to involve impulsive, opportunistic behavior occurring in the context of a dysfunctional family system.

Hypothesizing that individual men might show idiosyncratic patterns of arousal and that offender groups might be heterogeneous in their individual age-preference profiles, Barbaree and Marshall (1989) conducted an analysis of age preference profiles among forty extrafamilial child molesters who had offended against female children, twenty-one father-daughter incest offenders, and a group of twenty-two matched nonoffenders. In this study, a computer program was written to sort the profiles among five categories:

1. An adult profile in which subjects showed strong responses to adult females aged 20 years and older, moderate responses to 16- and 18-year-old targets, and minimal or no responses to targets below age 15.

2. A teen-adult profile in which subjects showed strong responses to female targets aged 13 and older, with a decreasing response to younger-aged targets.

3. A nondiscriminating profile in which subjects showed moderate arousal to targets of all ages.

4. A child-adult pattern in which subjects showed strong responses to targets 18 years and older and 11 years and younger but only weak responses to targets aged 12 to 14.

5. A child profile in which subjects showed strong responses to targets 11 years of age and younger but only minimal responses to targets aged 13 and older.

Almost 70 percent of nonoffenders showed response patterns categorized as adult profiles. The remainder of the nonoffenders were approximately evenly distributed between the teen-adult and nondiscriminating profiles. Of incest offenders, 40 percent showed an adult profile, and an equal number exhibited a nondiscriminating response pattern. Most of the remaining incest offenders showed a teen-adult profile, with only one incest offender showing a child-adult profile. None of the nonoffenders had profile shapes that indicated a sexual preference for children, and none of the incest offenders showed responses exclusively to children. In contrast, the child molesters showed remarkably heterogeneous patterns of response. The largest subgroup (35 percent) showed a child profile. The remainder of the child molester group was approximately equally distributed among the other four profile categories. It is clear from this close examination of individual profile shapes that child molesters do not uniformly show sexual preferences for children, and they certainly do not show sexual arousal only to children. Responders to children (the child and the child-adult profile groups) were found to have lower-than-average intelligence and lower socioeconomic status. Further, the men who exhibited the child profile had used more force in the commission of their offenses and reported having offended against a larger number of victims (Barbaree & Marshall 1989).

As these studies clearly show, men who sexually molest children are not necessarily pedophiles. Some data suggest a higher proportion of pedophiles in the group of men who target male children compared to female children and in extrafamilial offenders compared to incest offenders (Freund & Watson 1992). For example, the sensitivity of phallometric testing for pedophilic age preference, defined as the percentage of correctly classified child molesters, has been estimated as 44.5 percent for offenders against female children and 86.7 percent for offenders against male children; the corresponding specificity, defined as the percentage of correctly classified nonchild molesters, was 80.6 percent for men in the community and 96.9 percent for offenders against female adults (Freund & Watson 1991). Offenders against female adults were considered to be the better comparison group because they were more similar in the level of motivation not to exhibit deviant sexual arousal in the testing. The lower values for sensitivity compared to specificity indicate that the presence of sexual arousal to children is more informative than its absence, presumably because of faking (i.e., voluntary control over sexual arousal).

The simplest rational categorization of child molesters is based on the sex of the victim and the offender's relationship to the victim. This categorization appears to have discriminant and concurrent validity. There have also been attempts to develop more sophisticated classification schemes according to the behavioral topography of their offenses and inferences about their motivation for the offending behavior. Particularly noteworthy are the efforts of Knight and Prentky and their associates at the Massachusetts Treatment Center (MTC). (Knight & Prentky 1990). These investigators devised two separate taxonomies, one for child molesters and one for rapists. In the child molester typology, offenders are classified as either high or low in fixation on children. Highly fixated subjects are those whose thoughts, offense history, and social interactions suggest a pedophilic interest in children. Offenders low in fixation do not show the same focus on children. Although the term *fixation* has its origins in psychodynamic theory, behavioral criteria are used to make this judgment. A recent study supported the validity of the fixation distinction by showing that high-fixated child molesters scored lower on a psychopathy measure, had less extensive criminal histories, and showed stronger arousal to children than low-fixated child molesters (Barbaree, Seto & Serin 1994). In addition, the high-fixated child molesters showed a sexual preference for children as measured by phallometric testing.

CHANGING SEXUAL PREFERENCES

Having defined pedophilia as a sexual orientation and in preparation for a discussion of attempts at reorientation, it would be appropriate to discuss what we know of its etiology. For example, if we were to find that sexual orientation was learned, then it might be reasonable to expect that reorientation might be accomplished through some learning process. Unfortunately, we know very little because there are no informative empirical studies in the literature (see Quinsey, Rice, Harris & Reid 1993 for a review). Numerous authorities have been influential in their speculations concerning the origins of inappropriate age preferences and various other sexual disorders, basing their ideas on the assumption that the disorder results from a process of learning or conditioning (Kinsey, Pomeroy & Martin 1948; Kinsey, Pomeroy, Martin & Gebhard 1953; Storms 1981; Van Wyk & Geist 1984). There has been widespread acceptance of this view. Laws and Marshall (1990) recently presented a theory of the etiology and maintenance of deviant sexual preferences and behavior involving processes of Pavlovian (classical) conditioning (Pavlov 1960), instrumental learning (Skinner 1938, 1953), and social learning (Bandura 1973, 1977). Laws and Marshall's (1990) theory is certainly plausible, and their chapter, using examples, describes in detail how these disordered sexual orientations could develop. However, there is no empirical evidence to confirm that deviant orientations are learned.

O'Donohue and Plaud (1994) reviewed the evidence for conditioning or learning of stimulus control of sexual arousal responses. Several studies have demonstrated modest effects of classical conditioning of sexual arousal, particularly with unconditioned stimuli that elicit high levels of arousal (Rachman 1966, Langevin & Martin 1975). However, these effects were confounded, and there are obvious alternative explanations. O'Donohue and Plaud expressed concern that the studies they reviewed seldom used proper controls to account for non-specific effects of the learning procedure. For example, common control procedures such as backward conditioning and truly random control procedure were rarely used. Another major methodological concern in demonstrating classical conditioning of arousal is the possibility of voluntary control over arousal and subjects' awareness of procedures or the study's hypothesis. These, together with experimenter demands, may account for some of the positive findings. Studies of instrumental learning were also reviewed by O'Donohue and Plaud. Several studies support the effectiveness of this procedure, including increasing penile responding to slides by presentation of water (reinforcement) to a water-deprived subject (Quinn, Harbison & McAllister 1970) and increasing penile responses to explicit materials by allowing subjects to ejaculate (reinforcement) after being exposed to explicit materials (Schaefer & Colgan 1977). Although supportive, these studies are also confounded and the authors suggest the studies are open to alternative explanations. Finally, O'Donohue and Plaud reviewed clinical treatments based on learning models, some of which are also reviewed below. The authors suggest that these studies generally support the effectiveness of reorientation therapy in terms of changing sexual arousal patterns, but only limited conclusions can be made about the exact process responsible for changes because many components were often included in therapy. Other factors such as placebo effects and therapists' and clients' expectations, cannot be ruled out. The authors conclude that the scientific support for conditioning of sexual arousal is weak.

Early accounts of learning (Pavlov 1960; Skinner 1938) held that the learning process depended simply on the association of various stimuli and responses; the association learned was essentially arbitrary, depending on the arrangements between stimuli and responses that the experimenter or behavior therapist provided. Later research was more sensitive to the effects of the phylogenetic and ontogenetic histories of animal subjects. This research showed clearly that what was learned depended heavily on the animal's "preparedness" to learn that association (Seligman 1970). For example, whereas pigeons could learn in only a few trials to avoid electric shock by flapping their wings or hopping, they took many more trials to learn to avoid the same shock by pecking a key and sometimes could not learn this response at all (Bolles 1970). Similarly, rats can learn a taste aversion in one trial when the conditioned stimulus is a flavor paired with a nausea-producing agent, but learning is more difficult or even impossible to achieve when the conditioned stimulus is a flashing light (Garcia & Koelling 1966). It is now widely accepted that learning is constrained by the biology of the organism in question.

In making the point that learning of sexual arousal responses may be similarly constrained, Quinsey et al. (1993) suggest that evolutionary theory can be used to explain why some stimuli appear to be easier to connect to sexual arousal than others. These authors point to what they describe as a "striking restriction" of male sexual preferences. For males, paraphilias such as voyeurism, exhibitionism, frotteurism, and toucheurism can be viewed as variations in normative human courtship patterns (Freund 1990); other paraphilias involve dominance or submission, or stimuli associated with adult females (Quinsey 1984, 1986). Quinsey et al. note that it is unheard of for someone to develop a sexual interest in beds, despite the fact that so much sexual arousal is associated with them. They present an argument informed by evolutionary theory to explain sexual age preferences in normal males, based on the idea that men in the past were reproductively advantaged if they sought out, or showed a sexual preference for, young adult females as sexual partners, because these females were more likely to produce viable offspring. The development of a sexual preference for children can presumably be understood as a failure in the evolutionary mechanism (Feierman 1994).

Learning involved in sexual orientation may similarly be constrained by ontogenetic processes in which associations are more easily learned at particular stages of development and then relatively difficult to learn (or unlearn) at other stages. The best-known example of this in biology is imprinting (Hess 1958), in which precocial species of birds become imprinted to objects or other animals they are exposed to at a critical period in their early life. This phenomenon includes sexual imprinting, in which, for example, ducks raised by geese try to copulate with geese later in life and do not show normal, species-appropriate sexual behavior (Hess 1958). It has been suggested that early adolescence is a particularly sensitive time for learning of sexual responses in human males (Marshall & Eccles 1993).

Most of the serious attempts at achieving sexual reorientation have been based on the idea that sexual responses can be learned and unlearned. Changes in orientation may be difficult or impossible to achieve once an orientation has become established. The empirical data on learning of sexual responses and theoretical speculations concerning the etiology of sexual orientation support the idea that sexual orientation in adult males may be resistant to change using behavioral therapies.

MODIFYING SEXUAL AROUSAL TO CHILDREN

Behavioral approaches to the treatment of pedophiles have been directed toward the modification of patterns of stimulus control of sexual arousal by decreasing deviant arousal and increasing appropriate arousal. Quinsey and Marshall (1983) critically reviewed a broad range of studies examining various offensive and eccentric sexual behaviors. They concluded that while some of the procedures appeared to offer some hope, there was little in the way of clear, convincing evidence of their efficacy.

Aversive procedures take various forms, but basically they involve pairing the desired sexual stimulus (e.g., a child or coercive sex) with some aversive event. In overt aversive procedures, this aversive event has been one of a variety of physical stimuli such as a mild electric shock (Quinsey, Chaplin & Carrigan 1980) or a strong aversive odor (Laws, Meyer & Holmen 1978). In covert sensitization (covert aversion), the aversive event has been a negative imaginal event generated by the offender under instructions from the clinician. These negative imaginal cues have included physically aversive images such as thoughts about feces or vomit, or psychologically aversive images such as being discovered during the commission of deviant acts by a spouse, relatives, or friends (Levin, Barry, Gambaro, Wolfinsohn & Smith 1977).

Kelly (1982) reviewed thirty-two published studies of behavioral reorientation of pedophiliacs since 1960, with most of these studies using some form of aversion therapy. He evaluated the studies using a number of criteria, including design characteristics, therapy components, subject variables, assessment measures, treatment goals, outcome data, and follow-up. First, he reviewed sixteen uncontrolled case studies. A total of forty-six pedophiles were included. Most of the studies (75 percent) used some form of aversion therapy, the most common of which was electrical shock associated with arousal to deviant stimuli. The second most common was covert sensitization in which unpleasant scenes were paired with deviant fantasies. Finally, some other forms of aversion therapy such as noxious auditory feedback or shame aversion have been used as well. Some of these studies used a number of other therapies in combination with the aversion therapy, and these additional therapies included desensitization to adult females and assertiveness training. Each of the studies of aversion therapy reported some level of significant improvement.

Second, Kelly (1982) reviewed ten controlled case studies using multiple baseline designs, withdrawal procedures, or differential treatments as control procedures. Aversion therapy was the most often used treatment method here as well, with covert sensitization being the most common of these aversive methods. For example, Laws (1980) reported on a bisexual pedophile who used biofeedback to develop his own strategy (covert sensitization) of controlling sexual arousal to slides of young boys and girls.

Third, Kelly (1982) reviewed two uncontrolled group studies. In one of these two studies, Marshall (1973) reduced deviant sexual behavior in five pedophiles using a combination of aversion and organismic reconditioning; according to self-reports, four remained nondeviant in behavior after a three- to six-month follow-up. The second study, by Quinsey et al. (1976), found that a sample of ten pedophiles showed small positive shifts in arousal patterns (penile circumference changes) after twenty classical conditioning aversion trials. A follow-up to this study will be described below.

Fourth, Kelly (1982) reviewed four controlled group studies representing a total of ninety-nine treated pedophiles. A form of aversion therapy was used in three of the four studies. For example, Maletsky (1980) assessed self-referred (voluntary) and court-referred (involuntary) pedophiles and exhibitionists using multiple measures, including self-report, observer report, and penile plethysmography. The treatment involved a convert sensitization procedure run over twenty-four sessions and an additional twelve "booster" sessions. The treatment was effective for all groups, and no differences were observed between self-referred and court-referred patients. These results were maintained over follow-up times of six, twelve, eighteen, twenty-four, and thirty months. Kelly also reviewed Quinsey et al. (1980), in which a signaled punishment procedure plus biofeedback was found to be more effective than biofeedback alone in reducing penile responses to deviant stimuli in eighteen pedophiles. This study together with a follow-up will be described in more detail below.

Finally, Kelly (1982) presented a statistical summary of the studies reviewed. For example, 78 percent of all studies used some form of aversion therapy, although 56 percent employed a combination of treatments; 44 percent of the studies did not use any form of control procedure. The average age of the pedophiles was 32 years. Of these, 50 percent of were heterosexual, and 44 percent were homosexual in terms of their responses to adults. Eighty percent of those who made an attempt to decrease pedophilic arousal were successful to some degree, whereas only 66 percent were successful in their attempt to increase heterosexual arousal. Finally, only 81 percent of the studies had any follow-up data, and of those with follow-ups, the average duration was only seventeen months.

Although positive about the results and prospects of reorientation therapy, Kelly (1982) cautioned against interpreting these data too optimistically. Published reports are biased in favor of statistically significant findings. Only 56 percent of the studies had adequate controls, and many of the studies also included other sex offenders in the experimental samples. Assessment problems may have inflated success rates. For example, motivated subjects may lie on self-reports or try to fake penile responses. Finally, only 28 percent of the studies had follow-ups lasting longer than a year, and most of these assessments were based on self-report data only.

Perhaps the most helpful series of studies on aversion therapy in the treatment of pedophiles has been reported by Quinsey and his associates. Using a between-groups crossover design, Quinsey et al. (1980) compared biofeedback with an electrical aversion procedure in the reduction of pedophilic arousal. Eighteen heterosexual child molesters were exposed to pictures of adult and child female nudes while their erectile responses were monitored. All subjects were provided with feedback from their erectile responses. A blue signal light was activated whenever arousal surpassed a preset criterion during presentation of the adult stimuli, and a red signal light was activated whenever arousal surpassed a preset criterion during presentation of the child stimuli. Subjects were required to maximize the time the blue light was on and minimize the time the red light was on. Subjects were assigned to one of two conditions. In the aversive procedure (signaled punishment) condition, a mild electric shock was delivered to the subject's arm whenever the red light came on during presentation of the child stimulus. The biofeedback condition followed the same procedure without the shock. After a number of treatment sessions, the two groups were crossed over to the alternate treatment procedure. Data analysis was conducted on each subject individually, comparing pretreatment erectile measures with those taken after the first and then the second treatment procedure. Whereas only four of twelve offenders showed significant reductions in deviant arousal after the initial biofeedback procedure, five of six showed significant reductions as a result of the signaled punishment procedure. After the second treatment procedure, neither of two offenders showed improvement as a result of biofeedback, while five of eight showed improvement after the punishment procedure. This study constitutes the only well-controlled treatment study that convincingly shows the effectiveness of electrical aversion with child molesters.

The study on these aversive procedures conducted by Quinsey and his associates is also interesting because it is the only one of electrical aversion involving a long-term follow-up of the study participants. Rice, Quinsey, and Harris (1991) studied the recidivism of 136 extrafamilial child molesters who had received phallometric assessment in a maximum security psychiatric institution from

1972 to 1983. Recidivism was determined over an average 6.3-year follow-up. Fifty of these men had participated in behavorial treatment to alter inappropriate sexual age preferences, in the studies described earlier. Thirty-one percent of the men had been convicted of a new sex offense, 43 percent committed a violent or sexual offense, and 58 percent were arrested for some offense or returned to the institution. Compared with men who did not recidivate, men convicted of a new sex offense had previously committed more sex offenses, had been admitted to correctional institutions more frequently, were more likely to have been diagnosed as personality disordered, were more likely never to have married, and had shown more inappropriate sexual preferences in initial phallometric assessment than those who had not. Unfortunately, although behavioral treatment affected a reduction in deviant sexual arousal, it did not affect recidivism. Apparently change in pedophilic arousal is not sufficient to prevent future offending in these men.

MASTURBATORY RECONDITIONING

Laws and Marshall (1991) reviewed the evidence for masturbatory reconditioning with sexual deviates. Masturbatory reconditioning has advantages over other methods because it is a nonaversive and rewarding activity and can be done in "homework" (i.e., nonlaboratory) assignments. Four forms of this treatment methodology were reviewed. First, in thematic shift (sometimes called orgasmic reconditioning) the man masturbates to a deviant sexual fantasy until the point of orgasm, when he switches to a more appropriate fantasy. Seven studies were reviewed. Although some studies reported treatment effectiveness, it is difficult to attribute improvements to this procedure directly because additional treatments were used. The best controlled study (Conrad & Winzce 1976) failed to find positive effects using phallometric testing. The second form of this methodology is fantasy alternation, where the man changes or alters the content of his fantasies daily or weekly. Five studies were reviewed. Some studies were supportive, but one study found an increase in deviant arousal. The authors concluded that fantasy alternation is probably not an appropriate reconditioning method because any pairing of orgasm with deviant stimuli should be avoided. Third, the man is required to masturbate to the appropriate stimuli in directed masturbation. Five studies were reviewed. The authors concluded that this method is simple and straightforward and can be effective. Finally, the fourth method was satiation therapy, where the man masturbates and fantasizes aloud to deviant stimuli for a long period of time after ejaculation, ostensibly to produce boredom with the deviant fantasy. Seven studies were reviewed. There was some support for this procedure, particularly if it was combined with directed masturbation. Overall, Laws and Marshall concluded that although some promising results were reported in the literature, there was little available evidence that these techniques are effective in the long term.

Satiation is a behavioral method used to reduce deviant arousal that does not depend on the use of aversive procedures. Marshall (1979) used single case research methods to evaluate this procedure, which he had described earlier (Marshall & Lippens 1977). In this procedure, the man is required to masturbate to ejaculation while verbalizing aloud every imaginable variation of his deviant fantasy. Upon ejaculation and throughout the refractory period, he is instructed to continue to masturbate to the same fantasies over several hour-long sessions. Marshall (1979) examined two repetitive child molesters who showed considerable arousal to both children and other deviant stimuli (fetishes) and minimal arousal to adult females. In the first case, Marshall used a multiple baseline across behaviors design targeting arousal to female children aged 6 to 8 years, female children aged 11 to 13 years, footwear, and underwear, in sequence. As each category was treated, probes revealed that arousal to those stimuli decreased while arousal to the other stimuli remained relatively stable. In the second case, Marshall attempted to reduce pedophilic arousal by the sequential application of self-esteem training, electrical aversion therapy, and satiation. Pedophilic arousal was resistant to the first two interventions, whereas satiation rapidly reduced deviant responding. In both these patients, follow-up data are available over ten years after treatment, no relapses have occurred.

To summarize, two general approaches to treatment are in use in attempts to reduce pedophilic sexual arousal: aversion therapy and masturbatory reconditioning. However, the studies that attest to the effectiveness of these procedures are limited in number and methodological rigor. These studies have indicated that reductions in deviant arousal were recorded, and they have shown that these reductions in deviant arousal persist over weeks and months.

The studies reviewed here indicate that behavioral techniques directed at changing pedophilic response patterns do in fact reduce arousal to stimuli depicting children. Although these techniques have been based on conditioning models, the existing research does not permit the conclusion that these changes were due to conditioning or instrumental learning per se. The most important confound in most of these studies was that voluntary control over sexual arousal was not eliminated as a possible explanation of results. Some offenders are able to suppress their responses to preferred stimuli (Abel, Barlow, Blanchard & Mavissakalian 1975; Freund 1963; Wydra, Marshall, Laws & Barbaree 1983), and some nonoffenders are able to produce moderate levels of erectile response to nonpreferred stimuli (Quinsey & Bergersen 1976). Offenders are presumably highly motivated to avoid exhibiting deviant sexual arousal during phallometric testing. Some offenders have been observed using tactics such as manipulating the strain gauge, tensing the pelvic musculature, hyperventilating, or averting their gaze from the visual presentation (Laws & Holmen 1978; Laws & Rubin 1969; Quinsey & Bergersen 1976). These attempts at faking can be thwarted by monitoring offenders using a video camera or by requiring them to participate in a detection task that involves reporting a signal that randomly appears during the stimulus presentation (Laws & Rubin 1969). However, it is much more difficult to prevent cognitive control over sexual arousal. Geer and Fuhr (1976) demonstrated that sexual arousal is suppressed when men are required to engage in a complex cognitive task, and indeed, men instructed to suppress their responses to preferred stimuli report using this kind of tactic (Wydra et al. 1983).

Two published studies have attempted to prevent faking during phallometric testing. In the first study, Malcolm, Davidson, and Marshall (1985) suddenly switched to different deviant or nondeviant stimuli once nonoffender volunteers had been aroused to different levels (25, 50, and 75 percent of full erection) while watching another stimulus. Subjects were instructed to lose their erection completely as quickly as possible after the switch, while attending to the new stimulus. At 50 percent of full erection, subjects had the most difficulty detumescing to stimuli depicting a nude adult female, compared with deviant or neutral stimuli. A longer latency in detumescing to a deviant stimulus is presumably an indication of a deviant preference. In the second study, Quinsey and Chaplin (1988) asked nonoffenders to attend to a sexual stimulus under usual instructions, under instructions to fake, and under instructions to fake while participating in a semantic tracking task. This task required subjects to press one button when sexual activity was being depicted and another button when violence was being depicted. Quinsey and Chaplin's subjects were able to fake a deviant preference without a task but were unable to do so during the task. Proulx, Cote, and Achille (1993) recently attempted to replicate Quinsey and Chaplin's findings. Unfortunately, they found no difference in indexes of deviant arousal between the group of subjects assigned to the semantic tracking task and another group that was not. Overall it appears that subjects can fake their erectile responses, and attempts to prevent this faking have not been uniformly successful.

In their thoughtful review, Quinsey and Earls (1990) describe the process of change resulting from behavioral techniques for changing deviant arousal. They point to the large variation among procedures that have successfully produced changes and suggest that the common feature is repeated exposure to deviant stimuli in a social context that pressures offenders to suppress their deviant arousal. Quinsey and Earls concluded that treatment effects essentially represent learning to increase voluntary control over sexual responding in the laboratory. They then go on to argue that therapeutic gains can be maintained only if they are integrated into a comprehensive treatment approach.

COGNITIVE-BEHAVIORAL MODEL OF SEXUAL OFFENDING

A conceptual framework is presented in figure 17.1 to formalize and articulate the processes that are thought to give rise to sexually assaultive behavior. It forms the basis for characteristics of child molesters at the time of their offense into two broad categories: dysfunctions in social behavior and relationship skills (McFall 1990; Stermac, Segal & Gillis 1990) and dysphoria or emotional disturbances (Langevin et al. 1978).

Figure 17.1
The Cognitive-Behavioral Chain Leading to Offense in the Relapse Prevention Model

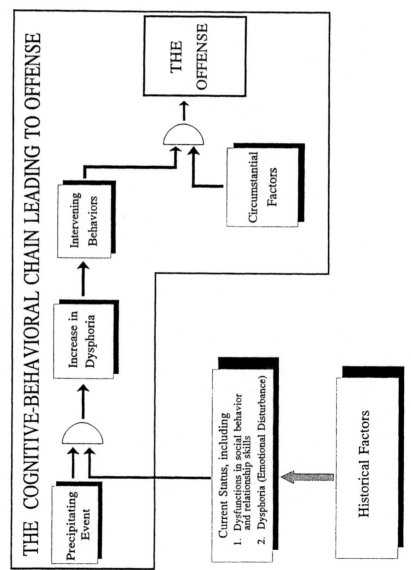
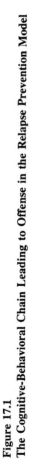

Table 17.1
Historical Precursors to Sexual Aggression

Precursor	Child Molesters
Familial chaos	49
Maternal	29
Parental marital discord	45
Paternal absence/neglect	54
Physically abused as a child	7
Prior arrest for nonsexual offense	15
Sexual victimization	
Prior to age 12	56
Between ages 12 & 18	6
Limited education (< grade 9 completed)	26

Source: Adapted from Pithers, Kashima, Cumming, Beal, and Buell (1988).

In a study of incarcerated sex offenders, Christie, Marshall, and Lanthier (1977) found that 57 percent of child molesters had received psychiatric attention for problems such as anxiety, depression, and psychotic episodes. The psychiatric disturbance was described as being severe "at one time or another" in the case of 26 percent of the child molesters. It is not known whether these difficulties were present at the time of the offense, although no doubt these difficulties were brought on, at least in part, by the stress of institutional life as experienced by sexual offenders. While it is not known what statistics would result if modern diagnostic criteria (DSM-IV) were to be applied systematically to the population, some educated guesses are possible from our own experiences and from observations reported by other researchers.

It is quite clear that apart from the paraphilias, serious Axis I disorders are infrequently observed in sex offenders. Abel, Mittleman, and Becker (1985) report that serious diagnosable mental disorders are found in less than 25 percent of sex offenders seen in an outpatient treatment setting. Laws (1981, cited in Knopp 1984) reports that no more than 10 percent of incarcerated offenders exhibit serious mental disorders. Some studies of incarcerated sex offenders

Table 17.2
Current Status Precursors to Sexual Aggression

Precursor	Child Molesters
Dysfunctions in Social Behaviour and Relationship Skills:	
Social skills deficit	50
Assertive skill deficit	23
Sexual knowledge deficit	52
Emotionally inhibited/overcontrolled	51
Interpersonal dependence	48
Personality disorder	35
Cognitive impairment	10
Dysphoria (Emotional Disturbance):	
Anxiety, generalized	46
Anxiety, social	39
Anxiety, sexual	58
Depression	38
Anger, generalized and global	32
Anger towards women	26
Boredom	28
Low self esteem	61

Source: Adapted from Pithers, Kashima, Cumming, Beal, and Buell (1988).

using standardized psychological tests have indicated a high rate of clinical symptoms. For example, Hall, Maiuro, Vitaliano, and Proctor (1986) examined the Minnesota Multiphasic Personality Inventory profiles of 406 institutionalized child molesters and found elevated means on all of the clinical scales. Sixty-five percent of the sample had a *T*-score over 70 on the Psychopathic Deviate

Table 17.3
Intervening Behavior as Precursors to Sexual Aggression

Precursor	Child Molesters
Paraphilic Behaviors:	
Cognitive distortions	65
Deviant sexual fantasies	51
Deviant sexual arousal	57
Planning of sexual offense	73
Pornography use	7
Driving car alone without destination	1
* Masturbation to deviant themes	
Non Paraphilic Behaviors (disinhibiting behaviors):	
Alcohol use/abuse	23
* Criminal thinking	
* Provoking conflict	

Source: Adapted from Pithers, Kashima, Cumming, Beal, and Buell (1988).
*Added to original Pithers et al. list.

scale. Similarly, approximately 50 percent of the sample had elevated scores on both the Schizophrenia and the Depression scales. Other reviews of the literature (Quinsey 1984, 1986) point out that child molesters show a peak on the Psychopathic Deviate scale (Langevin 1983; Panton 1979) but that this pattern of results is not different from that obtained from other groups of incarcerated offenders.

In summary, although serious diagnosable mental disorders are not frequently encountered among sex offenders, a significant degree of psychopathology is present. The role of this disturbance in their offenses is not understood; the psychological disturbance may have preceded and contributed to the offense, or it might be a consequence of the arrest and incarceration. However, it is more likely that for many sex offenders, some level of psychological disturbance was a contributing factor in their offense, and this disturbance was exacerbated by the judicial process and the stresses of incarceration.

Deficits in social skills among sex offenders are widely recognized. Reflecting the common acceptance of these deficits, social skills training is one of the most often prescribed treatments for sex offenders (McFall 1990). However, the nature of these deficits and the way in which these deficits contribute to the commission of sexual offenses are not well understood. Recent reviews of the literature on social skills assessment and training of sex offenders point to serious conceptual and methodological problems (Earls & Quinsey 1985; Stermac et al. 1990). And it is still too early to say that social skills deficits are characteristic of sex offenders (Stermac & Quinsey 1986; Stermac et al, 1990). McFall (1990) has argued that the conceptual and methodological weaknesses in the literature have presented an inadequate test of the hypothesis. In response, he has proposed an information-processing model of social skills designed to identify the social deficits that lead to sexual aggression. The model specifies three stages of social information processing. Decoding skills involve the psychological processes that lead to the reception, perception, and interpretation of incoming social information. Decision skills involve generating response options, matching these responses to task demands, selecting the best opinion, searching for that option in the behavioral repertoire, and evaluating likely outcomes of each option. Enactment skills involve carrying out the behavior selected in the preceding stage. Recent studies have found particular deficits in decoding abilities among sexual offenders in heterosexual social situations. Further, there is evidence that sex offenders are deficient in decision skills in social interactions. Conner (1988) examined the social problem-solving skills of child molesters and reported no deficiencies in child molesters' abilities at recognizing the existence of a problem or at generating alternative solutions. However, they tended to choose inappropriate solutions and did not recognize the negative outcomes of the solutions they chose. Finally, a number of studies have supported the notion of enactment deficits among sex offenders. Compared with community control subjects and rapists, child molesters have been found to be less effectively assertive (Segal & Marshall 1985; Overholser & Beck 1986).

Related to social misperceptions, cognitions that contribute to crimes among child molesters have been labeled cognitive distortions (Abel, Becker & Cunningham-Rathner 1984) and reflect mistaken beliefs about childhood sexuality and the nature of sexual interactions between an adult and a child. They include one or more of the following misperceptions: children are not harmed by sexual interactions with an adult; children benefit (in terms of sex education or in terms of affection and attention) through sexual interactions with an adult; children are capable of consenting to sexual interactions with an adult and often desire this (offenders frequently view the child as having been sexually provocative); and an adult male's sexual interactions with a child can be justified or rationalized in some way (i.e., it is not his fault). Stermac and Segal (1987) examined the judgments of offenders and nonoffenders regarding descriptions of adult-child sexual interactions. Child molesters pointed to the benefit of abuse for the child, attributed more blame to the victim, and tended to minimize the effects of sexual assault on children. Offenders also considered current punishment for offenders to be too severe.

Besides providing a set of practical and innovative techniques for treating sexual offenders, the relapse prevention approach, and the writing of Bill Pithers in particular (Pithers 1990; Pithers, Beal, Armstrong & Petty 1989), represents an important conceptual advance in the treatment of sexual offenders. A number of researchers have previously suggested that interactions between offenders' behavioral excesses or deficits and situational factors, particularly those immediately preceding the offense, are important in understanding sexual assault (Marshall & Barbaree 1984, 1990). Some experimental research has pointed to experimental manipulations of situational factors that increase sexual arousal to deviant cues, including alcohol intoxication (Barbaree, Marshall, Yates & Lightfoot 1983; Briddell et al. 1978), anger (Yates, Barbaree & Marshall 1984), and victim blame (Sundberg, Barbaree & Marshall 1991). Other authors have also pointed to the role of antecedent anger in contributing to sexual assault (Groth, Burgess & Holmstrom 1977).

Authors who adopt a relapse prevention approach in treating sexual offenders refer to cognitive-behavioral chains in the sexual offending (Pithers 1990). It is widely recognized that sexual offenses are not isolated events that are independent of other aspects of the offender's life. Instead, offenses are the terminal event in a long sequence of events (Nelson & Jackson 1989). In figure 17.1, elements of a typical cognitive-behavioral chain are contained inside the black border. The chain is a sequence of events, thoughts, emotional responses, and behaviors that precede the offense. For offenders who report more than one offense, the offense chains preceding different offenses often bear considerable similarity, and as a consequence the chain is often referred to as an offense cycle. It is recognized that the content of offense cycles is idiosyncratic and varies from offender to offender.

The behavioral chain begins with a precipitating event. Not surprising, given the dysfunctional social behavior of these men, the precipitating event is often an interpersonal conflict causing an increase in emotional disturbance. The offender's inability to resolve the interpersonal conflict leaves him feeling angry and frustrated, and vulnerable to continuing interpersonal conflict. In response to increased dysphoria, the offender engages in behaviors that are both an expression of the emotional disturbance he feels and intended in part to relieve his dysphoria. We have subdivided the intervening behaviors into two categories: paraphiliac and nonparaphiliac. Paraphiliac behaviors are deviant behaviors that serve to reduce the tension and frustration, or negative emotional state, he is feeling. Nonparaphiliac behaviors are often expressions of anger or disturbed social behaviors that denote anger and often lead to continuing interpersonal conflict. These nonparaphiliac behaviors also include those that serve to disinhibit deviant sexual behavior, such as heavy alcohol intake. Alcohol intoxication is frequently implicated in the commission of sexual offenses (see Seto & Barbaree 1994 for a review). Between 33 and 77 percent of child molesters report having been intoxicated at the time of the offense (Groth 1979; Wormith 1983). However, it is not known whether offender self-report of intoxication is exaggerated to reduce his culpability in the offense (Quinsey 1984; Seto & Barbaree 1994).

Paraphiliac behaviors are deviant behaviors that serve to reduce the tension and frustration the offender experiences. In a state of increased tension and dysphoria, offenders may engage in sexual fantasy with deviant themes, become aroused to these deviant themes and masturbate, or use pornography depicting deviant content. These offenders experience cognitive distortions that justify and normalize their own paraphiliac behaviors to themselves. As the cognitive-behavioral chain progresses, the offender's fantasies evolve into planning for an offense. In this situation, with the disturbed offender involved in continuing interpersonal conflict and engaging in sexually deviant approximations to actual offending, an offense becomes more likely. When the offender is presented with the opportunity, he offends, thereby temporarily reducing his tension and frustration.

The model can be flexibly applied to each offender. Not every offender shows problems in all components of the model. For example, for some offenders, paraphiliac behaviors appear to be absent, and the offense seems impulsive and unplanned. For others, the paraphiliac behavior is predominant and apparently occurs without a precipitating event. Nonetheless, the model offers a framework for understanding individual offending, assessing behavioral deficits and excesses that lead to the offense in each individual, and targeting behavior in treatment that will reduce the likelihood of his committing the offense in the future.

CONCLUSIONS

Reorientation methods described in this chapter, including aversion therapy and masturbatory reconditioning, have been shown to reduce deviant sexual arousal. The mechanism by which this change occurs is not known but likely involves the acquisition by the pedophile of effective self-control skills and strategies he can use to suppress arousal. These newly acquired abilities are integrated into a comprehensive cognitive-behavioral approach to treatment (Marshall & Barbaree 1990), which targets numerous factors that may lead to reoffense in the pedophile. Relapse prevention is then used to maintain the therapeutic gains achieved in treatment. One of the objectives of a relapse prevention approach is to teach offenders how to generalize this voluntary control from the laboratory to real-life settings.

Future research is needed to address the questions of the etiology of sexual orientation and the learning (and unlearning) of sexual response patterns. Quinsey et al. (1993) suggest that the development of sexual preferences can be fully understood only if sexual interests are studied in children and young adolescents. Future research also is required to assess the effects on long-term recidivism of the comprehensive cognitive-behavioral treatments with relapse prevention when they include sexual reorientation as an important component.

REFERENCES

Abel, G. G., Barlow, D. H., Blanchard, E. B., & Mavissakalian, M. (1975). Measurement of sexual arousal in male homosexuals: The effects of instructions and stimulus modality. *Archives of Sexual Behavior, 4,* 623–629.

Abel, G. G., Becker, J. V., & Cunningham-Rathner, J. (1984). Complications, consent and cognitions in sex between children and adults. *International Journal of Law and Psychiatry, 7,* 89–103.

Abel, G. G., Mittleman, M. S., & Becker, J. V. (1985). Sex offenders: Results of assessment and recommendations for treatment. In M. H. Ben-Aron, S. J. Hucker & C. D. Webster (Eds.), *Clinical criminology: The assessment and treatment of criminal behavior* (pp. 207–220). Toronto: M & M Graphics.

Abel, G. G., Becker, J. V., Mittleman, M., Cunningham-Rathner, J., Rouleau, J. L., & Murphy, W. D. (1987). Self-reported sex crimes of nonincarcerated paraphiliacs. *Journal of Interpersonal Violence, 2,* 3–25.

Adams, H. E., & Sturgis, E. T. (1977). Status of behavioral reorientation techniques in the modification of homosexuality: A review. *Psychological Bulletin, 84,* 1171–1188.

American Psychiatric Association. (1973). *Diagnostic and statistical manual of mental disorders* (2nd ed.). Washington, DC: Author.

American Psychiatric Association. (1994). *Diagnostic and statistical manual of mental disorders* (4th ed.). Washington, DC: Author.

Bandura, A. (1973). *Aggression: A social learning analysis.* Englewood Cliffs, NJ: Prentice-Hall.

Bandura, A. (1977). *Social learning theory.* Englewood Cliffs, NJ: Prentice-Hall.

Barbaree, H. E. (1990). Stimulus control of sexual arousal: Its role in sexual assault. In W. L. Marshall, D. R. Laws & H. E. Barbaree (Eds.), *Handbook of sexual assault: Issues, theories, and treatment of the offender* (pp. 115–142). New York: Plenum Press.

Barbaree, H. E., & Marshall, W. L. (1989). Erectile responses among heterosexual child molesters, father-daughter incest offenders, and matched non-offenders: Five distinct age preference profiles. *Canadian Journal of Behavioural Science, 21,* 70–82.

Barbaree, H. E., Marshall, W. L., Yates, E., & Lightfoot, L. O. (1983). Alcohol intoxication and deviant sexual arousal in male social drinkers. *Behaviour Research and Therapy, 21,* 365–373.

Barbaree, H. E., Seto, M. C., & Serin, R. C. (1994). *Comparisons of low- and high-fixated child molesters: Psychopathy, criminal history, and sexual arousal to children.* Manuscript submitted for publication.

Bard, L. A., Carter, D. L., Cerce, D. D., Knight, R. A., Rosenberg, R., & Schneider, B. (1987). A descriptive study of rapists and child molesters: Developmental, clinical, and criminal characteristics. *Behavioural Sciences and the Law, 5,* 203–220.

Baxter, D. J., Marshall, W. L., Barbaree, H. E., Davidson, P. R., & Malcolm, P. B. (1984). Deviant sexual behavior: Differentiating sex offenders by criminal and personal history, psychometric measures, and sexual response. *Criminal Justice and Behavior, 11,* 477–501.

Bolles, R. C. (1970). Species-specific defense reactions and avoidance learning. *Psychological Review, 77,* 32–48.

Briddell, D. W., Rimm, D. C., Caddy, G. R., Krawitz, G., Sholis, D., & Wunderlin, R. J. (1978). Effects of alcohol and cognitive set on sexual arousal to deviant stimuli. *Journal of Abnormal Psychology, 87,* 418–430.

Briere, J. (1988). The long-term clinical correlates of childhood sexual victimization. In R. A. Prentky, & V. L. Quinsey, (Eds.), *Human sexual aggression: Current perspectives* (pp. 327–334). New York: New York Academy of Sciences.

Christie, M. M., Marshall, W. L., & Lanthier, R. D. (1977). *A descriptive study of rapists and pedophiles.* Unpublished manuscript.

Conner, C. (1988). *Social problem solving in child molesters.* Unpublished honour thesis, Queen's University, Kingston, Ontario, Canada.

Conrad, S. R., & Wincze, J. P. (1976). Orgasmic reconditioning: A controlled study of its effects upon the sexual arousal and behavior of adult male homosexuals. *Behavior Therapy, 7,* 155–166.

Conte, J. R. (1988). The effects of sexual abuse on children: Results of a research project. In R. A. Prentky & V. L. Quinsey (Eds.), *Human sexual aggression: Current perspectives* (pp. 310–326). New York: New York Academy of Sciences.

Earls, C. M., & Marshall, W. L. (1983). The current state of technology in the laboratory assessment of sexual arousal patterns. In J. G. Greer & I. R. Stuart, (Eds.), *The sexual aggressor: Current perspectives on treatment* (pp. 336–362). New York: Van Nostrand Reinhold.

Earls, C. M., & Quinsey, V. L. (1985). What is to be done? Future research on the assessment and behavioral treatment of sex offenders. *Behavioral Sciences and the Law, 3,* 377–390.

Feierman, J. R. (1994). Pedophilia: Paraphilic attraction to children. In J. J. Krivasca & J. Money (Eds.), *The handbook of forensic sexology: Biomedical and criminological perspectives* (pp. 49–79). Amherst, NY: Prometheus.

Finkelhor, D., Hotaling, G., Lewis, I. A., & Smith, C. (1990). Sexual abuse in a national sample of adult men and women: Prevalence, characteristics, and risk factors. *Child Abuse and Neglect, 14,* 19–28.

Freund, K. (1963). A laboratory method of diagnosing predominance of homo- and hetero-erotic interest in the male. *Behavior Research and Therapy, 5,* 85–93.

Freund, K. (1967). Erotic preference in pedophilia. *Behavior Research and Therapy, 5,* 339–348.

Freund, K. (1981). Assessment of pedophilia. In M. Cook, & K. Howells, (Eds.), *Adult sexual interest in children* (pp. 139–179). London: Academic Press.

Freund, K. (1990). Courtship disorder. In W. L., Marshall, D. R. Laws, & H. E. Barbaree (Eds.), *Handbook of sexual assault: Issues, theories, and treatment of the offender* (pp. 195–207). New York: Plenum Press.

Freund, K., & Blanchard, R. (1981). Assessment of sexual dysfunction and deviation. In M. Hersen, & A. S. Bellack, (Eds.), *Behavioral assessment: A practical handbook* (2nd ed.) (pp. 427–455). New York: Pergamon Press.

Freund, K., & Blanchard, R. (1989). Phallometric diagnosis of pedophilia. *Journal of Consulting and Clinical Psychology, 57,* 100–105.

Freund, K., McKnight, C. K., Langevin, R., & Cibiri, S. (1972). The female child as a surrogate object. *Archives of Sexual Behavior, 2,* 119–133.

Freund, K., & Watson, R. J. (1991). Assessment of the sensitivity and specificity of a phallometric test: An update of phallometric diagnosis of pedophilia. *Psychological Assessment, 3,* 254–260.

Freund, K., & Watson, R. J. (1992). The proportions of heterosexual and homosexual pedophiles among sex offenders against children: An exploratory study. *Journal of Sex and Marital Therapy, 18,* 34–43.

Garcia, J., & Koelling, R. A. (1966). The relation of cue to consequence in avoidance learning. *Psychonomic Science, 4,* 123–124.

Geer, J. H., & Fuhr, R. (1976). Cognitive factors in sexual arousal: The role of distraction. *Journal of Consulting and Clinical Psychology, 44,* 238–243.

Groth, A. N. (1979). *Men who rape: The psychology of the offender.* New York: Plenum Press.

Groth, A. N., Burgess, A. W., & Holmstrom, L. L. (1977). Rape: Power, anger, and sexuality. *American Journal of Psychiatry, 134,* 1239–1243.

Haldeman, D. C. (1994). The practice and ethics of sexual orientation conversion therapy. *Journal of Consulting and Clinical Psychology, 62,* 221–227.

Hall, G. C. N., Maiuro, R. D., Vitaliano, P. P., & Proctor, W. C. (1986). The utility of the MMPI with men who have sexually assaulted children. *Journal of Consulting and Clinical Psychology, 54,* 493–496.

Hanson, R. K., Steffy, R. A., & Gauthier, R. (1993). Long-term recidivism of child molesters. *Journal of Consulting and Clinical Psychology, 61,* 646–652.

Hess, E. H. (1958). Imprinting in animals. *Scientific American, 198,* 82.

Kaplan, M. S., Abel, G. G., Cunningham-Rathner, J., & Mittleman, M. S. (1990). The impact of parolees' perception of confidentiality of their self-reported sex crimes. *Annals of Sex Research, 3,* 293–303.

Kelly, J. R. (1982). Behavioral reorientation of pedophiliacs: Can it be done? *Clinical Psychology Review, 2,* 387–408.

Kinsey, A. C., Pomeroy, W. B., & Martin, C. E. (1948). *Sexual behavior in the human male.* Philadelphia: W. B. Saunders.

Kinsey, A. C., Pomeroy, W. B., Martin, C. E., & Gebhard, P. H. (1953). *Sexual behavior in the human female.* Philadelphia: W. B. Saunders.

Knight, R. A., & Prentky, R. A. (1990). Classifying sexual offenders: The development and corroboration of taxonomic models. In W. L. Marshall, D. R. Laws, & H. E. Barbaree, (Eds.), *Handbook of sexual assault: Issues, theories, and treatment of the offender* (pp. 23–52). New York: Plenum Press.

Knopp, F. H. (1984). *Retraining adult sex offenders: Methods and models.* Syracuse, NY: Safer Society Press.

Langevin, R. (1983). *Sexual strands: Understanding and treating sexual anomalies in men.* London: Erlbaum.

Langevin, R., & Martin, M. (1975). Can erotic responses be classically conditioned? *Behavior Therapy, 6,* 350–355.

Laws, D. R. (1980). Treatment of bisexual pedophilia by a biofeedback-assisted self-control procedure. *Behavior Research and Therapy, 18,* 207–211.

Laws, D. R., & Holmen, M. L. (1978). Sexual response faking by pedophiles. *Criminal Justice and Behavior, 5,* 343–356.

Laws, D. R., & Marshall, W. L. (1990). A conditioning theory of the etiology and maintenance of deviant sexual preference and behavior. In W. L. Marshall, D. R. Laws, & H. E. Barbaree (Eds.), *Handbook of sexual assault: Issues, theories, and treatment of the offender* (pp. 209–229). New York: Plenum Press.

Laws, D. R., & Marshall, W. L. (1991). Masturbatory reconditioning with sexual deviates: An evaluative review. *Advances in Behavior Research and Therapy, 13,* 13–25.

Laws, D. R., Meyer, J., & Holmen, M. L. (1978). Reduction of sadistic sexual arousal by olfactory aversion: A case study. *Behavior Research and Therapy, 16,* 281–285.

Laws, D. R., & Osborn, C. A. (1983). How to build and operate a behavioral laboratory to evaluate and treat sexual deviance. In J. G. Greer, & I. R. Stuart, (Eds.), *The sexual aggressor: Current perspectives on treatment* (pp. 293–335). New York: Van Nostrand Reinhold.

Laws, D. R., & Rubin, H. B. (1969). Instructional control of an autonomic response. *Journal of Applied Behavior Analysis, 2,* 93–99.

Levin, S. M., Barry, S. M., Gambaro, S., Wolfinsohn, L., & Smith, A. (1977). Variations of covert sensitization in the treatment of pedophilic behavior: A case study. *Journal of Consulting and Clinical Psychology, 45,* 896–907.

McFall, R. M. (1990). The enhancement of social skills. In W. L. Marshall, D. R. Laws, & H. E. Barbaree, (Eds.), *Handbook of sexual assault: Issues, theories, and treatment of the offender* (pp. 311–330). New York: Plenum Press.

Malcolm, P. B., Davidson, P. R., & Marshall, W. L. (1985). Control of penile tumescence: The effects of arousal level and stimulus content. *Behaviour Research and Therapy, 23,* 273–280.

Maletsky, B. (1980). Self-referred versus court-referred sexually deviant patients: Success with assisted covert sensitization. *Behavior Therapy, 11,* 306–314.

Marques, J. K., Day, D. M., Nelson, C., & West, M. A. (1994). Effects of cognitive-behavioral treatment on sex offender recidivism: Preliminary results of a longitudinal study. *Criminal Justice and Behavior, 21,* 28–54.

Marquis, J. N. (1970). Orgasmic reconditioning: Changing sexual choice through controlling masturbatory fantasies. *Journal of Behavior Therapy and Experimental Psychiatry, 1,* 263–271.

Marshall, W. L. (1973). The modification of sexual fantasies: A combined treatment approach to the reduction of deviant sexual behavior. *Behaviour Research and Therapy, 11,* 557–564.

Marshall, W. L. (1979). Satiation therapy: A procedure for reducing deviant sexual arousal. *Journal of Applied Behavior Analysis, 12,* 377–389.

Marshall, W. L., & Barbaree, H. E. (1984). A behavioral view of rape. *International Journal of Law and Psychiatry, 7,* 51–77.

Marshall, W. L., & Barbaree, H. E. (1990). An integrated theory of the etiology of sexual offending. In W. L. Marshall, D. R. Laws & H. E. Barbaree (Eds.), *Handbook of sexual assault: Issues, theories, and treatment of the offender* (pp. 257–275). New York: Plenum Press.

Marshall, W. L., Barbaree, H. E., & Butt, J. (1988). Sexual offenders against male children: Sexual preferences for gender, age of victim, and type of behavior. *Behaviour Research and Therapy, 26,* 383–391.

Marshall, W. L., Barbaree, H. E., & Christophe, D. (1986). Sexual offenders against female children: Sexual preferences for age of victims and type of behaviour. *Canadian Journal of Behavioural Science, 18,* 424–439.

Marshall, W. L., & Eccles, A. (1993). Pavlovian conditioning processes in adolescent sex offenders. In H. E. Barbaree, W. L. Marshall & S. M. Hudson (Eds.), *The juvenile sex offender* (pp. 118–142). New York: Guilford.

Marshall, W. L., & Lippens, K. (1977). The clinical value of boredom: A procedure for reducing inappropriate sexual interests. *Journal of Nervous and Mental Disease, 165,* 283–287.

Murphy, W. D., Haynes, M. R., Stalgaitis, S. J., & Flanagan, B. (1986). Differential sexual responding among four groups of sexual offenders against children. *Journal of Psychopathology and Behavioral Assessment, 8,* 339–353.

Nelson, C., & Jackson, P. (1989). High-risk recognition: The cognitive-behavioral chain. In D. R. Laws (Ed.), *Relapse prevention with sex offenders* (pp. 167–177). New York: Guilford.

O'Donohue, W., & Plaud, J. J. (1994). The conditioning of human sexual arousal. *Archives of Sexual Behavior, 23,* 321–344.

Overholser, J. C., & Beck, S. (1986). Multimethod assessment of rapists, child molesters, and three control groups on behavioral and psychological measures. *Journal of Consulting and Clinical Psychology, 54,* 682–687.

Panton, J. H. (1979). MMPI profile configurations associated with incestuous and non-incestuous child molesting. *Psychological Reports, 45,* 335–338.

Pavlov, I. P. (1960). *Conditioned reflexes: An investigation of the physiological activity of the cerebral cortex* (2nd ed.). New York: Dover.

Pithers, W. D. (1990). Relapse prevention with sexual aggressors: A method for maintaining therapeutic gain and enhancing external supervision. In W. L. Marshall, D. R. Laws & H. E. Barbaree (Eds.), *Handbook of sexual assault: Issues, theories, and treatment of the offender* (pp. 343–361). New York: Plenum Press.

Pithers, W. D., Beal, L. S., Armstrong, J., & Petty, J. (1989). Identification of risk factors through clinical interviews and analysis of records. In D. R. Laws (Ed.), *Relapse prevention with sex offenders* (pp. 77–87). New York: Guilford.

Pithers, W. D., Kashima, K. M., Cumming, G. F., Beal, L. S., & Buell, M. M. (1988). Relapse prevention of sexual aggression. In R. A. Prentky & V. L. Quinsey (Eds.), *Human sexual aggression: Current perspectives* (pp. 244–260). New York: New York Academy of Sciences.

Proulx, J., Côté, G., and Achille, P. A. (1993). Prevention of voluntary control of penile response in homosexual pedophiles during phallometric testing. *Journal of Sex Research, 30,* 140–147.

Quinn, J. T., Harbison, J. J., & McAllister, H. (1970). An attempt to shape human penile responses. *Behaviour Research and Therapy, 8,* 213–216.

Quinsey, V. L. (1984). Sexual aggression: Studies of offenders against women. In D. N. Weisstub (Ed.), *Law and mental health: International perspectives* (Vol. 1, pp. 84–121). New York: Pergamon Press.

Quinsey, V. L. (1986). Men who have sex with children. In D. N. Weisstub (Ed.), *Law and mental health: International perspectives* (Vol. 2, pp. 140–172). New York: Pergamon Press.

Quinsey, V. L., & Bergersen, S. G. (1976). Instructional control of penile circumference in assessments of sexual preference. *Behavior Therapy, 7,* 489–493.

Quinsey, V. L., & Chaplin, T. C. (1988). Preventing faking in phallometric assessments of sexual preference. In R. Prentky & V. L. Quinsey (Eds.), *Human sexual aggression: Current perspectives* (pp. 49–58). New York: New York Academy of Sciences.

Quinsey, V. L., Chaplin, T. C., & Carrigan, W. F. (1979). Sexual preferences among incestuous and nonincestuous child molesters. *Behavior Therapy, 10,* 562–565.

Quinsey, V. L., Chaplin, T. C., & Carrigan, W. F. (1980). Biofeedback and signaled punishment in the modification of inappropriate sexual age preferences. *Behavior Therapy, 11,* 567–576.

Quinsey, V. L., & Earls, C. M. (1990). The modification of sexual preferences. In W. L. Marshall, D. R. Laws & H. E. Barbaree (Eds.), *Handbook of sexual assault: Issues, theories, and treatment of the offender* (pp. 279–295). New York: Plenum Press.

Quinsey, V. L., & Marshall, W. L. (1983). Procedures for reducing inappropriate sexual arousal: An evaluative review. In J. G. Greer & I. R. Stuart (Eds.), *The sexual aggressor: Current perspectives on treatment* (pp. 267–289). New York: Van Nostrand Reinhold.

Quinsey, V. L., Rice, M. E., Harris, G. T., & Reid, K. S. (1993). The phylogenetic and ontogenetic development of sexual age preferences in males: Conceptual and measurement issues. In H. E. Barbaree, W. L. Marshall & S. M. Hudson (Eds.), *The juvenile sex offender* (pp. 143–163). New York: Guilford.

Quinsey, V. L., Steinman, C. M., Bergersen, S. G., & Holmes, T. F. (1975). Penile circumference, skin conductance, and ranking responses of child molesters and "normals" to sexual and nonsexual visual stimuli. *Behavior Therapy, 6,* 213–219.

Rachman, S. (1966). Sexual fetishism: An experimental analogue. *Psychological Record, 16,* 293–296.

Rice, M. E., Quinsey, V. L., & Harris, G. T. (1991). Sexual recidivism among child molesters released from a maximum security psychiatric institution. *Journal of Consulting and Clinical Psychology, 59,* 381–386.

Schaefer, H. H., & Colgan, A. H. (1977). The effect of pornography on penile tumescence is a function of reinforcement and novelty. *Behaviour Therapy, 8,* 938–946.

Segal, Z. V., & Marshall, W. L. (1985). Self-report and behavioral assertion in two groups of sexual offenders. *Journal of Behavior Therapy and Experimental Psychiatry, 16,* 223–229.

Seghorn, T. K., Prentky, R. A., & Boucher, R. J. (1987). Childhood sexual abuse in the lives of sexually aggressive offenders. *Journal of the American Academy of Child and Adolescent Psychiatry, 26,* 262–267.

Seligman, M. (1970). On the generality of the laws of learning. *Psychological Review, 77,* 406–418.

Seto, M. C., & Barbaree, H. E. (1994). *The role of alcohol in sexual aggression.* Manuscript submitted for publication.

Skinner, B. F. (1938). *The behavior of organisms.* New York: Appleton-Century-Crofts.

Skinner, B. F. (1953). *Science and human behavior.* New York: Free Press.

Stermac, L. E., & Quinsey, V. L. (1986). Social competence among rapists. *Behavioral Assessment, 8,* 171–185.

Stermac, L. E., & Segal, Z. V. (1987). *Condoning or condemning adult sexual contact with children: A criterion group-based analysis.* Unpublished manuscript.

Stermac, L. E., Segal, Z. V., & Gillis, R. (1990). Social and cultural factors in sexual assault. In W. L. Marshall, D. R. Laws & H. E. Barbaree (Eds.), *Handbook of sexual assault: Issues, theories, and treatment of the offender* (pp. 143–159). New York: Plenum Press.

Storms, M. D. (1981). A theory of erotic orientation development. *Psychological Review, 88,* 340–353.

Sundberg, S., Barbaree, H. E., & Marshall, W. L. (1991). Victim blame and the disinhibition of sexual arousal to rape vignettes. *Violence and Victims, 6,* 103–120.

Van Wyk, P. H., & Geist, C. S. (1984). Psychosocial development of heterosexual, bisexual, and homosexual behavior. *Archives of Sexual Behavior, 13,* 505–544.

Williams, L. M., & Finkelhor, D. (1990). The characteristics of incestuous fathers: A review. In W. L. Marshall, D. R. Laws & H. E. Barbaree (Eds.), *Handbook of sexual assault: Issues, theories, and treatment of the offender* (pp. 231–255). New York: Plenum Press.

Wormith, J. (1983). A survey of incarcerated sexual offenders. *Canadian Journal of Criminology, 25,* 379–390.

Wydra, A., Marshall, W. L., Earls, C. M., & Barbaree, H. E. (1983). Identification of cues and control of sexual arousal by rapists. *Behaviour Research and Therapy, 21,* 469–476.

Yates, E., Barbaree, H. E., & Marshall, W. L. (1984). Anger and deviant sexual arousal. *Behavior Therapy, 15,* 287–294.

Zuckerman, M. (1971). Physiological measures of sexual arousal in the human. *Psychological Bulletin, 75,* 297–329.

18

Race and Sexuality in the United States: Sexuality and Sexual Preference in the African-American Population

Rupert A. Francis, Frederick A. Ernst, Jessy G. Devieux, and Joyce Perkins

Little is confidently known about the sexual practices of Americans, and even less is known about cross-cultural diversity of sexuality within the American population (Belcastro 1985; Janus & Janus 1993; Reiss 1993). Researching human sexuality is particularly problematic because there is no methodology for collecting data that is not subject to the bias of an individual's report about what he or she does in complete privacy. We describe here a review of studies relevant to sexuality and sexual preference among African-Americans and provide some preliminary new data collected in our own investigations. While we feel strongly that the term *African-American* is a more accurate characterization of our study population than *black*, we will use both terms interchangeably to describe our results because all of our data are comparative and whites do not typically provide ethnic information in response to a question asking for race, and in our experience, the majority of African-Americans continue to use the *black* descriptor in response to a question about race.

SEXUALITY

A recent review (Seidman & Reider 1994) concluded that reliable data concerning sexual behavioral norms are only now beginning to emerge. Despite the most ambitious effort to characterize American sexual practices and norms since the Kinsey report (Kinsey, Pomeroy & Martin 1948), Janus and Janus (1993) did not include comparisons between blacks and whites. Belcastro's (1985) investigation of black and white sexuality was restricted to college students, and his data are now more than ten years old. Other racial comparisons have been conducted on attitudes about sexuality (Oggins, Leber & Veroff 1994; Oggins, Veroff & Leber 1993), but there continues to be a paucity of cross-cultural information about preferences for specific sexual practices.

In the context of an effort to replicate a study performed in 1989 as an investigation of AIDS-related attitudes, we surveyed nearly 700 employees of the Tennessee Mental Health and Retardation System (MH&MR). We selected critical items concerning HIV/AIDS-related attitudes from the previous questionnaire for replication and added a section that assessed preferences for various broadly defined sexual activities on a three-point scale: "Always Prefer," "Sometimes Prefer," and "Never Prefer." While we recognized that respondents would be defensive about providing demographic data along with information about preferences of sexual activity, we believed that useful data comparing black and white responses might possibly be achieved if the rates of declining to answer at all were relatively the same for blacks and whites, while differences in responses were found between blacks and whites who did respond.

We recognized the validity of Mays and Jackson's (1991) assertion concerning the problematic nature of using traditional survey methodologies in the assessment of attitudes in the African-American community. However, our sample of MH&MR employees were all working and literate, thereby narrowing the socioeconomic gap that frequently prevents a black-white comparison. Moreover, Siegel, Krauss, and Karus (1994) provided evidence that a questionnaire is more likely than an interview to elicit disclosure of risky sexual behaviors (e.g., anal intercourse).

Survey Respondents

Six hundred eighty-seven employees completed all or a portion of the questionnaire while attending mandatory in-service training sessions on HIV/AIDS. Although this sample is one of convenience rather than random, we have found in previous research that a wide diversity of demographics is found in this working population, including a surprising number of subjects with less than a high school education (Ernst, Francis, Nevels & Lemeh 1991). While unemployed and extremely poor subjects tend not to be represented in the sample, other demographic similarities between whites and blacks allow for a reasonably confident assessment of black-white differences in knowledge, attitudes, and behavior.

The questionnaires were distributed prior to each in-service session, and it was emphasized that participation in the survey was entirely voluntary. Of 654 respondents who provided data concerning race, 265 (41 percent) were black and 389 (59 percent) were white. Twelve subjects described themselves as neither black nor white and were eliminated from the database. Of 664 respondents revealing gender, 211 (31 percent) were males and 453 (69 percent) were females. The mean age ($\pm$ standard error of measurement) of 664 respondents who provided age was 43.9 years (± 0.4).

The Questionnaire

The questionnaire was a brief two-page fold-out with demographic questions on the face page and survey questions on the inside page (see the chapter appendix). The first six items were statements to which the respondent was asked to agree or disagree on a six-point Likert scale. Questions concerning preferences for various broadly defined sexual activities followed but were preceded by a proclamation that respondents need not provide the information if they were not entirely comfortable with doing so. Those who chose to complete part or all of this section did so by circling "Always Prefer," "Sometimes Prefer," or "Never Prefer" in relation to vaginal intercourse, oral sex, anal intercourse, mutual masturbation, self-masturbation, abstinence, and the category "Other." Demographic data and responses to each section of the survey were entered on computer into STATISTICA, and questionnaires were subsequently destroyed by shredding.

Results

Statistical comparisons of response distributions by blacks and whites to each item were made using 2 × 3 chi-square analyses. Refusal to complete all items in this section of the questionnaire was 39.8 percent. This statistic is very close to the 39 percent of unreturned or inaccurately completed questionnaires reported by Janus and Janus (1993). Interestingly, there were no differences in the refusal rates of blacks and whites to any of the specific items (table 18.1). We also analyzed the demographic characteristics of the nearly 40 percent who refused to provide any information in the section of the questionnaire concerning preferences for sexual activities—those who skipped the entire section. There were no differences between blacks and whites in this measure of defensiveness (table 18.2), although there was a trend for black females to be less defensive about providing information than black males and whites ($p < .08$). Overall, these findings were interpreted as evidence that blacks and whites were not differentially defensive about providing information concerning their preferences for various sexual activities. An important extension of our interpretation, therefore, is that differences in defensiveness between blacks and whites could be ruled out as a source of differences in responses to the specific items of interest.

Nonresponders were also slightly older than responders (45.5 versus 42.9, $t = 3.15$, $p < .002$); no differences in religious preference were found between the two groups. Both of these findings are consistent with Wiederman's (1993) recent report. We also found no differences in responding between single, married, separated, divorced, and widowed subjects, although there was a trend for single subjects to be less defensive than married ones ($p < .06$).

Table 18.1

Responses of Blacks and Whites to Each Item of the Sexual Activity Survey

Activity Item	Response	Blacks	Whites	χ^2	P
Vaginal Intercourse	None	103 (39%)	172 (44%)	1.64	0.2
	Never Prefer	4 (2.5%)	8 (3%)		
	Sometimes Prefer	4 (2.5%)	12 (6%)		
	Always Prefer	154 (95%)	197 (91%)	2.68	0.44
Anal Intercourse	None	130 (49%)	197 (51%)	0.1	0.75
	Never Prefer	125 (93%)	168 (87.5%)		
	Sometimes Prefer	4 (3%)	22 (11.5%)		
	Always Prefer	6 (4%)	2 (1%)	12.3	0.002
Oral Sex	None	130 (46%)	189 (49%)	0.43	0.51
	Never Prefer	84 (58.3%)	58 (29%)		
	Sometimes Prefer	48 (33.3%)	108 (54%)		
	Always Prefer	12 (8.33%)	34 (17%)	31.44	.000001
Mutual Masturbation	None	129 (49%)	192 (49%)	0.01	0.93
	Never Prefer	92 (68%)	91 (46%)		
	Sometimes Prefer	34 (25%)	85 (43%)		
	Always Prefer	10 (7%)	21 (11%)	15.10	.0005
Self-Masturbation	None	131 (49%)	192 (49%)	0.00	0.95
	Never Prefer	110 (82%)	103 (52%)		
	Sometimes Prefer	23 (17%)	77 (39%)		
	Always Prefer	1 (1%)	17 (9%)	32.81	.000001
Abstinence	None	138 (52%)	204 (52%)	0.00	0.99
	Never Prefer	78 (62%)	115 (62%)		
	Sometimes Prefer	27 (21%)	54 (29%)		
	Always Prefer	22 (17%)	16 (9%)	6.48	.039

Note: Percentages for the three categories of response are based on the portion of the sample who provided information in that item of the survey section.

There were no racial differences in preferences for vaginal intercourse, but blacks were less likely than whites to prefer anal intercourse, oral sex, mutual masturbation, and self-masturbation and slightly more likely to prefer abstinence (table 18.1).

Anal Intercourse

Approximately 10 percent (10.49 percent) of our sample indicated some preference for anal intercourse. This is consistent with recent estimates that approximately 10 percent of the population probably engages in this behavior with

Table 18.2
Relative Preferences for Anal Intercourse

	Never Prefer	Sometimes Prefer	Always Prefer
Black Males	81%	6%	13%
White Males	80%	17%	3%
Black Females	96%	2%	2%
White Females	91%	9%	0%

some degree of regularity (Billy, Tanfer, Grady & Keplinger 1993; Seidman & Rieder 1994; Voeller 1991). Janus and Janus (1993) reported that anal sex was revealed as "very normal" or "all right" by 29 percent and 24 percent of men and women, respectively. However, two problems emerge in the interpretation of their data. First, some of their respondents may have wished to indicate that anal sex is "all right" for others without necessarily implying that it was "all right" for them. In other words, there is no indication that respondents who approved actually engaged in the practice. Second, anal sex may have been interpreted by some as any activity connected with stimulation of the anus, whereas anal intercourse for almost everyone implies penile insertion. In a different section of their questionnaire, 2 percent of males and no females revealed anal sex as their preferred method of achieving orgasm. This, again, is not a question that addresses whether anal intercourse is practiced at all.

Our data would suggest that blacks are slightly more conservative with regard to the practice of anal intercourse (overall 7 percent versus 12.5 percent), and the primary source of the difference between blacks and whites derives from a very low reported incidence among black females (3.9 percent). As can be seen in table 18.2, males prefer anal intercourse more frequently than females irrespective of race. Interestingly, of 126 white female respondents, not one indicated an exclusive preference for anal intercourse, which is somewhat consistent with the Janus and Janus (1993) finding. No attempt was made in our questionnaire to differentiate penetrative from receptive anal intercourse in males, nor did we ask directly about sexual preference. In light of this, it is recognized that the relatively greater preference for anal intercourse by males in both races may be an indirect result of unmeasured male homosexuality. In contrast to our findings, Fisher (1980) studied a small sample of middle-class women and found no differences between blacks and whites in reported frequency of anal intercourse. Frequency and preference, however, are not necessarily comparable.

Oral Sex

Rather dramatic differences were found between blacks and whites in the preferences for oral sex. Neither gender contributed disproportionately to this difference (table 18.3). However, the difference in preference between black and

Table 18.3
Relative Preferences for Oral Sex

	Never Prefer	Sometimes Prefer	Always Prefer
Black Males	56%	32%	12%
White Males	19%	59%	22%
Black Females	59%	34%	7%
White Females	33%	50%	16%

white females is consistent with Belcastro's (1985) finding that white females were more likely than black females to have performed fellatio. The range of 8 to 17 percent of exclusive preference is relatively consistent with Janus and Janus's (1993) report that 10 percent of men and 18 percent of women indicated oral sex as a preferred method of achieving orgasm.

Mutual Masturbation

Racial differences here were pronounced and again unaffected by gender (table 18.4). Again, the differences revealed by black and white females are consistent with Belcastro's (1985) findings that white females were more likely to have masturbated a partner.

Self-Masturbation

Preferences for self-masturbation were decidedly different. This practice would be expected to be affected by marital status (i.e., more common among unmarried persons). However, blacks were less likely to be married (53 percent versus 61 percent, $\chi^2 = 10.4$, $p < .001$), more likely to be single (31 percent versus 18 percent), and equally likely to be divorced (12 percent versus 18 percent, $\chi^2 = 1.72$, $p < .19$), but less likely than whites ever to prefer self-masturbation (18 percent versus 48 percent). The differences in preference for self-masturbation between blacks and whites, then, cannot be attributed to differences in marital status.

Janus and Janus (1993) reported that 5 percent of men and 8 percent of women prefer masturbation to achieve orgasm, and this is quite consistent with our findings. When blacks and whites are combined, we found that 4 percent of men and 14 percent of women "always prefer" masturbation. Fisher (1980), on the other hand, found no statistically significant differences in frequency of masturbation between black and white middle-class females. Here again, frequency and preference may not be entirely comparable.

Abstinence

Differences in preference for abstinence were minor although statistically significant. Table 18.1 reveals that 62 percent of blacks and whites never prefer

Table 18.4
Relative Preferences for Mutual Masturbation

	Never Prefer	Sometimes Prefer	Always Prefer
Black Males	70%	21%	9%
White Males	48%	40%	12%
Black Females	67%	26%	7%
White Females	45%	45%	10%

abstinence. A larger percentage of blacks did, however, indicate an exclusive preference for abstinence than whites, and this difference derives primarily from the responses of single and divorced black females.

HOMOSEXUALITY

Etiologic Factors

While there is increasing evidence that homosexuality is primarily a biologically determined, culturally invariant phenomenon, the data are not unequivocal (Byne & Parsons 1993; Diamond 1993; Gooren, Fliers & Courtney 1990; Whitam 1983). The extent to which exclusive homosexual preference is made public can and does vary from culture to culture, suggesting a biocultural interaction affecting the expression of this behavior (De Cecco & Elia 1993; Franklin 1993). In an extensive study of sexual preferences, Bell, Weinberg, and Hammersmith (1981) found differences in the developmental origins of homosexuality between black and white males. For black males, preadult sexual activities appeared to be a more important determinant of sexual preference later, whereas preadult sexual feelings appeared to be a more important determinant in white males. Developmental influences on black females, on the other hand, were considerably more similar to their white female counterparts.

Attitudes in the African-American Community about Homosexuality

Before the matter was investigated objectively, there had been a longstanding contention in the African-American community that homosexuality is socially less tolerated by blacks than by whites. Indeed, early in the history of the epidemic, HIV/AIDS was relatively ignored within the African-American community as a "gay, white problem" (Shilts 1987). We recently investigated black condemnation of homosexuality by comparing the extent of agreement by more than 2,000 blacks and whites to a statement hostile to homosexuality: "AIDS will help society by decreasing the number of homosexuals (gay people)" (Ernst

Figure 18.1
Responses of Blacks (B) and Whites (W) to a Statement Hostile to Homosexuality

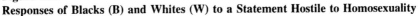
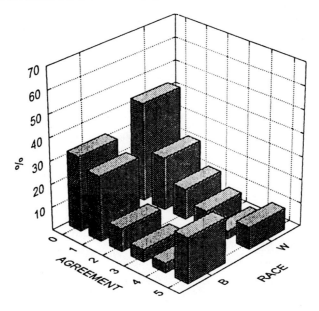

et al. 1991). We found that blacks were more likely than whites to endorse the statement and that the source of the black-white difference was primarily from greater endorsement by black females. With further inquiry, we concluded that black females were growing increasingly unhappy with the dwindling availability of black males because of integration, incarceration, violence, drug use, disease, and other causes that disproportionately affect black males. Male homosexuality was seen as yet another contributor to the overall problem of black male availability.

We included the same item in the questionnaire of our MH&ME investigation and found very similar results (figure 18.1). Blacks were more likely than whites to endorse the statement ($\chi^2 = 16.4$, $p < .006$). Here again, black females had the highest rate of strong endorsement (20 percent). This finding is consistent with our previous results and the observations of Mays, Cochran, and Rhue (1993), Cochran and Mays (1994), and Green (1994a) that black lesbians perceived the African-American community to be conservative in its view on homosexuality. Green (1994a, 1994b) employed the term *triple jeopardy* to describe the three identities through which black lesbians can receive prejudicial treatment: black, female, and lesbian. We would add to this an additional source of stress in that African-Americans may be even harsher in their treatment of homosexuality within their own community. As Green (1994a) pointed out, this creates a severe conflict in African-American homosexuals who perceive themselves as African-Americans first. Perhaps this, in part, may account for the fact that black homosexuals experience a higher level of depressive distress, as found by Cochran and Mays (1994). They also pointed out that the distress appears to be greater for women, further confirming the triple jeopardy phenomenon.

The relatively few empirical studies that have examined mental health issues of lesbians and gays have found that society's condemnatory attitudes play a role in the increased vulnerability of these groups to mental health problems (Green 1994a; Rothblum 1994).

Homosexuality in the African-American Community

An enormous literature on homosexuality has developed in recent years (see, for example, the comprehensive thirteen-volume series by Dynes & Donaldson 1992). But data concerning African-American homosexuality are still incredibly scarce (Berger 1992; Eldridge & Gilbert 1992; NIMH 1987; Zimmerman 1992). In part, this may be related to the historical underrepresentation of minorities in health research and to the relative scarcity of African-American scientists investigating these problems. Another possible source of data scarcity may derive from the reluctance of many African-Americans to volunteer for medical research, in part because African-Americans are well informed about the abuses of blacks in the history of medical research (e.g., the Tuskegee experience). It is well known that blacks are therefore likely to be more mistrusting of medical researchers, particularly if they are associated with majority institutions. In fact, we have data from two sources documenting greater mistrust of medical professionals by blacks (Ernst, Devieux, Perkins & Francis 1994).

Although there is no compelling reason to believe that there are fundamental differences in the nature or practice of homosexuality between blacks and whites, the matter still deserves empirical attention. However, in an exhaustive attempt, we were unable to locate a single published study in the scientific literature addressing the differences in sexual behaviors of black and white homosexuals. Most of the information available regarding sexual practices of African-American homosexuals can be found in the nonscientific literature. In fact, a lot of useful information about black and white homosexuality is available from these other sources, both books (Leyland 1991; Lorde, 1984; Shilts 1987, 1993; Smith 1983; Tripp 1975) and magazines (e.g., *Advocate, BLK,* or Poussaint 1990), most of which have originated in the gay and lesbian community.

SUMMARY AND CONCLUSIONS

We have found an alarming degree of neglect in the scientific literature concerning sexuality in the African-American population. The literature concerning sexual practices of black homosexuals is virtually nonexistent. The preliminary data reported here suggest pervasive conservatism in the African-American population with regard to sexual practices other than vaginal intercourse and acceptance of homosexuality. While conclusions drawn from our findings on sexual practices are limited by the use of questionnaire data to which nearly 40 percent did not respond, our findings concerning attitudes toward homosexuality fundamentally replicate those from a larger database established in our laboratory five years ago. It is clear that an enormous amount of research has yet to be performed if we hope ever to appreciate fully the cross-cultural influences on the expression of sexuality in the American population.

ACKNOWLEDGMENTS

This research was supported by a grant from the Association of Minority Health Professions Schools. Correspondence concerning this chapter should be addressed to F. A. Ernst, Ph.D., Department of Family and Preventive Medicine, Meharry Medical College, 1005 D. B. Todd Blvd., Nashville, TN 37208.

REFERENCES

Belcastro, P. A. (1985). Sexual behavior differences between black and white students. *Journal of Sex Research, 21,* 56–67.

Bell, A. P., Weinberg, M., & Hammersmith, S. (1981). *Sexual preference: Its development in men and women.* Bloomington: Indiana University Press.

Berger, R. M. (1992). Realities of gay and lesbian aging. In W. R. Dynes & S. Donaldson (Eds.), *Studies in homosexuality: Lesbianism* (Vol. 7, pp. 53–60). New York: Garland Publishing.

Billy, J. O., Tanfer, K., Grady, W. R., & Klepinger, D. H. (1993). The sexual behavior of men in the United States. *Family Planning Perspectives, 25,* 52–60.

Byne, W., & Parsons, B. (1993). Human sexual orientation: The biological theories reappraised. *Archives of General Psychiatry, 50,* 228–238.

Cochran, C. D., & Mays, V. M. (1994). Depressive distress among homosexually active African-American men and women. *American Journal of Psychiatry, 151,* 524–529.

De Cecco, J. P., & Elia, J. P. (1993). A critique and synthesis of biological essentialism and social constructionist views of sexuality and gender. *Journal of Homosexuality, 25,* 1–26.

Diamond, M. (1993). Homosexuality and bisexuality in different populations. *Archives of Sexual Behavior, 22,* 291–310.

Dynes, W. R., & Donaldson, S. (Eds.). (1992). *Studies in homosexuality: A 13-volume anthology of scholarly articles.* New York: Garland Publishing.

Eldridge, N. S., & Gilbert, L. A. (1992). Correlates of relationship satisfaction in lesbian couples. In W. R. Dynes & S. Donaldson (Eds.), *Studies in homosexuality: Lesbianism* (Vol. 7, pp. 73–92). New York: Garland Publishing.

Ernst, F. A., Devieux, J. G., Perkins, J., & Francis, R. A. (1994). *Pervasive mistrust of medical experts concerning AIDS-related information.* Unpublished manuscript in preparation for submittal.

Ernst, F. A., Francis, R. A., Nevels, H., & Lemeh, C. A. (1991). Condemnation of homosexuality in the black community: A gender-specific phenomenon? *Archives of Sexual Behavior, 20,* 579–585.

Fisher, S. (1980). Personality correlates of sexual behavior in black women. *Archives of Sexual Behavior, 9,* 27–35.

Franklin, S. (1993). Essentialism. Which essentialism? Some implications of reproductive and genetic techno-science. *Journal of Homosexuality, 25,* 27–39.

Gooren, L., Fliers, E., & Courtney, K. (1990). Biological determinants of sexual orientation. In J. Bancroft, C. M. Davis & D. Weinstein (Eds.), *Annual review of sex research: An integrative and interdisciplinary review* (Vol. 1). Lake Mills, IA: Society for the Scientific Study of Sex.

Green, B. (1994a). Ethnic-minority lesbians and gay men: Mental health treatment issues. *Journal of Consulting and Clinical Psychology, 62,* 243–251.

Green, B. (1994b). African American lesbians: Triple jeopardy. In A. Brown-Collins (Ed.), *The psychology of African American women.* New York: Guilford Press.

Janus, S. S., & Janus, C. L. (1993). *The Janus report on sexual behavior.* New York: John Wiley & Sons.

Kinsey, A. C., Pomeroy, W. B., & Martin, C. B. (1948). *Sexual behavior in the human male.* Philadelphia: W. B. Saunders.

Leyland, W. (Ed.). *Gay roots, twenty years of gay sunshine: An anthology of gay history, sex, politics, and culture.* San Francisco: Gay Sunshine Press.

Lorde, A. (1984). *Sister outsider.* Freedom, CA: Crossing Press.

Mays, V. M., Cochran, S. D., & Rhue, S. (1993). The impact of perceived discrimination on the intimate relationships of black lesbians. *Journal of Homosexuality, 25,* 1–12.

Mays, V. M., & Jackson, J. S. (1991). AIDS survey methodology with black Americans. *Social Science and Medicine, 33,* 47–54.

National Institute of Mental Health. (1987). *National lesbian health care survey.* Washington, DC: U.S. Department of Health and Human Services.

Oggins, J., Leber, D., & Veroff, J. (1994). Race and gender differences in black and white newlyweds' perceptions of sexual and marital relations. *Journal of Sex Research, 31,* 152–160.

Oggins, J., Veroff, J., & Leber, D. (1993). Perceptions of marital interaction among black and white newlyweds. *Journal of Personality and Social Psychology, 65,* 494–511.

Poussaint, A. F. (1990, September). An honest look at black gays and lesbians. *Ebony,* pp. 124, 126, 130, 131.

Reiss, I. L. (1993). The future of sex research and the meaning of science. *Journal of Sex Research, 30,* 3–11.

Rothblum, E. D. (1994). I only read about myself on bathroom walls: The need for research on the mental health of lesbian and gay men. *Journal of Consulting and Clinical Psychology, 62,* 213–220.

Seidman, S. N., & Rieder, R. O. (1994). A review of sexual behavior in the United States. *American Journal of Psychiatry, 151,* 330–341.

Shilts, R. (1987). *And the band played on: Politics, people, and the AIDS epidemic.* New York: St. Martin's Press.

Shilts, R. (1993). *Conduct unbecoming: Gays and lesbians in the U.S. military.* New York: Fawcett Columbine.

Siegel, K., Krauss, B. J., & Karus, D. (1994). Reporting recent sexual practices: Gay men's disclosure of HIV risk by questionnaire and interview. *Archives of Sexual Behavior, 23,* 217–230.

Smith, M. (Ed.). (1983). *Black men white men.* San Francisco: Gay Sunshine Press.

Tripp, C. A. (1975). *The homosexual matrix.* New York: McGraw-Hill.

Voeller, B. (1991). AIDS and heterosexual anal intercourse. *Archives of Sexual Behavior, 20,* 233–276.

Whitam, F. L. (1983). Culturally invariable properties of male homosexuality: Tentative conclusions from cross-cultural research. *Archives of Sexual Behavior, 12,* 207–226.

Wiederman, M. W. (1993). Demographic and sexual characteristics of nonresponders to sexual experience items in a national survey. *Journal of Sex Research, 30,* 1993, 27–35.

Zimmerman, B. (1992). What has never been: An overview of lesbian feminist literary criticism. In W. R. Dynes & S. Donaldson (Eds.), *Studies in homosexuality: Lesbianism* (Vol. 7, pp. 341–365). New York: Garland Publishing.

Appendix 18.A
Race and Sexuality Study Questionnaire

INFORMATION QUESTIONNAIRE
COVER SHEET

THANK YOU VERY MUCH FOR ASSISTING OUR RESEARCH PROGRAM BY AGREEING TO COMPLETE THIS BRIEF QUESTIONNAIRE DURING THIS IN-SERVICE TRAINING SESSION.

PLEASE REMEMBER THAT YOUR PARTICIPATION IS VOLUNTARY

THIS COVER SHEET IS PROVIDED TO KEEP YOUR ANSWERS COMPLETELY PRIVATE. **NO ONE IN YOUR WORKPLACE WILL HAVE ACCESS TO THIS QUESTIONNAIRE.** THE INFORMATION YOU PROVIDE WILL BE PUT ONTO A COMPUTER DATABASE BY DR. ERNST AND HIS RESEARCH ASSISTANT AND THE QUESTIONNAIRES WILL BE IMMEDIATELY DESTROYED BY SHREDDING.

AGE____ SEX____ RACE____ EDUCATION_____

OCCUPATION_____

MARITAL STATUS_____ NUMBER OF CHILDREN_____

NUMBER OF BROTHERS AND SISTERS YOU HAVE (HAD)_____

RELIGIOUS PREFERENCE_____

NOT INCLUDING A PATIENT, DO YOU KNOW ANYONE WHO HAS HIV/AIDS?

QUESTIONS BEGIN ON NEXT PAGE

Please **circle the number** which reflects the amount of your agreement or disagreement with each statement.

1. I have made changes in my personal habits to prevent being infected by the HIV/AIDS virus.

0	1	2	3	4	5
Strongly Disagree					Strongly Agree

2. Sterilized needles should be made available to needle-using drug abusers to prevent the spread of HIV/AIDS.

0	1	2	3	4	5
Strongly Disagree					Strongly Agree

3. HIV/AIDS will help society by decreasing the number of homosexuals (gay people).

0	1	2	3	4	5
Strongly Disagree					Strongly Agree

4. I find it easy to discuss sex-related issues with my partner.

0	1	2	3	4	5
Strongly Disagree					Strongly Agree

5. It is easier to catch the HIV/AIDS virus than the medical experts are leading us to believe.

0	1	2	3	4	5
Strongly Disagree					Strongly Agree

6. Please provide the following information <u>only</u> if you are comfortable doing so. Should you do so, we guarantee the privacy, confidentiality, and anonymity of your answers. **Circle** your degree of preference for each of the following general categories of sexual activity:

Vaginal Intercourse	Most Prefer	Sometimes Prefer	Never Prefer
Anal Intercourse	Most Prefer	Sometimes Prefer	Never Prefer
Oral Sex	Most Prefer	Sometimes Prefer	Never Prefer
Mutual Masturbation	Most Prefer	Sometimes Prefer	Never Prefer
Self Masturbation	Most Prefer	Sometimes Prefer	Never Prefer
Total Abstinence	Most Prefer	Sometimes Prefer	Never Prefer
Other_____	Most Prefer	Sometimes Prefer	Never Prefer

19

Sexuality and Disability

Stanley Ducharme and Kathleen M. Gill

For people with disabilities, the acceptance of sexuality as a justifiable and sanctioned area of rehabilitation has been controversial. Not surprisingly, people with disabilities often receive little or no information in the area of sexuality. In fact, they have generally been perceived as being nonsexual and incapable of achieving an intimate and sexual relationship with another person. This misperception has persisted in the general population and has been prevalent in the medical community as well.

Despite the fact that 10 percent of the general population is estimated to be homosexual, what limited information is provided to people with disabilities assumes heterosexuality, making the availability of sexual education and counseling services even more limited for gay men and lesbians with disabilities.

The history of sexuality services for people with disabilities dates back only to the mid-1970s when Theodore and Sandra Cole began their Sexual Attitude Reassessment Seminars at the University of Minnesota (Cole, Chilgren & Rosenberg 1973). The focus of these early workshops was on values clarification and communication. Their purpose was to increase the practitioner's level of comfort with and awareness of sexual issues among people with disabilities. To some extent, the idea of sexual education for people with disabilities was academic. People in rehabilitation were beginning to recognize the need for sexuality services, but there was little agreement as to how and when these services should be provided. Furthermore, for persons who had a disability and were gay, there was no awareness as to how issues of sexuality should be handled by the rehabilitation staff.

In many ways, the sexual functioning of people with disabilities is not so different from the able-bodied population. However, sexuality is a complex phenomenon, and a number of important variables should be considered: developmental aspects of sexuality for people with either heterosexual or homosexual orientations, adjustment and psychological issues, physical functioning, and issues of staff training and education.

SEXUALITY AS A DEVELOPMENTAL ISSUE

The theory of developmental tasks was originally discussed by the psychologist Eric Erickson (1953). These developmental stages represent the critical periods of development from birth to death. The first three stages of development, representing infancy and childhood, reflect the achievement of trust, autonomy through mobility, and the ability to explore the environment. Even at these early stages in life, sexual behaviors and curiosity are quite typical and expected. This is true for children with and without disabilities.

As individuals move through life, they encounter a number of tasks set by their cultural milieu and by themselves as biologic entities. These developmental tasks are particularly critical since they must be mastered if they are to develop more mature social and interpersonal skills. When disability occurs, not only are the current developmental tasks threatened, but the persons, at least temporarily, regress to an earlier stage of development, with broad implications for an individual's psychological and sexual adjustment. Because the person's sense of masculinity or femininity is an integral part of these developmental milestones, disability can create confusion and conflict in both gender identity and gender role, (identity and role are different aspects of the same process). For people with gay and lesbian orientations, both gender identity and role confusion can make the adjustment process more difficult, especially without adequate role models and sources of emotional support.

Gender identity is the inner experience of one's self as male or female; role is the outward expression of that identity. Without resolution of these conflicts, more complex tasks such as the formation of relationships and the achievement of a positive self-esteem may never occur (Ducharme & Ducharme 1983). Thus, for a person with a disability, a healthy sexual adjustment and the ability to achieve intimacy depend on successful resolution of the developmental tasks at the time of injury or onset of illness.

Superimposed on these developmental tasks are the specialized tasks of gay and lesbian identity formation. More than simply a matter of having a same-sex partner, gay and lesbian identity is similar in scope to ethnic or racial identity, involving identification with the values of a discrete subculture. The process of forming a gay or lesbian identity evolves in stages from confusion and conflict around the emerging awareness of same-sex urges to acceptance. Few individuals move effortlessly to acceptance in this culture given the negative stereotypes surrounding gay and lesbian issues. Furthermore, the presence of disability and the onset of illness or injury complicate this process with frequent regressions, further confusion, and psychological trauma.

Congenital disabilities often prevent the child from gaining essential information about the body. Overprotection by parents, discouragement of sexual exploration, and a lack of adequate socialization often add confusion to male and female roles. Since identity is formulated before the age of 3 years, confusion regarding sexuality lends itself to later feelings of inferiority and difficulty relating to members of the opposite sex. Children with a disability are often isolated from peers and may regard themselves as not equal to their playmates. These deficits in the early sexual education of a child can become more difficult to manage later in life.

During puberty and adolescence, the achievement of sexual identity and acceptance in peer group relationships are the goals to be accomplished. As the adolescent grows and enters young adulthood, one of the primary tasks is the development of intimacy and the concurrent strivings toward independence. Traumatic injury at this time threatens these important peer relationships and fosters dependency on the family unit. Adolescents with a disability often feel unattractive and ashamed of their bodies. Subsequently, they feel unwanted by the opposite sex and incapable of establishing a meaningful relationship. Without a sense of sexual identity, even late adolescents can lack the ability to make vocational and education decisions or to assume responsibility for their own behavior. Thus, future emotional growth is threatened.

Women in this culture are more likely than men to have conflicts around sexuality and to have been sexually coerced or abused. With two women in a relationship, there are greater chances of these issues being present and requiring some resolution prior to the development of a positive sexual adjustment (Nichols 1988). Gay men may also be the victims of childhood abuse and trauma; being able to establish intimacy with another man requires the resolution of any hostility and fear toward other men. In addition, gay men are subject to internalized homophobia (especially acute since the AIDS epidemic) and to stereotypical male sex roles that limit the formation of intimate relationships. Resolution of these internalized concerns is required by both partners if the men are to achieve an intimate relationship. In this regard, intimacy dysfunction can be defined as patterns of behaviors (including communication patterns and both intrapsychic and interpersonal stress) that can cause a person with sexual orientation confusion to rely on external agents (sex, drugs, alcohol, food, work, gambling, body building, or another person) for a positive sense of self. In the families of origin of gay men and lesbians, rejection and abandonment may be subtly conveyed if the family has a negative reaction to gender nonconformity. If sexual abuse is present, the risk of identity and intimacy problems increases (Coleman & Reece 1988).

Aging is also an often overlooked developmental stage. Although the reality is that elders can continue to be sexually active throughout the life span, internalized negative attitudes can inhibit sexual expression in later years. The stigma against aging is even greater in the gay community than in the culture at large and is experienced with fear at earlier ages than for straight men (Coleman & Reece 1988).

SEXUAL ADJUSTMENT

Adjustment to a physical disability or illness is a gradual process that occurs over an extended period of time. The individual must mourn the losses and ultimately develop coping strategies that will validate the meaningfulness of the new postinjury life. Successful adjustment depends on the recognition that choice is still available and is influenced by many factors, such as age at onset, quality of social supports, physical health, gender, and type of illness or injury (Ducharme & Ducharme 1983).

Successful sexual adjustment also requires the same gradual, and sometimes painful, emotional process. Losses need to be grieved so that the remaining strengths can be developed and nurtured. Because of different personality styles, however, not everyone completes this difficult adjustment. Gay men, for example, may have experienced more profound earlier periods of grief and trauma due to their sexuality. Often there were few available supports, and the grieving may have extended for prolonged periods of time. Gay men may also be at greater risk for unresolved grief as more of their friends are dying in the AIDS epidemic and because they may lack strong social support networks.

In addition to personality styles, cultural discrimination limits an individual's ability to adjust successfully. Although some progress in reducing discrimination against both people with disabilities and gay men and lesbians has taken place in the last twenty-five years, homosexuality is often viewed as a disability by gays and straights alike (Nichols 1989). Thus, the person who is gay and has a disability often is regarded as having a double disability. Regardless of disability, everyone has the ability to function sexually and to enjoy an intimate relationship.

After a traumatic disability, individuals frequently go through a period of reduced sexual drive or performance. Others go through a period of sexual acting out, presumably to validate their survival and sexual identity. However, substantial numbers of people fail to resume an active sex life after injury due to misinformation, problems of adjustment, or shame regarding body image and functioning. Those who do assume an active sex life after injury are often advised by rehabilitation staff members to keep separate the roles of sexual partner and care provider. Having one's sexual partner provide intimate medical care can be destructive to the relationship. Mixing these roles often places one member in a needy, helpless position while the other member is perceived as powerful and giving. Such an unequal balance of power in a relationship tends to dilute feelings of intimacy and to be the source of feelings of resentment and anger.

To the extent that persons with a disability can learn to value their new sexual abilities as opposed to trying to regain the same sexual expressions as before injury and to establish a positive level of communication, the person will achieve a satisfying sexual adjustment. These adjustments, however, often come slowly after a period of intense grieving and sadness. Sexual experimentation may or may not be a part of this adjustment process, depending on the individual's ability to take risk and tolerate feelings of vulnerability.

One advantage of gay and lesbian sexual identity may be that sex roles are not as rigid as in heterosexual couples. Penetration is not necessarily the goal, and the sexual repertoire of gay and lesbian couples may be much broader and more diverse. As a result, gay and lesbian couples with a disability may have more sexual alternatives available to them than their straight counterparts (Nichols 1989; Panzarino 1991).

People with disabilities who achieve success in their sexual functioning often do so because of increased communication and a willingness to experiment with developing romance and intimacy as well as technique. They are secure enough to realize that not every experiment will work, and they value nongenital erogenous zones. They are typically more comfortable with their own bodies and continue to feel a sense of self-worth and self-respect. As a result, partners also feel validated and perceive the sexual relationship as warm, caring, and a mutually enjoyable experience.

The importance of communication cannot be overstated. The development of skills in communication about sexual topics and methods of pleasure is the most critical aspect of successful sexual adjustment. Specific and immediate communication between partners can relieve intense feelings of anxiety, fears of rejection, and concerns about physical safety. For this reason, psychological counseling and education about sexuality while in rehabilitation must emphasize these areas and provide individuals with the opportunity to develop and strengthen these skills.

Although psychological considerations need to be addressed in all discussions regarding sexuality, physical functioning is equally important. Often in rehabilitation, it can be extremely supportive and helpful to patients if a sensitive discussion regarding physical capabilities is provided as soon as the individual is ready. Usually people will indicate their readiness by asking questions regarding attractiveness, dating, relationships, and intimacy. Even if the individual does not raise these concerns during hospitalization, it is usually appropriate for staff members to offer information if the patient seems interested and curious. Such topics as erections, orgasms, lubrication, fertility, mobility, sensation, and bladder functioning are all relevant to the sexual functioning of people with disabilities.

MALE SEXUAL FUNCTIONING

The capacity to achieve erections is often altered in most men who sustain damage to the central nervous system. This typically includes injuries such as spinal cord injury and stroke as well as progressive disabilities such as multiple sclerosis and diabetes. Interestingly, men with a head injury do not report similar impairments but often note changes in sexual desire and libido. (For men with a head injury, sexual expression is frequently compromised primarily because of changes in personality, cognition, and behavior). Men with congenital disabilities such as cerebral palsy and muscular dystrophy often retain the ability to achieve erections but more often report difficulties in mobility, positioning, and communication. If erections are altered, such as with spinal cord injury, the man may still be capable of reflexogenic erections. Although these may not be suitable for penetration, they can usually be achieved and sustained by ongoing manual stimulation of the genital area.

Sensory disturbances are also a prominent symptom in many of the disabilities that affect erectile functioning. For example, a man may be capable of a psychogenic or reflex erection but may be unable to feel his penis in response to his partner's stimulation. Other men may experience some sparing of sensation in the genital area, although these areas may not be as sensitive as prior to the injury. For example, the man may be able to differentiate hard touch but unable to experience soft touch or stroking. Areas of intact sensation, usually above the level of injury, are often hypersensitive and another source of erotic pleasure. These areas may be at the nipple line, for example, or in the vicinity of the ears, scalp, and neck.

In recent years, penile injections, implants, vacuum constrictive devices (that fit over the penis), and various surgical procedures have gained increased popularity for men with neurogenic erectile difficulties. One of the most promising forms of treatment, investigated in Denmark, utilized nitroglycerine plasters that were applied directly to the penile shaft, enabling men with spinal injuries to achieve erections sufficient for penetration (Sonksen & Biering-Sorenson 1992). Such noninvasive techniques represent a new wave of thinking in which medical science is offering a great deal of encouragement to men with disabilities.

Although of limited relevance to many gay men, the ability to diagnose and treat infertility in men is another area that continues to improve. For men with disabilities of the central nervous system, fertility rates have generally ranged anywhere from 1 to 10 percent. Reports of pregnancies were typically undocumented and anecdotal. Problems were due to either difficulties of sperm retrieval or poor sperm quality. Newer methods of retrieving sperm through electroejaculation and vibratory stimulation are demonstrating very positive results. In other cases, surgical sperm aspiration coupled with in vitro fertilization are offering new hope for couples wishing to have children. In other men, techniques to reduce testicular temperatures are having positive results on spermatogenesis and sperm production.

FEMALE SEXUAL FUNCTIONING

The literature on sexuality for women with disabilities tends to be minimal, lagging far behind the research being conducted for men with disabilities. Although a number of hypotheses have been made to explain this, the best answer may lie in the fact that most of the research in sexuality is conducted by male researchers, who are more interested in men's issues. There are still many unanswered questions, such as how female genital responses change at different levels of spinal cord trauma or specific questions regarding pregnancy or childbirth.

For the most part, changes in the female genital tract are most common after neurologic trauma or disease. These changes affect vaginal lubrication, labial swelling, clitoral swelling and regression, and a sequence of events at the time of orgasm that is similar to men with disabilities. Many aspects of a woman's sexuality may be altered after a traumatic injury, including libido or desire, arousal, response, and specific sexual behaviors. Complications encountered by women with traumatic disabilities include management of autonomic hyperreflexia (drastic changes in blood pressure), management of bowel and bladder continence, and management of spasticity. In some cases for women with multiple sclerosis and spinal injury, lubrication may become reflexogenic, facilitating penetration of the vagina. Changes in desire and arousal may result from the impact of changes in her physical status on her perception of herself, from role changes that may occur as a result of injury, or from the anger and depression that often accompany the onset of a disability (Gill & Ducharme 1992). As for fertility, women tend to remain fertile after disability, although it may take up to six months following trauma for menstruation to resume.

Current research on female sexuality appears to be exploring issues related to vaginal contractions, intensifying perception of orgasm, and stimulating vasodilation of the pelvic region. All require further investigation but seem to indicate a renewed interest in the field and a commitment to understanding female sexuality and disability. Most important, newer research is providing a renewed sense of hope for women with disabilities, offering important applications for clinical practice (Leyson, 1991).

STAFF TRAINING AND INSTITUTIONAL ISSUES

Staff training in sexuality is a critical feature of any comprehensive rehabilitation program. This must include programs aimed at values clarification as well as those that provide specific information on disability and sexuality. In addition to the training curriculum, administrative support of the sexuality program must be evident to staff members, families, and patients alike. This administrative approval establishes a positive therapeutic environment where openness, empowerment, and caring are the foundations of the rehabilitation process.

Although not all staff members need be sex counselors, all should feel comfortable with the topic of sexuality and communicate a sense of openness about the topic. This necessitates an awareness of one's own values and reactions to sexually related issues. Generally anxiety, shame, or discomfort about sexuality is common. Homophobia is also widespread, including among many individuals working in health and rehabilitation facilities. Putting this anxiety aside and becoming aware of personal reactions to sexual issues is a long process that requires sensitization, education, and practice. Often a first step in reducing this tension is acknowledging one's feelings to another person. In a work setting, a peer support group or discussion with a colleague can be especially helpful in overcoming personal barriers about sexuality.

In addition to processing personal feelings about sexuality, specific information on sexuality and disability must be taught to staff members. Without correct up-to-date information about sexuality, staff members will only add confusion to an already difficult topic. Worse, the patient and partner could be given incorrect information that will have a negative effect on their overall adjustment and relationship. An ongoing lecture series is often helpful in this regard. Typical issues addressed in such a program include sexual anatomy and physiology, effects of medications, physical functioning, treatment options such as penile injections and implants, counseling techniques, professional roles, and gay and lesbian issues.

Staff members should be able to facilitate positive sexual identity in both heterosexual and homosexual patients, including exposure to healthy role models. Patients require specific information on the norms of gay and lesbian culture, which have changed dramatically in the past ten years. In the gay community, sexual liberation had sometimes meant high-frequency, casual sexual contacts with an emphasis on genital pleasure. Partly as a result of AIDS, gay men are now exploring committed relationships with or without extrarelationship sexual encounters. In the lesbian community, liberation has traditionally meant freedom from patriarchy, and feminist lesbians have supported gentle, loving, egalitarian relationships. More recently, there has been a movement in the lesbian community to a more risky, exploratory sex for pleasure behavior. In order to prevent their own biases from being transmitted to patients, staff members need to be aware of their own values regarding these issues. They also need to supplement warnings about high-risk sexual behaviors with a more positive approach to appealing sexual alternatives that allow for intimacy and pleasure. Ultimately, community involvement in the gay and lesbian community can decrease the sense of powerlessness and provide access to more detailed and accurate information that may not be available from rehabilitation staff members (Coleman & Reece 1988).

The development of a sexuality committee within a facility is often the method of choice in addressing ongoing sexual issues and problems. Ideally, a member of the administration should serve on the committee to validate the committee's function and provide a sense of security, safety, and recognition to its members. The development of institutional guidelines and procedures is usually the first task of the committee and often its most important function. It is essential that the committee establish guidelines on some of the most sensitive interactions that occur in the day-to-day functioning of the institution. Typically issues to be addressed include such matters as whether to establish a privacy room, public versus private masturbation, partner sexual activity, dissemination of birth control information and supplies, prevention of sexual assault, prevention of sexually transmitted diseases, and policies concerning the relationships between patients and staff members.

Most often in-service education programs will raise concerns about staff-patient interactions. This is usually the primary area of staff anxiety, and sensitive discussion is most often welcomed and appreciated. In addition, an overview of behavior modification techniques can be helpful. This should be especially geared around sexual issues and should be combined with theoretical discussions of reinforcement schedules and behavioral contingencies. Finally, the importance of limit setting and professional boundaries should be discussed and emphasized.

UNIQUE ISSUES FACED BY GAY MEN AND LESBIANS WITH DISABILITIES

Health care providers need to become aware of the unique intrapersonal, interpersonal, and sociocultural issues that affect gay men and lesbians in order to provide them with adequate sexual rehabilitation services and information. Gay men and lesbians face the following problems, which may be unique to the homosexual community:

1. Homosexuals may be denied visitations in the hospital from their partners. This is especially true in intensive care units where only family members are typically permitted (Panzarino 1991). They may also be prevented from using privacy rooms, which in some facilities allow couples to be intimate while one member of the relationship is hospitalized. Sodomy laws in some states make it illegal for same-sex couples to engage in sexual practices. Therefore, access to these privacy rooms may be denied or discouraged because of cultural values or state laws.

2. One partner of a homosexual couple may not be included in discharge plans and may not be invited to participate in discharge planning meetings. If the staff member fails to inquire as to discharge plans and living arrangements, staff members may assume that the patient will be returning to the family's home. Particular problems may also arise if the patient has not revealed his sexual orientation to family members. In this case issues of confidentiality are critical, and the staff have an obligation to respect the rights of the patient (Ducharme, Gill, Biener-Bergman & Fertitta 1993).

3. The sexual information and videos available to patients may not adequately address the sexual concerns and questions of gay men and lesbian patients. This lack of information fixes the responsibility of disclosure on the patient, placing him or her in an unfair and compromising position. This focus on heterosexual issues alone conveys a bias against homosexual couples and again reflects the values of the staff members.

4. The patient's self-concept can suffer as a result of the double stigmatization still prevalent in the culture against both homosexuals and people with disabilities. This may be further intensified by the stereotypes against women who are both lesbians and have a disability.

5. The civil rights of gay men and lesbians with disability are often violated in the areas of cohabitation (disabled housing may prevent some same-sex partners from living together), credit, employment, tax benefits, medical insurance benefits, inheritance, child custody, adoption and fertility services, and vocational rehabilitation (Boston's Women's Health Book Collective 1984).

6. Meeting partners may be limited by the inaccessibility of social events and the discrimination against people with disabilities. Furthermore, much-needed support groups or self-help meetings such as Alcoholics Anonymous may not be accessible and open to gay men and lesbians.

7. Homophobia in the rehabilitation system prevents quality care in sexual rehabilitation services. Staff members are encouraged to explore and be aware of their biases and to provide to gay and lesbian patients role models who are successfully functioning in their sexual lives after the onset of disability. Staff members who themselves are homosexual may be very effective resource people to these patients and provide critical emotional support and acceptance.

CONCLUSION

For people with disabilities, there are multiple restrictions on the expression of sexuality. These stem from cultural biases, social ignorance, and unfounded fears regarding the person with a disability. For homosexual men and women, these fears and biases are significantly intensified, and there is a serious lack of information and resources available in the area of sexual health. The responsibility of medical professionals is to achieve a balance between protecting the rights and privacy of hospitalized patients and providing a safe and enriching environment. As staff attitudes are retrained away from control and from imposing restrictive values, a therapeutic environment that fosters self-esteem and sexual growth will unfold in the rehabilitation setting.

In the past decade, we have witnessed tremendous progress in the areas of sexuality and disability. However, there is much left to be done so that men and women of all sexual orientations are included in this revolution. What was a passing fad outside mainstream rehabilitation has now become an accepted standard of practice for the rehabilitation team. Education about sexuality is a critical component of the rehabilitation process. More important people with disabilities are now recognized as having the same rights, needs, and desires as all other people.

REFERENCES

Boston Women's Health Book Collective. (1984). *The new our bodies ourselves.* New York: Simon & Schuster.

Cole, T. M., Chilgren, R., & Rosenberg, P. (1973, August). A new program of sex education and counseling for spinal cord injured adults and health care professionals. *International Journal of Paraplegia,* 111–124.

Coleman, E., & Reece, R. (1988). Treating low sexual drive among gay men. In Leiblum & R. Rosen (Eds.), *Sexual desire disorders* (pp. 413–445). New York: Guilford Press.

Ducharme, S., & Ducharme, J. (1983) Sexual adaptation. *Seminars in Neurology, 3*(2), 135–140.

Ducharme, S., Gill, K. M., Biener-Bergman, S., & Fertitta, L. (1993). Sexual functioning: Medical and psychological aspects. In J. Delisa (Ed.), *Rehabilitation medicine: Principles and practice* (2nd ed.) (pp. 763–782). Philadelphia: J. B. Lippincott.

Erickson, E. (1953). *Childhood and society.* New York: W. W. Norton & Co.

Gill, K. M., & Ducharme, S. (1992). Female sexual functioning. In H. Frankel (Ed.), *Handbook of clinical neurology: Spinal cord trauma* (pp. 331–345). Amsterdam: Elsevier Science Publisher.

Leyson, J. F. J. (1991). Controversies and research in female sexuality. In J. F. J. Leyson (Ed.), *Sexual rehabilitation of the spinal cord injured patient* (pp. 465–481) Clifton, NJ: Humana Press.

Masters, W. H., & Johnson, V. E. (1966). *Human sexual response.* Boston: Little, Brown.

Nichols, M. (1988). Low sexual desire in lesbian couples. In S. Leiblum & R. Rosen (Eds.), *Sexual desire disorders* (pp. 387–412). New York: Guilford Press.

Nichols, M. (1989). Sex therapy with lesbians, gay men and bisexuals. In S. Leiblum & R. Rosen (Eds.), *Principles and practice of sex therapy: An update for the nineties* (pp. 269–297). New York: Guilford Press.

Panzarino, C. J. (1991). Female homosexuality. In J. F. J. Leyson (Ed.), *Sexual rehabilitation of the spinal cord injured patient* (pp. 379–387). Clifton, NJ: Humana Press.

Sonksen, J., & Biering-Sorensen, F. (1992). Transcutaneous nitroglycerin in the treatment of erectile dysfunction in spinal cord injured. *Paraplegia, 30,* 554–557.

20

Sexuality and Sexual Orientation in the Military and Other Social Institutions

Larry M. Lance

American culture, like other cultures in general, has been characterized by a heterosexual sexual orientation. As a result, there exist widespread homophobia and discrimination of the homosexual sexual orientation throughout social institutions—military, educational, family, religious, and political institutions, and beyond. For example, the governmental institution has traditionally dismissed gay people from the military based on their sexual orientation rather than their performance. Moreover, from the standpoint of the governmental institution, discrimination against the homosexual orientation is evident in the existing laws. In contemporary American society homosexual relations are illegal in about half of the states, with several states specifically singling out acts between persons of the same sex.

Gay marriages are not legally recognized by governmental institutions of any of the states. Further, for many people, linking lesbians and gays with the term *family* is a contradiction in terms. Many people take the position that "homosexuals are antifamily." However, research suggests that lesbians and gay males are as involved with family life as heterosexuals. Indeed, homosexuality in the family takes many forms. For example, there are traditional family structures where a member is homosexual as a parent, as a teenager, or as a grandparent.

With respect to the religious institution, many mainline Christian denominations and major Jewish bodies have made statements supporting civil rights for homosexuals. On the other hand, conservative religious groups and some segments of mainline Christian denominations continue to present the most vocal and unified opposition to these rights. It is easy to see why the relationship between the gay community and the religious institution is violent and unstable. It also is easy to understand why movements to modify the status quo of this strong division of beliefs between the gay community and the religious institutions produce sensitivities in each constituency.

With respect to the political institution, the impact of supporters of the gay sexual orientation continues to grow stronger. In addition to being active voters, gay people are becoming a constituency to be recognized. Evidence of the impact of gay people was recently shown when Bill Clinton proposed ending discrimination on the basis of sexual orientation in determining who may serve in the armed forces during the primary season. In 1993, President Clinton put his proposal into action by signing a memorandum directing the secretary of defense to submit a draft of an executive order ending discrimination on the basis of sexual orientation in determining who may serve in the armed forces. As a result of the memorandum, discrimination on the basis of sexual orientation in determining who may serve in the military institution is currently at the forefront of society.

This chapter focuses on the research conducted by RAND's National Defense Research Institute. This research included a review of public opinion involving the perspectives of current active-duty military personnel and examined the scientific literature on group cohesion, sexuality, several legal and enforcement issues, and the implementation of change in large organizations. In addition, an examination was conducted of the current literature dealing with the impact of sexual orientation on social institutions of society.

Sexuality research dealing with sexual orientation and social institutions, defined as the main areas of social life organized to meet basic human needs, is characterized by two key issues: one pertains to the meaning of sexual orientation, and the other is the quality of information available for understanding sexual orientation within the framework of social institutions. This discussion will first consider these two issues with respect to sexual orientation in the context of social institutions and then turn to sexuality research focusing on sexual orientation within the context of the military and other contemporary social institutions.

ASSESSMENT OF SEXUAL ORIENTATION

One of the key issues in the social research on sexual orientation with regard to social institutions is how to assess this orientation. Many methods have been used (Coleman 1987, 1990). Until the conclusion of the nineteenth century, sexual orientation was assessed in terms of two choices: homosexual or heterosexual. In recent times social researchers have pointed out that sexual orientation is not an either-or proposition. Based on research conducted by Kinsey, Pomeroy, and Martin (1948), sexual orientation is considered based on a continuum, consisting of a wide range with infinite degrees between the two extremes of exclusively heterosexual desire and exclusively homosexual desire. Kinsey, Pomeroy, and Martin (1948) pointed out that

the world is not divided into sheep and goats. Not all are black nor all things white. It is a fundamental of taxonomy that nature rarely deals with discrete categories and tries to force facts into separated pigeon holes. The living world is a continuum in each and every one of its aspects. The sooner we learn this concerning human sexual behavior the sooner we shall reach a sounder understanding of the realities of sex. (p. 639)

While assessing sexual orientation using the continuum approach was an improvement over the view that sexual orientation is dichotomous, it still is limiting for accurately describing a person's sexual orientation. This continuum approach assumes that sexual behavior or erotic responsiveness is the same within persons. In response to this limitation, Bell and Weinberg (1978) used two scales in their extensive investigation of homosexuality. They evaluated their respondents on two scales, one for sexual behavior and one for erotic fantasies. Their study yielded differences between ratings for the two scales. Paul (1983/1984) indicated that differences were found in about one-third of the homosexual samples. Most of the respondents perceived their behavior as more extensively homosexual than their erotic feelings.

Thus, in locating people along the continuum of orientation, it has been maintained that it is meaningful to stress each person's perceived attractions as well as his or her actual sexual partners. Further, research has indicated discrepancies between the sex of the partners a person prefers and the sex of a person's actual partners. For example, while some people prefer partners of the same sex, for reasons of social acceptability they restrict themselves to heterosexual relationships. This is true of some married people. On the other hand, people who prefer heterosexual relationships may have relationships with members of the same sex. This takes place in restrictive environments, such as prisons or the military. Thus, it has been maintained that the attractions a person feels are more significant in classifying sexual orientation than is the sex of that individual's sexual partners.

Yet another consideration in placing people along a continuum is that sexual orientation has been determined by social research to change over time. This notion is in opposition to the traditional belief that sexual orientation is firmly fixed for life at some point in a person's life. Thus, social research suggests it is possible for a person to move along the continuum with the passage of time. A good example of this change is the person who, when growing up, feels attracted to members of the same sex but as a result of social pressure becomes sexually involved with members of the opposite sex. Then, sometime later in life, he or she redirects his or her sexual activities from members of the opposite sex to members of the same sex to conform with his or her inner feelings of sexual attraction. Thus, instead of assessing sexual orientation as a dichotomous choice at one point in time, this approach expands on the Kinsey continuum of

Figure 20.1
**Expanded Kinsey Sexual Orientation Continuum Taking into Account Behavior
and Feelings of Attraction Early in Life**

```
Exclusively              Equal Amounts of          Exclusively
Heterosexual             Heterosexual and          Homosexual
Behavior                 Homosexual Behavior       Behavior

|------------X---------------|---------------------------|

                        Behavior

Exclusively              Equal Attraction          Exclusively
Heterosexual             to Heterosexuals          Homosexual
Attraction               and Homosexuals           Attraction

|---------------------------|---X----------------------|

                  Feelings of Attraction
```

sexual orientation. Rather than considering the Kinsey continuum, which focuses on the sex of the person(s) with whom sexual behavior is involved, this approach sees two continuums and takes into account who is involved in sexual behavior and feelings about who the person is interested in or attracted to over time. For a person growing up in a heterosexual society with feelings of attraction toward members of the same sex, responses to the two continuums might be as shown in figure 20.1. Then, after growing up and establishing stronger feelings of attraction toward members of the same sex, this person may tend to restrict adherence to the heterosexual social pressures of society and act upon the inner feelings of attraction. Thus, the responses to the continuums of sexual orientation may change to those shown in figure 20.2.

Other social researchers have offered additional dimensions of sexual orientation for consideration in future studies dealing with sexual orientations in the context of social institutions, Klein (1978, 1980) and Klein, Sepekoff, and Wolf (1985) defined several dimensions of sexual orientation, including sexual attraction, social preference, self-identification, and heterosexual or homosexual lifestyle preference. In total, respondents are asked to rate themselves on a seven-point scale for seven different dimensions. Contending that sexual orientation is not fixed or permanent, the Klein Sexual Orientation Grid (KSOG) asks people to provide ratings in a 7×3 matrix (figure 20.3). This matrix presents the seven sexual orientation dimensions and provides ratings for past, present, and the ideal choice of the person.

Further elaboration on the dimensions of sexual orientation was provided by Eli Coleman (1990). Coleman, also maintaining that Kinsey's continuum of sexual orientation is possibly overly simplistic and fails to reflect all of the components in sexual orientation, considered nine dimensions in sexual orientation:

Figure 20.2

Expanded Kinsey Sexual Orientation Continuum Taking into Account Behavior and Feelings of Attraction Later in Life

```
Exclusively              Equal Amounts of           Exclusively
Heterosexual             Heterosexual and           Homosexual
Behavior                 Homosexual Behavior        Behavior

|---------------------------|------------X--------------|
                        Behavior

Exclusively              Equal Attraction           Exclusively
Heterosexual             to Heterosexuals           Homosexual
Attraction               and Homosexuals            Attraction

|---------------------------|--------------------X-----|
                   Feelings of Attraction
```

1. Lifestyle or current relationship status.

2. Self-identification of current sexual orientation.

3. One's idealized sexual orientation.

4. Degree of self-acceptance of one's current sexual orientation identity.

5. Physical sexual identity.

6. Gender identity.

7. Sex role identity.

8. Current sexual behavior, fantasies, and emotional attachments.

9. Past and idealized future sexual identities.

To summarize, social researchers have discussed and elaborated on the view that sexual orientation is dichotomous and the view of Kinsey, Pomeroy, and Martin (1948) that sexual orientation can be assessed along a single continuum. Many suggestions for more precisely assessing sexual orientation have been proposed. Unfortunately, these suggestions have not found widespread use in studies of sexual orientation in the context of social institutions. These suggestions need to be considered in future research.

QUALITY OF SOCIAL INFORMATION

Regardless of whether the discussion is dealing with sexuality, sexual orientation and social institutions, or some other social aspect of society, it needs to be recognized that social research on sexual attitudes, behavior, and knowledge is characterized by serious limitations, many of them unlikely to be overcome in future research. For example, most of the social data from the research by Kinsey et al. (1948, 1953) until the present time has been collected using non-probability samples, which cannot be considered representative of the U.S. pop-

Figure 20.3
Assessment of Sexual Orientation Using the Klein Sexual Orientation Grid

	Rating Mode		
Sexual Orientation Dimension	Past	Present	Ideal
Sexual Attraction			
Sexual Behavior			
Sexual Fantasies			
Emotional Preference			
Social Preference			
Self Identification			
Hetero/Gay Lifestyle			

ulation and therefore are not generalizable to the U.S. population. Even recent social researchers, who have tried to use probability sampling techniques to achieve representation, have conducted studies characterized by other serious limitations. For instance, there are limitations as a result of sampling error, nonresponse bias, and several sources of measurement error, such as the respondent's skipping embarrassing questions, distortion of answers to fit a socially desirable image or denying incriminating behavior, or simple failure of memory to provide the correct information. As a result, there are no completely accurate studies of the occurrence of private sexual behaviors. However, data gathered by some social researchers do provide useful information on sexual orientation, whether self-identified sexual orientation and homosexual behavior are synonymous, and the occurrence of proscribed sexual behaviors among male and female heterosexuals and homosexuals.

Taking into account the variation in the quality of social research, the focus of this discussion is on the studies that yield the most objective empirical evidence. Most of the studies selected for discussion in this chapter are based on the following six criteria (National Defense Research Institute 1993):

1. With regard to sampling methods, probability sampling techniques that enable generalizations to a population of interest are preferred to nonprobability samples.

2. Studies were generally selected that provided specific, well-defined, objective measures of behavior. In other words, the ability to interpret self-reports of sexual behavior requires that the questions be clear and well defined so respondents are aware of what is being asked and researchers know the meaning of the response.

3. Studies were preferred that demonstrated a high quality of survey execution. In other words, it was considered desirable to have studies using appropriate procedures to safeguard privacy and to achieve adequate response rates.

4. The quality of the documentation of results was taken into account. That is, studies

were selected that reported key variables for subgroups as well as the entire sample, and evidence was given on the effects of nonresponse.

5. With respect to sample size, larger samples were preferred to small samples.

6. The recency of the research was taken into account. Recent investigations were considered as being more readily generalizable to the current policy context.

Sexuality and sexual orientations with respect to various social institutions are covered in the following discussion, although the focus is on the military social institution. While sexuality and sexual orientation are of concern with respect to several of the social institutions, as a result of a 1993 presidential memorandum directing Secretary of Defense Les Aspin to end discrimination on the basis of sexual orientation in the armed forces, the military as a social institution has been the center of attention. With this in mind, much of the following discussion focuses on a summary of material stemming from an investigation by a multidisciplinary team of researchers drawn from several research departments at RAND, a nonprofit institution that strives to enhance public policy through research and analysis. (Elaboration on the information provided on the military social institution with respect to sexual orientation can be obtained by consulting the report of the National Defense Research Institute 1993.)

SEXUAL ORIENTATION AND THE U.S. MILITARY SOCIAL INSTITUTION

In January 1993, President Clinton signed a memorandum requesting the secretary of defense to turn in before July 15, 1993, a draft of an executive order that would end discrimination on the grounds of sexual orientation in the determination of who may serve in the armed forces. By issuing this request, the president was carrying out a campaign promise to end the prohibition of homosexuals serving in the U.S. military. This proposed change in policy to permit homosexuals to serve is controversial, with opposition to the change being raised by many in the public and in Congress.

Attitudes of the Public

Gallup polls conducted in 1992 and 1993 determined that 40 to 60 percent of Americans did not support permitting homosexuals to serve in the U.S. military. The proportion of Americans supporting the rights of homosexuals to serve varied to some extent on the way the question was worded. When provided with a list of occupations and asked in which occupations homosexuals should be permitted to be employed, 57 percent stated that homosexuals should be permitted to be employed in the U.S. military. This is higher than the percentage of Americans who felt that homosexuals should be allowed to be doctors (53 percent), clergy (43 percent), high school and elementary school teachers (47 percent and 41 percent, respectively), or members of the president's cabinet (54 percent) but lower than the percentage who felt that homosexuals should be permitted to be salespersons (82 percent).

Results of a 1993 Gallup poll showed 53 percent responded positively to the question, "Should homosexuals be able to serve in the Armed Forces?" Also in 1993 an ABC News/Washington Post poll found 53 percent of the respondents agreeing that enlistees should not be asked about their sexual orientation. However, support dropped to 40 to 45 percent when people were asked if openly homosexual individuals should be allowed to serve. Also, when asked if they "approve or disapprove of ending the ban on homosexuals serving in the military," 43 percent of the participants approved.

Attitudes of the Church

Views of church bodies and organizations are mixed on the issue of permitting homosexuals to serve in the U.S. military. Some church bodies and religious organizations, such as the Evangelical Lutheran Church in America (ELCA) and the American Jewish Committee, favor removal of the ban against military service by homosexuals ("News: Church leaders on gay issue," 1993). Bishop Herbert Chilstrom of the ELCA related the issue to the ordination of homosexuals by stating that the ELCA does not ban homosexuals from becoming pastors but rather relies on a clear set of standards for those who are ordained. Judgment is made on the basis of behavior rather than on sexual orientation (Chilstrom 1993). In contrast, Southern Baptists have taken a position strongly against removing the ban. In accord with their opposition to extending civil rights to homosexuals, recently the Southern Baptist Christian Life Commission expressed opposition to the removal of the ban as a result of a concern for its effects on the military and because "lifting the ban will give approval and support to an immoral, harmful lifestyle" ("Baptists call for keeping military ban on gays," 1993).

Thus, there is a diversity in positions toward homosexuality among the churches and church organizations. Although the range of positions is as great as the range of denominations, positions have been generally summarized into three categories:

1. Those providing full acceptance to homosexual members, which may deal with performing or recognizing homosexual marriages, ordination of homosexual clergy, and incorporation of homosexual laity in other sacramental rights.

2. Those providing compassion and openness to individuals of homosexual orientation but maintaining moral prohibitions on homosexual behaviors because they fall outside the orthodox bounds of monogamous heterosexual marriage.

3. Those who are unable to locate acceptability of homosexual persons within their

religious doctrines and are condemnatory of homosexual acts or partnerships as a "lifestyle."

A majority of denominations fit into the second category (Melton 1991).

Attitudes in the Military

With respect to ending discrimination on the basis of sexual orientation in the military, data from military members who participated in social research indicate they are generally opposed to removing the restriction. This conclusion is based on a survey by the *Los Angeles Times* of 2,346 enlisted men and women during February 1993 and a survey of 2,804 enlisted personnel and officers between February and December 1992 by Charles Moskos and Laura Miller. There were limitations associated with these studies. First, nonprobability sampling was used in both surveys, so generalization of the findings to the entire military population is not possible. Second, since the surveys were conducted at a small number of army sites in the Moskos and Miller survey, there is limited geographic representation. Also, the Moskos and Miller survey did not involve senior officers. Regardless of these limitations, the survey data provide insights about the views and concerns of the survey respondents about lifting the ban (National Defense Research Institute 1993).

From these surveys 75 percent of the males and about 50 percent of the females in the military opposed permitting homosexuals to serve. Respondents in the *Los Angeles Times* poll opposing homosexuals expressed a fear of sharing quarters with homosexuals. In addition, they viewed homosexuality as immoral and opposed to their religious beliefs, and they were concerned that homosexuals contribute to the spread of AIDS. A large majority expressed the view that homosexuals would be subject to violence if restrictions on them were dropped (National Defense Research Institute 1993).

Prevalence of Homosexuality in the United States and the U.S. Military

From one perspective, prevalence of homosexual behavior in the U.S. population has no direct relevance on policy pertaining to military service by homosexuals. If homosexuality is not compatible with military service, then it is not compatible, no matter how many people are excluded from serving by the restriction. However, when attention is turned to ending the restriction, the prevalence of homosexual behavior becomes relevant from a practical standpoint. How many potential military people are under consideration? Moreover, occurrence of homosexual behavior in the military becomes a consideration for determining if a change in policy will create a rise in sexual behaviors related to health risks (National Defense Research Institute 1993).

Taking the recent major survey studies into account, about 2 to 8 percent of

Table 20.1

Estimates of Homosexual Behavior from U.S. Probability Studies

Study	Sample Characteristics	Prevalence of Same-Gender Sexual Contact Male Female	Methods of Data Collection	Response Rate
National Opinion Research Council, (NORC) 1970 (Fay et al., 1989)	1450 men aged 21 and older	Since age 20 6.7% N/A -------------- Last year 1.6-2.0% N/A	SAQ following face-to-face interview	N/A
General Social Survey (GSS)[a] 1989-91	1564 men and 1963 women aged 18 and older -------------- 1941 men and 2163 women aged 18 and older	Since age 18 5.0% 3.5% -------------- Last year 2.2% 0.7%	SAQ following face-to-face interview	74%-78% (1988-1991)
Louis Harris and Associates, 1988 (Taylor, 1993)	739 men 409 women aged 16-50	Last 5 years 4.4% 3.6% Last year 3.5% 2.9% Last month 1.8% 2.1%	SAQ following face-to-face interview; same sex interviewer	67%
Research Triangle Institute (Rogers and Turner, 1991)	660 male residents of Dallas County, TX, aged 21-54	Last 10 years 8.1% N/A -------------- Last year 4.6% N/A	SAQ	88%
National Survey of Men (NSM-1) (Billy et al., 1993)	3321 men aged 20-39	Last 10 years 2.3% N/A	Face-to-face interview; female interviewers	70%

Notes: N/A = not available; SAQ = self-administered questionnaire; [a] = Prevalence of male and female homosexuality calculated at RAND from General Social Surveys (Davis & Smith, 1991).

Source: National Defense Research Institute (1993).

adult American males report having engaged in sexual behaviors with another man during adulthood (table 20.1). The extent to which these percentages are affected by underreporting is not known. However, since homosexual behavior is highly stigmatized, this sexual behavior is probably more frequently under-reported than overreported. Since extensive time may pass between homosexual experiences for many males, the percentage of males who indicate such acts during the previous year is generally smaller than the percentage who indicate any such contact as adults. It has also been determined that a majority of the males who report homosexual experiences have also had sex with women (Rogers & Turner 1991). Therefore, the percentage of males who are exclusively homosexual in their adult sexual behavior is much lower than the percentage who ever have sex with other males.

Data pertaining to the prevalence of homosexuality among females are much more scarce than data for males. However, the data that are available suggest a prevalence lower than for males: about 1 to 6 percent of adult American females indicate having engaged in sexual acts with another woman during adulthood.

Information about homosexual activity among military personnel is also extremely limited. Generalizations about the prevalence of homosexual behavior in the military are restricted to one study (Rogers & Turner 1991). Its findings, based on three national probability samples that included data on prior military status, indicate that the prevalence of same-gender sexual behavior by males who have been in the military is at the high end of the range for the general population.

HOMOSEXUAL BEHAVIOR AMONG SELF-IDENTIFIED HETEROSEXUALS

Presently in the United States it appears that bisexuality is more common than exclusive homosexuality. Studies using probability sampling techniques, which are listed in table 20.1, indicate support for the notion that a majority of men who report male-male sexual contacts in adulthood also report female sexual partners in adulthood (Rogers & Turner 1991, pp. 505, 509). Blumstein and Schwartz (1976a, p. 342, 1976b), assessing the sex histories of respondents who had both heterosexual and homosexual experiences in adulthood, maintained that there may be a low coherent association between the amount and "mix" of homosexual and heterosexual behavior in a person's biography and that person's choice of label as heterosexual, bisexual, or homosexual. In general, the association between identity and behavior has not been well studied, since data have usually included measures of only behavior or identity or have been based on very small and nonprobability samples (National Defense Research Institute 1993). One study containing independent measures of behavior and identity on a large national sample of 56,600 males suggests that conduct and status are not synonymous (Lever et al. 1992).

Epidemiology and criminology research also illustrates the point that homosexual behavior does not occur only among people with homosexual identification. Epidemiologists (Doll et al. 1992) researched 209 HIV-seropositive male blood donors who reported having had sex with both males and females since 1978. Since males who have had sex with males are asked to refrain from donating blood, one might anticipate this sampling procedure to overrepresent males who do not have a homosexual self-identification. Of these, 45 percent identified themselves as homosexual, 30 percent as bisexual, and 25 percent as heterosexual.

Criminology research cites illustrations in prison of what social scientists conceptualize as situational homosexuality, defined as self-identified heterosexuals who engage in homosexual acts only in situations that preclude sex with females. In a major study of male-male sexual activity in a prison environment, the sexual aggressors considered themselves as "heterosexual"; their targets are males they assume are homosexual or younger heterosexual males who are not able to protect themselves (Wooden & Parker 1982). Most sexual aggressors claim no homosexual experience before prison, and those released claim to resume a life of strictly heterosexual relations. Of those who responded to the questionnaire, 10 percent self-identified as homosexual, 10 percent as bisexual, and the other 80 percent as heterosexual. More than half of the heterosexual group reported having engaged in homosexual activity in prison.

IMPLEMENTATION OF A MILITARY POLICY
THAT ENDS DISCRIMINATION ON THE BASIS
OF SEXUAL ORIENTATION

A policy for terminating discrimination on the basis of sexual orientation in the military will present implementation problems that go beyond those created by more usual structural or organizational changes. Similar to racial integration, accepting known homosexuals represents a social change that has an impact on strongly held social attitudes and moral beliefs. It makes no difference for many people if they come into contact with a homosexual serving in the military. However, changing the policy alters their perception of the organization in very basic ways. For these people, the main issue is morality rather than unit cohesion. Some might leave the organization as a result. For those who remain in the military, the challenge will be to implement the change in ways that maintain basic task cohesion and organizational effectiveness. Much greater elaboration of the implementation of a policy that ends discrimination in the military on the basis of sexual orientation, as well as other aspects, options, and assessment of sexual orientation and U.S. military personnel policy, is set out in National Defense Research Institute 1993.

SEXUAL ORIENTATION IN THE MILITARY AND OTHER
SOCIAL INSTITUTIONS

Military policies seem to be related to existing cultural, legal, medical, and religious factors. What factors perpetuate the U.S. military policy? Although homosexuality is no longer classified as an illness, major religious institutions consider it sinful, and half of the states maintain sodomy laws (Harris 1991). The origin of sodomy laws extends back to Emperor Justinian's sixth century A.D. Corpus juris civilis, in which the sin of homosexuality was codified as crime for the Judeo-Christian world (Bullough 1976).

The traditional American religious condemnation of homosexuality, and the larger concept of sin in Western civilization, is founded on a free will model. From this perspective, the rule is clear, and people may select to either obey or disobey. Thus, nonconformity is seen as both an act of contempt for moral principle and a social example that must be condemned (Hammersmith 1987). In the United States, this perspective of homosexuality is supported by a Puritan tradition of antisexuality, which has been ameliorated for heterosexuality only within the past fifty years (Gordon & Bernstein 1970; Weinberg, Swensson & Hammersmith 1983).

Since homosexuals and their families are raised in the same religious traditions as others (Bell, Weinberg & Hammersmith 1981), this moral condemnation may be a major drawback to their understanding and accepting homosexuality. However, assistance is available within many mainstream churches (Hammersmith 1987).

Before World War II, various religious, legal, and educational factors were involved in providing school administrators with the power to fire a gay teacher. Homosexuality was regarded as innately evil, and teachers were expected to be role models of exemplary behavior. School officials had almost unlimited power in hiring and retention decisions. Moreover, the cost of litigation was beyond reach for the person who might have thought about rising above the condemnation of society to argue for remaining an educator. However, in the past forty years social and legal consensus on the definition of "immoral" behavior has broken down as a result of changing sexual norms, expanding personal freedoms, and the emerging political identity of gay people (Harbeck 1991). As a result of the collective power of teachers' unions, special interest litigation organizations, and the gay and lesbian rights movement, a challenge has arisen, with a debate characterized by a California gubernatorial candidate as "the hottest social issue since Reconstruction" (Briggs 1978).

Perhaps the greatest advances lie in education, not litigation (Harbeck 1992). Social psychological research has shown that if a heterosexual individual knows a homosexual, acceptance rises as stereotypical responses diminish (Butler 1978; Bowman 1979; Glasser & Owen 1976; Hansen 1982; Millham et al. 1976; Weis & Dain 1979). Moreover, other social psychological studies indicate that heterosexual exposure and interaction with members of the gay community in classroom environments tends to reduce homophobia (Lance 1987, 1992, 1994).

In the educational institution, as well as the military and other social institutions, the past for gay men and lesbians has been a history characterized by a moral order aggressively antagonistic toward homosexual expression. However, there are now those who are optimistic that improvements lie ahead in the quality of life for gay people in the institution of higher education. This favorable outlook in our homophobic heterosexual society is based on a growing body of scholarship and pressure for gay studies programs; the creation of stable and permanent caucuses by academics in many disciplines; and the formulation of regional associations of gay student groups to reinforce groups already established on individual campuses. Moreover, the National Gay and Lesbian Task

Force in Washington, D.C., has developed a campus organizing project so that gay men and lesbians do not have to reinvent the wheel continually (D'Emilio 1990).

Also of great importance, administrators of educational institutions, as well as other social institutions, are going beyond the most basic issues of visibility and recognition. These administrators in education, the military, religion, and other social institutions are addressing the major areas of equal treatment and deep-rooted prejudice. This movement of all of the social institutions of our heterosexual society, which are characterized by a high degree of homophobia, is way overdue.

REFERENCES

Baptists call for keeping military ban on gays. (1993, June 5). *Los Angeles Times*, p. B4.

Bell, A. P., & Weinberg, M. S. (1978). *Homosexualities: A study of diversity among men and women.* New York: Simon and Schuster.

Bell, A. P., Weinberg, M. S., & Hammersmith, S. K. (1981). *Sexual preference: Its development in men and women.* Bloomington: Indiana University Press.

Billy, J. O. G., Tanfer, K., Grady, W. R., & Klepinger, D. H. (1993). The sexual behavior of men in the U.S. *Family Planning Perspectives, 25,* 52–60.

Blumstein, P. W., & Schwartz, P. (1976a). Bisexuality in men. *Urban Life, 5,* 339–358.

Blumstein, P. W., & Schwartz, P. (1976b). Bisexuality: Some social psychological issues. *Journal of Social Issues 33,* 30–45.

Bowman, R. (1979). Public attitudes toward homosexuality in New Zealand. *International Review of Modern Sociology, 9,* 229–238.

Briggs, John. (1978, September 28). In Ellen Goodman, Proposition fever. *Boston Globe.*

Bullough, V. L. (1976). *Sexual variance in society and history.* Chicago: University of Chicago Press.

Butler, K. (1978, 26 August). Perils for gays fighting Briggs initiative. *San Francisco Chronicle.*

Chilstrom, H. (1993, February 2). Letter to President Clinton.

Coleman, E. (1987). Assessment of sexual orientation. *Journal of Homosexuality, 14,* 9–25.

Coleman, E. (1990). Toward a synthetic understanding of sexual orientation. In *Homosexuality/Heterosexuality,* ed. David McWhirter, Stephanie Sanders & June Reinisch. New York: Oxford University Press.

Davis, J. A., & Smith, T. W., General Social Surveys, 1972–1991. (1991). Sponsored by National Science Foundation. Chicago: National Opinion Research Center.

D'Emilio, J. (Speaker). (1990). *Vision '90: The emergence of lesbian, gay, and bisexual visibility on campus* [videocassette recording]. Portland, OR: Community Information Center.

Doll, L. S., Petersen, L. R., White, C. R., Johnson, E. S., Ward, J. W. & the Blood Donor Study Group. (1992). Homosexually and nonhomosexually identified men who have sex with men: A behavioral comparison. *Journal of Sex Research, 29,* 1–14.

Faye, R. E., Turner, C. F., Klassen, A. D., & Gagnon, J. H. (1989). Prevalence and patterns of same-gender sexual contact among men. *Science, 243,* 338–348.

Glasser, B., & Own, C. (1976). Variations in attitudes toward homosexuality. *Cornell Journal of Social Relations, 11,* 161–176.

Gordon, M., & Bernstein, M. C. (1970). Mate choice and domestic life in the nineteenth-century marriage manual. *Journal of Marriage and the Family, 32,* 655–674.

Hammersmith, S. K. (1987). A sociological approach to counseling homosexual clients and their families. *Journal of Homosexuality, 14,* 173–191.

Hansen, G. (1982). Measuring prejudice against homosexuality (homosexism) among college students. *Journal of Social Psychology, 117,* 233–236.

Harbeck, K. M. (1991). Gay and lesbian educators: Past history/future prospects. *Journal of Homosexuality, 22,* 121–141.

Harris, S. E. (1991). Military policies regarding homosexual behavior: An international survey. *Journal of Homosexuality, 21,* 67–74.

Kinsey, A. C., Pomeroy, W. B., & Martin, C. E. (1948). *Sexual behavior in the human male.* Philadelphia: W. B. Saunders.

Kinsey, A. C., Pomeroy, W. B., Martin, C. E., & Gebhard, P. H. (1953). *Sexual behavior in the human female.* Philadelphia: W. B. Saunders.

Klein, F. (1978). *The bisexual option.* New York: Arbor House.

Klein, F. (1980, December). Are you sure you're heterosexual? or homosexual? or even bisexual? *Forum Magazine,* pp. 41–45.

Klein, F., Sepekoff, B., & Wolf, T. J. (1985). Sexual orientation: A multivariate dynamic process. *Journal of Homosexuality, 11,* 35–49.

Lance, L. M. (1987). The effects of interaction with gay persons on attitudes toward homosexuality. *Human Relations, 40,* 329–336.

Lance, L. M. (1992). Changes in homophobic views as related to interaction with gay persons: A study in the reduction of tensions. *International Journal of Group Tensions, 22,* 291–299.

Lance, L. M. (1994). Do reductions in homophobia from heterosexual interactions with gay persons continue? A study of social contact theory of intergroup tensions. *International Journal of Group Tensions, 24,* 423–434.

Lever, J., Kanouse, D. E., Rogers, W. H., Carson, S., & Hertz, R. (1992). Behavior patterns and sexual identity of bisexual males. *Journal of Sex Research, 29,* 141–167.

Melton, J. G. (1991). *The churches speak on homosexuality: Official statements from religious bodies and ecumenical organizations.* Detroit: Gale Research.

Miller, L. (1993, May). Moskos/Miller 1992 sociological survey of the Army. *Report to the RAND Corporation on Soldier Attitudes Toward Gays and Lesbians in the Military.* Northwestern University.

Millham, J., San Miguel, C. L., & Kellogg, R. (1976). A factor-analytic conceptualization of attitudes toward male and female homosexuals. *Journal of Homosexuality, 2*(1), 3–10.

Moskos, C. (1993, May 7). Discussion points on DOD policy options regarding gays and lesbians. Memorandum to Dr. Bernard Rostber.

National Defense Research Institute. (1993). *Sexual orientation and U.S. Military personnel policy: Options and assessment.* Santa Monica, CA: RAND.

News: Church leaders on gay issue. (1993, March 3). *Christian Century,* p. 233.

Paul, J. P. (1983–1984). The bisexual identity: An idea without social recognition. *Journal of Homosexuality, 9*, 45–63.

Rogers, S. M., & Turner, C. F. (1991). Male-male sexual contact in the U.S.A.: Findings from five sample surveys, 1970–1990. *Journal of Sex Research, 28*, 491–519.

Taylor, H. (1993). Number of gay men more than 4 times higher than the 1 percent reported in a recent survey. *The Harris Poll #20*, 1–4.

Weinberg, M. S., Swensson, R. G., & Hammersmith, S. K. (1983). Sexual autonomy and the status of women: Models of female sexuality in U.S. sex manuals from 1950–1980. *Social Problems, 30*, 312–324.

Weis, C., & Dain, R. (1979). Ego development and sex attitudes in heterosexual and homosexual men and women. *Archives of Sexual Behavior, 8*, 341–356.

Wooden, W. S., & Parker, J. (1982). *Men behind bars: Sexual exploitation in prison.* New York: Plenum.

21

The Development of Gender Roles: Societal Influences

Marjorie S. Hardy

From the moment we are born, the world holds certain expectations of us based exclusively on one factor, our gender. As we proceed through life, the social forces around us work to mold us into the "acceptable" role we are to take in society, as boys and girls, as men and women. How far-reaching are these social factors? Can these forces be so influential as to affect our physical, emotional, and social adjustment in life? Can gender socialization and degree of conformity to gender roles in childhood predict sexual orientation in adulthood? In this chapter, these issues will be explored, with emphasis on the gender socialization of children in particular, by their parents, teachers, and peers and by the media, and the effects such socialization can have on adjustment throughout the life span.

GENDER ROLE THEORY

Sex and *gender* are frequently used interchangeably to refer to one's assigned anatomical sex at birth. To avoid confusion with other meanings of the word *sex,* however, the word *gender* has gradually gained usage. *Gender identity* is the personal belief that one is either a male or a female, regardless of assigned gender. Thus, a male transsexual may have been assigned a male gender at birth, but his gender identity is female. *Gender role* refers to how a person behaves as a male or female—the relative masculine or feminine characteristics as perceived by self or by others. *Masculinity* and *femininity* are traditionally seen as polar opposite gender roles, with masculinity described as an instrumental trait and associated with such characteristics as independence, aggressiveness, and dominance, and femininity described as an expressive trait and associated with such characteristics as emotionality, warmth, and passivity. A *gender role stereotype* conforms to the polar distinction of masculinity and femininity by rigidly assigning certain oversimplified characteristics to all males and all females based solely on their gender. For example, the common belief that all men are interested in sex while all women are interested in love is a gender role stereotype.

Despite the fact that gender accounts for only 5 to 10 percent of differences in social behavior, nonconformity to gender stereotypes is often discouraged in children and adults (Eagly 1987). A person whose behavior conforms to traditional gender roles is said to be gender typed; a person whose behavior does not conform to society's gender stereotypes is said to exhibit gender-atypical or gender-nonconforming behavior. Prior to 1973, it was believed that psychological well-being was dependent on the congruence between one's gender and gender role; healthy women were expected to be feminine, and healthy men were expected to be masculine (Grimmell & Stern 1992). Constantinople (1973) questioned this traditional belief, and a flurry of subsequent research found little support for it (Brooks, Morgan & Scherer 1990; Whitley 1984). Since then, two views have arisen, one arguing that masculine traits are necessary for psychological health, and the other arguing that a combination of masculine and feminine traits, known as *androgyny,* is the healthiest (Basoff & Glass 1982; Bem 1975). Those who argue that masculinity is healthier point to the correlations between masculine behavior and self-esteem and psychological adjustment (Basoff & Glass 1982; Kelly & Worrell 1977; Silvern & Ryan 1979; Whitley 1983). Proponents of androgyny argue that the gender role of the person interacts with situations and that feminine characteristics are associated with greater resilience to stress and with positive adjustment in settings marked by interpersonal demands (Hoffman & Fidell 1979; Roos & Cohen 1987; Steenbarger & Greenberg 1990; Wells 1980). Moreover, Bem (1974) argues that androgyny is the ideal gender role because it enhances behavioral and information processing flexibility, and Quackenbush (1987) points out that masculinity leads to instrumental effectiveness while femininity leads to expressive competency, both desirable traits. In addition, others have demonstrated that masculine behaviors such as competitiveness, aggression, and hostility may actually place a person at risk for physical problems and that androgynous individuals report better health behaviors than do other individuals (Helgeson 1990; Shifren, Bauserman & Carter 1993). Finally, Doescher and Sugawara (1990) found that gender role flexibility in boys was associated with prosocial behaviors such as sharing, cooperation, and helping.

Many researchers have turned their attention to the development of gender roles, particularly in children. The cognitive social learning theorists have emphasized observable events and their consequences and have asserted that we acquire our gender role characteristics through interactions with others in which we model and are reinforced for certain behaviors. The cognitive developmental theorists stress the interpretation of messages we receive from others and assert that we conform to gender-specific behaviors because of an internal motivation to do so. Gender schema theory brings together these two positions and asserts that children form schemas—cognitive concepts of gender—based upon their social learning history. All three theories stress the socializing influence of others and largely discount the idea that gender role differences are biologically determined (Strong & DeVault 1994). The major socializing agents in our society are parents, teachers, peers, and the media.

PARENTAL INFLUENCE

Infancy

Despite the fact that most parents are not aware that they treat their sons and daughters differently or that their behaviors can have such a strong impact on their child's gender role development, research has suggested that the socialization of gender differences begins at birth (Culp, Cook & Houseley 1983). Parents are more likely to perceive their infant girls as softer, finer-featured, smaller, and more inattentive than their infant boys, even in the absence of objective differences (Rubin, Provenzano & Luria 1974). Parents also interact with their children differently on the basis of the children's gender; boys are touched more frequently and handled more roughly before the age of 3 months, whereas neonatal girls are treated as more fragile but touched more frequently than boys after 6 months of age (Lewis & Weinraub 1979; Maccoby & Jacklin 1974). This finding is paradoxical given that boys are actually less mature at birth and more vulnerable to disease and infant mortality (Minton, Kagan & Levine 1971; Moss 1967).

Perhaps to compensate for the lack of physical stimulation, girls are verbally stimulated more than boys, and mothers respond more consistently to their daughters' cries (Cherry & Lewis 1976; Moss 1967). Furthermore, mothers report that they demonstrate more affection and warmth toward their infant daughters, a finding supported by the daughters' retrospective reports years later (Hoffman & Saltzstein 1967; Sears, Maccoby & Levin 1957). Subsequent studies, however, have been inconsistent in showing this bias in the display of maternal warmth and affection toward female infants (Maccoby & Jacklin 1974).

Overall, a review of the gender labeling studies (in which adults are observed interacting with an infant whose gender is ambiguous) revealed that the most consistent effects of gender labeling were on an adult's interpretations of ambiguous infant behavior, perceptions of infant physical characteristics, and beliefs about appropriate infant activities. However, the studies were inconsistent with respect to the effect of gender labeling on adult attributions of the infants' personality traits (Stern & Karraker 1989).

The physical surroundings of infants also differ with regard to gender. A boy's room typically has more traditional boy colors (e.g, blue) and traditional boy toys (e.g., sports equipment, tools, cars and trucks), while a girl's room is likely to be pink and to contain more dolls, fictional characters, and children's furniture (Pomerleau, Bolduc, Malcuit & Cossette 1990). Boys are also more likely than girls to be provided with educational and art materials, as well as military toys (Rheingold & Cook 1975). Thus, from the moment of birth, the socialization of boys and girls is different.

Childhood

Parents continue to respond differentially to the behaviors and activities of boys and girls as they enter early childhood. Toddlers frequently exhibit dependent behavior, turning to their parents for response. In a summary of the findings in the area, Maccoby and Jacklin (1974) hypothesized that instrumental dependency (asking for help on a task) is more likely to be reinforced in boys and not in girls, while a girl's emotional displays of dependent behavior (either overdependence or independence) are more likely to be rewarded in comparison to a boy's displays of the same behaviors. In contrast, Fagot (1978, 1985) found that both emotional dependency and instrumental dependency were rewarded in girls but not in boys.

Parents also seem to respond differentially to assertions of independence by boys and girls, but the evidence is mixed. Newsom and Newsom (1968) found that more autonomy was typically given to girls in comparison to boys in early childhood, but that after the age of 7, girls were more likely to be chaperoned than boys. However, the majority of subsequent studies contradict these findings, showing instead that boys are allowed and encouraged to be more autonomous than girls throughout early childhood (Chodorow 1978; Fagot, Hagan, Leinbach & Kronsberg 1985; Hoffman 1977). Boys are also given more freedom and personal responsibility, for example, by being allowed to cross the street by themselves at a younger age, despite the finding that girls are more likely than boys to be more mature and less impulsive and thus more capable of independent behavior (Hoffman 1977). Independence is equally encouraged for boys and girls, however, if such independence is helpful to the mother (e.g., the child may be encouraged to dress himself or herself or to take care of a sibling).

Parents also react differentially to aggressive behavior in their children. Overall, boys are more aggressive than girls (Maccoby & Jacklin 1974), but whether this gender difference is the result or cause of differential treatment by parents is unclear. Mothers and fathers appear to react differently to their children's aggressive behavior; however, in general, aggression is expected and deemed more acceptable in boys than in girls (Minton, Kagan & Levine 1971; Sears, Maccoby & Levin 1957). Here also some controversy exists; other researchers have found no differences in parental responses to aggression by boys and girls (Sears, Ran & Alpert 1965). The discrepancy in findings may be due to a parent-child interaction effect. For example, Rothbart and Maccoby (1966) found that fathers were more accepting of aggression and "insolence" from their daughters than from their sons, while the reverse was true for mothers.

Perhaps because they are more aggressive and active, boys are more likely to be punished for misbehaviors than are girls. The amount and type of punishment also differs for boys and girls. While boys are more likely to be physically punished or to receive harsh reprimands, girls are more likely to be softly reprimanded and given a suggestion for an alternative activity (Minton, Kagan & Levine 1971). The reason for differential punishment is unclear. Perhaps parents view their daughters as more fragile and unable to tolerate corporal punishment. Alternatively, Minton, Kagan, and Levine (1971) suggest that boys may simply need to be punished more, since girls are more likely to desist upon an initial warning. Boys are less likely to do so, forcing the parent to resort to more severe punishment. Therefore, over time, a parent may resort immediately to a harsher punishment with a son, regardless of his misbehavior.

Some theorists argue that negative attention (punishment) is just one form of parental attention and that boys act out more often for the attention itself, perpetuating the cycle of misbehavior and punishment. However, researchers have found that boys are also more likely than girls to receive positive feedback from their parents (Bee, VanEgeren, Streissguth, Nyman & Leckie 1967). Thus, boys are the recipients of both more negative and positive attention from their parents in comparison to girls.

One of the most studied behaviors in the field of gender research is the reaction of parents to children's gender-typed play and activities. Most researchers agree that gender-typical play in children of both genders is rewarded by parents (Fagot 1978). As is the case with aggression, there appears to be an interactive effect in parental response to gender-atypical behavior in boys and girls. Fathers especially seem to discourage and be more concerned with their sons' gender-atypical behavior (Feinman 1981; Fling & Manosevitz 1972; Lansky 1967). Moreover, Langlois and Downs (1980) found that girls were rewarded for playing with doll houses and domestic toys and punished for playing with military toys and vehicles by both mothers and fathers, while boys were treated in the reverse manner by their fathers only.

Children quickly learn which toys and activities are gender conforming, and they tend to ask for and receive more gender-typed toys from their parents (Bradbard 1985; Bradbard & Parkman 1984; Downs 1983; Robinson & Morris 1986). Both preschool and elementary school children who ask for and receive gender-typed toys are also more likely to have same-gender friends and to engage in gender-typed play (Eisenberg-Berg, Boothby & Matson 1979; Robinson & Morris 1986). Moreover, they appear to be aware at an early age which behaviors are gender conforming and which are not. Boys will avoid gender-atypical toys when an experimenter is present, suggesting that they have learned the play behavior that is expected of them (Hartup & Moore 1963).

Finally, children are more likely to be assigned traditional gender role activities and chores at early ages. Mauldin and Meeks (1990) found that boys as young as 3 years of age were more likely to spend time in leisure activities, unstructured activities, active sports, and games, whereas girls were more likely to spend time in household activities, including meal preparation, clean-up, and personal care. These behaviors were observed in families regardless of factors such as family income and maternal employment and education. From their observations, White and Brinkerhoff (1981) reported that twice as many girls as boys cleaned the bathroom, washed clothes and dishes, cooked, and performed general household work. The boys, on the other hand, were twice as likely to mow the lawn, shovel snow, take out the garbage, and work outside on the farm. Gender differences were not found for keeping one's room straight, picking up after oneself, and feeding pets. Interestingly, the tasks that were required of boys were later rewarded monetarily outside the home (e.g., mow their neighbor's lawn for money), while girls were not taught such tasks. Thus, it appears that from an early age, girls are taught skills that benefit others, whereas boys are taught skills that are more beneficial to them personally (Goodnow 1988).

TEACHER INFLUENCE

Parents are not the only ones who react to their children in a gender-typed manner. From the time children enter school, they are met with the expectations of their teachers, many based on the child's gender or gender role rather than on any objective behavior of the child.

Overall, boys and girls are treated differently by teachers, and the gender role messages conveyed in the academic setting tend to be quite traditional (Wynn & Fletcher 1987). In comparison to girls, boys appear to receive more attention from teachers, especially female teachers, are more likely to receive positive feedback and to be rewarded when demonstrating instrumental dependency, and are reprimanded and physically restrained more often when misbehaving (Alfgren, Aries & Olver 1979; Serbin, O'Leary, Kent & Tonick 1973). Boys are also more likely to be called upon to answer and to be given work-related activities, although girls are more likely than boys to be reprimanded for not competently performing a task (Etaugh & Harlow 1975; Good, Sikes & Brophy 1973; Minton, Kagan & Levine 1971; Serbin et al. 1973). The majority of these studies were conducted primarily with female teachers. In comparison, it appears that male teachers attend more equally to boys and girls (Alfgren et al. 1979).

When Rosenthal and Jacobson (1968) demonstrated the power of teachers' expectations on children's performance, researchers wondered if teachers held different expectations for boys and girls. The results of the research were surprising: teachers often attributed the success of boys to ability and the success of girls to luck. On the other hand, the failures of boys were typically blamed on sloppiness or lack of effort, while the failures of girls were blamed on lack of ability (Dweck, Davidson, Nelson & Enna 1978; Heller & Parsons 1981). Furthermore, teachers' expectations seem to generate a self-fulfilling prophecy;

children adopted these attributions, with girls attributing failure to a lack of ability and success to luck, and boys attributing successful performance to ability and failure to external factors (Deaux & Emswiller 1974).

Teachers also hold different expectations about the relative abilities and interests of boys and girls. For example, Phillips (1980) found that teachers viewed early elementary school–aged boys as more aggressive than girls as well as more interested in science and math. Girls, on the other hand, were viewed as more emotional and more interested in art and literature. The expectations were unwarranted, since research has shown that boys and girls do not actually differ in their preference of school subjects and typically perform equally well in school (Rogers 1987; Stein 1971). Nonetheless, boys tend to take harder courses (math and physics) and maintain higher expectations for their own performance, perhaps in response to their parents' and teachers' expectations (Entwisle & Baker 1983).

Dusek and Joseph (1983), in a meta-analysis of various studies of teacher expectancies, concluded that differences in teacher expectations based on children's gender are not as strong as originally believed. Rather, it appears that teachers' expectations are more strongly influenced by their perceptions of the child's gender role. For example, high-achieving students are expected to be masculine or androgynous but not necessarily male, and low-achieving students are expected to be feminine or undifferentiated (possessing neither masculine nor feminine traits) but not necessarily female (Benz, Pfeiffer & Newman 1981). Moreover, teachers view students with cross-gender role behavior (males with feminine characteristics and females with masculine characteristics) as more intelligent and independent than those with traditional gender roles (Bernard 1979). Even in an academic setting, masculinity is associated with intelligence, independence, logical thinking, and academic success, while femininity is associated with warmth and concern. Furthermore, Bernard (1979) found that male and female teachers possessed a different set of expectations and norms of gender role behaviors of students.

PEER INFLUENCE

Children have been shown to respond more stereotypically in gender-labeling studies, yet peer influence on gender role development has been largely ignored by researchers (Stern & Karraker 1989). Such a dearth of studies is surprising given the role that peers play on the development of social attitudes and behaviors of one another. From the time children enter school, peers become a dominant force in children's lives. In fact, it appears that the influence of peers may be more important than that of adults at times. Dweck and Bush (1976) found that when given failure feedback from adults, girls demonstrated little improvement in performance on a task, but when given feedback from peers, they demonstrated both improved and sustained performance. Notably the opposite was found for boys. Moreover, girls were more likely to attribute failure to a lack of ability when the evaluator was an adult and/or female, while boys were more likely to do so when the evaluator was a peer.

Peers are also an influential agent in children's gender-based play and behavior. Young children reinforce traditional gender role behavior and punish gender-atypical behavior, particularly in boys (Carter & McCloskey 1984; Fagot 1977; Lamb & Roopnarine 1979). While masculine characteristics (e.g., athletic prowess, competitiveness, and "toughness") are correlates of popularity in elementary school–aged boys, boys who act in gender-atypical ways are typically rejected by their peers, criticized more frequently, and receive less positive feedback (Adler, Kless & Adler 1992; Fagot 1977). Such rejection by peers may lead to later psychological problems (Cowen, Pederson, Babigian, Izzo & Trost 1973). Therefore, there is significant pressure to conform to gender roles defined as desirable by peers.

MEDIA INFLUENCES

Children ages 2 to 18 typically spend more than three hours a day watching television—twenty-five hours in a single week, or more time than they spend in any other single activity, including going to school and interacting with family and peers (Nielsen Television Services 1985). The televised role models to which children are exposed exhibit traditional and often exaggerated gender role stereotypes. Women are portrayed as dependent, submissive, and emotional characters who live to serve men and children and are typically cast as housewives, teachers, secretaries, and nurses. Men, on the other hand, are depicted as active, dominant, and rational characters who make important decisions and provide the family income and are typically depicted in professional and law enforcement roles (Doyle 1991; Macklin & Kolbe 1984). Furthermore, when female characters are cast in nontraditional roles, it is often in an obviously humorous manner not to be taken seriously (Macionis 1989). Although it is widely assumed that the media have become less stereotyped over time, researchers have found that in fact the presentation of gender role stereotypes has remained relatively unchanged over the past ten to fifteen years (Signorielli 1989).

The impact of television on the development of gender roles is significant. Ross, Anderson, and Wisocki (1982) found that college students who reported greater exposure to television as children were more likely to hold stereotypical attitudes of males and females than were subjects who were exposed to less television. Longitudinal findings also support the assertion that television viewing is associated with gender-stereotypical beliefs among elementary and high school students (Morgan 1982, 1987). Finally, Davidson, Yasuna, and Tower (1979) found that 5- and 6-year-old children who viewed highly gender-stereotyped cartoons were more likely to give stereotyped answers to questions about the qualities of men and women.

Children are exposed to gender-stereotypical messages not only on television but in movies, on billboards, and in magazines and books. The effect of such widespread exposure has not been systematically studied, but one can imagine that the impact is tremendous.

IMPACT OF GENDER ROLE SOCIALIZATION

Although most behaviors are the result of the interaction of biological and psychosocial factors, the impact of gender socialization on the behaviors, attitudes, and psychological functioning of children and adults is sometimes remarkable. In this chapter, the effect of gender socialization on depression and achievement in females and aggression in males will be addressed; the impact of socialization on sexual orientation and behaviors will be covered in other chapters in this book.

Depression in Females

In infancy, parents frequently imitate or match their children's affective state, which conveys to the child a sense of control and effectance (Watson & Rame 1972). However, studies have shown that mothers match fewer of their daughters' than their sons' affective displays (Robinson, Little & Zeynep 1993). Allessandri and Lewis (1993) found that parents were more likely to use negative evaluations with 3-year-old daughters and more positive evaluations with their 3-year-old sons in a dyadic problem-solving task. The negative evaluative statements were positively correlated with feelings of shame in the female child.

In what way does this negative socialization affect young children, especially girls? Silvern and Katz (1986) found that gender-stereotypical self-concepts were related to disruptive, aggressive, and noncompliant behavior in boys and social immaturity, depression, social isolation, and lowered self-esteem in girls. The effects can be long-lasting as well. Women are twice as likely as men to experience depression, and gender role factors are strongly implicated (Nolem-Hoeksema 1990). Conditioned early in life to attribute their failures to a lack of ability and their successes to luck, women are more prone to learned helplessness, or a feeling of loss of control over outcomes in their environment. Such a feeling of learned helplessness is believed to be associated more with the feminine gender role than with the actual female gender (Baucom & Danker-Brown 1979; Radloff & Rae 1981). Sayers, Baucom, and Tierney (1993) investigated the impact of gender role on persuasive ability and depressive mood following a two-person persuasion task. In this task, the uninformed subject was told that the purpose of the study was to arrive jointly at the best answer to a question; the informed subject was told that the purpose was to persuade his or her partner that the correct answer was the informed subject's own. The researchers found that the subjects who scored high in masculinity and low in femininity were able to gain interpersonal control, regardless of the gender role characteristics of their partners. Conversely, women with feminine characteristics were more likely to give up control. Furthermore, femininity was related to increases in depressed mood in situations requiring the exercise of control.

Depression in women has also been linked with the tendency to self-focus and ruminate on depressive thoughts and feelings (Ingram, Cruet, Johnson & Wisnicki 1988; Nolem-Hoeksema 1987). In contrast, men are more likely to distract themselves in response to feelings of sadness (Nolem-Hoeksema 1987). Research indicates that such responses to depressive situations are also more a function of gender role than of actual gender (Babl 1979; Conway, Giannopoulos & Stiefenhofer 1990; Ingram et al. 1988). Specifically, high femininity is associated with rumination, self-focus, and a greater awareness of distress, while high masculinity is associated with distraction, antisocial behavior, and the alienation of others as a protection against self-distress.

Achievement in Females

The impact of differential expectations of males and females in a scholastic setting appears to have a strong impact on children's later achievement. Overall, girls generally have lower expectations for their own success and decreased achievement striving under failure or evaluative pressure, and they are more likely to assume personal responsibility for failure than are boys (Maccoby & Jacklin 1974; Parsons, Rubble, Hodges & Small 1976). Furthermore, because girls are more likely to attribute failure to a lack of ability when that failure is evaluated by an adult (in comparison to boys, who attribute failure to ability only when the evaluator is a peer), they are at greater risk for feelings of learned helplessness and low achievement striving in an academic setting (Dweck & Bush 1976).

Other researchers have suggested that gender stereotypes restrict children's behavior by limiting their competence (ability to perform) rather than their actual performance, which is motivated by reward and punishment (Martin & Halverson 1981). Bradbard and Endsley (1983) found that preschool children were less likely to explore, ask questions about, and recall the names of objects that were labeled for the opposite gender in comparison to objects that were labeled for their own gender. In an extension of the research, Bradbard and his colleagues (Bradbard, Martin, Endsley & Halverson 1986) found that even when given incentives for recalling information about opposite-gender objects, children were less successful in doing so in comparison to their recall of objects labeled for the same gender. This pattern of differential recall was present by the age of 3 and increased across age as children's concept of gender roles became more constant (Stangor & Ruble 1989). It appears, therefore, that we subtly affect children's competence, their ability to acquire and/or retain information, through gender typing early in life and that the effect becomes stronger as they mature.

Aggression in Males

Because boys are more aggressive than girls as children and because such aggression appears to be at least tolerated in boys by fathers and reinforced by peers, it is not surprising that boys are more likely to be referred for mental health services for the treatment of behavior problems (Achenbach & Edelbrock 1981). Silvern and Katz (1986) found that gender role and gender-stereotypical concepts actually play a greater role than biological gender in displays of aggressive behavior in children. Boys who were androgynous in their play and had feminine self-concepts were more likely to present with internalizing problems (e.g., depression and anxiety) than externalizing ones (e.g., conduct and attentional).

The impact of gender socialization on aggression in males appears to be long-lasting, as men are also more likely to instigate aggression as adults (Gaebelein 1977). Other researchers too have found that males are more likely to describe themselves as aggressive, despite the fact that there are often no actual gender differences in displays of aggression when provoked (Frodi, Macaulay & Thome 1977). Overall, men are more likely to be the perpetrators of violent crime (Megargee 1993).

SEXUAL ORIENTATION

The role of social factors and gender role conformity in the development of sexual orientation is controversial. Despite the fact that gender role stereotypes are widespread, little research has been conducted to evaluate the validity of these beliefs. One common assumption of the general public is that homosexuality is associated with gender role nonconformity: gay men are more feminine than their heterosexual counterparts, and lesbians are more masculine than heterosexual females. Thus, homosexuality is believed to be associated with a failure to conform to traditional gender roles (DeCecco & Elia 1993). Is there some truth to the public's perception? The findings are inconclusive. While evidence suggests that some gay men and women exhibit nonconforming gender role characteristics, it is unclear whether they do so because they believe that they should act in such a manner or whether the characteristics are innate (Strong & DeVault 1994).

Perhaps due to the stereotype that homosexuals exhibit gender-atypical behaviors, parents and others differentially reinforce and punish gender conformity and nonconformity in children's play. Whether the gender conformity of children's behavior has a bearing on future sexual orientation has been the focus of several studies. Retrospective reports of some homosexuals suggest early onset and enduring atypical gender-typed behaviors in childhood (Bell, Weinberg & Hammersmith 1981). Furthermore, mothers of homosexual males and females also retrospectively report gender-atypical behaviors in their children. In one study, this finding was biased in the lesbian sample by the mothers' knowledge of their daughters' sexual orientation; however, the same bias was not found for the male homosexual sample (Bailey, Miller & Willerman 1993). Other researchers have found that it is the absence of masculine traits, rather than the presence of feminine traits, that may predict future homosexuality (Hockenberry & Billingham 1987). Finally, Phillips and Over (1992) noted that while many homosexuals recall exhibiting gender-atypical behavior during childhood, it is important to keep in mind that such findings are not universal. In fact, the retrospective reports by homosexuals in their study revealed more diversity in gender conformity than among heterosexuals.

Prospective data are uncommon but also support the relationship between gender nonconformity in childhood and later homosexuality. Green (1985, 1987) found that 75 percent of boys described as feminine by their parents later reported homosexual fantasies (in comparison to none of the boys described as masculine), and 75 to 80 percent reported a homosexual or bisexual orientation in adulthood. However, these studies have been criticized on the grounds that the samples were unrepresentative of the population of gay men and women (Bailey, Miller & Willerman 1993).

The interplay of gender role development and sexual orientation is complex. The limited data suggest several hypotheses that merit further empirical study. Gender nonconformity is more commonly reported in retrospective studies of gay men and possibly lesbians. However, these findings are not universal since many homosexuals display gender-typical roles as children. The role of parents and other social agents also needs to be studied. It is unclear whether gender nonconformity among gay men and lesbians is subtly shaped by others or whether it reflects more innate characteristics. Some homosexuals, upon learning the cultural stereotypes about homosexual gender roles, may adopt these behaviors as a self-fulfilling prophecy. Finally, the direction of effect is unclear: Does gender nonconformity in childhood lead to homosexuality, or is a homosexual orientation the precipitating factor in gender-nonconforming behaviors?

CONCLUSION

There are several methodological concerns regarding the studies of gender roles. The research is mostly correlational in design, and thus it cannot be assumed that any one social agent causes the adoption of a particular gender role in children. Furthermore, the studies have investigated various social agents apart from one another, and the additive effect of gender socialization by the various agents is unknown. Additionally, much of the research concerning the effects of gender role stereotypes on depression in women and aggression in men has been conducted using nonclinical samples. In clinical populations, it is possible that gender role plays a less prominent role and that other factors are much more influential. Finally, little attention has been directed to cross-cultural issues. Study of various ethnic groups as well as investigation of gender role development in other cultures may help to shed some light on our understanding of gender role socialization.

Despite the methodological concerns, decades of research have supported the assertion that boys and girls are differentially treated and that social forces strongly influence the development of certain behaviors, characteristics, and attitudes in children and adults. Parents, teachers, peers, and the media all work in the same direction to shape children's development of and attitudes toward traditional and nontraditional gender roles. Boys are encouraged to be independent, strong, and unemotional, and girls are taught to be passive, dependent, and nurturing. Despite the findings that gender-atypical characteristics may actually be both psychologically and physically healthier, social forces continue to shape children to adopt gender-typed roles. Fortunately, these attitudes are changing somewhat, as is evident in the merging of gender role stereotypes over time. Today, more women are viewed as independent and competitive, and more men are viewed as warm and emotional (Deaux 1984).

Perhaps it is not conformity to a particular gender role that is healthier but rather society's encouragement and acceptance of flexibility that engenders positive characteristics in its members. Each culture has the opportunity to determine the acceptability of particular gender roles. Among the Arapesh of New Guinea, both men and women are passive, cooperative, peaceful, and nurturing, and fathers hold the same responsibility as do mothers for raising the children (Mead 1975). Grimmell and Stern (1992) argue that personal and societal values define what is healthy and that masculine traits are simply more valued in the American culture whereas feminine traits are devalued. In a study of perceived and ideal gender roles, subjects who endorsed feminine traits as being descriptive of themselves while holding masculine traits as the ideal were more hostile than those who did not demonstrate such discrepancies. Grimmell and Stern (1992) thus proposed a social conflict model that stipulates that adjustment may actually be better predicted by the congruence between one's self-ratings of masculinity and femininity and one's gender role ideals rather than by the adoption of any one particular gender role. We must consider, then, that if it is society that sets such ideals, then society bears the responsibility for setting the standards of healthiness for its own members.

REFERENCES

Achenbach, T. M., & Edelbrock, C. S. (1981). Behavioral problems and competencies reported by parents of normal and disturbed children aged 4 through 16. *Monographs of the Society for Research in Child Development, 46* (Serial No. 188).

Adler, P. A., Kless, S. J., & Adler, P. (1992). Socialization to gender roles: Popularity among elementary school boys and girls. *Sociology of Education, 65,* 169–187.

Alfgren, S. H., Aries, E. J., & Oliver, R. R. (1979). Sex differences in the interaction of adults and preschool children. *Psychological Reports, 44,* 115–118.

Allessandri, S. M., & Lewis, M. (1993). Parental evaluation and its relation to shame and pride in young children. *Sex Roles, 29,* 335–343.

Babl, J. D. (1979). Compensatory masculine response as a function of sex role. *Journal of Consulting and Clinical Psychology, 47,* 252–257.

Bailey, J. M., Miller, J. S., & Willerman, L. (1993). Maternally rated childhood gender nonconformity in homosexuals and heterosexuals. *Archives of Sexual Behavior, 22,* 461–469.

Basoff, E. S., & Glass, G. V. (1982). The relationship between sex roles and mental health: A meta-analysis of 26 studies. *Counseling Psychologist, 10,* 105–112.

Baucom, D. H., & Danker-Brown, P. (1979). Influence of sex roles on the development of learned helplessness. *Journal of Consulting and Clinical Psychology, 47,* 928–936.

Bee, H. L., VanEgeren, L. F., Streissguth, A. P., Nyman, B. A., & Leckie, M. S. (1967). Social class differences in maternal teaching strategies and speech patterns. *Developmental Psychology, 1,* 726–734.

Bell, A. P., Weinberg, M. S., & Hammersmith, S. K. (1981). *Sexual preference: Its development in men and women.* Bloomington: Indiana University Press.

Bem, S. L. (1974). The measurement of psychological androgyny. *Journal of Consulting and Clinical Psychology, 42,* 155–162.

Bem, S. L. (1975). Sex role adaptability: One consequence of psychological androgyny. *Journal of Personality and Social Psychology, 31,* 634–643.

Benz, C., Pfeiffer, I., & Newman, I. (1981). Sex role expectations of classroom teachers, Grades 1–12. *American Educational Research Journal, 18,* 289–302.

Bernard, M. (1979). Does sex role behavior influence the way teachers evaluate students? *Journal of Educational Psychology, 71,* 553–562.

Bradbard, M. R. (1985). Sex differences in adults' gifts and children's toy requests at Christmas. *Psychological Reports, 56,* 969–970.

Bradbard, M. R., & Endsley, R. C. (1983). The effects of sex-typed labeling on preschool children's information seeking and retention. *Sex Roles, 9,* 247–260.

Bradbard, M. R., Martin, C. L., Endsley, R. C., & Halverson, C. F. (1986). Influence of sex stereotypes on children's exploration and memory: A competence versus performance distinction. *Developmental Psychology, 22,* 481–486.

Bradbard, M. R., & Parkman, S. A. (1984). Gender differences in preschool children's toy requests. *Journal of Genetic Psychology, 145,* 283–284.

Brooks, P. R., Morgan, G. S., & Scherer, R. F. (1990). Sex role orientation and type of stressful situation: Effects on coping behavior. *Journal of Social Behavior and Personality, 5,* 627–639.

Carter, D. B., & McCloskey, L. A. (1984). and the maintenance of sex-typed behavior: The development of children's conceptions of cross-gender behavior in their peers. *Social Cognition, 2,* 294–314.

Cherry, L., & Lewis, M. (1976). Mothers and two-year-olds: A study of sex-differentiated aspects of verbal interaction. *Developmental Psychology, 12,* 278–282.

Chodorow, N. (1978). *The reproduction of mothering: Psychoanalysis and the sociology of gender.* Berkeley: University of California Press.

Constantinople, A. (1973). Masculinity-femininity: An exception to the famous dictum? *Psychological Bulletin, 80,* 389–407.

Conway, M., Giannopoulos, C., & Stiefenhofer, K. (1990). Response styles to sadness are related to sex and sex-role orientation. *Sex Roles, 22,* 579–587.

Cowen, E., Pederson, A., Babigian, H., Izzo, L., & Trost, N. (1973). Long term follow-up of early detected vulnerable children. *Journal of Consulting and Clinical Psychology, 41*, 438–446.

Culp, R. E., Cook, A. S., & Houseley, P. C. (1983). A comparison of observed and reported adult-infant interactions: Effects of perceived sex. *Sex Roles, 9*, 475–479.

Davidson, E. S., Yasuna, A., & Tower, A. (1979). The effect of television cartoons on sex-role stereotyping in young girls. *Child Development, 50*, 597–600.

Deaux, K. (1984). From individual differences to social categories: Analysis of a decade's research on gender. *American Psychologist, 39*, 105–116.

Deaux, K., & Emswiller, T. (1974). Explanations of successful performance on sex-linked tasks: What is skill for the male is luck for the female. *Journal of Personality and Social Psychology, 29*, 80–85.

DeCecco, J. P., & Elia, J. P. (1993). A critique and synthesis of biological essentialism and social constructionist views of sexuality and gender: Introduction. *Journal of Homosexuality, 24*, 1–26.

Doescher, S. M., & Sugawara, A. I. (1990). Sex role flexibility and prosocial behavior among preschool children. *Sex Roles, 22*, 111–123.

Downs, A. C. (1983). Letters to Santa Claus: Elementary school-age children's sex-typed toy preferences in a natural setting. *Sex Roles, 9*, 159–163.

Doyle, J. (1991). *The male experience* (2nd ed.). Dubuque, IA: Brown & Benchmark.

Dusek, J. B., & Joseph. G. (1983). The bases of teacher expectancies: A meta-analysis. *Journal of Educational Psychology, 75*, 327–346.

Dweck, C. S., & Bush, E. S. (1976). Sex differences in learned helplessness: I, Differential debilitation with peer and adult evaluators. *Developmental Psychology, 12*, 147–156.

Dweck, C. S., Davidson, W., Nelson, S., & Enna, B. (1978). Sex differences in learned helplessness: II, The contingencies of evaluative feedback in the classroom, and III, An experimental analysis. *Developmental Psychology, 14*, 268–276.

Eagly, A. H. (1987). *Sex differences in social behavior: A social-role interpretation.* Hillsdale, NJ: Erlbaum.

Eisenberg-Berg, N., Boothby, R., & Matson, T. (1979). Correlates of girls' feminine and masculine toy preferences. *Developmental Psychology, 15*, 354–355.

Entwisle, D. R., & Baker, D. P. (1983). Gender and young children's expectations for performance in arithmetic. *Developmental Psychology, 19*, 200–209.

Etaugh, C., & Harlow, H. (1975). Behaviors of male and female teachers as related to behaviors and attitudes of elementary school children. *Journal of Genetic Psychology, 127*, 163–170.

Fagot, B. I. (1977). Consequences of moderate cross-gender behavior in preschool children. *Child Development, 48*, 902–907.

Fagot, B. I. (1978). The influence of sex of child on parental reactions to toddler children. *Child Development, 49*, 459–465.

Fagot, B. I. (1985). Beyond the reinforcement principle. *Developmental Psychology, 21*, 1097–1104.

Fagot, B. I., Hagan, R., Leinbach, M. E., & Kronsberg, S. (1985). Differential reactions to assertive and communicative acts of toddler boys and girls. *Child Development, 56*, 1499–1505.

Feinman, S. (1981). Why is cross-sex-role behavior more approved for girls than boys? A status characteristic approach. *Sex Roles, 7*, 289–299.

Fling, S., & Manosevitz, M. (1972). Sex typing in nursery school children's play interests. *Developmental Psychology, 7*, 146–152.

Frodi, A., Macaulay, J., & Thome, P. (1977). Are women always less aggressive than men? *Psychological Bulletin, 84*, 634–660.

Gaebelein, J. (1977). Sex differences in instigative aggression. *Journal of Research in Personality, 11*, 466–474.

Good, T. L., Sikes, J. N., & Brophy, J. E. (1973). Effects of teacher sex and student sex on classroom interaction. *Journal of Educational Psychology, 65*, 74–87.

Goodnow, J. J. (1988). Children's household work: Its nature and functions. *Psychological Bulletin, 103*, 5–26.

Green, R. (1985). Gender identity in childhood and later sexual orientation: Follow-up of 78 males. *American Journal of Psychiatry, 142*, 339–341.

Green, R. (1987). *The "sissy boy syndrome" and the development of homosexuality.* New Haven: Yale University Press.

Grimmell, D., & Stern, G. S. (1992). The relationship between gender role ideals and psychological well-being. *Sex Roles, 27*, 487–497.

Hartup, W. W., & Moore, S. G. (1963). Avoidance of inappropriate sex typing by young children. *Journal of Consulting Psychology, 27*, 467–473.

Helgeson, V. S. (1990). The role of masculinity in a prognostic predictor of heart attack severity. *Sex Roles, 22*, 755–774.

Heller, K. A., & Parsons, J. E. (1981). Sex differences in teachers' evaluative feedback and students' expectancies for success in mathematics. *Child Development, 52*, 1015–1019.

Hockenberry, S. L., & Billingham, R. E. (1987). Sexual orientation and boyhood gender conformity: Development of the boyhood gender conformity scale (BGCS). *Archives of Sexual Behavior, 16*, 475–492.

Hoffman, L. W. (1977). Changes in family roles, socialization, and sex differences. *American Psychologist, 32*, 644–657.

Hoffman, D. M., & Fidell, L. S. (1979). Characteristics of androgynous, undifferentiated, masculine, and feminine middle-class women. *Sex Roles, 5*, 765–781.

Hoffman, M. C., & Saltzstein, H. D. (1967). Parent discipline and the child's moral development. *Journal of Personality and Social Psychology, 5*, 45–57.

Ingram, R. E., Cruet, D., Johnson, B. R., & Wisnicki, K. S. (1988). Self-focused attention, gender, gender role, and vulnerability to negative affect. *Journal of Personality and Social Psychology, 55*, 967–978.

Kelly, J. A., & Worell, J. (1977). New formulations of sex roles and androgyny: A critical review. *Journal of Consulting and Clinical Psychology, 45*, 1101–1115.

Lamb, M. E., & Roopnarine, J. L. (1979). Peer influences on sex-role development in preschoolers. *Child Development, 50*, 1219–1222.

Langlois, J. H., & Downs, A. C. (1980). Mothers, fathers, and as socialization agents of sex-typed play behavior in young children. *Child Development, 51*, 1237–1247.

Lansky, L. M. (1967). The family structure also affects the model: Sex role attitudes in parents of preschool children. *Merrill-Palmer Quarterly, 13*, 139–150.

Lewis, M., & Weinraub, M. (1979). Origins of early sex-role development. *Sex Roles, 5*, 135–153.

Maccoby, E. E., & Jacklin, C. N. (1974). *The psychology of sex differences.* Stanford: Stanford University Press.

Macionis, J. (1989). *Sociology* (2nd ed.). Englewood Cliffs, NJ: Prentice-Hall.

Macklin, M. C., & Kolbe, R. H. (1984). Sex role stereotyping in children's advertising: Current and past trends. *Journal of Advertising, 13,* 34–42.

Martin, C. L., & Halverson, C. F., Jr. (1981). A schematic processing model of sex typing and stereotyping in children. *Child Development, 52,*1119–1134.

Mauldin, T., & Meeks, C. B. (1990). Sex differences in children's time use. *Sex Roles, 22,* 537–554.

Mead, M. (1975). *Male and female.* New York: William Morrow.

Megargee, E. I. (1993). Aggression and violence. In P. B. Sutker & H. E. Adams (Eds.), *Comprehensive handbook of psychopathology* (pp. 617–644). New York: Plenum Press.

Minton, C., Kagan, J., & Levine, J. A. (1971). Maternal control and obedience in the two-year-old. *Child Development, 42,* 1873–1894.

Morgan, M. (1982). Television and adolescents' sex stereotypes: A longitudinal study. *Journal of Personality and Social Psychology, 43,* 947–955.

Morgan, M. (1987). Television, sex-role attitudes, and sex-role behavior. *Journal of Early Adolescence, 7,* 269–282.

Moss, H. A. (1967). Sex, age and state as determinants of mother-infant interaction. *Merrill-Palmer Quarterly, 13,* 19–36.

Newsom, J., & Newsom, E. (1968). *Four years old in an urban community.* Harmondsworth, England: Pelican Books.

Nielsen Television Services. (1985). *Nielsen report on television.* Northbrook, IL: A. C. Nielsen.

Nolem-Hoeksema, S. (1987). Sex differences in unipolar depression: Evidence and theory. *Psychological Bulletin, 191,* 259–282.

Nolem-Hoeksema, S. (1990). *Sex differences in depression.* Stanford: Stanford University Press.

Parsons, J. E., Rubble, D. N., Hodges, K. L., & Small, A. W. (1976). Cognitive-developmental factors in emerging sex differences in achievement-related expectancies. *Journal of Social Issues, 32,* 47–61.

Phillips, G., & Over, R. (1992). Adult sexual orientation in relation to memories of childhood gender conforming and gender nonconforming behaviors. *Archives of Sexual Behavior, 21,* 543–558.

Phillips, R. (1980). Teachers' reported expectations of children's sex-roles and evaluations of sexist teaching. *Dissertation Abstracts International, 41,* 995–996A.

Pomerleau, A., Bolduc, D., Malcuit, G., & Cossette, L. (1990). Pink or blue: Environmental gender stereotypes in the first two years of life. *Sex Roles, 22,* 359–367.

Quackenbush, R. L. (1987). Sex roles and social perception. *Human Relations, 40,* 659–670.

Radloff, L. S., & Rae, D. S. (1981). Components of the sex difference in depression. *Research in Community and Mental Health, 2,* 111–137.

Rheingold, H. L., & Cook, K. V. (1975). The contents of boys' and girls' rooms as an index of parents' behavior. *Child Development, 46,* 459–463.

Robinson, C. C., & Morris, J. T. (1986). The gender-stereotyped nature of Christmas toys received by 36-, 48-, and 60-month-old children: A comparison between requested and nonrequested toys. *Sex Roles, 15,* 21–32.

Robinson, J., Little, C., & Zeynep, B. (1993). Emotional communication in mother-toddler relationships: Evidence for early gender differentiation. *Merrill-Palmer Quarterly, 39,* 496–517.

Rogers, C. (1987). Sex roles in education. In D. J. Hargreaves & A. M. Colley (Eds.), *The psychology of sex roles* (pp. 159–175). New York: Hemisphere Publishing.

Roos, P., & Cohen, L. (1987). Sex roles and social support as moderator of life stress adjustment. *Journal of Personality and Social Psychology, 52,* 576–585.

Rosenthal, R., & Jacobson, L. (1968). *Pygmalion in the classroom.* New York: Holt, Rinehart, & Winston.

Ross, L., Anderson, D. R., & Wisocki, P. A. (1982). Television viewing and adult sex-role attitudes. *Sex Roles, 8,* 589–592.

Rothbart, M. K., & Maccoby, E. E. (1966). Parents' differential reactions to sons and daughters. *Journal of Personality and Social Psychology, 4,* 237–243.

Rubin, J., Provenzano, R., & Luria, Z. (1974). The eye of the beholder: Parents' views on sex of newborns. *American Journal of Orthopsychiatry, 44,* 512–519.

Sayers, S. L., Baucom, D. H., & Tierney, A. M. (1993). Sex roles, interpersonal control, and depression: Who can get their way? *Journal of Research in Personality, 27,* 377–395.

Sears, R. R., Maccoby, E. E., & Levin, H. (1957). *Patterns of child rearing.* Evanston, IL: Row & Peterson.

Sears, R. R., Ran, L., & Alpert, R. (1965). *Identification and child rearing.* Stanford: Stanford University Press.

Serbin, L. A., O'Leary, K. D., Kent, R. N., & Tonick, I. J. (1973). A comparison of teacher response to the pre-academic and problem behavior of boys and girls. *Child Development, 44,* 796–804.

Shifren, K., Bauserman, R., & Carter, D. B. (1993). Gender role orientation and physical health: A study among young adults. *Sex Roles, 29,* 421–431.

Signorielli, N. (1989). Television and conceptions about sex roles: Maintaining conventionality and the status quo. *Sex Roles, 21,* 341–360.

Silvern, L. E., & Katz, P. A. (1986). Gender roles and adjustment in elementary-school children: A multidimensional approach. *Sex Roles, 14,* 181–202.

Silvern, L. E., & Ryan, V. L. (1979). Self-rated adjustment and sex-typing on the Bem Sex-Role Inventory: Is masculinity the primary predictor of adjustment? *Sex Roles, 5,* 739–763.

Stangor, C., & Ruble, D. N. (1989). Differential influences of gender schemata and gender constancy on children's information processing and behavior. *Social Cognition, 7,* 353–372.

Steenbarger, B. N., & Greenberg, R. P. (1990). Sex roles, stress, and distress: A study of person by situation. *Sex Roles, 22,* 59–68.

Stein, A. H. (1971). The effects of sex-role standards for achievement and sex-role preference on three determinants of achievement motivation. *Developmental Psychology, 4,* 219–231.

Stern, M., & Karraker, K. H. (1989). Sex stereotyping of infants: A review of gender labeling studies. *Sex Roles, 20,* 501–522.

Strong, B., & DeVault, C. (1994). *Human sexuality.* Mountain View, CA: Mayfield Publishing Company.

Watson, J. S., & Rame, C. (1972). Reactions to response-contingent stimulation in early infancy. *Merrill-Palmer Quarterly, 18,* 219–227.

Wells, K. (1980). Gender-role identity and psychological adjustment in adolescence. *Journal of Youth and Adolescence, 9,* 59–73.

White, L. K., & Brinkerhoff, D. B. (1981). The sexual division of labor: Evidence from childhood. *Social Forces, 60,* 170–181.

Whitley, B. E. (1983). Sex-role orientation and self-esteem: A critical meta-analytic review. *Journal of Personality and Social Psychology, 44,* 765–778.

Whitley, B. E. (1984). Sex-role orientation and psychological well-being: Two meta-analyses. *Sex Roles, 12,* 207–222.

Wynn, R., & Fletcher, C. (1987). Sex role development and early educational experiences. In D. B. Carter (Ed.), *Current conceptions of sex roles and sex typing.* New York: Praeger.

22

Sexuality and Religion

Vern L. Bullough

It has sometimes been said that human beings are incurably religious, an epi-
grammatic tribute to its wide dispersion. When attempts are made to define what
is meant by the term *religion,* however, there is little agreement. The disagreement is an old one, as emphasized by the disputed etymology of the word itself,
which is derived either from *relegere,* ''to read again,'' or from *religare,* ''to
bind.'' Moreover, each successive broadening of human intellectual horizons
through exploration and discovery has usually led to a redefinition of religion
to include the new and to discard some of the old. For example, traditional
Western ideas of religion usually included the necessity for the existence of a
god or gods, but Western confrontation with Buddhism, Confucianism, and Hinduism made it clear that theism as traditionally posited was by no means a
universal tenet of religions. In the United States, some humanists define themselves as religious humanists, while others, attempting to escape the connotation
of religion, adopt the term *secular humanists.* This division exists because of
one current definition of religion: the attempt to hold the encompassing alle-
giance of a group or organization through which individuals define their identity.
Secular humanists refuse to accept this definition; those who consider humanism
a religion adopt it.

Indeed, many scholars insist that to be defined as a religion, some common
elements must be present, including at least some of the following: rituals to
perform, formulas to recite, tales to narrate, objects to manipulate, places to
frequent or avoid, holy days to keep, natural phenomena by which to predict

the future, charismatic leaders to follow, truths to affirm, a literature to ponder, and precepts to obey. Many fall under the category of worship, perhaps the most universal of religious categories—such activities as prayer, sacrifice, contemplation, magic, and incantation.

Closely associated with worship is conduct, correctly following the precepts inherent in the worship, and it is in this category that sexuality looms important. James Brundage, a historian of canon law, has found that canon or church law gave much more emphasis to sexual activities (slightly over 10 percent) than did civil law (about 6 percent). He also found that the greatest emphasis was in the earlier canon law than in the later (Brundage 1982), as if it was necessary to assert right sexual conduct from the beginning, and once established it was easier to maintain. What is true for Catholic Christianity is true for other major religions: the regulation or control of sexuality, or even permission giving, has been an important aspect of religious regulations regarding conduct.

Generally, such regulations are based on theological explanations, which guide religious conduct in other areas as well. The basis for such explanations lies in the distant past and is often derived from assumptions and beliefs that would not be accepted by modern science. Since different cultures gave different answers to basic questions, religious concepts of right conduct in sexual matters came to differ early in human history, and they continue to do so. Of necessity, in a single chapter, a discussion of these differences must be limited to some of the major religious traditions: Christianity, Judaism, Islam, Hinduism, Taoism, and Buddhism. The emphasis is put on the dominant tradition; dissenting opinions about sexual conduct are not discussed.

JUDAISM

One of the oldest traditions is Judaism, which had some influence upon both Christianity and Islam. The first recorded divine commandment to humans, according to the Jewish Scripture, was to "be fruitful and multiply" (Genesis 1: 22), a statement often repeated (Genesis 1:28; 8:17; 9:7; 35:11, etc.). At the same time there were various forms of prohibited sexual relations, most of them mentioned in Leviticus. Prohibited sex fell mainly into three categories as Judaism developed, based on prohibition found in the Bible and expanded in the Talmud (compiled from about 1150 B.C.E. to 500 C.E.), the legal codes, and the *Responsa* literature (published legal opinions and ethical and philosophical guidance of rabbis up to the present day).

The first category prohibited are sexual acts based on propinquity or relationship (e.g., those of a mother with her son). A stipulated contradiction is the levirate marriage, under which a surviving widow has claim on her husband's brother to marry her and to try to provide her with child. The second category of prohibited sexual relations are those considered unnatural or contrary to physical nature, as between a human and animals or lesbianism and homosexuality. The third category of prohibited sexual activities are those contrary to law (e.g., adultery). Sex is also prohibited during menstruation because the contact with the catamenial blood according to Jewish law is a source of ritual impurity. On the other hand, Jewish law regards certain sexual activity as a mitzvah, a good deed, since it is fulfilling the will of God. Sexual intercourse on the Sabbath is one such act since the Sabbath is the most precious of days, and having sex would make it even more so. Some sexual activities reflect considerable ambivalence. There are, for example, relatively few references to masturbation in Jewish law, perhaps because it was such a solitary act. There is, however, much uplifting homiletic and instructive literature that looks upon masturbation as a corrupting practice, although it is also sometimes seen as an acceptable release of tensions in a situation where other releases are not possible. In many other ways the Jewish attitude seems fairly tolerant. Once the commandment to reproduce had been met by having at least two children, contraception was allowable. Similarly, abortion was not condemned since under Jewish jurisprudence the majority opinion did not view the fetus as an individual but as part of the mother and therefore with no independent human rights as such (Bullough 1976; Felman 1968; Gittelsohn 1980; Podet 1994; Roth & Wigoder 1972).

CHRISTIANITY

Growing out of the Jewish tradition, Christianity adopted radically different views about sexuality. In part, the Christian views were a reflection of the world in which it found itself, one in which ascetic views were strong, pushed by the neo-Platonists, the Stoics, and some of the rivals of Christianity, such as Gnosticism and Manicheanism. Although there was considerable debate among the church fathers, the theologians who formulated Christian doctrine, the dominant voice in the West came from St. Augustine of Hippo (died 430 C.E.).

Augustine had been an adherent of the Manichean religion, which emphasized abstinence from all sexual activities for the adept, elect members who had reached the highest level of the religion. Procreation for them was an evil act since it imprisoned spirits in a material body and denied them the wisdom of the true light. Although those who were already born could lessen their imprisonment by abstaining from eating any product of sexual union and living an exemplary life, they were also enjoined to abstain from sexual intercourse. Augustine as a young man had been converted to Manicheanism but never became a full-fledged member or an adept. Instead, he was a believer, an auditor, living with a mistress, and striving to overcome his sexual urges. Unhappy for his inability to do so, he decided to recognize his sexual needs and get married; he sent away his mistress and his son and became betrothed to a girl not yet of marriageable age. Still unable to deny his sexual urges while awaiting marriage, he underwent a crisis that eventually resulted in his conversion to Christianity, the religion of his mother. He found that with this second conversion, he was freed from his incessant sexual needs and could finally become celibate. He rose rapidly in the Christian church hierarchy, becoming bishop of Hippo and the major theological spokesman for what became Western Christianity.

In interpreting and establishing Christian doctrine, Augustine was influenced by his Manichean background and held that sexual abstinence was the highest of moral goods. Such a view ran contrary to the Jewish (and increasingly Christian) scriptural tradition of being fruitful and multiplying and was also contrary to the teachings of Jesus, whose presence at a marriage feast gave a Christian sanction to marriage and family. After struggling over these contradictions, Augustine adhered to the greater virtue of celibacy but also held that marriage could be permitted for those unable to remain celibate and that sexual intercourse in marriage was permitted as long as it met the commandment to procreate. Marriage, he argued, managed to transform coitus from simply a satisfaction of animal lust to a necessary duty, although it still remained the channel by which the guilt of concupiscence was transmitted from parents to children, a sin that could be removed only by baptism.

Augustine went into great detail about sexual intercourse and emphasized that it should only be engaged in between a married couple with the woman on the bottom and the man on the top and only in the orifice (vagina) with the instrument (penis) that God had given humans. All intercourse between the unmarried, even if it resulted in conception, was condemned by Augustine. Masturbation was an even greater sin, as was the use of any barrier contraception. He equated homosexuality with the destruction of Sodom, and fellatio and other sexual activities were condemned (Bullough 1976). In sum, all sexual activities except sex for procreation were sins.

Sin in the early Christian church involved penance—technically the reconciling of a sinner with God. Originally in the early Christian church, this reconciliation had been accomplished through open and public confession in an effort of the Christian congregations to retain their purity amid the evils of the secular world. The three principal sins were idolatry or reversion to paganism, sexual impurity, and homicide. Those who committed any of these sins were excluded from communion and from the fellowship of the church; they could be restored only by submitting to a strict regimen of public penance for a set number of years.

As the Christian community grew in numbers and influence, public penance fell into disuse, and a system of private penance and recurrent confession was instituted. This movement started in the monasteries and spread to the secular church, and penance came to be regarded as healing medicine for the soul, with the priest confessor probing into the festering sins of his congregation. Penitential collections offered a listing and categorizing of the level of sins. A hierarchy of sexual sins was established with corresponding periods of penance. Papal edicts and council decisions were codified into canon law, which continues to elucidate on the sexual sins.

As the medieval Christian church developed, its theology, particularly in the thirteenth century, was elaborated on by St. Thomas Aquinas, who rationalized

Christianity while retaining the Augustinian sexual attitudes. The modern Catholic church essentially follows Aquinas, though not in all ways. Aquinas, for example, held that early abortions were allowed because life did not begin until quickening, a common belief of the time (Bullough 1976). Celibacy was still held to be the highest virtue, even for the married; many Christians, not only those who were monks or nuns or clergy, emphasized the importance of celibacy, and some, like King Edward the Confessor of England and his wife, swore to abstain from sex.

Aquinas's version of Christianity was challenged by Martin Luther, John Calvin, and others, who turned to a renewed emphasis on scriptural authority over the scholastic theology of Aquinas. The result was a deemphasis on celibacy and a greater emphasis on marriage. There was also a greater recognition of the pleasures of sexual intercourse by both Luther and Calvin, although in other ways, traditional ideas about sex remained. Increasingly, however, in both Catholic countries and Protestant ones, religious sins came to be regarded as crimes when the law became secularized.

ISLAM

Islam, which also accepts much of the Jewish Scriptures as part of its sacred book, the Koran, drew more from the Jewish tradition in its attitudes toward sex than from the Christians. Islamic law, however, also drew from pre-Islamic Arabic attitudes, and this is particularly true of laws relating to marriage, divorce, fornication, and other aspects of sexual behavior. Muhammad regarded sexual intercourse as one of the joys of life, even though much of Islamic writing on the joys of sex seems to be even more male centered than in Judaism. Muhammad intended to defend women in his attempt to limit the numbers of wives a husband might have (four at any one time), making it difficult to accuse a woman of adultery, and emphasizing the importance of treating wives with kindness. The Koran has a whole section on the rights of women. Women were regarded as erotic creatures, however, and were advised to stay behind curtains when male guests who were not relatives were present in order for them to remain pure.

Generally Islam emphasizes that sexuality should take place within the family, where men and women are the shepherds, responsible for the well-being of society. Sexuality is not so much an end in itself as a means to achieve certain biological, familial, and societal objectives. Muslims emphasize that there is punishment in this world and the next for failing to follow the commands given by God, but they also emphasize that God is merciful.

In terms of general sexual morals, the chief virtue in Islam seems to be to avoid excess. Traditionally, Islamic scholars regard all heterosexual intercourse between persons not in a state of legal matrimony or concubinage as a sin. This includes adultery, fornication between unmarried persons, and same-sex relations. Adultery is particularly abhorred, but unless the individuals are caught in the act or for some reason confess to committing adultery, proving adultery in the Islamic world is almost impossible since the Koran requires four unimpeachable eyewitnesses to testify to the act. Muhammad also held that lust itself was a sin, but some Islamic writings revealed ways around some prohibitions, for example, by allowing for temporary marriage (*Mut'a*), which could be arranged for a set number of hours or as long as the caravan travel lasted.

Various rules of sexual hygiene are stipulated in the Koran. A menstruating woman is regarded as ritually impure as she is in Judaism, and men are forbidden from having intercourse with a woman during this time. Discharge of semen through masturbation results in impurity also and requires the believer to cleanse himself in ways similar to those required of women following their menses. It is not, however, a sin, and though even nocturnal emissions require a cleansing afterward, there is nothing wrong with having an involuntary emission. Islam teaches that the clitoris is the source and wellspring of all female passions.

Homosexuality is not particularly condemned in the Koran, although it certainly is looked upon with disfavor, particularly if it seems to be so all-consuming that it excludes heterosexual relationships. As in Christianity, it is often equated with the sins of Sodom and Gomorrah, but not to the same extent since the emphasis is on the power of God and his ability to be merciful. Elsewhere, I have called Islam a sex-positive religion as contrasted to the sex-negative aspects of traditional Christianity, and certainly both Islam and Muhammad have been looked upon by the West as less concerned with sexual sins than Christians were. Even bestiality might be tolerated if it served the purpose of preventing the person from committing a greater crime. Cross-dressing was institutionalized in some areas of the Islamic world to perform the women's role in public, since proper women were not to expose themselves. Generally, Islam emphasized tolerance toward sexual peccadilloes (but not adultery which was a crime against property). Believers who strayed were never entirely regarded as lost souls, provided they repented and did not flaunt their excesses (Bullough 1976).

HINDUISM

Hinduism has many sects since it is a complex product of the amalgamation of various cults and beliefs within a common social framework. It does not conceive of itself as a separate religion but rather as a pattern of living, controlled by what was taken to be a correct interpretation of ancient tradition. This makes it difficult to give a unifying portrait of concepts of sexuality. Moreover, like Judaism, it has given birth to religions that have taken separate paths. Jainism, one of the oldest, retains a social structure much like Hinduism but stresses asceticism and heroic self-mortification, which will carry adherents upward in the long path to liberation in future lives. Buddhism, another offshoot, emphasizes how suffering and mortality, the common lot of humanity, can be transcended and a new state of being achieved. Sikhism, which started as a movement to seek unity between the best in Islam and the best in Hinduism, has evolved a distinctive religious culture of its own.

At the core of Hindi ideas about sexuality is the belief that the literature of love and sex is of divine origin, derived from a collection of all knowledge compiled in some 100,000 chapters by Prajāpati, the supreme god, creator of heaven and earth. Included in this collection was *kāma*, or the pursuit of pleasure, particularly sexual pleasure. The transmission of this knowledge to humans was a complicated process, but eventually it was put down in writing by Vātsyāna (fl. 450 C.E.) in the Kāmasūtra ("love text"). Included in its contents are most aspects of human courtship and mating, including positions in intercourse. It was followed by a series of other love texts over the next several centuries, some of them quite crude, more or less giving out the same information. The number of erotic classics suggests that the peoples of the Indian subcontinent did not hold the fear of sex that some of their Western counterparts did. In fact, unlike the Judeo-Christian description of the creation of humanity as an asexual affair, Hindus put creation itself in sexual terms, and the "Hymn of Creation" in the *Rig Veda* attributes the beginning to sex desire. Most Hindu religious documents such as the *Athana Veda*, the fourth of the Hindu *Vedas*, include many magical formulations and incantations to help or hinder lovemaking.

Although Hinduism condemned bestiality, some sects practiced it. Incest, rape, and adultery were also condemned, and there are prohibitions against having sex with a woman during her menses and against having sex with someone from the wrong caste. The ultimate ends of men and women—salvation, bliss, knowledge, and pleasure—can be achieved by following any number of different paths, which vary according to the cult, creed, sect, and system. Usually no single path is all sufficient, a blending of two or more being regarded as essential. Sexual activity is important. The *yoni*—narrowly the vagina, but in a broader sense including pubic hair, the opening or cleft of the labia, and the uterus—is considered to have a life of its own and is a sacred area, worthy of reverence, and a symbol of the cosmic mysteries. The penis, called the *linga*, is also an object of veneration.

Copulation itself can bring about supernatural power, but only if the practitioner has learned to transcend the carnal state of sexual activity and rise above passion. Hindu cultism is most active in this aspect of sex. Some cults worship the *linga*, others the *yoni*. One cult, the Sakhibhava, holds that only the godhead, Krishna, was truly male, while every other creature in the world was female, subject to the pleasure of Krishna. They worship Radha, the favorite consort of Krishna, and the object of their devotion is to become a female attendant upon her. Female followers of this sect grant sexual favors freely to anyone because they believe that all their sexual partners are Krishna himself. Male followers dress like women and effect the behavior, movements, and habits of women. In the past, many of them emasculated themselves, and all were supposed to play the female part during sexual intercourse. The technical term *hijra* is applied to these men, and there are colonies of them in India today.

In the tantric sects, literally those who follow a collection of scriptures known as Tantras, which explain ways to "expand" or "extend" knowledge, sexual activity plays a particularly important role. Essentially, tantric sects are antinomians; that is, they hold that individuals are not bound by the moral law and can reach a state that takes them so far beyond its purview that they can cease to obey its precepts. In both Hinduism and Buddhism these antinomian groups are known quite literally as "the left," although some scholars derive the term from *yama,* meaning "women." The tantric cults hold that spiritual union with the god can best be attained through sexual union in the flesh. During intercourse, an individual is able to contemplate reality face to face, and the supreme bliss that proceeds from ritual sexuality is the height of religious experience. In this stage of nonduality, all differences vanish, and everything—high and low, good and bad, ugly and beautiful—becomes the same. In this pose, the couple is able to comprehend the mystery of the whole cosmic process and taste the transcendent bliss of divine experience.

Anal intercourse, between either a woman and a man or two men, was held to be one of the main expedients for utilizing the potencies of the rectal center, whose animation was believed to energize the artistic, poetic, and mystical faculties. Some medieval writers wrote of it as quite common. Certainly concentration on the anus—the introduction of wooden plugs into the rectum during meditation, digital insertion during sex-magic rites, constriction of the anal sphincter, and stimulation of the regions during mystical poses—is common yogic practice. Oral-genital sexual activity, either between the same sex or opposites, was condemned by some lawgivers but not by Hindu erotic writers, who held that the mouth is pure for purposes of sexual congress. In harems, cunnilingus was widely practiced by the women, and it also is described in Hindu erotic manuals (Walker 1968).

Among tantric believers, promiscuous intercourse is usually regarded as an act of devotion to the deity, since it is through the union of male and female semen that the primordial male and female elements can be united into the nondual state of Absolute Reality. There is also another extreme in the Tantras, as emphasized by Jainism, which subscribes to the tantric idea that sex is a gateway to salvation, but it regards sexual indulgence itself as a weakness and an evil to overcome because it is the chief manifestation of lust. Hindu temples, particularly those built before the Muslim conquests and the entry of the British into India, often portray sexually symbolic scenes. The gods themselves were very sexual, emphasizing only that religion has offered many approaches to sexuality (Bullough 1976; Walker 1968).

BUDDHISM

Buddhism was founded by Siddhartha Gautama, the Buddha who lived in northern India (560–480 B.C.E.). His followers seek to emulate his example of perfect morality, wisdom, and compassion, culminating in a transformation of consciousness known as the enlightenment. Buddhism is based on Buddha's Four Noble Truths, the last of which is the Eightfold Path by which enlightenment may be attained and the individual self-annihilated in nirvana.

It is common to divide Buddhism into two main branches. The Theravada (Way of the Elders) is the more conservative of the two, and it is dominant in Sri Lanka, Burma, and Thailand. The Mahayana (Great Vehicle) is more diverse and liberal and is found mainly in China, Korea, and Japan and among Tibetan peoples, where it is distinguished by its emphasis on the Buddhist Tantras, where it retains strong similarity to the tantric beliefs of the Hindus. In fact, some religious scholars believe that Tantrism was a separate pan-Indian movement whose ideas were assimilitated into the major Indian religions including Hinduism, Buddhism, and Jainism, and thereby lost its separate identity.

Most Buddhist schools deemphasize sexual desire, and traditionally Buddhist monks have been celibate. This is not true of the tantric schools of Mitsung (Mantrayana), the True Word school (Chen-yen Tsung), or the Esoteric school of Buddhism. The main emphasis of Buddhist Tantrism is on the development of the devotee's dominant psychophysical powers by means of special meditations and ritual techniques. These are essentially esoteric and must be passed on personally from master to initiate and include the use of symbolic gesture (*mudras*), the uttering of potent formulas (*mantras*), and the entering through meditation of sacred diagrams (*mandalas*) and *yantras* (the mediator's creative visualization of and identification with specific divine forms). Although the particulars of practice vary between the groups, they are similar to the Hindu Tantras in that they stress the realization of the union of polar opposites (e.g., male and female). At the same time, within tantric Buddhism some of the same ideas about homosexuality and lesbianism exist as among the esoteric cults of Hinduism (Bullough 1976; Ruan 1991).

TAOISM

Tantric beliefs were also present in Taoism, the traditional religion of China that dates from the I Ching composed in the first millennium B.C.E. It appears first as a philosophical movement in the fifth century B.C.E. in the writings of Lao-tzu, who offered a practical way of life. His teachings later came to be incorporated into a popular religion called Tao-chiao, which in the West is mistakenly called Taoism (and includes both the philosophy and the religion).

The historical founder of the Taoist religion was Chang Ling, who lived in the second century C.E. In terms of sexuality, Taoism incorporates many of the tantric ideas into a unique Chinese formulation. The major Taoist sexual belief is that longevity or immortality is attainable by sexual activity. One way for men to achieve this is by having intercourse with virgins, particularly young virgins. There was also a belief in the desirability of multiple sexual partners. Key to longevity was the ability to control ejaculation, and this was true for women as well as men. For men, this was called *cai Yin pu Yang* (gathering a woman's yin to nourish a man's yang) and for women *cai Yang pu Yin* (gathering a man's yang to nourish a woman's yin). This comes from the Chinese belief that perfect harmony results from the intermingling of heaven and earth, symbolized by yin and yang. Though both sexes have yin and yang essences within them, yang is more important in women, yin in man, although in each there needs to be a proper balance. At birth the individual is filled with the principle of primordial yang and yin, and as the body matures both the yin and yang increase, but after maturity the yang force in males begins to decrease unless steps are taken to restore it. The yin force in women, however, does not decrease. If the imbalance becomes too great, the individual will die. The secret of long life, then, is to try to retain as much yang as possible in men, and this can be achieved by practicing coitus reservatus while bringing the women to orgasm.

It is important for the male to understand the female's sexual responses so he can penetrate her at the appropriate time and use the correct sexual postures, positions, and movements, which include controlled breathing, preventing ejaculation by stopping and pressuring the base of the penis, and achieving sexual satisfaction by coitus without ejaculation. Women, for their part, had their techniques to encourage the male to ejaculate while preserving her own yin, but these are not written down (Bullough 1976; Ruan 1991).

Following the concepts of yin and yang, however, the Chinese tolerated, if they did not encourage, lesbianism. With their unlimited supply of the yin substance, masturbation was harmless, and so was mutual masturbation between two women. Within the large polygamous households, lesbian relations were recognized as inevitable, and some of the Chinese sex manuals include instructions for two women and one man and even for two women without a man. Attitudes toward male homosexuality were more ambivalent, with some writers glorifying it and others condemning it, and attitudes tended to reflect not so much religious ones as the position of those in power. From the eighteenth to the twentieth centuries, discussion of the topic of homosexuality went underground (Bullough & Ruan 1993; Ruan 1991).

RELIGION AND SEX

Religious writings are a major source of information about ancient, or for that matter modern, sexual practices. In some religions, much of the writing about sex is an attempt to control and prohibit sexual activities. Other religions look upon sex as one of the enjoyments of life, something to be treasured, although in moderation. Others see sex itself as a way of achieving union with the gods. Still others see it as a way of achieving a long life.

These religious ideas remain important because they are still held by large segments of the population. Religious concepts, though they might have derived from myths as well as physiological assumptions not accepted in today's world, still play a crucial role in what might be called moral consciousness. The practice of traditional rituals or the recitation of an accepted yet unproven canon does seem to imply that what is being enacted or affirmed is a revelation of divine truth.

In the twentieth century, the study of theology and religion, previously left to theological, literary, or philosophically oriented scholars, has seen an influx of researchers from the social sciences: anthropology, sociology, psychology, and history. Many historians, for example, have seen early religion as sort of a primitive science, and just as astrology preceded astronomy, this primitive set of beliefs would be replaced by more sophisticated ones. To some extent this has happened, and there has always been an ongoing reinterpretation of ancient moral commandments in the light of new experiences or through the need to deal with previously unknown problems.

Just as the interpretations of St. Augustine were reexamined and codified by St. Thomas Aquinas, and Aquinas by John Calvin, Martin Luther, and the Catholic neo-Scholastics, and by a whole host of theologians in the twentieth century, the progress of change has been slow. Religious authorities traditionally have been suspicious of change. Even the writings of Aquinas were prohibited for a time from being taught at the University of Paris, the major theological school of the Middle Ages. Although this prohibition was soon reversed and Aquinas was canonized shortly after his death, the story emphasizes that even Catholic saints have difficulty. The real problem with Aquinas, however, was not foreseen by his contemporaries: he based many of his assumptions on the existence of a geocentric universe. This meant that when the heliocentric universe came to be promulgated, the Catholic church found itself in a quandary. One result was the forced recantation of Galileo and a condemnation of the whole concept, and though the condemnations grew less strident as time passed, it was not until the twentieth century and the pontificate of John Paul II that the Catholic church admitted that it had been wrong.

The criticisms of Martin Luther, John Calvin, and others were also challenges to the scholasticism of Aquinas and led to the development of Protestantism when the papacy was unable to resolve the differences brought about by the new scholarship. Still, in spite of the reluctance to change, Christian history has seen radical revision of basic concepts. Early in the church, killing of any kind, even by soldiers in time of war, was labeled murder. Eventually the church accepted war as a fact of life, and the pacifism of the early church continues to exist only as a minority movement, most of it today concentrated in the so-called peace churches, such as the Society of Friends and the Mennonites. The Christian prohibition against usury was reinterpreted in the later Middle Ages by adding the concept of just interest and distinguishing it from usury. This change allowed the development of banking and what we know as capitalism. The belief that life began at quickening was reinterpreted by the pope in the nineteenth century to say that life began at conception. The general condemnation of contraception by all Christian groups has been gradually reinterpreted in the nineteenth and twentieth centuries to allow various forms of family planning. One of the more recent radical changes took place in Mormonism when the church officials changed their prohibitions about allowing individuals of African descent to hold the priesthood. The list could go on, but the battles are ongoing.

The most bitter controversies in the history of religions have been fought by strict constructionists, who have adhered to traditional prescriptions, and by revisionists, who have sought to adapt both moral and ceremonial requirements to the changing situations. At times religious authorities have appeared to equate all of religion with its moral imperatives, reducing its other constituents to supports for the ethical. Although such reductionism ignores the full scope and profound subtleties of the religious experiences of individuals and communities, it remains a means of control by religious authorities. Their ability to exercise such control, which varies in different religious groupings, emphasizes the importance of the need for sexologists to understand our religious traditions.

Many of the battles in religious communities today are being fought on sex and gender issues. The debate of the place of women in the various organized churches led to the exodus of a number of congregations and individuals from the Anglican church when the archbishop of Canterbury proclaimed women's right to be ordained. Discussions of homosexuality have split the Presbyterians, the Lutherans, and many other denominations that have tried to issue statements on the topic. Abortion has put church people against church people, both within and between religious groupings. Yet at the same time, some of the issues that seemed so important to religious groups in the past, such as divorce and contraception, have become far less controversial.

Interestingly, some of the most rigid of Christian pentecostal and fundamentalist churches are those that are growing most rapidly, while those seemingly willing to adjust more to the modern world, the so-called established churches, have not been growing, and some are declining. At the same time there has been an increasing growth of nonbelievers and secularists or people who are only nominally church members. In effect, if sexual conduct is any judge, religious influence on decision making has been declining throughout the twentieth century. In spite of Catholic opposition to most forms of family planning, attitudes of American Catholics toward contraception reflect public opinion on the topic. Even on abortion, the ranks of Catholics do not agree with official church dogma.

Still, large numbers of people continue to go through the motions of religion long after they have transferred their personal loyalty and trust to objects other than those of traditional observance. Consciously or unconsciously, they still retain some of the old belief structure, and in the Western countries such as the United States, this belief structure adds to the guilt that many people feel about sex. Many so burdened turn to clergy for pastoral counseling, but in today's secular world, large numbers still burdened by their guilt furnish a significant part of the clientele for the various professional counselors: psychologists, psychiatric social workers and nurses, marriage and family counselors, and psychiatrists. In short, religion remains influential in forming attitudes toward sex, and any professional in the sex field who ignores it ignores a significant component in the human psyche. It is essential, however, that the different religious traditions be taken into account in this multicultural country.

REFERENCES

Brundage, J. (1982). Sex and canon law. In V. L. Bullough & J. Brundage (Eds.), *Sexual practices and the medieval church* (pp. 89–101). Buffalo, NY: Prometheus Books.

Bullough, V. L. (1976). *Sexual variance in society and history.* Chicago: University of Chicago Press.

Bullough, V. L., & Bullough, B. (Eds.). (1994). *Human sexuality: An encyclopedia.* New York: Garland.

Bullough, V. L., & Ruan, F. F. (1993). Same-sex love in contemporary China. In A. Hendricks, R. Tielman & E. van der Veen (Eds.), *The third pink book* (pp. 46–53). Buffalo, NY: Prometheus.

Felman, D. M. (1968). *Marital relations, birth control and abortion in Jewish law.* New York: New York University Press.

Gittelson, R. B. (1980). *Love, sex and marriage.* New York: Union of Hebrew Congregations.

Nugent, R., & Gramick, J. (1989). Homosexuality: Protestant, Catholic and Jewish issues: A fishbone tale. *Journal of Homosexuality, 18,* 7–46.

Podet, A. H. (1994). Judaism and sexuality. In V. L. Bullough & B. Bullough (Eds.), *Human sexuality: An encyclopedia* (pp. 325–330). New York: Garland.

Roth C., & Wigoder, G. (Eds.). (1972). *Encyclopedia Judaica.* Jerusalem: Keter.

Ruan, F. F. (1991). *Sex in China.* New York: Plenum Press.

Walker, B. (1968). *The Hindu world* (2 vols.). New York: Praeger.

23

Sexuality and Sexual Orientation: Adjustments to Aging

Kelly B. Kyes

As a sex educator, I have found that one of the most predictable ways to generate a reaction of discomfort in my students has been to ask them to imagine their parents or even their grandparents engaged in sexual activity. This reaction seems typical of college students (Pocs & Godaw 1977). The reason seems to be that our youth-oriented society has reinforced the belief that old people are not interested in sex. Little has been done to contradict the belief. We see older people in commercials advertising vitamins, laxatives, and incontinence undergarments. We rarely see them in advertisements for products intended to enhance sex appeal, such as cosmetics or cologne. We also receive many messages that tell us "young and smooth is beautiful; old, wrinkled and gray is ugly." The abundance of moisturizers, hair dyes, and other products designed to help us look younger reinforces these messages. These messages, combined with the reluctance to talk about sexuality in general, lead many to assume that older people are not interested in sex because they are sick, tired, and unattractive. If they are believed to be sexually active, they may be perceived as abnormal (La Torre & Kear 1977).

MYTHS AND STEREOTYPES ABOUT AGING AND SEXUALITY

For many years, research on sexuality in the elderly gave evidence that supported the belief that the aged are not interested in sex. Kinsey, Pomeroy, and

Martin (1948) reported that the frequency of intercourse among their older male participants was lower than that of their middle-aged and young adults, leading many to assume that the differences were due to maturation. More recent studies have also documented lower levels of sexual activity in older adults compared to middle-aged and young adult samples (Mulligan & Moss 1991), which has led to the conclusion that sexual activity and interest decline with age. Other evidence, however, suggests that these data probably reflected cohort, and not age, differences. George and Weiler (1981) collected longitudinal data showing that the frequency of sexual intercourse remained the same for the majority of their respondents over a six-year period. Starr and Weiner (1981), interviewing hundreds of elderly adults about their past and present sexual behavior, found that the frequency of sexual activity tended to remain the same for the majority of respondents. Thus, rather than significantly decreasing their sexual activity, the older adults interviewed in Kinsey's study may have always had a relatively low frequency of sexual intercourse. In support of this theory, Hobson (1984) reported that many of those who believed sex was improper during old age never enjoyed sex in the first place due to feelings of guilt or shame. Since Kinsey's old adults were children during the Victorian era, when attitudes about sex were repressive, this is not surprising.

Other research dealing with sexual activity and aging has shown that although many experienced a decline in sexual activity, they did not cease sexual activity altogether. Additionally, their level of sexual interest and satisfaction remained the same with age (Schiavi, Schreiner-Engel, Mandeli, Schanzer & Cohen 1990; Winn & Newton 1982). In a study of 106 cultures, Winn and Newton (1982) reported that the women often became more sexually expressive in a variety of ways (e.g., jokes, conversation content) as they approached old age. This may have been because the women felt freer to enjoy sex once menopause had passed and pregnancy was no longer a concern. In studies that have reported a cessation of sexual activity in older populations, generally the reasons have been due to lack of a sexual partner (Cavallaro 1991; Malatesta, Chambless, Pollack & Cantor 1988; Janus & Janus 1993) or because of the man's lack of interest and/or sexual function (George & Weiler 1981).

The current evidence does not answer definitively the question of whether sexual activity declines with age. Certainly there is evidence that, compared to middle-aged and young adults, the aged engage in sexual activity less frequently. However, it is impossible to determine whether their level of sexual activity has always been lower than subsequent generations or whether there is an actual decline with age. In any case, there does not seem to be a general lack of interest, and sexual activity does not typically cease completely with age.

Another belief is that sexual dysfunction experienced in old age is inevitable and irreversible. This comes from the myth that our sex life is the first thing to go as we age. In reality, it is the last function to deteriorate as part of the aging process (Kaplan 1990). Masters and Johnson (1966) reported that the older adults in their studies were just as responsive to treatment as the younger adults.

The evidence that older couples who experience sexual dysfunction seek treatment shows that their capacity for sexual expression is important to them. For example, Masters and Johnson (1966) reported that they treated clients as old as 93 years for sexual dysfunction. A report on sexual dysfunction from a Loyola University clinic showed that 30 percent of the clients were at least 50 years old (Renshaw 1984).

The reality is that older people are interested in sex. Equally noteworthy is the fact that many are sexually active. Starr and Weiner (1981) reported that 82 percent of the 665 older respondents in their study were sexually active, even into their 90s. Many reported finding their partner attractive and reported engaging in a wide variety of sexual techniques, including oral sex. Even among those who suffered from failing health, sexual expression was an important part of their lives. Nearly half (46 percent) reported that they masturbated at least occasionally. In a more recent survey, Janus and Janus (1993) reported that generally the rate of sexual activity actually increased for women after age 65.

If we realize that growing old does not mean becoming asexual and that sexual satisfaction for many increases with age, perhaps we will be less likely to fear the aging process.

BIOLOGICAL CHANGES IN THE REPRODUCTIVE ORGANS AS A RESULT OF AGING

Although it is normal for adults to maintain an interest in sex and a sexually active lifestyle as they age, aging does produce physical changes in the reproductive organs. Rather than seeing these changes as the beginning of the end of sexual expression, many members of the elderly population simply adapt their sexual behavior to the changes in their bodies instead of believing that they must stop being sexually active altogether.

Changes in Women's Reproductive Organs

Menopause

Women experience a relatively abrupt change in their bodies compared to men because of menopause, when the ovaries cease to produce the hormones that have contributed to ovulation and menstruation during the woman's reproductive life. Women usually notice the onset of menopause when they stop having menstrual periods, typically between the ages of 48 to 52 (Masters, Johnson & Kolodny 1992). However, the changes associated with menopause can be experienced as young as age 35, and signs of menopause can continue well into the 50s (Leiblum 1990). Perhaps the most noticeable change to the woman is decreased skin elasticity, which results from the reduction of estrogen in her body. Although the woman's adrenal glands will continue to produce estrogen in small amounts, the reduction of this hormone will result in several changes. Her breasts may sag more noticeably, and she will probably experience a decrease in the amount of vaginal lubrication during sexual arousal. The walls of her vagina will start to thin and become more susceptible to abrasions during intercourse (Kaplan 1990; Leiblum 1990; Masters, Johnson & Kolodny 1992). Some women find that coitus becomes uncomfortable because of the lack of lubrication and atrophy of the vagina.

Rather than signaling an end to her sexual activity, many women and their partners have learned to take these changes in stride and make small adjustments in their lovemaking technique so that sexual activity continues to be enjoyable for both. The use of an artificial lubricant such as K-Y jelly is helpful for solving the lubrication deficiency problem (Kaplan 1990; Leiblum 1990). Kaplan (1990) notes that taking more time during foreplay allows women to become sufficiently lubricated to enjoy intercourse. A woman's partner can also help her by using gentler touches and gentler thrusting during coitus so as not to irritate her vagina.

Finally, many women are receiving estrogen replacement therapy (ERT), which seems to slow or stop altogether the effects of the loss of her own estrogen. Although ERT is still considered somewhat controversial because of uncertainties about long-term health risks, Leiblum (1990) believes that it is safe and effective. Besides controlling the problem of vaginal dryness, ERT is also reported to reduce the risk and/or development of osteoporosis. A potential risk of ERT is endometrial cancer (cancer of the uterus); however, taking progesterone supplements in addition to the estrogen appears to protect against this risk (Leiblum 1990).

One interesting finding from Masters and Johnson's (1966) data on older women was that those who remained sexually active were less likely to report problems with insufficient vaginal lubrication after menopause. These same women also were found to have less atrophy of the vaginal muscles than women who had become less active as they aged. Because this relationship between vaginal condition and frequency of sexual activity is correlational, it is inappropriate to conclude that this relationship is causal or even directional (Libman 1989). It is tempting to conclude that maintaining an active sex life helped these women to maintain healthy vaginas, as Masters and Johnson (1966) did. However, it is equally likely that they continued to be sexually active because they did not experience the decrease in lubrication after menopause that the less active women experienced. Nevertheless, it could do no harm to assume the former with the expectation that the vagina might stay healthy with continued sexual activity. If this outcome is not realized for an individual woman, she can make use of artificial lubricants.

Changes in Men's Reproductive Organs

It is generally believed that men do not experience a male version of menopause. Nevertheless, men's bodies do change as a result of aging, and the sexual response of most men is affected to some degree.

Many men notice that their erections are not as full as they once were and that they require direct physical stimulation of the penis to acquire or maintain an erection (Kaplan 1990). This can be disconcerting to those who are not aware that this is a normal occurrence in older men, especially for those who in the past attained erections at the mere sight or thought of their partner (Kaplan 1990).

Another noticeable change in men is that their refractory period—the time after an orgasm during which a man cannot ejaculate again (Masters & Johnson 1966)—becomes longer as they get older. For the man who is not aware that this is normal, the increased refractory period can be misinterpreted as erectile dysfunction or impotence. Masters, Johnson, and Kolodny (1992) point out that many men are unrealistic in their expectation that their sexual functioning will remain virtually unchanged as they age: "While they wouldn't expect to run a mile as fast at age 65 as they did at age 25 (or to recuperate from their exertion as quickly), they expect to get rock-hard erections instantly in all sexual situations and are worried when they can't make love twice in one evening" (p. 259).

Along with the increased refractory length during waking hours, many older men do not attain as many nocturnal erections as they did when they were younger. Libman (1988) reported, however, that frequency of nocturnal erections was not predictive of reported coital frequency or of reported erectile functioning. One problem with Libman's survey was that the reports of nocturnal erections were self-reported and not objectively measured. Because nocturnal erections occur while the man is asleep, it seems doubtful that he would know every time he experiences such an erection. Probably not quite as noticeable to most men is the decrease in the amount of semen produced at each ejaculation. However, men are typically fertile throughout adulthood (Masters, Johnson & Kolodny 1992).

Finally, most men find that they require more time to reach orgasm than before (Masters, Johnson & Kolodny 1992). This can actually be a welcome change to many men and their partners because it allows them more time to enjoy coitus before ejaculation occurs.

As in women, the changes in sexual functioning that accompany the aging process need not be considered a signal to stop sexual activity altogether. In fact, some find that these changes, when approached with a positive, open attitude, pave the way for more intimate, satisfying sexual encounters than they experienced earlier in their lives.

One strategy for adjusting to the physical changes in men is for his partner to increase the amount of genital stimulation (Kaplan 1990). This may help the man to attain and maintain an erection. Although there is no known solution for shortening a refractory period, couples may do well to realize that an erect penis is not needed to enjoy an intimate sexual experience. For those who do not enjoy the longer time required to reach orgasm, increased stimulation of the penis before coitus may be helpful.

Kaplan (1990) recommends that couples learn to take the focus off intercourse and focus instead on the pleasurable sensations that they can experience with other parts of their bodies. Even if he does not get an erection, a man may enjoy having his genitals caressed, or he may caress his partner's genitals to orgasm. Also, the couple may discover for the first time erogenous zones on other parts of their bodies that went unnoticed previously.

SEXUAL DESIRE IN OLDER WOMEN AND MEN

Some older adults experience a decrease in sexual desire as they age. Low sexual desire refers to a lack of interest in sexual activity and is typically accompanied by a low frequency of thinking about or initiating sex.

Low sexual desire is not a problem that is limited to the older population by any means, but it may be more common in this age group. While low desire can have many causes, among postmenopausal women and their male counterparts, it is sometimes attributed to a deficiency in testosterone production (Schiavi, Schreiner-Engel, White & Mandeli 1991).

Testosterone, the hormone responsible for controlling the sex drive, is produced in women and in men from the adrenal glands and the gonads (ovaries and testes), with men producing twelve to sixteen times more testosterone than women. Interestingly, women are much more sensitive to the effects of testosterone than men are, which probably explains the relative similarity in sex drive between the sexes (Masters, Johnson & Kolodny 1992).

Because of menopause and its process of reducing the quantity of hormones produced by the ovaries, women experience a reduction in testosterone production. Typically the reduction is not enough to affect the overall sex drive in women, but in some women it may be noticeable.

While men typically do not experience a reduction in testicular production of testosterone, some men do (Kaplan 1990). This reduction could be thought of as a kind of male menopause. For those who are willing to try it, testosterone replacement therapy seems to bring blood concentrations of testosterone up to a normal range, and with it, a return to normal levels of sexual desire (Davidson 1989).

Low sexual desire may be caused by a number of factors. Abnormally low testosterone levels is only one possible cause. Many psychosocial factors can create the belief that one ought not to be sexually active when "old." A new perspective on aging and sexuality can reduce these factors and bring about a return of the desire.

AGING IN THE GAY MALE AND LESBIAN POPULATIONS

Myths about Aging Homosexuals

The beliefs and stereotypes about aging usually carry a negative connotation. Another prejudice found in our society is homophobia (Herek 1988). When ageism and homophobia come together, they result in a set of stereotypes and beliefs about aging homosexual women and men that is very negative.

Generally aging gay men are stereotyped as unattractive and lonely. Supposedly they crave sex with younger men but are unable to attract such a partner; they are perceived as dissatisfied with their sex lives (Kelly 1977). The stereotype also portrays aging homosexual men as paying for young male prostitutes (Gray & Dressel 1985), unable to develop long-term relationships, and looking for sexual encounters in a "tearoom" or public toilet (Kelly 1977). They are believed to live a secretive life for fear of others' finding out about their "perversion" of homosexuality (Kelly 1977).

Although the literature on lesbian women is not as extensive as it is on gay men, evidence suggests that the stereotypes of aging lesbians and aging gay men are quite similar. Typically, lesbians are perceived as lonely and unattractive, as well as a social embarrassment (Kehoe 1986).

The data available on the behavioral changes and concerns of aging homosexual men and women are even rarer than those for aging heterosexual women and men. Kimmel (1978) asserted that the lack of information about homosexual adult development has contributed to homophobia. Nevertheless, the evidence uncovered thus far suggests that virtually all of the stereotypes reported about aging lesbians and gay men are false.

Kelly (1977), in conducting one of the earliest studies on aging gay men, found that among those who visited "tearooms," the majority were below the age of 36—hardly fitting the image of the "perverted old man" that the stereotype conveys. Additionally, the partners of the men surveyed were usually in the 25 to 44 year age range, and few reported having very young partners. The oldest men in the study were most likely to have partners who were closer to their own age (Kelly 1977). Gray and Dressel (1985) conducted a survey of older gay men and found that having paid for sex was related most strongly to length of time of having been homosexually active rather than age per se. They speculated that the same relationship would likely be found for heterosexual men. In other words, the longer one has been sexually active, whether in a heterosexual or a homosexual orientation, the greater the likelihood is that one would have at some time paid for sex (Gray & Dressel 1985). As homosexual men age, they are also reported to continue a moderately active social life (Gray & Dressel 1985; Kelly 1977), in contradiction of the stereotype of the gay man's becoming increasingly lonely as he ages.

Similarities in Aging Homosexual and Heterosexual Adults

Although many might believe that aging homosexual adults are very different from their heterosexual counterparts, the reality is that the two populations are very similar in terms of the issues that they face as they age. First, there is no evidence to suggest that the changes in sexual functioning in homosexuals are any different from those reported in heterosexuals. Masters and Johnson (1966) could not document any difference in sexual responding for the two groups.

It also seems that the perceived advantages and disadvantages due to changes in sexual physiology are virtually the same for homosexual and heterosexual adults. In a survey of middle-aged homosexual men, Pope and Schulz (1991) reported that increasing age did not predict any change in sexual interest. Over 90 percent of the men in all age groups were moderately to strongly interested in sex. As in the studies of heterosexuals reported earlier in this chapter, cross-sectional comparisons of age groups showed that the older respondents engaged in sex less frequently than the middle-aged respondents did. Kelly (1977) reported that most of the older gay men in his study described their sex lives as satisfactory, a finding consistent with the literature on older heterosexual men and women (Starr & Weiner 1981).

Homosexual adults also seem to be no less susceptible to the doubts about their sexual functioning that sometimes occur when their bodies do not respond they way they used to when they were younger. For instance, Friend (1987) reported that as some gay men age, they may begin to avoid sex or at least become anxious about it. The anxiety seems to come from the changes in erectile function that are normal for all aging men. Friend also postulated that if a gay man and his partner believe the myth that the goal of sex should be orgasm and ejaculation, then they may have problems adjusting to the physiological changes in erectile function that occurs. Some older lesbians are also reluctant to continue to express their sexual feelings, especially after menopause, because they may believe the myths about aging and sexuality (Friend 1987). However, Cole and Rothblum (1990) reported that lesbian women in their survey found that sex was more enjoyable after menopause. One respondent felt that if women were not burdened by ageism, there would be many more reports of sex being better after menopause. Friend (1987) opined that education could resolve most of these anxieties and concerns about sex that accompany aging. Although there are virtually no studies that make direct comparison of homosexuals and het-erosexuals on the psychological adjustment to changes in sexual functioning, studies done on these two populations separately suggest that the concerns are extremely similar, if not the same.

Nonsexual Concerns of Gay Men and Lesbians

Other research on adjustments to aging in the homosexual population suggests that their concerns are very similar to those of heterosexuals. Several surveys of homosexual women and men have been conducted to determine the problems that they have encountered as they have grown older (Kelly 1977; Quam & Whitford 1992). The most frequently reported concern among aging homosex-uals has been their health (Quam & Whitford 1992), undeniably an important concern for aging heterosexuals as well. Other concerns that aging homosexuals and heterosexuals seem to share include loneliness due to the death of friends and relatives, finances, and retirement.

One common concern that crosses gender lines when comparing heterosexuals and homosexuals is the concept known as accelerated aging, a term that refers to an individual's defining himself or herself as old before his or her same-age peers define themselves as old. Friend (1987) hypothesized that gay men are more likely than heterosexual men to experience accelerated aging, which makes the transition to old age more difficult. He also speculated that this phenomenon may be the result of gender role expression rather than sexual orientation. In other words, accelerated aging may occur more among those who hope to be sexually attractive to men. If this is true, then heterosexual women should be affected by accelerated aging as well. Friend's (1987) argument is supported by Laner's (1979) comparison of heterosexual and lesbian women's personal ads. She concluded that the heterosexual women displayed more symptoms of accelerated aging than the lesbian women did.

There is still some disagreement in the literature about whether accelerated aging exists at all for homosexual men. Contrary to Friend's (1987) speculations, Minnigerode (1976) found no evidence to support the notion that gay men are more likely to experience accelerated aging than heterosexual men are. Harry (1982) collected data strongly suggesting that accelerated aging is a developmental issue rather than a premature labeling of the self as old. He found that gay men in their 40s were more likely than either younger or older gay men to be concerned about their age. Thus, this accelerated aging may be a symptom of a midlife crisis.

The one issue that is a unique concern for homosexuals is discrimination based on their sexual orientation. For example, some insurance companies have refused to sell life insurance to gay men once their sexual orientation is discovered (Kelly 1977). Another area in which discrimination becomes a problem is when the death of a lover or close homosexual friend occurs. Because the lovers and friends are often excluded from funeral arrangements and services, the death can be particularly devastating (Friend 1987). This problem has become more noticeable because of the high rate of gay men who have died from AIDS. Hence, it appears that the problems that are of special concern to aging homosexuals are not the result of being homosexual per se but rather the result of being homosexual in a homophobic society (Adelman 1991).

The Advantages of Being an Aging Homosexual

Some evidence suggests that homosexuals who are overt (open) about their sexual orientation may actually have an advantage over heterosexuals and covert ("closeted") homosexuals when dealing with the changes and prejudices associated with aging. Because they have had to cope with the crisis of revealing their homosexuality, they have had the opportunity to develop important coping skills for accepting major upheavals in their lives. These skills play an important role in accepting the many changes that occur as we age, including personal changes and changes in society's perception of us.

Richard Friend (1991) has developed a theory of healthy aging in homosexuals in which he identifies three types of homosexuals: stereotypic, passing, and affirmative. Stereotypic gays are those who accept the negative views held by society of homosexuals and are fearful that their homosexuality will be discovered. They feel guilt, self-hatred, and low self-esteem. Passing homosexuals marginally accept their homosexuality but still believe the heterosexist view of society. Many manage this conflict by distancing themselves from anything that smacks of homosexual lifestyle, including entering into heterosexual marriages so that they can "pass" as straight. Affirmative older lesbians and gay men openly accept their homosexuality. They manage heterosexism by reevaluating homosexuality as something positive.

Friend (1991) theorized that the affirmative group moves into old age more smoothly because they have developed social, cognitive, and behavioral coping techniques that help them to deal with the transition to old age in our youth-oriented society. For example, dealing with the loss of family and friends through relocation or death may be easier because affirmatives have developed crisis competence. By "coming out," they probably lost some friends and family members who could not deal with their sexual orientation. Having dealt successfully with this, they are better equipped to manage the inevitable losses encountered as one ages.

Another reason that affirmative gay men and lesbians adapt to aging so well may be that they have challenged arbitrary gender role behavior. Heterosexuals who have never taken on nontraditional gender role behavior are suddenly forced to do so when their spouse dies. Homosexuals may have challenged these nontraditional gender role behaviors years ago and so are more flexible in handling these adjustments.

Having redefined homosexuality into something positive despite prevalent homophobia and heterosexism, affirmatives may be more equipped to deal with ageism by redefining aging into something positive, too (Adelman 1991; Friend 1991).

Finally, as people age, their circle of family and friends may become smaller due to moving or death, and so their support network becomes smaller and more fragile. Affirmative homosexuals very often develop surrogate families and have a large network of friends, so they are less likely to be left completely alone (Friend 1991).

The evidence and speculation found in the literature to date overwhelmingly suggest that having weathered the consequences of revealing their homosexuality to others and having defined their sexual orientation in a positive manner contribute to the development of skills in homosexual women and men that encourage acceptance of aging in an ageist society (Adelman 1991; Friend 1991, 1987). Quam and Whitford (1992) reported that one respondent experienced an enhanced state of psychological and spiritual well-being because of having weathered the coming-out process in an homophobic society.

Does Friend's (1991) theory imply that heterosexuals are incapable of developing the coping skills necessary for adjusting comfortably to the aging process and the events that accompany it? Hardly. Friend is suggesting only that being homosexual in a heterosexist society does result in an advantage for those who are willing to accept themselves and insist that others do so as well. That advantage is the ability to cope in the face of adversity. Because Friend (1991) defines several categories of homosexuals, he implies variability in adjustment levels within the homosexual community. It is likely that this type of diversity exists in the heterosexual population as well. In other words, among heterosexuals there are likely those who adjust well to aging and those who do not adjust well. Heterosexuals who adjust relatively easily to aging in a youth-oriented society may have had the opportunity to develop healthy coping skills because they faced adversity at some time in their lives, just as the affirmative lesbians and gay men did.

Some evidence in support of this hypothesis comes form Beard's study on centenarians (reviewed by Lee 1992). Beard found that those who lived to be 100 years or older had several characteristics in common, among them the tendency to look ''at the brighter side of life'' (Lee 1992, p. 85). This tendency could be considered an aspect of crisis competence. People who live this length of time are certain to have lost many friends and relatives, perhaps even their own children, to death. Perhaps their reaction to their losses enabled them to develop this sense of crisis competence that is also found among affirmative homosexuals. Beard also found that they were likely to be involved in activities important to them, such as church or volunteer work (Lee 1992), providing them with an extended network of friends who help create a sense of belonging and give emotional support when needed. Similarly, Friend (1991) and others have suggested that the support network that gays and lesbians often develop when they are open about their sexual orientation may provide them with an extended family of many ages that helps to keep them from being alone. One possibility for future research might be to operationalize the concepts in Friend's (1991) theory to determine if they do predict successful aging in both homosexual and heterosexual populations.

SUGGESTIONS FOR RESEARCH

The greatest weakness in the literature on aging and sexual orientation is the relative lack of information compared to that on young heterosexuals. If we are ever to comprehend completely the aging process and the adjustments that accompany it, it is imperative that more research be conducted. Three areas are particularly noticeable in their absence of information.

First is the lack of research on lesbian women. This is not surprising considering that women have typically been overlooked in psychological and medical research. As Kehoe (1986) pointed out, aging lesbians have three strikes against them that make them particularly invisible in the literature: they are women, they are homosexual, and they are old. Society's persistence in ignoring any one of these groups has made it unlikely that women who belong to all three groups will get much attention in the scientific literature (Kehoe 1986).

Another problem with studies on homosexuals is that samples are typically drawn from those who are moderately to highly involved in gay community activities. This may predispose the results to show good adjustment to aging (Quam & Whitford 1992). The community as a whole would be well served by knowing precisely why they have adapted so well. The simplest means to answer this question is to compare them to those who have not adjusted well, and these people are typically more difficult to find. We also need to know if adjustment has anything to do with the disclosure of sexual orientation. Therefore, more effort should be made to locate maladjusted overt homosexuals and well-adjusted covert homosexuals so that proper comparisons can be made.

Finally, very few studies exist in which direct comparisons are made of homosexual and heterosexual aging adults. Many of the comparisons that I have drawn in this chapter were based on studies that showed similar results for the two populations separately. I have maintained throughout that the two groups are likely more similar than different, but confirming research should be done. Considering the evidence that sexual orientation is biologically, and not psychosocially, determined (Dorner 1968; Money & Schwartz 1977) it is important to discover whether these biological differences manifest in psychosocial differences in adjustment to crises.

CONCLUSIONS

Aging is not synonymous with asexuality. The stereotype is that after middle age, adults are not interested, or should not be interested, in sex. The evidence shows very clearly that sex is physically possible and is desired into very old age. Although there are some obvious differences in some of the mechanics of sex for homosexuals and heterosexuals, there are many more similarities between the two groups, and their concerns and fears about aging and sexual functioning are virtually the same. It may be that affirmative homosexuals have an advantage overall in the transition to old age because of the crisis endured during the coming-out process in a homophobic society. This does not mean that heterosexuals cannot or do not have the same advantage. Heterosexuals who are facing their first real crisis, such as aging in an ageist society, will have to develop coping skills to help with their adjustment to old age. In all likelihood, those who have weathered other crises earlier in their lives may adjust more easily. Hence, as there is variability in the homosexual segment of our society with regard to these coping skills, there is likely to be variability in the heterosexual segment of society as well. Thus, once again, homosexuals and heterosexuals may be more alike than different.

REFERENCES

Adelman, M. (1991). Stigma, gay lifestyles, and adjustment to aging: A study of later-life gay men and lesbians. *Journal of Homosexuality, 20* (3–4), 7–32.

Cavallaro, M. L. (1991). Curriculum guidelines and strategies on counseling older women for incorporation into gerontology and counseling coursework. *Educational Gerontology, 17,* 157–166.

Cole, E., & Rothblum, E. (1990). Commentary on "Sexuality and the midlife woman." *Psychology of Women Quarterly, 14,* 509–512.

Davidson, J. (1989). Sexual emotions, hormones, and behavior. *Advances, 6,* 56–58.

Dorner, G. (1968). Hormonal induction and prevention of female homosexuality. *Journal of Endocrinology, 42,* 163–164.

Friend, R. A. (1987). The individual and social psychology of aging: Clinical implications for lesbians and gay men. *Journal of Homosexuality, 14* (1–2), 307–331.

Friend, R. A. (1991). Older lesbian and gay people: A theory of successful aging. *Journal of Homosexuality, 20* (3–4), 99–118.

George, L. K., & Weiler, S. J. (1981). Sexuality in middle and late life. *Archives of General Psychiatry, 38,* 919–923.

Gray, H., & Dressel, P. (1985). Alternative interpretations of aging among gay males. *Gerontologist, 25,* 83–87.

Harry, J. (1982). *Gay children grown up.* New York: Praeger.

Herek, G. M. (1988). Heterosexuals' attitudes toward lesbians and gay men: Correlates and gender differences. *Journal of Sex Research, 25,* 451–477.

Hobson, K. G. (1984). The effects of aging on sexuality. *Health and Social Work, 9* (1), 25–35.

Janus, S. S., & Janus, C. L. (1993). *The Janus report on sexual behavior.* New York: John Wiley & Sons.

Kaplan, H. S. (1990). Sex, intimacy, and the aging process. *Journal of the American Academy of Psychoanalysis, 18,* 185–205.

Kehoe, M. (1986). Lesbians over 65: A triply invisible minority. *Journal of Homosexuality, 12* (3–4), 139–152.

Kelly, J. (1977). The aging male homosexual: Myth and reality. *Gerontologist, 17,* 328–332.

Kimmel, D. C. (1978). Adult development and aging: A gay perspective. *Journal of Social Issues, 34,* 113–130.

Kinsey, A. C., Pomeroy, W. B., & Martin, C. E. (1948). *Sexual behavior in the human male.* Philadelphia: Saunders.

Laner, M. R. (1979). Growing older female: Heterosexual and homosexual. *Journal of Homosexuality, 4,* 267–275.

La Torre, R. P., & Kear K. A. (1977). Attitudes toward sex in the aged. *Archives of Sexual Behavior, 6,* 203–213.

Lee, E. S. (1992). Book review on *Centenarians: The new generation,* by B. B. Beard. *International Journal of Aging and Human Development, 34,* 83–86.

Leiblum, S. R. (1990). Sexuality and the midlife woman. *Psychology of Women Quarterly, 14,* 495–508.

Libman, E. (1989). Sociocultural and cognitive factors in aging and sexual expression: Conceptual and research issues. *Canadian Psychology, 30,* 560–567.

Malatesta, V. J., Chambless, D. L., Pollack, M., & Cantor, A. (1988). Widowhood, sexuality, and aging: A lifespan analysis. *Journal of Sex and Marital Therapy, 14,* 49–62.

Masters, W. H., & Johnson, V. E. (1966). *Human sexual response.* Boston: Little, Brown.

Masters, W. H., Johnson, V. E., & Kolodny, R. C. (1992). *Human sexuality* (4th ed.). New York: HarperCollins.

Minnigerode, F. A. (1976). Age status labeling in homosexual men. *Journal of Homosexuality, 1* (13), 273–276.

Money, J., & Schwartz, M. (1977). Dating, romantic and nonromantic friendships, and sexuality in 17 early-treated adrenogenital females, aged 16–25. In P. A. Lee et al. (Eds.), *Congenital adrenal hyperplasia.* Baltimore: University Park Press.

Mulligan, T., & Moss, C. R. (1991). Sexuality and aging in male veterans: A cross-sectional study of interest, ability, and activity. *Archives of Sexual Behavior, 20,* 17–25.

Pocs, O., & Godow, A. G. (1977). Can students view parents as sexual beings? *Family Coordinator, 26* (1), 31–36.

Pope, M. and Schulz, R. (1991). Sexual attitudes and behavior in midlife and aging homosexual males. *Journal of Homosexuality, 20* (3–4), 169–177.

Quam, J. K., & Whitford, G. S. (1992). Adaptation and age-related expectations of older gay and lesbian adults. *Gerontologist, 32,* 367–374.

Renshaw, D. C. (1984). Geriatric sex problems. *Journal of Geriatric Psychiatry, 17* (2), 123–138.

Schiavi, R. C., Schreiner-Engel, P., Mandeli, J., Schanzer, H., & Cohen, E. (1990). Healthy aging and male sexual function. *American Journal of Psychiatry, 147,* 766–771.

Schiavi, R. C., Schreiner-Engel, P., White, D., & Mandeli, J. (1991). The relationship between pituitary-gonadal function and sexual behavior in healthy aging men. *Psychosomatic Medicine, 53,* 363–374.

Starr, B. D., & Weiner, M. B. (1981). *On sex and sexuality in the mature years.* New York: Stein & Day.

Winn, R. L., & Newton, N. (1982). Sexuality in aging: A study of 106 cultures. *Archives of Sexual Behavior, 11,* 283–298.

24

Gender, Sexuality, and Sexual Behavior in an Age of Sexual Epidemic

Nancy L. Roth and Raul Goyo-Shields

The late twentieth century has been characterized as an era of sexual epidemic that represents a historical moment when not only has HIV/AIDS reached pandemic proportions but sickness and health have come to be the dominant metaphors of the age. Other sexual "viruses," including unwanted pregnancy and sexual violence, have come to be called "epidemic" (Singer 1993). HIV/AIDS has become a dominant signifier of sexual epidemic (Treichler 1988b, 1992). Certain sexual behaviors have been identified as primary avenues of transmission, the syndrome is widely associated with homosexuality in European contexts, and no vaccine or cure has been discovered. In the grips of sexual epidemic, society struggles to find interventions to stem the spread of both the physical virus (HIV) that is the putative cause of AIDS and the social "viruses" associated with it.

Safer sex education has emerged as a key strategy in stemming the transmission of HIV in the absence of a cure or vaccine, though it has been suggested that even if a cure or vaccine was found, it would not reduce the spread of the virus, as continued transmission has as much to do with the social stigmas that prevent effective prevention and treatment as with the lack of a medical "magic bullet" (Brandt 1985). Such programs have brought to the fore in public arenas questions about what is meant by the terms *gender, sexuality,* and *sexual behavior.* Such questions challenge both academic theories about gender and sexuality and identity politics.

This chapter explores previous theoretical conceptions of gender, sexuality, and sexual behavior and highlights an alternative theory that overcomes some of their limitations. Using safer sex brochures published around the world from the mid-1980s to the present time, we argue that while safer sex discourses can be shown to be decentering some oppressive sexuality norms, they reproduce oppressive gender norms.

SOME THEORETICAL CONCEPTIONS OF GENDER AND SEXUALITY

Freud's Psychological Understanding of Gender

Freud's interpretation of gender is biologically and psychologically based. He suggested that the biological sex drive is at the root of human needs to create and procreate and that gender preference is psychologically based. Although humans tend to develop a preference for members of a particular sex when they enter puberty, they have a general predisposition toward bisexuality. He argued that all humans are capable of making "a homosexual object-choice and have in fact made one in their unconscious" (Freud 1962). However, he did not consider the possibility of homosexual object choice in his discussions of incestuous desires. Because Freud based his arguments about gender on his discussion of incest rather than on his discussion of homosexual object choice, his gender theory makes no allowances for homosexuality (Butler 1990).

Lacan's Discursive Understanding of Gender

Lacan disagreed with Freud's argument that gender is rooted in biology and psychology. He offered a perception of gender as discursive: gender is produced and reproduced linguistically within social structures that both contribute to, and are in turn affected by, the ways in which gender is constructed. He further suggested that the social structures that construct gender are oppressive. In this system, women can never be acting subjects because they lack the only attribute that marks gender: the phallus (Lacan 1977).

Kristeva's Semiotic Alternative

Kristeva accepted Lacan's assertion of the power of oppressive discourse in constructing gender but suggested that gender can also be constructed at a pre-discursive level she calls semiotic. At that level, gender can be constructed as multidimensional and therefore open to multiple interpretations. In this way, her argument questioned Lacan's founding of gender in a single discourse: the having or lack of a phallus. However, as she based her critique of Lacan in an argument about the fundamental nature of maternity, she fell into the same discursive trap, though from women's perspective (Kristeva 1986).

Wittig's Subversion of the Heterosexual Construct of Gender

While Kristeva disputed Lacan's perception of gender as defined in a single discourse, Wittig challenged the assumptions of heterosexuality implied in both authors' works. Wittig argued that gender is discursively created and conceals the power structures that privilege one group at the expense of another. The patterns of domination that lead to oppression are the source of the artifacts we know as masculine and feminine. Furthermore, she argued that gender is truly applicable to women since only they are marked; men are seen as the norm, or the universally human, and women as deviations from it. Wittig argued for the need to eradicate gender so that women can achieve the status of acting subject, a status currently reserved only for men.

In Wittig's theory, gender is seen as a construction of a heterosexual society that seeks to define women within the narrow confines of reproducer of the species. This definition not only limits the range of possibilities for women but simultaneously perpetuates the heterosexual power structure. Consequently, Wittig's political agenda involves the undermining of gender by manipulating language and thereby challenging the assumption that gender is essentially binary in nature (Wittig 1992).

Problematizing the Binary Understanding of Gender

Recent theorists have offered critiques of the gender theories of Freud, Lacan, Kristeva, and Wittig. Butler's (1990) comprehensive critique builds on the strengths of each theory and leads to construction of an alternative gender theory (Butler 1993) that informs our analysis of safer sex pamphlets in this chapter. Butler used Lacan's concept of gender as discursive to challenge Freud's suggestion of biological and psychological bases for gender and employed Wittig to challenge Freud's assumption of compulsory heterosexuality underlying the incest taboo. She adopted Kristeva's notion of multiple meanings for gender to challenge Lacan's view of gender as in a single discourse. Butler in turn questioned Kristeva's semiotic alternative because it is rooted in her perception of the maternal construct and critiqued Wittig for ignoring the preformative nature of discourse—the extent to which labeling in discourse renders something as existing—for example, gender.

AN ALTERNATIVE THEORY OF GENDER, SEXUALITY, AND SEXUAL BEHAVIOR

Based on her critiques of previous gender theories, Butler (1990, 1993) offered an alternative theory of gender that overcomes the limitations of earlier theories. The paragraphs that follow highlight the salient features of Butler's alternative gender theory and then show how it can be extended to address the issues of sexuality and sexual behavior that are central to discussions of HIV prevention in an age of sexual epidemic.

Butler's Alternative Gender Theory

Gender Is Not Grounded in Biology or Psychology

Following Lacan, an alternative theory of gender would remove biological sex and psychological features of individuals as grounds for gender distinctions, leaving gender as a concept that has meaning only because of the social forces that produce and reproduce sedimented or established meanings. The argument that gender is grounded in biological sex began to be questioned by Lacan (1977) and Money and Ehrhardt (1972), who suggested that a person's sex is biologically determined but that gender is a social construction. This work offered an important boost to feminists who wished to argue against biological determinism and to assert that the gender roles to which women and men were expected to conform were socially constructed roles that were originally grounded in biological differences but in their current form had little or no basis in the biological differences between the two sexes (Friedan 1974; Maccoby & Jacklin 1974; Morgan 1977; Scott 1992; Sterling & Balaban 1993).

That argument encountered limitations, however. If there is no necessary association between biological sex and gender, how did gender construction come to be so closely associated with biological sex? Foucault (1978) argued that biological sex and gender are both discursive; the perception that there are two biological sexes is constructed through the same set of social forces that suggest that there are two genders. There is no particular reason that certain physical characteristics are selected as signifying sex or a particular sex; some of those omitted from the determining bundle could just as easily be seen as significant and might result in a classification scheme quite different from the currently accepted male-female. In addition, certain chromosomal anomalies highlight the important role of social construction in our understanding of sex. In cases where genital characteristics categorize a person as one sex but chromosomal characteristics suggest another or are anomalous, the determination of which characteristics should predominate is often left to physicians and parents (Butler 1990; Foucault 1978, 1980b; Sterling & Balaban 1993).

The argument against psychological foundations for gender is similar to the argument against biological foundations. Psychological constructions of gender are based in the incest taboo. When the incest taboo is fully explicated, it can be seen that underlying it is an assumption of heterosexuality. The incest taboo has meaning only if it is assumed that the desires being prohibited are heterosexual. Compulsory heterosexuality can be seen as a social construction, and the same social forces that produce and reproduce compulsory heterosexuality can be shown to produce the incest taboo. This would suggest that theories that ground gender differences in psychological models that posit the incest taboo as the basis for gender are also founded on a social construction of difference that has no "real" basis. The assumption of a psychological base for gender is no more solid than the assumption of a biological base (Butler 1990; Weeks 1985). Gender may come to be meaningful without grounding in any other sphere, and our understanding of psychology, biology, and other spheres may in fact be mediated by gender.

Gender Is Discursively Performative

In the absence of biological or psychological bases for the construction of gender, Butler (1990, 1993) argued that gender is discursively performative. That is, in the process of naming sets of ritualized acts as gender, gender is produced. Through repetitive acts, gender norms are established. Norms are to be understood in this case as averages. Just as when the average height of a group of people is calculated, no single member of the group may be the "average height," gender norms can be understood as an average that no single person may reify. The norms are sedimented by repeated citation—when formulaic sets of behaviors that have come to mean a particular gender are reiterated (Butler 1993).

Gender Identity Exists Only at Moments in Time

If gender is discursively performative, then particular gender identities are ephemeral. They exist only at moments in time and change as the norm is decentered by repetition of behaviors that are further from the norm. Just as outlying data points can have a strong pull on the average, reiteration of behaviors sanctioned by the norm but varying from the norm change the norm itself. Under such conditions, there is a possibility for limited agency (Butler 1990). Such agency should not be seen as the act of a choosing subject; rather it is constrained to the behaviors that are sanctioned (Butler 1993). When identity is viewed in this more fluid way, it becomes clear that strict identification with a particular set of characteristics can become politically constraining. By claiming a particular set of characteristics, identity politics limits the possibilities for variation and in so doing reinforces the very norms that they are attempting to displace (Butler 1990).

Therefore, Butler's political project is not about whether to repeat the actions through which gender derives its meaning but rather how to repeat them in order to subvert and finally displace entrenched notions of gender. She suggests that cultural practices and configurations that blur the gender lines (homosexuality, bisexuality, etc.) can operate in this manner. In addition, she suggests that both parody and citation can be used subversively to undermine sedimented gender norms.

Gender Is Performed Within Existing Power Relations

Butler warns against postulating about a normative sexuality that somehow exists outside the realm of power relations. Since sexuality is produced within discursive practices, any attempt at theorizing about sexuality that precedes discourse "is a cultural impossibility":

If subversion is possible, it will be a subversion from within the terms of the law, through the possibilities that emerge when the law turns against itself and spawns unexpected permutations of itself. The culturally constructed body will then be liberated, neither to its "natural" past, nor to its original pleasures, put to an open future of cultural possibilities. (Butler 1990, p. 93)

Implications of Alternative Gender Theory for Theories of Sexuality

Carried to its limits, the alternative gender theory calls into question categories of sexuality as they are commonly understood in European-white contexts. If biological sex and gender are both discursively performative, then categories of sexuality that are based on the sameness or difference of the sexes (or genders) of the participants become meaningless. Possibilities of varied performances of sexuality proliferate or multiply; not only does the sex or gender of the participants become meaningless, but a plethora of other possible ways of categorizing sexuality become possible. Sexuality could be characterized by the number of people who participate, by the types of acts engaged in, by the extent to which affectional bonds are present, or by the extent to which sexual activity is limited to a particular partner or partners (Sterling & Balaban 1993). More important, such categories would be multiple and fluid so that participation in one would not preclude participation in another. Political action would not be tied to identification with any particular category but rather would inhere in the subversive repetition of activities that call into question the norms through parody or citation.

Implications of Alternative Gender Theory for Theories of Sexual Practice

The alternative gender theory also brings to the fore questions concerning what constitutes sexual practice. Exposing the heterosexual assumption behind the incest taboo highlights the assumptions of compulsory heterosexuality that undergird conceptions of what constitutes sexual practice. Implicit in compulsory heterosexuality is a view of sexual activity as having the possibility of leading to procreation. In the absence of such assumptions, a wider range of activity might be viewed as sexual. Notions of sexual activity that do not involve mixed-sex pairs, penile penetration, ejaculation, genital stimulation, and so forth can proliferate (Weeks, 1985).

THE DISCOURSES OF GENDER, SEXUALITY, AND SEXUAL BEHAVIOR IN AN AGE OF SEXUAL EPIDEMIC

The alternative gender theory can help to inform questions of gender, sexuality, and sexual practice that have emerged in this era of sexual epidemic. While medical scientists have sought information about the epidemiology, etiology, virology, and immunology related to HIV/AIDS, community activists, and more recently public health officials, have sought means to reduce transmission (reception) of the virus. Among the earliest attempts to reduce transmission in the United States were efforts by gay activist Larry Kramer to convince gay men not to have sex. (Kramer 1978 was an argument against viewing gay liberation as a sexual liberation. It was followed by a series of editorials in gay community newspapers, particularly in the *New York Native,* that framed the argument in terms of HIV transmission prevention.)

Kramer's efforts met with resistance similar in some ways to the resistance against Nancy Reagan's "just say no" (to drugs) campaign. But there was a particular resistance to Larry Kramer's message in gay male communities. Gay men were just coming to see themselves as an identity group drawn together by the opinion that gay sex is good sex. Prohibitions against gay sex resembled the vitriol spewed against gay men by their detractors and ran counter to the sexual proliferation—pushing the boundaries of definitions of behaviors considered to be sexual, experimenting with various types and quantities of relationships, disassociating gender from biological sex, selecting sexual partners without reference to gender—that characterized some gay political and social movements at the time the community began to be aware of HIV/AIDS (Altman 1986; Patton 1990, 1994).

One response to Kramer's version of the campaign was the promotion of safer sex. As it became understood that HIV can be transmitted through various sexual activities, activists in the gay communities (and later, community clinics partially funded with local, state, and federal dollars and public health agencies) developed a variety of pamphlets designed to promote "safer sex." A repository of such pamphlets is held by the Centers for Disease Control and Prevention National AIDS Clearinghouse. To investigate how the alternative gender theory presented in this chapter informs understanding of the discourses of gender, sexuality, and sexual behavior in an age of sexual epidemic, we performed an analysis of 336 safer sex pamphlets produced by governments, health agencies, and activists from the mid-1980s through the early 1990s. We examined the historical context of the pamphlets' creation (which is understood through the discourses that constitute the present-day conceptions of history), the pressing concerns of the sexual epidemic, and the extent to which oppressive norms are reproduced or decentered in these discourses (Weedon 1987).

Gender

Representations of gender in the safer sex pamphlets studied reproduce oppressive gendered discourses. As noted by Kristeva, gender is portrayed as necessarily binary. Men are depicted as the norm and women as "other." Women who do not conform to social norms are seen "not real women."

The general public is white, male, and heterosexual and does not inject drugs. The pamphlets are obviously targeted toward particular audiences. Their cover photos or graphics pictorially depict the intended audience; in cases where the targeted audience's first language may not be English, another language is used; and except in cases of pamphlets targeted toward gay men, the intended audience is identified verbally on the front cover. (This may be due to the fact that pamphlets produced using U.S. federal funds are prohibited by the Helms amendment of 1988 from promoting homosexuality.) Brochures produced in the United States, for example, are targeted at gay men (or men who have sex with men), women, African-Americans, Native Americans, Latinos, Asian-Americans, injecting drug users, and the general public. Among the sample examined for this chapter, there is only one brochure targeted specifically toward generic men. This absence would suggest that within the existing power structure, it is assumed that the general public is white, heterosexual, and male and does not inject drugs. Materials that are not addressed to a specific identity group can be assumed to be addressed primarily to white men (Wittig 1992). Watney (1987) notes a similar phenomenon with regard to mass media representations in general.

Women are sexually passive. Women are represented as sexual partners of men and as mothers of infants. For example, a Hennepin County (Minnesota) 1986 brochure entitled *AIDS: What Women Should Know,* answers the question, "Who has AIDS?" by stating that "People at higher risk are":

- Men who have sex with other men, and men who have sex with both men and women.
- Intravenous drug users, specifically people who share needles.
- *Women who are sexual partners of persons at high risk.*
- *Children born to women infected with the AIDS virus* (Hennepin County, December 1986, emphasis added).

This phenomenon reflects and reinforces societal notions that women are passive in sexual encounters. If a woman becomes infected during intercourse with a man, she is the passive partner of an infected man, not a full participant (Patton 1994).

Some women are not women. In seeming contradiction, a few brochures represent particular categories of women—women of color and sex workers—as people who have active sex lives or sexual desires. An example is one produced by the Hispanic AIDS Forum (1988), which says to women: "HIV can be transmitted through sexual contact. If you're sexually active, you may become infected with the virus and infect others, even if you have no symptoms." The contrast between this representation of Latinas as sexually active and the earlier example of European and other white women as passive raises the possibility that Latinas are not perceived to be members of the category women; if Latinas are sexually active and "real" women are not, then, by definition, Latinas become "not women." Such a reading is informed by historical precedent; people of color are seen as sexually exotic, and "color" is perceived as spectacle (Reid-Pharr 1993).

The pamphlets suggest that female sex workers actively transmit the virus to their unsuspecting male customers. "Real" women are passive; "prostitutes" are active and dangerous. Yet medical evidence suggests that male-to-female transmission is more likely than female-to-male transmission (Corea 1992; Patton 1993, 1994). The incongruence becomes particularly striking when one considers that the pamphlets addressed to women do not warn female sex workers of the dangers of transmission to them by their male clients, but those addressed to the general public note the dangers of "having sex with prostitutes." For example, in a pamphlet produced by the Louisiana Department of Public Health that has one side addressed to men and another addressed to women, the side for women suggests that a woman can be exposed to HIV if her "sex partner has had sex with a prostitute." The side for men suggests that a man can be exposed to HIV if he has "had sex with a prostitute" (Louisiana 1987). Such discursive construction suggests that in the current heterosexual power structure, women who do sex work are not considered to be women and are therefore not worthy of being protected from the virus, but men who have sex with prostitutes are "men" and must be protected.

Some must be protected and others must be policed. Pamphlets targeted toward the general public emphasize the importance of choosing one's partner carefully (Metts & Fitzpatrick 1992). "You cannot tell if someone is infected with the AIDS virus by looking at him or her," warns a pamphlet from the Michigan Department of Health (1987). Therefore it is important for the general public to know their sexual partners. They are warned to

find out about a person's sexual history before you have sex. . . . Remember that people who are in high-risk groups, who have had partners in high risk groups, or who have had many different partners have a much higher risk of being infected than people who have had only one or a few partners in low risk groups. (Massachusetts 1988)

On the other hand, gay men are warned to avoid risky behavior and adopt routine use of condoms. For example, the Lesbian and Gay Health Project of North Carolina (1989) offers a pamphlet entitled *Guidelines for AIDS Risk Reduction.* Typical of pamphlets produced by gay community organizations at the time, it labels a variety of sexual behaviors as "safest," "probably safe, possibly unsafe," and "unsafe." Patton (1994) suggests that the differences between pamphlets produced for the general public and those produced for gay men produce and reproduce societal norms that label gay sex as deviant and general public sex as normal. Such discourse implies that if members of the general public are simply careful enough to avoid having sex with deviants, they will protect themselves, but gay men must police their own behavior to avoid transmitting the virus.

Discussion

Representations of gender in safer sex pamphlets highlight the importance of Foucault's admonition not to view proliferation of discourse as necessarily liberatory (Foucault 1980a; Singer 1993). Safer sex discourses reproduce many societal norms: they cast non–drug using, white, male, heterosexuals as the gender norm, sexually passive females as the only females worthy of the label, and compulsory heterosexuality as the only acceptable expression of sexuality. As predicted by the alternative theory, gendered discourses in this time of sexual epidemic are constrained by the same social forces that construct sex and gender in general: the perceived necessary binary nature of gender and compulsory heterosexuality. It should be noted, however, that many of the pamphlets cited in this section are from the late 1980s. Pamphlets of the early 1990s portray a shift in some discursive norms, as described in the next section.

Sexuality

While oppressive gender norms are reproduced in the safer sex pamphlets studied, there has been some decentering of sexuality norms. As suggested by Butler (1993), repetition of discourse that cites the norm but deviates from it shifts the norm. Sexuality, which in the early years of the epidemic was represented as binary group membership (one was a member of a group or not—for example, heterosexual or not), is represented in more recent pamphlets as a spectrum of (sexual) behaviors.

Sexuality as Group Membership

Safer sex pamphlets produced in the mid- to late 1980s represented sexuality as group identity. Pamphlets suggested that only people who belong to certain groups identified as being at high risk of transmitting the virus, or those having sex with members of high-risk groups, needed to be concerned about safer sex. Those who were not members of high-risk groups were simply warned to screen their potential partners carefully for membership in such groups. A pamphlet produced by the U.S. Department of Health and Human Services (1987) is typical:

Persons at increased risk of [HIV] infection include homosexual and bisexual men; present or past intravenous drug users; persons with clinical or laboratory evidence of infection such as signs or symptoms compatible with AIDS or AIDS-related illnesses; persons born in countries where heterosexual transmission is thought to play a major role in the spread of [HIV] (for example, Haiti and Central African countries); male or female prostitutes and their sex partners, sex partners of infected persons or persons at increased risk; persons with hemophilia who have received clotting factor products; and newborn infants of high-risk or infected mothers. . . . Communities can help prevent AIDS by vigorous efforts to educate and inform their populations about the illness, with special emphasis on educational activities for members of high risk groups.

Such pamphlets reflect use of the Centers for Disease Control and Prevention (CDC) epidemiological categories to define sexuality categories for the purposes of prevention education. CDC first noted the signs of the syndrome that has come to be known as HIV/AIDS among homosexuals, heroin users, hemophiliacs, and Haitians (Shilts 1987), and those became the reporting categories for physicians who had patients with the relevant symptoms to inform the CDC. The fact that the first people to evidence symptoms in mass numbers were homosexual men led many epidemiologists to believe that the syndrome was a result of certain lifestyle features. Early research investigated correlations between the use of certain inhalants popular in the gay male community and AIDS and suggested that others who became infected engaged in "deviant" activities similar to those engaged in by gay men (Patton 1994). By the time that HIV was identified in 1984, and blood and semen had been identified as the main vectors of transmission, the message that HIV/AIDS was associated with certain high-risk groups had been well established.

Sexuality as a Spectrum of Sexual Behaviors

A shift in the discourse of safer sex pamphlets occurred after the publication of the surgeon general's report on AIDS (1988). That report represented the first government move from a discussion of membership or nonmembership in high-risk groups to a discussion of a range of sexual behaviors that carry various levels of risk. Pamphlets produced after 1990 tend to mirror this change and to carry further the separation between group membership and sexual behavior. For example, a 1989 pamphlet from AIDS Project Utah states:

AIDS is transmitted through certain kinds of sexual contact, receiving certain contaminated blood products, and sharing needles. Despite certain risks, physical intimacy (as well as emotional intimacy) is important for overall health. The safe expression of intimacy comes from knowing that specific risks are related to certain sexual practices.

A wallet-sized card distributed by the San Mateo County (California) AIDS Project and funded by the California Department of Health Services (1990) says:

Unless you are absolutely certain that neither you nor your partner have been exposed to AIDS, you should:

1. *Always* use a condom during vaginal and anal intercourse. If you can't or don't wish to use a condom, engage in *other* activities only.
2. Do *not* use IV drugs, but if you must, don't share your works, but if you do, clean your works with bleach between users.
3. Because AIDS can be transmitted from a pregnant woman to a fetus, if you are considering pregnancy, consult your physician for more information.

The move from sexuality as binary group membership to sexuality as a spectrum of sexual behaviors was spurred by recognition by activists working in gay community–based HIV/AIDS programs that simply "being" homosexual did not increase one's risk for HIV infection. Indeed, "doing" certain sexual activities was what increased a person's risk—and all homosexually active men did not engage in risky sex. Because sex that involves penile penetration and ejaculation without (condom) protection is the most effective sexual transmitter of HIV, the mistaken assumption that "homosexual lifestyle" increased one's risk of HIV infection may have been based in part in a transference of heterosexual norms about what constitutes sex onto same-gender sex. In heterosexual circles, an activity is often not considered to be sex unless it involves penile penetration (Singer 1993). By extension, it could be assumed that gay male sex must also involve analogous penile penetration. However, research associated with HIV/AIDS prevention has found that a variety of activities are considered to constitute gay male sex; anal sex is not the defining feature for all gay men (see, for example, Ross & Rosser 1991). The move to discussion of multiple behaviors with a range of risk begins to ameliorate the conflation of group membership and behavior found in the earlier brochures.

In addition, gay identity politics turned on reclamation of a negative group identity through a variety of discursive moves that accentuated the positive. In the late 1970s, homosexual identity groups adopted the term *gay* to describe themselves in the face of social norms that termed homosexuality as dismal and homosexuals as depressed (Chesebro 1980; Darsey 1981, 1991). In the 1990s, activists have reclaimed the derisive *queer,* a move that can be interpreted as a subversive, parodic repetition of the norm so as to decenter it (Abelove, Barale & Halperin 1993; Ringer 1994; Signorile 1993). Using the positive identity as a focal point for targeting safer sex messages offered the possibility for both positive and negative consequences for gay activists. On one hand, it might consolidate group identification; on the other hand, it might reinfect group identification with the already existing social norm that to be homosexual was to be a "risky" person (Crimp 1988; Patton, 1994; Treichler, 1988a, 1992).

The move from risk group membership to multiple behaviors was also spurred by a realization among AIDS activists that use of identity group labels in targeting safer sex messages was keeping the messages from being perceived as relevant by certain groups of people. As Rist (1993) noted, there are men across the United States who do not consider themselves to be "gay," "queer," or "bisexual" but who engage with other men in behaviors that can transmit the virus. Such men would not heed messages targeted toward gay men because they do not consider themselves to be gay.

Similarly, there are a number of customs characteristic of certain contexts where men engage in acts that elsewhere might be labeled sex but in those contexts have other labels (for example, prison sex or the domestic arrangements found among migrant workers; Patton 1994). Further, many women who identify themselves as lesbians have had sex with men in the past or have sex with men currently. Simple identification as a lesbian does not mean that a woman has not engaged in behaviors that might transmit or receive the virus, as is popularly believed (Hollingbaugh 1994; Patton 1994). Indeed, a 1989 New Zealand pamphlet for women identifies lesbians as "low-risk partners."

Discussion

The displacement of risk group membership discourse by risk behavior discourse is not complete. Pamphlets continue to note that although the syndrome was first identified among certain groups, it is now spreading to others. This displacement may be due to the fact that although the discourse in safe sex brochures has changed, that found in the popular media tends to reinforce the earlier conception (Patton 1994). In addition, there appears to be a strong pattern toward disassociating the subject from "others" who get sick (Roth in press; Roth & Stephenson in press).

However, the move from constructing sexuality as binary—in terms of the group (heterosexual) to which a person does or does not belong—to constructing it as multiple—in terms of the variety of behaviors engaged in—may be interpreted as an example of a decentering of the norm by repetition of a sanctioned position that cites the norm but does not reproduce it exactly. During the era when public health officials were discussing risk groups, AIDS activists in the gay communities were beginning to discuss risk in terms of a spectrum of behavior rather than binary group membership. When the surgeon general invited representatives of gay communities to provide input into the surgeon general's report on AIDS (1988), they emphasized the importance of highlighting risk behaviors rather than groups and demonstrated how this was already being done within gay communities (Roth 1988). The surgeon general and his staff took this advice; the norm was decentered, though it is still very much in evidence.

Representing sexuality as multiple behaviors rather than as binary group membership can also be interpreted as a move toward viewing sexuality as performative. Such a representation is consistent with that suggested in the alternative theory. In addition, the move away from using identity groups as markers for sexuality reinforces the argument that group identification can be limiting when change is important. Under the pressure to promote behaviors that would save lives, AIDS activists, many involved with gay identity group politics, found it more efficacious to use behavior discourse that provided more opportunities for variation than to use the confining discourse of group identity (Holligbaugh 1994). The move from discussion of risk group membership to multiple behaviors of varying risk can begin to address the issue of men who have sex with men, but it does not resolve those associated with "what counts as sex, with whom, and in what context," which is addressed in the next section.

Sexual Behavior

As the discourse of multiple sexual behaviors began to decenter sexuality norms, an additional range of terms came to be contested. Issues concerning which behaviors could be characterized as sexual, with whom they were performed, what constituted safety, and for whom became important. To date there has been insufficient analysis of these issues.

Some Sexual Behavior Is Not Sex

The change is discourse norms from sexuality as group membership to behaviors was based, in part, on the assumption that a wider range of people would identify with the behaviors identified as risky than with the groups so identified. However, research suggests that individuals who engage in risky behaviors perceive themselves as being at lower risk of negative outcomes than the average person who engages in such behavior (Roth & Stephenson in press; Weinstein 1987, 1989). Individuals rationalize their risk in a number of ways. In the case of sexual epidemic, such rationalizations may include individual determinations that engaging in certain behaviors with certain people does not constitute sexual behavior.

The pamphlets' discourse suggests an underlying belief that engaging in any of the behaviors listed, with any partner, in any context, constitutes sexual behavior. Many provide long lists of activities in terms of their level of risk. For example, a Krames Publications (California, 1991) pamphlet lists:

No-Risk Sex
—Masturbating yourself
—Fantasy, phone sex, using (not sharing) sex toys

Very Low-Risk Sex
—Kissing with your lips closed
—Caressing, sensual massage
—Hugging and rubbing bodies together
—Masturbating your partner using a rubber barrier

Low-Risk Sex
—Vaginal intercourse using a latex condom
—Oral sex on partner using a latex barrier
—Wet kissing with your lips open
—Urine contacting partner's skin ("watersports")

Moderate-Risk Sex
—Oral/anal contact ("rimming")
—Oral sex on a woman without a barrier
—Anal intercourse using a condom
—Inserting fingers, hand or fist into anus or vagina
—Masturbating your partner without using a barrier

High-Risk Sex
—Anal or vaginal sex without a condom
—Sexual activity that causes bleeding or injury
—Oral sex on a man without a condom

First, not all of these would be considered to be sexual activities by all people. Under the influence of compulsory heterosexuality, many consider only those that involve penile penetration to be "real sex."

Second, preliminary research suggests that people who use lower-risk or safer sex practices use them with some partners and not others. For example, female sex workers report using condoms with clients but not with their primary sex partners (Bellis 1990; Campbell 1991; Patton 1994), and intravenous drug users report using condoms with casual sex partners but not with their primary sex partners (Ross, Wodak & Gold 1992). Some men who have female primary partners and engage in casual sex with males call the casual encounters "messing around," which is considered to be a different category of activity from the sexual behaviors engaged in with their female primary partners (Humphreys 1970; Patton 1990). These data suggest that the context of the behavior, the gender of the partner, and the type of relationship, in addition to the type of behavior, may be factors in people's constructions of what counts as sexual behavior and therefore may enter in decisions about the safety precautions. Such distinctions are not found in the safer sex pamphlets analyzed.

Monogamy Is Not Always Exclusive

Many of the pamphlets suggest that sex within mutually monogamous relationships is safe. For example, a 1993 pamphlet from the Whitman Walker Clinic in Washington, D.C., notes, "For individuals who know their HIV status and who are not infected, a faithful, mutually monogamous relationship will prevent infection." Yet monogamy means different things to different people. For example, Patton (1994) cites the case of a person who considered monogamy to be geographically bounded. Research on women sex workers suggested that some consider themselves to be monogamous if they do not have sex without recompense with anyone but their primary sexual partner (Campbell 1991). Research with gay men found that some consider themselves to be monogamous if they do not have ongoing relationships with others beside their primary partners (Hollingbaugh 1994; Ross & Rosser 1988). The safer sex pamphlets studied do not take into account varying constructions of what constitutes monogamy in giving advice about safer sexual behaviors.

Safety Is Not Always Safe

Safer sex pamphlets make the assumption that sexual behaviors that preclude transmission of the HIV virus are safe, low risk, or at least safer for all involved. An Allen County, Ohio (1987), brochure answers the question "What is safer sex?" by stating that safer sex:

- is deciding whether or not to have intercourse. Abstinence (not having intercourse) is the surest way not to get AIDS.
- is respecting yourself and your partner.
- can prevent AIDS as well as other sexually transmitted diseases.
- is limiting the number of sexual partners.
- is knowing the sexual history of your partner.

- is the proper use of condoms before and during any sexual activity.
- is preventing the exchange of body fluids:
  semen
  vaginal fluids
  blood
  feces
- is avoiding unprotected anal, vaginal and oral intercourse.

This brochure, though produced by Planned Parenthood of Central Ohio, ignores features of sex that have made sex unsafe for many women throughout
history: risks of pregnancy (for women who have sex with men), violence,
misogyny, nonconsensual domination, and abuse (Corea 1992; Patton 1994;
Singer 1993). These omissions raise the question of for whom safer sex cam-
paigns were intended to keep sex safe. As women have often felt at a power
disadvantage in mixed-sex situations and occasionally in same-sex situations, it
would seem that powerful gender relation norms are reproduced in safer sex
pamphlets. The assumption that stemming virus transmission alone will make
sex safe suggests that the safety of women is not of primary concern. Even
pamphlets addressed to women mention the possibility of pregnancy only in the
context of possible transmission of HIV to fetuses during pregnancy and do not
mention concerns about violence, though research suggests that some women
who request that their male partners use condoms are subjected to violence as
a result (Fullilove, Fullilove, Haynes & Gross 1990).

Discussion

Defining behaviors that count as sex, monogamy, and safer sex in an age of
sexual epidemic is working in contested areas as discursive norms shift. That
the issues are arising at all, and in public health, education, and political arenas,
can be explained by the alternative gender theory presented in this chapter. The
theory describes the movement from sexuality as binary to sexuality as multiple
as decentering a number of norms. Sex and gender or partners become irrelevant
to sexuality; sexual behaviors are described in terms of whether they involve a
sheet of latex, not whether they involve mixed-gender partners. The brochures
emphasize the doing of behaviors and in so doing name them as sexual behaviors, thus demonstrating that gender and sexuality can be seen as discursively
performative.

However, the issue of what constitutes safer sex resurfaces the heterosexual
power structure. That existing norms allow unwanted pregnancy and violence
to be ignored in discussions about making sex safer suggests that existing social
forces value men more than women; it is important to stem the spread of a virus
that may kill males, but staunching the excess of violence and unwanted pregnancy that kill females is not to be included in the list of what makes sex safe.
Singer (1993) extends this argument to suggest that safer sex pamphlets send

the message that heterosexual family values constitute safer sex. All one needs to do to be safe is to conform to the heterosexual norm. The strong currents of compulsory heterosexuality that underlie safer sex pamphlets are indicators that many norms have yet to be decentered.

CONCLUSION

Summary

In this era of sexual epidemic, gender, sexuality, and sexual behavior discourses have proliferated. Risk and safety are dominant metaphors in efforts to stem the spread of both the medical virus known as HIV and the social viruses of unwanted pregnancy and sexual violence. In the absence of a medical magic bullet for HIV/AIDS, promoting safer sex is seen as a primary way to contain HIV, but our study suggests that it does not address the social viruses that also constitute sexual epidemic.

The alternative gender theory presented in this chapter suggests that discourse can produce and reproduce sedimented societal norms and/or can serve to decenter the norms through subversive repetition of discourse sanctioned by the norm but distinct from it. Our analysis of safer sex pamphlets suggests that the pamphlets reinforce some norms, particularly those that concern gender, decenter some sexuality norms, and highlight contested sexual behavior norms.

Many of the social norms surrounding gender appear to be firmly entrenched, as exemplified by representations of the general public as white and male and "real" women as sexually passive. In contrast, some of the social norms surrounding sexuality have begun to be decentered, as evidenced by the move from discussions of binary group membership to a spectrum of possible sexual behaviors that are associated with a range of risks. However, other sexuality norms continue to be reinforced, as seen in the differing emphases of safer sex pamphlets targeted toward men who have sex with men and those targeted at the general public: gay men are urged to police their behavior, the general public to choose partners carefully to protect themselves from deviant others. In addition, several terms are still being contested, as demonstrated by research suggesting that some behaviors are considered to be sexual only under certain circumstances, monogamy is not always exclusive, and safer sex applies only to the medical (HIV) epidemic, not to the social (unwanted pregnancy, sexual violence) epidemics.

Limitations

Our research discusses representations of gender, sexuality, and sexual behavior in safer sex pamphlets produced in the United States and other European-white contexts. A fuller understanding of these discourses would require exploration of additional media and of materials from a wider range of cultures.

In addition, comparisons between safer sex materials designed to stem HIV transmission with those designed to reduce the spread of social viruses would provide an added dimension to our understanding of gender discourse in a time of sexual epidemic.

This research reinforces Butler's (1990, 1993) assertion that agency inheres in the repetition of behaviors sanctioned by norms but different from them. This notion of agency is a limited one—only behaviors that are possible under existing norms can be repeated—though their repetition may decenter the original norm, thereby opening up the possibility for adding new sanctioned behaviors. The decentering of sexuality norms detected in the safer sex pamphlets analyzed is an instance of such limited agency. The norm of compulsory heterosexuality that categorizes sexuality as binary (heterosexual or not) is moved off center by describing a range of sexual activities in terms of their relative safety rather than by the gender of the participants. The activities mentioned as sexual behaviors are sanctioned by the compulsory heterosexuality norm, but their repetition moves the norm from categorization by group membership to categorization by type of behavior.

However, as might be predicted by Butler's conception of limited agency, the decentering of the norm is incomplete. Increasingly, the discourse of safer sex pamphlets reflects the changed norm; however, discourses of sexuality in other media do not. Future research should explore the diffusion of norm decentering across media and should examine more directly the extent to which and how agency is limited and how it is not.

This research also raises issues that should be addressed by HIV/AIDS prevention educators. The power differences reinforced by compulsory heterosexuality make it impossible for many women to follow the pamphlets' advice and negotiate the use of latex barriers to prevent the spread of HIV because they fear sexual violence. Thus, discussion of violence and pregnancy in HIV prevention materials is integral to the ability of women to negotiate sex that is safer from both a medical and a social perspective.

Perhaps the efficacy of safer sex pamphlets would be increased if they decentered additional norms. For example, they could:

- Decenter the norm of compulsory heterosexuality by not labeling heterosexual white men who do not use intravenous drugs as the "general public."
- Decenter gender norms by not assuming that women are sexually passive and by not assuming that those women who are sexually active are somehow not "real" women.
- Decenter gender norms by promoting sex that is safer for all participants by acknowledging how violence and pregnancy contribute to sexual risk.
- Decenter sexual behavior norms by addressing specific behaviors in specific contexts (e.g., prisons, migrant settings, boarding schools) and clarifying such currently contested terms as *monogamy*.

These additional decenterings are required to make safer sex education more effective. The move from sexuality as binary to sexuality as a spectrum of behaviors can serve as a model for the suggested discursive changes. Decentering norms of compulsory heterosexuality, gender, and sexual behavior that reproduce gender-based power differentials may be the magic bullet that will stem the spread not only of HIV/AIDS but of the sexual epidemic that plagues our society.

ACKNOWLEDGMENTS

The authors acknowledge the invaluable assistance of Beth M. Wescott, Veronica Thomas, and John Watson of the CDC National AIDS Clearinghouse in conducting the research for this project. We are also most grateful to Stan Deetz, Karen Foss, Katie Hogan, and Michael Ross who provided comments on earlier drafts of this chapter.

SAFER SEX PAMPHLETS

All pamphlets referred to are available from:

CDC National AIDS Clearinghouse
P. O. Box 6003
Rockville, MD 20849-6003
800-458-5231

The AD number in parentheses is the clearinghouse accession number.

California. (1991). *Prevent AIDS and other STDs: Safer sex.* (AD10969)

Hispanic AIDS Forum. (1988). *Let's talk in confidence about AIDS: Woman to woman.* (AD2313)

Louisiana. (1987). *Women: What's the connection with AIDS. Men: What's the connection with AIDS.* (AD2070)

Massachusetts. (1988). *Protect yourself from AIDS.* (AD1381)

Michigan. (1987). *AIDS and everyone.* (AD1961)

Minnesota. (1986). *AIDS: What women should know.* (AD3255)

North Carolina. (1990). *Acquired immune deficiency syndrome.* (AD1013)

Ohio. (1987). *Safer sex, condoms and AIDS, AIDS, AIDS, AIDS.* (AD2112)

San Mateo, CA. (1990). *AIDS risk reduction guidelines.* (AD5906)

The lesbian and gay health project of North Carolina. (1989). *Guidelines for AIDS risk reduction.* (AD2622)

U.S. Department of Health and Human Services. (1987). *Facts about AIDS.* (AD0013)

Utah. (1989). *AIDS: Guidelines for risk reduction.* (AD3202)

Washington, DC. (1993). *AIDS: The basics.* (AD15931)

REFERENCES

Abelove, H., Barale, M. A., & Halpern, D. M. (Eds.). (1993). *The lesbian and gay studies reader.* New York: Routledge.

Altman, D. (1986). *AIDS in the mind of America: The social, political, and psychological impact of a new epidemic.* Garden City, NY: Anchor Press/Doubleday.

Bellis, D. J. (1990). Fear of AIDS and risk reduction among heroin-addicted female street prostitutes: Personal interviews with 72 southern California subjects. *Journal of Alcohol and Drug Education, 35,* 26–37.

Brandt, A. M. (1985). *No magic bullet: A social history of venereal disease in the United States since 1880.* New York: Oxford University Press.

Butler, J. (1990). *Gender trouble: Feminism and the subversion of identity.* New York: Routledge.

Butler, J. (1993). *Bodies that matter: On the discursive limits of "sex."* New York: Routledge.

Butler, J., & Scott, J. W. (Eds). (1992). *Feminists theorize the political.* New York: Routledge.

Campbell, C. E. (1991). Prostitution, AIDS, and preventive health behavior. *Social Science and Medicine, 32,* 1367–1378.

Chesebro, J. W. (1980). Paradoxical views of "homosexuality" in the rhetoric of social scientists: A fantasy theme analysis. *Quarterly Journal of Speech, 66,* 127–139.

Chesebro, J. W. (Ed.). (1981). *GaySpeak: Gay male and lesbian communication.* New York: Pilgrim Press.

Corea, G. (1992). *The invisible epidemic: The story of women and AIDS.* New York: HarperCollins.

Crimp, D. (Ed.). (1988). *AIDS: Cultural analysis, cultural activism.* Cambridge, MA: MIT Press.

Darsey, J. (1981). From "commies" and "queers" to "gay is good." In J. W. Chesebro (Ed.), *GaySpeak: Gay male and lesbian communication* (pp. 224–247). New York: Pilgrim Press.

Darsey, J. (1991). From "gay is good" to the scourge of AIDS: The evolution of gay liberation rhetoric, 1977–1990. *Communication Studies, 42*(1), 43–66.

Foucault, M. (1978). *The history of sexuality: An introduction.* New York: Vintage Books.

Foucault, M. (1980a). *Power/knowledge.* New York: Pantheon.

Foucault, M. (Ed.). (1980b). *Herculine Barbin, being the recently discovered memoirs of a nineteenth century hermaphrodite.* New York: Colophon.

Freud, S. (1962). *Three essays on the theory of sexuality.* James Strachey (Trans.). New York: Basic Books.

Friedan, B. (1974). *Feminine mistique.* New York: Dell.

Fullilove, M. T., Fullilove, R. E., Haynes, K., & Gross, S. (1990). Black women and

AIDS prevention: A view toward understanding the gender rules. *Journal of Sex Research, 27,* 47–64.

Holligbaugh, A. (1994). Transmission, transmission, where's the transmission? *Sojourner, 19,* 5–8.

Humphreys, R. A. L. (1970). *Tearoom trade: A study of homosexual encounters in public places.* London: Duckworth.

Kramer, L. (1978). *Faggots.* New York: Random House.

Kristeva, J. (1982). *Desire in language.* Leon Roudiez (Trans.). New York: Columbia University Press.

Kristeva, J. (1984). *Revolution in poetic language.* Leon Roudiez (Trans.). New York: Columbia University Press.

Kristeva, J. (1986). *The Kristeva reader.* Toril Moi (Ed.). Oxford: Blackwell.

Lacan, J. (1977). *Ecrits: A selection.* Alan Bass (Trans.). New York: W. W. Norton.

Lacan, J. (1982). *Feminine sexuality.* Juliet Mitchell & Jackeline Rose (Eds.). Jackeline Rose (Trans.). New York: W. W. Norton.

Maccoby, E. E., & Jacklin, C. N. (1974). *The psychology of sex differences.* Stanford: Stanford University Press.

Metts, S., & Fitzpatrick, M. A. (1992). Thinking about safer sex: The risky business of "know your partner" advice. In T. Edgar, M. A. Fitzpatrick & V. S. Freimuth (Eds.), *AIDS: A communication perspective* (pp. 1–20) Hillsdale, NJ: Lawrence Erlbaum Associates.

Money, J., & Ehrhardt, A. A. (1972). *Man and woman, boy and girl: Differentiation and dimorphism of gender identity from conception to maturity.* Baltimore: Johns Hopkins University Press.

Morgan, R. (1977). *Going too far: The personal chronicle of a feminist.* New York: Random House.

Patton, C. (1990). *Inventing AIDS.* New York: Routledge, Chapman, and Hall.

Patton, C. (1993). With champagne and roses: Women at risk from/in AIDS discourse. In Corinne Squire (Ed.), *Women and AIDS.* Newbury Park, CA: Sage.

Patton, C. (1994). *Last served? Gendering the HIV epidemic.* Bristol, PA: Taylor & Francis.

Public Health Service. (1988). *Understanding AIDS.* Washington, DC: U.S. Department of Health and Human Services.

Radtke, L. H., & Stam, H. J. (Eds.). (1994). *Power/gender: Social relations in theory and practice.* Newbury Park, CA: Sage.

Reid-Phar, R. F. (1993). The spectacle of blackness. *Radical America, 24*(4), 57–65.

Ringer, J. (Ed.). (1994). *Queer words, queer images: Communication and the construction of homosexuality.* New York: New York University Press.

Rist, D. Y. (1993). *Heartlands: A gay man's odyssey across America.* New York: Plum/Penguin Books.

Ross, M. W. (1988). Prevalence of classes of risk behaviors for HIV infection in a randomly selected Australian population. *Journal of Sex Research, 25*(4), 441–450.

Ross, M. W., & Rosser, S. (1988). Monogamy is . . . *Genitourinary Medicine, 64,* 65–66.

Ross, M. W., & Rosser, S. (1991). Dimensions of sexual behavior in homosexual men: Replicability across time and country. *Psychological Reports, 68,* 607–612.

Ross, M. W., Wodak, A., & Gold, J. (1992). Sexual behavior in injecting drug users. *Journal of Psychology and Human Sexuality, 5,* 89–104.

Roth, N. (in press). Identity, subjectivity, and agency in conversations about disease. In H. Mokros (Ed.), *Interaction and identity: Information and behavior* (Vol. 5, pp. 215–248). New Brunswick, NJ: Transactions Press.

Roth, N. (1988). Organizational learning about AIDS: The federal response. *Proceedings of the third annual Texas conference on organizations.* Austin, TX: University of Texas.

Roth, N., & Stephenson, H. (in press). The structuration of self, disease, and conversation in communication about communicable diseases. In L. K. Fuller & L. McP. Shilling (Eds.), *Communicating about communicable diseases.* Amherst, MA: HRD Press.

Ruben, G. (1992). Thinking sex: Notes for a radical theory of the politics of sexuality. In C. S. Vance (Ed.), *Pleasure and danger: Exploring female sexuality* (pp. 267–319). London: Pandora Press.

Scott, J. (1992). Experience. In J. Butler and J. W. Scott. (Eds.), *Feminists theorize the political.* New York: Routledge.

Shilts, R. (1987). *And the band played on: Politics, people, and the AIDS epidemic.* New York: St. Martin's Press.

Signorile, M. (1993). *Queer in America: Sex, the media, and the closets of power.* New York: Random House.

Singer, L. (1993). *Erotic welfare: Sexual theory and politics in the age of epidemic.* New York: Routledge.

Squire, C. (1993). *Women and AIDS.* Newbury Park, CA: Sage.

Sterling, A. F., & Balaban, E. (1993). Genetics and male sexual orientation. *Science, 261,* 1257.

Treichler, P. A. (1988a). AIDS, gender and biomedical discourse: Current contests of meaning. In E. Fee & D. M. Fox (Eds.), *AIDS: The burdens of history* (pp. 12–32). Berkeley: University of California Press.

Treichler, P. A. (1988b). AIDS, homophobia and biomedical discourse: An epidemic of signification. In D. Crimp (Ed.), *AIDS: Cultural analysis, cultural activism* (pp. 31–70). Cambridge, MA: MIT Press.

Treichler, P. A. (1992). AIDS, HIV, and the cultural construction of reality. In G. Herdt & S. Lindenbaum (Eds.), *The time of AIDS: Social analysis, theory, and method* (pp. 65–97). Newbury Park, CA: Sage.

Watney, S. (1987). *Policing desire: Pornography, AIDS and the media.* Minneapolis: University of Minnesota Press.

Weedon, C. (1987). *Feminist practice and poststructuralist theory.* Cambridge, MA: Blackwell.

Weeks, J. (1985). *Sexuality and its discontents: Meaning, myths, and modern sexualities.* New York: Routledge.

Weinstein, N. D. (1987). Unrealistic optimism about susceptibility to health problems: Conclusions from a community-wide sample. *Journal of Behavioral Medicine, 10*(5), 481–501.

Weinstein, N. D. (1989). Optimistic biases about personal risks. *Science, 246,* 1232–1233.

Wittig, M. (1992). *Straight mind and other essays.* Boston: Beacon Press.

25

Sexual Orientation and the Law

Michael H. McGee

The debate about the legal status of gays and lesbians is intense and very positional, with a large bloc of people and institutions declaring that any sexual orientation other than the traditional male-female pairing is a sin and a crime and should not be tolerated under any circumstances. On the other side is an increasingly large number of persons who are proclaiming that sexual orientation should not be a basis for punishment, shunning, or discrimination and that the gay and lesbian minority class should have all of the legal rights and protections accorded to the heterosexual population, without any distinction or limit. In the middle of all of this are most of the people, who do not personally have any very strong feelings either way and for the most part wish that the debate would just go away or feel vaguely that homosexuals should just be left alone to live their own lives privately and in peace, as long as they do not bother anybody else.

There will not be much additional change in the laws or in the culture with regard to gays and lesbians until the heterosexual majority sees the need for change. Groups with minimal voting power fare poorly in a democracy unless they are allied with other blocs of voters. Few blocs of voters have wanted to be identified with or support gay and lesbian issues. Therefore this chapter also attempts to demonstrate those analytical perspectives that would be particularly persuasive to the majority community, including the elected officials and judges, who will ultimately be making the changes.

THE USE OF THE LAW TO KEEP HOMOSEXUALS QUIET

Some members of the public fear that the culture will change if legal rights are given to gays and lesbians. This fear may have some basis in reality. When persons with differing sexual orientations are free to express themselves and participate fully in the society, their influence will alter the culture. Consider the new influences that have entered the culture in the last thirty years as gays and lesbians have slowly and carefully stepped out of the closet. Much more can be expected if the legal repression is lifted entirely.

Great Britain offers an example of what can be expected when the laws are changed. In 1967, Great Britain passed the Sexual Offences Act, which made homosexuality partially lawful. The consequences were apparently unexpected, even by those who voted in favor of the legislation:

Within five years a social revolution which had been simmering behind closed doors had exploded on to the streets. There were openly gay bars, gay clubs, gay social organisations, gay newspapers and even gay demonstrations. Homosexual men and women in Britain were publicly identifying themselves as gay, and were demanding to be recognised on their own, gay, terms, This had not been the intention of Parliament. (Burns, 1983, p. 213)

In the city of Charlotte, North Carolina, homosexuality is illegal. But perhaps more in the United States, even in the South, than in Great Britain, people are willing to ignore the laws that limit their freedom of expression. In many regions, gay institutions are secretive. The effect on the culture at large is thus minimal. Although Charlotte, a southern Bible Belt city, has a visible gay and lesbian sub-culture, having laws that make homosexual activity a criminal offense maintains a degree of secretiveness.

This would change if the threat of arrest and imprisonment, of termination from employment, and of police indifference to violence against gays was removed. The cultural climate would change if a portion of the population publicly identified themselves as gay and demanded to be recognized on their own terms.

Thus, it may be postulated that one major purpose of the existing laws that restrict consenting adult gay and lesbian activity is to inhibit the free expression of a minority portion of our population; the direct intent is not to allow the majority culture to be altered by the open presence of persons with a different approach, which the majority finds unacceptable.

To illustrate, one only needs look at another culture within our own and see how it fears influences from outside sources. There has been an ongoing debate in our country about whether the law should permit the adoption of black children by white parents. For more than twenty years, black organizations have actively opposed such interracial adoptions. The concern is that their culture will be altered:

In 1972, the National Association for Black Social Workers likened the adoption of black children by white parents to "cultural genocide," fearing that in widespread practice, it would destroy the racial identity of black kids. Ever since, there has been an emotional debate over that contention. (Jones 1994b)

In this case, black professionals are using the word *genocide* to describe the alteration of their culture by the injection of white middle-class values and cultural norms.

It took over twenty years after that statement was made before the Congress passed the Multiethnic Placement Act to prevent child welfare agencies from discriminating against prospective parents solely on the basis of race. During those twenty years, thousands of black children went unadopted, although there were many white families eager to adopt some of them. All of this resistance was in the name of the preservation of black cultural norms and traditions.

Would the heterosexual culture be any less fearful of the potential alteration of its cultural norms by the introduction of gay and lesbian social values? There are laws on the books whose primary purpose is to keep gays and lesbians quiet and to keep their values suppressed.

Lawmakers may think otherwise and truly believe that having the laws in place will prevent otherwise law-abiding individuals from engaging in the "criminal" acts of gay and lesbian sexual behavior. There is one major legal clue that the prevention of criminal activity is not the purpose of these laws. These laws against such behavior are rarely or never enforced by actual prosecution and imprisonment. The laws are kept in place to keep people quiet about such things and to "protect the culture."

The U.S. Supreme Court, in the 1986 landmark case *Bowers* v. *Hardwick*, discussed the constitutionality of the felony criminal homosexual sodomy statute of the state of Georgia (Sodomy was defined as including either oral or anal sexual penetration of a male by another male). The Court found that such statutes were constitutional and could be enforced. One of the notes in the opinion, however, was that the Georgia prosecutor had elected not to prosecute the defendant in the case, a male who was accused of criminal sodomy in a private residence with a consenting adult male.

The Georgia attorney general was quoted as saying that the last case he could recall being prosecuted in the state under this law "was back in the 1930s or '40s" (The Court's decision was in 1986.) But the law was and is still on the books. Why? To protect the culture from people getting too open about their sexual orientation. This is obviously not a proper purpose for a criminal statute. Footnote 12 of Justice John Paul Stevens's dissent in the case says, "It is, of course, possible to argue that a statute has a purely symbolic role. . . .Since the Georgia Attorney General does not even defend the statute as written, however . . . , the State cannot possibly rest on the notion that the statute may be defended for its symbolic message."

Further on the issue of selective prosecution, the Court noted that the Georgia sodomy statute applied only to male homosexual sodomy, and not to lesbian or heterosexual sodomy. A man and a woman, or two women, can practice the same "criminal" sexual acts as two men, but this is not unlawful in Georgia.

The Supreme Court perhaps did not consider the First Amendment free speech issues and the Fifth and Fourteenth amendment due process and equal protection issues relating to selective prosecution because those issues were not directly before it. (The Court normally does not deal with issues that are not before it.) The dissent written by Justice Stevens does raise the question, although no satisfactory resolution is provided:

If the Georgia statute cannot be enforced as it is written—if the conduct it seeks to prohibit is a protected form of liberty for the vast majority of Georgia's citizens—the State must assume the burden of justifying a selective application of its law. Either the persons to whom Georgia seeks to apply its statute do not have the same interest in "liberty" that others have, or there must be a reason why the State may be permitted to apply a generally applicable law to certain persons that it does not apply to others. . . . A policy of selective application must be supported by a neutral and legitimate interest—something more substantial than a habitual dislike for, or ignorance about, the disfavored group. Neither the State nor the Court has identified any such interest in this case. . . . Nor, indeed, does the Georgia prosecutor even believe that all homosexuals who violate this statute should be punished. This conclusion is evident from the fact that the . . . [defendant] in this very case has formally acknowledged . . . that he intends to continue to engage, in the prohibited conduct, yet the State has elected not to process criminal charges against him.

U.S. Supreme Court justice Joseph Story, in a commentary published in 1851, discussed the Alien and Sedition Acts of 1798, which among other things made it a criminal offense to speak against the president or congress then in office; he pointed out that the demise of these acts was in part due to the selective enforcement of the laws. Referring to the selective enforcement aspect of the laws, Justice Story concluded: "The Sedition Act was clearly in the highest degree impolitic, and, as the prosecutions under it showed, was susceptible of being used for the purposes of oppression and terrorism" (Story 1851, pp. 172–176).

The Fifth Amendment states that the federal government shall not permit any person to "be deprived of life, liberty, or property, without due process of law," and the Fourteenth Amendment applies this prohibition to the states. It is quite possible that a successful argument could be made to a court by presenting evidence of a pervasive policy of not enforcing a law that is on the books or of selectively enforcing the law only at the whim of a prosecutor, creating an atmosphere of "oppression and terrorism."

This argument would have to be coupled with psychological and sociological data demonstrating that the purpose of the laws in question is not to eliminate criminal behavior but to serve a symbolic purpose of keeping a certain group of people quiet. Such an argument could possibly demonstrate that such a law violates not only the Fifth and the Fourteenth amendments but also offends the First Amendment protection of freedom of speech. Freedom of speech arguments have not been directly addressed by the U.S. Supreme Court in this context. Siegel (1991) analyzed the case law on the issue of free speech in the context of homosexual rights and found no cases relating directly to the issue of whether the selective enforcement of criminal laws could be per se a vehicle to suppress constitutional free speech rights.

A homosexual who is living under such a law would be highly intimidated—indeed, would feel "oppressed and terrorized"—at the prospect of speaking up about his or her sexual orientation or of defending in public the right to have a gay sexual orientation, if he or she fears that a prosecutor might at any time charge him or her with a felony that could be punishable by up to ten years in jail. Therefore this person's free speech interests and due process interests are unquestionably violated.

Additionally, if gays or lesbians let their orientation be known, then the threat of prosecution may be the least of their worries. The biggest problem is that the police will not protect that person or may actually participate in systematic harassment since the person is violating the criminal laws of the state. A gay man, for example, may be assaulted by "normal" persons, and he will be either afraid to report the incident to the police or the police will not investigate his complaint because he is a known "criminal." He may actually find himself the target of abuse and harassment by police officers who are only "doing their job" by keeping known "criminals" off the streets and in their place.

One common practice was for an otherwise law-abiding heterosexual man to go downtown and hang out on the streets or in bars until a gay man approached him. The heterosexual man would go with the gay man, pretending to be interested, until they were in a secluded place, where the heterosexual man would assault and rob the gay man. This activity was called "rolling queers" and was considered to be a legitimate activity by the heterosexual men who participated in it. These men were confident that their victims would not report the crime to the police.

Another consequence of the criminalization of homosexual behavior is opportunity for blackmail. When a person can technically be subject to a prison sentence of ten years because of sexual orientation, opportunities exist for unscrupulous persons to abuse homosexual individuals through threats of exposure. And there are much worse things that happen when gays and lesbians are forced to live outside the protection of the law.

James Madison, in a letter to Thomas Jefferson dated October 17, 1788, correctly predicted at the time the Constitution was being written the type of problems that would come up if majoritarian abuses of power were not contained: "In our government the real power lies in the majority of the community, and the invasion of private rights is chiefly to be apprehended, not from acts of government contrary to the sense of its constituents, but from acts in which the government is the mere instrument of the majority" (Madison 1900).

KEEPING THE LEGAL ISSUES CLEAR
AND WELL DEFINED

The assumption that gays and lesbians should be entitled to constitutional rights is likely to be recognized by the courts only if one operates under the further assumptions that the status of being gay or lesbian itself is not intrinsically criminal in nature and deserving of criminal prosecution, and that homosexual sexual activities are not abominable and detestable criminal choices but instead are the normal sexual expression of an identifiable minority portion of the population. This is where the courts are confused and have not acted decisively, where the input of mental health and social science professionals can be useful.

One point must be made clear from the outset. If there is to be any acceptance by the courts of a constitutional due process right, or a right to privacy, of persons whose sexual orientation is gay or lesbian, it is going to be established in a situation involving consenting sexual behavior between two adults in private. If other issues are introduced, it is likely that the argument will get muddled and the courts will be distracted by these other (often extraneous and irrelevant) issues and ignore the core issue at stake. Consequently, the courts will have difficulty accepting the principles of freedom that are being argued. For example, it is important to avoid bringing along irrelevant or peripheral issues such as pedophilia, homosexual rape, solicitation in public facilities, prostitution, bestiality, or any form of psychiatrically recognized deviant behavior. This is a trap that religion and the law as a whole have fallen into throughout history.

Looking at the primary current legal reference work for North Carolina law, *Strong's North Carolina Index 4th,* there is a title known as Crime Against Nature (Schwartz 1990). This criminal offense is defined in North Carolina as consisting of sexual acts "contrary to the order of nature" committed with either a human or with an animal. Notice that even in the essential definition, two totally unrelated actions are grouped together. The first is oral or anal sex with a human (including heterosexual acts), and the second is sex of any kind with an animal. As long as homosexual activity is linked in that way with bestiality, then no analyst can be objective in seeing any essential basis for a right to freedom and privacy. No legal scholar will be willing to argue that the right to privacy extends to having sex with a goat, regardless of its gender.

Immediately after this overinclusive definition of the crime, the commentary goes on to address the sexual molestation of children. The first substantive commentary involves two full pages of cases involving oral or anal sex with children. Once again, it is certain that no legal scholar will argue in favor of a right of privacy to have sex with a child.

The commentary then immediately continues with a discussion of sodomy committed in the course of a rape or an assault of another person. One case cited as an illustration describes how "Galbreath threatened him with a violent death if he did not perform fellatio upon him." Once again, no legal scholar will argue in favor of a right of privacy where rape or assault is involved.

Indeed, in the fifteen pages of commentary in the North Carolina *Strong's* index, there are only two paragraphs that refer to the plain and simple issue of homosexual acts between consenting adults in private, and this collapsing of distinctions is not necessarily the fault of the author. The courts of North Carolina, as well as the legislature, have grouped these definitions at all times since the founding of the state; the commentary is simply reflecting and describing the law as it exists. A review of a recent national survey of laws (Theuman 1983) indicates that most legal scholars in most states do in fact group these diverse definitions as is done in North Carolina.

Indeed, the very name *sodomy* comes from a biblical description of homosexual gang rape. The city of Sodom was destroyed by God as being unredeemably evil for, among other things, the following behavior toward two male guests in Lot's home in Sodom:

Before the guests went to bed, the men of Sodom surrounded the house. All the men of the city, both young and old, were there. They called out to Lot and asked, "Where are the men who came to stay with you tonight? Bring them out to us!" The men of Sodom wanted to have sex with them. Lot went outside and closed the door behind him. He said to them, "Friends, I beg you, don't do such a wicked thing!" (Genesis 19:4–11)

Biblical scholars since the third century A.D. have interpreted that story to mean that the destruction of Sodom was due to the single fact that these men of the city were homosexual (McNeill 1988, pp. 36–50, 78–80). These scholars have collapsed the defined behavior in much the same way as the author of *Strong's* index has done. The plain language of the Bible, though, as can be seen very clearly from this modern translation, refers to homosexual gang rape (McSpadden 1993). There is no legal or religious scholar who would contend that gang rape should be legalized.

This grouping of unrelated issues is sometimes done by advocates of gay and lesbian rights. One error is to introduce the issue of the right of privacy for AIDS victims into the debate over the right of privacy for consenting homosexual behavior between two adults in private. If the AIDS issue is brought in along with the core issue, it is likely that the argument will get muddled and the courts will tend to focus on the AIDS issue. Again, the risk is that the core issue will be ignored because a distracting issue has been introduced along with it.

An example of the collapsing of the basic privacy issue with the AIDS issue may be found in a book entitled *The Right to Privacy: Gays, Lesbians, and the Constitution:*

Can a gay or lesbian person validly claim that the constitutional right to privacy is violated when he or she is forced from a job because of sexual orientation or when the state enacts a sodomy statute prohibiting sexual relations among same-sex individuals?

Does a person with AIDS or a person who is HIV positive have the constitutional right not to be forced into quarantine or to have his or her body tattooed or name included on a governmental list of infected and potentially dangerous individuals if no other person is endangered? (Sammar 1991)

In a single paragraph, defensible issues are inextricably linked with what many legal scholars would say are indefensible issues. The proposed constitutional right to privacy for homosexual activity between consenting adults is inextricably linked with some supposed corollary constitutional right to privacy for persons who are infected with the AIDS virus. Those who expect to make progress before the courts should treat this linking as the most dangerous obstacle to the establishment of a constitutional decriminalization of homosexual activity between consenting adults.

This collapsing of issues is being done not only by the majoritarian scholars but also by some gay and lesbian activists. Each time these often unrelated issues are grouped, the more firmly it becomes ingrained in the legal system and in the culture that being gay or lesbian means having AIDS. This reinforces the prevailing homophobia in a phenomenally effective way.

Associating peripheral and controversial issues with the basic constitutional claim of a right of privacy for homosexual acts by consenting adults is ineffective. The result in court is most likely to result in the proverbial throwing out the baby with the bathwater. Doing so will also most certainly lead to an early and catastrophic end to majoritarian sympathy for the basic rights of homosexuals. (For a discussion of a similar problem with uses of the term *sexual orientation,* see Diamant, this volume.)

STATUS HOMOSEXUALITY: CHOICE OR DESTINY?

In this analysis, all references are to English common law, the source and substance of our current common law system and the source of the statutory law of the United States. It is beyond the range of this chapter to do a cross-cultural analysis because such analyses are available (Boswell 1994; Brzek & Hubalek 1988).

The first English statute criminalizing any behavior related to homosexuality was passed by King Henry VIII in 1533 (Warner 1983). That statute provided for the death penalty for buggery—male anal penetration—but criminalized no other act. Therefore, there is evidence that all other gay and lesbian acts were legal in England until 1885, when male homosexual acts generally were made criminal offenses. This law was effectively repealed by the 1967 Sexual Offences Act. Since that time adult male homosexuality has been decriminalized in England. At no time in the history of England does it appear that lesbian activity has been considered illegal (Warner 1983).

Even the U.S. Supreme Court in the landmark case of *Bowers* v. *Hardwick* made the error of collapsing the distinction between various forms of homosexual conduct. After looking at ancient precedent, the majority found that the laws of the thirteen original colonies were patterned after the English common law, referring to Henry VIII's original sodomy law. However, that original sodomy law and the English common law up until 1885 prohibited only male anal penetration, while the Supreme Court seemed to lump together all oral and anal acts, whether done by males or females, or by homosexuals or heterosexuals; this was clearly unwarranted on the basis of the English common law. The Supreme Court also failed to note that all sodomy laws between consenting adults were repealed in England in 1986.

What has really happened is that the United States has gone beyond the English common law precedents in declaring any form of homosexual conduct to be criminal and at the same time making heterosexual oral sex illegal as well. Either there was no argument on these issues in the briefs submitted to the Supreme Court in *Bowers* v. *Hardwick,* or the Supreme Court after research and analysis did not agree that English common law was so limited. It is likely that the former was the case.

In any case, the goal of persons concerned with creating a zone of legal privacy for consenting homosexual acts among adults, which is also expressed as a decriminalization of homosexual activity, involves several sorts of analyses. The first of these analyses may be to look at the ancient precedents with more specificity. Another may be to look at the purposes of the laws, which appear to require homosexuals to remain invisible in the culture. All of these have been discussed.

Another area of analysis is primarily psychological in nature and has to do with whether homosexuality is a freely chosen orientation and lifestyle or a matter over which an individual has little or no choice; it is a matter of destiny, be it genetic or psychosocial. It does not appear that the American Psychological Association in its *amicus* (friend of the court) brief in *Bowers* v. *Hardwick* addressed this issue directly (Bersoff & Ogden 1991; Cameron & Cameron 1988). The issue must be addressed directly in any further challenges to criminal prohibitions against homosexuality. As will be demonstrated in this section, the justices of the Supreme Court will definitely listen to scientific evidence, but it must be reliable and relevant to the issues at stake.

Many opinion makers in this country, particularly those of the religious right, view homosexuality as an abominable and criminal (sinful) choice that a person makes voluntarily and with full knowledge of the consequences. The consequences are that by making such a choice, they are committing a crime. The fear is that if we do not retain the criminal laws, then more people will make this choice, and civilization will be devastated, as was the ancient city of Sodom. The alternative point of view is that homosexual orientation is present at birth or developed very early in life and never changes thereafter. Attempting to persuade a homosexual to switch to being a heterosexual may be akin to asking a black man to change his mind and become a white man.

The research for this chapter was done from a legal rather than psychological perspective. Combing the legal literature on the subject reveals no reference to such studies about the origins of sexual orientation. In order to convince courts, lawyers will require studies that are methodologically sound and draw the conclusions herein asserted. In the absence of such studies, a lawyer cannot make much of an argument for a fundamental constitutional right to privacy that is any different from that which has already been rejected by the U.S. Supreme Court in *Bowers* and in a string of employment cases involving the military. If in fact homosexuality is as much of a choice as whether to have long hair or short hair, then the courts will not grant that choice much respect as a constitutional right. This is not to say that the courts will not at some time in the future grant to citizens the constitutional right to choose their sexual preference. It is just not likely.

The American Psychological Association filed an *amicus* brief in *Bowers* when it was before the Supreme Court. A review of two articles concerning their brief shows that it did not focus on the issue of choice or destiny at all or did so only tangentially. And there are three possible reasons that the association did not so focus. The first is that the association in 1986 did not really believe that homosexuality was other than a freely chosen activity. Another possible reason is that there were at the time no, or few, conclusive and sound studies stating conclusively that homosexuality was not a choice for most persons. A third possible reason could have been that the lawyers who developed the strategy did not consider such arguments to be necessary for winning the case. For example, one argument advanced by the American Psychological Association in its brief to the Court was:

Because neither same-gender sexual orientation nor the prohibited sexual conduct is pathological, preventing the development of same-gender sexual orientation and deterring the conduct could not be defended as proper mental health goals, even if the statute could have such effects (which it could not). (Bersoff & Ogden, 1991)

Such language or jargon may have meaning to psychologists. To lawyers in general and more especially to Supreme Court justices, that kind of language will be perceived as incomprehensible. Embedded within the statement is a possible assumption that it may be possible to "prevent" the development of homosexual orientation. What is seems to say is that although homosexual orientation can be prevented, doing so is not a proper "mental health" goal since someone who is homosexual is not defined by psychologists as maladjusted. A lawyer or judge will likely say that this reasoning is not a valid reason to overturn centuries of legal precedent.

The brief of the American Psychological Association devoted much text to analyzing the extent to which early childhood homosexual activity was related to later sexual orientation and concluded that there was no correlation. The brief also noted that prehomosexual boys reached orgasm for the first time at earlier ages than their heterosexual counterparts (Cameron & Cameron 1988).

Lawyers and judges, and justices, are much more pragmatic and people oriented than many people believe. They want to hear about real people's lives and case studies of patients to decide if valid conclusions can be drawn as to whether homosexual orientation is choice or destiny. When legal minds are distracted with studies of the orgasms of young boys, these minds shut like steel traps. These kinds of studies raise images of child molesting and the exploitation of children, and lawyers know of these crimes only too well.

What is likely to be more persuasive is the testing of hypotheses such as assertions that persons who are homosexuals as adults were inevitably led in that direction by their own inner drive and physical-psychological makeup; or a hypothesis that one can study a group of children and determine which of the children are likely to become homosexual as they mature; or a study that examines the likelihood of conversion of adult homosexuals to a heterosexual orientation, including marriage to a member of the opposite sex and the creation of a traditional family.

As an example of the type of study that a lawyer or judge may be better able to understand, here is a quotation from an article authored jointly by a physician and a psychologist in the former Czechoslovakia:

If homosexual men are to adapt appropriately to marriage and parenthood, the following conditions should be met. First, the individual's motivation should be strong and authentic. . . . Second, after spending considerable time with a suitable woman, the homosexual male patient should experience a continued sense of well-being. He should not feel annoyance, discomfort, or otherwise unexplained fatigue. Third, there should be an exceptionally good rapport between the patient and his spouse in the non-sexual sphere. Fourth, the patient should be capable of frequent coital activity with his spouse without dysfunction. And fifth, in the course of living with his spouse, the patient should be capable of giving up even incidental homosexual contacts. . . . The therapist cannot significantly strengthen the patient's capacity to adapt. His main function is the prevention of maladaptation. For this reason, few homosexuals successfully adapt to heterosexual life as the direct result of therapy. Most such therapeutic attempts end with the patient realizing that he is incapable of such an adjustment, and subsequently returning to the homosexual subculture. . . . Because most male homosexual patients are not capable of authentic heterosexual and matrimonial adaptation, their contacts with . . . clinical psychologists are limited to supportive therapy which helps them accept their sexual orientation, discover their own homosexual identity, and improve their lives. Our ultimate goal has been to help homosexuals establish permanent love partnerships. (Brzek & Hubalek 1988)

In addition to studies on the question of whether homosexuality is a choice or destiny, one more type of study may be useful in convincing a court: studies that objectively demonstrate the individual and social harm of exclusion of homosexuals from the cultural mainstream through the application of criminal sanctions.

If one assumes that consenting homosexual activity between consenting adults in private is normal (i.e., non-pathological) and that homosexuals have no choice about their sexual orientation, then it follows that there must be psychological harm that results when such persons are labeled criminals, persecuted by governments, or forced to live secretive lives. In addition, with those same assumptions, it could follow that children who are predisposed to be homosexual are severely psychologically harmed by being reared in the present antihomosexual social and legal environment. Such studies demonstrating harm due to prejudice on the basis of sexual orientation would be useful evidence in any future case designed to gain constitutional status for homosexuals.

Such studies were very important in *Brown* v. *Board of Education* (1954), the landmark case in which the U.S. Supreme Court reversed the doctrine of "separate but equal" schools for blacks and whites. The Court stated as follows:

We come to the question presented: Does segregation of children in public schools solely on the basis of race, even though the physical facilities and other "tangible" factors may be equal, deprive the children of the minority group of equal educational opportunities? We believe that it does. . . . To separate them from others of similar age and qualifications solely because of their race generates a feeling of inferiority as to their status in the community that may affect their hearts and minds in a way unlikely ever to be undone. . . . Whatever may have been the extent of psychological knowledge at the time of *Plessy* v. *Ferguson* [decided in about 1896], this finding is amply supported by modern authority.

The Court then in a footnote cited the modern authority that justified their conclusions: seven or eight psychological and sociological treatises. In addition, the Court in other parts of the opinion referred to psychological studies of whether black children were harmed by the separate but equal doctrine; these studies were conducted for the specific purpose of introducing expert evidence at the trials of the cases that led to the matter's coming before the Supreme Court.

Note that the Supreme Court is entirely willing and able to consider competent and well-documented psychological authority that is pertinent to the question at hand and deals with real people. It is, moreover, entirely likely that the psychological studies turned the tide on racial segregation with the justices of the Supreme Court. The Court's discussion of these studies is primary in the Court's written decision, and the pivotal point of overruling the "separate but equal" doctrine occurs in the written opinion in the very next paragraph after the above-quoted reference to modern psychological authority.

EQUAL EMPLOYMENT AND ACCOMMODATIONS FOR HOMOSEXUALS

Decriminalizing homosexual status and eliminating formal governmental prejudice against homosexuals will not necessarily resolve all the discrimination problems. There is still a need for legislation in order to protect gays and lesbians from the common prejudices of employers and other citizens and from the public at large. It is very clear that race, sex, national origin, religion, age, and disability discrimination in employment was not eliminated by the Court's statements that these classes of persons were entitled to full citizenship status and to constitutional rights.

One of the bedrock principles of the common law in the United States is often referred to as the employment-at-will doctrine: employers may employ, promote, terminate, or otherwise deal with any and all employees as they will, with or without having a reason for actions taken, or even if a bad reason is given, without any interference or constraint from the government or from the courts. This doctrine has been modified in some states, but in many states, particularly those in the South, it still stands. As recently as 1993 in North Carolina, the doctrine was restated by the North Carolina Court of Appeals in the case of *Boesche* v. *Raleigh-Durham Airport Authority:* "Generally, North Carolina adheres to the employee-at-will doctrine which holds that absent a contract of employment for a definite term, the employee-employer relationship can be terminated by either party at any time for any reason or for no reason."

Although this was a discharge case, the courts in other cases have made it abundantly clear that the same doctrine applies to hiring, promotion, and other types of employment cases. This principle means in practice that an employer can refuse to hire a homosexual, even if the Supreme Court decriminalizes behavior, and an employer can still fire a person if he or she becomes aware that the person is gay or lesbian. There then remains a fear that disclosure will have severe economic consequences. Thus, homosexual will still be vulnerable to exploitation and blackmail because their jobs can still be arbitrarily taken away by employers.

It was not until the U.S. Congress enacted Title VII of the Civil Rights Act of 1964 that employment discrimination began to come to a very slow, yet incomplete, end for blacks, women, Hispanics, and religious minorities. And it was not until much later, in 1967 for persons over the age of 40 and in 1993 for persons with disabilities, that overt discrimination against these categories of persons began to be illegal by statute. Not until the statutes were passed by Congress, providing penalties for noncompliance, did any substantial change occur in the behavior of employers and private citizens whose behavior was motivated by private prejudices.

The same can be said for the question of day-to-day discrimination against gays and lesbians. Even if the Court formally decriminalizes homosexual activity, discrimination will not formally end until Congress acts to amend the current laws by adding sexual orientation as a protected category.

It is much more likely that Congress will act to prohibit employment discrimination against homosexuals if the Supreme Court fully decriminalizes homosexual behavior. As it is now, members of Congress could be accused by their constituents of actively promoting unlawful activities if they pass a blanket prohibition against homosexual employment discrimination because many states still have valid laws declaring homosexual activity to be unlawful and criminal.

Nevertheless, if Congress chooses, it can act without waiting for the courts. All that is necessary to end job discrimination against homosexuals are two amendments to Title VII of the Civil Rights Act of 1964.

The first would be to add language prohibiting discrimination because of a person's sexual orientation, to the same degree that discrimination based on race, religion, sex, and national origin is prohibited. This amendment would enact into law a blanket prohibition of discrimination against homosexuals in employment. It would give homosexuals not only a legal right but a means to enforce that right through a federal administrative agency and through the federal courts.

Under such an amendment, any person who was known to be homosexual and believed that he or she had been denied employment, or discriminated against on the job, or who had been terminated because of sexual orientation, would have a right to file a charge of discrimination with the Equal Employment Opportunity Commission. The charge must be filed within 180 days, or 300 days if there is a state enforcement agency that also prohibits such discrimination, and the employer must employ more than fifteen employees.

The Equal Employment Opportunity Commission would conduct an investigation of the charge and make a determination as to whether the alleged discrimination had in fact occurred. If the commission determined that the charging party had in fact been discriminated against, the agency could, using its own staff of attorneys and at no cost to the charging party, file a lawsuit in the federal courts to remedy the alleged violation of the law. A very high proportion of charges filed with the Equal Employment Opportunity Commission are settled privately to the satisfaction of the charging party without the necessity of having to go to court; this is especially true when the preliminary evidence indicates that the allegation of discrimination is justified.

Upon filing a charge and giving the agency 180 days to conduct an investigation, an individual also has the right to take the matter into the federal courts with the assistance of a private attorney. A person who files a valid and provable charge of discrimination has the right to be hired, promoted, or transferred into the position he or she was denied because of homosexuality. A person who is discharged has a right to reinstatement. There is a right to back pay for wages that may have been lost due to the discrimination and a right to an award of attorney's fees if a private attorney was employed. Additionally, there is a right to receive an award of up to $300,000 in damages, depending on the size of the organization, for pain and suffering and as punitive damages (Schlei & Grossman 1983).

This prohibition, using the language *sexual orientation* as the prohibited basis for discrimination, would also prohibit discrimination against heterosexuals by homosexuals.

The second amendment, which is unnecessary to secure the basic employment right but would make the initial prohibition more palatable to politicians and the public, would be a section prohibiting any law or regulation that would purport to establish employer hiring or promotion goals or quotas based on sexual orientation. This amendment would defuse one of the major fears of opponents of legislation protecting homosexual employment rights.

This fear concerning goals or quotas is very real since there are thirty years of cases interpreting Title VII that permit the courts to use statistics to prove discrimination and that permit and sometimes require employers to set goals of having a certain percentage of blacks or females or Hispanics in their workforce by a certain date. These goals or quotas place an affirmative obligation on the employer to make special efforts to recruit persons in the protected groups and place a burden on the employer to show a great deal of documentation demonstrating why he or she has not met a goal or quota.

There do not seem to be any public policy reasons to require employers to recruit and give preference to homosexuals until their workforce reaches a certain percentage of homosexual employees. Others may wish to make the argument that such is appropriate, but Congress will have a tough time politically with prohibiting discrimination against homosexuals unless goals and quotas are explicitly prohibited. It is worth noting that there is little or no case law approving goals or quotas for religion, age, or disability status. Goals and quotas have usually been reserved for blacks, females, and Hispanics. Thus, there would be no fundamental unfairness in an explicit prohibition of goals and quotas for homosexuals.

Other titles of the Civil Rights Act of 1964, and numerous other federal laws, contain provisions prohibiting discrimination in public accommodations and facilities, education, and other areas of life. All of these laws should also be amended to add sexual orientation as a prohibited category of discrimination.

Additionally, more than half of the states, as well as many cities and counties, have "fair employment laws," which prohibit discrimination and provide for state law penalties and a right to legal action in the state courts for persons who believe that they are being or have been discriminated against in employment, accommodations, or education. A few local laws already prohibit discrimination based on sexual preference. All of these state and local laws should be amended to include sexual preference as a protected category. This will have to be done by each city, county, and state separately, and local politics is probably more heavily dominated by homophobic constituencies than is national politics.

FAMILY AND PARTNER ISSUES

No state in the United States grants legal recognition to marriage between people of the same sex. And even if *Bowers* v. *Hardwick* is overruled by a future Supreme Court decision and homosexuality is decriminalized, and even if Congress makes employment and other forms of discrimination against homosexuals unlawful by statute, there is no known legal theory that would require any state to alter its family laws to accommodate same-sex marriage or same-sex family rights and obligations. Marriage and family laws are created by and are totally within the control of the state legislatures, without any direct control by the federal government. And there is no constitutional provision that would require the states to change their family laws to accommodate same-sex couples.

About the most that the federal government could do would be to threaten to withhold federal funds from states that did not alter their laws. That method has been very successful in several areas of the law, such as reducing the speed limit nationally to 55 mph with the threat of withholding federal highway funds. It is unlikely that Congress will take this radical step at any time in the near future, though.

Rather, family and same-sex partner issues will have to be dealt with through the political process in each state separately, and the likelihood of the states' changing their marriage and family laws in the near term is slim at best. For change to occur, there would have to be a breakthrough in changing the laws of one or more states and time to see what actual effects those changes had on the populace at large. Then other states might follow suit slowly.

A marriage that is made valid in any one state by legislation or court decision is presumptively entitled under the U.S. Constitution to validity in every other state:

Full Faith and Credit shall be given in each State to the Public Acts, Records, and Judicial Proceeding of every other State. And the Congress may by general Laws prescribe the Manner in which such Acts, Records and Proceedings shall be proved, and the Effect thereof. (Constitution, Art. IV, sec. 1)

Thus, if even one state allows same-sex marriages, couples from all over the country could travel to that state to be married and return to their home states and start legal actions to have the marriage from the other state be declared valid and entitled to full faith and credit. Thus, the first state to pass such laws would see a major upsurge in its homosexual population; second, a major upsurge in same-sex couples visiting that state in order to marry would follow; and third, other states would protest being required to address the full faith and credit issue. The courts may or may not accept the argument, but the presumption of validity would attach to any such marriage (Jones 1994a).

The state that is perhaps closest to recognizing same-sex marriage is Hawaii, where the state supreme court recently ruled that there is no constitutional reason that a same-sex couple should be denied the right to marry. Further court proceedings are underway:

"If we get a favorable ruling in Hawaii, the law will apply to every U.S. state," says Evan Wolfson, co-counsel in the case and senior attorney for the Lambda Legal Defense and Education Fund, a gay rights group. "You don't have to get your marriage visa stamped when you cross the state line." (Jones 1994a)

This development should not yet be viewed with too much significance because the fact that the Constitution "does not prohibit" same-sex marriages is not the same as a finding that the Constitution requires a certain action. In such a situation, the state legislature would in all likelihood still have the right to overrule the court decision by passing a law specifically prohibiting same-sex marriages. This scenario is discussed solely to give life to the full faith and credit issue as it is being worked out in a legal controversy.

Same-sex marriages, or their equivalent, are recognized by some foreign countries. Denmark recognizes "registered partnerships," which confer on same-sex couples most of the rights of married heterosexual couples. Sweden and the Netherlands have similar laws recognizing same-sex couples (Hunter, Michaelson & Stoddard 1992).

An interesting question would be whether a same-sex couple could go to one of these countries and be married according to the laws of that country, then return to the United States and ask that this legally binding union be recognized as valid in the United States for all purposes provided under the foreign law. The answer probably is that such a marriage would not be recognized. A state has a right to refuse to recognize foreign marriages or other contracts that would violate its own public policy (e.g., polygamy).

So far there is no known case where a legally valid foreign same-sex marriage has been recognized in the United States. Conversely, there are no published cases where such a marriage has been declared invalid. It is not, therefore, a forgone conclusion that each and all of the fifty states would find that a legally valid foreign same-sex marriage would violate the public policy of that state. Hawaii, parts of California, and New York, for example, have fairly liberal public policies making homosexuality legal and forbidding discrimination based on sexual orientation, and it is conceivable, although not likely, that their courts could find that the state had no public policy prohibiting same-sex marriage (Hunter, Michaelson & Stoddard 1992).

Conservative scholars have for years attacked homosexuals and homosexual rights groups for being "antifamily" and for contributing to the breakdown of family values in the United States. It would be more accurate, though, to state that homosexuals are not permitted by law to form families, or that they wish to reject the traditional concept of family for themselves. It is entirely possible for a person to support family values for society at large and for the majority heterosexual population and yet reject that lifestyle for himself or herself. It is also entirely consistent for any person to be a strong supporter of the family and family values and yet acknowledge that the homosexual minority in our society is not required to live in a traditional family setting.

The further corollary is that were it not for the state laws prohibiting same-sex marriage, laws that were passed by mostly heterosexual and pro-family legislators, a significant portion of the gay and lesbian population might settle down into stable, long-term, committed family units.

If same-sex couples are granted the legal right to unite for life in marriage or in a civil ceremony corollary to marriage, then these couples will have the opportunity to enjoy all of the benefits of marriage, including rights to a statutory share of their partner's estate on that partner's death, the right to own property as a family unit, and the right to share in any pension, insurance, or other employee or government benefits of their partner. Such couples will also be entitled to alimony for a dependent partner and a right of property division upon a severing of the union.

CONCLUSION

The current legal climate is such that homosexuals have virtually no legal rights other than scattered partial legal rights granted voluntarily by city councils, county commissions, state legislatures, and Congress, and scattered protections voluntarily granted by public or private employers. The corollary is that any of these rights may be taken away as easily as they are granted, as homosexuals have no present right to protection under the Constitution of the United States. There is a legal basis for prosecuting homosexual behavior as criminal activity.

Researchers need to understand that their work could be the vehicle for making changes in the interpretation of the status of homosexuals under the U.S. Constitution. Contemporary laws relevant to sexual orientation are based on archaic and obscure beliefs and traditions. Methodologically sound research is needed in order to challenge the fallacies about sexual orientation that are evident in the existing laws.

REFERENCES

Bersoff, D. N., & Ogden, D. W. (1991). APA amicus curiae briefs: Furthering lesbian and gay male civil rights. *American Psychologist, 46,* 950–956.

Boesche v. Raleigh-Durham Airport Authority. (1993). 111 N. C. App. 149, 432 S. E. 2d 137.

Boswell, J. (1994). *Same-sex unions in premodern Europe.* New York: Villiard Books.

Bowers v. Hardwick. (1986). 478 U.S. 186.

Brown v. Board of Education. (1954). 347 U. S. 483.

Brzek, A., & Hubalek, S. (1988). Homosexuals in Eastern Europe: Mental health and psychiatric issues. *Journal of Homosexuality, 15,* 153–162.

Burns, R. (1983). The fight for equality. In B. Galloway (Ed.), *Prejudice and pride: Discrimination against gay people in modern Britain* (pp. 213–228). London: Routledge & Kegan Paul.

Cameron, P., & Cameron, K. (1988). Did the American Psychological Association misrepresent scientific material to the US Supreme Court? *Psychological Reports, 63,* 255–270.

Hunter, N. D., Michaelson, S. E., & Stoddard, T. B. (1992). *The rights of lesbians and gay men.* Carbondale: Southern Illinois University.

Jones, R. (1994a, September 28). *The next two years should tell if same-sex marriages will be legal in the United States.* New York: Associated Press Wire Service.

Jones, R. (1994b, October 6). Interracial adoption bill passed. *Charlotte Observer,* p. 1A.

Madison, J. (1900). Letter to Thomas Jefferson, October 17, 1788. In G. Hunt (Ed.), *The writings of James Madison* (Vol. 5, p. 272). New York: G. P. Putnam's Sons.

McNeill, J. J. (1988). *The church and the homosexual.* Boston: Beacon Press.

McSpadden, J. R., Jr. (1993). Homosexuality and the church. In L. Diamant (Ed.), *Homosexual issues in the workplace* (pp. 91–103). Washington, DC: Taylor & Francis.

Samar, V. J. (1991). *The right to privacy: Gays, lesbians and the Constitution.* Philadelphia: Temple University.

Schlei, B. L., & Grossman, P. (1983). *Employment discrimination law.* Washington, DC: Bureau of National Affairs.

Schwartz, A. L. (1990). Crime against nature. In *Strong's North Carolina Index 4th* (Vol. 6, pp. 729–743). Rochester: Lawyer's Cooperative Publishing Co.

Siegel, P. (1991). Lesbian and gay rights as a free speech issue: A review of relevant case law. *Journal of Homosexuality, 21,* 203–259.

Story, J. (1851). *Commentaries on the Constitution of the United States.* Boston: Little, Brown.

Theuman, J. E. (1983). Validity of statute making sodomy a criminal offense. *American Law Reports* (Vol. 20, pp. 1009–1068). Rochester, NY: Lawyer's Cooperative Publishing.

Title VII of the Civil Rights Act of 1964, as amended, 42 U. S. C. 2000e *et seq.*

Warner, N. (1983). Parliament and the law. In B. Galloway (Ed.), *Prejudice and pride: Discrimination against gay people in modern Britain* (pp. 78–86). London: Routledge & Kegan Paul.

Index

About the Editors

LOUIS DIAMANT is Professor Emeritus of Psychology, having served as Chair and Professor in the Department of Psychology at the University of North Carolina at Charlotte. In addition, he serves as psychologist for intercollegiate athletics and has a private practice in clinical psychology. His research interests include sexual orientation, sexual identification, and the psychology of sports and fitness. Previous publications include *Male and Female Homosexuality: Psychological Approaches* (1987) and *Homosexual Issues in the Workplace* (1993).

RICHARD D. McANULTY is Assistant Professor of Psychology at the University of North Carolina at Charlotte. He received his doctorate in clinical psychology from the University of Georgia. His research interests include problems of sexuality, the paraphilias, and issues in classification and assessment. He has served as consulting editor for several journals including the *Journal of Sex Research.*

ISBN 0-313-28501-2

90000>

EAN

9 780313 285011

HARDCOVER BAR CODE